Corporate Value Creation

The Wiley Corporate F&A series provides information, tools, and insights to corporate professionals responsible for issues affecting the profitability of their company, from accounting and finance to internal controls and performance management.

Founded in 1807, John Wiley & Sons is the oldest independent publishing company in the United States. With offices in North America, Europe, Asia, and Australia, Wiley is globally committed to developing and marketing print and electronic products and services for our customers' professional and personal knowledge and understanding.

Corporate Value Creation

An Operations Framework for Nonfinancial Managers

LAWRENCE C. KARLSON

To Mike
Best Wishes
Lawrence Karlson

WILEY

Cover image: © iStock.com/kentoh

Cover design: Wiley

Published by John Wiley & Sons, Inc., Hoboken, New Jersey.

Published simultaneously in Canada.

Library of Congress Cataloging-in-Publication Data:

Karlson, Lawrence C., 1942–
Corporate value creation : an operations framework for nonfinancial managers / Lawrence C. Karlson.
pages cm. — (The Wiley corporate F&A series)
Includes index.
ISBN 978-1-118-99752-9 (cloth); 978-1-118-99715-4 (ePDF); 978-1-119-00044-0 (ePub)
1. Corporations—Valuation. 2. Corporations—Finance. 3. Stockholder wealth. I. Title.
HG4028.V3K364 2015
658.15′5—dc23

2014041590

Printed in the United States of America

10 9 8 7 6 5 4 3 2 1

This book is dedicated to my family. Without their support over these many years, this work would not have been possible.

Special thanks to my editor, Patrick L. Edsell, whose tireless efforts throughout numerous revisions have made this book much better than it otherwise would have been.

Contents

Preface

DURING MY CAREER I have been involved in numerous businesses in various industries: some doing well and others in need of drastic attention. At an early stage in my career, I realized that many businesses could improve their performance if shown how. So I began to develop presentations addressing some of the aspects of creating value in a business. I then systematically presented my thoughts to the various management teams I was involved with. The outcome was dramatic in many cases. Performing businesses did better. Turnarounds became profitable. The first codification of this material was documented in a series of VHS tapes I did in 1990 titled "A Smile Is Not Enough," which have been used as training material for several firms.

When I stepped down as executive chairman of Spectra Physics I was no longer responsible for any day-to-day operations. While I had many board opportunities to keep me busy I still had "time on my hands," so to speak. Given this state of affairs I decided to write a book that addressed what I perceived to be a need to combine the essence of sound business practices with an analytical framework that managers and executives who don't have an MBA could use to make better decisions and advance their careers.

I would like to thank all of the organizations and people I have worked with who have made this work possible. In particular I must give credit to my dear friend and editor, Patrick Edsell. Pat is a very capable executive and was my business partner when he was CFO of Pharos AB and later CEO of Spectra Physics Inc. He devoted an enormous amount of time editing many revisions, including some of the earlier manuscripts (which must have been painful). In fact his contributions have made this a much better book than it would have been otherwise. Others who have played a significant role in the preparation of this book are: Yuanshun Li, PhD, Assistant Professor of Finance, Ryerson University, who did a detailed edit of a final manuscript; James Gabriel, retired CEO of the Harris Group Inc., who also edited a final version; Jason Spera, CEO of Aegis Software Inc., who tirelessly edited the sections on the Internet in Chapter 6; Dennis Pizzica, VP and Treasurer of Berwind Corporation, who made numerous helpful suggestions during his review of Chapter 9; and Steven Ritter, partner, KPMG LLP, who provided advice on accounting-related matters. Finally this book would not have been possible without the support of my family, who never complained about my periodic absences from events and preoccupation with the manuscript. In particular I must thank my wife, Deborah, who read numerous manuscripts, made many helpful suggestions, and who didn't have to ask what I was doing when passing my office for the past many years.

ABOUT THIS BOOK

While there is material in all chapters that is very readable, a level of comfort with algebra is required in order to appreciate much of what is presented. Conventional wisdom would suggest that value creation would include at least three business activities: operations, investment, and financing. Within these milieus, management is expected to find the optimum combination of debt and equity to minimize the firm's cost of capital and to provide adequate working capital. In addition, one of their prime objectives is to grow the organization's revenue and profit by identifying and making investments in Research and Development; Property, Plant, and Equipment; Operations; Marketing; Sales; Human Resources; Systems; Procurement; and Finance and Administration. This book addresses these issues by offering an analytical operations framework that management can use to optimize the impact of their investment decisions on operations and to create value through the growth of the firm.

Chapters 1 through 3 lay the groundwork for subsequent chapters.

Chapter 1 is dedicated to explaining the Income Statement, Balance Sheet, and Cash Flow Statement, how they interact, and the importance of a thorough understanding of these statements in decision making. The concept of measuring value is introduced early to give the reader an appreciation of what's involved. Also the notion of Required Revenue is defined and discussed to give the reader an appreciation of the role Revenue plays in covering all the expenses and taxes incurred by a company. The case study is built around a manager who has just returned from a training program and proceeds to use his new skills to analyze his company's financial statements.

Chapter 2 builds on the concepts developed in Chapter 1 and establishes the need for a model that enables management to make quick estimates of performance based on various assumptions about the business environment. To this end, the Envelope Equations that permit quick estimates of profit and cash flow are introduced. Their use is illustrated by various examples. The power of the way of thinking developed in the chapter is demonstrated in the case study where the chair of a corporation wrestles with an investment decision.

In Chapter 3, the issues associated with a company's cost of capital broadly known as the Weighted Average Cost of Capital are discussed. Beta is introduced, which leads into a discussion of the Capital Asset Pricing Model. The focus of the theory and examples is on investment decision making. For those who need a refresher, it includes an illustration of the concept of Present Value. The case study tells the story of a CEO of a successful company who, against the advice of his board of directors, makes a serious mistake but goes on to fix it and regains the confidence of his management team and directors.

Chapter 4 provides an introduction to the valuation of Cash Flows. It begins by defining forecast and post-forecast cash flows, and then takes the reader through a series of models that, depending on the circumstances, can be arranged to suit a particular operating environment. The chapter concludes with several examples, including single and multi-stage cash flow business models, and a case study in which a young group of managers is given an opportunity to value the largest acquisition their company has ever contemplated.

Chapter 5 introduces the concept of Return on Capital Employed (ROCE), a widely used measure of the returns management generates relative to the capital employed in the business. This is followed by introducing the Income Statement and Balance Sheet accounts into the ROCE expression, and via these analytics the drivers of ROCE are identified. Several examples are cited and followed in a discussion of the practical aspects of managing ROCE. The case study tells the story of a management team that purchases a troubled company and then proceeds to fix it using a combination of the CEO's experience and the ROCE driver model.

Chapter 6 outlines strategies and best practices for managing ROCE and it is the most qualitative chapter in the book. Because it is largely qualitative this chapter is a prime example of the attribution problem referred to in the "Selected References" section of this book.

The chapter begins with a discussion of basic pricing-driven models that is followed by a dialogue that defines and characterizes the attributes of several value-added models. A detailed discussion of the factors that affect the cost of goods sold follows the business models that have been introduced with the objective of identifying what can be done to maximize Gross Margin. Operating Expenses are examined next in the context of viewing expenditures on Sales, Marketing, Human Resources, and so on as investments rather than expenses. Considerable space is devoted to the Internet and its impact on business and strategies. A model for estimating R&D expenses is illustrated by way of an example as are other concepts introduced in the chapter. A discussion and analysis of the strategies and best practices associated with balance sheet–related topics is included. It concludes with a case study in which a board of directors decides management's business model is broken and appoints an energetic, experienced director to develop and implement a plan to reinvent the business.

Chapter 7 is solely devoted to the measurement of Productivity and Operating Margin and the role they play in the long-term performance of a firm. A model that quantifies productivity is developed first. Then in order to make it a useful tool for estimating profitability, it is modified to incorporate the concept of operating margin, a predictor of future performance. The models are then explained in terms of manufacturing and service environments. Examples are used to illustrate the power of the concepts that have been introduced. The chapter concludes with a case study that portrays how a management team systematically developed productivity and operating margin improvement plans for an underperforming company.

Chapter 8 examines the question of maximizing profitability from another perspective. It is based on the premise that there is a relationship between what a customer is prepared to pay for a deliverable and how a company should be spending its money. It starts with a definition of the Expense Coverage Ratio (ExpCR) and then systematically goes through a process of creating alignment between the value a customer perceives in a deliverable and the money the company spends responding to the customers' needs. Examples that illustrate how the ratio can be used to predict future performance are included, as are strategies and best practices for managing the ExpCR. The concluding case study illustrates how a management team used the concepts embedded in the ExpCR to dramatically improve the company's performance.

Chapter 9 examines Leverage. It begins with a dialogue on debt and leverage and then proceeds to outline how interest rates for business loans are priced using something called the "London Inter-Bank Offered Rate" (LIBOR). A discussion of creditworthiness, security, covenants, financial performance, tenor, and priority is followed by an introduction to the various forms of debt financing. The import of creditworthiness in establishing the ultimate pricing of a security is addressed as is the role played by the various credit rating agencies. The concept of Return on Equity (ROE) is introduced, followed by the development of the ROE driver equation and various examples that illustrate the tradeoffs involved by various capital structures involving debt and equity. The chapter is all about capital structure. The case study illustrates how a management team went about financing future growth.

Chapter 10, the concluding chapter, is designed to bring together the concepts associated with understanding financial statements; how the management's day-to-day operational strategies (including financial and investment strategies) discussed throughout this book can influence value creation; and how all of this can be used to build or modify a business plan. It begins with a review of the key elements of financial performance and the financial statements. This is followed by a case study that portrays how a potential investor takes data that is presented to her in an investment prospectus, carefully reviews its contents, and then proceeds to modify the business plan based on her assumptions. She then builds a set of financial statements that reflect what she perceives to be a risk-adjusted view of the possible financial performance of the investment opportunity.

Lawrence C. Karlson
Palm Beach Gardens, Florida
February 2015

Acknowledgments

THE FOLLOWING PEOPLE REVIEWED the entire manuscript and provided the author with numerous comments and suggestions:

Patrick L. Edsell, Private Investor and Business Consultant
James A. Gabriel, Director, Harris Group, Inc.
Yuanshun Li, PhD, Assistant Professor of Finance, Ryerson University
Deborah Lee Karlson, BA

Portions of the manuscript were reviewed by:

Jason Spera, CEO at Aegis Software Inc.
Dennis Pizzica, Vice President and Treasurer at Berwind Corporation
Graydon Karlson, Senior Manager at Ernst &Young LLP

Foreword

ALMOST EVERY SUCCESSFUL PERSON I know will tell you their success was, in many ways, the result of having a mentor or role model early in their life or career. That was certainly the case for me.

I met Lawrence in the fall of 1984 when he was hiring a CFO for Bofors Electronics, a small technology company of which he had recently become CEO. I had sent my resume to Heidrick and Struggles, where it happened to land on the desk of the recruiter who was doing the search for Lawrence. It was my lucky day. The recruiter was a West Point graduate and a GE alumnus, and I was an Air Force Academy graduate and a GE alumnus, so my background resonated with the recruiter and he presented it to Lawrence. Of course, there were several qualified candidates, but Lawrence wanted a CFO who was "light but bright" and selected me for the job. That was the beginning of an incredible business and life experience for me.

Lawrence is the quintessential success story. He grew up in a small town in Canada and worked his way through Ryerson University, graduating from the engineering program. From there, he focused his energy, ambition, and talent on a career that, in a few short years, led to becoming President of Fisher and Porter's U.S. operations, while earning an MBA from Wharton along the way. Soon thereafter, Lawrence would join Bofors Electronics and hire me to work with him.

The thing that struck me immediately was that Lawrence had developed a comprehensive model for running businesses. With an MBA and a Master's in Economics, I had a pretty good education and a fair amount of experience when I joined Lawrence, but I had never put it all together into a model for running businesses as he had. His model made an incredible amount of sense and, more importantly, it worked. Lawrence used his model to manage the Bofors Electronics companies and subsequently the Pharos AB and Spectra-Physics AB companies. In every case, these companies produced exceptional returns for the owners and shareholders.

Lawrence's business acumen impressed a lot of other people as well. After selling one of our companies to Berwind Corporation, he was asked to join their Board. Subsequently, a number of other companies, including AmeriSource Inc., Campbell Soup Company, CDI Corporation, and H & E Equipment Services Inc., invited Lawrence to join their boards. All of these companies recognized the power and effectiveness of Lawrence's approach to business.

That brings us to this book. It started out in 1990 as a presentation he made to the key employees and leadership team of Spectra-Physics, a company we had recently acquired. Spectra-Physics was a major acquisition for our company, and it was critical that it be successful. We knew that for that to happen we would have to instill our management philosophy and culture quickly. So Lawrence created a presentation that he gave to several hundred key employees in the United States, Europe, and Asia over a couple of months. In his usual charismatic style, he explained his philosophy for creating value and articulated a business model for making it happen. That worldwide presentation was a catalyst for the success of the acquisition, not only because the overall concepts were understandable and appealing to his audience, but because Lawrence had the ability to make people believe that they, too, would be successful if his concepts were implemented.

Over the years, Lawrence has continued to refine his thoughts, with this book being the culmination of that effort. The reader should recognize three things. First, Lawrence supports his ideas rigorously through equations and mathematical models. While you don't need to understand the quantitative aspects of the book to extract value from it, if you do, you will have a better understanding of how everything fits together. Second, by working through the case studies and examples, you will get a thorough understanding of the business model that Lawrence used throughout his incredibly successful career. Finally, pay close attention to the *takeaways* at the beginning of every chapter. These represent the basic principles that underlie Lawrence's business model.

While many successful people write autobiographies, it's not often that an accomplished business leader takes the time and makes the effort to put his entire approach to business in writing. At times, Lawrence's ideas may seem unconventional, but I'm sure you will have many "Aha" moments as you read his detailed descriptions of what makes a business tick. Keep reading, and you'll soon understand what Lawrence taught me over the past 30 years.

Patrick L. Edsell
Menlo Park, California

CHAPTER ONE

Basic Concepts*

CHAPTER 1 TAKEAWAYS

- There are only two business reasons to own or invest in a company. One is because the company will grow its earnings and therefore value. The other is to receive dividends from the cash flow. In practice, it is often a combination of both.
- Management teams perform better if they are measured against some set of criteria. One of the criteria that is of interest to investors is the return provided by funds invested in the business. A measurement of this is Return on Capital Employed (ROCE).
- In a general sense, managers are tasked with two key objectives: (1) Find attractive investments, and (2) deliver attractive returns. Since ROCE compares what management delivers (Net Operating Profit after Tax) to what has been invested in the company (Capital Employed), it is a good measure of management's effectiveness.
- In some instances, a decline in cash flow can be avoided by cutting costs. In fact, management can increase cash flow by disinvesting in the business. However, in today's business climate, increasing cash flow by expense control doesn't work for very long. Eventually cost cutting is a dead end and the only remaining road to increasing shareholder value is growth. Growth opportunities don't just come along. A company has to be committed to investing for growth in order to get it and even then success is highly uncertain. Unlike sustaining investments, investments focused on growth inherently involve more risk. The upside is, of course, the possibility of a better return.
- Making a choice between sustaining or growth investments or investing for both is not simply a matter of money. In practice it (money) frequently turns out to be the least important resource. Investments directed at growth require

(continued)

*The reader may notice minor discrepancies in the calculations in this chapter. When this occurs, it is the result of rounding.

ideas and sometimes new technologies. Furthermore, it's not very often that a management team that is outstanding when it comes to cost control and optimizing the productive level of sustaining investments is also good at managing a company for growth. While managing the process and resources associated with putting a company on a growth track can be learned, it takes time—often lots of time and many lessons learned. In practice, most companies make both sustaining and growth investments at the same time. Successful companies have learned that each category of investment has its own prerequisites and culture and therefore staff and manage accordingly.

- The key drivers of Cash Flow are Net Income, Investments, and Return on Capital Employed.
- Without Net Income, a company doesn't generate any cash from operations.
- The first thing that one should notice when examining a Cash Flow Statement is that "Cash" is missing. The reason for this is when it comes to the Cash Flow Statement the "Change in Cash" is what the statement determines.
- When considering the impact that Working Capital has on the Cash Flow Statement, it's the changes (Δ) in the various accounts that are important.

INTRODUCTION

The underlying assumption for the preparation of the material in this chapter is that the reader has limited comfort and experience with the financial statements and the language of business. The chapter begins the education process by creating a general expression for Net Income (NI), followed by a discussion of Earnings before Interest and Taxes (EBIT) and Earnings before Interest, Taxes and Depreciation (EBITDA).

Next the Balance Sheet is used to define Capital Employed (CE) and Return on Capital Employed (ROCE) and then to combine these expressions with the equation(s) developed for Net Income (NI). After a brief discussion of the kinds of Investments a company makes, the Cash Flow Statement is introduced to help define cash flow in terms of Cash Flow from Operating Activities (CFfOA), Cash Flow after Investing Activities (CFaIA), and Cash Generated/Used (CGU).[1] Finally the Income Statement is worked backward, so to speak, where an expression is developed that describes the Required Revenue necessary to generate a given level of Net Income using the various components of the Income Statement.

FINANCIAL STATEMENTS

When one opens a financial report or a set of financial statements, the first statement encountered is usually the Income Statement, followed by a Balance Sheet and Cash Flow Statement. There isn't anything sacrosanct about this order of presentation. In fact they could be presented in any order. One of the reasons the presentation conventions have evolved in this manner is by doing so they present the financial affairs in a logical order. Stated simply, the Income Statement presents how a business has done during a period

[1] Other terminology used includes: CFF (cash flow from financing), CFI (cash flow from investing), and CFO (cash flow from operations).

of time (usually the most recent period, i.e., month, quarter, or year). The Balance Sheet is a presentation of the Company's capital structure and ability to make investments. The Cash Flow Statement shows where the business generated cash and what it did with it and is developed from the accounts in the Income Statement and Balance Sheet. In the discussion that follows, the definitions implied by the simplified financial statements shown in Tables 1-1, 1-3, and 1-5 will be used.[2]

As its title implies, this chapter deals with basic concepts. The intent is to quickly move through the basic concepts associated with financial statements such as the Income Statement, Balance Sheet, and Cash Flow Statement and give the reader an overview. An in-depth discussion of this material and more will be provided in the chapters that follow.

THE INCOME STATEMENT

By inspecting Table 1-1, it's apparent that the Net Income (NI) can be expressed as

$$\begin{aligned} \mathit{Net\ Income} = {} & \mathit{Revenue} - \mathit{Cost\ of\ Goods\ Sold} - \mathit{Operating\ Expenses} \\ & - \mathit{Depreciation\ \&\ Amortization} + \mathit{Interest\ Income} \\ & - \mathit{Interest\ Expense} - \mathit{Taxes\ Paid} \end{aligned} \qquad [1\text{-}1]^{3}$$

or

$$NI = Rev - COGS - OpExp - D\ \&\ A \pm NetInt - TaxesPaid \qquad [1\text{-}2]$$

where:

$\pm$ *NetInt* is a short form way of expressing "+ *Interest Income* – *Interest Expense*"

TABLE 1-1 Basic Income Statement

Period Ending DD/MM/YYYY $(000)'s		
Revenues (Rev)		100,000
Cost of Goods Sold (COGS)		(40,000)
Gross Margin (GM)		60,000
Operating Expenses (OpExp)		(43,500)
Earnings before Interest, Taxes, and D&A (EBITDA)		16,500
Depreciation and Amortization (D&A)		(5,000)
Earnings before Interest and Taxes (EBIT)		11,500
Net Interest Income/Expense (NetInt)		0
Earnings before Tax (EBT)		11,500
Taxes Paid (TaxesPaid) @	40%	(4,600)
Net Income (NI)		6,900

[2]The numbers used in Tables 1-1, 1-3, and 1-5 are illustrative only and not intended to represent a typical company.

[3]Revenue (Rev) and Net Revenues (NetRev) will be used interchangeably throughout this book.

While Equation [1-2] is a solid definition of Net Income, it is often more useful to break it into its various constituents such as Earnings before Interest, Taxes, Depreciation and Amortization (EBITDA), Earnings before Interest and Taxes (EBIT), Earnings before Taxes (EBT), and Net Income (NI).

The EBITDA, EBIT, EBT, and Net Income Relationships

Again referring to Table 1-1, it should be clear that the Gross Margin (GM) can be defined in terms of the Revenues (Rev) and the Cost of Goods Sold (COGS).

Revenues represent the dollar amount the Company has charged its customers for its deliverable. The Cost of Goods Sold is the cost the company incurred producing the deliverable, and Gross Margin is what the Company has left over to cover Operating Expenses, Depreciation, Amortization, Interest, Taxes, and Profit.

$$GM = Rev - COGS \qquad [1\text{-}3]$$

In addition to the cost incurred to produce the deliverable, the Company also incurred costs such as Sales, Marketing, Research and Development, and Administration. These costs are known as Operating Expenses. The difference between the GM and OpExp is called Earnings before Interest, Taxes, and Depreciation and Amortization (EBITDA).

$$EBITDA = GM - OpExp \qquad [1\text{-}4]$$

Depreciation represents a charge to the Income Statement for Property, Plant and Equipment (PP&E) that has been purchased and is being expensed over its useful life. Amortization is similar except that it pertains to Intangible Assets the Company may have purchased such as patents, which, like PP&E, are expensed over their useful life. The difference between EBITDA and Depreciation and Amortization is the Earnings before Interest and Taxes (EBIT).[4]

$$EBIT = EBITDA - D\,\&\,A \qquad [1\text{-}5]$$

Then allowing for the impact of Net Interest[5] (NetInt) on Earnings before Interest and Taxes provides Earnings before Taxes (EBT).

$$EBT = EBIT \pm NetInt \qquad [1\text{-}6]$$

[4] For an explanation of how Depreciation and Amortization are calculated and treated refer to the section in this chapter that deals with the Balance Sheet.

[5] There are two types of interest. Interest Income (interest earned on cash and investments) and Interest Expense (interest paid on debt). Net Interest can be either positive (interest income > interest expense) or negative (interest expense > interest income), hence the term ± NetInt.

Subtracting Taxes Paid[6] (TaxesPaid) from the Earnings before Taxes yields the Company's Net Income (NI).

$$NI = EBT - TaxesPaid \tag{1-7}$$

Since Taxes Paid are a function of the Earnings before Tax and the Tax Rate (TR), then

$$TaxesPaid = (EBT)(TR) \tag{1-8}$$

Substituting in Equation [1-7],

$$NI = EBT - (EBT)(TR) \tag{1-9}$$

Simplifying,

$$NI = (EBT)(1 - TR) \tag{1-10}$$

NI can be expressed in terms of EBIT or EBITDA. Substituting the results of Equation [1-6] for EBT in Equation [1-10] gives an expression for NI in terms of EBIT.

$$NI = (EBIT \pm NetInt)(1 - TR) \tag{1-11}$$

To get an NI expression in terms of EBITDA it is necessary to once again refer to Table 1-1 and Equation [1-5] and then substitute for EBIT in Equation [1-11].

$$EBIT = EBITDA - D\ \&\ A \tag{1-5}$$

$$NI = (EBITDA - D\ \&\ A \pm NetInt)(1 - TR) \tag{1-12}$$

Equation [1-12] says that for any given EBITDA, a company's Net Income is a function of the Depreciation and Amortization associated with investments made in prior periods, any interest paid or received and taxes.

This is not a book about taxes. So, other than going on record stating that management should employ the best professionals they can afford to help them minimize taxes there will be little more said on the subject.

Interest is of course a consequence of cash on hand or debt, which is a component of the company's capital structure (how the business is financed by the owners). Debt and its implications will be revisited when leverage is discussed in Chapter 9.

Depreciation and Amortization, as stated earlier, is a period expense that results from depreciating or amortizing assets over their useful life. Once money is spent on an investment, the investment is capitalized on the company's balance sheet and then written off by periodic charges to the D&A account on the Balance Sheet via the Income Statement over the asset's useful life. Successful management teams consistently make

[6]Taxes Paid consist primarily of federal and state income taxes. Taxes such as municipal, wage, property, and so on are normally included in Cost of Goods Sold or Operating Expenses.

investments that provide a recurring contribution to income greater than the associated periodic D & A.[7]

Special Case: Ignoring the Interest Component

While debt and associated costs must be thoughtfully managed, when it comes to creating value, management's prime responsibility is to focus on what happens to the money invested in the business. In fact well-managed private and public companies don't want their management teams spending a lot of time on financial engineering. As far as management is concerned capital structure need only be addressed periodically when the company needs funds to finance such things as a major acquisition. Investors want their team to concentrate on creating value, which is done by growing the top and bottom lines of the Income Statement. When it's appropriate to ignore the "Interest" component, then Equations [1-11] and [1-12] become Equations [1-13] and [1-14] respectively.[8]

$$NI = (EBIT)(1 - TR) \quad [1\text{-}13]$$

$$NI = (EBITDA - D \,\&\, A)(1 - TR) \quad [1\text{-}14]$$

Example 1-1: Calculating Net Income

Using the data in Table 1-1 and Equations [1-2], [1-11], and [1-12] show that the Net Income in each case is $6,900,000.

Applying Equation [1-2] and substituting values for each of the terms from Table 1-1 gives an NI of $6,900,000 as expected.

$$NI = Rev - COGS - OpExp - D \,\&\, A \pm NetInt - TaxesPaid \quad [1\text{-}2]$$

$$NI = 100{,}000{,}000 - 40{,}000{,}000 - 43{,}500{,}000 - 5{,}000{,}000 - 4{,}600{,}000 = \$6{,}900{,}000$$

Similarly, applying Equation [1-11] gives the same result.

$$NI = (EBIT \pm NetInt)(1 - TR) \quad [1\text{-}11]$$

$$NI = (11{,}500{,}000 - 0)(1 - 0.40) = (11{,}500{,}000)(0.60) = \$6{,}900{,}000$$

Finally, substituting in Equation [1-12] shows that all three equations yield the same amount for the Net Income.

$$NI = (EBITDA - D \,\&\, A \pm NetInt)(1 - TR) \quad [1\text{-}12]$$

$$NI = (16{,}500{,}000 - 5{,}000{,}000 - 0)(1 - 0.40) = (11{,}500{,}000)(0.60) = \$6{,}900{,}000$$

---

[7] Depreciation and Amortization are discussed in more detail in subsequent chapters.

[8] This assumption is almost always valid during the initial stages of the business planning process.

Why EBITDA?

The reader may have noticed that after analyzing the Income Statement in terms of various definitional equations the discussion seems to have settled on a couple of equations built around EBITDA. As will be seen later, it turns out that EBITDA is often an excellent proxy for a company's ability to generate cash flow.

There are only two business reasons to own or invest in a company. One is that the company will grow its earnings and therefore value. The other is to receive dividends from the cash flow. In practice, it is often a combination of both. In order to generate cash a company must be profitable and have Net Income.[9]

Furthermore, because of the correlation between EBITDA and Cash Flow, EBITDA can be used as a proxy for Cash Flow and therefore it is useful in valuing a business. The valuation of companies is the subject of Chapter 4. However, since Chapter 4 is several chapters away, the role that EBITDA plays in valuation is illustrated by Example 1-2. Before moving on to the example it's necessary to say a few words about something called an *industry multiple*.

Industry Multiple

Briefly, an industry multiple is an indication of the value investors assign to the industrial sector a particular company serves and the company's ability to create EBITDA and future cash flows. These multiples can vary over a wide range from near "1+" to "20+." For the purpose of this example the industry multiple is assumed to be nine (9).

Example 1-2: Using EBITDA to Value a Company

Companies can be valued in a number of ways, including the present value of cash flows and/or an appropriate industry multiple. When the applicable multiple is known, the value calculation is straightforward. There are instances where the multiple isn't readily available, nor for that matter are the cash flows. In instances such as this, an estimate of an industry multiple can be made by making use of historical and forecasted financial statements and using the Revenue and EBITDA growth rates to estimate a suitable multiple.

(a) Valuing a Company Using the Industry Multiple

In its simplest form a company can be valued by using the following relationship:

$$Value = (EBITDA)(Industry\ Multiple) - Debt + Excess\ Cash \qquad [1\text{-}15]$$

---

[9] Here the reference is to cash flow from operations. As will be seen later, cash can be generated from working capital by reducing accounts receivable and inventory and extending accounts payable. However, once working capital has been optimized, no further cash can be generated and in this sense this cash flow is nonrecurring.

In the interest of simplicity it is assumed that the cash shown on the balance sheet in the following and other examples is necessary for the day-to-day operations of the company and therefore the excess cash is zero and Equation [1-15] becomes Equation [1-16].

$$Value = (EBITDA)(Industry\ Multiple) - Debt \tag{1-16}$$

The company represented by the Income Statement (Table 1-1) has an EBITDA of $16,500,000. According to the Balance Sheet (Table 1-3) the company doesn't have any Debt. Since the industry multiple is 9, an indication of the company's value is obtained by substituting in Equation [1-16].

$$Value = (16{,}500{,}000)(9) - 0 = \$148{,}500{,}000$$

If the company had $10,000,000 of debt, then the value would be

$$Value = (16{,}500{,}000)(9) - 10{,}000{,}000 = 148{,}500{,}000 - 10{,}000{,}000 = \$138{,}500{,}000$$

Why is debt subtracted? Consider the following. Assume someone purchased the company for $148,500,000 and rather than zero debt, it had $30,000,000 of debt. The buyer would be assuming responsibility for the $30,000,000 obligation. Since this debt ultimately has to be paid off, the total cost to the buyer would be $178,500,000. Now, one may note that the company has cash and it's reasonable to ask who gets the cash when a company is sold. The answer is, it all depends. Typically if the cash is necessary to fund the day-to-day operations (Working Capital), then it stays with the company. If there is excess cash, the seller normally keeps the excess.

(b) Valuing the Company If the Industry Multiple Isn't Known

The valuation in Part (a) of this example is only an indication of value. The correct way to value a business is to calculate the present value (PV) of future cash flows. However, since present value techniques are the subject of a future chapter, this method is not available at this time. So absent a PV valuation, other indications of value are the Revenue and EBITDA growth rates. The historical and projected Revenue and the EBITDAs for the Company with the Income Statement presented in Table 1-1 are shown in Table 1-2.

TABLE 1-2 Valuing a Company If the Industry Multiple Is Unknown

Historical and Projected Year Revenue and EBITDA in $(000)'s						
Year	***n* – 2**	***n* – 1**	***n***	***n* + 1**	***n* + 2**	***n* + 3**
Revenue	87,000	93,000	100,000	109,000	120,000	130,000
EBITDA	12,200	14,000	16,500	17,600	19,000	21,400

Assuming the forecast for Year *n* is accurate and using the data in Table 1-2, the Historical Compound Annual Growth Rate of Revenue, $CAGR_{HR}$, is calculated with the assistance of Equation [1-17]:[10]

$$CAGR_{HR} = \left[\left(\frac{Rev_n}{Rev_{n-2}}\right)^{1/years} - 1\right] \quad [1\text{-}17]$$

Substituting in Equation [1-17]

$$CAGR_{HR} = \left[\left(\frac{Rev_n}{Rev_{n-2}}\right)^{1/years} - 1\right] = \left[\left(\frac{100,000,000}{87,000,000}\right)^{1/2} - 1\right]$$

$$= \sqrt[2]{1.149} - 1 = 1.0721 - 1.0 = 0.0721$$

$$\%CAGR_{HR} = 7.2\%$$

Similarly, the Forecasted Compound Annual Growth Rate of Revenue ($CAGR_{FR}$) is calculated by using Equation [1-18].

$$CAGR_{FR} = \left[\left(\frac{Rev_{n+3}}{Rev_n}\right)^{1/years} - 1\right] \quad [1\text{-}18]$$

Substituting in Equation [1-18]

$$CAGR_{FR} = \left[\left(\frac{Rev_{n+3}}{Rev_n}\right)^{1/years} - 1\right] = \left[\left(\frac{130,000,000}{100,000,000}\right)^{1/3} - 1\right]$$

$$= \sqrt[3]{1.3} - 1 = 1.0914 - 1.0 = 0.0914$$

$$\%CAGR_{FR} = 9.1\%$$

Assuming the historical growth rate has been a steady 7.2% and the projected Revenue growth rate of 9.1% is credible, these growth rates can be helpful in estimating the Company's value to the extent they are reasonable proxies for an industry multiple. The historical growth rate is a fact. The question is: Is the projected growth rate believable? If it is forecasted to come about as a result of increased investment year by year in Sales and Marketing, Research and Development, Plant and Equipment, and Administration during the forecast period (implying that management intends to spur growth by investment) rather than grow Operating Expenses at a slower rate to increase the bottom line, then a growth rate of 9.1% is realistic. On the other hand, it does represent a healthy increase and a prudent buyer would take this into account. Be that as it may, given the information at hand, the only conclusion that can be reached by applying this methodology is to assume the growth rates are indicative of a suitable multiple and that the multiple range in this case can be said to be a range of 7 to 9.

The average EBITDA for the period $n-2$ to n is

$$Average\ EBITDA_H = \frac{(12,200,000 + 14,000,000 + 16,500,00)}{3} = \$14,233,000$$

[10] See Appendix C for the development of this relationship.

And for the period n to $n+3$, EBITDA is

$$Average\ EDBITDA_F = \frac{(16,500,00 + 17,600,00 + 19,000,000 + 21,400,00)}{4}$$
$$= \$18,625,000$$

Recalling Equation [1-16],

$$Value = (EBITDA)(Industry\ Multiple) - Debt \quad [1\text{-}16]$$

The company doesn't have any debt or excess cash, hence the implied value is

$$Value = (EBITDA)(7\ to\ 9) - 0 = (EBITDA)(7\ to\ 9)$$

The EBITDA to use can get a little complicated depending on the buyer and what they are comfortable with. One way of coming up with an EBITDA is to assume the average of the Historical and Forecasted EBITDAs. Since the EBITDA proposed is the average of the two averages, one might be tempted to use an average of the multiple range (8). However, this company is very profitable and has demonstrated it can grow, and grow consistently, hence there is a strong argument for using the high end of the range. Hence:

$$Value = (EBITDA)(9) = \left(\frac{(14,233,000 + 18,625,000)}{2}\right)(9) = (16,429,000)(9)$$
$$= \$147,861,000$$

or approximately $148 million using these assumptions.

However, as can be seen, the averaging method previously chosen yields an average EBITDA of $16,429,000, which is almost the same as the current year's EBITDA of $16,500,000, so one could argue that a value of $148 million is at the low end of the value range. If the average of the future EBITDAs were used and a multiple of 9 applied, the value would be closer to $168 million.

$$Value = (EBITDA)(9) = (18,625,000)(9) = \$167,625,000$$

THE BALANCE SHEET

The first thing to note about the Balance Sheet shown in Table 1-3 is by definition:

$$Total\ Assets = Total\ Liabilities + Total\ Shareholders'\ Equity\ (TSHE) \quad [1\text{-}19]$$

or

$$Total\ Assets = Total\ Liabilities + TSHE \quad [1\text{-}20]$$

TABLE 1-3 Basic Balance Sheet

DD/MM/YYYY $(000)'s			
Current Assets		**Current Liabilities**	
Cash	750	Accounts Payable	2,500
Accounts Receivable	6,250	Taxes Payable	0
Inventory	5,000	Short-Term Debt	0
Total Current Assets	12,000	**Total Current Liabilities**	2,500
Fixed Assets			
PP&E at Cost	30,000	**Long-Term Debt**	0
Less Accumulated Depreciation	5,000		
Net Fixed Assets	25,000	**Total Liabilities**	2,500
Intangible Assets		**Shareholders' Equity**	
Goodwill and Other Intangible Assets	0	Paid-in Capital	50,000
Less Accumulated Amortization	0	Retained Earnings	(15,500)
Net Intangible Assets	0	**Total Shareholders' Equity**	34,500
Total Assets	37,000	**Total Liabilities + TSHE**	37,000

If Equation [1-19] isn't satisfied, the Balance Sheet isn't balanced and there is something wrong with the numbers.

Following the model used when analyzing the Basic Income Statement, an inspection of the Balance Sheet in Table 1-3 results in a number of equations that describe the relationships between the various accounts.

$$\textit{Total Assets} = \textit{Total Current Liabilities} + \textit{Net Fixed Assets} + \textit{Net Intangible Assets} \quad [1\text{-}21]$$

Current Assets consists of Cash, Accounts Receivable (money customers owe the company), and Inventory. Therefore:

$$\textit{Current Assets} = \textit{Cash} + \textit{Accounts Receivable} + \textit{Inventory} \quad [1\text{-}22]$$

Similarly, Fixed Assets consists of Property, Plant, and Equipment (PP&E), which represent the fixed assets the Company needs to produce its deliverable, and Accumulated Depreciation, which represents how much of these assets have been expensed through the Income Statement as they wear out.

For example, if a hard asset is purchased for $5,000,000 and has an estimated useful life of 10 years, then the amount the asset would be depreciated each year would be $500,000 ($5,000,000/10)[11] and after two years the accumulated depreciation for this asset would be $1,000,000 ($500,000 * 2).

All of this can be expressed as

$$\textit{Net Fixed Assets} = \textit{PP\&E at Cost} - \textit{Accumulated Depreciation} \quad [1\text{-}23]$$

[11] This is known as the *straight line* method of depreciation. Others include the *declining balance* and *units of production* methods.

Intangible Assets includes such things as Goodwill, which is created when an Asset is purchased at a price in excess of its book value. Other Intangible Assets are such things as patents, non-competes, and customer lists if acquired as part of an M&A transaction.[12]

Again an example may be helpful. If a patent acquired as part of an acquisition of a company was valued at $3,000,000 and had 10 years remaining before expiring, it would be amortized at a rate of $300,000 ($3,000,000/10) per year for 10 years and at such time the accumulated amortization associated with the patent would be $3,000,000, leaving a net tangible value for this asset of zero.

Net Intangible Assets can be defined by Equation [1-24]:

$$\begin{aligned} \textit{Net Intangible Assets} = {} & \textit{Goodwill \& Other Intangible Assets} \\ & - \textit{Accumulated Amortization} \end{aligned} \qquad [1\text{-}24]$$

Applying the same process to the Liability side of the Balance sheet:

$$\begin{aligned} \textit{Total Liabilities} + \textit{TSHE} = {} & \textit{Total Current Liabilities} + \textit{Long-Term Debt} \\ & + \textit{Total Shareholders' Equity} \end{aligned} \qquad [1\text{-}25]$$

Current Liabilities consists of Accounts Payable,[13] which is money the company owes its suppliers, Taxes Payable, and Short-Term Debt, which is interest-bearing debt that has to be repaid in less than one year.

$$\begin{aligned} \textit{Total Current Liabilities} = {} & \textit{Accounts Payable} + \textit{Taxes Payable} \\ & + \textit{Short-Term Debt} \end{aligned} \qquad [1\text{-}26]$$

Long-Term Debt is interest-bearing debt and has a tenor of more than one year before it has to be repaid or rolled over.

Total Shareholders' Equity is the sum of the money the company took in when it raised capital by selling shares in the Company to investors and Retained Earnings, which is the sum of all the profits and losses of the Company since inception minus any dividends that have been paid.

$$\textit{Total Shareholders' Equity} = \textit{Paid-in Capital} + \textit{Retained Earnings} \qquad [1\text{-}27]$$

Return on Capital Employed

Management teams perform better if they are measured against some set of criteria. One of the criteria that is of interest to investors is the return provided by funds invested

---

[12] A lot has been said here about Fixed and Intangible Assets. Don't be concerned if it strikes you as being confusing. The purpose is to expose the reader to the terminology and nothing more. All of this will be discussed in more detail in subsequent chapters.

[13] Accrued Liabilities are assumed to be included in Accounts Payable to simplify the discussion.

in the business. A measurement of this is "Return on Capital Employed." The classical definition for Return on Capital Employed (ROCE) is:

$$ROCE = \frac{NOPAT}{CE} \quad [1\text{-}28]$$

where:

NOPAT = Net Operating Profit after Tax and *CE* = Capital Employed

Before Equation [1-28] can be used it's necessary to define NOPAT in terms of Income Statement terminology. The Income Statement in Table 1-1 has several line items such as EBITDA, EBIT, and EBT that state income at different levels. EBITDA and EBIT are clearly operations oriented. EBT is not, because it would include the impact of any interest expense or income. Interest is a result of capital structure (Debt the company takes on to its balance sheet) or interest income generated by any excess cash and isn't operating income per se. Therefore, the income classification that states the Operating Profit is EBIT. To comply with the definition it has to be tax affected, hence the expression for ROCE becomes

$$ROCE = \frac{EBIT - TaxesPaid}{\text{CE}} = \frac{EBIT - (EBIT)(TaxRate)}{CE}$$

$$ROCE = \frac{EBIT - (EBIT)(TR)}{CE} \quad [1\text{-}29]$$

or

$$ROCE = \frac{(EBIT)(1 - TR)}{CE} \quad [1\text{-}30]$$

In a general sense, managers are tasked with two key objectives: (1) Find attractive investments, and (2) deliver attractive returns. Since ROCE compares what management delivers (Net Operating Profit after Tax) to what has been invested in the company (Capital Employed), ROCE is a key measure of how well management is performing and is often used in the annual evaluation process of management teams.

Capital Employed

Capital Employed (CE) can be defined with the assistance of the Balance Sheet (Table 1-3).

By definition, the Capital Employed in a business is the capital provided by equity holders and holders of equity-like instruments, earnings retained in the business, and interest-bearing debt (such as bank loans, bonds, private placements, and so on). Liabilities such as Accounts Payable and Taxes Payable and so forth are not considered as Capital Employed because they do not result in any financing cost to the company.

As can be seen by referring to Table 1-3, the capital provided by the equity holders is Total Shareholders' Equity plus the interest-bearing capital provided by debt holders (Short-Term Debt[14] and Long-Term Debt):

$$CE = \textit{Total Shareholders' Equity} + \textit{Short-Term Debt} + \textit{Long-Term Debt} \quad [1\text{-}31]^{15}$$

or

$$CE = TSHE + STD + LTD \quad [1\text{-}32]$$

or

$$CE = TSHE + IBD \quad [1\text{-}33]$$

where:

TSHE = Total Shareholders' Equity, *STD* = Short-Term Debt, *LTD* = Long-Term Debt, and *IBD* = STD + LTD or Interest Bearing Debt

It is worthwhile to note that Accounts Payable and Taxes Payable (and other similar accounts) are also debt. They are excluded from Capital Employed because normally they are not interest bearing.

Example 1-3: Calculating ROCE

The Income Statement (Table 1-1) states the EBIT for year *n* is $11,500,000. The Balance Sheet (Table 1-3) shows that Total Shareholders' Equity is $34,500,000 and that the company is debt free.

Substituting in Equation [1-32] the Capital Employed is calculated to be

$$CE = TSHE + STD + LTD \quad [1\text{-}32]$$

$$CE = 34{,}500{,}000 + 0 + 0 = \$34{,}500{,}000$$

Substituting for EBIT, Tax Rate (TR), and CE in Equation [1-30],

$$ROCE = \frac{(EBIT)(1-TR)}{CE} \quad [1\text{-}30]$$

$$ROCE = \frac{(11{,}500{,}000)(1-0.40)}{34{,}500{,}000} = \frac{(11{,}500{,}000)(0.60)}{34{,}500{,}000} = 0.20^{16}$$

$$ROCE = 20\%$$

Drivers of Return on Capital Employed

If ROCE is to be used as a measurement of performance, then it seems logical that management would want to understand what drives ROCE. A more insightful understanding

[14] Debt due for repayment in one year or less.

[15] Capital Employed can also be defined as: CE = Total Assets – Current Liabilities + Short-Term Debt.

[16] An ROCE of this magnitude produced on a consistent basis would be attractive to many investors.

of the drivers of ROCE can be obtained by examining the relationships between ROCE and the Income Statement accounts.

Recall that Equation [1-30] defined ROCE as

$$ROCE = \frac{(EBIT)(1-TR)}{CE} \quad [1\text{-}30]$$

To introduce EBITDA it's necessary to recall Equation [1-5], which defined EBIT as

$$EBIT = EBITDA - D \,\&\, A \quad [1\text{-}5]$$

Substituting for EBIT in Equation [1-30] gives an expression for ROCE in terms of Income Statement variables and Capital Employed.

$$ROCE = \frac{(EBITDA - D \,\&\, A)(1-TR)}{CE} \quad [1\text{-}34]$$ [17]

Since

$$CE = TSHE + STD + LTD \quad [1\text{-}32]$$

then

$$ROCE = \frac{(EBITDA - D \,\&\, A)(1-TR)}{TSHE + STD + LTD} \quad [1\text{-}35]$$

Equation [1-34] defines the impact EBITDA, Depreciation and Amortization, Taxes, and Capital Employed have on the Return on Capital Employed. Managers have the ability to impact all of these variables. As mentioned earlier, tax minimization is best handled by getting good advice. Depreciation and Amortization is the price paid for making investments to drive Revenue, *EBIT*, and ultimately Net Income. The amount of Capital Employed is a consequence of the capital structure (combination of debt and equity) and how well management manages the company's balance sheet. Equation [1-35] clearly spells out how important it is for management to do its homework up front, select the best investment opportunities, and aggressively manage them and the balance sheet if they are to deliver returns in line with expectations.

Now that the groundwork for understanding the drivers of the Return on Capital Employed has been laid, it's appropriate to turn attention to cash flow and what drives it. However, before that is done another kind of capital needs to be discussed.

Working Capital

Working Capital (WC) is defined as

$$WC = Current\ Assets - Current\ Liabilities \quad [1\text{-}36]$$

---

[17] The reader can check the result of Equation [1-34] by entering the appropriate values for EBITDA, D&A, NetInt, TR, and CE from Tables 1-1 and 1-3.

It is the Capital that the Company works with on a daily basis to produce its deliverable, collect money, and pay its bills. Equation [1-22] defines Current Assets as consisting of Cash, Accounts Receivable (AR), and Inventory (Inv):

$$Current\ Assets = Cash + Accounts\ Receivable + Inventory \qquad [1\text{-}22]$$

or

$$CA = Cash + AR + Inv \qquad [1\text{-}37]$$

Similarly, Equation [1-26] defines Current Liabilities as consisting of Accounts Payable (AP), Taxes Payable (TP), and Short-Term Debt (STD):

$$Current\ Liabilities = Accounts\ Payable + Taxes\ Payable + Short\text{-}Term\ Debt \qquad [1\text{-}26]$$

or

$$CL = AP + TP + STD \qquad [1\text{-}38]$$

Substituting Equations [1-37] and [1-38] in Equation [1-36] creates an expression for WC in terms of its Balance Sheet accounts.

$$WC = (Cash + AR + Inv) - (AP + TP + STD) \qquad [1\text{-}39]$$

Example 1-4: Calculating the Working Capital for a Company

The Working Capital for the Company represented by the Balance Sheet shown in Table 1-3 can be calculated by using Equation [1-39].

Substituting the values for Cash, Accounts Receivable, Inventory, Accounts Payable, Taxes Payable, and Short-Term Debt into Equation [1-39] gives a value of $9,500,000 for Working Capital.

$$WC = (Cash + AR + Inv) - (AP + TP + STD) \qquad [1\text{-}39]$$

$$WC = (750{,}000 + 6{,}250{,}000 + 5{,}000{,}000) - (2{,}500{,}000 + 0 + 0)$$

$$WC = 12{,}000{,}000 - 2{,}500{,}000 = \$9{,}500{,}000$$

As can be seen from this, calculating the Working Capital employed in a company is a straightforward exercise. However, when it comes to the Cash Flow Statement, dealing with Working Capital is a little more complicated.[18] This will be illustrated in the following example.

---

[18] It's important to note that when calculating the Working Capital for a company from its Balance Sheet "Cash" is included. When it comes to the Cash Flow Statements the Changes in Working Capital do not include cash because one of the objectives of the Cash Flow Statement is to show the impact that changes in Working Capital have on "Cash."

TABLE 1-4 Calculating the Change in Working Capital

$(000)'s	Prior Year	Current Year	Change
Accounts Receivable	5,550	6,250	(700)
Inventory	4,350	5,000	(650)
Accounts Payable	2,400	2,500	100
Taxes Payable	0	0	0
Short-Term Debt	0	0	0
Change in Working Capital			(1,250)

Example 1-5: Calculating the Change in Working Capital

Table 1-4 shows the Working Capital accounts for the company represented by the Balance Sheet shown in Table 1-3 for the Current and Prior Years.

The first thing that one should notice is that "Cash" is missing. The reason for this is when it comes to the Cash Flow Statement the "Change in Cash" is what the statement determines, so there is no need to be concerned about it here. More on how this works later.

When considering the impact that Working Capital has on the Cash Flow Statement, it's the change (Δ) in the various accounts that is important. The usual procedure used to determine the impact of any change in the "Asset" Working Capital accounts is to subtract the "Current Year" from the "Prior Year" to get the correct sign. When this definition is applied to the Accounts Receivable, Equation [1-40] is obtained.

$$\Delta AR = AR_{(PriorYear)} - AR_{(CurrentYear)} \quad [1\text{-}40]$$

Substituting

$$\Delta AR = 5{,}550{,}000 - 6{,}250{,}000 = -\ \$700{,}000$$

Accounts Receivable increased by $700,000. This is $700,000 of Revenues the Company didn't collect during the period covered by the financial statements and represents a use of cash and hence the negative sign.[19] Similarly,

$$\Delta Inv = Inventory_{(PriorYear)} - Inventory_{(CurrentYear)} \quad [1\text{-}41]$$

and

$$\Delta Inv = 4{,}350{,}000 - 5{,}000{,}000 = -\$650{,}000$$

Here the story is the same except this time it's Inventory that increased by $650,000 from the Prior to the Current Year. Cash was used to accumulate the incremental inventory and so this represents another use of cash.

[19] Similarly, if prior and current year Accounts Receivable balances were the same, this would mean that Cash collections equaled Revenues during the year and the impact Accounts Receivable had on Cash would be neutral.

When it comes to changes in the "Liability" Working Capital Accounts the convention is to subtract "Prior Year" from the "Current Year" in order to get the sign correct. The Change in Accounts Payable is calculated with the use of Equation [1-42],

$$\Delta AP = AP_{(CurrentYear)} - AP_{(PriorYear)} \quad [1\text{-}42]$$

and

$$\Delta AP = 2{,}500{,}000 - 2{,}400{,}000 = +\$100{,}000$$

Accounts Payable increased by $100,000. This happened because the Company didn't pay some vendors. By not paying vendors, the Company saved $100,000 in cash.

There is no change in the Taxes Payable or Short-Term Debt, so they don't have any impact on Cash. If there had been a change, the analysis would be the same as for the other Working Capital Accounts.

When calculating The Cash Generated or Used by Working Capital, there is need for a convention. A use of Cash (in this case Accounts Receivable and Inventory) is preceded by a negative sign and a Source of Cash is preceded by a plus sign. Applying the proper sign to each term the ΔWC is simply the algebraic sum of all of the Δ's as shown in Equation [1-43].

$$\Delta WC = \pm\Delta AR \pm \Delta Inv \pm \Delta AP \quad [1\text{-}43]$$

Substituting the calculated values with the appropriate sign in Equation [1-43] gives the Change in Working Capital.

$$\Delta WC = -700{,}000 - 650{,}000 + 100{,}000 = -\$1{,}250{,}000$$

This result agrees with the Change in Working Capital shown in the Cash Flow Statement (Table 1-5).

THE CASH FLOW STATEMENT

Of the three financial statements, the one that seems to trouble managers the most is the Cash Flow Statement. In the section that follows, a very basic statement is introduced. The purpose is to begin a process that will ultimately result in the reader achieving a high level of comfort with this statement. The reader shouldn't be concerned if everything about the statement isn't crystal clear. It will become increasingly so as the reader progresses through this book.

What Drives Cash Flow and Value?

In the chapters that follow, considerable time is devoted to showing why and how "value" is driven by cash flow and how to quantify it using the discounted cash flow

TABLE 1-5 Basic Cash Flow Statement

Period Ending DD/MM/YYYY $(000)'s	
Operating Activities	
Operations	
Net Income (Loss) (NI)	6,900
Depreciation and Amortization (D&A)	5,000
Net Cash Flow from Operations	11,900
Working Capital Accounts	
Change in Current Assets (ΔCA)	(1,350)
Change in Current Liabilities (ΔCL)	100
Net Change in Working Capital	(1,250)
Cash Flow from Operating Activities (CFfOA)	10,650
Investing Activities	
Fixed Asset Additions	(10,000)
Cash Flow after Investing Activities (CFaIA)	**650**
Financing Activities	
Increase (Decrease) in Long-Term Debt	0
Proceeds Purchase) of Common Stock	0
Dividends Paid (DP)	0
Cash Generated (Used) (CGU)	650

methodology.[20] Therefore, if cash flow drives value, the logical question is: What drives cash flow? More importantly, what can a manager do to increase cash flow and thereby increase value?

A careful examination of the Cash Flow Statement shown in Table 1-5 indicates that without Net Income a company doesn't generate any cash from operations other than the cash that can be squeezed out of working capital. Hence it is clear that Net Income drives Cash Flow. Also, since one of management's key tasks is to make investments that result in a future increase in earnings, it would seem logical to add investments to the list of Cash Flow drivers. However, as Table 1-5 indicates, there are other activities that impact cash flow (i.e., changes in working capital, changes in long-term debt, proceeds from the sale of equity, buybacks of equity, and dividends). A better understanding of how all of these activities impact cash flow is facilitated by a careful inspection of Table 1-5.

The next section deals with quantifying these drivers in terms of their relationship to the Income, Balance Sheet, and Cash Flow Statements and this point is intended to briefly expose the reader to the concept of Cash Flow. Everything discussed in the

[20] The discounted cash flow method (explained in detail later in this book) is one of the most widely used methods for valuing a business and considered by many to be the theoretically correct methodology.

following section is developed in more detail in the chapters that follow, so the reader shouldn't be concerned if some of the concepts aren't crystal clear.

Defining Cash Flow

Inspection of the Cash Flow Statement (Table 1-5) indicates that Cash Flow from Operations (CFfO) is a function of Net Income, Depreciation and Amortization, whereas Cash Flow from Operating Activities (CFfOA) is comprised of Cash Flow from Operations and Changes in Current Assets and Current Liabilities. These relationships are expressed in Equations [1-44] and [1-45]:

$$CFfO = NI + D\,\&\,A \tag{1-44}$$

$$CFfOA = NI + D\,\&\,A \pm \Delta CA \pm \Delta CL \tag{1-45}$$

or

$$CFfOA = NI + D\,\&\,A \pm \Delta WC \tag{1-46}$$

where:

$$\Delta WC = \text{Change in Working Capital} = \pm\,\Delta\text{CA} \pm \Delta\text{CL}$$

Since NI is the ultimate driver of Cash Flow, all Cash Flow Statements start with the current period's Net Income and then make adjustments for the impact other factors have had on the period's Cash Flow from Operations. The first step in adjusting Net Income for non-cash charges is to add back the Depreciation and Amortization that was incorporated into the Income Statement for the current period.

The reason for this is: D&A represents Depreciation and Amortization of assets purchased and paid for during a prior period and that therefore don't have any current cash impact. It should be noted that even if the asset being depreciated or amortized was purchased during the current year and still not paid for, it's D or A would still be treated as a non-cash item because the amount the Company owes the supplier is accounted for in Accounts Payable and the cash has not left the company.

The role the change in Working Capital plays in CFfOA may not be so obvious. Recall that Working Capital is defined as Current Assets – Current Liabilities, and, as shown in the preceding section, when calculating Cash Flow it is the Change in the Working Capital (ΔWC) accounts (excluding cash) between the current and prior period that is of interest. The discussion on Working Capital showed that when the Change in Current Assets increases between the Current and Prior Year this represents a use of cash and this amount has to be subtracted from CFfOA. Conversely, when the Change in Current Liabilities increases from one year to the next this represents a source of cash and this amount has to be added back to properly reflect the impact this source of cash has on the Cash Flow from Operating Activities.[21]

---

[21] Of the three financial statements, the Cash Flow Statement can be the most difficult to understand. Considerable time is spent in Chapter 10 on preparing financial statements for a company and explaining the concepts that have been covered here and subsequent chapters in more detail.

Table 1-5 also suggests that CFfOA is available for making investments in the business (Investments), "Financing Activities" (servicing/repaying debt), and paying dividends to shareholders (Dividends Paid). The following relationships can be deduced by working down the Cash Flow Statement.

Cash Flow after Investing Activities (CFaIA):

$$CFaIA = CFfOA - Investments \quad [1\text{-}47]$$

Cash Flow after Financing Activities (CFaFA):

$$CFaFA = CFaIA \pm Financing\ Activities \quad [1\text{-}48]$$

Cash Flow after Dividends Paid:

$$CFaDP = CFaFA - Dividends\ Paid \quad [1\text{-}49]$$

At the end of the day managers and investors alike are interested in whether the business generates or uses cash, hence the interest in the "Cash Generated (Used)" by the business, which can be expressed as:

$$Cash\ Generated\ (Used) = CFfOA - Investments \pm Financing - Dividends\ Paid \quad [1\text{-}50]$$

Another way to think about this is to look at the uses of Cash Flow from Operating Activities. The uses can be expressed as follows:

$$CFfOA = (CF\ for\ Investments)\ \&\ (CF\ for\ Debt\ Holders)\ \&\ (CF\ for\ Shareholders) \quad [1\text{-}51]$$

Equation [1-51] says that the Cash Flow from Operating Activities caters to two constituencies. The first is shareholders. The shareholders (by virtue of the board of directors) decide how much is invested in the business to generate future cash flows, and how much, if any, is paid out in dividends. The board also decides on the capital structure of the business (debt vs. equity) and thereby obliges the company to make interest payments on debt and repay money the company has borrowed from the second constituency, the debt holders.

Investments and Cash Flow after Investing Activities

While there are numerous kinds of investments made by all companies, they broadly fall into two categories:

1. *Sustaining investments:* These are investments necessary to sustain or improve the company's productive asset base as part of an effort to maintain the existing stream of Net Income and Cash Flow.

2. *Growth investments:* Unlike the sustaining investments, growth investments are investments in new capacity, business areas, or technologies and are directed at increasing the company's rate of Revenue, Net Income, and Cash Flow growth.

Every company needs to make "sustaining investments" to stay alive. Those that don't will go into a period of decline. While it may take many years, decline, if unchecked, is ultimately terminal. Unfortunately, while sustaining investments are necessary, they usually aren't sufficient. This is because growth will ultimately slow down and demand in the company's niche or market will sooner or later stabilize or decline as the market matures. In terms of a company's value, decline is a disaster. As far as investors are concerned, when market growth or sales decline, this is quickly seen in the value of the Company's shares.

In some instances, a decline in cash flow can be avoided by cutting costs. In fact, management can increase cash flow by disinvesting in the business. However, in today's business climate, increasing cash flow by expense control doesn't work for very long. Eventually cost cutting is a dead end and the only remaining road to increasing shareholder value is growth. Growth opportunities don't just come along. A company has to be committed to investing for growth in order to get it and even then success is highly uncertain. Unlike sustaining investments, investments focused on growth inherently involve more risk. The upside is, of course, the possibility of a better return.

Making a choice between sustaining or growth investments or investing for both is not simply a matter of money. In practice it (money) frequently turns out to be the least important resource. Investments directed at growth require ideas and sometimes new technologies. Furthermore, it's not very often that a management team that is outstanding when it comes to cost control and optimizing the productive level of sustaining investments is also good at managing a company for growth. While managing the process and resources associated with putting a company on a growth track can be learned, it takes time—often lots of time and many lessons learned. In practice, most companies make both sustaining and growth investments at the same time. Successful companies have learned that each category of investment has its own prerequisites and culture and therefore staff and manage accordingly.

As far as the Cash Flow Statement is concerned there isn't any need to be concerned with the kind or category of investment but rather how investments are treated financially and the impact investments have on Cash Flow after Investing Activities (CFaIA).

Recalling that earlier in this chapter Equation [1-46] defined Cash Flow from Operating Activities (CFfOA) as:

$$CFfOA = NI + D\ \&\ A \pm \Delta WC \qquad [1\text{-}46]$$

and that Cash Flow after Investing Activities (CFaIA) can be expressed as:

$$CFaIA = CFfOA - Investments \qquad [1\text{-}47]$$

substituting [1-46] for CFfOA in [1-47] produces an equation for CFaIA expressed in terms of operating cash flows and investments.

$$CFaIA = NI + D\,\&\,A \pm \Delta WC - Investments \qquad [1\text{-}52]$$

Example 1-6: Calculating CFaIA and CGU

Cash Flow after Investing Activities for the company represented by the Cash Flow Statement (Table 1-5) in Year *n* can be determined by substituting the values for NI, D&A, ΔWC, and Investments in Equation [1-52].

$$CFaIA = 6{,}900{,}000 + 5{,}000{,}000 - 1{,}250{,}000 - 10{,}000{,}000 = \$650{,}000$$

The CGU is calculated with the use of Equation [1-50]

$$Cash\ Generated\ (Used) = CFfOA - Investments \pm Financing - Dividends\ Paid \qquad [1\text{-}50]$$

Substituting values from Table 1-5 for CFfOA, Investments, Financing, and Dividends Paid the CGU is calculated to be:

$$Cash\ Generated\ (Used) = 10{,}650{,}000 - 10{,}000{,}000 \pm 0 - 0 = \$650{,}000$$

It may be helpful to look at the Cash Generated/Used from another perspective. Recall that

$$CFaIA = CFfOA - Investments \qquad [1\text{-}47]$$

Rearranging,

$$CFfOA = CFaIA + Investments \qquad [1\text{-}53]$$

Substituting the results of Equation [1-53] for CfaOA in Equation [1-50] yields

$$Cash\ Generated\ (Used) = CFaOA + Investments - Investments \pm Financing - Dividends\ Paid \qquad [1\text{-}54]$$

or

$$Cash\ Generated\ (Used) = CFaIA \pm Financing - Dividends\ Paid \qquad [1\text{-}55]$$

Substituting,

$$Cash\ Generated\ (Used) = 650{,}000 \pm 0 - 0 = \$650{,}000$$

It is worthwhile to note that since no Equity was sold to investors and no dividends were paid, the CGU is the same as the Cash Flow after Investing Activities.

So if $650,000 of Cash was generated during this period, the question is: How much cash will the company have at the end of the period? If you assume the Balance Sheet shown in Table 1-3 is the balance sheet at the end of a month (January), then the

TABLE 1-6 Period Cash Balances $(000)'s

Beginning Cash Balance	750
Cash Generated/(Used)	650
Ending Cash Balance	1,400

cash balance at the beginning of the next month (February) will be the same as the cash balance at the end of January, or $750,000. Then if the Cash Flow Statement shown in Table 1-5 is the statement for the month of February, the Cash Generated during February will be $650,000 and the cash balance at the end of February would be as shown in Table 1-6.[22]

REQUIRED REVENUE FOR A GIVEN LEVEL OF NET INCOME[23]

So far the primary focus has been on Net Income and Cash Flow and what drives them. One issue that hasn't been addressed is the role Revenue plays in covering all the expenses incurred by a business. For example, for any given level of Net Income the Revenue must be adequate to cover the Cost of Goods Sold, Operating Expenses, Depreciation and Amortization, Net Interest, and Taxes. In this section, instead of starting with Revenue, the Income Statement will be worked backward, so to speak, and start with Net Income and end up with the Required Revenue to support the Net Income.

The analysis of Required Revenue begins by referring to Table 1-7 and then letting "RR" represent the Required Revenue to drive a level of Net Income.

By inspection:

$$NI = Rev - COGS - OpExp - D\ \&\ A \pm NetInt - TaxesPaid \tag{1-56}$$

or

$$NI = Rev - (COGSRatio)(Rev) - (OpExpRatio)(Rev) - D\ \&\ A \pm NetInt - TaxesPaid \tag{1-57}$$

where:

$$COGS = (COGSRatio)(Rev) \text{ and } OpExp = (OpExpRatio)(Rev)$$

If Rev is the Required Revenue (RR) to deliver Net Income NI, then

$$NI = RR - (COGSRatio)(RR) - (OpExpRatio)(RR) - D\ \&\ A \pm NetInt - TaxesPaid \tag{1-58}$$

[22] Table 1-6 is actually known as the "Cash Flow Proof" and usually appended to Cash Flow Statements as will be shown in Chapter 10.

[23] T. E. Copeland, T. Koller, and J. Murrin, *Valuation: Measuring and Managing the Value of Companies*, 2nd ed. (New York: John Wiley & Sons, 1995), 166, "ROIC Tree."

TABLE 1-7 Income Statement for Calculating Required Revenue

Period Ending DD/MM/YYYY $(000's)			
		$	Ratio
Revenues (Rev)		100,000	1.000
Cost of Goods Sold (COGS)		(40,000)	–0.400
Gross Margin (GM)		60,000	0.600
Operating Expenses (OpExp)		(43,500)	–0.435
Earnings Before Interest, Taxes, and D&A (EBITDA)		16,500	0.165
Depreciation and Amortization (D&A)		(5,000)	–0.050
Earnings Before Interest and Taxes (EBIT)		11,500	0.115
Interest Income/(Expense) (NetInt)		0	0.000
Earnings Before Tax (EBT)		11,500	0.115
Taxes Paid (TaxesPaid) @	40%	(4,600)	–0.046
Net Income (NI)		6,900	0.069

Factoring,

$$NI = (RR)(1 - COGSRatio - OpExpRatio) - D\,\&\,A \pm NetInt - TaxesPaid \quad [1\text{-}59]$$

Rearranging,

$$RR(1 - COGS\ Ratio - OpExpRatio) = NI + D\,\&\,A \pm NetInt + TaxesPaid \quad [1\text{-}60]$$

Dividing both sides of [1-60] by (1 – COGSRatio – OpExpRatio),

$$RR = \frac{NI + D\,\&\,A \pm NetInt + TaxesPaid}{(1 - COGSRatio - OpExpRatio)} \quad [1\text{-}61]$$

Again by inspection of Table 1-7 it can be seen that

$$(1 - COGSRatio - OpExpRatio) = EBITDARatio \quad [1\text{-}62]$$

Substituting [1-62] in Equation [1-61], the revenue required (Required Revenue) to support a given level of Net Income is obtained:

$$RR = \frac{NI + D\,\&\,A \pm NetInt + TaxesPaid}{EBITDARatio} \quad [1\text{-}63]$$

or

$$RR = \frac{NI}{EBITDARatio} + \frac{D\,\&\,A}{EBITDARatio} \pm \frac{NetInt}{EBITDARatio} + \frac{TaxesPaid}{EBITDARatio} \quad [1\text{-}64]$$

Equation [1-64] tells an interesting story. It says that for a given level of financial performance the Revenue must be sufficient to cover the expected Net Income, Depreciation and Amortization, any Interest Expense, and Taxes Paid.[24]

Also, since

$$TaxesPaid = (EBT)(TR) \quad [1\text{-}8]$$

then another form of Equation [1-64] is

$$RR = \frac{NI}{EBITDARatio} + \frac{D\&A}{EBITDARatio} \pm \frac{NetInt}{EBITDARatio} + \frac{(EBT)(TR)}{EBITDARatio} \quad [1\text{-}65]$$

Example 1-7: Calculating Required Revenue

Del Rey Corporation has a budgeted Net Income of $2,495,000 in Year 1 of its operating plan with an EBITDA of 11.5%. If Depreciation and Amortization, Net Interest, and Taxes Paid are $1,735,000, $0, and $1,828,000 respectively, calculate the Required Revenue for each term in Equation [1-65] and the Total Required Revenue for Year 1 of the operating plan (Table 1-8).

The Required Revenue to support the Net Income NI_1 of $2,495,000 is

$$RR_{(NI_1)} = \frac{NI_1}{EBITDARatio_1} = \frac{2,495,000}{0.115} = \$21,696,000$$

Repeating this process, the Required Revenue for D&A, NetInt, and TaxPaid can be calculated.

$$RR_{(D\&A_1)} = \frac{D\&A_1}{EBITDARatio_1} = \frac{1,735,000}{0.115} = \$15,087,000$$

$$RR_{(NetInt_1)} = \frac{NetInt_1}{EBITDARatio_1} = \frac{0}{0.115} = \$0$$

$$RR_{(TaxPaid_1)} = \frac{TaxesPaid_1}{EBITDARatio_1} = \frac{1,828,000}{0.115} = \$15,896,000$$

TABLE 1-8 Condensed Income Statement for Del Rey Corporation

	Year 1 ($'s and %)
Net Income	2,495,000
EBITDA	11.50%
EBITDA Ratio	0.115
Depreciation and Amortization	1,735,000
Net Interest	0
Taxes Paid	1,828,000

[24] It can actually get a little more complicated. If the company in question has interest-bearing cash or investments, the associated interest income would give the Required Revenue some assistance and actually reduce the Revenue required to support a given level of Net Income.

Substituting in Equation [1-65] gives the Required Revenue in Year 1.

$$RR_1 = 21{,}696{,}000 + 15{,}087{,}000 + 0 + 15{,}896{,}000$$
$$RR_1 = \$52{,}679{,}000$$

As can be seen from the example, approximately $15 million and $16 million of Revenue are required to cover Depreciation and Amortization and Taxes respectively, whereas roughly $21,700,000 of revenue is required to deliver the Year 1 Net Income in the operating plan.[25]

CASE STUDY: ADVANCED SOLAR SYSTEMS CORPORATION

Ms. Engel has just returned from completing an Executive Management Program at the University of Pennsylvania's Wharton School. In keeping with the school's reputation the program had an emphasis on developing quantitative skills, which wasn't a problem for Ms. Engel since she had a degree in electrical engineering. The assignment from the Professor of Finance who conducted the concluding session was for all participants to do an analysis of their company's financial statements using the skills they had just developed when they returned to their offices.

Ms. Engel's employer is Advanced Solar Systems Corporation. As the name would suggest, the Company specializes in systems that utilize solar technology to build power sources for the military and aerospace industries. One of the things that was stressed by the professors conducting the program was that while all students should have a solid grasp of the relationships they were taught that defined the financial statements, they should also remember that the statements are logical, and with a little practice they can be analyzed by running some simple calculations based on inspection rather than rigorous mathematical treatment. With this in mind and after scanning the Solar Systems Income Statement, Ms. Engel did a comparative analysis of the actual results for the Prior Year and the forecast for the Current Year. The Income Statement including the analysis is shown in Table CS 1-1.

After looking at the Comparative Analysis, Ms Engel concluded:

- Revenue increased 12% on a year-over-year basis driven by the demand for the company's products, what one expects of a growth company.
- The Cost of Goods Sold (COGS) had increased by 100 basis points (1%) from 56% to 57%. While this is a movement in the wrong direction, it was not unexpected given the startup costs associated with the products that had been released to production at the end of the Prior Year.
- As a result of the deterioration in the COGS, the Gross Margin (GM) decreased to 43%.
- Operating Expense decreased from 27% to 24.5% but in absolute terms increased slightly to $307,632,000. The reduction in percentage terms was to be expected given the Revenue Growth. The modest increase was made possible by the reduction

[25] The reader may wish to refer to the "Takeaways" section at the beginning of this chapter before proceeding to the next chapter.

TABLE CS 1-1 Advanced Solar Systems Comparative Income Statement

Period Ending DD/MM/YYYY $(000)'s				
Year	**PriYr % Rev**	**Prior**	**Current**	**CurYr % Rev**
Revenues (Rev)		1,121,108	1,255,641	12.00%
Cost of Goods Sold (COGS)	–56.00%	(627,820)	(715,715)	–57.00%
Gross Margin (GM)	44.00%	493,288	539,926	43.00%
Operating Expenses (OpExp)	–27.00%	(302,699)	(307,632)	–24.50%
Earnings Before Interest, Taxes, and D&A (EBITDA)	17.00%	190,588	232,294	18.50%
Depreciation and Amortization (D&A)	–3.00%	(33,633)	(40,181)	–3.20%
Earnings Before Interest and Taxes (EBIT)	14.00%	156,955	192,113	15.30%
Interest Income/(Expense) (NetInt)	0.02%	227	455	0.04%
Earnings Before Tax (EBT)	14.02%	157,183	192,568	15.34%
Taxes Paid (TaxesPaid) @	–37.00%	(58,158)	(67,399)	–35.00%
Net Income (NI)	8.83%	99,025	125,169	9.97%

in R&D expenses associated with the new products that were released to production at the end of Prior Year.

- Driven by the Revenue and OpExp the EBITDA increased 150 basis points (1.5%) to 18.5%, which is in keeping with the operating leverage obtained by managing the Operating Expenses while increasing Revenue.
- Depreciation increased from 3% to 3.2% of Revenue as the company continued to invest to keep up with demand and technology.
- Since the company was debt-free there was no interest expense. Management preferred to remain very liquid, so all cash on hand was invested in money market funds. The outcome of this was that very little interest was earned from the available cash.
- As expected (driven by Revenue and Operating Expenses), the Earnings before Taxes increased from 14.02% to 15.34% of Revenue.
- For the last two years the company's CFO and VP of Tax had been working on a program to reduce the company's taxes. This effort is expected to pay off in the Current Year and contribute substantially to the company's Net Income, which is forecasted to grow to nearly 10% of Revenue.

After thinking about the Income Statement Analysis she just finished, Ms. Engel concluded that overall the company had a great year and management should continue to focus on growing Revenue, reducing the Cost of Goods Sold, and carefully managing Operating Expenses.

She then moved on to the Balance Sheet. She knew from her Wharton Program that the preferred way to think about Working Capital was in terms of Days Outstanding, Inventory Turns, and so forth. However, given that she was primarily interested in what was happening directionally with Working Capital, she thought this was an unnecessary complication, and made some annotations using percentages of revenue. The result of her work is included in the Balance Sheet, Table CS 1-2.

TABLE CS 1-2 Advanced Solar Systems Comparative Balance Sheet

DD/MM/YYYY $(000)'s									
	PriYr % Rev	**Prior**	**Current**	**CurYr % Rev**		**PriYr % Rev**	**Prior**	**Current**	**CurYr % Rev**
Current Assets					**Current Liabilities**				
Cash		45,479	130,865		Accounts Payable	**14%**	156,955	182,673	**16%**
Accounts Receivable	**21%**	230,613	263,685	**24%**	Taxes Payable		0	0	
Inventory	**14%**	156,955	174,565	**16%**	Short-Term Debt (STD)		0	0	
Total Current Assets		433,047	569,115		**Total Current Liabilities**		156,955	182,673	
Fixed Assets									
At Cost		637,889	692,889		**Long-Term Debt (LTD)**		0	0	
Less Depreciation	**−19%**	(216,892)	(257,073)	**−23%**					
Net Fixed Assets		420,997	435,816						
					Shareholder's Equity (TSHE)				
Other Assets					Paid-in Capital		150,000	150,000	
Goodwill net of Amortization		0	0		Retained Earnings		547,089	672,258	
Net Other Assets		0	0		**Total Shareholders' Equity**		697,089	822,258	
Total Assets		854,044	1,004,931		**Total Liabilities + TSHE**		854,044	1,004,931	

- Her first observation was that Advanced Solar's Balance Sheet was expanding rapidly.
- Her second observation was that Cash was building and if this continued, the company would be in a position to finance a major new program, do an acquisition, and pay a dividend or some combination thereof.
- Accounts Receivable needed attention, having increased from 21% to 24% of Revenue.
- The same could also be true for inventory, which had increased from 14% to 16% of Revenue. Given her experience in engineering and manufacturing she knew that if this was a result of a deterioration in inventory management as opposed to a temporary build associated with the new products, a major write-off could be in the offing since in Advanced Solar's business product enhancements and obsolescence were a way of life.
- Depreciation also increased as a percentage of Revenue driven by investments in plant and equipment. After some thought she concluded that this was not a concern because the spike could be a result of the timing associated with purchases and useful life assumptions but primarily because Depreciation as a percentage of Revenue was fairly stable in the range of 3%.
- Since the company didn't have any Short-Term or Long-Term Debt, the only thing of note on the Liabilities and Total Shareholders' Equity side was the Accounts Payable, which had increased as a percentage of Revenue to16 percent.

The take-home value from her analysis of the Balance Sheet was: Management needed to understand why Receivables and Inventory were increasing and take appropriate action. As for Accounts Payable, they needed to make sure they were paying suppliers on a timely basis since they fed Solar's manufacturing plant and played a huge role in product quality, product cost, and delivery performance.

Next, and primarily out of curiosity, she decided to take a closer look at Working Capital and the impact the changes had on the company's Cash Flow. The results are tabulated in Table CS 1-3.

After studying Table CS 1-3 Ms. Engel observed the following:

- Accounts Receivable increased by $33,072,000 and since this was cash the company had not collected, the impact on the company's Cash was negative or a "Use of Cash."
- Inventory increased by $17,610,000 and this inventory build had to be paid for. So like Accounts Receivable the impact on Cash was negative and also a "Use of Cash."

TABLE CS 1-3 Working Capital Analysis $(000)'s

Year	Prior	Current	Change	CashEffect
Accounts Receivable	230,613	263,685	33,072	(33,072)
Inventory	156,955	174,565	17,610	(17,610)
Accounts Payable	156,955	182,673	25,718	25,718
Taxes Payable	0	0	0	0
Short-Term Debt	0	0	0	0
Change in Working Capital (ΔWC)				(24,963)

- Accounts Payable was a different matter. They increased by $25,718,000 and this indicated the company had made purchases that they hadn't paid for and in a sense was using their suppliers to finance their operations. From an accounting perspective the Cash impact was a positive $25,718,000 and a "Source of Cash."
- The company's practice was to pay all taxes by year-end. Hence, there was no change from one year to the next, so there wasn't any Taxes Payable impact on Working Capital.
- The impact of Short-Term Debt on the change in Working Capital is zero since the company didn't expect to have debt of any kind on its Balance Sheet at the end of either year.
- The net Cash impact of the changes in the company's Working Capital was a negative $24,963,000.

Ms. Engel recalled that of the three financial statements, the one that caused the most difficulty for many of the managers who attended the training program was the Cash Flow Statement. So she decided to see if she could work her way through Solar's Current Year Cash Flow Statement[26] that was part of the management reporting package (Table CS 1-4).

When it came to cash flow from operations, the first entry was Net Income ($125,169,000). This was logical because Net Income is what the company earned during the year and the major source of Cash Flow from Operating Activities. Depreciation ($40,181,000) was added back since it represented a charge in the Income Statement for assets that were being depleted and, since they were paid for in a prior period, didn't have any Cash impact. Interest Income ($455,000) was a different matter. It was a Source of Cash but since it wasn't generated from operations it had to be deducted. The Change in Working Capital ($24,963,000, according to the analysis she had completed and tabulated in Table CS 1-3) was a use of cash so it should be deducted when determining the Cash Flow from Operating Activities.

TABLE CS 1-4 Advanced Solar Systems Cash Flow Statement $(000)'s

Year	**Current**
Net Income (NI)	125,169
Depreciation and Amortization (D&A)	40,181
Interest Income (Expense) (NetInt)	(455)
Change in Working Capital (ΔWC)	(24,963)
Cash Flow from Operating Activities (CFfOA)	139,932
Investments (Investments)	(55,000)
Cash Flow after Investing Activities (CFaIA)	84,932
Dividends Paid to Shareholders	0
Interest Income (Expense)	455
Increase (Decrease) in Long-Term Debt	0
Shareholders' Contribution	0
Cash Generated (Used) (CGU)	85,386

[26] She wasn't able to do the Cash Flow Statement for the Prior Year because data for the year before the Prior Year was not at hand.

In summary, the Cash Flow from Operating Activities ($139,932,000) was obtained by starting with the Net Income, adding back the Depreciation, subtracting the Interest Income, and deducting the Change in Working Capital.

Ms. Engel then proceeded to the Investment section of the Cash Flow Statement. Initially she was puzzled by where the $55,000,000 of "Investments" came from. After thinking about it she concluded that since it was most probably an investment in assets, it had to be on the Balance Sheet. Sure enough, after subtracting the "Fixed Assets at Cost" at the end of the Prior Year from the forecasted "Fixed Assets at Cost" at the end of the Current Year ($692,889,000 – 637,889,000 = $55,000,000) she found the source of the $55,000,000 entry.

With this information the Cash Flow after Investing Activities ($84,932,000) was easily obtained by subtracting the $55,000,000 investment in Fixed Assets from the Cash Flow from Operating Activities ($139,932,000).

Since Solar didn't pay any dividends there wasn't any impact on Cash Flow.

When it came to Financing, Ms. Engel was fine with no impact from Debt or Shareholders' Contributions on the Cash Flow Statement since the company didn't borrow any money during the year or raise any capital from shareholders. However, she was puzzled for a moment to see the $455,000 of Interest Income entered in this section of the Cash Flow Statement. Then she realized that since it had been deducted in the operating section of the statement because it wasn't a source of operating cash it was a source of cash and had to be added back to obtain the Cash Generated ($85,386,000) during the period.

Having worked her way through the financial statements she was now at a point where she could finish her analysis by calculating the Return on Capital Employed (ROCE) and the Required Revenue (RR).

After checking her notes she recalled that the ROCE could be calculated by applying Equations [1-30] and [1-32].

$$ROCE = \frac{(EBIT)(1-TR)}{CE} \qquad [1\text{-}30]$$

where

$$CE = TSHE + STD + LTD \qquad [1\text{-}32]$$

Substituting values from Tables CS 1-1 and CS 1-2 the ROCE's for Prior and Current Years were obtained:

$$ROCE_{PriorYear} = \frac{156{,}955{,}000 * (1-0.37)}{(697{,}089{,}000+0+0)} = \frac{156{,}955{,}000 * (0.63)}{697{,}089{,}000} = \frac{98{,}882{,}000}{697{,}089{,}000}$$

$$= 0.1418$$

$$ROCE_{PriorYear} = 14.2\%$$

or

$$ROCE_{CurrentYear} = \frac{192{,}113{,}000 * (1-0.35)}{(822{,}258{,}000+0+0)} = \frac{192{,}113{,}000 * (0.65)}{822{,}258{,}000} = \frac{124{,}874{,}000}{822{,}258{,}000}$$

$$= 0.152$$

$$ROCE_{CurrentYear} = 15.2\%$$

Ms. Engel noted that the ROCE was moving in the right direction, but she wasn't sure how these returns compared to other companies in the industry. Given the company's profitability she intuitively expected them to be higher. Also she noted that since the company was beginning to accumulate cash it could drastically increase the ROCE by paying a dividend to decrease the Total Shareholders' Equity, and concluded that maybe she should begin to purchase shares in the company as and when she had excess cash.

To deal with the question of Required Revenue she once again consulted her notes to refresh her memory. The result was the Required Revenue equation, Equation [1-65].

$$RR = \frac{NI}{EBITDARatio} + \frac{D\&A}{EBITDARatio} \pm \frac{NetInt}{EBITDARatio} + \frac{(EBT)(TR)}{EBITDARatio} \quad [1\text{-}65]$$

Since she planned to use the material she was preparing in a training program for her staff, she decided to only deal with the Current Year and prepared Table CS 1-5 because she felt it would simplify the process associated with applying the Required Revenue equation.

She then proceeded to use this data and calculated each of the terms.

$$RR_{NICurrentYr} = \frac{NI}{EBITDARatio} = \frac{125,169,000}{0.185} = \$676,589,000$$

$$RR_{D\&ACurrentYr} = \frac{D\&A}{EBITDARatio} = \frac{40,181,000}{0.185} = \$217,195,000$$

$$RR_{NetIntCurrentYr} = \frac{NetInt}{EBITDARatio} = \frac{455,000}{0.185} = \$2,459,000$$

$$RR_{TaxesPaidCurYr} = \frac{(EBT)(TR)}{EBITDARatio} = \frac{192,568,000 * 0.35}{0.185} = \frac{67,399,000}{0.185} = \$364,318,000$$

TABLE CS 1-5 Required Revenue $'s and %

Year	Prior	Current
Net Income	99,025	125,169
EBITDA	17.00%	18.50%
EBITDA Ratio	0.1700	0.1850
Depreciation and Amortization	(33,633)	(40,181)
Net Interest	227	455
Taxes Paid	(58,158)	(67,399)

Ms. Engel then substituted the calculated values for each of the terms in Equation [1-65], which gave her a Required Revenue for the Current Year of $1,260,561,000, which didn't agree with the Revenue shown for the Current Year in the Income Statement ($1,255,643,000).

$$RR_{CurrentYear} = 676{,}589{,}000 + 217{,}195{,}000 + 2{,}459{,}000 + 364{,}318{,}000$$
$$= \$1{,}260{,}558{,}000$$

She quickly realized her mistake. The Interest Income of $455,000 actually reduced the Revenue required to cover the Net Income, Depreciation, and Taxes Paid. The correct answer was then obtained by changing the sign on the NetInt term in the Required Revenue expression.

$$RR_{CurrentYear} = 676{,}589{,}000 + 217{,}195{,}000 - 2{,}459{,}000 + 364{,}318{,}000$$
$$= \$1{,}255{,}643{,}000$$

While staring at the result of applying the Required Revenue equation she was struck by the fact that in order to create $125 million of Net Income, the company had to generate $364 million of Revenue to pay the taxes and $217 million of Revenue to cover Depreciation and Amortization, and only after $581 million of Revenue had been produced did the next dollar of Revenue contribute to profit.

CHAPTER TWO

The Envelope Equations*

CHAPTER 2 TAKEAWAYS

- In addition to new plant and equipment and software, companies routinely invest in quality control programs, productivity programs, research and development, marketing, sales, and administration. Companies also spend money on consultants, lawyers, accountants, investment bankers, and acquisitions. Expenditures of this type are also investments because the reason for such expenditures is to add or preserve value. If not, why would the company spend the money?
- One could argue that any expenditure that isn't an investment is a waste of money. "Operating Expenses" are really poorly named as such and perhaps "Operating Investments" would be more appropriate.
- Accounting for changes in Working Capital during the formulation stages of building a business plan is often not worth the effort. However, the importance of properly accounting for Working Capital requirements in the later versions of the business plan and managing Working Capital should not be minimized. There are many examples of companies that have gone out of business because they didn't manage their Working Capital (uncollectable receivables and poor inventory management) and ultimately ran out of cash.
- To a significant extent, this book is about Cash Flow since cash is the basic resource required by a business. In the long run, Net Income is the only source of cash and so its importance cannot be overemphasized.
- The amount of debt a company takes on is a function of its capital structure and this is ultimately decided by the owners of the business (shareholders) via the board of directors. In practice, however, the CEO and his management team are responsible for everything that happens in a business. Therefore, the management team can't get a free pass and hide behind the board of directors

(continued)

*The reader may notice minor discrepancies in the calculations in this chapter. When this occurs, it is the result of rounding.

when it comes to capital structure. Stated simply, they have to deal with the hand that has been dealt and improve it over time.

- One could argue that management should not be primarily judged by how well they manage excess cash, nor should they be penalized for having to cope with excessive debt. A company takes on debt to leverage the return to equity holders and this debt has to be serviced. However, other than the case of a highly leveraged company created in a leveraged buyout[1] or a string of poor management decisions, management are not hired to service debt per se. They are hired and should be incentivized to create value, not through financial engineering but through growth. As far as management is concerned, capital structure is only important periodically for such things as financing a major acquisition, and so on. In other words, it's extremely important for operating management, as the stewards of the shareholders' assets, to focus on value creation.

INTRODUCTION

In Chapter 1 the basic relationships between the Income, Balance Sheet, and Cash Flow statements were explored. The concepts and equations that were developed are basic to understanding what drives Cash Flow and Value. However, there are other ways of looking at what drives Cash Flow in a company and one of these involves a set of equations called the *Envelope Equations*. These equations enable the user to make quick estimates of Net Income and Cash Flow, in a sense on the "back of an envelope," hence the name.

In this chapter, the study of the Envelope Equations begins by defining and discussing Net Investments (NetInvest) and the Investment Rate (IR). These concepts are then incorporated into the equation developed in Chapter 1 for CFaIA. This is followed by the development of a more general form of the Cash Flow equation incorporating the concept of Net Income Return on Capital Employed (NiROCE). Then, based on the observation that the IR and NiROCE vary little from year to year for many companies, the equations are simplified and then abridged further by focusing on Operational Cash Flows. Next, equations for the Cash Flow and Net Income growth rates, CFaIAg and NIg, respectively, are discussed. Finally, the growth equations are simplified by assuming constant IR's and NiROCE's, and included in the family of Envelope Equations, which are then used in a series of examples and a case study that illustrate how they can be used.

ROCE AND NiROCE

In Chapter 1, the Return on Capital Employed (ROCE) was defined as:

$$ROCE = \frac{NOPAT}{Capital\ Employed} = \frac{(EBIT)(1-TR)}{TSHE + Interest\ Bearing\ Debt} = \frac{(EBIT)(1-TR)}{TSHE + IBD} \quad [1\text{-}29]$$

[1] In a leveraged buyout environment, management should and will focus on debt reduction. However, everyone involved, management and shareholders alike, will be striving to minimize the period during which they manage for cash and get to a point where they can focus on creating value through growth.

Since the objective of the Envelope Equations is to make quick estimates of Net Income and Cash Flow, the classical definition of ROCE needs to be modified because it deals with EBIT, and to get to Net Income involves introducing additional complexity that isn't warranted given the objective of making quick estimates of NI and CFaIA. To get around this, the definition of ROCE in this chapter is modified to use Net Income in place of NOPAT (Net Operating Profit after Tax) and as a result, the term "Net Income Return on Capital Employed (NiROCE)" is introduced and defined as:

$$NiROCE = \frac{(EBT)(1 - TR)}{CE} = \frac{NI}{TSHE + Interest\ Bearing\ Debt} = \frac{NI}{TSHE + IBD} \qquad [2\text{-}1]$$

At this point it may be worthwhile to comment on why ROCE uses NOPAT. The reason is: It excludes the impact of interest income or expense and since the cause of interest is the debt on the balance sheet (and it is already included in the denominator as part of Interest Bearing Debt), using NI would, in a sense, be double counting because it understates the NOPAT by an amount equal to the after-tax impact of interest. To the extent there is any interest expense, NiROCE would be less than ROCE, and vice versa. If there isn't any interest, the NiROCE and ROCE would be the same.

Underlying Assumptions

In their simplest form, the Envelope Equations are centered around the notion that Net Income and Cash Flow are driven by investments in property, plant, equipment, software, and the like and do not reflect the results of other operational improvements. The assumptions that are important to understand are:

- The underlying assets that generated Year 1's Net Income will continue to do so for the estimating horizon and beyond.
- Investments made during Year 1 don't provide an immediate return but take time, and the incremental Net Income from these investments is generated in Year 2.
- Year 2's Net Income is the sum of the repeating Year 1's Net Income and the Incremental Net Income generated by the investments made in Year 1.
- Like Year 1's Net Income, the investments that generated Year 2's Incremental Net Income will also produce a stream of equal Net Incomes during the subsequent years.

Applying the Equations

Since using the Envelope Equations involves a series of steps, it may be helpful to start the discussion with the end in mind and define the process involved in using the equations before defining the variables and developing the key relationships. Hopefully, by doing so the reader will have an appreciation of where all of this is headed.

As stated earlier, the Envelope Equations provide a way of making rapid estimates of Net Income and Cash Flow. They are built around the concepts of Net Investments

(NetInvest), Investment Rate (IR), and Net Income Return on Capital Employed (NiROCE).[2] To use the equations, it's necessary to have (or make) estimates for the IR and NiROCE, assume some initial level of Net Income, and then sequentially apply the appropriate equation to calculate the Net Incomes and Cash Flows for the years in question. The way it works is as follows:

- Establish the Investment Rate (IR) and Net Income Return on Capital Employed (NiROCE) that are to be used.
- Start with or make an estimate of the Current Year's (Year 1) Net Income:

$$\textit{Net Income in Year } 1 = NI_1$$

- Using the Investment Rate calculate the Net Investment (NetInvest) during Year 1:

$$NetInvest_1 = (NI_1)(IR_1)$$

- With this information, estimate the Cash Flow for Year 1:

$$CFaIA_1 = NI_1 - NetInvest_1 \pm NetInt_1 \pm \Delta WC_1$$

- Using the NiROCE the company expects from the Net Investment made during Year 1 (the return on the investment is expected to take place the following year), calculate the incremental Net Income (ΔNI_2) for the following year (Year 2):

$$\Delta NI_2 = (NetInvest_1)(NiROCE_2)$$

- The Net Income for Year 2 is the sum of NI_1 and ΔNI_2.

$$NI_2 = NI_1 + (NetInvest_1)(NiROCE_2)$$

- With this information, estimate the Cash Flow for Year 2:

$$CFaIA_2 = NI_2 - NetInvest_2 \pm NetInt_2 \pm \Delta WC_2$$

- Repeating the procedure provides estimates of subsequent years' Net Incomes and Cash Flows.[3]

At this point the reader shouldn't be troubled by the fact that the relationships given in the above procedure are not understood. In fact it would be surprising if this wasn't the case. All of the above relationships are a subset of the Envelope Equations. To give

[2]The basics of ROCE were covered in Chapter 1.

[3]Later, expressions for Net Income and Cash Flow after Investing Activities will be developed in terms of the Investment Rate and Net Income Return on Capital Employed.

the reader some idea of what the complete set looks like and what will be developed in subsequent sections of this chapter and Appendix D, the complete set is shown here.

$$NetInvest_n = (NI_n)(IR_n) \quad [2\text{-}8]$$

$$NI_{(n+1)} = NI_n + Netinvest_n\,(NiROCE_{(n+1)}) \quad [2\text{-}12]$$

$$NI_{(n+1)} = (NI_n)[1 + (IR_n)(NiROCE_{(n+1)})] \quad [2\text{-}14]$$

$$CFaIA_n = NI_n - NetInvest_n \pm NetInt \pm \Delta WC \quad [2\text{-}16]$$

$$CFaIA_n = (NI_n)(1 - IR_n) \pm NetInt_n \pm WC_n \quad [2\text{-}18]$$

$$CFaIAg_n = \frac{[1 + (IR_{(n-1)})(NiROCE_n)](1 - IR_n)}{(1 - IR_{(n-1)})} - 1 \quad [2\text{-}40]$$

$$NIg_n = (IR_{(n-1)})(NiROCE_n) \quad [2\text{-}43]$$

With the assumptions defined and the application process illustrated, it is now time to develop the Envelope Equations. This process begins with a discussion of Net Investments.

NET INVESTMENTS[4,5]

The equation for Cash Flow after Investing Activities that was introduced in Chapter 1, modified to include the impact of interest income and interest expense (NetInt), is:

$$CFaIA = NI + D\,\&\,A \pm NetInt \pm \Delta WC - Investments \quad [2\text{-}2]$$

Usually investments are considered to be a "positive" or a good thing for a business. To accommodate this notion Equation [2-2] can be rewritten as:

$$CFaIA = NI - (Investments - D\,\&\,A) \pm NetInt \pm \Delta WC \quad [2\text{-}3]$$

Now, when Investments > D & A, the term (Investments – D & A) is positive. The term (Investments – D & A) is also known as "Net Investments" where

$$NetInvest = Investments - D\,\&\,A \quad [2\text{-}4]$$

---

[4]T. E. Copeland, T. Koller, and J. Murrin, *Valuation: Measuring and Managing the Value of Companies*, 2nd ed. (New York: John Wiley & Sons, 1995), 137, "What Drives Cash Flow and Value."

[5]T. Koller, R. Dobbs, and B. Huyett, *The Four Cornerstones of Corporate Finance*, McKinsey and Company (Hoboken, NJ: John Wiley & Sons, 2011), 237, "Appendix A."

Substituting NetInvest for the term (Investments – D & A), Equation [2-3] becomes:

$$CFaIA = NI - NetInvest \pm NetInt \pm \Delta WC \qquad [2\text{-}5]$$

The magnitude and sign of the Net Investments term is of interest because it may give an indication of what's going on with the cash flow–producing assets of the business. For example, three ways of looking at this term are:

1. If Investments = D & A, then the net investment is zero. This may indicate the company is replacing its cash flow–producing assets at the same rate as they are wearing out or being depleted.
2. If Investments < D & A, then the net investment is negative (adding to the Cash Flow) and the cash flow–generating assets may not be being replaced as quickly as they are being written off.
3. If Investments > D & A, then the net investment is positive and the management team is making investments that in total are greater than the sum of depreciation and amortization and thereby increasing the company's future cash flow–generating assets.

However, a lot of other things could also be going on. For example: If NetInvest equals zero, it doesn't necessarily follow that the cash flow–producing assets are simply being replaced. It could be that the existing assets aren't in need of replacement and the investments that are being made are intended to generate future cash flows from another product line or service. Similarly, if NetInvest is negative, it could signify that once again there is no need to replace all existing assets at the rate they are being depreciated. It could simply be that the investments being made are for a new product line or service but the investment is less than the depreciation of assets on the books. Finally, if NetInvest is positive, it could signify that existing assets are being replaced with assets that have more capacity or the assets aren't being replaced at all but rather the investments are in a new product line or service or investments are being made at an accelerated pace for a period of time.

The point is: The term NetInvest only indicates the magnitude of investments being made relative to the depreciation and amortization that is taking place. It also quantifies the net magnitude of expenditures that will have an impact on Net Income and Cash Flow for many periods. In and by itself, it doesn't say anything about the kind of investments that management have chosen to make.

For this reason there is also a need to focus and understand investments that are being made and not reflected in the definition of Investments (capitalized investments) but can have an impact on Revenue, Net Income, and Cash Flow.

Investments that are typically capitalized and depreciated over time are:

- *New plant and equipment:* Maintenance can perhaps extend equipment life indefinitely. However, at some point it becomes inefficient. In addition, equipment manufacturers are continuously improving their product. This results in the next generation being able to perform better, cheaper, and faster. Equipment is purchased for various reasons. Whether it represents a replacement for a worn-out machine or new technology, it is an investment.

- *New or upgraded software:* While there aren't any technical reasons why software can't last forever, developers continue to develop more powerful releases and new applications. This results in decisions to discontinue factory support for older versions. Upgrading isn't a trivial project. Systems that control the enterprise or parts thereof are very sophisticated and any change involves risk. To offset this risk considerable planning takes place, which results in detailed implementation plans that can turn upgrades into a major investment.
- *Acquisitions:* Growth strategies are often based on acquiring cash flow, products, technologies, companies, and so on, which involve goodwill, non-competes, patents, and so on, all of which represent an investment.

Expenditures that are not capitalized because the expected result is too difficult to quantify over time are:

- *Research and development:* In most companies it's mostly "D" with little "R" and when R does exist it is usually "r." In well-run organizations the R&D budget represents an investment in products, services, and cost reduction.[6]
- *Quality control program:* This is an investment in cost reduction, risk management, and happy customers.
- *Productivity program:* Companies cannot count on price increases to offset cost increases. To maintain or improve gross margin, a company has to continuously invest in improving its productivity.
- *Marketing:* Depending on the organization this can be large "M" or small "m." Be that as it may, marketing represents an investment in placing the company's product or service top of mind with consumers.
- *Sales:* This may not traditionally be considered an investment, but it is one nevertheless. Whether the contact is in person, by telephone, or via the Internet, the objective is always to get an order for a product or service at an attractive price from either new or repeat customers in existing or new markets. This doesn't just happen. To capture the customers' wallet takes an investment in time and money.
- *Administration:* Investments are made all the time in this area in both people and systems. The objective is to provide efficient infrastructure and services to the various operating entities. To do so, a company must continually strive to be best in class and this takes resources that require investments.[7]

---

[6]From a Cash Flow point of view, companies prefer to write off all expenses as period expenses. Tax rules can require some kinds of R&D expenditure to be capitalized. As stated elsewhere this is not a text on tax treatment and for our purposes it is assumed that all expenses except plant, equipment, and software that are utilized over multiple periods are written off (expensed) as incurred.

[7]When investments in this area involve accounting and enterprise software they are usually capitalized.

- *Lawyers:* While not always viewed as such, the legal profession has a role to play, and experience has shown that it pays to invest in legal advice up front as opposed to fighting it out in court.[8]
- *Accountants:* This is an investment by the owners of the business in getting an independent assessment of the company's financial condition, and for public companies is a legal requirement. In addition, management will often call on accountants for specialized advice on such things as improving the control environment and minimizing taxes. Both of these represent value to the business. The first reduces risk by providing advice on best practices. The second results in more after-tax cash flow.[9]
- *Investment bankers:* Companies frequently require capital and such services as strategic advice. Bankers provide these (and other) services for a fee, which can represent an investment in improving the capital structure of the company and/or maximizing shareholder value by considering various strategic alternatives.[10]

The list goes on. The point is: Investments are not merely expenditures that offset depreciation or amortizing assets. Investments, in the context of this discussion, include select items in several categories.[11]

$$\begin{aligned} \textit{Investments} = \textit{Property} + \textit{Plant} + \textit{Equipment} + \textit{Software} + \textit{Acquisitions} \\ + \textit{Intangibles} + \textit{Operating Investments} \end{aligned} \qquad [2\text{-}6]$$

So, in summary, Investments are not merely the difference between the D&A of existing assets and expenditure on like kinds of assets. They include those just discussed and much more. However, to simplify the discussion, the investments discussed in the context of Net Investments refer to investments that are capitalized, such as facilities, equipment, and software.

Since Investments are what ultimately drive growth and cash flow, the rate at which they are made is of interest. For example, if a project that involves $1,000,000 of investment is completed in three years, its impact on the company's growth will be different than if it was completed in two years, all other things being equal. Hence, the rate at which a company invests money or the "Investment Rate" is a concept that needs to be explored.

INVESTMENT RATE

There is a strong correlation between investments and Net Income in most companies. Therefore, rather than think of Net Investments as an absolute number, it is often more convenient to think of it as a percentage of net income, especially when preparing

---

[8] Legal costs associated with such things as patents and acquisitions can be capitalized and amortized.

[9] When accounting advice involves a merger or acquisition, the costs are capitalized.

[10] Like lawyers, investment bankers' fees that are associated with a transaction are capitalized.

[11] One could argue that any expenditure that isn't an investment is a waste of money. In a later chapter the observation is made that "Operating Expenses" are really poorly named as such and perhaps "Operating Investments" would be more appropriate.

pro-forma financial statements for business plans, preparing cash flow streams for present value analysis, and so forth.

This is done by defining the Investment Rate IR in Year *n* as the ratio of $NetInvest_n$ in Year *n* to Net Income NI_n in Year *n* (Equation [2-7]).

$$IR_n = \frac{NetInvest_n}{NI_n} \quad [2\text{-}7]$$

Rearranging, Equation [2-7] becomes:

$$NetInvest_n = (NI_n)(IR_n) \quad [2\text{-}8]$$

Equation [2-8] is the First Envelope Equation. It is the cornerstone of the Net Investment Version of the Envelope Equations because it defines Net Investment in terms of Net Income and the Investment Rate and will surface many times in the following sections.

Special Case: Constant Investment Rate

Equation [2-7] is a solid definition for the Investment Rate under all circumstances. As will be seen, its more useful form is Equation [2-8].[12] However, in many companies the Investment Rate doesn't change much from one year to the next and, therefore, in numerous situations or as a first approximation the IR can be viewed as a constant. Dropping the subscript on IR accomplishes this. Hence, under these conditions Equation [2-8] becomes

$$NetInvest_n = (NI_n)(IR) \quad [2\text{-}9]$$

INCORPORATING THE IR AND NiROCE INTO THE EXPRESSION FOR NET INCOME[13]

To a significant extent, this book is about Cash Flow since cash is the basic resource required by a business. In the long run Net Income is the only source of cash and so its importance cannot be overemphasized.

Having made an unequivocal statement about the source of cash, the next step in understanding the power of the Envelope Equations is to incorporate IR and ROCE into the Net Income and Cash Flow equations, which is done by starting with the ultimate driver of Cash Flow—Net Income.

[12] Even if the historical Investment Rate has varied considerably, a company will often assume a constant rate going forward for business planning and preparing pro-forma financial statements.

[13] The material in this and the following sections is taken from Appendix D.

The assumptions are: The Net Income for Year n is NI_n and during the year the company makes $NetInvest_n$ at a rate of IR_n of Year n's Net Income. Since it takes time for investments to produce results this investment provides a return of $ROCE_{n+1}$ in the following year.[14] Given these assumptions and Equation [2-8], the amount of Year n's Net Income invested in assets that will generate future cash flows is:

$$NetInvest_n = (NI_n)(IR_n) \qquad [2\text{-}8]$$

Since $NetInvest_n$ provides a return of $ROCE_{(n+1)}$ the following year, then the Incremental Net Income in Year $n+1$ will be:

$$\Delta NI_{(n+1)} = (NetInvest_n)(NiROCE_{(n+1)}) \qquad [2\text{-}10]$$

The NI in Year $n+1$ is the sum of the NI from Year n and ΔNI in Year $n+1$. Therefore, the NI in Year $n+1$ is:

$$NI_{(n+1)} = NI_n + \Delta NI_{(n+1)} \qquad [2\text{-}11]$$

Substituting the results of Equation [2-10] into Equation [2-11] creates an expression for NI in terms of NetInvest and ROCE:

$$NI_{(n+1)} = NI_n + (NetInvest_n)(NiROCE_{(n+1)}) \qquad [2\text{-}12]$$ [15]

Equation [2-12] is the Second Envelope Equation. It enables the calculation of Any Year's Net Income by simply knowing the Current Year's Net Income, Net Investment, and Net Income Return on Capital Employed, thus enabling the calculation of the Cash Flow after Investing Activities for the year in question.

The Investment Rate IR can be incorporated into Equation [2-12] by substituting the results of Equation [2-8] for the term NetInvest in Equation [2-12].

$$NI_{(n+1)} = NI_n + (NI_n)(IR_n)(NiROCE_{(n+1)}) \qquad [2\text{-}13]$$

Factoring [2-13] gives an equation that defines NI in terms of IR and NiROCE.

$$NI_{(n+1)} = (NI_n)[1 + (IR_n)(NiROCE_{(n+1)})] \qquad [2\text{-}14]$$

---

[14] This is an important set of assumptions, especially the notion of $NetInvest_n$ providing a Net Income Return on Capital Employed of $NiROCE_{n+1}$ the following year.

[15] It is important to understand the basis for this equation as well as [2-13] and [2-14]. The Net Income in Year $n+1$ is the sum of the Net Income in Year n and the incremental Net Income is generated by the Net Investment made in Year n in Year $n+1$. This implies that the assets that provided the Net Income in Year n will continue to provide the same level of Net Income in the subsequent years of the planning window. This is also true for the incremental Net Income provided in Year $n+1$ by the Net Income Return on Capital Employed on the Net Investments made in Year n.

Equation [2-14] is the Third Envelope Equation and differs from Equation [2-12] in the sense that it calculates a Future Year's Net Income by using the Current Year's Net Income in combination with the Investment Rate and Net income Return on Capital Employed.

In Year $n+1$, investments are also being made and the magnitude of the NetInvest in Year $n+1$ is:

$$NetInvest_{(n+1)} = (NI_{(n+1)})(IR_{(n+1)}) \qquad [2\text{-}15]$$

which will prove to be a useful expression when estimating the Incremental Net Income and so forth in Year $n+2$.

Equations [2-12] and [2-14] are powerful tools for doing quick estimates of a stream of Net Incomes that are the result of investments with expected returns. These equations together with Equation [2-8] constitute three of a set of five equations that are useful for predicting Net Income. The other two equations have to do with Cash Flow. They will be derived in the following section.

INCORPORATING IR INTO THE EXPRESSION FOR CASH FLOW AFTER INVESTING ACTIVITIES

Incorporating the Investment Rate, IR, into the expression for Cash Flow is done as follows.

Recall Equation [2-5]:

$$CFaIA = NI - NetInvest \pm NetInt \pm \Delta WC \qquad [2\text{-}5]$$

This equation can be generalized by defining CFaIA for Year n as a function of the NI and NetInvest in Year n:

$$CFaIA_n = NI_n - NetInvest_n \pm NetInt_n \pm \Delta WC_n \qquad [2\text{-}16]$$

Equation [2-16] is the Fourth Envelope Equation and is very significant because it allows the user to calculate the Cash Flow after Investing Activities directly by knowing the Net Income, Net Investment, Net Interest, and Change in Working Capital.

Substituting the results of Equation [2-8] for $NetInvest_n$ in Equation [2-16] gives CFaIA for Year n as a function of NI, the Net Income in Year n, and IR, the Investment Rate.

$$CFaIA_n = NI_n - (NI_n)(IR_n) \pm NetInt_n \pm \Delta WC_n \qquad [2\text{-}17]$$

Factoring,

$$CFaIA_n = (NI_n)(1 - IR_n) \pm NetInt_n \pm \Delta WC_n \qquad [2\text{-}18]$$

Equation [2-18] is the Fifth Envelope Equation and it allows one to calculate the Cash Flow after Investing Activities by knowing the Net Income, Investment Rate, and Net Interest and Change in Working Capital. It differs from Equation [2-16] by using the Investment Rate in place of the Net Investment.

In summary, starting with a level of Net Income and values for the Investment Rate and Return on Capital Employed, by using equation [2-8] the Net Investment for any year can be calculated. Then with either Equation [2-12] or [2-14] Net Income for any year is obtained. The Cash Flow for any year is given by using Equation [2-16] or [2-18]. Together these five equations will enable the user to quickly create a stream of pro-forma net incomes and cash flows and constitute five of the seven equations known as the Envelope Equations. The remaining two equations are developed in Appendix C and discussed in a later section of this chapter.

Going through the process of deriving somewhat general equations like those previously listed is a useful exercise because it provides insights into the Envelope Equation framework and the range of their application. However, the methodology involved in calculating Net Income and Cash Flow after Investing Activities using the Investment Rate, IR, and Net Income Return on Capital Employed, NiROCE can take some time to fully appreciate. Therefore, before the remaining Envelope Equations are discussed (sixth and seventh), it's important to make sure that the assumptions underlying these equations are well understood. This will be accomplished by working through the process of applying them over a three-year period, doing away with the *n*'s, and using numbered years in their place.[16]

NI AND CFaIA—A SEQUENTIAL YEAR-BY-YEAR ANALYSIS

Once more, here is a summary of the requirements and process involved in order for these equations to give meaningful results.

- The Net Income for Year 1 is assumed or known.
- Historical values for the Investment Rate (IR) and Net Income Return on Capital Employed (NiROCE) are assumed to be reasonable estimates for future years or arbitrary numbers based on some rationale.
- The underlying assets that generated Year 1's Net Income will continue to do so for the estimating horizon.

[16] Readers who are comfortable with their grasp of the material covered so far can skip the next two sections.

- Net Investments (NetInvest) made during Year 1 don't provide an immediate return but take time and this incremental Net Income is generated in Year 2.
- Year 2's Net Income is the sum of the repeating Year 1's Net Income and the Incremental Net Income in Year 2.
- Like Year 1's Net Income, the incremental assets that generated Year 2's Incremental Net Income will also produce a stream of equal Net Incomes during subsequent years.
- The Cash Flow estimates for each year don't suffer this complication and are relatively straightforward.

The operative equations are:

$$NetInvest_n = (NI_n)(IR_n) \quad [2\text{-}8]$$

$$NI_{(n+1)} = NI_n + (NetInvest_n)(NiROCE_{(n+1)}) \quad [2\text{-}12]$$

$$NI_{(n+1)} = (NI_n)[1 + (IR_n)(NiROCE_{(n+1)})] \quad [2\text{-}14]$$

$$CFaIA_n = NI_n - NetInvest_n \pm NetInt_n \pm \Delta WC_n \quad [2\text{-}16]$$

$$CFaIA_n = (NI_n)(1 - IR_n) \pm NetInt_n \pm \Delta WC_n \quad [2\text{-}18]$$

These equations can be also classified according to the variables used and in the case study at the end of this chapter are referred to as such.

Net Investment (NetInvest) Model or Form

Equations [2-12] and [2-16] constitute the Net Investment Model.

$$NI_{(n+1)} = NI_n + (NetInvest_n)(NiROCE_{(n+1)}) \quad [2\text{-}12]$$

$$CFaIA_n = NI_n - NetInvest_n \pm NetInt_n \pm \Delta WC_n \quad [2\text{-}16]$$

Investment Rate (IR) Model or Form

Equations [2-14] and [2-18] constitute the Investment Rate Model.

$$NI_{(n+1)} = (NI_n)\ [1 + (IR_n)(NiROCE_{(n+1)})] \quad [2\text{-}14]$$

$$CFaIA_n = (NI_n)(1 - IR_n) \pm NetInt_n \pm \Delta WC_n \quad [2\text{-}18]$$

Year 1:

Recalling Equation [2-8],

$$NetInvest_n = (NI_n)(IR_n) \quad [2\text{-}8]$$

if NI_1 is the Net Income for Year 1 in a company that has a Investment Rate IR_1, then by Equation [2-8] the Net Investment in Year 1 is:

$$NetInvest_1 = (NI_1)(IR_1) \quad [2\text{-}19]$$

The Cash Flow in Year 1 is given by the use of Equation [2-16]:

$$CFaIA_n = NI_n - NetInvest_n \pm NetInt_n \pm \Delta WC_n \quad [2\text{-}16]$$

Substituting subscripts in Equation [2-16] the Cash Flow after Investing Activities, CFaIA for Year 1 in terms of Net Income and Net Investments is:

$$CFaIA_1 = NI_1 - NetInvest_1 \pm NetInt_1 \pm \Delta WC_1 \quad [2\text{-}20]$$

Or by using Equation [2-18] and making suitable substitutes for *n* the CFaIA in Year 1 is calculated knowing the Net Income and the Investment Rate IR_1[17]

$$CFaIA_1 = (NI_1)(1 - IR_1) \pm NetInt_1 \pm \Delta WC_1 \quad [2\text{-}21]$$

Year 2:

Year 2's Net Income can be calculated with either Equation [2-12] or [2-14] after making suitable adjustments to the subscripts.[18]

$$NI_2 = NI_1 \pm (NetInvest_1)(NiROCE_2) \quad [2\text{-}22]$$

Or:

$$NI_2 = (NI_1)[1 + (IR_1)(NiROCE_2)] \quad [2\text{-}23]$$

In Year 2 investments are made at a rate IR_2, therefore the Net Investment in Year 2, $NetInvest_2$, is:

$$NetInvest_2 = NI_2(IR_2) \quad [2\text{-}24]$$

And following the same logic that resulted in Equations [2-20] and [2-21] the $CFaIA_2$ for Year 2 is calculated by:

$$CFaIA_2 = NI_2 - NetInvest_2 \pm NetInt_2 \pm \Delta WC_2 \quad [2\text{-}25]$$

or

$$CFaIA_2 = (NI_2)(1 - IR_2) \pm NetInt_2 \pm \Delta WC_2 \quad [2\text{-}26]$$

---

[17] Equations [2-20] and [2-21] both define CFaIA. The user is free to choose the one he or she prefers.

[18] At this point it's worthwhile to recall the assumptions made about NI_2. Specifically, the Net Income in Year 2 is the sum of the Net Income in Year 1 plus ΔNI_2, which is the incremental income produced by the $NiROCE_2$ acting on Year 1's investment.

Year 3:

Repeating the above process for Year 3 produces the Net Income in Year 3 in terms of Net Investments and Net Income Return on Capital Employed:

$$NI_3 = NI_2 + (NetInvest_2)(NiROCE_3) \quad [2\text{-}27]$$

or Year 3 Net Income in terms of the Investment Rate and Net Income Return on Capital Employed:

$$NI_3 = (NI_2)[1 + (IR_2)(NiROCE_3)] \quad [2\text{-}28]$$

The Year 3 CFaIA equations are:

$$CFaIA_3 = NI_3 - NetInvest_3 \pm NetInt_3 \pm \Delta WC_3 \quad [2\text{-}29]$$

$$CFaIA_3 = (NI_3)(1 - IR_3) \pm NetInt_3 \pm \Delta WC_3 \quad [2\text{-}30]$$

and so on.

NI AND CFaIA—THE GENERAL MODEL

The preceding section provided a progressive year-by-year development of a year-specific set of the Envelope Equations that can be used to predict Net Incomes and Cash Flows for such things as a first cut at a multiyear business plan. The rigor involved is probably adequate for most readers. However, there are always those who also like to see the general treatment or at least would like to have it available for reference. The equations for Year n and Year $n+1$ will hopefully be familiar since they have been derived in detail in the preceding sections. The equations for Years $n+2$ and so on are the subject of Appendix D.

If NI_n is the Net Income for Year n in a company that has a Net Investment Rate of IR_n and a Net Income Return on Capital Employed of $NiROCE_n$, then in Appendix D it is demonstrated that:

For Year *n*

$$Net\ Income\ in\ Year\ n = NI_n$$

Net Invest *n* $\quad NetInvest_n = (NI_n)(IR_n) \quad$ [2-8]

Cash Flow *n* $\quad CFaIA_n = NI_n - NetInvest_n \pm NetInt_n \pm \Delta WC_n \quad$ [2-16]

Or $\quad CFaIA_n = (NI_n)(1 - IR_n) \pm NetInt_n \pm \Delta WC_n \quad$ [2-18]

For Year *n* + 1

Net Invest *n* + 1 $NetInvest_{(n+1)} = (NI_{(n+1)})(IR_{(n+1)})$ [2-15]

Net Income *n* + 1 $NI_{(n+1)} = NI_n + (NetInvest_n)(ROCE_{(n+1)})$ [2-12]

Or $NI_{(n+1)} = (NI_n)[1 + (IR_n)(NiROCE_{(n+1)})$ [2-14]

Cash Flow *n* + 1 $CFaIA_{(n+1)} = NI_{(n+1)} - NetInvest_{(n+1)} \pm NetInt_{(n+1)} \pm \Delta WC_{(n+1)}$ [2-31]

Or $CFaIA_{(n+1)} = (NI_{(n+1)})(1 - IR_{(n+1)}) \pm NetInt_{(n+1)} \pm \Delta WC_{(n+1)}$ [2-32]

For Year *n* + 2

Net Invest *n* + 2 $NetInvest_{(n+2)} = (NI_{(n+2)})(IR_{(n+2)})$ [2-33]

Net Income *n* + 2 $NI_{(n+2)} = NI_{(n+1)} + (NetInvest_{(n+1)})(NiROCE_{(n+2)})$ [2-34]

Or $NI_{(n+2)} = (NI_{(n+1)})[1 + (IR_{(n+1)})(NiROCE_{(n+2)})]$ [2-35]

Cash Flow *n* + 2 $CFaIA_{(n+2)} = NI_{(n+2)} - NetInvest_{(n+2)} \pm NetInt_{(n+2)} \pm \Delta WC_{(n+2)}$ [2-36]

Or $CFaIA_{(n+2)} = (NI_{(n+2)})(1 - IR_{(n+2)}) \pm NetInt_{(n+2)} \pm \Delta WC_{(n+2)}$ [2-37]

and so on.

The discussion in Appendix D of these equations makes it clear that the equations that were derived did not place any restriction on what the Investment Rate and Net Income Return on Capital Employed must be in any year or relative to any other year. In other words, they are completely general.

Special Case: Constant Investment Rate and Net Income Return on Capital Employed

Earlier it was mentioned that over time IR and NiROCE often tend to be relatively stable. Therefore, in situations where the Investment Rate and/or Net Income Return on Capital Employed don't change from year to year, the subscripts on these terms can be dropped and they can be treated as constants. It's possible to restate Equations [2-8], [2-16], [2-18], [2-15], [2-12], [2-14], and [2-31]–[2-37] with IR constant and NiROCE variable, IR variable and NiROCE constant, and both IR and NiROCE constant. See Appendix D for details.

Special Case: Focus on Operational Cash Flows

The equations in the "General Model" deal with Operational Cash Flows as well as Interest (Capital Structure) and Changes in Working Capital (Balance Sheet). In some situations the impact of Interest and Changes in Working Capital can be ignored. Here are some of the considerations.

±NetInt: The amount of debt a company takes on is a function of its capital structure and in the final analysis this is decided by the owners of the business (shareholders) via the board of directors. In practice, however, the CEO and his management team are responsible for everything that happens in a business. Therefore the management team can't get a free pass and hide behind the board of directors when it comes to capital structure. Stated simply, they have to deal with the hand that has been dealt and improve it over time and provide sound proposals for financing growth.

Theoretically one could argue that management should not be primarily judged by how well they manage excess cash nor should they be penalized for having to cope with excessive debt. A company takes on debt to leverage the return to equity holders and this debt has to be serviced.[19] Therefore, in the real world, cash and debt management are part of the management task. Having said that, management is not hired to manage debt, per se. Their job is to profitably grow the business. They are hired and should be incentivized to create value, not through financial engineering but through growth. As far as management is concerned, capital structure is only important periodically to finance such things as a major acquisition. The point being made is: Management's job is to find investments that provide growth in net income and cash flow. In other words, it's extremely important for operating management, as the stewards of the shareholders' assets, to focus on value creation.

±ΔWC: In a practical sense and certainly in the long run, there is a limit to the amount of cash that can be generated by reducing Working Capital. At some point the Working Capital employed in a business bottoms out and thereafter fluctuates in some relationship to revenue and changes in market conditions. Therefore, once the Balance Sheet is optimized, Working Capital is no longer a source of cash flow from operations. In those instances where more precision is desired in estimating Cash Flows, Changes in Working Capital need to be considered. This can be done in a variety of ways. The simplest is to assume it is stable at some percentage of revenue.

In summary, while it is recognized that Net Interest and Working Capital are important to every business, they do not generate operating cash flow. Consequently, in instances where the focus is on recurring operational activities that impact cash flow, management may not need to be concerned with ±NetInt and ±ΔWC and, in such instances, these terms can be eliminated to further simplify the equations. For a thorough treatment of this assumption, refer to Appendix D.

It's now time to complete the set of Envelope Equations by turning attention to what drives Net Income and Cash Flow Growth in the context of the IR and NiROCE.

---

[19]In a leveraged buyout environment, management should and will focus on debt reduction. However, everyone involved, management and shareholders alike, will be striving to minimize the period during which they manage for cash and get to a point where they can focus on creating value through growth.

ESTIMATING GROWTH RATES OF CASH FLOW AFTER INVESTING ACTIVITIES AND NET INCOME

Up to this point, time and effort have been spent developing general equations for Net Income and Cash Flow and then simplifying them for special cases. The next topic to be investigated is growth. Similar to the approach used in the preceding section, the results of work done in Appendix C will be used in place of developing the growth equations in detail here and it is suggested the reader refer to the appendix as needed.

The Growth Rate of CFaIA over any period is simply the percentage change between the years in question, as shown in Equation [2-38].

$$\%\ CFaIA\ Growth = \left(\frac{CFaIA_n - CFaIA_{(n-1)}}{CFaIA_{(n-1)}}\right)(100) \qquad [2\text{-}38]$$

The growth in CFaIA can also be expressed in terms of the Investment Rate (IR) and Net Income Return on Capital Employed (NiROCE). The first step is to generalize Equation [2-38] and define CFaIAg, the Growth Rate of CFaIA, between any two years as:

$$CFaIAg_n = \frac{CFaIA_n - CFaIA_{(n-1)}}{CFaIA_{(n-1)}} \qquad [2\text{-}39]$$

In Appendix C general expressions for $CFaIA_n$ and $CFaIA_{(n-1)}$ are developed in terms of IR and NiROCE and substituted into the equivalent of Equation [2-39] and after simplifying end up with an equation for the Growth of Cash Flow after Investing Activities (CFaIAg), which is repeated here as Equation [2-40].

$$CFaIAg_n = \frac{[1+(IR_{(n-1)})(NiROCE_n)](1-IR_n)}{(1-IR_{(n-1)})} - 1 \qquad [2\text{-}40]$$

> Equation [2-40] is the Sixth Envelope Equation and is very helpful because it calculates the growth rate for the Cash Flow after Investing Activities for the Current Year directly by using the Investment Rate and Net income Return on Capital Employed without the need for the Prior Year's Cash Flow after Investing Activities.

GROWTH RATE OF CFaIAg WITH CONSTANT IR AND NiROCE

After a general expression for CFaIAg was derived in Appendix C, the next step was to consider a special case for Equation [2-40] by assuming that both the Investment Rate and Net Income Return on Capital Employed are constant and defined as IR and NiROCE, respectively. This effort yielded a much simplified expression.

$$CFaIAg = (IR)(NiROCE) \qquad [2\text{-}41]$$

Equation [2-41] is quite remarkable. It says that if one simply knows or makes an estimate of a company's IR and NiROCE, the growth rate of the company can be predicted.

While Equation [2-40] is a little more complicated than Equation [2-41] they both say the same thing and confirm what has already been demonstrated. That is, two of the drivers of cash flow growth and therefore of cash flow are:

- The Investment Rate (IR), which is the amount by which investments exceed depreciation compared to Net Income.
- The Net Income Return on Capital Employed (NiROCE), which is the Net Income resulting from these investments compared to the Capital Employed in the business.

The first thing these equations emphasize is that even if the IR is substantial, the impact it will have on CFaIAg depends on the Net Income Return on Capital Employed on the Net Investments.

They also point out that if all a company does is replace its assets at the same rate as they are wearing out (Investments = Depreciation), then the Net Investment (NetInvest) and Investment Rate (IR) are zero and CFaIAg is zero.

At first this conclusion may seem to conflict with what one would expect. But keep in mind that the equations are based on the notion that Cash Flow is investment driven. Experience has shown that for a period of time Cash Flow can be grown without any Net Investment or, for that matter, negative Net Investment. However, this comes about as a result of management getting more out of the existing assets and promoting Cash Flow Growth through increased Revenue, higher Gross Margin, lower spending on Operating Expenses, or any combination thereof. When this happens management isn't defying the principles inherent in these expressions. Instead they are focusing on getting underperforming resources to perform at a higher level via productivity increases.

Another example would be "Moore's Law."[20] The law is named after Intel co-founder Gordon E. Moore, who described the trend in his 1965 paper. The paper noted that the number of components in integrated circuits had doubled every year from the invention of the integrated circuit in 1958 until 1965 and predicted that the trend would continue "for at least 10 years." His prediction has proved to be uncannily accurate, in part because the law is now used in the semiconductor industry to guide long-term planning and to set targets for research and development.

This trend has continued for more than half a century. However, recent studies have shown that growth is slowing and after 2013, transistor counts and densities are forecasted to double only every three years. The implication of all of this may be that additional investment in R&D and equipment will be required to accommodate the higher densities.

[20]Gordon Moore, "Cramming More Components onto Integrated Circuits," *Electronics* 38, no. 8 (April 19, 1965): 82–85.

As evidenced by the implications of Moore's Law, this process can go on for quite a long time. However, at some point the assets or operating resources won't be able to produce anymore and at that time cash flow can't grow without significant additional investment. Furthermore, if the assets aren't maintained, they will ultimately become outdated and inefficient. When this happens, cash flow will begin to decrease and Cash Flow Growth will be negative.

An example of a different strategy would be a highly levered, *leveraged buyout*. To pay off the debt, management focuses on Cash Flow. Counting on increasing Revenue alone to generate more cash is risky. Therefore management often chooses as part of its strategy a more certain path and cuts investments, squeezes excess cash out of the balance sheet, focuses R&D on cost reduction, and cuts Operating Expenses. This works for a while, but ultimately Net Investments will have to be positive and at that time getting the innovation engine going can be problematic.

GROWTH RATE OF NET INCOME (NIg)

As important as the Investment Rate and Net Income Return on Capital Employed are to Cash Flow Growth, nothing happens without Net Income. Therefore, the next topic is how Net Income Growth, NIg, ties in with CFaIAg.

If NIg_n is the Growth Rate of NI between any two years, then in any Year *n*, NIg_n can be expressed by:

$$NIg_n = \frac{NI_n - NI_{(n-1)}}{NI_{(n-1)}} \qquad [2\text{-}42]$$

Once again in Appendix C general expressions for NI_n and $NI_{(n-1)}$ are derived and substituted in the equivalent of Equation [2-42]. After simplifying, the relationship expressed by Equation [2-43] is produced.

$$NIg_n = (IR_{(n-1)})(NiROCE_n) \qquad [2\text{-}43]$$

> *Equation [2-43] is the Seventh Envelope Equation. It says the Net Income growth rate in any Year n is the product of the Investment Rate IR during the Prior Year and the Net income Return on Capital Employed that an investment is expected to return the following year.*

NET INCOME GROWTH RATE (*NIg*) WITH CONSTANT IR AND NiROCE

The Net Income growth equation can be further simplified by assuming that both the Investment Rate and Net Income Return on Capital Employed are constant from year to year and defined as IR and NiROCE respectively. This results in a special case of Equation [2-43]: Equation [2-44].

$$NIg = (IR)(NiROCE) \qquad [2\text{-}44]$$

Recalling the special case for the CFaIAg growth equation in which it was assumed that the Investment Rate and Net Income Return on Capital Employed were constant from year to year the CFaIAg was given by:

$$CFaIAg = (IR)(NiROCE) \qquad [2\text{-}41]$$

Hence, Equation [2-41] equals Equation [2-44] and

$$CFaIAg = NIg$$

and the growth in CFaIAg and NIg are the same and expressed by (IR)(NiROCE).

Much of what has been said about the impact of IR and NiROCE on CFaIAg also applies to NIg. Because without Net Income, there can't be any long-term cash flow. By comparing Equations [2-40] and [2-43] it should be noted that the expression for NIg, the Growth in Net Income, is much simpler than the expression for CFaIAg, the Growth in Cash Flow after Investing Activities. This is because CFaIA (in addition to NiROCE) is impacted by the IRs for Years *n* and *n* – 1. Specifically, CFaIAg is positively impacted by the additional cash flow that eventuates in Year *n* from investments made in Year *n* – 1 and negatively impacted by the investments made in Year *n*, whereas NIg, the Growth in Net Income, in Year *n* compared to Year *n* – 1 is dependent on the additional earnings that arise from the investment made in Year *n* – 1 and the return this investment provides in Year *n*.

Perhaps this is a little easier to see by making some assumptions about Equation [2-40]:

$$CFaIAg_n = \frac{[1+(IR_{(n-1)}(NiROCE_n)](1-IR_n)}{(1-IR_{(n-1)})} - 1 \qquad [2\text{-}40]$$

In the preceding paragraph it was said that the reason the expression for CFaIAg was more complicated than the expression for NIg was that the growth in CFaIAg is driven by both the current and prior year's IRs. If this statement is correct, then by assuming the IR in Year *n* is the same as the IR in Year *n* – 1 ($IR_n = IR_{(n-1)}$) and reworking Equation [2-40] the assertion should be demonstrated.

Substituting in Equation [2-40] and simplifying:

$$CFaIAg_n = \frac{[1+(IR_{(n-1)}(NiROCE_n)](1-IR_{(n-1)})}{(1-IR_{(n-1)})} - 1 = [1+(IR_{(n-1)})(NiROCE_n)] - 1 \qquad [2\text{-}45]$$

Canceling the 1s:

$$CFaIAg_n = (IR_{(n-1)})(NiROCE_n) \qquad [2\text{-}46]$$

However, since $IR_n = IR_{(n-1)}$ or simply IR

$$CFaIAg = (IR)(NiROCE) \qquad [2\text{-}41]$$

which is the same as the expression for NIg_n given by Equation [2-43] for a constant IR.

ENVELOPE EQUATIONS METHODOLOGY FOR ESTIMATING NET INCOME, CASH FLOW AFTER INVESTING ACTIVITIES, AND GROWTH RATES

The point has now been reached where the material covered in this chapter can be drawn together. Recall that when the relationships for Net Income and Cash Flow were developed based on the Investment Rate (IR) and Net Income Return on Capital Employed (NiROCE), an important assumption was made: The growth in NI and CFaIA is driven by Net Investments and NiROCE. It was also decided to call these relationships "Envelope Equations" because once the user has become familiar with them, rapid estimates of Net Income and Cash Flow can be made literally on the "back of an envelope." This will be demonstrated in the material that is covered in the rest of this chapter.

When it comes to equations, less is more. For this reason it is suggested that the reader become thoroughly familiar with the equations in general form and adapt them as circumstances require. The examples in the next section rely heavily on the Envelope Equations. To assist readers working their way through the examples, a summary of the Envelope Equations in general form is provided in this section. These are the same equations listed in the General Model with the addition of the Cash Flow and Net Income Growth Equations discussed in the preceding sections. The form these equations take in the examples varies depending on what is given and said about IR, NiROCE, ±NetInt, and ±ΔWC.

Net Investment $NetInvest_n = (NI_n)(IR_n)$ [2-8]

NI Net Investment Model $NI_{(n+1)} = NI_n + NetInvest_n\,(NiROCE_{(n+1)})$ [2-12]

NI Investment Rate Model $NI_{(n+1)} = (NI_n)[1 + (IR_n)(NiROCE_{(n+1)})]$ [2-14]

CFaIA Net Investment Model $CFaIA_n = NI_n - NetInvest_n \pm NetInt \pm \Delta WC$ [2-16]

CFaIA Investment Rate Model $CFaIA_n = (NI_n)(1 - IR_n) \pm NetInt_n \pm \Delta WC_n$ [2-18]

For any interval

Cash Flow Growth

$$CFaIAg_n = \frac{[1+(IR_{(n-1)}(NiROCE_n)](1-IR_n)}{(1-IR_{(n-1)})} - 1 \qquad [2\text{-}40]$$

Net Income Growth $NIg_n = (IR_{(n-1)})(NiROCE_n)$ [2-43]

EXAMPLE 2-1: IMPACT OF NET INCOME RETURN ON CAPITAL EMPLOYED AND INVESTMENT RATE ON CASH FLOW AFTER INVESTING ACTIVITIES WHEN NiROCE AND IR ARE CONSTANT

Company A's management has decided to update their five-year business plan. For the purpose of preparing a financial model, they have assumed that the Company will generate \$1,000,000 of Net Income NI_1 during Year 1. An examination of historical Investment Rates and Net Income Returns on Capital Employed convinces management they have held steady at about 30% and 25% respectively. Management feel that they should maintain an IR of 30% (Investments > Depreciation) and believe that if they do so, they will realize the historical Net Income Return on Capital Employed (NiROCE) of 25%. (These assumptions are summarized in Table 2-1.) The company is debt free and management feel they have minimized Working Capital and any incremental increases that would be required as a result of growth can be ignored at this stage of the planning process.[21]

The management team is very "value" oriented and so the first question that crosses their mind is: Based on these assumptions, how much CFaIA (Cash Flow after Investing Activities) will the company generate during each of the five years?

The Envelope Equations used to answer this question are:

$$NetInvest_n = (NI_n)(IR_n) \quad [2\text{-}8]$$

$$CFaIA_n = (NI_n)(1 - IR_n) \pm NetInt_n \pm WC_n \quad [2\text{-}18]$$

$$NI_{(n+1)} = NI_n + (NetInvest_n)(NiROCE_{(n+1)}) \quad [2\text{-}12]$$

From Equation [2-8][22], the Net Investment in Year 1 is:

$$NetInvest_1 = (NI_1)(IR) = (1,000,000)(0.30) = \$300,000$$

And from Equation [2-18] (after dropping ±NetInt and ±ΔWC terms), the Cash Flow after Investing Activities CFaIA for Year 1 is:

$$CFaIA_1 = (NI_1)(1 - IR) = (1,000,000)(1 - 0.30) = (1,000,000)(0.70) = \$700,000$$

TABLE 2-1 Company A Plan 1 Assumptions and Requirements \$'s and %

	Year 1 NI	NiROCE	IR	CFaIAg	Find
Given	1,000,000	25.00%	30.00%	7.50%	CFaIA

[21] If ±NetInt and/or ±ΔWC are not to be considered, they can be dropped from the equation.

[22] When the general equations are used and both IR and ROCE are constant, the subscript *n* can be dropped from these terms.

TABLE 2-2 Company A Plan 1 $'s and %

	Year				
	1	2	3	4	5
Net Income (NI)	1,000,000	1,075,000	1,155,625	1,242,297	1,335,469
Growth Rate of NI	n/a	7.50%	7.50%	7.50%	7.50%
Net Investment (NetInvest)	300,000	322,500	346,688	372,689	400,641
CF after Investing Activities (CFaIA)	700,000	752,500	808,938	869,608	934,828
Growth Rate of CFaIA	n/a	7.50%	7.50%	7.50%	7.50%

The $300,000 invested in the business in Year 1 provides a 25% NiROCE in Year 2. Using Equation [2-12] the Net Income NI_2 in Year 2 is calculated to be:

$$NI_2 = NI_1 + (NetInvest_1)(NiROCE) = 1{,}000{,}000 + (300{,}000)(0.25) = \$1{,}075{,}000$$

Once more 30% of Year 2's Net Income is invested. The Net Investment in Year 2 is given by applying Equation [2-8].

$$NetInvest_2 = (NI_2)(IR) = (1{,}075{,}000)(0.30) = \$322{,}500$$

And using Equation [2-18], the CFaIA for Year 2 is:

$$CFaIA_2 = (NI_2)(1 - IR) = (1{,}075{,}000)(1 - 0.30) = \$752{,}500$$

Similarly, by using Equations [2-12], [2-8], and [2-18]:

$$NI_3 = NI_2 + (NetInvest_2)(NiROCE) = 1{,}075{,}000 + (322{,}500)(0.25) = \$1{,}155{,}625$$

$$NetInvest_3 = (NI_3)(IR) = (1{,}155{,}625)(0.30) = \$346{,}688$$

$$CFaIA_3 = (NI_3)(1 - IR) = (1{,}155{,}625)(1 - 0.30) = \$808{,}938$$

The reader can use the above process to calculate the CFaIA for Years 4 and 5. The results for all years are tabulated in Table 2-2.

As can be seen from Example 2-1, Cash Flow is easily estimated if a company's starting NI and expected IR and NiROCE are known. Also note the drivers of cash flow are Net Income (NI), Investment Rate (IR), and Net Income Return on Capital Employed (NiROCE).

EXAMPLE 2-2: IMPACT OF VARIABLE NiROCE AND IR ON CFaIA

After reviewing the results of their model, the management of Company A decided that since they had many ideas for new products and services and enhancements to existing offerings they should consider increasing the Investment Rate. After

TABLE 2-3 Company A Plan 2 Assumptions $'s and %

	Year				
	1	2	3	4	5
Net Income (NI)	1,000,000				
Investment Rate (IR)	31%	32%	33%	33%	33%
Net Income ROCE (NiROCE)	25%	26%	28%	30%	31%

considerable discussion they concluded if they did this, they should be able to leverage the company's assets and systematically improve the Net Income Return on Capital Employed by several points over time. The assumptions for this plan are tabulated in Table 2-3.

Being very cash flow oriented they once again proceeded to run the numbers using Equations [2-8], [2-18], and [2-12]. The process and results are as follows.

$$NetInvest_n = (NI_n)(IR_n) \quad [2\text{-}8]$$

$$CFaIA_n = (NI_n)(1 - IR_n) \pm NetInt_n \pm WC_n \quad [2\text{-}18]$$

$$NI_{(n+1)} = NI_n + (NetInvest_n)(NiROCE_{(n+1)}) \quad [2\text{-}12]$$

Using Equations [2-8] and [2-18] (after dropping the NetInt and WC terms), the Net Investment in Year 1 and Cash Flow after Investing Activities are calculated to be:

$$NetInvest_1 = (NI_1)(IR_1) = (1{,}000{,}000)(0.31) = \$310{,}000$$

$$CFaIA_1 = (NI_1)(1 - IR_1) = (1{,}000{,}000)(1 - 0.31) = (1{,}000{,}000)(0.69) = \$690{,}000$$

With Equations [2-12], [2-8], and [2-18], the NI_2, $NetInvest_2$ and $CFaIA_2$ for Year 2 are calculated.

The $310,000 invested in the business in Year 1 provides a 26% ROCE in Year 2. Therefore, the Net Income in Year 2 is:

$$NI_2 = NI_1 + (NetInvest_1)(NiROCE_2) = 1{,}000{,}000 + (310{,}000)(0.26) = \$1{,}080{,}600$$

In Year 2, 32% of Net Income is invested. The Net Investment in Year 2 is obtained by applying Equation [2-8].

$$NetInvest_2 = (NI_2)(IR_2) = (1{,}080{,}600)(0.32) = \$345{,}792$$

And $CFaIA_2$ for Year 2 is (Equation [2-18]):

$$CFaIA_2 = (NI_2)(1 - IR_2) = (1{,}080{,}600)(1 - 0.32) = \$734{,}808$$

The corresponding NI and CFaIA growth rates are:

$$NIg_2 = \frac{NI_2 - NI_1}{NI_1} = \frac{1{,}080{,}600 - 1{,}000{,}000}{1{,}000{,}000} = 0.0806$$

$$NIg_2 = 8.06\%$$

$$CFaIAg_2 = \frac{CFaIA_2 - CFaIA_1}{CFaIA_1} = \frac{734{,}808 - 690{,}000}{690{,}000} = .0649$$

$$CFaIAg_2 = 6.49\%$$

Similarly, by using Equations [2-12], [2-8], [2-18], and the data in Table 2-3, the Net Income, Net Investment, and Cash Flow after Investing Activities for Year 3 are:

$$NI_3 = NI_2 + (NetInvest_2)(NiROCE_3) = 1{,}080{,}600 + (345{,}793)(0.28) = \$1{,}177{,}422$$

$$NetInvest_3 = (NI_3)(IR_3) = (1{,}177{,}422)(0.33) = \$388{,}549$$

$$CFaIA_3 = (NI_3)(1 - IR_3) = (1{,}177{,}422)(1 - 0.33) = \$788{,}873$$

The corresponding NI and CFaIA growth rates are:

$$NIg_3 = \frac{NI_3 - NI_2}{NI_2} = \frac{1{,}177{,}422 - 1{,}080{,}600}{1{,}080{,}600} = 0.0896 = 8.96\%$$

$$NIg_3 = 8.96\%$$

$$CFaIAg_3 = \frac{CFaIA_3 - CFaIA_2}{CFaIA_2} = \frac{788{,}873 - 734{,}808}{734{,}808} = .0736$$

$$CFaIAg_3 = 7.36\%$$

Once again it is left to the reader to calculate the NI, NetInvest, CFaIA, NIg, and CFaIAg for Years 4 and 5.

The results for all years are tabulated in Table 2-4.

TABLE 2-4 Company A Plan 2 $'s and %

	Year				
	1	2	3	4	5
Net Income (NI)	1,000,000	1,080,600	1,177,422	1,293,987	1,426,361
Growth Rate of NI	n/a	8.06%	8.96%	9.90%	10.23%
Investment (NetInvest)	310,000	345,792	388,549	427,016	470,699
CF after Investing Activities (CFaIA)	690,000	734,808	788,873	866,971	955,662
Growth Rate of CFaIA	n/a	6.49%	7.36%	9.90%	10.23%

When the management of Company A got the results tabulated in Tables 2-2 and 2-4, there was considerable controversy as to whether they should opt for one plan or the other. In Chapter 4, Company A's business plans will be subjected to a present value analysis to help answer this question.

Also, when Tables 2-2 and 2-4 are compared and when the Investment Rate and Net Income Return on Capital Employed are constant, the growth rates of Net Income and Cash Flow after Investing Activities are the same and constant from year to year. When the IR and NiROCE fluctuate from one year to the next the growth rates are different and vary between years. In the next example the issues associated with growth rates and how they are driven will be examined.

EXAMPLE 2-3: CALCULATING THE GROWTH RATE OF NI AND CFaIA KNOWING IR AND NiROCE

Equations [2-40] and [2-43] can be validated by using the data in Table 2-3 to calculate the growth in Cash Flow after Investing Activities and Net Income for any year. For example, consider Year 3.

Applying Equation [2-40] with suitable subscripts, the growth in $CFaIA_3$ is given by

$$CFaIAg_3 = \frac{[1 + (IR_2)(NiROCE_3)](1 - IR_3)}{(1 - IR_2)} - 1 \qquad [2\text{-}40]$$

Substituting,

$$\%CFaIAg_3 = \frac{[1 + 0.32(0.28)](1 - 0.33)}{(1 - 0.32)} - 1 = \frac{(1 + 0.0896)(0.67)}{0.68} - 1$$
$$= 1.0736 - 1 = 0.0736 = 7.36\%$$

which agrees with the result obtained in Example 2-2.

Next consider Year 4 in Table 2-5.

TABLE 2-5 Company A Plan 2 (Growth Verification) $'s and %

	Year				
	1	2	3	4	5
Net Income (NI)	1,000,000	1,080,600	1,177,422	1,293,987	1,426,361
Growth Rate of NI	n/a	8.06%	8.96%	9.90%	10.23%
Investment (NetInvest)	310,000	345,792	388,549	427,016	470,699
CF after Investing Activities (CFaIA)	690,000	734,808	788,873	866,971	955,662
Growth Rate of CFaIA	n/a	6.49%	7.36%	9.90%	10.23%

Applying Equation [2-43] with suitable subscripts the growth in NI_4 is given by

$$NIg_4 = (IR_3)(NiROCE_4) \qquad [2\text{-}43]$$

Substituting,

$$\%NIg_4 = (IR_3)(NiROCE_4)(100) = (0.33)(0.30)(100) = 9.90\%$$

At this point one might wonder about the advantage of using Equation [2-40] or [2-43] as opposed to the method used in Example 2-2 where the approach was to simply take the difference between the NI or CFaIA for any two years compared to the first year in the difference. The answer is: By using Equation [2-40] or [2-43] the growth rates are obtained directly using the relevant IR and NiROCE without calculating the corresponding NI or CFaIA.

The results for $CFaIAg_3$ and NIg_4 are tabulated in Table 2-5 and are identical to those in Table 2-4, which were calculated using the actual cash flows $CFaIA_2$ and $CFaIA_3$ and Net Incomes NI_3 and NI_4.

Similarly, Equations [2-41] and [2-44] can be validated and confirm the result of the calculations for CFaIAg and NIg in Example 2-1 shown in Table 2-2.

$$CFaIAg = (IR)(NiROCE) \qquad [2\text{-}41]$$

$$NIg = (IR)(NiROCE) \qquad [2\text{-}44]$$

Applying Equations [2-41] and [2-44] and substituting IR = 30% and NiROCE = 25%,

$$\%CFaIAg = \%NIg = (IR)(NiROCE)(100) = (0.30)(0.25)(100) = 7.5\%$$

Hence. if the Investment Rate and Net Income Return on Capital Employed are relatively constant, quick estimates of a company's expected growth rate can be made by only knowing the IR and ROCE.

The relationship between CFaIAg, IR, NiROCE, and CFaIA is further illustrated in Example 2-4.

EXAMPLE 2-4: IMPACT OF NiROCE AND TARGET NET INCOME GROWTH RATES ON THE INVESTMENT RATE AND CASH FLOW AFTER INVESTING ACTIVITIES

Company B is a keen competitor of Company A. It's the same size as A and is also projecting a Net Income of $1,000,000 in Year 1 of their business plan. The management of Company B have learned that Company A has been growing faster than Company B as of late. Not wanting to be left behind, they are determined to grow the Company's Net Income at the same rate as Company A, which it has just announced in one of its press releases as being 7.5% per year compounded. They know their

TABLE 2-6 Company B Assumptions and Requirements

	NiROCE	IR	CFaIAg	Find	Find
Given	18.75%	40.00%	7.50%	NI	CFaIA

historical Net Income Return on Capital Employed is 18.75% and believe they can maintain this rate going forward. The question they are asking themselves is: How much will they have to consistently invest to keep up with A's growth and what will this do to their cash flow?[23]

The first step is to calculate the Investment rate Company B needs to achieve its goal and it's obtained by applying Equation [2-41], which can be rearranged as:

$$IR = \frac{CFaIAg}{NiROCE} \qquad [2\text{-}47]$$

If CFaIAg = NIg = 7.5%, for constant IR and NiROCE and NiROCE = 18.5%, then the Investment Rate Company B must have to grow its Net Income at the same rate as Company A is:

$$\%IR = \left(\frac{CFaIAg}{NiROCE}\right)(100) = \left(\frac{7.5}{18.75}\right)(100) = 40\%$$

Proceeding as in the earlier example and ignoring ±ΔWC and ±NetInt, the Net Investment in Year 1 is:

$$NetInvest_1 = (NI_1)(IR_1) \qquad [2\text{-}8]$$

$$NetInvest_1 = (1{,}000{,}000)(0.40) = \$400{,}000$$

And the Cash Flow after Investing Activities for Year 1 is:

$$CFaIA_1 = (NI_1)(1 - IR_1) \qquad [2\text{-}18]$$

$$CFaIA_1 = (1{,}000{,}000)(1 - 0.40) = (1{,}000{,}000)(0.60) = \$600{,}000$$

The \$400,000 invested in the business in Year 1 provides an 18.75% NiROCE in Year 2. Therefore, the Net Income in Year 2 is, according to Equation [2-12]:

$$NI_2 = NI_1 + (NetInvest_1)(NiROCE_2) \qquad [2\text{-}12]$$

$$NI_2 = 1{,}000{,}000 + (400{,}000)(0.1875) = \$1{,}075{,}000$$

[23] In these calculations the ±NetInt and ±WC terms are once again ignored.

Since 40% of Year 2's Net Income is invested, the Net Investment in Year 2 is (Equation [2-8]):

$$NetInvest_2 = (NI_2)(IR_2) \quad [2\text{-}8]$$

$$NetInvest_2 = (1{,}075{,}000)(0.40) = \$430{,}000$$

And the Cash Flow after Investing Activities for Year 2 is (Equation [2-18]):

$$CFaIA_2 = (NI_2)(1 - IR_2) \quad [2\text{-}18]$$

$$CFaIA_2 = (1{,}075{,}000)(1 - 0.40) = (1{,}075{,}000)(0.60) = \$645{,}000$$

Similarly, by applying Equations [2-12], [2-8], and [2-18] the NI, NetInvest, and CFaIA for Year 3 are:

$$NI_3 = NI_2 + (NetInvest_2)(NiROCE_3) = 1{,}075{,}000 + (430{,}000)(0.1875) = \$1{,}155{,}625$$

$$NetInvest_3 = (NI_3)(IR_3) = (1{,}155{,}625)(0.40) = \$462{,}250$$

$$CFIA_3 = (NI_3)(1 - IR_3) = (1{,}155{,}625)(1 - 0.40) = (1{,}155{,}625)(0.60) = \$693{,}375$$

The results for Years 4 and 5 are obtained by proceeding as above.

The assumptions and requirements are summarized in Table 2-6. Table 2-7 tabulates the impact that Company B's lower Net Income Return on Capital Employed and correspondingly higher Investment Rate have on its Cash Flow after Investing Activities in order to emulate Company A's growth rate.

TABLE 2-7 Company B $'s and %

	Year				
	1	**2**	**3**	**4**	**5**
Net Income (NI)	1,000,000	1,075,000	1,155,625	1,242,297	1,335,469
Growth Rate of NI	n/a	7.50%	7.50%	7.50%	7.50%
Net Investment (NetInvest)	400,000	430,000	462,250	496,919	534,188
CF after Investing Activities (CFaIA)	600,000	645,000	693,375	745,378	801,281
Growth Rate of CFaIA	n/a	7.50%	7.50%	7.50%	7.50%

TABLE 2-1 Company A Plan 1 Assumptions and Requirements $'s and %

	Year 1 NI	NiROCE	IR	CFaIAg	Find
Given	1,000,000	25.00%	30.00%	7.50%	CFaIA

Tables 2-1 and 2-2 are reproduced here for convenience. The objective is to draw some additional conclusions about Companies A and B and the impact that growth rates, Net Investments, Investment Rate, and Net Income Return on Capital Employed have on Cash Flow after Investing Activities

By comparing Tables 2-2 and 2-7 it can be seen that:

- If two companies have the same growth rates for CFaIA and net income NI but different NiROCEs, the company with the higher NiROCE will have the higher CFaIA (i.e., if a company has a better return and makes more money on its investments, it will have more cash flow after making these investments).
- CFaIA tracks Net Income.
- If a company has a lower NiROCE (than its competitors) and wishes to grow NI at the same rate as its competitor(s), it will have to invest more and this will result in a higher IR and lower CFaIA.

The one question that a comparison of Tables 2-2 and 2-7 doesn't answer is: Which company (A or B) has a higher value? Based on intuition, investors would probably prefer to own Company A's stock rather than Company B's because A has a higher Net Income Return on Capital Employed and Cash Flow after Investing Activities and therefore is probably better managed.

In the following chapters different models will be used to value several companies, including Companies A and B, and thereby get a quantitative answer to the question just posed.

TABLE 2-2 Company A Plan 1 $'s and %

	Year				
	1	2	3	4	5
Net Income (NI)	1,000,000	1,075,000	1,155,625	1,242,297	1,335,469
Growth Rate of NI	n/a	7.50%	7.50%	7.50%	7.50%
Net Investment (NetInvest)	300,000	322,500	346,688	372,689	400,641
CF after Investing Activities (CFaIA)	700,000	752,500	808,938	869,608	934,828
Growth Rate of CFaIA	n/a	7.50%	7.50%	7.50%	7.50%

REQUIRED REVENUE REVISITED

In Chapter 1 the level of Required Revenue (RR) for a targeted level of Net Income was discussed and Equations [1-64] and [1-65] were developed and renumbered here as [2-48] and [2-49].

$$RR = \frac{NI}{EBITDARatio} + \frac{D\,\&\,A}{EBITDARatio} \pm \frac{NetInt}{EBITDARatio} + \frac{TaxesPaid}{EBITDARatio} \qquad [1\text{-}64][2\text{-}48]$$

$$RR = \frac{NI}{EBITDARatio} + \frac{D\,\&\,A}{EBITDARatio} \pm \frac{NetInt}{EBITDARatio} + \frac{(EBT)(TR)}{EBITDARatio} \qquad [1\text{-}65][2\text{-}49]$$

Where the term $\frac{NI}{EBITDARatio}$ is the Revenue Required to support the Net Income,

NI and $\frac{D\,\&\,A}{EBITDARatio}$ is the Required Revenue to cover the D & A, etc.

These equations can be modified to introduce the concept of Net Income as developed in the discussion of the Envelope Equations. The idea is that the Net Income in any year is repeated in subsequent years and that Incremental Net Income in any year is the product of investments made during the prior year and the Return on those investments expected in the following year. Furthermore, any Incremental Income is also repeated in subsequent years.

The first step in this process is to recall the earlier discussion on "investments" whereby if in Year 1 a company invests $NetInvest_1$ with an expected Net Income Return on Capital Employed, $NiROCE_2$, then the expected Incremental Net Income produced in Year 2 from this investment would be:

$$\Delta NI_2 = (NetInvest_1)(NiROCE_2) \qquad [2\text{-}10]$$

Hence the additional Revenue necessary in Year 2 to cover the additional Net Income produced as a result of the Net Investment in Year 1 would be ($RR_2\Delta NI$) where:

$$(RR_2\Delta NI) = \frac{\Delta NI_2}{EBITDARatio_2} \qquad [2\text{-}50]$$

Since the Net Income from any period is expected to repeat during the following year, if that year is Year 2, then $NI_2 = NI_1 + \Delta NI_2$ and the Required Revenue in Year 2 necessary to support $NI_1 + \Delta NI_2$ is (RR_2NI) where:

$$(RR_2NI) = \frac{NI_1}{EBITDARatio_2} + \frac{\Delta NI_2}{EBITDARatio_2} \qquad [2\text{-}51]$$

Substituting Equation [2-51] for the first term in Equation [2-48] yields an expression for the Required Revenue in Year 2 incorporating the concept of Incremental Income ΔNI

$$RR_2 = \frac{NI_1}{EBITDARatio_2} + \frac{\Delta NI_2}{EBITDARatio_2} + \frac{D\,\&\,A_2}{EBITDARatio_2} \pm \frac{NetInt_2}{EBITDARatio_2} + \frac{TaxesPaid_2}{EBITDARatio_2} \quad [2\text{-}52]$$

Or since

$$TaxesPaid = (EBT)(TR) \quad [1\text{-}8]$$

then

$$RR_2 = \frac{NI_1}{EBITDARatio_2} + \frac{\Delta NI_2}{EBITDARatio_2} + \frac{D\,\&\,A_2}{EBITDARatio_2} \pm \frac{NetInt_2}{EBITDARatio_2} + \frac{(EBT_2)(TR)}{EBITDARatio_2} \quad [2\text{-}53]$$

EXAMPLE 2-5: CALCULATING REQUIRED REVENUE FOR THE STEPHENSON CORPORATION

Stephenson Corporation, a small manufacturing company, had a Net Income in Year 1 of $4,500,000 and Net Investments of $1,000,000 that are expected to generate an NiROCE of 25% in Year 2. In Year 2 the D&A, EBT, Tax Rate, and %EBITDA are $3,300,000, $7,916,667, 40%, and 18.5% respectively. In Year 2 the Company makes a Net Investment of $1,200,000 with an expected return on this investment in Year 3 of 30% NiROCE. Also during Year 3 the company expects to incur $3,500,000 of D&A expenses and produce $8,516,667 of EBT, which is taxed at the 40% rate. The Year 3 %EBITDA is expected to remain constant at the Year 2 level. This data is summarized in Table 2-8.

TABLE 2-8 Stephenson Corporation Statistics $'s and %

	Year 1	Year 2	Year 3
Net Income	4,500,000		
Net Investments	1,000,000	1,200,000	
NiROCE	25%	30%	
EBITDA		18.5%	18.5%
Depreciation & Amortization		3,300,000	3,500,000
EBT		7,916,667	8,516,667
Tax Rate		40%	40%

Given this information and using Equation [2-53], calculate the Required Revenue to support this level of performance in Year 2 and Year 3.

Recalling the general expression for Required Revenue developed in the preceding section, the next step is to calculate each of the "RR" components.

$$RR_2 = \frac{NI_1}{EBITDARatio_2} + \frac{\Delta NI_2}{RatioEBITDA_2} + \frac{D\ \&\ A_2}{EBITDARatio_2} \pm \frac{NetInt_2}{EBITDARatio_2} + \frac{(EBT_2)(TR_2)}{EBITDARatio_2} \qquad [2\text{-}53]$$

To simply replace the Year 1 Net Income in Year 2, the Required Revenue in Year 2 (RR_2NI_1) would have to be:

$$(RR_2NI_1) = \frac{NI_1}{EBITDARatio_2} = \frac{4{,}500{,}000}{0.185} = \$24{,}324{,}324$$ [24]

The Net Investment made during Year 1 with a 25% NiROCE in Year 2 will produce an incremental Net Income during Year 2 of:

$$\Delta NI_2 = (NetInvest_1)(ROCE_2) = (1{,}000{,}000)(0.25) = \$250{,}000$$

And the Incremental Revenue, $\Delta Rev_2(\Delta NI_2)$, necessary to produce the incremental NI of $250,000 would be

$$(RR_2\Delta NI_2) = \frac{\Delta NI_2}{EBITDARatio_2} = \frac{250{,}000}{0.185} = \$1{,}351{,}351$$

which says that the $1,000,000 of Net Investment in Year 1 that is expected to return a NiROCE of 25% in Year 2 will require $1,351,351 of Revenue to produce an 18.5% EBITDA.

The Depreciation and Amortization also has to be covered by the Year 2's Revenue if an 18.5% EBITDA is to be produced. Hence,

$$(RR_2\, D\ \&\ A_2) = \frac{D\ \&\ A_2}{EBITDARatio_2} = \frac{3{,}300{,}000}{0.185} = \$17{,}837{,}838$$

The Taxes Paid on an EBT of $7,916,667 at a 40% tax rate is:

$$TaxesPaid_2 = (EBT_2)(TR_2) = (7{,}916{,}667)(0.40) = \$3{,}166{,}667$$

---

[24] This may be a surprising result but keep in mind the assumption is that previous investments generate the returns for at least the length of the planning horizon. Also, in the absence of any D&A or Taxes an 18.5% EBITDA would be produced by $24,324,324 of Revenue since EBITDA is what is left after subtracting the Cost of Goods Sold and Operating Expenses from Revenue (EBITDA = Revenue – COGS – OpExp).

If the 18.5% EBITDA is to be maintained, then the Taxes Paid in Year 2 also has to be covered by Year 2 Revenue. Hence:

$$(RR_2 TaxesPaid_2) = \frac{(EBT_2)(TR_2)}{EBITDARatio_2} = \frac{3,166,667}{0.185} = \$17,117,117$$

Modifying Equation [2-52] with the terminology used above creates Equation [2-54].

$$RR_2 = (RR_2NI_1) + (RR_2\Delta NI_2) + (RR_2D \,\&\, A_2) + (RR_2 TaxesPaid_2) \qquad [2\text{-}54]$$

Substituting the calculated values,

$$RR_2 = 24,324,324 + 1,351,351 + 17,837,838 + 17,117,117 = \$60,630,631$$

Now, if the Revenue generating assets that were in place at the end of Year 2 are to produce Year 2's Net Income in Year 3, then the Required Revenue (RR_3NI_2) will be:

$$(RR_3NI_2) = \frac{NI_2}{EBITDARatio_2} = \frac{(4,500,000 + 250,000)}{0.185} = \frac{4,750,000}{0.185} = \$25,675,676$$

where $NI_2 = NI_1 + \Delta NI_2$

In Year 2 the Company makes a Net Investment of $1,200,000 with the expectation that it will return a 30% NiROCE in Year 3. Then the expected Incremental Income from this investment in Year 3 is:

$$\Delta NI_3 = (NetInvest_2)(NiROCE_3) = (1,200,000)(0.30) = \$360,000$$

And the incremental Revenue in Year 3 that is required to produce an incremental Net Income of $360,000 with an EBITDA of 18.5% is:

$$(\Delta RR_3\Delta NI_3) = \frac{\Delta NI_3}{EBITDARatio_3} = \frac{360,000}{0.185} = \$1,945,946$$

Similarly, if the Year 3 D&A and EBT are $3,500,000 and $8,516,667 respectively, then:

$$(RR_3D \,\&\, A_3) = \frac{D \,\&\, A_3}{EBITDARatio_3} = \frac{3,500,000}{0.185} = \$18,918,919$$

and

$$(RR_3 TaxesPaid_3) = \frac{(EBT_3)(TR_3)}{EBITDARatio_3} = \frac{(8,516,667)(0.40)}{0.185} = \frac{3,406,667}{0.185} = \$18,414,414$$

For Year 3, Equation [2-54] becomes:

$$RR_3 = (RR_3NI_2) + (\Delta RR_3\Delta NI_3) + (RR_3D \,\&\, A_3) + (RR_3 TaxesPaid_3) \qquad [2\text{-}55]$$

Substituting the Required Revenue for Year 3,

$$RR_3 = 25{,}675{,}676 + 1{,}945{,}946 + 18{,}918{,}919 + 18{,}414{,}414 = \$64{,}954{,}955$$

Finally, the year-over-year Revenue growth is

$$\%Rev\ Growth = \left(\frac{Rev_3 - Rev_2}{Rev_2}\right)(100) = \left(\frac{64{,}954{,}955 - 60{,}630{,}631}{60{,}630{,}631}\right)(100) = 7.13\%$$

The assumptions and results of the above calculations are summarized in Table 2-9.

A little more information can be wrung from this example by using the material in Table 2-9 to construct Income Statements for Stephenson Corporation. Starting with Year 2, the only variables missing are EBITDA and (COGS + OpExp), which are calculated as follows.

$$EBITDA_2 = (Revenue_2)(EBITDARatio_2) = (60{,}630{,}631)(0.185) = \$11{,}216{,}667$$

$$(COGS + OpExp)_2 = Revenue_2 - EBITDA_2 = 60{,}630{,}631 - 11{,}216{,}667 = \$49{,}413{,}964$$

The same is true for Year 3. Hence:

$$EBITDA_3 = (Revenue_3)(EBITDARatio_3) = (64{,}954{,}955)(0.185) = \$12{,}016{,}667$$

and

$$(COGS + OpExp)_3 = Revenue_3 - EBITDA_3 = 64{,}954{,}955 - 12{,}016{,}667 = \$52{,}938{,}288$$

TABLE 2-9 Stephenson Corporation Revenue Components for Given Ni, ROCE, and EBITDA $'s and %

	Year 1	Year 2	Year 2 RR	Year 2	Year 3	Year 3 RR
Prior Year Net Income	4,500,000	4,500,000	24,324,324		4,750,000	25,675,676
Net Investment	1,000,000			1,200,000		
NiROCE (Realized in Y2 & Y3)	25.00%			30%		
ΔNI		250,000	1,351,351		360,000	1,945,946
Depreciation & Amortization		3,300,000	17,837,838		3,500,000	18,918,919
EBT		7,916,667			8,516,667	
TR		40.00%			40.00%	
TR*EBIT		3,166,667	17,117,117		3,406,667	18,414,414
% EBITDA		18.50%			18.50%	
Total Revenue			60,630,631			64,954,955
Revenue Growth						7.13%

TABLE 2-10 Stephenson Corporation Income Statement $'s and %

	Year 2 RR	Year 3 RR	Growth
Required Revenue	60,630,631	64,954,955	7.13%
Cost of Goods Sold + Operating Expenses	(49,413,964)	(52,938,288)	7.13%
EBITDA	11,216,667	12,016,667	7.13%
Depreciation and Amortization	(3,300,000)	(3,500,000)	6.06%
Taxes Paid	(3,166,667)	(3,406,667)	7.58%
Net Income	4,750,000	5,110,000	7.58%

Using the previous results and the Depreciation and Amortization, Earnings before Tax, and Taxes Paid shown in Table 2-9 yields the Income Statements for Years 2 and 3 (Table 2-10).

Review of Table 2-10 shows that Net Income grows faster at 7.58% than the Revenue (7.13%), which is what you expect because the Depreciation and Amortization didn't grow as fast as Revenue. The moral of the story is: In order for NI to grow faster than Revenue some combination of (COGS + OpExp) and Depreciation and Amortization must grow slower than Revenue. A tax strategy that reduced Taxes Paid would also help.

GROWING THE NET INCOME

Up to this point the Net Income resulting from Net Investments and the associated Net income Return on Capital Employed has simply repeated in the following years. While this approach is helpful in getting comfortable with applying the Envelope Equations, it is unlikely management would be attracted to making investments that were static and did not grow Net Income. In the case study that follows, the methodology involved when Net Income grows at some rate is demonstrated.

CASE STUDY: AMERICAN TECHNOLOGY CORPORATION

Katherine Novak, chair of American Technology, has had a busy week—three full days of board and committee meetings and the usual private meetings with the CEO and various board members. The meetings went more or less as expected with two exceptions. At the Finance Committee meeting management had proposed a major acquisition and a stock buyback program. In most corporations these topics surface regularly. In fact she had encountered both many times in the various boards she had served on over the years. For some reason, she was troubled by this development at American Technology. After thinking about it for a while she concluded these proposals signaled a change. Rather than continue to grow the business by investing in the company's core businesses, management were proposing to purchase growth via acquisitions and improve earnings per share by buying back the company's stock. She also wondered what had brought this about. It seemed to her that based on the presentations made by marketing and research and development, the company had numerous options and ideas to mine. Initially she was tempted to discuss her concerns with management but decided she needed to think this through and if possible develop some options before doing so. To this end she decided to contact an investment banking friend, Carl Louis, with the express purpose of sharing her thoughts and exploring options with him on a confidential basis.

At their first meeting she outlined what happened at the meeting and her reaction to what was proposed and presented a copy of the most recent forecasted Income Statement and Balance Sheet for the Current Year (Tables CS 2-1 and CS 2-2).

She began the discussion by pointing out what was perhaps obvious to Louis. Her objective in doing this was to lay the groundwork for what was to follow. She made two points: This was a well-managed company, the leading player in its industry with Revenues in excess of $8.5 billion, and extremely profitable with a Net Income in excess of $1 billion and percentage-wise (12.6%) the highest in the industry. She then moved on to the Estimated Balance Sheet for the Current Year and pointed out that the company had no debt and over $400 million of Cash. Carl responded by reminding Katherine that being familiar with companies like American Technologies was imbedded in his job description. She acknowledged Carl's assertion and said, "Now I will get to what is bothering me."

Katherine continued, "American Technologies is a great company in all respects save one. The days of rapid growth have become a thing of the past and I'm having difficulty trying to understand why with a host of investment options available to

TABLE CS 2-1 American Technologies Estimated Income Statement for Current Year $(000)'s

Revenues (Rev)		8,547,390
Cost of Goods Sold (COGS)		(3,333,482)
Gross Margin (GM)		5,213,908
Operating Expenses (OpExp)		(3,258,692)
Earnings Before Interest, Taxes, and D&A (EBITDA)		1,955,215
Depreciation and Amortization (D&A)		(341,896)
Earnings Before Interest and Taxes (EBIT)		1,613,320
Interest Income/(Expense) (NetInt)		(4,274)
Earnings Before Tax (EBT)		1,609,046
Taxes Paid (TaxesPaid) @	33.00%	(530,985)
Net Income (NI)		1,078,061

TABLE CS 2-2 American Technologies Estimated Balance Sheet for Current Year $(000)'s

Current Assets		**Current Liabilities**	
Cash	427,370	Accounts Payable	324,089
Accounts Receivable	830,996	Taxes Payable	132,746
Inventory	666,696	Short-Term Debt (STD)	0
Total Current Assets	1,925,062	**Total Current Liabilities**	456,835
Fixed Assets			
At Cost	11,022,714		
Less Depreciation	(3,555,714)		
Net Fixed Assets	7,467,000	**Long-Term Debt (LTD)**	0
Other Assets		**Shareholders' Equity (TSHE)**	
Goodwill net of Amortization	0	Paid-in Capital	600,000
		Retained Earnings	8,335,227
Net Other Assets	0	**Total Shareholders' Equity**	8,935,227
Total Assets	9,392,062	**Total Liabilities + TSHE**	9,392,062

them, management have decided to take the acquisition and stock repurchase option at this fork in the road. It seems to me that the soft option will always be there, and why the management team doesn't opt for funding highly attractive projects is a mystery to me."

Carl responded, "If you can get me a forward-looking cash flow statement, perhaps I can help you with this."

Katherine had anticipated this request, and since a five-year forward-looking cash flow wasn't available she did her best to prepare one and handed Carl Table CS 2-3 as well. As she did so she said, "As you know, I'm no accountant, so it's important that you understand how I put this forecast together, so please bear with me while I go through the process that got me here."

She began by explaining that analysts were forecasting American's Revenue and Net Income to grow at 4% and 6% for the foreseeable future and she used these growth rates to forecast Revenue and Net Income. She continued and explained that after looking at some historical data she noted that 4% of Revenue was a good proxy for Depreciation and Amortization.

Her approach to Interest Income was a little more scientific and after a call with the CFO it seemed that in this low-interest-rate environment a 1% rate was suitable. The estimated interest was then calculated by taking 1% of the cash at the beginning of the year. She knew that a better way would have been to take the cash at the beginning of the year, add 50% of the cash generated during the year (on the assumption the cash was generated throughout the year and 50% of the cash generated during the year would be the average cash), and then 1% of the sum. Since this would have resulted in a circular calculation she decided not to unnecessarily complicate the document.

$$InterestIncome_{Year\ C+1} = (CashBeginning\ of\ Year_{Year\ C+1})(0.01)$$

$$InterestIncome_{Year\ C+1} = (427{,}370{,}000)*(0.01) = \$4{,}274{,}000$$

As for Working Capital, it has run at 20% of Revenue as of late so to get the Change in Working Capital for Year C +1, she took the estimated Revenue for Year C + 1, subtracted from it the estimated Revenue for the Current Year, and took 20% of the difference:

$$\Delta WC_{C+1} = (Revenue_{C+1} - Revenue_{CurrentYear})(0.20)$$

$$\Delta WC_{C+1} = (8{,}889{,}296{,}000 - 8{,}547{,}390{,}000)(0.20) = \$68{,}379{,}000$$

The Change in Working Capital was of course a use of cash since more working capital would be required to support the increased Revenue in Year C + 1.

As for the Cash Flow from Operating Activities, it was simply the algebraic sum of the Net Income, Depreciation and Amortization, Interest Income, and the change in Working Capital.[25]

$$CFfOA_{C+1} = Net\ Income_{C+1} + Depreciation_{C+1} - Interest\ Income_{C+1} - Change\ in\ Working\ Capital_{C+1}$$

$$CFfOA_{C+1} = 1{,}142{,}745{,}000 + 355{,}571{,}000 - 4{,}274{,}000 - 68{,}379{,}000$$

$$CFfOA_{C+1} = \$1{,}425{,}663{,}000$$

Continuing, she explained that historically Investments in Plant and Equipment, Systems, Software, and so on amounted to approximately 5% of Revenue and this was the basis for the investment figures used in the document. This resulted in investments totaling $444,464,000 and Cash Flow after Investing Activities (CFaIA) for Year C + 1 of $981,199,000.

$$CFaIA_{C+1} = CFfOA_{C+1} - Investment_{C+1}$$

$$CFaFA_{C+1} = 1{,}425{,}663{,}000 - 444{,}464{,}000$$

$$CFaFA_{C+1} = \$981{,}199{,}000$$

As for Dividends and Stock Repurchases, the Dividends Paid had been set at 40% of CFfOA for some time and the Stock Repurchase was based on data contained in management's presentation at the board meeting. For Year C + 1 the dividend the company would pay if the CFfOA was achieved would be $570,265,000. As for the

[25] Interest income is subtracted because it isn't operating income. Working capital is also subtracted because it represents an increase in Accounts Receivable and Inventory partially offset by an increase in Accounts Payable, resulting in a Change in Working Capital that represents a net use of cash.

Stock Repurchase it was penciled in at $300,000,000 and growing by $10,000,000 thereafter. Since the company didn't have any debt or need to raise capital there weren't any entries for these categories. This resulted in a Cash Flow after Financing Activities of $115,207,000.[26]

$$CFaFA_{C+1} = CFaIA_{C+1} - DividendsPaid_{C+1} + InterestEarned_{C+1} - StockRepurchase_{C+1}$$

$$CFaFA_{C+1} = 981{,}199{,}000 - 570{,}265{,}000 + 4{,}274{,}000 - 300{,}000{,}000$$

$$CFaFA_{C+1} = \$115{,}207{,}000$$

After reviewing the document, Carl commented, "This is very adequate for our purposes and I must commend you on having tackled this." Continuing, he said, "I gather from your earlier comments that you feel the Company should be using its cash to invest

TABLE CS 2-3 American Technologies Forecasted Cash Flow Statement (Base Case) $(000)'s

Year	C + 1	C + 2	C + 3	C + 4	C + 5	Assumption
Revenue	8,889,286	9,244,857	9,614,651	9,999,237	10,399,207	4%
NetInc	1,142,745	1,211,309	1,283,988	1,361,027	1,442,689	6%
D&A	355,571	369,794	384,586	399,969	415,968	4%
IntInc[25]	(4,274)	(5,426)	(6,785)	(8,372)	(11,282)	1%
ΔWC	(68,379)	(71,114)	(73,959)	(76,917)	(79,994)	20%
CFfOA	1,425,663	1,504,563	1,587,830	1,675,707	1,767,381	Sum
Invest	(444,464)	(462,243)	(480,733)	(499,962)	(519,960)	5%
CFaIA	981,199	1,042,321	1,107,097	1,175,745	1,247,421	Sum
DivPaid	(570,265)	(601,825)	(635,132)	(670,283)	(706,952)	40%
IntInc[26]	4,274	5,426	6,785	8,372	11,282	1%
StockPurch	(300,000)	(310,000)	(320,000)	(330,000)	(340,000)	+10,000/yr
IntLTD	0	0	0	0	0	
SH Cont	0	0	0	0	0	
CFaFA	115,207	135,921	158,750	183,835	211,750	Sum
CGU	115,207	135,921	158,750	183,835	211,750	CFaFA
CashBegYr	427,370	542,577	678,498	837,248	1,021,083	
CGU	115,207	135,921	158,750	183,835	211,750	
CashEndYr	542,577	678,498	837,248	1,021,083	1,232,833	

[26]Interest Earned is added back, because even though it doesn't contribute to Cash Flow from Operating Activities, it is cash the company has received.

in the most attractive projects that were presented by marketing and engineering during the board meeting."

"Yes," she responded, adding, "I would like to see the impact of investing an additional $100,000,000 per year on the Income Statement and Cash Flow."

Carl then said, "In order to do that we need to estimate the Net Income Return on Capital Employed (NiROCE) this additional investment will return."

She responded, "I did research on that. The NiROCE for the company based on estimated Income Statement and Balance Sheet for the current year is 12% ((1,078,061)/(8,935,227) (100)). Historically when new products have been introduced they did much better for the first five years and in the vicinity of 25%. However, I think for our purposes we should be conservative and assume five points less and use 20%."

To this, Carl responded, "I can work with that but before I answer your question, I need to know the Net Income growth rate you would expect for the products for the first five years after introduction."

Katherine had anticipated this question and answered, "10%." With this information Carl excused himself and 30 minutes later came back with several tables. The first table he referred to was Table CS 2-4.

Carl began by explaining he used a set of relationships described as the "Envelope Equations" to develop Table CS 2-4 and the other material he planned to discuss. Continuing, he explained, "The first thing I calculated was the impact each $100 million investment had on Net Income for each of the years and to do that I used the following equation.

$$\Delta NI_{n+1} = (NetInvest_n)(NiROCE_{n+1}) \quad [2\text{-}10]$$

TABLE CS 2-4 Proposed Incremental Investments and Impact on Net Income $(000)'s

Year	**C + 1**	**C + 2**	**C + 3**	**C + 4**	**C + 5**
Net Investment C + 1	(100,000)				
Net Income C + 2		20,000	22,000	24,200	26,620
Net Investment C + 2		(100,000)			
Net Income C + 3			20,000	22,000	24,200
Net Investment C + 3			(100,000)		
Net Income C + 4				20,000	22,000
Net Investment C + 4				(100,000)	
Net Income C + 5					20,000
Net Investment C + 5					(100,000)
Total Δ Net Income	0	20,000	42,000	66,200	92,820
Net Investment	(100,000)	(100,000)	(100,000)	(100,000)	(100,000)
CFaIA	(100,000)	(80,000)	(58,000)	(33,800)	(7,180)
Cumulative CFaIA	(100,000)	(180,000)	(238,000)	(271,800)	(278,980)

"This says that if you know the Net Investment ($NetInvest_n$) and Net Income Return on Capital Employed ($NiROCE_{n+2}$), the incremental Net Income associated with that investment can be calculated. For example, for Year C + 2 the equation would look like this."

$$\Delta NI_{C+2} = (NetInvest_{C+1})(NiROCE_{C+2})$$

He continued, "While the message this equation sends is simple it's very important to keep in mind that it assumes investments take time to have an impact and that any investment made in C + 1 would only have an impact on Net Income in Year C + 2 and the proper NiROCE to use is the one that will occur in Year C + 2. Then, substituting $100,000,000 and 20% for NetInvest and NiROCE respectively, the Incremental Net Income (ΔNI_{C+2}) in Year C + 2 is calculated to be $20,000,000."

$$\Delta NI_{C+2} = (100{,}000{,}000)(0.20) = \$20{,}000{,}000$$

Next he explained that since ΔNI_{c+2} was expected to grow at a compound rate of 10% the contribution of this investment for Years C + 3, C + 4, and C + 5 would be $22,000,000, $24,200,000, and $26,620,000 respectively, and by applying this model the Net Income portion of Table CS 2-4 was completed.

Continuing, he pointed out: "The data in CS 2-4 also deals with the impact the investments have on cash flow for each of the years and these calculations were based on the Envelope Equation that deals with the Cash Flow after Investing Activities for any year ($CFaIA_n$).

$$CFaIA_n = NI_n - NetInvest_n \pm NetInt_n \pm \Delta WC_n \qquad [2\text{-}16]$$

"Which, when applied to Year C + 1, would look like this.

$$CFaIA_{C+1} = NI_{C+1} - NetInvest_{C+1} \pm NetInt_{C+1} \pm \Delta WC_{C+1}$$

"And given the accuracy of the model the NetInt and ΔWC terms can be dropped.

$$CFaIA_{C+1} = NI_{C+1} - NetInvest_{C+1}$$

"Applying the equation for Year C + 1 was moot since there wasn't any Net Income. However, it is appropriate to apply the equation for Year C + 2 and subsequent years."

$$CFaIA_{C+2} = \Delta NI_{C+2} - NetInvest_{C+2}$$

He did this for Year C + 2 and calculated the Cash Flow after Investing Activities for the year to be –$80,000,000.

$$CFaIA_{C+2} = 20{,}000{,}000 - 100{,}000{,}000 = -\$80{,}000{,}000$$

TABLE CS 2-5 Forecasted CFaIA and Cash at End of Year $(000)'s

Year	C + 1	C + 2	C + 3	C + 4	C + 5
Net Income	1,142,745	1,211,309	1,283,988	1,361,027	1,442,689
CFfOA	1,425,663	1,504,563	1,587,830	1,675,707	1,767,381
Investments	(444,464)	(462,243)	(480,733)	(499,962)	(519,960)
CFaIA	981,199	1,042,321	1,107,097	1,175,745	1,247,421
Cash Beginning of Year	427,370	542,577	678,498	837,248	1,021,083
CGU	115,207	135,921	158,750	183,835	211,750
Cash at End of Year	542,577	678,498	837,248	1,021,083	1,232,833

At this point, Katherine interjected that she had never seen this model before and that "it certainly is a very simple way to calculate Net Income and Cash Flows resulting from investments." Continuing, she stated, "I assume this data will be helpful in getting to the question at hand, which is what impact these investments will have on Net Income and Cash Flow for the company as a whole."

Carl answered, "Absolutely," and produced Tables CS 2-5 and CS 2-6.

TABLE CS 2-6 Forecasted CFaIA and Cash at End of Year with Additional $100,000,000 of Investment Each Year $(000)'s

Year	C + 1	C + 2	C + 3	C + 4	C + 5
Net Income	1,142,745	1,211,309	1,283,988	1,361,027	1,442,689
CFaIA					
Δ Net Income	0	20,000	41,600	64,928	90,122
Total Net Income	1,142,745	1,231,309	1,325,588	1,425,955	1,532,811
% Δ NI Over Base Case	0.00%	1.65%	3.24%	4.77%	6.25%
CFfOA	1,425,663	1,524,563	1,629,430	1,740,635	1,857,503
Investments	(444,464)	(462,243)	(480,733)	(499,962)	(519,960)
Additional Investments	(100,000)	(100,000)	(100,000)	(100,000)	(100,000)
CFaIA	881,199	962,321	1,048,697	1,140,673	1,237,543
Cash at End of Year					
Cash Beginning of Year	427,370	442,577	498,498	598,848	747,611
CGU Base Case	115,207	135,921	158,750	183,835	211,750
Impact of Δ Net Income	0	20,000	41,600	64,928	90,122
Additional Investments	(100,000)	(100,000)	(100,000)	(100,000)	(100,000)
Cash at End of Year	442,577	498,498	598,848	747,611	949,484
Comparative Change in Cash at End of Year	(100,000)	(180,000)	(238,400)	(273,472)	(283,350)

Carl started with Table CS 2-5 and said, "Since we are primarily interested in Net Income and Cash Flow I thought it would be helpful for comparison purposes to have a Base Case table (Table CS 2-5) that presented a summary of the material you prepared; however, the real message is in Table CS 2-6."

Katherine studied Table CS 2-6 for several minutes and then said, "Carl, I would like to tell you what this table tells me." Continuing, she said the following:

- "First the Net Income for each year's investment is $20,000,000 and compounds at 10% yielding an incremental Net Income of $90,122,000 in the fifth year and this represents an increase of approximately 6.25% in Net Income for the fifth year compared to the Base Case.
- "Second, the CFfOA in every year of the Additional Investment Case is improved by the incremental Net Income compared to the Base Case.
- "The CFaIA for any year is adversely affected by the $100 million of additional investments offset somewhat by the incremental Net Income.
- "The differential in Cash at the End of the Year is most severe in the beginning years but deteriorates at a slower rate as the Net Income created by the investments takes hold."

Carl answered, "Yes; that is the essence of Table CS 2-6."

After taking a breath Katherine said, "This is all great, but what's not clear to me is while the additional Net Income is attractive, is this something the company should do?"

Carl responded by producing Table CS 2-7.

Katherine's reaction was, "These returns are very attractive."

Carl agreed and went on to say, "I hope you realize the company can well afford to do this, and with American's Balance Sheet, it can do much more—including acquisitions and stock repurchases."

TABLE CS 2-7 Annual Return on Additional Investment $'s and %

Cumulative Δ Net Income	0	20,000	41,600	64,928	90,122
Cumulative Δ Investment	(100,000)	(200,000)	(300,000)	(400,000)	(500,000)
Annual % NI Return	0.00%	10.00%	13.87%	16.23%	18.02%

CHAPTER THREE

The Weighted Average Cost of Capital*

CHAPTER 3 TAKEAWAYS

- Being able to estimate a company's cost of capital is important for several reasons. First recall that creating value is all about cash flow and growing cash flow. Next a company's value can be estimated by calculating the present value of future cash flows (this is what the price of a public company's stock represents) and then combining the present value with any long-term debt and excess cash to obtain an enterprise value. The use of this technique requires that a discount rate be established to discount the future cash flows to a present value. The Weighted Average Cost of Capital is fundamental in this regard.
- Well-run companies generally have good cash flow and strong balance sheets with low debt-to-equity ratios and qualify for investment-grade debt ratings. Among other things this means that there is substantial equity and cash flow standing behind the debt, thus greatly reducing the risk associated with the debt to a level where it can be viewed as nearly risk free and thereby fulfilling one of the assumptions that form the basis for the Beta framework.
- Taken as a whole, cash flows from projects or investments must provide funds that will pay interest on debt, repay debt in accordance with the debt amortization schedule, provide for any dividends for shareholders the board may declare, and provide cash to reinvest in the business.
- The Weighted Average Cost of Capital is also known as a *hurdle rate*. The only time a particular WACC is appropriate for evaluating a prospective investment is when the risk associated with the investment is the same as the risk environment for which the WACC was calculated, which is usually for the mainstream business and expansion investments. Relative to expansion investments, the risk involved in the replacement and repair of existing equipment is much

(continued)

*The reader may notice minor discrepancies in the calculations in this chapter. When this occurs, it is the result of rounding.

lower because the future cash flows are well understood. Companies also make investments in cost reduction. However, whether the cost reduction program will actually generate the forecasted cash flows is not nearly as certain and involves increased risk when compared to replacement or repair. Investments in new products usually involve more risk and therefore would justify a higher WACC than for expansion of the business. Acquisition of a company is probably the riskiest of all, requiring the WACC be adjusted accordingly.

- A close look at the results of the examples and calculations made in this chapter points out several characteristics of the WACC.
  - If the WACC isn't calculated realistically, the result can be either paying too much or deciding not to pursue the investment opportunity.
  - When using a particular WACC to calculate a present value, the presumption is that the risk associated with the cash flow stream and the risk implied in the WACC are one and the same.
  - Experienced managers have learned that most investments don't play out as expected and therefore it is necessary to adjust the discount rate upward to take into account risks not inherently implied in the WACC calculation.
  - Management creates value when an investment provides a return greater than the WACC.
  - Management destroys value when it engages in investments that earn less than the WACC.
  - Management is neither creating nor destroying value when an investment returns the WACC but rather providing debt and equity holders with the returns they expect.

WHY IS A COMPANY'S WEIGHTED AVERAGE COST OF CAPITAL IMPORTANT?

Being able to estimate a company's cost of capital is important for several reasons. First recall that creating value is all about cash flow and growing cash flow. Next a company's value can be estimated by calculating the present value of future cash flows (this is what the price of a public company's stock represents) and then combining the present value with any long-term debt and excess cash to obtain an enterprise value. The use of this technique requires that a discount rate be established to discount the future cash flows to a present value. The Weighted Average Cost of Capital is fundamental in this regard.

A hypothetical prototype may be helpful in illustrating the second point, which has to do with investments made by management. Assume a management team thinks that any project that yields more than the company's cost of debt is attractive. To see the fallacy in this kind of thinking assume that a company's cost of debt financing is 8% and the cost of equity is 12%. To them it would seem that a project promising 9% is attractive because it exceeds the marginal cost of debt. However, this kind of thinking is flawed for at least two reasons: (1) As the company takes on more debt to finance 9% projects, the *debt-to-equity ratio* will increase as will the interest rate on recent tranches and at some point no more debt financing will be available. (2) It ignores the cost of equity. When the company runs out of debt financing it now looks at the cost of equity and this would require they only approve projects that promise returns in excess of the cost of equity. Unfortunately by this time the cost of equity will have increased as a result of the debt load to some higher level, say (14%). The problem this creates is an investment with a 13% return should be turned down because it would have to be financed with the 14% cost of equity. To avoid this situation, management needs to take into consideration all of the components of the company's capital structure when making investment decisions and its cost of capital should be calculated as a weighted average of the cost of debt and equity used in the business. This concept is known as the Weighted Average Cost of Capital (WACC).

Much theoretical work has been done in this area and therefore calculating a company's WACC can be either an involved or a relatively simple process. The approach taken in this chapter is a middle-of-the-road approach.

WEIGHTED AVERAGE COST OF CAPITAL DEFINED

As its name implies, the WACC is a weighted average of the cost of the various kinds of capital a company uses to finance its operations. Generally speaking it is the weighted average of two kinds of capital: debt and equity.

A generalized equation for estimating a company's WACC is:[1]

$$k_{WACC} = \sum_{i=1}^{n} k_i w_i \qquad [3\text{-}1]$$

where:

k_i is the cost of the ith component of the capital structure and w_i is the weighting of the ith type of capital

If a firm's capital structure consisted of one class of debt, preferred equity, and common equity, then the generalized equation would reduce to:

$$k_{WACC} = k_B w_B + k_{PE} w_{PE} + k_{CE} w_{CE} \qquad [3\text{-}2]$$

where:

the subscripts B, PE, and CE refer to debt, preferred equity, and common equity respectively

When a company has only one class of debt and no preferred equity, Equation [3-2] becomes:

$$k_{WACC} = k_B w_B + k_E w_E \qquad [3\text{-}3]$$

where:

k_B = The company's cost of debt
k_E = The company's cost of equity
w_B = The debt or debt equivalent proportion of the company's capital structure
w_E = The equity proportion of the company's capital structure

Before moving on to a consideration of the weighting of the Components of the Capital Structure, a brief discussion of leases is in order, especially capital leases since they represent a special kind of debt.

[1] T. E. Copeland and J. F. Watson, *Financial Theory and Corporate Policy* (Reading MA: Addison-Wesley, 1979), 710, "Weighted Average or Composite Cost of Capital."

OPERATING AND CAPITAL LEASES

Basically there are two types of leases, operating and capital. Operating leases are those where the company has little if any ownership risk and simply pays a rental fee on some periodic basis. Normally, operating leases are not a material part of a company's financial obligations and therefore little value is added by going through a process to value them. In most cases they are considered as part of the cost of goods sold and expensed through the Income Statement. An example of an Operating lease is a lease for a building or space therein where at the end of the lease the ownership of the building remains with the lessor.

Capital leases according to the Financial Accounting Standards Board are leases that transfer most of the ownership risk of the asset to the lessee. In this sense, capital leases are really another form of debt and should be valued by computing the present value of all of the lease obligations using an appropriate discount rate. Determining the "appropriate" discount rate can involve considerable effort or one can capitalize the lease obligations by using the company's marginal cost of debt financing. In many situations little is added by going through this laborious process and using the cost of debt is adequate. Obviously such an approach is inappropriate in instances where the magnitude of a company's capital lease obligations starts to impact its ability to secure debt financing at existing rates. Examples of capital leases are leases on equipment such as copiers where the ownership of the equipment transfers to the lessee at the end of the lease.

WEIGHTING OF THE COMPONENTS OF CAPITAL STRUCTURE

The first step when estimating the WACC for a company or business unit is to determine the fractional market value w_i of each of the components of the capital structure and weigh each of these as a function of the enterprise value. This can be done by using the relationships for w_B and w_E expressed by Equations [3-4] and [3-5] respectively.

$$w_B = \frac{B}{B+E} = \frac{B}{EV} \tag{3-4}$$

$$w_B = \frac{E}{B+E} = \frac{E}{EV} \tag{3-5}$$

where:

B = The market value of the company's debt
E = The market value of the company's equity
EV = The Enterprise Value of the company
$EV = B + E +$ Excess Cash (sum of the market value of the company's debt, equity, and excess cash)[2]
$EV = E + B$ (when the cash in the company is required for working capital)

[2]By definition the Enterprise Value of a firm is the sum of the market value of its debt, equity, and excess cash. The reason "excess cash" is part of the enterprise value calculation is that should an acquirer purchase the stock of the company, any excess cash (cash that isn't required for working capital) can be paid out as a dividend and thus reduce the purchase price. When the cash in a company is required for working capital, EV = E + B and this definition of enterprise value is used throughout this book.

Substituting for w_B and w_E in Equation [3-3] creates expressions that define the WACC in terms of Debt, Equity, k_B and k_E, and Enterprise Value.

$$k_{WACC} = (k_B)\left(\frac{B}{B+E}\right) + (k_E)\left(\frac{E}{B+E}\right) \quad [3\text{-}6]$$

or

$$k_{WACC} = (k_B)\left(\frac{B}{EV}\right) + (k_E)\left(\frac{E}{EV}\right) \quad [3\text{-}7]$$

In situations where the debt consists of several kinds of debt obligations, the cost of debt k_B is the weighted average of the various components of debt. For example, if a company has three classes of debt, bank debt (B_{BD}), capital lease obligations (B_{CLO}), and public debt (B_{PD}), then the market value of the debt is expressed by Equation [3-8].

$$B = B_{BD} = B_{CLO} + B_{PD} \quad [3\text{-}8]$$

And the weighted average is:

$$k_B = (k_{BD})\left(\frac{B_{BD}}{B}\right) + (k_{CLO})\left(\frac{B_{CLO}}{B}\right) + (k_{PD})\left(\frac{B_{PD}}{B}\right) \quad [3\text{-}9]$$

where:

k_{BD}, k_{CLO} and k_{PD} are the interest rates (or implied costs) associated with B_{BD}, B_{CLO}, and B_{PD} respectively

MARKET VALUE OF DEBT AND EQUITY

As defined, B, E, and EV seem simple enough to understand. However, in practice they have to be calculated with some care. Furthermore, the procedure differs for public and non-public companies. The nomenclature used to consider the issues associated with the market value of the various classes of debt and equity is as follows:

B = One class of debt
B_{BD} = Bank debt
B_{CLO} = Present value of capital lease obligations
B_{PD} = Market value of public debt
B_{ID} = Market value of institutional debt
E = One class of equity
E_{CE} = Common equity
E_{PE} = Preferred equity

Public Companies

If the company is public and only has bank debt, one class of equity, and no excess cash, then the enterprise value of the company is:

$$EV = B + E \quad [3\text{-}10]$$

or

$$EV = \textit{Bank Debt} + (\textit{Number of Shares Outstanding})(\textit{Price per Share}) \quad [3\text{-}11]$$

If there are capital lease obligations on the company's balance sheet, then there is a need to estimate the present value of the capital lease payments. If they are material, then the present value should be included in the debt structure. In this case the debt component of a company's capital structure would be:

$$B = B_{BD} + B_{CLO} = \text{Bank Debt} + \text{Present Value of Capital Lease Obligations} \quad [3\text{-}12]$$

Substituting Equation [3-12] for Bank Debt in Equation [3-11] creates an expression for the enterprise value of a company with bank debt, capital lease obligations, and one class of equity.

$$\begin{aligned} EV = {} & \text{Bank Debt} + \text{Present Value of Capital Lease Obligations} \\ & + (\text{Number of Shares Outstanding})\,(\text{Price per Share}) \end{aligned} \quad [3\text{-}13]$$

If the company has public debt (bonds), then the market value of the public debt must be included in the debt component of the capital structure, as shown in Equation [3-14].

$$\begin{aligned} B = B_{BD} + B_{CLO} + B_{PD} = {} & \text{Bank Debt} + \text{Present Value of Capital Lease Obligations} \\ & + \text{Market Value of Public Debt} \end{aligned} \quad [3\text{-}14]$$

And once again substituting Equation [3-14] for Bank Debt in Equation [3-11] expresses the enterprise value of a company with these three kinds of debt and one class of equity.

$$\begin{aligned} EV = {} & \text{Bank Debt} + \text{Present Value of Capital Lease Obligations} \\ & + \text{Market Value of Public Debt} \\ & + (\text{Number of Shares Outstanding})\,(\text{Price per Share}) \end{aligned} \quad [3\text{-}15]$$

Non-Public Companies or Business Units

Most companies are not publicly traded. In these cases the market value of the equity needs to be estimated. There are several ways that this can be done and these methods are illustrated elsewhere in this chapter. One of the most straightforward ways is to calculate the present value of the business's future cash flows.[3] In order to make this calculation, cash flow forecasts for the company or business unit are required, and in addition an appropriate discount rate. The "appropriate" discount rate for this calculation is the company's WACC (or in some cases a discount rate based on the WACC). Since calculating the WACC requires knowledge of the company's capital structure, a dilemma exists. To solve this, the usual procedure is to look at comparable public companies and thereby gain insight into competitive capital structures. Then, based on this information, assume a capital structure for the private business

[3]The concepts associated with the Present Value of Future Cash Flows are dealt with in great detail in Chapter 4. Also refer to Appendix A.

or business unit in question, estimate the WACC, calculate a market value of the equity, and then through an iterative process refine the capital structure, WACC, and market value of the equity.

Often private companies have institutional debt in addition to bank debt and capital lease obligations.

Then if

$$B = Bank\ Debt + Present\ Value\ of\ Capital\ Lease\ Obligations + Institutional\ Debt \quad [3\text{-}16]$$

and if E_{FCF} is the value of the company's equity where:

$$E_{FCF} = Present\ Value\ of\ the\ Equity\ Holders'\ Future\ Cash\ Flow \quad [3\text{-}17]$$

Then, the Enterprise Value of a private company can be expressed by Equations [3-18] and [3-19].

$$EV = B + E_{FCF} \quad [3\text{-}18]$$

or

$$EV = Bank\ Debt + Present\ Value\ of\ Capital\ Lease\ Obligations + Institutional\ Debt + Present\ Value\ of\ the\ Equity\ Holders'\ Future\ Cash\ Flows \quad [3\text{-}19]$$

IMPACT OF TAXES ON THE WEIGHTED AVERAGE COST OF CAPITAL

Equations [3-3] and [3-6] do not reflect the fact that interest on debt is deductible for tax purposes. This is an important consideration because at the Net Income line, the impact of interest on taxes paid actually reduces the cost of debt and therefore the amount the debt component in the company's capital structure adds to the Weighted Average Cost of Capital.

The fact that interest on debt is deductible for tax purposes results in the interest cost being reduced by the amount of taxes saved. Therefore, if the cost of debt is k_B and a company's tax rate is TR, then the interest rate saved (so to speak) is $(k_B)(TR)$ and the cost of debt interest is $k_B - (k_B)(TR)$ and the after-tax cost of debt k_{BAT} is

$$k_{BAT} = (k_B)(1 - TR) \quad [3\text{-}20]$$

The after-tax Weighted Average Cost of Capital is obtained by substituting [3-20] into Equation [3-3].

$$k_{WACC} = (k_B)(1 - TR)(w_B) + k_E w_E \quad [3\text{-}21]$$

Substituting the proportion of the market value of debt and equity for w_B and w_E in Equation [3-21] modifies Equations [3-6] and [3-7] to include the impact of interest on the WACC.

$$k_{WACC} = (k_B)(1 - TR)\left(\frac{B}{B+E}\right) + (k_e)\left(\frac{E}{B+E}\right) \quad [3\text{-}22]$$

or

$$k_{WACC} = (k_B)(1 - TR)\left(\frac{B}{EV}\right) + (k_E)\left(\frac{E}{EV}\right) \quad [3\text{-}23]$$

If the only debt a company has is bank debt, it is relatively easy to estimate the cost of debt (i.e., the interest rate charged by the bank).[4] However, it's not so simple to estimate the cost of equity.

ESTIMATING THE COST OF DEBT AND EQUITY AND THE CAPITAL ASSET PRICING MODEL

Until this point k_B has been considered to simply be the "all-up rate" or the interest rate the lender requires to make a loan. When a bank makes a loan it takes into consideration several factors. Among these are the security the borrower provides and the borrower's ability to repay the loan. Logically if adequate security is provided by the borrower, then the risk the bank takes on is less than if the loan is unsecured. This implies that the all-up rate is a little more complicated than it appears and is dependent on several factors. Another way to look at this is to consider k_B to be the "marginal cost of borrowing"; if the lender is asked to provide more financing, then the risk associated with the loan increases and the lender will demand a premium for taking on the additional risk.

Therefore, when considering k_B it is often useful to think of it as consisting of two components: the risk-free rate for debt k_{rf} and a debt risk premium k_{rp}. Using this model the cost of debt financing can be expressed as:

$$k_B = k_{rf} + k_{rp} \quad [3\text{-}24]$$

It wasn't until 1964 when William Sharp first published his seminal work on the Capital Asset Pricing Model (CAPM)[5] that there was a unified theory on how to estimate the cost of equity. The CAPM is used to determine a theoretically appropriate required rate of return for an asset or investment assuming that it's financed entirely by equity.

---

[4]Sometimes this is not as simple as it seems. For example, if the rate the bank has agreed to for a $100 million line of credit is 8% and the company wants to extend the line to $200 million, the interest rate the bank will want to charge (assuming it wants to extend the line) will be several basis or interest points higher because its collection risk has changed.

[5]William Sharp, "Capital Asset Prices: A Theory of Market Equilibrium Under Conditions of Risk," *Journal of Finance* 19 (1964): 425–442.

The model takes into account the asset's inherent sensitivity to systematic[6,7] risk represented by the quantity *Beta* as well as the expected return of the market as a whole and a risk-free asset. Beta[8] is typically established using statistical techniques that look at data representing a company's total return compared to the market going back 5 to 10 years.

According to the Capital Asset Pricing Model the cost of equity k_E (like debt) can also be broken into its component parts. During the discussion of debt, the risk-free rate was defined as (k_{rf}). If $E(k_m)$[9] is the expected rate of return on the market as a whole, then the market risk premium is simply the expected rate of return on the market minus the risk-free rate or $[E(k_m) - k_{rf}]$.

The market risk premium is the premium an investor would expect from investing in the market as a whole as opposed to risk-free securities. However, it doesn't take into account the risk associated with investing in any individual company. To do this the market risk premium needs to be adjusted for a particular company's systematic risk. This systematic risk is expressed by Beta. The Capital Asset Pricing Model ties all of this together. According to the CAPM the cost of equity k_E is expressed mathematically as:

$$k_E = k_{rf} + [E(k_m) - k_{rf}](Beta) \qquad [3\text{-}25]$$

where once again:

k_{rf} = The risk-free rate of return

$E(k_m)$ = The expected rate of return on the overall market portfolio

$[E(k_m) - k_{rf}]$ = The market risk premium (the price of risk)

Beta = The systematic risk of the company under consideration

Estimating the various components of the CAPM can be effort intensive. However, it doesn't have to be that way in most cases. Here are some suggestions.

- The interest rate for 10- to 30-year U.S. Treasury Bills is typically used to estimate k_{rf}, the risk-free rate of return, which has characteristically had a value of 4–6% for U.S. companies.[10]
- k_{rp} is the premium above the risk-free rate (k_{rf}) that lenders charge for a particular class of debt. This rate is usually available from lenders or is given as an all-up rate, that is, $k_{rf} + k_{rp}$. In such a case k_{rp} is easily calculated by subtracting k_{rf} from the all-up rate.
- $[E(k_m) - k_{rf}]$, the market risk premium, is the difference between the risk-free rate and the expected rate of return on the market as a whole, which has historically run at 9–11%.
- There are several sources of published Betas for publicly traded companies (and industries), *Value Line* being among the better known.

[6]Systematic risk, sometimes called *market risk, aggregate risk*, or *undiversifiable risk*, is the risk associated with aggregate market returns. By contrast, unsystematic risk, sometimes called *specific risk, idiosyncratic risk, residual risk*, or *diversifiable risk*, is the company-specific or industry-specific risk in a portfolio, which is uncorrelated with aggregate market returns. Unsystematic risk can be mitigated through diversification, whereas systematic risk cannot be diversified away.

[7]Systematic risk should not be confused with *systemic* risk, which is the risk of loss from some catastrophic event that collapses the entire financial system.

[8]See the discussion of Beta in the next section of this chapter.

[9]In this case "E" is read as "Expected" and should not be confused with "E" when used to denote equity.

[10]The past decade has seen somewhat lower rates but it is yet to be seen if these rates are indicative of future long-term rates.

GENERAL EQUATIONS FOR ESTIMATING THE WACC FOR A COMPANY WITH ONE CLASS OF DEBT AND EQUITY

As stated previously the capital structure of a large number of companies consists of one class of debt and one class of equity. By using the equations developed in the preceding sections it is a simple matter to update these expressions for the WACC of a company with this capital structure to include the CAPM.

Substituting for k_B (Equation [3-24]) and k_E (Equation [3-25]) into Equation [3-21] creates an expression that can be used to estimate a company's WACC by using the risk-free and risk premium rates, market risk premium, and Beta.

$$k_{WACC} = (k_{rf} + k_{rp})(1 - TR)(w_B) + \{k_{rf} + [E(k_m) - k_{rf}](Beta)\}(w_E) \quad [3\text{-}26]$$

Similarly, substituting for k_B (Equation [3-24]) and k_E (Equation [3-25]) in Equation [3-22] modifies Equation [3-26] to include the debt and equity components.

$$k_{WACC} = (k_{rf} + k_{rp})(1 - TR)\left(\frac{B}{B+E}\right) + \{k_{rf} + [E(k_m) - k_{rf}](Beta)\}\left(\frac{E}{B+E}\right) \quad [3\text{-}27]$$

Finally, substituting for k_B (Equation [3-24]) and k_E (Equation [3-25]) in Equation [3-23] adjusts Equation ([3-26]) to include the notion of enterprise value.

$$k_{WACC} = (k_{rf} + k_{rp})(1 - TR)\left(\frac{B}{EV}\right) + \{k_{rf} + [E(k_m) - k_{rf}](Beta)\}\left(\frac{E}{EV}\right) \quad [3\text{-}28]$$

where:

k_{rf} = The risk-free rate of return
k_{rp} = The debt risk premium
TR = The corporate tax rate
$E(k_m)$ = The expected rate of return on the overall market portfolio
$[E(k_m) - k_{rf}]$ = The market risk premium
$Beta$ = The systematic risk of the company under consideration
B = The market value of the company's debt
E = The market value of the company's equity
EV = The Enterprise Value of the company
$EV = B + E$ (sum of the market value of the company's debt and equity)

LEVERED AND UNLEVERED BETAS[11]

Before Equations [3-26]–[3-28] are used to calculate a company's WACC it is necessary to make sure that the reader has a basic understanding of Beta and levered and unlevered Betas.

[11] T. E. Copeland, T. Koller, and J. Murrin, *Valuation, Measuring and Managing the Value of Companies*, 2nd ed. (New York: John Wiley & Sons, 1995), 329, "Business-Unit Capital Structure and Cost of Capital."

The definition of Beta involves a statistical term, *covariance*, which is simply a measurement of how the variances (read *variability*) of two variables are related. If the two variables tend to increase together, then the covariance is positive. If one tends to decrease in relation to the other, then the covariance is negative. When the two variables are unrelated the covariance is zero. Also, a large covariance (positive or negative) indicates a relationship but does not suggest what may have caused the relationship.

When the concept of covariance is used in determining the Beta of a security it is the measurement of the variance of a security (such as IBM stock) to the variance of the market portfolio divided by the variance of the market portfolio. Statistically, Beta (β) is defined as:

$$\beta_i = \frac{\sigma_m}{\sigma_m^2} \qquad [3\text{-}29]$$

where:

β_i = Beta of security *i*, σ_{im} = covariance between the security *i* and the market portfolio *m*, and σ_m^2 = variance of the market portfolio

Statistically σ_{im} can be expressed as COV(R_i, R_m) and σ_m^2 as VAR(R_m) where R_i and R_m are the expected return of security *i* and the expected return of the market portfolio *m* respectively. Substituting these expressions in Equation [3-29] yields the usual definition of Beta.

$$Beta = \frac{COV(R_i, R_m)}{VAR(R_m)} \qquad [3\text{-}30]$$

A detailed discussion of Beta as defined by Equations [3-29] and [3-30] is beyond the scope of this book. This is not necessarily a problem since our prime concern is to understand what Beta means and how to use it. So at this point the statistical discussion is abandoned. Instead the focus is on the key points necessary for understanding and using Beta. To this end, the following summary should help.

- Beta is a number.
- Stated simply, the Beta for the market as a whole is defined as 1.
- The Beta for a company depends on the industry characteristics and how the company's returns vary in relationship to fluctuations in the market as a whole.
- Industry characteristics usually evolve over time, whereas management's strategy can change overnight and therefore is more likely to impact Beta in the short run.
- There are Betas for industries and companies.
- Divisions of multi-division companies can have different Betas with the Beta for the conglomerate reflecting the weighted average of the Betas of all the divisions.
- You can think of Beta as a number that reflects the volatility of the returns of a company's securities compared to the market returns.
- When the systematic risk (total return) of a company is the same as the total return of the index, its Beta = 1.
- Stated differently, a stock that moves in unison with the market will have a Beta = 1.

- If the volatility of the returns of a particular company's stock is high, then it will have a higher Beta than a company with a security that has more stable returns.[12]
- Companies with securities that have above-average volatility of returns will have a Beta > 1.
- Companies with securities that have below-average volatility of returns will have a Beta <1.
- Companies with securities that move in the same direction as the market have a +Beta.
- Conversely, companies with securities that move in a direction opposite to the market as a whole would have a –Beta.[13]
- In practical terms, if a company has a Beta of 1.2, then the return on that company's security varies 1.2% for every 1% change in the index.

As a company takes on debt, it places obligations ahead of the equity holders. The interest and debt amortization have to be serviced from the company's cash flow. This results in an increase in the company's systematic risk and a corresponding increase in the company's Beta. A company with no debt has an *unlevered* equity Beta. Conversely, a company with debt has a *levered* equity Beta.

The relationship between the unlevered and levered Betas is expressed by Equations [3-31] and [3-32]:[14]

$$Beta_L = \left[1 + (1 - TR)\left(\frac{B}{E}\right)\right](Beta_U) \qquad [3\text{-}31]$$

$$Beta_U = \frac{Beta_L}{\left[1 + (1 - TR)\left(\frac{B}{E}\right)\right]} \qquad [3\text{-}32]$$

where:

$Beta_L$ = The levered equity Beta
$Beta_U$ = The unlevered equity Beta
TR = The marginal tax rate of the corporation
B = Market value of the debt of the company under consideration
E = Market value of the equity of the company under consideration

As can be seen from these equations, if the company doesn't have any debt, the value of $B/E = 0$, $Beta_U = Beta_L$, and there is no need to be concerned about which Beta one is talking about. However, in the real world, companies have debt and as the B/E ratio increases, the risk profile of the company changes and Beta increases as a result of the leverage.

[12] For example, the Beta for Emerson Electric Co. is 1.19 compared to 1.60 for General Electric Co.
[13] An example of this is gold and related stocks, which generally move in a direction opposite to the market.
[14] Once again, derivation is not a prime concern. The use of the $Beta_L$ and $Beta_U$ equations is demonstrated in Example 3-1 and other examples in this chapter.

ESTIMATING BETA FOR NON-PUBLIC COMPANIES OR BUSINESS UNITS

As mentioned earlier, Beta for public companies is readily available from various sources. Obtaining a value for Beta can be problematic if the company in question is not publicly traded. Two of the most straightforward techniques that can be used to estimate a Beta for a division, business unit, or private company are "industry comparisons" and "comparable companies." More sophisticated techniques such as "multiple regression" and "covariance of earnings" exist but are beyond the scope of this book.

Industry Comparisons

This technique is quite simple. A group of managers are asked to look at a list of industries and select the industry with the risk profile most like their own business or division. After an iterative process, the group usually agrees on the most appropriate industry. Using this technique, the Beta of the industry selected by the managers is the levered Beta of their business or division. (The industry Beta will almost always be levered because it is composed of a wide cross-section of companies, many of which will have debt.) Once the levered Beta has been established the next step is to decide on what the tax rate and ratio of debt to equity this industry Beta represents. This can be done by taking an average of the industry companies that you think are most representative of the business or division in question and then using Equation [3-32] to calculate the unlevered Beta of the representative companies. This is the unlevered Beta for the company or division in question. If the company or division under consideration has debt, then the levered Beta is obtained by substituting the relevant Debt-to-Equity ratio and Tax Rate into Equation [3-31].

Comparable Companies

This approach is similar to that for the industry comparison except management is asked to identify public companies that are most similar to their division or business. The Beta of these companies is looked up and the Beta of the one that is perceived to have similar risk is used as a *starting point*. *Starting point* is emphasized because the comparison company selected will almost always employ different leverage than that used in the business under consideration. To get around this complication the comparison company's Beta has to be unlevered and then using the company or business in question's leverage, calculate the levered Beta for the business being analyzed. An example may clarify the process.

EXAMPLE 3-1: ESTIMATING BETA USING THE COMPARABLE COMPANY METHOD

The management of DLK Enterprises has decided to update its strategic plan. It has been several years since they have reviewed their Weighted Average Cost of Capital. In order to update their WACC they need to know their Beta. The company is not publicly traded so management looks for comparable public companies. After agreeing on a comparable company, management looked up the comparables data and found that it had a levered

TABLE 3-1 DLK Enterprises Data and Requirements

	Comparable Company	DLK Enterprises
Levered Beta	1.25	?
Debt to Equity	0.60	0.50
Marginal Tax Rate	0.35	0.40
Unlevered Beta	?	?

Beta ($Beta_L$) of 1.25, a debt-to-equity ratio (B/E) of 60%, and a marginal tax rate (TR) of 35%. This data is summarized in Table 3-1.

As indicated in the preceding section the first step in calculating the levered Beta for DLK Enterprises is to determine the unlevered Beta for the comparable company. The relationship between levered and unlevered Betas is given by Equation [3-32].

$$Beta_U = \frac{Beta_L}{\left[1+(1-TR)\left(\frac{B}{E}\right)\right]} \qquad [3\text{-}32]$$

By applying Equation [3-32], DLK Enterprises management was able to calculate the unlevered Beta ($Beta_U$) for the comparable company to be 0.90.

$$Beta_U = \frac{1.25}{[1+(1-0.35)(0.60)]} = \frac{1.25}{[1+(0.65)(0.60)]} = \frac{1.25}{1+0.39} = \frac{1.25}{1.39} = 0.90$$

Next, using 0.90 as the unlevered Beta of DLK Enterprises, management used Equation [3-31] to calculate the levered Beta of their business and determined it to be 1.17.

$$Beta_L = \left[1+(1-TR)\left(\frac{B}{E}\right)\right](Beta_U) \qquad [3\text{-}31]$$

$$Beta_L = [1 + (1 - 0.4)(0.50)](0.90) = [1 + (0.60)(0.50)](0.90)$$
$$= [1 + 0.30](0.90) = 1.30(0.90) = 1.17$$

The results of these calculations are tabulated in Table 3-2.

TABLE 3-2 DLK Enterprises Calculated Betas

	Comparable Company	DLK Enterprises
Levered Beta	1.25	1.17
Debt to Equity	0.60	0.50
Marginal Tax Rate	0.35	0.40
Unlevered Beta	0.90	0.90

An important point needs to be made before moving on from the discussion of unlevered and levered Betas. Equations [3-31] and [3-32] should be used with care because unlevering and levering Betas can become very complicated in situations where the debt-to-equity ratio is very high. One of the reasons for this is that these equations assume that the debt in question is risk free, which is rarely the case.[15] Sensibly applied, these formulas can be of great assistance when working through the process of calculating the WACC of divisions, business units, or private companies.

SIGNIFICANCE AND USES OF THE WACC

By definition the Weighted Average Cost of Capital is the blended cost of capital to the company for a given capital structure that reflects the risk-adjusted returns required by lenders and equity holders. Using the WACC as a discount rate for a stream of certain cash flows makes sure that as a minimum, the cash flow stream will be burdened with a discount rate that represents the combined financial expectations of all of the debt and equity stakeholders.

The point made in the preceding paragraph should not be glossed over. Each project or investment has its own risk characteristics. A project that simply involves increasing production of an existing product is probably well understood and since it constitutes an expansion of existing business using the company's WACC as a hurdle rate is probably appropriate. Putting a new product into production or buying a company is a different matter. In both of these cases there are numerous assumptions and unknowns and therefore the WACC has to be adjusted to reflect the additional risk. Adjusting the Weighted Average Cost of Capital to reflect additional risk is a topic of its own and will be covered in a subsequent chapter.

The Weighted Average Cost of Capital concept has numerous applications. Some of the more common uses are:

- Establishing a hurdle rate for internal projects that have a risk profile that is the same as the company's existing business
- It is also applicable in those cases where a company needs to calculate the maximum price it should pay for a stream of cash flows that are perceived to involve the same amount of risk as that imbedded in the WACC
- Establishing a starting point from which it is possible to logically develop a hurdle rate for projects, investments, and so on that involve different risk profiles
- Establishing a reference point from which to judge the impact that various projects could have on the value of the firm

Using the Weighted Average Cost of Capital as a reference point has several implications. Taken as a whole, cash flows from projects or investments must provide funds that

---

[15]Well-run companies generally have good cash flow and strong balance sheets with low debt-to-equity ratios and qualify for investment-grade debt ratings. Among other things this means that there is substantial equity and cash flow standing behind the debt thus greatly reducing the risk associated with the debt to a level where it can be viewed as "nearly risk free" and thereby fulfilling one of the assumptions that form the basis for the Beta framework.

will pay interest on debt, repay debt in accordance with the debt amortization schedule, provide for any dividends for shareholders the board may declare, and provide cash to reinvest in the business. In general, returns on projects or investments fall into three categories.

Rate of Return from a Project or Investment = WACC

When the returns from a project or investment equal the WACC, then the returns required by debt and shareholders are just met and no value beyond this is created.

Rate of Return from a Project or Investment < WACC

If the return is less than the WACC, the requirements of debt and shareholders will not be met. In fact shareholder wealth is diminished because cash flow will have to be taken from elsewhere in the corporation to meet obligations.

Rate of Return from a Project or Investment > WACC

Only when the returns from a project or investment exceed the WACC will shareholder value increase. In this case, returns satisfy debt and equity holders' expectations and provide a source of cash flow to reinvest in the business and/or for other uses that management and the board of directors consider appropriate.

The examples following the next section should help bring together the various factors involved in estimating a company's Weighted Average Cost of Capital. But first there is a need to spend some time trying to understand where the coefficients that are used in calculating WACCs originate.

ORIGIN OF THE COEFFICIENTS USED IN CALCULATING A WACC

Stated simply, they come from the markets.

The risk-free rate (k_{rf}) is generally considered to be the interest rate on long-term U.S. Treasury Bills.

As can be seen from Table 3-3 the rates for U.S. Treasury Bills vary from 3.0 to 4.75 percent depending on the duration. And the return of the S&P 500 has varied from 4.66 to 10.55 over the past 5 to 30 years.

Now there are some issues associated with these numbers. At the time this book was written Treasury Bill and interest rates in general were at relatively low levels. Companies

TABLE 3-3 Current and Historical Interest Rates and Returns

5-Year U.S. Treasury Notes	3.00%	5-Year S&P 500 Return	4.66%
10-Year U.S. Treasury Notes	3.85%	10-Year S&P 500 Return	0.60%
20-Year U.S. Treasury Notes	4.40%	20-Year S&P 500 Return	10.16%
30-Year U.S. Treasury Notes	4.75%	30-Year S&P 500 Return	10.55%

TABLE 3-4 Market Return, Risk-Free Rate, and Market Premium

	Market Return	Risk-Free Int Rate	Market Premium
	$E(k_m)$	k_{rf}	$(E(k_m) - k_{rf})$
5-Year	4.66%	3.00%	1.66%
10-Year	0.60%	3.85%	–3.25%
20-Year	10.16%	4.40%	5.76%
30-Year	10.55%	4.75%	5.80%

typically use the 10- to 30-year Treasury Bill rates as a proxy for the risk-free rate, which characteristically have been in the range of 4 to 6%. In this case, since the rate environment is so low it would appear to be appropriate to pick the 30-year rate of 4.75%, which is just below the midpoint of the historical range of 4 to 6%.

The S&P 500 data is also problematic. The data in Table 3-3 indicates that S&P returns can be all highly variable depending on the time horizon selected and short-term horizons such as 5 and 10 years may not be particularly helpful when estimating market performance. The returns on markets over long periods of time have characteristically been in the 9 to 11% range and so it would seem that the 20- or 30-year market returns are more indicative of what investors expect.

Table 3-4 provides another perspective of the coefficients. As can be seen from the data in the table, if the 5-year numbers are used, the Market Risk Premium ($E(k_m)$) is only 1.66%, which is hardly enough to convince most investors to be in the market and way below what investors have historically demanded. The 10-year statistic is even worse because it implies that an investor should expect to lose money by investing in the market. The only credible coefficients that are indicative of what investors expect are the 20- and 30-year numbers, which indicate a Market Premium in the vicinity of 5.8%.

So in summary the 20 (4.40%) and 30 (4.75%) year Treasury Bill rates in Table 3-3 approximate the midpoint of the historical range of 4–6% for k_{rf}. The range that is characteristic of the Market Return ($E(k_m)$) is 9–11%. From Table 3-4 it can be seen that based on this data Market returns of 10.16% (4.40 + 5.76 =10.16%) and 10.55% (4.75 + 5.80 = 10.55%) for the 20- and 30-year time horizons respectively fall into this range.[16]

However, this discussion should not end here. The dilemma that one can face by using the wrong rates for k_{rf} and $E(k_m)$ is illustrated by the following example.

EXAMPLE 3-2: CALCULATING THE COST OF EQUITY USING MARKET DATA FOR HOPE INC.

The CEO of Hope Incorporated has decided the company should be more aggressive in the acquisition arena. The board of directors is receptive to the idea but before it gives approval requests that the company update its Weighted Average Cost of Capital. Since the

[16] In the examples that follow we will use various rates within these ranges.

company is debt free and has a cash-rich balance sheet, the WACC is the cost of equity and so acting on instructions from the CEO, the CFO proceeds to update his data on the company's Beta, risk-free rates, and market returns. According to *Value Line* the company's Beta is 1.36. Reference to the Treasury Bill rates in the *Wall Street Journal* for 5-, 10-, and 20-year notes indicates that the relevant rates are 1.8%, 2.78%, and 3.66% respectively. After consulting the performance of the S&P 500 he determines that the market performance over the same periods is 4.66%, 0.60%, and 10.16%. Using Equation [3-25] the CFO estimates the cost of equity based on the 5-, 10-, and 20-year statistics.

$$k_E = k_{rf} + [E(k_m) - k_{rf}](Beta) \qquad [3\text{-}25]$$

5-Year Horizon

$$k_E = 1.80 + [4.66 - 1.80](1.36) = 5.70\%$$

10-Year Horizon

$$k_E = 2.78 + [0.60 - 2.78](1.36) = -0.18\%$$

20-Year Horizon

$$k_E = 3.66 + [10.16 - 3.66](1.36) = 12.50\%$$

Clearly almost any investment would pass a 5.7% hurdle rate. Making investments that would produce a loss was out of the question. The 12.5% hurdle rate was the only one that made any sense and so the CFO decided to propose it to the board and CEO with the caveat that if risk-free rates increased and all other things remained equal, the cost of equity would go up and the hurdle rate would have to be revisited at that time.

EXAMPLE 3-3: ESTIMATING THE WACC OF A COMPANY WITH ONE CLASS OF DEBT AND EQUITY

Assume k_{rf}, the risk-free rate of return is 5.28%, and that a company has a market value of debt to enterprise value B/EV of 29%, market risk premium $[E(k_m) - k_{rf}]$ of 5.0%, levered Beta of 1.15, debt risk premium (k_{rp}) of 2.09%, and a tax rate (TR) of 35%. This data is summarized in Table 3-5.

TABLE 3-5 Calculating the WACC for a Company with One Class of Debt and Equity

Risk-Free Rate	k_{rf}	5.28%
Market Value of Debt/Enterprise Value	B/EV	0.29
Market Risk Premium	$[E(k_m) - k_{rf}]$	5.00%
Levered Beta	$Beta_L$	1.15
Debt Risk Premium	k_{rp}	2.09%
Tax Rate	TR	35.00%
Weighted Average Cost of Capital	WACC	?

Based on these assumptions, the company's WACC can be calculated as follows.

The Equity to Enterprise ratio is not given. Therefore the first step is to calculate this ratio. Recall that

$$EV = B + E \qquad [3\text{-}10]$$

Dividing both sides of Equation [3-10] by the Enterprise Value EV

$$\frac{EV}{EV} = \frac{B}{EV} = \frac{E}{EV} \qquad [3\text{-}33]$$

Simplifying and rearranging,

$$\frac{B}{EV} = \frac{E}{EV} = 1 \qquad [3\text{-}34]$$

which can be rearranged as:

$$\frac{E}{EV} = 1 - \frac{B}{EV} \qquad [3\text{-}35][17]$$

Now, since the market value of debt to enterprise value is 29%, then B/EV = 0.29 and by Equation [3-35]

$$\frac{E}{EV} = 1 - \frac{B}{EV} = 1 - 0.29$$

and

$$\frac{E}{EV} = 0.71$$

which of course is exactly what you would expect since the sum of the debt and equity fractions must equal 1.

Next, recall Equation [3-28]:

$$k_{WACC} = (k_{rf} + k_{rp})(1 - TR)\left(\frac{B}{EV}\right) + \{k_{rf} + [E(k_m) - k_{rf}](Beta)\}\left(\frac{E}{EV}\right) \qquad [3\text{-}28]$$

By substituting values from Table 3-5 for the variables in Equation [3-28] the company's WACC is obtained.

$$k_{WACC} = (5.28 + 2.09)(1 - 0.35)(0.29) + \{5.28 + [(5.0)(1.15)]\}(0.71)$$

$$k_{WACC} = (7.37)(0.65)(0.29) + [5.28 + 5.75](0.71)$$

$$k_{WACC} = (1.39) + [11.03](0.71) = 1.39 + 7.83$$

$$k_{WACC} = 9.22\%$$

[17] This equation can also be expressed as B/EV = 1 – B/EV.

A few observations are in order:

- While the company's cost of debt and equity financing was not calculated, it should be clear that the company's pretax cost of debt is 7.37% (5.28 + 2.09), the after-tax cost of debt k_{BAT} is 4.79% ((7.37)(1 – 0.35))[18] and the cost of equity k_E is 11.03% [5.28 + (5.0)(1.15)].
- If the company's capital structure consisted of 100% equity, it would only be able to consider projects that had returns in excess of 11.03%.
- By including debt in the capital structure, the company's cost of capital has been reduced and management is able to consider projects with returns exceeding 9.22%.
- Taking on more debt could reduce the Weighted Average Cost of Capital further. However, as the amount of debt increases, the cost of debt would also increase and at some point no more debt would be available without more equity standing below it. Also, as the debt in a company increases, the levered Beta would increase and thereby increase the company's cost of equity financing. All of this suggests that there is an optimal capital structure for a company and once you go beyond it leverage works against you.[19]

There is another way to look at the impact of leverage on the WACC. When leverage is increased the risk shouldered by shareholders also increases. Shareholders are risk averse and react by demanding a higher return on their investment. Hence, k_E and to a lesser extent k_B rise as leverage increases. The result is that increased leverage reduces the WACC, but this reduction is offset somewhat by the increase in the cost of equity and the cost of debt that results from the increase in leverage.

MULTIPLE HURDLE RATES

The Weighted Average Cost of Capital is also known as a hurdle rate. Previously it was stated that the only time a particular WACC is appropriate for evaluating a prospective investment is when the risk associated with the investment is the same as the risk environment for which the WACC was calculated, which is usually for the mainstream business and expansion investments. Relative to expansion investments, the risk involved in the replacement and repair of existing equipment is much lower because the future cash flows are well understood. Companies also make investments in cost reduction. However, whether the cost reduction program will actually generate the forecasted cash flows is not nearly as certain and involves increased risk when compared to replacement or repair. Investments in new products usually involve more risk and therefore would justify a higher WACC than for expansion of the business. Acquisition of a company is probably the riskiest of all, requiring the WACC be adjusted accordingly. Table 3-6 represents hypothetical hurdle rates for a company with a WACC of 11.5.

[18] See "Impact of Taxes on the Weighted Average Cost of Capital" in a previous section of this chapter.

[19] This is true. There are many models out there that optimize capital structure. Dealing with this complex issue is beyond the scope of this book.

TABLE 3-6 Multiple Hurdle Rates

Category of Investment	WACC
Replacement or Repair	9.5%
Cost Reduction	10.5%
Business Expansion	11.5%
New Products	13.0%
Acquisitions	15.0%

EXAMPLE 3-4: RETAIL CORPORATION'S WACC

Retail Corporation is a company with $300 million of debt on its balance sheet for which it pays an all-up interest rate of 8.8%. It has 250 million shares outstanding with an average price per share of $70.00. The Beta is 0.96 and Treasury Bills are fetching 5.6%. The market risk premium is 5.2%, and the tax rate is 37%. The data given in Example 3-4 is summarized in Table 3-7.

Using this data Retail's CFO calculated the firm's WACC to be 10.5% by using the following process.

The equity of the firm is calculated by recalling that[20]

$$E = (Number\ of\ Shares\ Outstanding)(Price\ per\ Share) \tag{3-36}$$

$$E = (250{,}000{,}000)(70.00) = \$17{,}500{,}000{,}000$$

Since the debt is $300,000,000 the enterprise value is (Equation [3-10]):

$$EV = B + E \tag{3-10}$$

$$EV = 300{,}000{,}000 + 17{,}500{,}000{,}000 = \$17{,}800{,}000{,}000$$

Substituting in Equation [3-25], the cost of equity k_E is:

$$k_E = k_{rf} + [E(k_m) - k_{rf}](Beta) \tag{3-25}$$

$$k_E = 5.6 + (5.2)(0.96) = 5.6 + 4.99 = 10.59\%$$

The debt risk premium k_{rp} is calculated with the aid of Equation [3-24].

$$k_B = k_{rf} + k_{rp} \tag{3-24}$$

$$k_{rp} = 8.8 - 5.6 = 3.2\%$$

[20]Refer to the section titled "Weighting of the Components of Capital Structure" earlier in this chapter.

TABLE 3-7 Retail Corporation Data

(M = $000,000)'s			
Debt (B)	$300 M	Beta	0.96
Interest Rate on Debt B	8.80%	Treasury Bill Rate	5.60%
Shares Outstanding	250 M	Market Risk Premium	5.20%
Share Price	$70.00	Tax Rate	37.00%

Recall that the after-tax cost of debt interest k_{BAT} can be calculated with the assistance of Equation [3-20].

$$k_{BAT} = (k_B)(1 - TR) \qquad [3\text{-}20]$$

Therefore, if the pretax cost of debt is 8.8% and the tax rate is 37%, then using Equation [3-20] the after-tax cost of debt is:

$$k_{BAT} = (8.8)(1 - .37) = 8.8(0.63) = 5.54\%$$

Finally, with the assistance of Equation [3-23] the WACC is obtained:

$$k_{WACC} = (k_B)(1-TR)\left(\frac{B}{EV}\right)+(k_E)\left(\frac{E}{EV}\right) \qquad [3\text{-}23]$$

$$k_{WACC} = (8.8)(1-0.37)\left(\frac{300}{17{,}800}\right)+(10.6)\left(\frac{17{,}500}{17{,}800}\right)$$

$$k_{WACC} = (8.8)(0.63)(0.017) + (10.6)(0.983) = 0.094 + 10.42 = 10.514$$

$$k_{WACC} = 10.5\%$$

The results of the calculations are presented in Table 3-8.

TABLE 3-8 Retail Corporation Data and Calculated Statistics

(M = $000,000, B = $000,000,000)'s			
	Data		Calculated
Debt (B)	$300 M	Equity Value (E)	$17,500 B
Interest Rate on B (kB)	8.80%	Enterprise Value (EV)	$17,800 B
Shares Outstanding	250 M	Cost of Equity (k_E)	10.59%
Share Price	$70.00	Debt Risk Premium (k_{rp})	3.20%
Beta	0.96	After-Tax Cost of Debt	5.54%
Treasury Bill Rate	5.60%	WACC (k_{WACC})	10.51%
Market Risk Premium	5.20%		
Tax Rate	37.00%		

This example illustrates a few points.

- The debt risk premium k_{rp} at 3.2% is relatively small for this well-capitalized company, which is what you would expect for a company with so much equity standing behind the debt.
- Once again the tax shield provided by the fact interest is tax deductible has the effect of lowering the company's cost of debt from 8.8% to an after-tax cost of 5.54%.
- The company's debt is so low compared to the enterprise value (1.7%) it has negligible effect on the company's WACC.
- With a B/EV of .017 or 1.7% the company's Beta = 0.96 is essentially an unlevered beta.

EXAMPLE 3-5: RETAIL CORPORATION DECIDES TO ACCESS THE DEBT MARKETS

The management of Retail Corporation becomes aware that one of its key competitors is not making investments in the next generation of packaging and sees an opportunity to increase its market share by bringing to market, on an accelerated basis, their contemplated line of aseptic packaging that is highly attractive to consumers. To do this they need to increase the level of R&D spending substantially and install the new packaging equipment in their factories. After numerous engineering studies and meetings, management concludes that in order for the company to pursue this opportunity they will have to find an additional $3 billion to fund the project. They had a couple of choices. One was to fund it from current cash flows. The problem with this was the project would be spread over several years and the dividend paid to shareholders would have to be cut significantly. Another option was to raise additional equity. Neither of these were attractive options.

While the matter of financing the project was being considered the economy began to slow and the Federal Reserve took action to reduce interest rates with the result that U.S. Treasuries were now yielding 4.6%. Given the company's negligible debt position, an AAA+ debt rating, and attractive interest rates the management decided to recommend to the board that the project be financed by going to the debt markets. Discussions with investment bankers indicated a high level of confidence in being able to place the debt with a 10-year balloon at 8.0%. Management also considered what to do about the $300 million of 8.8% debt. Since there were five years left before maturity and the 80 basis points they were paying in excess of the current market rate was less than the cost of terminating the loan, they decided to leave it in place. The company's stock is now trading at an average of $77 per share. The number of shares outstanding is unchanged, as is the market risk premium.

The CFO was tasked by the board to analyze the impact the debt under consideration would have on the WACC. Out of curiosity she ran a couple of scenarios. She first analyzed what the new WACC would be if only the additional debt was considered (but otherwise using the data in Example 3-4). The second incorporated the new debt and current market conditions. Both estimated the impact the new debt would have on the: enterprise value, levered Beta, cost of equity, cost of debt, debt risk premium, after-tax cost of debt, and the WACC.

Example 3-5A: Impact on Retail Corporation's WACC If Only New Debt Is Considered

The impact additional debt would have on Retail Corp's WACC can be illustrated by assuming that only the debt on Retail's Balance Sheet has changed. This is highlighted in the shaded area in Table 3-9.

The market value of the equity E is obtained by the use of Equation [3-36] and multiplying the number of shares outstanding by price per share. Note: In this Example, the average share price ($70) is used. In the Example that follows, the current share price ($77) will be used.

$$E = (250{,}000{,}000)(70.00) = \$17{,}500{,}000{,}000$$

And with the assistance of [3-10] the enterprise value EV is calculated to be:

$$\begin{aligned} EV = B + E &= (300{,}000{,}000 + 3{,}000{,}000{,}000) + 17{,}500{,}000{,}000 \\ &= \$20{,}800{,}000{,}000 \end{aligned}$$

Recall that one of the conclusions reached from Example 3-3 was that at a debt level of $300 million the Beta was essentially unlevered at 0.96. The new debt level changes things and therefore before the new cost of equity is calculated a check on what has happened to Beta with the additional leverage is necessary.

Utilizing Equation [3-31] the levered Beta is calculated

$$Beta_L = \left[1 + (1 - TR)\left(\frac{B}{E}\right)\right](Beta_U) = \left[1 + (1 - 0.37)\left(\frac{300 + 3{,}000}{17{,}500}\right)\right](0.96)$$

$$Beta_L = [1 + (0.63)(0.189)](0.96) = 1.074$$

With the levered Beta in hand, the cost of equity k_E is obtained with the use of Equation [3-25]:

$$k_E = k_{rf} + [E(k_m) - k_{rf}](Beta) = 5.6 + [5.2](1.074) = 5.6 + 5.59 = 11.19$$

TABLE 3-9 Retail Corporation Data Example 3-5A

(M = $000,000)'s			
	Data		Data
Debt (B_1)	$300 M	Share Price	$70.00
Interest Rate on B_1 (k_{B1})	8.80%	Beta Unlevered	0.96
Debt (B_2)	$3,000 M	Treasury Bill Rate	5.60%
Interest Rate on B_2 (k_{B2})	8.00%	Market Risk Premium	5.20%
Shares Outstanding	250 M	Tax Rate	37.00%

The new cost of debt is obtained by calculating the weighted average of the two classes of debt as shown in Equation [3-37].

$$k_B = (k_{B1})\left(\frac{B_1}{B_1 + B_2}\right) + (k_{B2})\left(\frac{B_2}{B_1 + B_2}\right) \quad [3\text{-}37]$$

Substituting in Equation [3-37],

$$k_B = (8.8)\left(\frac{300}{3,300}\right) + (8.0)\left(\frac{3,000}{3,300}\right) = (8.8)(0.091) + (8.0)(0.901)$$

$$= 0.80 + 7.27 = 8.07\%$$

Then with the use of Equation [3-24] expressed in terms of k_{rp} the debt risk premium is derived.

$$k_B = k_{rf} + k_{rp} \quad [3\text{-}24]$$

$$k_{rp} = k_B - k_{rf} = 8.07 - 5.6 = 2.47\%$$

Since there are two classes of debt, Equation [3-20] needs to be modified to be a weighted average of debts B_1 (\$300 million) and B_2 (\$3,000 million) before the after-tax cost of debt k_{BAT} can be calculated.

$$k_{BAT} = (k_{B1})(1 - TR)\left(\frac{B_1}{B_1 + B_2}\right) + (k_{B2})(1 - TR)\left(\frac{B_2}{B_1 + B_2}\right) \quad [3\text{-}38]$$

Substituting in Equation [3-38],

$$k_{BAT} = (8.8)(1 - .37)\left(\frac{300}{3,300}\right) + (8.0)(1 - .37)\left(\frac{3,000}{3,300}\right)$$

$$k_{BAT} = (8.8)(0.63)(0.091) + (8)(0.63)(0.909) = 0.504 + 4.58$$

$$k_{BAT} = 5.09\%$$

Similarly Equation [3-23] needs to be modified to incorporate the two types of debt in order to calculate the WACC. See Equation [3-39].

$$k_{WACC} = (k_{B1})(1 - TR)\left(\frac{B_1}{EV}\right) + (k_{B2})(1 - TR)\left(\frac{B_2}{EV}\right) + (k_E)\left(\frac{E}{EV}\right) \quad [3\text{-}39]$$

Substituting,

$$k_{WACC} = (8.8)(1-.37)\left(\frac{300}{20,800}\right) + (8.0)(1-.37)\left(\frac{3,000}{20,800}\right) + (11.19)\left(\frac{17,500}{20,800}\right)$$

$$k_{WACC} = (8.8)(0.63)(0.0144) + (8.0)(0.63)(0.144) + (11.19)(0.841)$$
$$k_{BAT} = 0.0798 + 0.7258 + 9.41$$
$$k_{WACC} = 10.22\%$$

It should be noted that the same result would have been obtained by using the after-tax weighted average of debt and Equation [3-40]:

$$k_{WACC} = (k_{BAT})\left(\frac{B_1 + B_2}{EV}\right) + (k_E)\left(\frac{E}{EV}\right) \qquad [3\text{-}40]$$

$$k_{WACC} = (5.09)\left(\frac{300 + 3,000}{20,800}\right) + (11.19)\left(\frac{17,500}{20,800}\right)$$

$$k_{BAT} = (5.09)\left(\frac{3,300}{20,800}\right) + (11.19)\left(\frac{17,500}{20,800}\right)$$

$$k_{BAT} = (5.09)(0.1587) + (11.9)(0.8414)$$
$$k_{BAT} = 0.808 + 9.415 = 10.223$$
$$k_{WACC} = 10.22\%$$

The results are tabulated in Table 3-10.

TABLE 3-10 Retail Corporation Data and Calculated Statistics Example 3-5A

(M = \$000,000, B = \$000,000,000)'s			
	Data		**Calculated**
Debt (B_1)	\$300 M	Equity Value (E)	\$17,500 B
Interest Rate on $B_1(k_{B1})$	8.80%	Enterprise Value (EV)	\$20,800 B
Debt (B_2)	\$3,000 M	Beta ($Beta_L$)	1.074
Interest Rate on $B_2(k_{B2})$	8.00%	Cost of Equity (k_E)	11.19%
Shares Outstanding	250 M	Cost of Debt (k_B)	8.07%
Share Price	\$70.00	Debt Risk Premium (k_{rp})	2.47%
Beta ($Beta_U$)	0.96	After-Tax Cost of Debt	5.09%
Treasury Bill Rate	5.60%	WACC (k_{WACC})	10.22%
Market Risk Premium	5.20%		
Tax Rate	37.00%		

Example 3-5B: Calculating Retail's New WACC by Incorporating All Current Market Data

After satisfying her curiosity about the impact the new debt would have on Retail's previously calculated WACC, the CFO proceeded to calculate the WACC with the new debt and current market conditions.

Refer to the data in Table 3-11.

Once again the market value of the equity E is calculated with the assistance of Equation [3-36] but this time using the current market share price of $77.00.

$$E = (250{,}000{,}000)(77) = \$19{,}250{,}000{,}000$$

Then using Equation [3-10] the enterprise value EV is calculated to be:

$$EV = B + E = (300{,}000{,}000 + 3{,}000{,}000{,}000) + 19{,}250{,}000{,}000 = \$22{,}550{,}000{,}000$$

The impact of leverage on Beta given the new debt and change in EV is calculated with the aid of Equation [3-31] and the data in Table 3-11.

$$Beta_L = \left[1 + (1 - TR)\left(\frac{B}{E}\right)\right](Beta_U) = \left[1 + (1 - 0.37)\left(\frac{3,300}{19,250}\right)\right](0.96)$$

$$Beta_L = [1 + (0.63)(0.171)](0.96) = 1.064$$

k_E the cost of equity is obtained by applying Equation [3-25]

$$k_E = k_{rf} + [E(k_m) - k_{rf}](Beta) \quad [3\text{-}25]$$

$$k_E = 4.6 + [5.2]\,(1.064) = 4.6 + 5.53 = 10.13$$

The weighted average cost of debt is once again calculated by substituting data from Table 3-11 in Equation [3-37].

$$k_B = (k_{B1})\left(\frac{B_1}{B_1 + B_2}\right) + (k_{B2})\left(\frac{B_2}{B_1 + B_2}\right) \quad [3\text{-}37]$$

$$k_B = (8.8)\left(\frac{300}{3,300}\right) + (8.0)\left(\frac{3,000}{3,300}\right) = 0.80 + 7.27 = 8.073$$

$$k_B = 8.07\%$$

TABLE 3-11 Retail Corporation Data Example 3-5B

(M = $000,000)'s			
	Data		**Data**
Debt (B_1)	$300 M	Share Price	$77.00
Interest Rate on B_1 (k_{B1})	8.80%	Beta ($Beta_U$)	0.96
Debt (B_2)	$3,000 M	Treasury Bill Rate	4.60%
Interest Rate on B_2 (k_{B2})	8.00%	Market Risk Premium	5.20%
Shares Outstanding	250 M	Tax Rate	37.00%

The debt risk premium is obtained by rearranging and applying Equation [3-24]:

$$k_B = k_{rf} + k_{rp} \quad [3\text{-}24]$$

$$k_B = 8.07 - 4.6 = 3.47\%$$

In part A of this example, the after-tax cost of debt was calculated using Equation [3-38]. A simpler solution that would have yielded the same result would have been to use Equation [3-20] where k_B is the weighted average cost of debt.

$$k_{BAT} = k_B\,(1 - TR) \quad [3\text{-}20]$$

$$k_{BAT} = (8.073)(1 - 0.37) = (8.073)(0.63) = 5.09\%$$

The WACC for Retail Corporation with $3 billion of new debt on its balance sheet is obtained by once again applying Equation [3-39].

$$k_{WACC} = (k_{B1})(1 - TR)\left(\frac{B_1}{EV}\right) + (k_{B2})(1 - TR)\left(\frac{B_2}{EV}\right) + (k_E)\left(\frac{E}{EV}\right) \quad [3\text{-}39]$$

$$k_{WACC} = (8.8)(0.63)\left(\frac{300}{22{,}500}\right) + (8.0)(0.63)\left(\frac{3{,}000}{22{,}500}\right) + (10.13)\left(\frac{19{,}250}{22{,}500}\right)$$

$$k_{WACC} = (8.8)(0.63)(0.01330) + (8.0)(0.63)(0.1330) + (10.13)(0.8537)$$

$$k_{WACC} = 0.07374 + 0.6703 + 8.6477 = 9.3917$$

$$k_{WACC} = 9.40\%$$

The results are tabulated in Table 3-12.

TABLE 3-12 Retail Corporation Data and Calculated Statistics Example 3-5B

(M = \$000,000, B = \$000,000,000)'s			
	Data		**Calculated**
Debt (B_1)	\$300 M	Equity Value (E)	\$19,250 B
Interest Rate on B_1 (K_{B1})	8.80%	Enterprise Value (EV)	\$22,550 B
Debt (B_2)	\$3,000 M	Beta ($Beta_L$)	1.064
Interest Rate on B_1 (K_{B1})	8.00%	Cost of Equity (k_E)	10.13%
Shares Outstanding	250 M	Cost of Debt (k_B)	8.07%
Share Price	\$77.00	Debt Risk Premium (k_{rp})	3.47%
Beta ($Beta_U$)	0.96	After-Tax Cost of Debt	5.09%
Treasury Bill Rate	4.60%	WACC (k_{WACC})	9.40%
Market Risk Premium	5.20%		
Tax Rate	37.00%		

EXAMPLE 3-6: COMPARISON OF RETAIL CORPORATION'S WACCS

When her work on the prospective Weighted Average Cost of Capital was completed the CFO of Retail Corporation prepared Table 3-13 to compare the results of the various scenarios considered.

After completing the table the CFO forwarded it to her CEO with the following observations.[21]

- Equity value in Example 3-5B increases by virtue of the fact the share price has increased from $70.00 to $77.00
- Enterprise value in Example 3-5A increases due to the additional $3 billion of debt and increases further in Example 3-5B as a result of the higher equity value.
- Beta increases from 0.96 to 1.07 in Example 3-5A due to the increased debt. It reduces modestly in Example 3-5B due to the increased value of the equity.

TABLE 3-13 Retail Corporation: Comparison of Data and Calculated Statistics for Examples 3-4, 3-5A, and 3-5B

(M = $000,000, B = $000,000,000)'s			
	Example 3-4	Example 3-5A	Example 3-5B
Debt (B_1)	$300 M	$300 M	$300 M
Interest Rate on B_1 (k_{B1})	8.80%	8.80%	8.80%
Debt (B_2)	n/a	$3,000 M	$3,000 M
Interest Rate on B_2 (k_{B2})	n/a	8.00%	8.00%
Shares Outstanding	250 M	250 M	250 M
Share Price	$70.00	$70.00	$77.00
Beta ($Beta_U$)	$0.96	$0.96	0.96
Treasury Bill Rate	5.60%	5.60%	4.60%
Market Risk Premium	5.20%	5.20%	5.20%
Tax Rate	37.00%	37.00%	37.00%
Equity Value (E)	$17,500 B	$17,500 B	$19,250 B
Enterprise Value (EV)	$17,800 B	$20,800 B	$22,550 B
Beta ($Beta_U$)	0.96	–	–
Beta ($Beta_L$)	–	1.074	1.064
Cost of Equity (k_E)	10.59%	11.19%	10.13%
Debt Risk Premium (k_{rp})	3.20%	2.47%	3.47%
After-Tax Cost of Debt	5.54%	5.09%	5.09%
WACC (k_{WACC})	10.51%	10.22%	9.40%

[21] The only difference between Examples 3-4 and 3-5A is that in 3-5A, $3 billion of 8% debt is hypothetically taken on by the company whereas in 3-5B the share price increased and the risk-free rate decreased compared to Example 3-4.

- Cost of equity in Example 3-5A increases to 11.19% due to the increase in Beta and reduces in Example 3-5B primarily due to the decrease in the risk-free rate.
- Debt risk premium decreases to 2.47% in Example 3-5A due to the lower weighted average cost of debt and then increases with the decrease in the risk-free rate from 5.6% to 4.6% in Example 3-5B.
- After-tax cost of debt decreases to 5.09% due to the lower weighted average cost of debt.
- WACC decreases in Example 3-5A due to the leverage effect of the additional $3 billion of debt and then decreases further as a result of the lower cost of equity in Example 3-5B.

The CEO congratulated his CFO on a job well done and asked her to work with the Investment Bankers and prepare a term sheet to be presented at the next board meeting for approval.

INTRODUCTION TO PRESENT VALUE

At this point it is necessary to introduce the concept of present value (PV) in order to use the Weighted Average Cost of Capital to assist in making an investment decision. PV is covered in great detail in Appendix A. What follows is a simplistic consideration to educate those who are not familiar with the concept, or rekindle memory in those that worked with PV some time ago.

The concept of the present value of a cash flow stream is fundamental to any analytical approach to measuring value. In its simplest form, it can be used to calculate the value today of a stream of payments to be received in the future.

To illustrate this point, assume that you won a small lottery and are entitled to receive $100,000 per year for the next five years. You are given the option of taking a lump sum or receiving five annual payments on January 1 of each year. If you can safely earn interest of 10% per annum on any deposits, what would you do? Well, applying the concept of present value will help you decide.

Year 1 is trivial. You simply take the money and put it in the 10%-interest-bearing account.

Year 2 is a little trickier. If you wait until January 1 of Year 2, then you would have lost one year of interest. However, if you ask yourself, What discount will I take to get the money now?, the answer is: How much money do I need now that I can deposit at 10% and end up with $100,000 at the beginning of Year 2?

If x_2 is that amount, then:

$$(x_2)(1 + 10\%) = \$100{,}000$$

or

$$(x_2)(1 + 0.10) = \$100{,}000$$

and

$$x_2 = \frac{100{,}000}{(1 + 0.10)} = \frac{100{,}000}{1.10} = \$90{,}909$$

If you deposited the $90,909 in the 10% account at the beginning of Year 1, one year later (beginning of Year 2) the $90,909 would have grown to:

$$(90{,}909)(1.10) = \$100{,}000$$

That is to say that the present value of Year 2's cash flow is $90,909.

Furthermore, $90,909 is the least you should take if you want to end up revenue neutral. If you negotiated a deal and got more than $90,909, you would end up with more than $100,000 at the end of Year 1. If you negotiated less, you would not do as well (but it may be worth it to have the money in your account because the collection risk has been eliminated).

Similarly if you also want the Year 3 money at the beginning of Year 1, the least you should take would be:

$$(x_3)(1 + 10\%)(1 + 10\%) = \$100{,}000$$

Rearranging,

$$x_3 = \frac{100{,}000}{(1 + 10\%)\,(1 + 10\%)}$$

$$x_3 = \frac{100{,}000}{(1 + 0.10)\,(1 + 0.10)} = \frac{100{,}000}{(1 + 0.10)^2} = \frac{100{,}000}{1.21} = \$82{,}645$$

because

$$(82{,}645)(1.1)(1.1) = \$100{,}000$$

Finally, x_4 and x_5 would be

$$x_4 = \frac{100{,}000}{(1 + 0.10)^3} = \frac{100{,}000}{1.331} = \$75{,}131$$

$$x_5 = \frac{100{,}000}{(1 + 0.10)^4} = \frac{100{,}000}{1.464} = \$68{,}301$$

The total of the present values for years $x_1 \ldots x_5$ is $416,986.

From this illustration a more general expression for present value can be developed by asking: What is the total value of the five-year stream of cash flows discounted at 10%?

$$\textit{Total Value} = x_1 + x_2 + x_3 + x_4 + x_5$$

Substituting for each of the cash flows we get

$$\textit{Total Value} = 100{,}000 + \frac{100{,}000}{(1 + 0.10)} + \frac{100{,}000}{(1 + 0.10)^2} + \frac{100{,}000}{(1 + 0.10)^3} + \frac{100{,}000}{(1 + 0.10)^4}$$

Expressed this way the total value is really the present value and in sigma notation can be written as:

$$Present\ Value = \sum_{i=1}^{n} \frac{E_i}{(1+k)^{i-1}} \qquad [3\text{-}41]$$

where the present value, PV, is the sum of all of the cash flows E_i for the Years i discounted at rate k.

Equation [3-41] can be checked by substituting $E_i = 100{,}000$, $i = 5$, and $k = 10\%$ from the illustration.

$$PV = \frac{100{,}000}{(1+0.10)^{(1-1)}} + \frac{100{,}000}{(1+0.10)^{(2-1)}} + \frac{100{,}000}{(1+0.10)^{(3-1)}} + \frac{100{,}000}{(1+0.10)^{(4-1)}} + \frac{100{,}000}{(1+0.10)^{(5-1)}}$$

$$PV = \frac{100{,}000}{(1+0.10)^{0}} + \frac{100{,}000}{(1+0.10)^{1}} + \frac{100{,}000}{(1+0.10)^{2}} + \frac{100{,}000}{(1+0.10)^{3}} + \frac{100{,}000}{(1+0.10)^{4}}$$

$$PV = \frac{100{,}000}{1} + \frac{100{,}000}{1.10} + \frac{100{,}000}{1.210} + \frac{100{,}000}{1.331} + \frac{100{,}000}{1.464}$$

$$PV = 100{,}000 + 90{,}909 + 82{,}645 + 75{,}131 + 68{,}301$$

$$PV = \$416{,}986$$

This is identical to the result obtained in the illustration.

It should be noted that the expression just developed by deduction applies to cash flows that start at the beginning of a year. If the cash flow takes place at the end of a year, then it needs to be modified to allow for this and becomes:

$$Present\ Value = \sum_{i=1}^{n} \frac{E_i}{(1+k)^{i}} \qquad [A\text{-}1]^{22}\ [3\text{-}42]$$

Once again the reader is reminded that the concepts of present value as applied to various cash flow scenarios are presented in detail in Appendix A. Anyone in need of further review might consider looking at this appendix before proceeding.

[22] See Appendix A, Equation [A-1].

EXAMPLE 3-7: CALCULATING THE VALUE OF A STREAM OF CASH FLOWS USING THE WACC

"NewCo" is considering purchasing a product line from "OldCo." The product line is believed to have five years remaining in its life.[23] The estimated cash flows for the product line under consideration are tabulated in Table 3-14. The cash flows are assumed to take place at the end of each year.[24] If NewCo's Weighted Average Cost of Capital is 15%, what is the maximum price that NewCo should pay for OldCo's product line?

By using Equation [A-1] or [3-42] the present value of the cash flows forecasted for OldCo's product line can be calculated.

$$PV = \sum_{i=1}^{n} \frac{E_i}{(1+k)^i} \qquad \text{[A-1] [3-42]}$$

Expanding, Equation [A-1] becomes [A-2] and [3-42] becomes [3-43][25] where $E_i = CFaIA_i$ and $k = WACC$:

$$PV = \frac{CFaIA_1}{(1+WACC)} + \frac{CFaIA_2}{(1+WACC)^2} + \cdots + \frac{CFaIA_5}{(1+WACC)^5} \qquad \text{[A-2] [3-43]}$$

Substituting the values from Table 3-14 in Equation [3-43] produces the PV of the stream of cash flows under consideration.

$$PV = \frac{732{,}500}{1.15} + \frac{659{,}250}{1.15^2} + \frac{593{,}325}{1.15^3} + \frac{533{,}993}{1.15^4} + \frac{480{,}593}{1.15^5}$$

$$PV = 636{,}957 + 498{,}488 + 390{,}121 + 305{,}312 + 238{,}940$$

$$PV = \$2{,}069{,}817$$

A little more mileage can be obtained from this example by observing that this stream of cash flows $CFaIA_i$ decreases at a constant rate $g = -10\%$. Therefore, it should

TABLE 3-14 OldCo's Product Line Forecasted Cash Flows $'s and %

	Year				
	1	**2**	**3**	**4**	**5**
Cash Flow (CFaIA)	732,500	659,250	593,325	533,993	480,593
Growth Rate of Cash Flows	n/a	−10.00%	−10.00%	−10.00%	−10.00%

[23]In practice it is highly unlikely that a cash flow stream would end so abruptly. A more practical case would be one in which cash flows from the product line go into further decline after Year 5.

[24]In the preceding section the cash flows were assumed to take place at the beginning of the year; hence, there wasn't any need to discount the first year's cash flow.

[25]Using the WACC as a discount rate in this case is appropriate because we are calculating a price that provides—as a minimum—the returns expected by debt and equity holders.

be possible to calculate the PV of this cash flow stream by applying Equation [A-35] from Appendix A renumbered here as Equation [3-44].

$$PV = \frac{E}{1+k} + \frac{(E)(1+g)\left[1-\left(\frac{1+g}{1+k}\right)^{(n-1)}\right]}{(k-g)(1+k)} \qquad \text{[A-35]}^{26}\ \text{[3-44]}$$

Where:

$E = CFalA_1$, $k = WACC$, (15%), n = the number of periods (5), and g = the constant rate at which the cash flow stream decreases (negative growth) (–10%)

Substituting in Equation [3-44] yields the PV of OldCo's stream of cash flows discounted at NewCo's WACC.

$$PV = \frac{732,500}{1+0.15} + \frac{(732,500)(1-0.10)\left[1-\left(\frac{1-0.10}{1+0.15}\right)^{(5-1)}\right]}{(0.15+0.10)(1+0.15)}$$

$$PV = \frac{732,500}{1.15} + \frac{(732,500)(0.90)\left[1-\left(\frac{0.90}{1.15}\right)^{(4)}\right]}{(0.25)(1.15)}$$

$$= 636,957 + \frac{(659,250)(1-0.37513)}{(0.28750)}$$

$$PV = 636,957 + \frac{(659,250)(0.624873)}{(0.28750)} = 636,957 + 1,432,860$$

$$PV = \$2,069,817^{27}$$

Either approach gives the same answer. NewCo should not pay more than $2,069,817 for the cash flow from OldCo's product line if it wants to earn at least its Weighted Average Cost of Capital.

A close look at the results of the present value calculation points out several characteristics of the WACC.

- If the WACC isn't calculated realistically, the result can be either paying too much or deciding not to pursue the investment opportunity.
- When using a particular WACC to calculate a present value, the presumption is that the risk associated with the cash flow stream and the risk implied in the WACC are one and the same.

[26] See Appendix A, Equation [A-35].

[27] The equivalency of the two formulas [A-1] and [A-35] is demonstrated. This example, like all others in this book, is calculated in a spreadsheet. If you work through the example step by step with a calculator, you may end up with a small difference between the two results. If so, this would be a consequence of rounding.

- Experienced managers have learned that most investments don't play out as expected and therefore it is necessary to adjust the discount rate upward to take into account risks not inherently implied in the WACC calculation.
- Management creates value when an investment provides a return greater than the WACC.
- Management destroys value when it engages in investments that earn less than the WACC.
- Management is neither creating nor destroying value when an investment returns the WACC but rather providing debt and equity holders with the returns they expect.

Having worked through the basics of the WACC and touched on "Value," it is time to move on to Chapter 4 and explore valuation methods in more detail.

CASE STUDY: OMEGA CORPORATION

It has been over 20 years since Ron Myers had started his company and as he prepared for the special board meeting scheduled for next week, he took some to think about how he was going to approach the board on the subject matter he was contemplating. Ron and his engineering team had been working on an idea that could revolutionize how medium-sized businesses manufacture product, control costs, improve product quality, and better manage logistics.

Omega was started around a simple idea. The company's mission statement, way back when, was to become the industry leader in software that could trace the path of any component from its genesis to the user. In addition it was designed so that it could be readily interfaced with all major manufacturing systems. Their targeted customers were the military contractors and electronics industry that had a need for such a system. The first few years were difficult but Ron and his team persevered and about five years ago, Year (C – 5) achieved a landmark in their business plan. That was to achieve $25,000,000 in revenue (See Table CS 3-1).

TABLE CS 3-1 Omega Corporation Comparative Income Statements

December 31, 20XX $(000)'s						
Year	**C – 5**	**C – 4**	**C – 3**	**C – 2**	**C – 1**	**Current**
Revenues (Rev)	25,789	28,368	24,113	22,907	26,114	28,987
Cost of Goods Sold (COGS)	(3,868)	(4,539)	(4,099)	(4,123)	(4,701)	(4,638)
Gross Margin (GM)	21,921	23,829	20,014	18,784	21,414	24,349
Operating Expenses (OpExp)	(12,895)	(7,092)	(14,468)	(13,515)	(14,102)	(14,493)
EBITDA	9,026	16,737	5,546	5,269	7,312	9,855
Depreciation and Amortization (D&A)	(516)	(567)	(597)	(622)	(642)	(661)
EBIT	8,510	16,170	4,949	4,647	6,670	9,194
Interest Income/(Expense) (NetInt)	6	6	5	5	6	7
Earnings before Tax (EBT)	8,516	16,176	4,954	4,652	6,676	9,201
Taxes (TaxesPaid) @	(3,406)	(6,470)	(1,982)	(1,861)	(2,670)	(3,680)
Net Income (NI)	5,110	9,706	2,973	2,791	4,005	5,521

Like many high-value-added companies the EBIT and Net Income for Omega were very attractive at approximately 33% and 20% respectively. Ron and his team had labored for many years with modest take-home incomes and were very anxious to take some money off the table. Over the years they had many discussions with their board members about this subject and always ended up convinced that now was not the time. The discussions always ended with a statement from the chair to the effect, "With your gross margin (85%) the company's income can be most anything you want it to be by reducing operating expenses but be careful when it comes to operating expenses because they are driving the company's revenue." Of course this was hard to argue with and so the discussions ended in a continuation of the historical spending pattern.

However, when the company achieved $25 million in revenue, Ron decided it was time to "take some money off the table" and convinced the board against their better judgment that the company could cut expenses for a time and the revenue would continue to grow, although perhaps at a more modest rate. The operating expenses were cut from 50% of Revenue (Year C – 5) to 25% for Year C – 4 and the outcome had been as Ron predicted. The EBIT and Net Income hit a record high of $16,170,000 and $9,706,000 respectively and the Revenue continued to grow another 10% to approximately $28,400,000.

However, the following year (Year C – 3) was another story. It started strong but later in the year Revenue slowed dramatically. This of course set off alarm bells for the management team because with Omega's strong Gross Margin the impact was felt immediately at the bottom line. Ron persuaded himself that this was temporary and was only convinced early in the third quarter that the cause was delays in new releases of their product offering brought on by the cut in operating expenses. Then, and only then, with broad agreement of his management team, did he once again start pouring money into R&D and all related activities. The result was too little too late. The year ended with a 15% drop in Revenue and the associated impact on the bottom line.

The restoration of Operating Expenses to an appropriate level required time to take effect with the result that Year C – 2 ended up being the worst year in the past 10 as Revenue dropped an additional 5% and EBIT and Net Income fell to $4,647,000 and $2,791,000 respectively. Recovery continued into Year C – 1 with the company achieving slightly more than Year C – 5's Revenue ($26,114,000) and Net Income just north of $4,000,000. In fact the result was much worse than the story the numbers told. Omega had created a window of opportunity for their largest competitor, which now enjoyed the number-one position in the industry.

Ron shuddered every time he thought about this costly mistake and was determined to once again achieve industry leadership.

To be sure, the board had lost some faith in Ron's judgment even though he and his team had led the company back to a growth environment. He knew that the presentation he was about to make had to be both flawless and compelling. The idea he and his team had developed a novel way of building a manufacturing system incorporating Omega's highly regarded traceability, quality, and productivity modules and user-friendly interface into one that would be compelling from a cost aspect to mid-size manufacturing and assembly companies with Revenues less than a billion dollars. The project was to be unique in many respects, including modules that would permit numerous assembly/manufacturing lines to

TABLE CS 3-2 Investment and Pretax Cash Flow $(000)'s

Year	C + 1	C + 2	C + 3	C + 4	C + 5	C + 6	C + 7
Investment	(2,500)	(3,900)	(6,000)	(5,000)	(2,900)	(2,200)	(1,100)
Cash Flow	0	0	2,800	5,800	9,200	19,000	39,000

be operated simultaneously, driven by a "scheduler" that would prioritize which line should run what product based on parameters set by the user. The catch was the project would cost a lot of money and had to be operational within two years.

The project team discussed the project at length and, while there was broad agreement that the project was essential to growing Omega, there was also consensus on the fact that this would be the biggest investment the company ever made, and so every aspect of the presentation must be very professional. With the assistance of the company's CFO, Ron was able to put together the required investment and resulting cash flows (Table CS 3-2).

While this table was interesting, it wasn't helpful in determining the attractiveness of the investment. In order to evaluate the investment, the present value of this stream of cash flows needed to be determined. This required an estimate of the company's Weighted Average Cost of Capital.

The WACC was determined with the aid of the Capital Asset Pricing Model (Equation [3-25]) and Equation [3-28].

$$k_E = k_{rf} + [E(k_m) - k_{rf}](Beta) \quad [3\text{-}25]$$

$$k_{WACC} = (k_{rf} + k_{rp})(1 - TR)\left(\frac{B}{EV}\right) + \{k_{rf} + [E(k_m) - k_{rf}](Beta)\}\left(\frac{E}{EV}\right) \quad [3\text{-}28]$$

From readily available financial data the CFO determined that the Risk-Free Rate k_{rf} and Market Premium $[E(k_m) - k_{rf}]$ were 3.85% and 4.70% respectively. The next step was to determine Omega's Beta. By using the comparable companies method the CFO concluded the levered Beta for this group of companies to be 1.10 with a debt-to-equity ratio (B/E) of 10% and Tax Rate of 40%. With this information and using Equation [3-32] the unlevered Beta for Omega Corporation was calculated to be 1.038.

$$Beta_U = \frac{Beta_L}{\left[1 + (1 - TR)\left(\frac{B}{E}\right)\right]} \quad [3\text{-}32]$$

$$Beta_U = \frac{1.10}{[1 + (1 - 0.40)(0.10)]} = \frac{1.10}{1 + (0.6)(0.10)} = \frac{1.10}{1.06} = 1.038$$

Management had managed Omega's cash flow very well over the years and this had produced a balance sheet with no debt. While according to the projections Omega could finance this project with internally generated cash flow, the CFO argued that if they had a blip in Revenues or a major problem in the field implementing the new software, this could quickly change the cash flow picture. Therefore, it would be prudent to buttress their cash position and take on some debt. Furthermore with interest rates being near an all-time low (premium above the risk-free rate of 1.5 percentage points) this was a low-cost source of financing and the breathing room afforded by the loan would more than offset the cost, not to mention the favorable impact on the WACC. Ultimately it was decided to negotiate a 10-year-term loan in the amount of \$4,000,000. Determining the market value of Omega's equity proved to be a problem. The reason was that in the last several years the company had shown little growth. The CFO discussed the problem with the company's investment banker. She agreed that the normal approach would be to take the present value of the company's future cash flows and to that add the present value of the terminal value. However, given the company's recent performance she felt that was unrealistic and would be a hard sell to investors if the company went to the market to raise capital. After some work, she advised the CFO that market value of the company's equity was about \$30,000,000, or roughly one time the current year's revenue. With this data and Equation [3-31] the levered Beta for Omega was estimated to be 1.12 (which made sense since Omega's debt to equity was approximately one third higher than the comparable companies).

$$Beta_L = \left[1+(1-TR)\left(\frac{B}{E}\right)\right](Beta_U) \qquad [3\text{-}31]$$

$$Beta_L = \left[1+(1-0.40)\left(\frac{4{,}000{,}000}{30{,}000{,}000}\right)\right](1.038)$$

$$= [1+(0.60)(0.133)](1.038) = (1.08)(1.038) = 1.121$$

$$\text{Beta}_L = 1.12$$

Having estimated Omega's levered Beta, the CFO was now in a position to calculate the WACC. To assist in this regard he prepared Table CS 3-3, which consolidated the data he would need for the calculation.

TABLE CS 3-3 Omega Corporation Weighted Average Cost of Capital Data

	\$'s Unless Stated Otherwise	
k_{rf}	Risk-Free Rate of Return	3.85%
k_{RP}	Debt Risk Premium	1.50%
TR	Corporate Tax Rate	40.00%
$[E(km) - k_{rf}]$	Market Risk Premium	4.70%
Beta	Company's Beta	1.12
B	Market Value of Company's Debt	4,000,000
E	Market Value of Company's Equity	30,000,000
EV	Company's Enterprise Value, Sum of Debt and Equity	34,000,000

He began by breaking Equation [3-28] into its Debt and Equity components.

$$\textit{Debt Component of WACC} = (k_{rf} + k_{rp})(1 - TR)\left(\frac{B}{EV}\right)$$

$$\textit{Equity Component of WACC} = \{k_{rf} + [E(k_m) - k_{rf}](Beta)\}\left(\frac{E}{EV}\right)$$

Substituting values from Table CS 3-3 for the variables in the component equations the Debt and Equity components of the WACC were calculated to be:

$$\textit{Debt Component of WACC} = (k_{rf} + k_{rp})(1 - TR)\left(\frac{B}{EV}\right)$$

$$= (3.85 + 1.50)(1 - 0.40)\left(\frac{4{,}000{,}000}{34{,}000{,}000}\right)$$

$$= (5.35)(0.60)(0.118) = 0.00376$$

$$\textit{Debt Component of WACC} = 0.38\%$$

$$\textit{Equity Component of WACC} = \{3.85 + [4.7](1.12)\}\left(\frac{30{,}000{,}000}{34{,}000{,}000}\right)$$

$$= (3.850 + 5.264)(0.8824)$$

$$= (9.114)(0.8824) = 8.042$$

$$\textit{Equity Component of WACC} = 8.04\%$$

The sum of the two gives the WACC for Omega Corporation.

$$k_{WACC} = \textit{Debt Component of WACC} + \textit{Equity Component of WACC}$$
$$= 0.38 + 8.04 = 8.42$$
$$k_{WACC} = 8.4\%$$

At this point the CFO had to think about exactly what this number meant. He concluded that it was a discount rate that was appropriate for the company's core business. Since the project that was to be funded was riskier than their current offering, the rate had to be adjusted to reflect the additional risk. After some discussion with the CEO they settled on a WACC for this undertaking of 10%. At this point the CFO had everything he needed to complete the presentation to be made to the board of directors.

In addition to Ron and the independent directors, the chief financial officer, VP of Research and Development (R&D), and VP of Marketing were present at the meeting. Ron thanked everyone for coming to this special meeting, which had been called to consider an investment proposal, which, if approved, would be the largest investment the company had ever made. He began with an overview of the proposed investment, outlining its unique features and various attributes. This was followed by a presentation by the VP of R&D, who, in anticipation of the difficulty the board may have in grasping the essence of the investment, had prepared a clear and simplified step-by-step presentation of the new technology, scheduler, flexibility, and risks associated with the proposed investment. Next a discussion was led by the VP of Marketing, who, by using a Q&A format, took the directors through a series of charts that quantified the value to the customer. At the conclusion the CFO presented Table CS 3-4.

With the assistance of the table the CFO explained that the project required a considerable investment over a 7-year period totaling $23,600,000 and that the cash flow from the revenues the product would generate wouldn't commence until the third year. He also explained that while the company's cash position was adequate to fund the investment, it wouldn't be generating any cash for the next couple of years. Therefore, as part of the strategy associated with the investment, the company proposed to enter into a 10-year-term loan. The loan, in addition to providing extra liquidity should they need it, had the added advantage of reducing the company's WACC, which they had calculated to be 8.4% for the existing business, and this had been topped up to 10% to reflect the additional risk presented by this opportunity. Finally he pointed out that the Net Present Value of the proposed investment was $25,490,000 and the cash flow payback would take place just after Year C + 5, the third year of the product's life cycle, which was expected to be more than 10 years.

At this point the CEO stepped forward and addressed the board: "Gentlemen, we have before us a game-changing opportunity for Omega Corporation. It certainly has risks but in management's view, and hopefully the board's, risks worth taking. When this project is fully implemented, Omega will be a different company and once again the unquestioned leader in our industry. Tables CS 3-5 and CS 3-6 tell a great story."

Continuing, "As you can see, seven years into the program, we will have Revenues of nearly $120,000,000, a company growing at 20% per year, and a Net Income of approximately $23,700,000."

There was some discussion about the growth rates. The concern was they may be too aggressive and produce unrealistic pro-forma projections, especially insofar as cash

TABLE CS 3-4 Omega Corporation Present Value Analysis of Cash Flows

$(000)'s Unless Stated Otherwise							
Year	**C + 1**	**C + 2**	**C + 3**	**C + 4**	**C + 5**	**C + 6**	**C + 7**
Investment	(2,500)	(3,900)	(6,000)	(5,000)	(2,900)	(2,200)	(1,100)
Cash Flow	0	0	2,800	5,800	9,200	19,000	39,000
CF Net of Investment	(2,500)	(3,900)	(3,200)	800	6,300	16,800	37,900
Discount Term	1/(1 + *k*)	1/(1 + *k*)^2	1/(1 + *k*)^3	1/(1 + *k*)^4	1/(1 + *k*)^5	1/(1 + *k*)^6	1/(1 + *k*)^7
Discount Factor	0.9091	0.8264	0.7513	0.6830	0.6209	0.5645	0.5132
Present Value	(2,273)	(3,223)	(2,404)	546	3,912	9,483	19,449
Net Present Value	25,490						

TABLE CS 3-5 Omega Corporation Comparative Projected Income Statements

December 31, 20XX $(000)'s								
Year	**Current**	**C + 1**	**C + 2**	**C + 3**	**C + 4**	**C + 5**	**C + 6**	**C + 7**
Revenues (Rev)	28,987	31,885	35,074	42,089	54,715	76,601	99,582	119,498
Cost of Goods Sold (COGS)	(4,638)	(5,102)	(5,436)	(8,418)	(9,302)	(10,724)	(13,941)	(16,730)
Gross Margin (GM)	24,349	26,784	29,637	33,671	45,414	65,877	85,640	102,768
Operating Expenses (OpExp)	(14,493)	(19,769)	(23,499)	(27,358)	(32,829)	(38,301)	(49,791)	(59,749)
EBITDA	9,855	7,015	6,138	6,313	12,584	27,576	35,849	43,019
Depreciation and Amortization (D&A)	(661)	(797)	(1,052)	(1,263)	(1,641)	(2,298)	(2,987)	(3,585)
EBIT	9,194	6,218	5,086	5,051	10,943	25,278	32,862	39,434
Interest Income/ (Expense) (NetInt)	7	8	8	8	9	9	11	14
Earnings before Tax (EBT)	9,201	6,226	5,094	5,059	10,952	25,287	32,873	39,448
Taxes Paid (TaxesPaid) @	(3,680)	(2,490)	(2,037)	(2,023)	(4,381)	(10,115)	(13,149)	(15,779)
Net Income (NI)	5,521	3,735	3,056	3,035	6,571	15,172	19,724	23,669

flow was concerned. The CFO responded by producing Table CS 3-7 and pointed out that in this table the Cash Flow had been discounted by 25% and even then the Net Present Value is approximately $14,900,000 with the payback period stretched out somewhat but still between the third and fourth years after the product's release for sale.

At this point the CEO commented, "A 3-plus-year payback period after release isn't great, but based on my experience, such a period is fairly common for projects of this type." He reminded the board that the growth rates and the implied payback period suggested by the material presented were typical of what the company had achieved with prior product releases, but admittedly not of this scale, during earlier periods in Omega's history.

At this point one of the directors asked a question. "Ron, this all looks very good but what would our company's performance look like if we didn't invest as you suggest

TABLE CS 3-6 Omega Corporation Projected Performance Statistics

$(000)'s Unless Stated Otherwise								
Year	**Current**	**C + 1**	**C + 2**	**C + 3**	**C + 4**	**C + 5**	**C + 6**	**C + 7**
Revenue	28,987	31,885	35,074	42,089	54,715	76,601	99,582	119,498
% Revenue Growth		10%	10%	20%	30%	40%	30%	20%
Net Income	5,521	3,735	3,056	3,035	6,571	15,172	19,724	23,669
Net Income % Revenue	19%	12%	9%	7%	12%	20%	20%	20%

TABLE CS 3-7 Omega Corporation Present Value Analysis of Cash Flows Reduced by 25% $(000)'s

Year	C + 1	C + 2	C + 3	C + 4	C + 5	C + 6	C + 7
Investment	(2,500)	(3,900)	(6,000)	(5,000)	(2,900)	(2,200)	(1,100)
Cash Flow	0	0	2,100	4,350	6,900	14,250	29,250
CF Net of Investment	(2,500)	(3,900)	(3,900)	(650)	4,000	12,050	28,150
Discount Term	1/(1 + *k*)	1/(1 + *k*)^2	1/(1 + *k*)^3	1/(1 + *k*)^4	1/(1 + *k*)^5	1/(1 + *k*)^6	1/(1 + *k*)^7
Discount Factor	0.9091	0.8264	0.7513	0.6830	0.6209	0.5645	0.5132
Present Value	(2,273)	(3,223)	(2,930)	(444)	2,484	6,802	14,445
Net Present Value	14,861						
Accumulated Invest					(20,300)	(22,500)	
Accumulated CF					13,350	27,600	
Total Accum Invest	(2,500)	(6,400)	(12,400)	(17,400)	(20,300)	(22,500)	(23,600)
Total Accumulated CF	0	0	2,100	6,450	13,350	27,600	56,850

and instead continue to implement our current strategy?" Ron's response was: "We ran that scenario. Revenue and Net Income would climb to about $57,000,000 and $11,000,000, respectively, which would be less than half of what we can achieve if we make this investment. However that's not the whole story. In my view, continuing as we are now is riskier than making the investments we are proposing because a competitor has overtaken us with a very good product and they will make it difficult for us to achieve the numbers I just gave you." The director thanked Ron for his response and a brief discussion followed.

After a brief period the chair decided to bring the meeting to a decision point. "We have had a thorough discussion of this investment opportunity and I would like to commend management for an excellent presentation and discussion. Before I call for a vote on funding this investment I would like to know if there are any more questions."

The CEO responded by saying, "I don't have a question, but I do have a final comment. You may have noted that in the seventh year of the pro-forma projections (Table CS 3-5) the EBITDA is projected to be approximately $43,000,000. A company like Omega would typically command a multiple of at least 10 and probably higher. This would value the company at about $430,000,000. As I recall, the members of the board own 40% of Omega. I would think that the possibility of achieving a valuation exceeding $400 million makes this investment opportunity very interesting for all of us and puts management and the board on the same page."

The chair called for the vote on the resolution to authorize the funding. The vote was a unanimous *yes*.

CHAPTER FOUR

4

Introduction to Valuation Models*

CHAPTER 4 TAKEAWAYS

- The valuation model for an enterprise can consist of a series of cash flows or a combination of a *forecast series* followed by a *post-forecast series* of cash flows and is modeled by the expression

  PV (Cash Flows) = PV (Forecast Period Cash Flows) + PV (Post Forecast Cash Flows)

- The present value of forecast period cash flows is valued by

$$PV_{FP} = \sum_{i=1}^{n} \frac{E_i}{(1+k)^i}$$

  This in expanded form becomes

$$PV_{FP} = \sum_{i=1}^{n} \frac{E_i}{(1+k)^i} = \frac{E_1}{(1+k)^1} + \cdots + \frac{E_{n-1}}{(1+k)^{i-1}} + \frac{E_n}{(1+k)^i}$$

- Post-forecast-period cash flows can be valued in a number of ways. The model selected depends on the assumptions made about the post-forecast cash flows.
- The five models together with the associated assumptions are:

(1) Perpetual Fixed Model (PXM)

$$PV_{PXM_N} = \frac{E_{PX}}{k(1+k)^N}$$

This model assumes a fixed (constant) stream of cash flow that continues forever. It's hard to think of a company's post-forecast-period cash flows that would suit this model and therefore it's seldom if ever used.

(continued)

*The reader may notice minor discrepancies in the calculations in this chapter. When this occurs, it is the result of rounding.

(2) Finite Fixed Model (FXM)

$$PV_{FXM_N} = \frac{E_{FX}\left[1-(1+k)^{-NX}\right]}{k(1+k)^N}$$

Unlike the perpetual fixed model this model values a fixed cash flow stream for a finite period of *NX* years. Again it's unlikely to be a realistic prototype for valuing post-forecast-period cash flows. However, it is useful for valuing a fixed annuity and finds its greatest use in this application.

(3) Perpetual Growth Model (PGM)

$$PV_{PGM_N} = \frac{E_{PG}}{(k-g_{PG})(1+k)^N}$$

This model assumes that a cash flow stream grows at some fixed rate g_{PG} forever and since companies generally strive to grow cash flow year after year it can be a reasonable model to use for post-forecast-period cash flows. The fact that no company will continue to increase its cash flow forever doesn't invalidate the model because the outlying years don't contribute much to the present value. The discount rate to use can be difficult to establish. However, an examination of a company's historical performance will provide insight into an appropriate number that then needs to be tempered with judgment. There is no such thing as a typical number, but one often sees growth rates in the 3–4% range when this model is used. In fact there are many mature companies that grow at a rate near and correlated to the Gross National Product, which in developed economies averages something like 3%.

(4) Finite Growth Model (FGM)

$$PV_{FGM_N} = \frac{E_{FG}\left[1-\left(\frac{1+g_{FG}}{1+k}\right)^{NG}\right]}{(k-g_{FG})(1+k)^N}$$

Unlike the perpetual growth model this model assumes the cash flow grows at some constant rate g_{FG} for a finite period of *NG* years. It can be used in place of the perpetual growth model when the number of years of growth is relatively high, say 25+ years. It is most frequently used in *multi-stage models* where a cash flow is expected to grow at one rate for a period of years and then to be followed by a series of cash flows that grow at another rate. This model yields the best results when there is sufficient data available to enable the user to make educated estimates of the *finite growth rate* and *finite period*.

(5) Terminal Value Model (TVM)

$$PV_{TVM_N} = \frac{E_{TY}(TVM)}{(1+k)^N}$$

The company is assumed to be sold at the end of the forecast period. This is by far the most frequently used model when valuing post-forecast-period cash flows. It simply requires an estimate of a suitable multiplier, which can be deduced from readily available industry data or obtained from professionals/organizations that have accumulated this type of data and developed valuation expertise.

In instances where an industry-based TVM isn't available, an estimate can be made by using the expression,

$$TVM = \frac{1}{k - g_{PG}}$$

However, do so with care and keep in mind the constraints placed on k and g.

1. If $g_{PG} > k$, it will give a nonsensical result.
2. If $g_{PG} = k$, the result is indeterminate.
3. When these models were developed, the constraint placed was that $g_{PG} < k$. For any given level of cash flow, the value implied by the perpetual or finite growth models is controlled by $k - g_{PG}$. When the difference is small, the impact is large and small changes in g_{PG} will have a large impact. As the difference increases, the effect of any given change in g_{PG} diminishes.

Single-stage valuation models

The following two models are the most frequently used to value companies:

1. Forecast Period + Terminal Value Model

$$PV_{FP+TV} = \sum_{i=1}^{n} \frac{E_i}{(1+k)^i} + \frac{E_{TY}(TVM)}{(1+k)^N}$$

2. Forecast Period + Perpetual Growth Model

$$PV_{FP+PG} = \sum_{i=1}^{n} \frac{E_i}{(1+k)^i} + \frac{E_{PG}}{(k - g_{PG})(1+k)^N}$$

The model to use depends on the information that is available and the objective of the valuation. If the business is not a long-term hold, then the terminal value model is generally used. Management teams of businesses that are characterized by cash flows that are expected to continue for a long period of time would be inclined to use the perpetual growth model. Large consumer packaged goods companies (CPG) that grow with the economy are examples of companies that could use the perpetual growth model to value post-forecast-period cash flows.

Equivalence of the Single-Stage Models

A case can be made for the TVM being equivalent to $\frac{1}{k - g_{PG}}$ in certain circumstances and hence the implied equivalence of the two models. However, the distinction between the two must be kept in mind. When applying the terminal value model the preferred TVM is one determined by industry data. If industry data is not available, the single-stage TVM model defaults to the perpetual growth model.

INTRODUCTION TO ESTIMATING VALUE[1,2]

In Chapter 3 the concept of *Enterprise Value* was introduced and defined as:

$$EV = B + E \quad [3\text{-}10]$$

where for a public company:
B = The market value of the company's debt
E = The market value of the company's equity
= (Number of Shares Outstanding) (Price per Share)

The Enterprise Value of a private company was defined as:

$$EV = B + E_{FCF} \quad [3\text{-}18]$$

where:
B = The market value of a company's debt
E_{FCF} = The value of a private company's equity

And E_{FCF} the value of the private company's equity is given by:

$$E_{FCF} = \textit{Present Value of Company's Future Cash Flows} \quad [3\text{-}17]$$

When businesspeople talk about the value of a company they are usually talking about Enterprise Value. Equations [3-10] and [3-18] are definitions of Enterprise Value and consist of the sum of the market value of debt and equity. Valuing a public company's debt is usually not a problem since data on bank debt, capital lease obligations, public debt, and so forth is readily available. Private companies often have public debt and when this is the case their debt is also easily valued. Obviously, if a company is debt free, the enterprise value and market value of equity are one and the same. This chapter focuses on valuing cash flows and therefore unless stated otherwise the assumption is that the company is debt free, and other than briefly describing how the market value of debt can be quantified, any discussion of the impact that debt has on value is left to subsequent chapters.

---

[1]As the name implies, this chapter is about valuation of cash flows. The material used in this chapter relies heavily on Appendixes A and B. In Appendix A the equations are developed in detail. Appendix B summarizes the material developed in A with commentary on the suitability of the various models. All readers are advised to familiarize themselves with the material in both of these appendixes.

[2]As pointed out in Chapter 3, the Enterprise Value is technically defined as the sum of the value of the company's debt and equity less excess cash. In the interest of simplicity it is assumed that any cash on a company's balance sheet is required for working capital purposes and therefore ignored when calculating enterprise values.

Equation [3-17] is the theoretically correct way to value the equity of any company. When it comes to a public company the markets do the work and the value of a company's equity is the market's perception of the present value of the company's future cash flows. Private companies are another matter and valuing their equity has to be achieved through other means.

As just stated, the market decides the price of a public company's equity by valuing the price of the company's shares. This price times the number of shares outstanding is the market value of the equity.

The value of a private company's equity is not so easily obtained. Doing the calculations implied by Equation [3-17] is one way of valuing a private company's equity. Other methods utilize techniques involving *comparable companies* and *comparable transactions*. While on the subject of Equation [3-17] it should be noted that this equation is also widely used to value a division or business unit of a company (public or private) or, for that matter, investments in general.

One of the objectives of this chapter is to develop a framework that will help managers focus on creating value that is ultimately reflected in the value of the enterprise. The *comparable companies* and *comparable transactions* methods are important and widely used by professionals in valuing companies and will be discussed later in this book but aren't especially helpful in this regard. Why? They are too far removed from the everyday tools that managers have at their disposal. One of the things managers can do is focus on cash flow and therefore the Present Value of Future Cash Flows method is the most suitable for our purpose of valuing an enterprise at this time.

The Present Value of Cash Flows methodology implied by Equation [3-17] requires that someone (often management) estimate future cash flows. Some people think the longer the forecast period, the better the estimate of value. Experience doesn't support this. In this rapidly changing global business environment, many people would be thrilled if they could forecast with some accuracy what was going to happen next quarter or next year, never mind trying to forecast what will happen 10, 25, 50, or 75 years from now. However, just because it may be difficult to estimate cash flows with any certainty beyond some relatively short period of time doesn't mean these estimates don't have value. They do! The issue is: How do you incorporate distant cash flows into a cash flow valuation model? The usual method is to forecast cash flows for a 3-to-5-year period and then make some assumption(s) about what happens thereafter. The assumption(s) you make on what happens during the post-forecast period will determine which of the post-forecast valuation models presented in this chapter you will use.

Based on the foregoing discussion, it would seem logical to conclude that the Present Value of a Company's Future Cash Flows (PV_{FCF}) consists of the present value of the cash flows that take place during the forecast period and the present value of cash flows after the forecast period. This notion can be expressed as shown in Equation [4-1].

$$\begin{aligned} PV_{FCF} = {} & PV\,(Cash\ Flows\ during\ the\ Forecast\ Period) \\ & + PV\,(Cash\ Flows\ after\ the\ Forecast\ Period) \end{aligned} \qquad [4\text{-}1]$$

Present Value of Cash Flows during the Forecast Period

The pro-forma cash flows during the forecast period will usually consist of a series of distinct estimates for each period in the series. The present value of a discrete series of cash flows can be calculated by using the valuation model represented by Equations [A-1] and [A-2] in Appendix A.[3] To some, Equation [A-1] is troubling. It shouldn't be since it's just a convenient way of expressing [A-2], which is the essence of present value analysis.[4]

$$PV_{FP} = \sum_{i=1}^{n} \frac{E_i}{(1+k)^i} \qquad \text{[A-1]}$$

$$PV_{FP} = \frac{E_1}{(1+k)^1} + \frac{E_2}{(1+k)^2} + \frac{E_3}{(1+k)^3} + \ldots + \frac{E_n}{(1+k)^n} \qquad \text{[A-2]}$$

where:

PV_{FP} = Present value of the discrete cash flows during the forecast period

$\sum_{i=1}^{n}$ = Sum of the periodic cash flows out to year n in increments i

n = The last period for which cash flow is expected:

E_i = Expected cash flow in the ith period in the future

k = Discount rate (the market rate of return for other investments of comparable risk)

i = The period (usually in years) in the future in which the prospective cash flow is expected to be received

For example, if the forecast period is five years, then Equation [A-2] becomes:

$$PV_{FP} = \frac{E_1}{(1+k)^1} + \frac{E_2}{(1+k)^2} + \frac{E_3}{(1+k)^3} + \frac{E_4}{(1+k)^4} + \frac{E_5}{(1+k)^5} \qquad \text{[4-2]}$$

Present Value of Cash Flow Models after the Forecast Period

Estimating the value of post-forecast period cash flows isn't quite as straightforward as it is for the forecast period. The most common approaches include the following.

---

[3]After examining Appendix A one could properly conclude there are numerous models in addition to the ones quantified by Equations [A-1] and [A-2] that could be used for calculating the present value of a stream of cash flows during the forecast period. In fact various models are used throughout this book just to make this point. However, in practice the forecasted stream of cash flows is typically three to five years in duration and in these cases it's usually expedient to use either [A-1] or [A-2] even if other models apply.

[4]In Chapter 3 there is a section titled "Introduction to Present Value," which may be helpful to those in need of a review.

(1) Perpetual Fixed Model (PXM)

This model assumes that a constant cash flow stream continues forever. The present value of this cash flow stream that takes place in Year N is given by Equation [A-15], which for convenience is designated Equation [4-3].

$$PV_{PXM} = \frac{E_{PX}}{k} \qquad [4\text{-}3]^{5}$$

where:

PV_{PXM} is the present value of the perpetual fixed cash flows E_{PX}

Refer to Figure 4-1.

The perpetual stream of cash flows, E_{PX} takes place after the last forecasted cash flow at the end of period N (the period during which cash flows are forecasted). Also when the expression E_{PF}/k was derived it was present valued to time T_N. In order to present value Equation [4-3] to the beginning of the forecasted cash flow stream, it has to be multiplied by the term $1/(1+k)^N$. Hence, PV_{PXM_N} the present value of a perpetual stream of fixed cash flows commencing at the end of period N present valued to the beginning of the forecast period is given by:

$$PV_{PXM_N} = \frac{E_{PX}}{k(1+k)^N} \qquad [4\text{-}4]$$

Finally it's important to note that E_{PX} can be the same as E_N or some other cash flow as long as E_{PX} is fixed at some level of cash flow.

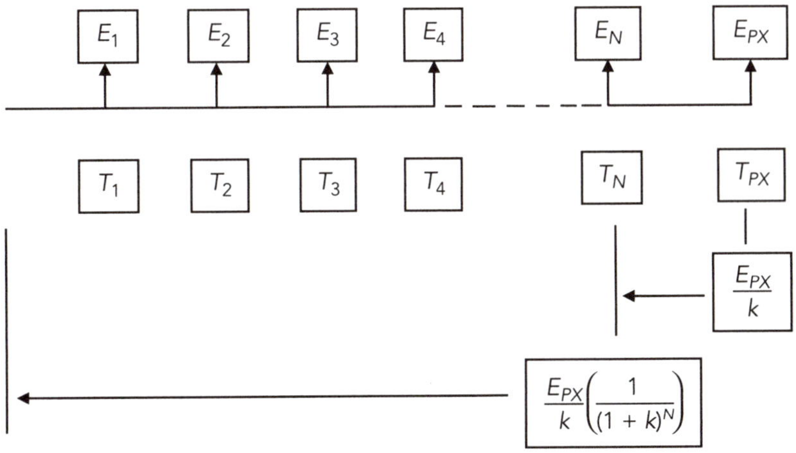

FIGURE 4-1 Perpetual Fixed Model

[5] See Appendix A, "Present Value of a Fixed Stream of Cash Flows in Perpetuity" (n = infinity).

(2) Finite Fixed Model (FXM)

This model is a little different from model (1). It assumes that a constant cash flow stream continues for *NX* periods (a limited number of years) and thereafter is zero. The present value of this type of cash flow stream is given by Equation [A-14], which is renumbered as Equation [4-5].

$$PV_{FXM} = \frac{E_{FX}\left[1-(1+k)^{-NX}\right]}{k} \qquad [4\text{-}5]^{6}$$

where:

PV_{FFM} is the PV of the finite fixed cash flow stream for *NX* years and E_{FX} is the first cash flow in the stream

Refer to Figure 4-2.

Again, the finite constant stream of cash flows E_{FX} that continues for *NX* years takes place after the last forecasted cash flow that occurs at the end of *N* periods. As in model (1), when Equation [4-5] was developed it was present valued to time T_N. In order to present value Equation [4-5] to the beginning of the forecasted cash flow stream, multiply it by $1/(1+k)^N$. Hence, PV_{FXM_N} , the present value of the finite stream of constant cash flows commencing at the end of period *N*, present valued to the beginning of the forecast period is given by:

$$PV_{FXM_N} = \frac{E_{FX}\left[1-(1+k)^{-NX}\right]}{k(1+k)^N} \qquad [4\text{-}6]$$

Again like E_{PX} there is no requirement that E_{FX} equal E_N. The only requirement is that whatever value E_{FX} has, it is constant throughout the period of *NX* years.

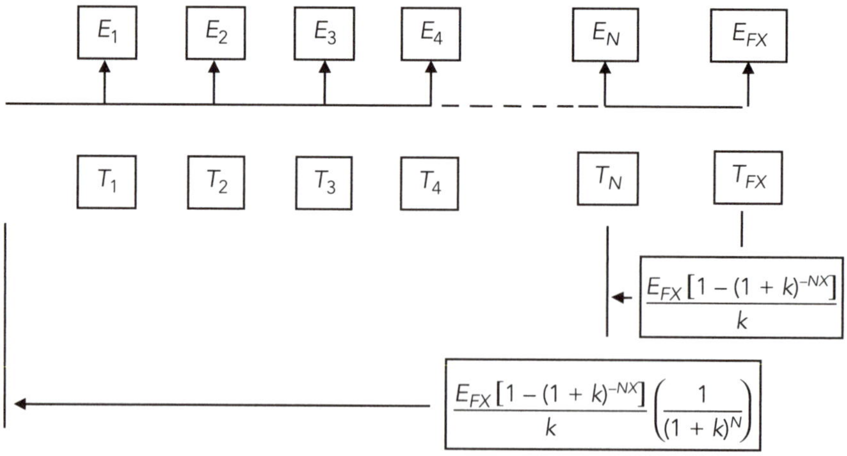

FIGURE 4-2 Finite Fixed Model

[6] See Appendix A, "Present Value of a Stream of Fixed Cash Flows E for *n* Years."

(3) Perpetual Growth Model (PGM)

This model assumes that the cash flow stream grows at a constant rate g_{PG} after the period of forecasted cash flows in perpetuity and the present value of the cash flow stream is defined by Equation [A-30] and designated here as [4-7].

$$PV_{PGM} = \frac{E_{PG}}{k - g_{PG}} \quad [4\text{-}7]$$ [7]

where:

PV_{PGM} is the PV of the cash flow stream that grows at a constant rate g_{PG} in perpetuity and E_{PG} is the first cash flow in the stream

Refer to Figure 4-3.

Just as in the previous models, the stream of cash flows E_{PG} that grow at rate g_{PG} in perpetuity takes place after the last forecasted cash flow at the end of period N. Once again, when this expression was developed it was present valued to time T_N. As in the previous models, in order to present value Equation [4-7] to the beginning of the forecasted cash flow period it has to be multiplied by $1/(1 + k)^N$. Hence, PV_{PGM_N}, the present value of the stream of constant cash flows that grow at rate g_{PG} in perpetuity, present valued to the beginning of the forecast period is given by:

$$PV_{PGM_N} = \frac{E_{PG}}{(k - g_{PG})(1+k)^N} \quad [4\text{-}8]$$

When using this model it's important to get the value of E_{PG} correct. As stated earlier, when this model was developed it was assumed that E_{PG} takes place one period after E_N has occurred. So if E_N grows at rate g_{PG}, then:

$$E_{PG} = E_N (1 + g_{PG}) \quad [4\text{-}9]$$

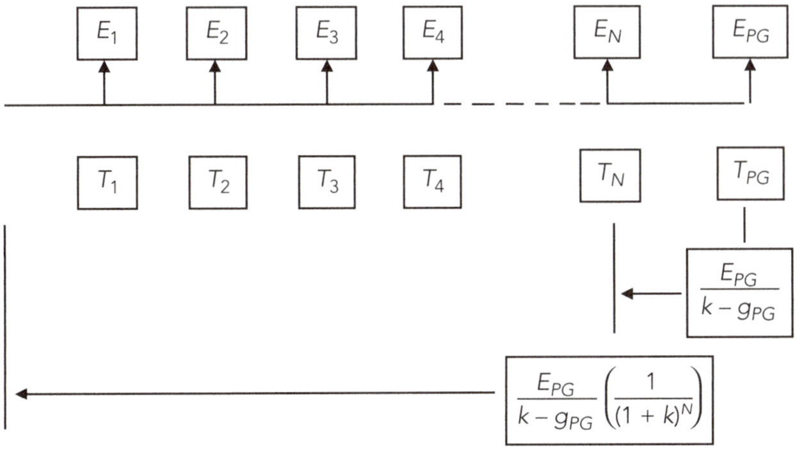

FIGURE 4-3 Perpetual Growth Model

[7] See Appendix A, "Present Value of a Stream of Cash Flows That Grow at a Fixed Rate in Perpetuity."

When Equation [4-9] represents the first cash flow that takes place in the perpetual growth model, then Equation [4-8] becomes

$$PV_{PGM_N} = \frac{E_N(1+g_{PG})}{(k-g_{PG})(1+k)^N} \tag{4-10}$$

Again, like E_{PX} and E_{FX}, there is no requirement that E_{PG} equal E_N. The only requirement is that whatever starting value E_N has, it grows at a fixed rate in perpetuity.

(4) Finite Growth Model (FGM)

This model is different from model (2). It assumes a cash flow stream that grows at a constant rate g_{FG} for NG years (a finite number) and thereafter is zero. The present value of this type of cash flow stream is given by Equation [A-29], which is renumbered as Equation [4-11].

$$PV_{FGM} = \frac{E_{FG}\left[1-\left(\frac{1+g_{FG}}{1+k}\right)^{NG}\right]}{(k-g_{FG})} \quad [4\text{-}11]^{8}$$

where:

PV_{FGM} is the PV of the finite constant cash flow stream for NG Years and E_{FG} is the first cash flow in the stream

Refer to Figure 4-4.

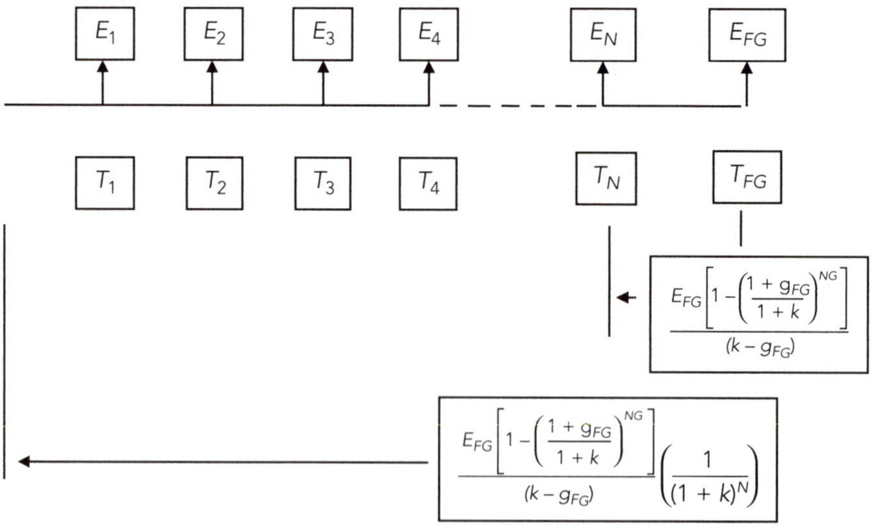

FIGURE 4-4 Finite Growth Model

[8]See Appendix A, "Present Value of a Stream of Cash Flows That Grow at a Fixed Rate g for a Finite Period."

As in the previous models, the finite stream of cash flows E_{FG} growing at rate g_{FG} for NG years takes place after the last forecasted cash flow that occurs at the end of N periods. As in model (2), when Equation [4-11] was developed it was present valued to time T_N. In order to present value [4-11] to the beginning of the forecasted cash flow stream it has to be multiplied by $1/(1 + k)^N$. Hence, PV_{FGM_N}, the present value of the finite stream of cash flows growing at a rate g_{FG} commencing at the end of period N, continuing for NG years, and discounted back to the beginning of the period of forecasted cash flows is given by:

$$PV_{FGM_N} = \frac{E_{FG}\left[1-\left(\dfrac{1+g_{FG}}{1+k}\right)^{NG}\right]}{(k-g_{FG})(1+k)^N} \qquad [4\text{-}12]$$

Just as in the perpetual growth model just discussed it's important to use the right value for E_{FG}. If E_N grows at a rate g_{FG} for the first period after time T_N, then:

$$E_{FG} = E_N\,(1 + g_{FG}) \qquad [4\text{-}13]$$

and Equation [4-12] can be modified to become:

$$PV_{FGM_N} = \frac{E_N(1+g_{FG})\left[1-\left(\dfrac{1+g_{FG}}{1+k}\right)^{NG}\right]}{(k-g_{FG})(1+k)^N} \qquad [4\text{-}14]$$

(5) Terminal Value Model (TVM)

Unlike the previous four models, this model doesn't make any assumption about future cash flows. It assumes the company is sold at the end of the forecast period for some multiple of cash flow. Equation [A-5] (designated here as [4-15]) gives the present value of this hypothetical transaction.

$$PV_{TVM_N} = \frac{E_{TY}(TVM)}{(1+k)^N} \qquad [4\text{-}15][9]$$

where:

PV_{TVM_N} is the PV of the product of the cash flows in the terminal year E_{TY}, and
TVM is the terminal year multiplier

Refer to Figure 4-5.

Note, in this case there isn't a need to make any adjustment to Equation [4-15] to present value it to the beginning of the period of forecasted cash flows. This was done

[9]See Appendix A, "Present Value of the Terminal Value of a Cash Flow at the End of Year *n*."

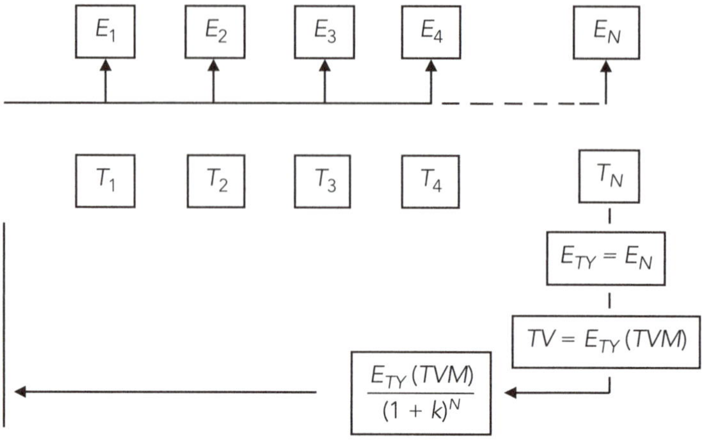

FIGURE 4-5 Terminal Value Model

when Equation [A-5] was derived in Appendix A. The process by which this was done is easily repeated. If E_{TY}(TVM) is the value of the company at time T_N, then it is present valued back to the beginning of the cash flow stream by multiplying it by $1/(1 + k)^N$.

Table 4-1 summarizes the forecast period and the five post-forecast period cash flow models just discussed.

Single-Stage Models

When a period of forecasted cash flows is followed by a post-forecast period and one of the post-forecast models is used to value the post-forecast-period cash flows, this is known as a *single-stage model.* In addition to using models 1–5 in single-stage valuations, they can be used in multi-stage models by applying them in various combinations.

Multi-Stage Models

For example, it's entirely possible that a management team could estimate that the post-forecast-period cash flows will be followed by a period of high growth as a new product line gains momentum, and when the cash flow from the new product line has leveled off the company will experience a period of slower growth. This could be modeled by a *two-stage growth model* by applying the *finite growth cash flow model* twice or the *finite growth model* followed by the *perpetual growth model.* In either case the first stage would have a growth rate of g_1 followed by a second stage of growth g_2. Another possibility would be to calculate the final cash flow occurring at the end of stage 1 and value the post–stage 1 cash flows by using the terminal value multiplier (more on this later).

Applying the Present Value Equations

As the treatments of the various subjects associated with valuation are refined, many different valuation expressions will be developed and used. However, almost all of these

TABLE 4-1 Summary of PVs of Cash Flows during the Forecast and Post-Forecast Periods in General Form

Model Used for Calculating the PV of: Cash Flows during Forecast Period	Model Used for Calculating the PV of: Cash Flows after Forecast Period
Stream of Distinct Cash Flows Model $PV_{FP} = \sum_{i=1}^{n} \frac{E_i}{(1+k)^i}$ [A-1]	Perpetual Fixed Cash Flow Model $PV_{PXM_N} = \frac{E_{PX}}{k(1+k)^N}$ [4-4]
	Finite Fixed Cash Flow Model $PV_{FXM_N} = \frac{E_{FX}\left[1-(1+k)^{-NX}\right]}{k(1+k)^N}$ [4-6]
	Perpetual Growth Cash Flow Model $PV_{PGM_N} = \frac{E_{PG}}{(k-g_{PG})(1+k)^N}$ [4-8]
	Finite Growth Cash Flow Model $PV_{FGM_N} = \frac{E_{FG}\left[1-\left(\frac{1+g_{FG}}{1+k}\right)^{NG}\right]}{(k-g_{FG})(1+k)^N}$ [4-12]
	Terminal Value Cash Flow Model $PV_{TVM_N} = \frac{E_{TY}(TVM)}{(1+k)^N}$ [4-15]

equations are based on the six models just presented (one for the forecast period and five for the post-forecast period). Therefore, readers would be well advised to take a little extra time now to make sure they feel completely comfortable with the material and concepts just presented. Doing so will pay big dividends later.

When applying Equation [4-1] the basic idea is to first value the stream of forecasted cash flows and then value the post-forecast-period cash flows. The sum of the two is the value of the cash flow stream being modeled.

$$PV_{FCF} = PV\,(Cash\ Flows\ during\ the\ Forecast\ Period) + PV\,(Cash\ Flows\ after\ the\ Forecast\ Period) \qquad [4\text{-}1]$$

The early examples in this chapter are intended to calculate the present value of the post-forecast-period cash flows by using all five models. This is done to illustrate how the expressions are applied and perhaps more importantly create an opportunity for the reader to begin to develop a feel for when to use one model or another. In later examples only those models that are considered to be appropriate will be used. In practice, because of their simplicity, models (3) and (5) and the perpetual growth and terminal value models, respectively, are perhaps the most widely used when valuing post-forecast-period cash flows. However, instances do occur that lend themselves to multi-stage models that involve the use of model (4), the finite growth model, and this model should be used when it contributes to a more realistic and comprehensible valuation.

Discount Rate *k*

All present value equations require that the user apply an "appropriate" discount rate. While it is easy to talk about the appropriate discount rate as an abstraction, it is a different matter when one is faced with quantification. Discount rates were discussed in Chapter 3 and will be revisited in considerable detail later. For now recall that the discount rate *k* can be viewed as consisting of two components. The first is the return implied by the capital structure of the business (WACC). The second is a premium that allows for the risk perceived with the cash flow stream in question when that risk isn't reflected in the WACC. In the examples that follow, various discount rates will be used and, when instructive, time will be spent explaining the rationale.

EXAMPLE 4-1: VALUING A&D INCORPORATED'S FORECASTED CASH FLOWS

A&D Incorporated has a forecasted stream of Cash Flow after Investing Activities as indicated in Table 4-2. The owners of the business are interested in what their Company might be worth if the Company achieves the forecasted cash flows. They are familiar enough with how companies are valued to know that they can get an answer to their question by using various techniques such as comparable companies, comparable transactions, and present value techniques. They decide on using a discounted cash flow analysis, at least as a starting point.

The first issue they are confronted with is selecting an appropriate discount rate. Since they are interested in what the business would be worth to someone else, they conclude that their Weighted Average Cost of Capital is not relevant. They decide to take the issue up with one of their business advisers. The adviser tells them that the highest valuation would come from a strategic buyer and in the current market such an investor would be looking for a return in excess of 15%. This rate struck them as being on the high side but based on this advice and after considerable discussion they decide to use a 16% discount rate.

TABLE 4-2 A&D Incorporated Forecasted Cash Flows

	Year $'s				
	1	2	3	4	5
CF after Investing Activities	1,050,000	1,113,000	1,179,780	1,250,567	1,325,601

The owners realize that Equation [A-1] in conjunction with one or more of Equations [4-4], [4-6], [4-8], [4-12], and [4-15] can be used to value their company. They begin by letting E_i, the expected cash flow in a particular period, be equal to $CFaIA_i$, the Cash Flow after Investing Activities for that period. (Based on this designation, Equations [A-1], [4-4], [4-6], [4-8], [4-12], and [4-15] become Equations [4-16]–[4-21]).

Present Value of Cash Flows during the Forecast Period

Discrete Cash Flow Model:

$$PV_{FP} = \sum_{i=1}^{n} \frac{CFaIA_i}{(1+k)^i} \qquad [4\text{-}16]$$

Present Value of Cash Flows after the Forecast Period

(1) Perpetual Fixed Model:

$$PV_{PXM_N} = \frac{CFaIA_{PX}}{k(1+k)^N} \qquad [4\text{-}17]$$

(2) Finite Fixed Model:

$$PV_{FXM_N} = \frac{CFaIA_{FX}\left[1-(1+k)^{-NX}\right]}{k(1+k)^N} \qquad [4\text{-}18]$$

(3) Perpetual Growth Model:

$$PV_{PGM_N} = \frac{CFaIA_{PG}}{(k-g_{PG})(1+k)^N} \qquad [4\text{-}19]$$

(4) Finite Growth Model:

$$PV_{FGM_N} = \frac{CFaIA_{FG}\left[1-\left(\frac{1+g_{FG}}{1+k}\right)^{NG}\right]}{(k-g_{FG})(1+k)^N} \qquad [4\text{-}20]$$

(5) Terminal Value Model:

$$PV_{TVM_N} = \frac{CFaIA_{TY}(TVM)}{(1+k)^N} \qquad [4\text{-}21]$$

Being aware of the notion that the value of a company is the sum of the present values of the company's forecast and post-forecast-period cash flows,[10] they realized that the five post-forecast models they were considering using suggested that their Company could be valued five different ways. The various combinations are summarized in Table 4-3.

[10] See Equation [4-1].

TABLE 4-3 Various Valuations of Forecast and Post-Forecast Period Cash Flows

Value Equation	Forecast Period		Post-Forecast Period
$E_1 = PV_{FP} + PV_{PFM_N}$	PV of Discrete Cash Flows	+	PV of Perpetual Fixed Cash Flows
$E_2 = PV_{FP} + PV_{FFM_N}$	PV of Discrete Cash Flows	+	PV of Finite Fixed Cash Flows
$E_3 = PV_{FP} + PV_{PGM_N}$	PV of Discrete Cash Flows	+	PV of Perpetual Growth Cash Flows
$E_4 = PV_{FP} + PV_{FGM_N}$	PV of Discrete Cash Flows	+	PV of Finite Growth Cash Flows
$E_5 = PV_{FP} + PV_{TVM_N}$	PV of Discrete Cash Flows	+	PV of Terminal Value Cash Flow

Since the first term in each of the Value Equations is the same, they decided that the first step would be to value the stream of discrete cash flows during the forecast period. This was done as follows.

Expanding Equation [4-16] and substituting $k = 16\%$ and the five values of CFaIA_i from Table 4-2 gave the present value of the forecasted cash flows:

$$PV_{FP} = \sum_{i=1}^{5} \frac{CFaIA_i}{(1+k)^i} = \frac{CFaIA_1}{(1+k)^1} + \frac{CFaIA_2}{(1+k)^2} + \frac{CFaIA_3}{(1+k)^3} + \frac{CFaIA_4}{(1+k)^4} + \frac{CFaIA_5}{(1+k)^5}$$

$$PV_{FP} = \frac{1{,}050{,}000}{(1+0.16)^1} + \frac{1{,}113{,}000}{(1+0.16)^2} + \frac{1{,}179{,}780}{(1+0.16)^3} + \frac{1{,}250{,}567}{(1+0.16)^4} + \frac{1{,}325{,}601}{(1+0.16)^5}$$

$$PV_{FP} = \frac{1{,}050{,}000}{1.16} + \frac{1{,}113{,}000}{1.3456} + \frac{1{,}179{,}780}{1.5609} + \frac{1{,}250{,}567}{1.8106} + \frac{1{,}325{,}601}{2.1003}$$

$$PV_{FP} = 905{,}172 + 827{,}140 + 755{,}835 + 690{,}677 + 631{,}136$$

$$PV_{FP} = \$3{,}809{,}961$$

They then proceeded to calculate five different values for the post-forecast-period cash flows by using Equations [4-17]–[4-21] and understood that by doing so, they would be making different assumptions about what each of these post-forecast-period cash flows would look like.

(1) Perpetual Fixed Cash Flow Model

By using this model to value the post-forecast cash flows, the owners of A&D Incorporated would be assuming that the cash flow in Year 6 and thereafter remains constant. They chose the last cash flow in the forecast period, Year 5.[11] While there was much

[11] Year 6's cash flow could be set at any level. The point is that the value used in Year 6 is the value used in perpetuity.

concern about the applicability of a model that valued flat cash flows forever, they decided in the interest of completeness to include it in their valuation project.

$$PV_{PXM_N} = \frac{CFaIA_{PX}}{k(1+k)^N} \tag{4-17}$$

Substituting $CFaIA_{PX} = 1{,}325{,}601$, $k = 0.16$ and $N = 5$ in Equation [4-17],

$$PV_{PXM_N} = \frac{1{,}325{,}601}{(0.16)(1.16)^5} = \frac{1{,}325{,}601}{(0.16)(2.1003)} = \frac{1{,}325{,}601}{0.33605}$$

$$PV_{PXM_N} = \$3{,}944{,}599$$

(2) Finite Fixed Cash Flow Model

This model assumes that the post-forecast-period cash flows continue at the Year 5 level for a finite period of time and then become zero. Since this model has a fixed time horizon the team agreed that it was somewhat more realistic than model (1) but still suffered from the fact that cash flows were static over the finite period. Despite this limitation they decided to use it in the analysis. Management discussed intervals from 5 years at the low end to 25 years at the high end. It was quickly concluded that five years would certainly produce a result that was an outlier and not meaningful. This prompted a discussion that reminded all that both models (1) and (2) would produce questionable results because they were based on flat cash flows. Despite concerns about the validity and usefulness of the model, they decided to press on and after much discussion they selected $NX = 20$ years.

$$PV_{FXM_N} = \frac{CFaIA_{FX}\left[1-(1+k)^{-NX}\right]}{k(1+k)^N} \tag{4-18}$$

Substituting $CFaIA_{FX} = 1{,}325{,}601$, $k = 0.16$, $N = 5$, and $NX = 20$ in Equation [4-18],

$$PV_{FXM_N} = \frac{(1{,}325{,}601)\left[1-(1+0.16)^{-20}\right]}{(0.16)(1+0.16)^5} = \frac{(1{,}325{,}601)[1-.0514]}{(0.16)(2.1003)} = \frac{(1{,}325{,}601)[0.9486]}{0.3361}$$

$$PV_{FXM_N} = \$3{,}741{,}904$$

(3) Perpetual Growth Model

The perpetual growth model assumes that the Year 5 cash flow grows at a constant rate g_{PG} forever. There was more enthusiasm for this model since it wasn't dependent on static cash flow. The low end of the company's historical growth rate was in the range of 5%. However, since the cash flow in this model was expected to grow forever, the owners of A&D Incorporated decided that in order for them to be able to justify the assumption the cash flow growth during the post-forecast period would have to be scaled back. They ultimately agreed on a growth rate of 3%, which was the rate at which their industry was forecasted to grow.

$$PV_{PGM_N} = \frac{CFalA_{PG}}{(k - g_{PG})(1+k)^N} \quad [4\text{-}19]$$

Since the first cash flow in this model is the one that occurs after Year 5 it's necessary to grow the Year 5 cash flow by the perpetual growth rate (which in this case is 3%) and this is the cash flow that is grown in perpetuity. Hence,

$$\begin{aligned} CFalA_{PG} &= \text{Year5}_{CF}\,(1 + g_{PG}) = (1{,}325{,}601)(1 + 0.03) \\ &= (1{,}325{,}601)(1.03) = \$1{,}365{,}369 \end{aligned}$$

Substituting $CFalA_{PG} = 1{,}365{,}369$, $k = 0.16$, $N = 5$, and $g_{PG} = 0.03$ in Equation [4-19],

$$PV_{PGM_N} = \frac{1{,}365{,}369}{(0.16-0.03)(1.16)^5} = \frac{1{,}365{,}369}{(0.13)(2.1003)} = \frac{1{,}365{,}369}{0.27304}$$

$$PV_{PGM_N} = \$5{,}000{,}537$$

(4) Finite Growth Cash Flow Model

Unlike the perpetual growth model, the finite model assumes that the cash flow beginning in the sixth year grows at a rate g_{FG} for NG years and thereafter is zero. This particular model sparked a new discussion. Some on the management team argued that this model was more realistic than models (1)–(3) because the period was fixed and if they could agree on a period of time, the growth rate could be increased to something closer to their historical growth rate. Periods of 15–20 years were considered. Some were comfortable with 20 years. Others felt 20 years was too long because the company had never demonstrated it could grow at a consistent rate for such an extended period of time. However, there was broad agreement that the company was currently better positioned for growth than it had been in recent history. This led to a discussion of the growth rate, g_{FG}. Those who felt 20 years was too long said they could get comfortable with a 15-year period if the growth rate was explainable. Finally, agreement was reached on a 15-year period with a growth rate of 5%, which was at the low end of the company's historical growth rate.

$$PV_{FGM_N} = \frac{CFalA_{FG}\left[1-\left(\frac{1+g_{FG}}{1+k}\right)^{NG}\right]}{(k - g_{FG})(1+k)^N} \quad [4\text{-}20]$$

Like the perpetual growth model, the cash flow that drives the finite growth model is the cash flow that takes place immediately after the forecast period, which in this case is the Year 5 cash flow adjusted for the finite growth rate g_{FG}. Hence:

$$\begin{aligned} CFalA_{FG} &= Year5_{CF}\,(1 + g_{FG}) = (1{,}325{,}601)(1 + 0.05) \\ &= (1{,}325{,}601)(1.05) = \$1{,}391{,}881 \end{aligned}$$

Substituting $CFalA_{FG}$ = 1,391,881, k = 0.16, N = 5, g_{FG} = .05, and NG = 15 in Equation [4-20],

$$PV_{FGM_N} = \frac{(1,391,881)\left[1-\left(\frac{1+0.05}{1+0.16}\right)^{15}\right]}{(0.16-.05)(1+0.16)^5} = \frac{(1,391,881)[1-0.2244]}{(0.11)(2.1003)} = \frac{1,079,581}{0.2310}$$

$$PV_{FGM_N} = \$4,672,751$$

(5) Terminal Value Model

The terminal value model is different from the previous models in that it assumes that the business is sold for a multiple of Year 5's cash flow at the end of Year 5.

This model was very appealing to management because it's based on market multiples and eliminates much of the arbitrary decisions involved in establishing parameters for other models. After taking advice from industry experts the terminal value multiplier TVM was set at 7.5.[12]

$$PV_{TVM_N} = \frac{CFalA_{TY}(TVM)}{(1+k)^N} \qquad [4\text{-}21]$$

Substituting $CFalA_{TY}$ = 1,325,601, k = 0.16, N = 5, and TVM = 7.5 in Equation [4-21],

$$PV_{TVM_N} = \frac{(1,325,601)(7.5)}{(1+0.16)^5} = \frac{9,942,008}{2.1003}$$

$$PV_{TVM_N} = \$4,733,518$$

Having exhausted the models under consideration, the results of the various valuations were summarized in Table 4-4.

TABLE 4-4 Summary of PVs of Models Used to Value the Cash Flows of A&D Incorporated $'s

	Discrete Cash Flow Model	Perpetual Constant Cash Flow Model	Finite Constant Cash Flow Model	Constant Growth Model	Finite Growth Cash Flow Model	Terminal Value Model	Value of A&D Inc.
(1) FPeriod + Perpetual Fixed	3,809,961	3,944,599					7,754,559
(2) FPeriod + Finite Fixed	3,809,961		3,741,904				7,551,864
(3) FPeriod + Perpetual Growth	3,809,961			5,000,537			8,810,498
(4) FPeriod + Finite Growth	3,809,961				4,672,751		8,482,711
(5) FPeriod + Terminal Value	3,809,961					4,733,518	8,543,479

[12] As will be shown later, under some conditions and in the absence of market data, the expression $1/(k-g)$ can be used as an indicator of a suitable TVM. In this case the implied TVM would be 7.7 [1/(0.16 – 0.03) = 7.7], which is in line with that suggested by the industry experts.

The data in Table 4-4 allowed the owners of A&D Incorporated to make some observations.

- As expected, model (2) yielded the lowest value because the cash flow doesn't grow and is limited to a 20-year stream of post-forecast cash flows.
- Model (1), which also had a fixed stream of post-forecast-period cash flows, gave a higher value than model (2) because it assumed that the constant cash flow stream continued forever.
- If the finite period in model (2) was increased, it would yield a result that is closer to the value obtained by using model (1). And in the limit, if the period used for model (2) was infinite ($NX \rightarrow \infty$), (1) and (2) would have the same value.
- Management concluded neither model (1) nor (2) was appropriate for valuing the post-forecast-period cash flows because these models essentially calculated the present value of an annuity and did not model management's goal of systematically increasing year-over-year cash flows.
- They observed models (4) and (5) yielded similar values. In their opinion, the fact that model (5) gave a higher value than (4) was not of any particular significance.
- All felt that the results of model (4) were worthy of consideration because they had grown the company at 5% for several years and while 15 years was a long time it wasn't unrealistic. Furthermore, if they had used 20 years in place of 15, the valuation would have been $9,013,056, very much in line with model (3).
- The average of models (3), (4), and (5) is $8,612, 229 or approximately $8,600,000. Since the discount rate used for the calculations was within the range of what they had been advised a strategic investor would use, management concluded that $8.6 million was representative of the value of the company.

Valuing a Cash Flow Stream Expressed in Terms of the Drivers of Cash Flow

All of the models presented so far for valuing a business during and after the forecast period are expressed in terms of the Expected Cash Flow E_i or Cash Flow after Investing Activities $CFaIA_i$. In many instances the cash flows are known and these equations can be applied directly. In other cases it is helpful to have cash flow defined in terms of the drivers of the business as described by the Envelope Equations in Chapter 2 (i.e., NI, IR, CFaIAg, NIg, and NiROCE).

Present Value of Cash Flows during the Forecast Period Using NI and IR

Equation [4-16] is the starting point.

$$PV_{FP} = \sum_{i=1}^{n} \frac{CFaIA_i}{(1+k)^i} \qquad [4\text{-}16]$$

In Chapter 2 it was demonstrated that if the Net Income NI_i grows at a constant rate NIg and the company has a constant Investment Rate IR, then the Cash Flow after Investing Activities $CFaIA_i$ can be expressed as:

$$CFaIA_i = NI_i\,(1 - IR) \qquad [2\text{-}18]$$[13]

Substituting the results of Equation [2-18] for $CFaIA_i$ into Equation [4-16] creates Equation [4-22], which calculates the present value of a discrete cash flow stream expressed in terms of NI_i *and* IR.

$$PV_{FP} = \sum_{i=1}^{n} \frac{NI_i(1-IR)}{(1+k)^i} \qquad [4\text{-}22]$$

Present Value of Cash Flows after the Forecast Period Using NI and IR

Perpetual Fixed Cash Flow Model: A constant cash flow stream continues forever.

Recall Equation [4-17].

$$PV_{PXM_N} = \frac{CFaIA_{PX}}{k(1+k)^N} \qquad [4\text{-}17]$$

Substituting $CFaIA_{PX} = NI_{PX}\,(1 - IR)$ in Equation [4-17] produces an expression that calculates the present value of cash flows expressed in terms of NI_{PX} *and* IR.

$$PV_{PXM_N} = \frac{NI_{PX}(1-IR)}{k(1+k)^N} \qquad [4\text{-}23]$$

Similarly, by substituting $CFaIA_i = NI_i\,(1 - IR)$ in Equations [4-18], [4-19], [4-20], and [4-21] expressions are obtained that calculate the present value of cash flows expressed in terms of NI_i *and* IR for each of the other four models.

Finite Fixed Cash Flow Model: A stream of constant cash flows continues for a finite period of *NX* years.

$$PV_{FXM_N} = \frac{NI_{FX}(1-IR)\left[1-(1+k)^{-NX}\right]}{k(1+k)^N} \qquad [4\text{-}24]$$

Perpetual Growth Cash Flow Model: The cash flow stream grows at a constant rate g_{PG} in perpetuity.

$$PV_{PGM_N} = \frac{NI_{PG}(1-IR)}{(k-g_{PG})(1+k)^N} \qquad [4\text{-}25]$$

[13]This equation is based on [2-18] in Chapter 2 and has been modified to exclude changes in working capital and net interest.

Finite Growth Cash Flow Model: The cash flow is assumed to grow at a rate g_{FG} for a finite period of *NG* years.

$$PV_{FGM_N} = \frac{NI_{FG}(1-IR)\left[1-\left(\frac{1+g_{FG}}{1+k}\right)^{NG}\right]}{(k-g_{FG})(1+k)^N} \quad [4\text{-}26]$$

Terminal Value Model: The Company is assumed to be sold at the end of the forecast period.

$$PV_{TVM_N} = \frac{NI_{TY}(1-IR)(TVM)}{(1+k)^N} \quad [4\text{-}27]$$

Table 4-5 provides a summary of the post-forecast-period cash flow equations expressed in terms of NI and IR.

TABLE 4-5 Summary of PVs of the Cash Flows during the Forecast and Post-Forecast Periods Using NI and IR

Model Used for Calculating the PV of: Cash Flows during Forecast Period	**Model Used for Calculating the PV of: Cash Flows after Forecast Period**
Stream of Distinct Cash Flows Model $PV_{FP} = \sum_{i=1}^{n} \frac{NI_i(1-IR)}{(1+k)^i}$ [4-22] where: NI_i can have any value and IR is constant	Perpetual Fixed Cash Flow Model $PV_{PXM_N} = \frac{NI_{PX}(1-IR)}{k(1+k)^N}$ [4-23]
	Finite Fixed Cash Flow Model $PV_{FXM_N} = \frac{NI_{FX}(1-IR)[1-(1+k)^{-NX}]}{k(1+k)^N}$ [4-24]
	Perpetual Growth Cash Flow Model $PV_{PGM_N} = \frac{NI_{PG}(1-IR)}{(k-g_{PG})(1+k)^N}$ [4-25]
	Finite Growth Cash Flow Model $PV_{FGM_N} = \frac{NI_{FG}(1-IR)\left[1-\left(\frac{1+g_{FG}}{1+k}\right)^{NG}\right]}{(k-g_{FG})(1+k)^N}$ [4-26]
	Terminal Value Model $PV_{TVM_N} = \frac{NI_{TY}(1-IR)(TVM)}{(1+k)^N}$ [4-27]

Present Value of Cash Flows during the Forecast Period Using NI, NIg, and NiROCE

Again beginning with Equation [4-16]

$$PV_{FP} = \sum_{i=1}^{n} \frac{CFaIA_i}{(1+k)^i} \quad [4\text{-}16]$$

In Appendix C it was demonstrated that if the Investment Rate (IR) and the Net Income Return on Capital Employed (NiROCE)[14] are constant, then the Net Income (NI) grows at a constant rate NIg where NIg = IR(NiROCE)[15] or $IR = \frac{NIg}{NiROCE}$. Recalling Equation [2-18],

$$CFaIA_i = NI_i\,(1 - IR) \quad [2\text{-}18]$$

Substituting NIg/ROCE for IR in Equation [2-18], the Cash Flow after Investing Activities $CFaIA_i$ can be expressed as:

$$CFaIA_i = NI_i \left(1 - \frac{NIg}{NiROCE}\right) \quad [4\text{-}28]$$

Substituting the results of Equation [4-28] into Equation [4-16] creates Equation [4-29], which can be used to calculate the present value of a cash flow stream expressed in terms of NI_i, NIg, and ROCE.

$$PV_{FP} = \sum_{i=1}^{n} \frac{NI_i \left(1 - \frac{NIg}{NiROCE}\right)}{(1+k)^i} \quad [4\text{-}29]$$

Present Value of Cash Flows after the Forecast Period Using NI, NIg, and NiROCE

Similarly, by substituting $NI_i \left(1 - \frac{NIg}{NiROCE}\right)$ for $CFaIA_i$ in Equations [4-17]–[4-21] creates expressions that calculate the present value of cash flows expressed in terms of NI_i, NIg, and NiROCE for the various post-forecast-period cash flow models.

[14] Refer to Chapter 2 for the rationale and definition of NiROCE and how it differs from ROCE.

[15] Appendix C, Equation [C-36].

Perpetual Fixed Cash Flow Model: A constant cash flow stream continues forever.

$$PV_{PXM_N} = \frac{NI_{PX}\left(1 - \frac{NIg}{NiROCE}\right)}{k(1+k)^N} \quad [4\text{-}30]$$

Finite Fixed Cash Flow Model: A stream of constant cash flows continues for a finite period of *NX* years.

$$PV_{FXM_N} = \frac{NI_{FX}\left(1 - \frac{NIg}{NiROCE}\right)\left[1-(1+k)^{-NX}\right]}{k(1+k)^N} \quad [4\text{-}31]$$

Perpetual Growth Model: The cash flow stream grows at a constant rate g_{PG} in perpetuity.

$$PV_{PGM_N} = \frac{NI_{PG}\left(1 - \frac{NIg}{NiROCE}\right)}{(k - g_{PG})(1+k)^N} \quad [4\text{-}32]$$

Finite Growth Cash Flow Model:

$$PV_{FGM_N} = \frac{NI_{FG}\left(1 - \frac{NIg}{NiROCE}\right)\left[1 - \left(\frac{1+g_{FG}}{1+k}\right)^{NG}\right]}{(k - g_{FG})(1+k)^N} \quad [4\text{-}33]$$

Terminal Value Model: The Company is assumed to be sold at the end of the forecast period.

$$PV_{TVM_N} = \frac{NI_{TY}\left(1 - \frac{NIg}{NiROCE}\right)(TVM)}{(1+k)^N} \quad [4\text{-}34]$$

A summary of post-forecast-period cash flows using NI, NIg, and NiROCE is provided in Table 4-6.

Now that various valuation models have been developed it's appropriate to go back and take another look at Company C and its consideration of the acquisition of Company A.[16]

---

[16]See Chapter 2, Example 2-1.

TABLE 4-6 Summary of PVs of Cash Flows during the Forecast and Post-Forecast Periods Using NI, NIg, and NiROCE

Model Used for Calculating the PV of: Cash Flows during Forecast Period	Model Used for Calculating the PV of: Cash Flows after Forecast Period
Stream of Distinct Cash Flows Model $$PV_{FP} = \sum_{i=1}^{n} \frac{NI_i\left(1 - \frac{NIg}{NiROCE}\right)}{(1+k)^i} \quad [4\text{-}29]$$	Perpetual Fixed Cash Flow Model $$PV_{PXM_N} = \frac{NI_{PX}\left(1 - \frac{NIg}{NiROCE}\right)}{k(1+k)^N} \quad [4\text{-}30]$$
where: NI_i can have any value and NIg and $NiROCE$ are constant	Finite Fixed Cash Flow Mode $$PV_{FXM_N} = \frac{NI_{FX}\left(1 - \frac{NIg}{NiROCE}\right)[1-(1+k)^{-NX}]}{k(1+k)^N} \quad [4\text{-}31]$$
	Perpetual Growth Cash Flow Model $$PV_{PGM_N} = \frac{NI_{PG}\left(1 - \frac{NIg}{NiROCE}\right)}{(k-g_{PG})(1+k)^N} \quad [4\text{-}32]$$
	Finite Growth Cash Flow Model: $$PV_{FGM_N} = \frac{NI_{FG}\left(1 - \frac{NIg}{NiROCE}\right)\left[1 - \left(\frac{1+g_{FG}}{1+k}\right)^{NG}\right]}{(k-g_{FG})(1+k)^N} \quad [4\text{-}33]$$
	Terminal Value Model $$PV_{TVM_N} = \frac{NI_{TY}\left(1 - \frac{NIg}{NiROCE}\right)(TVM)}{(1+k)^N} \quad [4\text{-}34]$$

EXAMPLE 4-2: COMPANY C'S VALUATION OF ACQUISITION TARGET COMPANY A

Company C is considering the acquisition of Company A. The management of Company A has provided Company C's leadership team with the basics of their plan 1. In this plan, the management of Company A forecasted it would generate $1,000,000 of Net Income in Year 1 (NI = $1,000,000), realize a Net Income Return on Capital Employed of 25% (NiROCE = 0.25), have an Investment Rate of 30% (IR = 0.30%), and grow Net Income 7.5% (NIg = 0.075) per year in Years 2–5. The data is summarized in Table 4-7.

TABLE 4-7 Data Provided by Company A to Management of Company C

	Year 1 NI	NiROCE	IR	NIg
Given	$1,000,000	25%	30%	7.5%

Company A has not made any forecast beyond Year 5 ($N = 5$). For this reason the management of Company C had to make assumptions about what happened after the forecast period. The question for the management of Company C was: If the WACC was 15% and indicative of the risk involved in purchasing Company A, what is the most they should consider paying for Company A?

Present Value of Cash Flows during and after the Forecast Period of Company A

There isn't one right answer to this question. However, a range of values can be calculated that represents the maximum price Company C should pay for Company A. This is done with the aid of Equation [4-29] to value the cash flows during the forecast period in combination with the models represented by Equations [4-30]–[4-34] for valuing cash flows after the forecast period.

(1) Perpetual Fixed Cash Flow Model

The CFO of Company C starts by letting PV_{FP+PF} represent the sum of the present values of the discrete cash flows during and post the forecast period where the post-forecast cash flows are assumed to follow the perpetual fixed cash flow model. Hence,

$$PV_{FP+PXM_N} = PV_{FP} + PV_{PXM_N} \qquad [4\text{-}35]$$

where:

PV_{FP} = Present value of discrete cash flows during the forecast period

PV_{PXM_N} = Present value of the perpetual fixed cash flows after the forecast period

Substituting the results of Equations [4-29] and [4-30] for PV_{FP} and PV_{PXM_N} into Equation [4-35], Equation [4-36] is obtained:

$$PV_{FP+PXM_N} = \sum_{i=1}^{n} \frac{NI_i\left(1-\dfrac{NIg}{NiROCE}\right)}{(1+k)^i} + \frac{NI_{PX}\left(1-\dfrac{NIg}{NiROCE}\right)}{k(1+k)^N} \qquad [4\text{-}36]$$

The first term in Equation [4-36] expands to become:

$$PV_{FP} = \left[\frac{NI_1}{(1+k)} + \frac{NI_2}{(1+k)^2} + \frac{NI_3}{(1+k)^3} + \frac{NI_4}{(1+k)^4} + \frac{NI_5}{(1+k)^5}\right]\left(1-\frac{NIg}{NiROCE}\right) \qquad [4\text{-}37]$$

But

$$NI_2 = NI_1(1 + NIg) \tag{4-38}$$

and

$$NI_3 = NI_2(1 + NIg) \tag{4-39}$$

Substituting the results of Equation [4-38] for NI_2 in Equation [4-39] yields an expression for NI_3 in terms of NI_1 and NIg,

$$NI_3 = NI_1(1 + NIg)^2 \tag{4-40}$$

Similarly,

$$NI_4 = NI_1(1 + NIg)^3 \tag{4-41}$$

and

$$NI_5 = NI_1(1 + NIg)^4 \tag{4-42}$$

Substituting for $NI_1 \ldots NI_5$ in Equation [4-37] and factoring the common term $NI_1/(1 + k)$ creates an expression for Company A's stream of forecasted cash flows.

$$PV_{FP} = \frac{NI_1}{(1+k)}\left[1+\frac{(1+NIg)}{(1+k)}+\frac{(1+NIg)^2}{(1+k)^2}+\frac{(1+NIg)^3}{(1+k)^3} + \frac{(1+NIg)^4}{(1+k)^4}\right]\left(1-\frac{NIg}{NiROCE}\right) \tag{4-43}$$

Substituting $NI_1 = 1{,}000{,}000$, $NIg = 0.075$, $NiROCE = 0.25$, and $k = \text{WACC} = 0.15$ the present value of A's forecasted cash flows is obtained.

$$PV_{FP} = \frac{(1{,}000{,}000)}{(1+0.15)}\left[1+\frac{(1+0.075)}{(1+0.15)}+\frac{(1+0.075)^2}{(1+0.15)^2}+\frac{(1+0.075)^3}{(1+0.15)^3} + \frac{(1+0.075)^4}{(1+0.15)^4}\right]\left(1-\frac{0.075}{0.25}\right)$$

$$PV_{FP} = (869{,}565)[1+.9348+.8738+.8168+.7636](0.70)$$

$$PV_{FP} = (869{,}565)[4.3890](0.70)$$

$$PV_{FP} = \$2{,}671{,}600$$

Next the CFO valued the second term in Equation [4-36]:

$$PV_{PXM_N} = \frac{NI_{PX}\left(1-\frac{NIg}{NiROCE}\right)}{k(1+k)^N} \tag{4-30}$$

By using this model, Company C has assumed that the cash flow in Year 5 continues forever. Therefore, substituting $NI_{PX} = NI_5 = NI_1\ (1 + NIg)^4 = 1{,}335{,}469$, $NIg = 0.075$, $NiROCE = 0.25$, $N = 5$, and $k = 0.15$ in Equation [4-30] gave the CFO the PV of a stream of cash flows that grows at 7.5% until Year 5 and then stays constant forever.

$$PV_{PXM_N} = \frac{(1{,}335{,}469)\left(1-\dfrac{0.075}{0.25}\right)}{(0.15)(1+.15)^5} = \frac{(1{,}335{,}468)(0.70)}{0.3017}$$

$$PV_{PXM_N} = \$3{,}098{,}500$$

Recalling Equation [4-35] and substituting, the CFO was able to come up with his first estimate of A's value.

$$PV_{FP+PXM_N} = PV_{FP} + PV_{PXM_N} = 2{,}671{,}600 + 3{,}098{,}500$$

$$PV_{FP+PX} = \$5{,}770{,}100$$

(2) Finite Fixed Cash Flow Model

The finite fixed cash flow model was considered next by letting PV_{FP+FGM_N} represent the sum of the present values of the discrete cash flows during and post the forecast period where the post-forecast cash flows are assumed to follow the finite fixed cash flow model. In this case:

$$PV_{FP+FXM_N} = PV_{FP} + PV_{FXM_N} \qquad [4\text{-}44]$$

where:

PV_{FP} = PV of the discrete cash flows during the forecast period
PV_{FXM_N} = PV of the constant cash flow that take place for a finite period after the forecast period

Substituting the results of Equations [4-29] and [4-31] into Equation [4-44] creates an equation for calculating the value of this model in general form:

$$PV_{FP+FXM_N} = \sum_{i=1}^{n} \frac{NI_i\left(1-\dfrac{NIg}{NiROCE}\right)}{(1+k)^i} + \frac{NI_{FX}\left(1-\dfrac{NIg}{NiROCE}\right)\left[1-(1+k)^{-NX}\right]}{k(1+k)^N} \qquad [4\text{-}45]$$

Since the present value of the stream of cash flows during the forecast period is identical to those calculated in part (1) of this example, then:

$$PV_{FP} = \$2{,}671{,}600$$

The second term in Equation [4-45] is of course defined by:

$$PV_{FXM_N} = \frac{NI_{FX}\left(1-\frac{NIg}{NiROCE}\right)\left[1-(1+k)^{-NX}\right]}{k(1+k)^N} \quad [4\text{-}31]$$

In order to use this model, Company C had to make some assumptions about the level and length (period) of post-forecast cash flows. Having limited experience with this model and lacking in-depth insight into Company A's operations they decided, as a starting point, that after Year 5, the cash flow would continue for an additional 20 years at the Year 5 level and then become zero. Hence the following

$NI_{FX} = NI_5 = NI_1\,(1 + NIg)^4 = 1{,}335{,}469$, $NIg = 0.075$, $NiROCE = 0.25$, $N = 5$, $NX = 20$, and $k = WACC = 0.15$

was substituted in Equation [4-31].

$$PV_{FXM_N} = \frac{(1{,}335{,}469)\left(1-\frac{0.075}{0.25}\right)\left[1-(1+0.15)^{-20}\right]}{0.15(1+0.15)^5}$$

$$PV_{FXM_N} = \frac{(1{,}335{,}469)(0.70)[1-.0611]}{0.15(1+.15)^5} = \frac{(1{,}335{,}469)(0.70)[0.9389]}{0.3017}$$

$$PV_{FXM_N} = \$2{,}909{,}200$$

Again recalling the expression for PV_{FP+FGM_N} and substituting, the CFO obtained the second valuation of Company A.

$$PV_{FP+FXM_N} = PV_{FP} + PV_{FXM_N} = 2{,}671{,}600 + 2{,}909{,}200$$

$$PV_{FP+FX} = \$5{,}580{,}800$$

(3) Perpetual Growth Cash Flow Model

To get the third valuation the CFO let PV_{FP+PGM_N} represent the sum of the present value of the discrete cash flows during the forecast period and a stream of cash flows that grows at a perpetual rate forever after. Mathematically he expressed this as:

$$PV_{FP+PGM_N} = PV_{FP} + PV_{PGM_N} \quad [4\text{-}46]$$

where:

PV_{FP} = PV of the discrete cash flows during the forecast period

PV_{PGM_N} = PV of the cash flows that grow at a constant rate g_{PG} forever after the forecast period

Once again substituting the results of Equations [4-29] and [4-32] into Equation [4-46] gave the desired expression.

$$PV_{FP+PGM_N} = \sum_{i=1}^{n} \frac{NI_i\left(1 - \frac{NIg}{NiROCE}\right)}{(1+k)^i} + \frac{NI_{PG}\left(1 - \frac{NIg}{NiROCE}\right)}{(k - g_{PG})(1+k)^N} \qquad [4\text{-}47]$$

Since the present value of the stream of cash flows during the forecast period is identical to those calculated in parts (1) and (2) the CFO made note of the PV and moved on to calculate the value of the second term (Equation [4-32]).

$$PV_{FP} = \$2,671,600$$

$$PV_{PGM_N} = \frac{NI_{PG}\left(1 - \frac{NIg}{NiROCE}\right)}{(k - g_{PG})(1+k)^N} \qquad [4\text{-}32]$$

Since the Net Income was projected to grow at a rate of 7.5% until Year 5, the NI_5 in Year 5 is:

$$NI_5 = NI_1\ (1 + NIg)^4 = (1,000,000)(1 + 0.075)^4 = 1,335,469$$

However, while \$1,335,469 is the Net Income for Year 5, it isn't the Net Income for the first year of the perpetual growth model, which as explained previously has to be adjusted for one year of perpetual growth, which is assumed to be 3%. Hence,

$$NI_{PG} = (NI_5)(1 + g_{PG}) = (1,335,469)(1 + 0.03) = (1,335,469)(1.03) = 1,375,533$$

and

$NI_{PG} = 1,375,533$, $NIg = 0.075$, $NiROCE = 0.25$, $N = 5$, $g_{PG} = 0.03$, and $k = \text{WACC} = 0.15$

Substituting into Equation [4-32],

$$PV_{PGM_N} = \frac{(1,375,533)\left(1 - \frac{0.075}{0.25}\right)}{(0.15 - 0.03)(1 + 0.15)^5} = \frac{(1,375,533)(0.70)}{(0.12)(2.0114)} = \frac{(1,375,533)(0.70)}{(0.2414)}$$

$$PV_{PGM_N} = \$3,988,700$$

And by using the expression for PV_{FP+PGM_N} that he established earlier the CFO obtained the third valuation.

$$PV_{FP+PGM_N} = PV_{FP} + PV_{PGM_N} = 2,671,559 + 3,988,700$$

$$PV_{FP+PGM_N} = \$6,660,300$$

(4) Finite Growth Cash Flow Model

For this model PV_{FP+FGM_N} was designated as the sum of the present values of the cash flows during the forecast period and a stream of cash flows that grow at a finite rate for *NG* years after the forecast period and was expressed as:

$$PV_{FP+FGM_N} = PV_{FP} + PV_{FGM_N} \quad [4\text{-}48]$$

where:

PV_{FP} = PV of the discrete cash flows during the forecast period

PV_{FGM_N} = PV of the terminal value of the cash flows at the end of the forecast period

By substituting Equations [4-29] and [4-33] into Equation [4-48] the CFO once again obtained a general expression for the valuation he was seeking.

$$PV_{FP+FGM_N} = \sum_{i=1}^{n} \frac{NI_i\left(1-\dfrac{NIg}{NiROCE}\right)}{(1+k)^i} + \frac{NI_{FG}\left(1-\dfrac{NIg}{NiROCE}\right)\left[1-\left(\dfrac{1+g_{FG}}{1+k}\right)^{NG}\right]}{(k-g_{FG})(1+k)^N} \quad [4\text{-}49]$$

As was the case in the previous three valuations, the present value of the stream of cash flows during the forecast period remained unchanged. Therefore:

$$PV_{FP} = \$2{,}671{,}600$$

To complete this valuation the CFO proceeded to value the second term in Equation [4-49]:

$$PV_{FGM_N} = \frac{NI_{FG}\left(1-\dfrac{NIg}{NiROCE}\right)\left[1-\left(\dfrac{1+g_{FG}}{1+k}\right)^{NG}\right]}{(k-g_{FG})(1+k)^N} \quad [4\text{-}33]$$

To use the finite growth model the CFO needed to decide on a growth rate and the number of years of growth. Since he was dealing with finite growth as opposed to perpetual growth he became comfortable with a growth rate of 5% for a period of 15 years. He also needed to calculate the Net Income for the first year of the finite growth model. Therefore:

$$NG = 15,\ g_{FG} = 0.05,\ NIg = 0.075,\ NiROCE = 0.25,\ N = 5,\ k = WACC = 0.15$$

Recall that the Net Income for Year 5 was calculated to be \$1,335,469

and

$$NI_{FG} = (NI_5)(1 + g_{FG}) = (1{,}335{,}469)(1 + 0.05) = (1{,}335{,}469)(1.05) = 1{,}402{,}243$$

Substituting,

$$PV_{FGM_N} = \frac{(1,402,243)\left(1-\frac{0.075}{0.25}\right)\left[1-\left(\frac{1+0.05}{1+0.15}\right)^{15}\right]}{(0.15-0.05)(1+0.15)^5}$$

$$PV_{FGM_N} = \frac{(1,402,243)(1-0.3)[1-0.2555]}{(0.10)(2.0114)} = \frac{(1,402,243)(0.70)[0.7445]}{0.20114} = \frac{730,790}{0.20114}$$

$$PV_{FGM_N} = \$3,663,200$$

Recalling the expression for PV_{FP+FGM_N} and substituting, the CFO obtained his fourth valuation.

$$PV_{FP+FGM_N} = PV_{FP} + PV_{FGM_N} = 2,671,600 + 3,663,200$$
$$PV_{FP+FGM_N} = \$6,334,800$$

(5) Terminal Value Model

To construct the final model the CFO let PV_{FP+TV} equal the sum of the present values of the cash flows during the forecast period and the terminal value. Hence:

$$PV_{FP+TVM_N} = PV_{FP} + PV_{TVM_N} \qquad [4\text{-}50]$$

where:

PV_{FP} = PV of the discrete cash flows during the forecast period

PV_{TVM_N} = PV of the terminal value of the cash flow at the end of the forecast period

Substituting Equations [4-29] and [4-34] in Equation [4-50] creates a general expression for this valuation model.

$$PV_{FP+TVM_N} = \sum_{i=1}^{n} \frac{NI_i\left(1-\frac{NIg}{NiROCE}\right)}{(1+k)^i} + \frac{NI_{TY}\left(1-\frac{NIg}{NiROCE}\right)(TVM)}{(1+k)^N} \qquad [4\text{-}51]$$

Once again the present value of the stream of cash flows during the forecast period in Equation [4-51] is identical to those in parts (1), (2), (3), and (4) so the CFO proceeds to value the second term:

$$PV_{FP} = \$2,671,600$$

$$PV_{TVM_N} = \frac{NI_{TY}\left(1-\frac{NIg}{NiROCE}\right)(TVM)}{(1+k)^N} \qquad [4\text{-}34]$$

To use the terminal value model, the CFO of Company C had to decide on what multiple of cash flow Company A would sell for at the end of Year 5. He believes C's management will be able to improve the business considerably during the five-year period and therefore the company's value at the end of year 5 could be at the higher end of the multiple range, which had been suggested by their adviser to be as much as 10 depending on how the company was positioned for growth. However, he didn't want to pay the owners of A for value C's management team would create. For this reason and until he had more insight and comfort with Company A's cash flow projections the CFO decided to be conservative and use a *terminal value multiplier* of 8. Using this multiplier and data from earlier models the value of PV_{TVM_N} was obtained by substituting in Equation [4-34].

$$NI_{TY} = NI_5 = NI_1\,(1 + NIg)^4 = 1{,}335{,}469,\ NIg = 0.075,\ NiROCE = 0.25,$$
$$N = 5,\ TVM = 8,\text{ and } k = WACC = 0.15$$

$$PV_{TVM_N} = \frac{(1{,}335{,}469)\left(1 - \dfrac{0.075}{0.25}\right)(8)}{(1+0.15)^5} = \frac{(1{,}335{,}469)(0.70)(8)}{(2.0114)}$$

$$PV_{TVM_N} = \$3{,}718{,}100$$

With the aid of the expression for PV_{FP+TVM_N} (Equation [4-50]) the CFO estimated the fifth valuation for Company A.

$$PV_{FP+TVM_N} = PV_{FP} + PV_{TVM_N} = 2{,}671{,}600 + 3{,}718{,}100$$

$$PV_{FP+TV} = \$6{,}389{,}700$$

Table 4-8, a summary of the various values calculated for Company A, was then prepared.

TABLE 4-8 Summary of Valuations of Company A Plan 1 Using Ni, Ng, and NiROCE $'s

	Discrete Cash Flow Model	Perpetual Fixed Cash Flow Model	Finite Fixed Cash Flow Model	Perpetual Growth Model	Finite Growth Cash Flow Model	Terminal Value Model	Value of Company A
(1) FPeriod + Perpetual Fixed	2,671,600	3,098,500					5,770,100
(2) FPeriod + Finite Fixed	2,671,600		2,909,200				5,580,800
(3) FPeriod + Perpetual Growth	2,671,600			3,988,700			6,660,300
(4) FPeriod + Finite Growth	2,671,600				3,663,200		6,334,800
(5) FPeriod + Terminal Value	2,671,600					3,718,100	6,389,700

Discussion of the CFO's Valuation of Company A

One of the purposes of this example was to answer the question: What is the most that Company C should consider paying for Company A? While the results tabulated in Table 4-8 are helpful, the answer to the question is not immediately evident. The reason for this is: The maximum price that C should pay depends on which of the post-forecast-period cash flows the management team feels is the most relevant.

In practice it is unlikely that the management of Company C would buy a company that had flat cash flows forever beginning in Year 6 let alone one that had flat cash flows for a finite period of 20 years and then zero. Hence, absent exceptional circumstances and other than perhaps quantifying the downside range of what Company A's value may be, the results of models (1) and (2) valuations are not particularly helpful. The values derived from models (4) and (5) are almost the same. Model (3) is within a couple hundred thousand of model (5) and can be viewed as the high end of a value range from $6,300,000 to $6,700,000.

Therefore, if Company C wants to earn at least its Weighted Average Cost of Capital, it should not pay more than some number in this range, say $6,500,000, for Company A.[17] Also recall that when Company C was determining the terminal value multiplier it should use it was assumed they could improve A's operations. Therefore, while the management of C may not want to pay A for the work they plan to do improving A's cash flow, they may have to pay the owners of Company A some of it for the opportunity to buy the company.

Equivalency of the Envelope Equation and Cash Flow Models

In this example Company A was valued by using A's Net Income, Growth Rate, and Net Income Return on Capital Employed. The company could also have been valued by using Company A's cash flows. In Chapter 2, Company A's cash flows were calculated and are repeated here in Table 4-9. The equivalency of the Envelope Equation and Cash Flow models for valuations will now be demonstrated.

TABLE 4-9 Company A Plan 1 Calculated Cash Flows

	Year $'s				
	1	2	3	4	5
CF after Investing Activities (CFaIA)	700,000	752,500	808,938	869,608	934,828

[17] Most companies would not be satisfied to make an investment that only offered the prospect of earning their weighted average cost of capital. They would expect a return in excess of the WACC. Also they would most likely add something to their WACC to account for the risk perceived to be associated with Company A's forecast and their assumptions about the post-forecast cash flow. The result of this would be to lower the value it would be prudent for Company C to pay for A. The methodology by which this is usually done is described in a later chapter.

Recall that the present value of the cash flows during the forecast period is given by Equation [4-16].

$$PV_{FP} = \sum_{i=1}^{n} \frac{CFaIA_i}{(1+k)^i} \qquad [4\text{-}16]$$

Expanding Equation [4-16] and substituting for $CFaIA_1 \ldots CFaIA_5$ from Table 4-9 and $k = 15\%$ the PV of the forecast period cash flows is:

$$PV_{FP} = \frac{700{,}000}{(1.15)} + \frac{752{,}500}{(1.15)^2} + \frac{808{,}938}{(1.15)^3} + \frac{869{,}608}{(1.15)^4} + \frac{934{,}828}{(1.15)^5} = \$2{,}671{,}600$$

The present value of the cash flows during the post-forecast period is given by Equations [4-17]–[4-21].

(1) Perpetual Fixed Cash Flow Model

$$PV_{PXM_N} = \frac{CFaIA_{PX}}{k(1+k)^N} \qquad [4\text{-}17]$$

Substituting $CFaIA_{PX} = \$934{,}828$, $k = 15\%$ and $N = 5$ in Equation [4-17],

$$PV_{PXM_N} = \frac{934{,}828}{(0.15)(1+0.15)^5} = \$3{,}098{,}500$$

(2) Finite Fixed Cash Flow Model

$$PV_{FXM_N} = \frac{CFaIA_{FX}\left[1-(1+k)^{-NX}\right]}{k(1+k)^N} \qquad [4\text{-}18]$$

Substituting $CFaIA_{FX} = 934{,}828$, $k = 15\%$, $N = 5$, and $NX = 20$ in Equation [4-18],

$$PV_{FXM_N} = \frac{(934{,}828)\left[1-(1+.15)^{-20}\right]}{(0.15)(1+.15)^5} = \$2{,}909{,}200$$

(3) Perpetual Growth Model

$$PV_{PGM_N} = \frac{CFaIA_{PG}}{(k-g_{PG})(1+k)^N} \qquad [4\text{-}19]$$

Substituting $CFaIA_{PG} = (\$934{,}828)(1 + g_{PG})$, $k = 15\%$, $N = 5$, and $g_{PG} = 3\%$ in Equation [4-19],

$$PV_{PGM_N} = \frac{(934{,}828)(1+.03)}{(0.15-0.03)(1.15)^5} = \$3{,}988{,}700$$

(4) Finite Growth Cash Flow Model

$$PV_{FGM_N} = \frac{CFalA_{FG}\left[1-\left(\frac{1+g_{FG}}{1+k}\right)^{NG}\right]}{(k-g_{FG})(1+k)^N} \quad [4\text{-}20]$$

Substituting $CFalA_{FG} = (\$934{,}828)(1 + g_{FG})$, $k = 15\%$, $N = 5$ years, $NG = 15$ years, and $g_{FG} = 5\%$ in Equation [4-20],

$$PV_{FGM_N} = \frac{(934{,}828)(1+.05)\left[1-\left(\frac{1+0.05}{1+0.15}\right)^{15}\right]}{(0.15-0.05)(1+0.15)^5} = \$3{,}663{,}200$$

(5) Terminal Value Model

$$PV_{TVM_N} = \frac{CFalA_{TY}(TVM)}{(1+k)^N} \quad [4\text{-}21]$$

Substituting $CFalA_{TY} = \$934{,}828$, $k = 15\%$, $N = 5$, and $TVM = 8$ in Equation [4-21],

$$PV_{TVM_N} = \frac{(934{,}828)(8)}{(1.15)^5} = \$3{,}718{,}200$$

The results of these calculations are tabulated in Table 4-10.

TABLE 4-10 Summary of the Valuations of Company A Plan 1 Using CFalA $'s

Valuation Model Used to Value the Cash Flows of Company A	Discrete Cash Flow Model	Perpetual Fixed Cash Flow Model	Finite Fixed Cash Flow Model	Perpetual Growth Model	Finite Growth Model	Terminal Value Model	Value of Company A
(1) FPeriod + Perpetual Fixed CFM	2,671,600	3,098,500					5,770,100
(2) FPeriod + Finite Fixed CFM	2,671,600		2,909,200				5,580,800
(3) FPeriod + Perpetual Growth CFM	2,671,600			3,988,700			6,660,300
(4) FPeriod + Finite Growth CFM	2,671,600				3,633,200		6,334,800
(5) FPeriod + Terminal Value CFM	2,671,600					3,718,100	6,389,700

A comparison of Tables 4-8 and 4-10 will show that the results are identical. It's fair to note at this point that the post-forecast cash flow equations expressed in terms of cash flow are less complicated than those using Envelope Equations and easier to use. Therefore, some readers may have a preference for the direct cash flow model. This may suggest the highest and best use of the Envelope Equations is to prepare quick estimates of cash flow as opposed to present value analysis.

EXAMPLE 4-3: COMPANY A VALUES VARIOUS BUSINESS PLANS

The reader may recall that in Chapter 2 the management of Company A was considering two business plans and was having some difficulty trying to decide which plan would create more value. The pro-forma results of these plans were summarized in tables in Chapter 2. In the interest of convenience, these tables are repeated here as Tables 4-11 and 4-12.

In order to decide which plan will create more value, the cash flows for both plans have to be valued. However, before doing so a discount rate for *k* has to be established. The management of Company A initially determined the risk associated with both plans to be about the same and decided to use a common discount rate for the valuations.

TABLE 4-11 Company A Plan 1

	Year $'s and %				
	1	**2**	**3**	**4**	**5**
Net Income (NI)	1,000,000	1,075,000	1,155,625	1,242,297	1,335,469
Growth Rate of NI (NIg)	n/a	7.50%	7.50%	7.50%	7.50%
Net Investment (NetInvest)	300,000	322,500	346,688	372,689	400,641
CF after Investing Activities (CFaIA)	700,000	752,500	808,938	869,608	934,828
Growth Rate of CFaIA	n/a	7.50%	7.50%	7.50%	7.50%

TABLE 4-12 Company A Plan 2

	Year $'s and %				
	1	**2**	**3**	**4**	**5**
Net Income (NI)	1,000,000	1,080,600	1,177,422	1,293,987	1,426,361
Growth Rate of NI (NIg)	n/a	8.06%	8.96%	9.90%	10.23%
Investment (NetInvest)	310,000	345,792	388,549	427,016	470,699
CF after Investing Activities (CFaIA)	690,000	734,808	788,873	866,971	955,662
Growth Rate of CFaIA	n/a	6.49%	7.36%	9.90%	10.23%

The discount rate that the management of Company A should use depends on their objective. If they:

- Only want a relative comparison, almost any reasonable rate will do.
- Are interested in how the plans play out if they earn their cost of capital, then $k = \text{WACC}$.
- Want to know the market value of the plans, they should use a discount rate that reflects the expected returns of investors.

Management decided that a relative comparison served their purpose and set k at 15% (which is their Weighted Average Cost of Capital).

The results of valuing Company A's plan 1 cash flows at $k = 15\%$ are presented in Table 4-10. The rationale and value of plan 2's cash flows as calculated by the CFO follow.

Valuation 1 of Company A's Plan 2

The present value of Company A's plan 2 cash flows during the forecast period is calculated by using Equation [4-16]:

$$PV_{FP} = \sum_{i=1}^{n} \frac{CFaIA_i}{(1+k)^i} \qquad [4\text{-}16]$$

Expanding and substituting for $CFaIA_1 \ldots CFaIA_5$ from Table 4-12 and $k = WACC = 15\%$,

$$PV_{FP} = \frac{690{,}000}{(1.15)} + \frac{734{,}808}{(1.15)^2} + \frac{788{,}873}{(1.15)^3} + \frac{866{,}971}{(1.15)^4} + \frac{955{,}662}{(1.15)^5} = \$2{,}645{,}143$$

The present value of Company A's plan 2 cash flows during the post-forecast period were calculated by using Equations [4-17]–[4-21].

(1) Perpetual Fixed Cash Flow Model

$$PV_{PXM_N} = \frac{CFaIA_{PX}}{k(1+k)^N} \qquad [4\text{-}17]$$

Substituting $CFaIA_{PX} = 955{,}662$, $k = 15\%$, and $N = 5$ in Equation [4-17],

$$PV_{PXM_N} = \frac{955{,}662}{(0.15)(1+.15)^5} = \$3{,}167{,}553$$

(2) Finite Fixed Cash Flow Model

$$PV_{FXM_N} = \frac{CFaIA_{FX}\left[1-(1+k)^{-NX}\right]}{k(1+k)^N} \qquad [4\text{-}18]$$

Substituting $CFalA_{FX} = 955{,}662$, $k = 15\%$, $N = 5$, and $NX = 20$ in Equation [4-18],

$$PV_{FXM_N} = \frac{(955{,}662)\left[1-(1+.15)^{-20}\right]}{(0.15)(1+.15)^5} = \$2{,}974{,}015$$

(3) Perpetual Growth Model

In the scenario envisaged in plan 2, the management of Company A will be investing at a higher rate than in plan 1. The result of the higher rate of investment presented a dilemma for the management team because according to Table 4-12 the CFalA Year 5 growth would be 10.23%. While they were comfortable this could be achieved, no one believed it could be sustained. The CFO pointed out that they were in an industry predicted to grow at about 3–4% per year. The management team felt they could do better than that because of their history of innovation and decided on a post-forecast-period constant growth rate g_{PG} of 4.5%.

$$PV_{PGM_N} = \frac{CFalA_{PG}}{(k-g_{PG})(1+k)^N} \qquad [4\text{-}19]$$

Substituting $CFalA_{PG}$ = (\$955,662)(1 + g_{PG}), k = 15%, N = 5, and g_{PG} = 4.5% in Equation [4-19],

$$PV_{PGM_N} = \frac{(955{,}662)(1+0.045)}{(0.15-0.045)(1.15)^5} = \$4{,}728{,}704$$

(4) Finite Growth Cash Flow Model

Once again to use this model management had to agree on the various parameters. They were fine with k =15%, N = 5 years, and NG = 15 years. The appropriate value to use for g_{FG} required a discussion. There was broad agreement on the notion that the higher growth rate in the later years of plan 2 and the prospects going forward should result in a growth rate for the finite model that was higher than the perpetual growth rate used in model (3). Ultimately it was agreed that 6% was a reasonable number to use.

$$PV_{FGM_N} = \frac{CFalA_{FG}\left[1-\left(\frac{1+g_{FG}}{1+k}\right)^{NG}\right]}{(k-g_{FG})(1+k)^N} \qquad [4\text{-}20]$$

Substituting $CFalA_{FG}$ = (\$955,662) (1 + g_{FG}), k = 15%, N = 5 years, NG = 15 years, and g_{FG} = 6% in Equation [4-20],

$$PV_{FGM_N} = \frac{(955{,}662)(1+.06)\left[1-\left(\frac{1+0.06}{1+0.15}\right)^{15}\right]}{(0.15-0.06)(1+0.15)^5} = \$3{,}947{,}852$$

(5) Terminal Value Model

Following the reasoning applied to the finite growth model, the management of Company A also felt that the higher growth rate in the later years of plan 2 and the prospects going forward would command a higher terminal value multiplier. After some discussion and advice from an investment banker they decide that the appropriate TVM for plan 2 is 10.

$$PV_{TVM_N} = \frac{CFalA_{TY}(TVM)}{(1+k)^N} \qquad [4\text{-}21]$$

Substituting $CFalA_{TY} = 955{,}662$, $k = 15\%$, $N = 5$, and $TVM = 10$ in Equation [4-21],

$$PV_{TVM_N} = \frac{(955{,}662)(10)}{(1.15)^5} = \$4{,}751{,}330$$

The results of this valuation of Company A's plan 2 are summarized in Table 4-13.

After comparing the results in Tables 4-10 and 4-13 management made the following observations:

- There is little difference in the valuation of the forecast period cash flows. This seemed logical since the cash flows in both plans are similar, with plan 1 having slightly higher cash flows during the early years and plan 2 having a higher cash flow during the final year.
- The values calculated by the perpetual fixed and finite fixed cash flow models for plan 2 are somewhat higher than plan 1 because plan 2's cash flow during the fifth year is greater than the corresponding cash flow for plan 1. Furthermore, neither of these post-forecast-period models is appropriate because they don't reflect the impact of the cash flow momentum the company will have achieved at the end of Year 5.

TABLE 4-13 Summary of Company A Plan 2 Valuation 1 $'s

Valuation Model Used to Value the Cash Flows of Company A	Discrete Cash Flow Model	Perpetual Fixed Cash Flow Model	Finite Fixed Cash Flow Model	Perpetual Growth Model	Finite Growth Model	Terminal Value Model	Company A, Plan 2 Value 1
(1) FPeriod + Perpetual Fixed CFM	2,645,143	3,167,553					5,812,696
(2) FPeriod + Finite Fixed CFM	2,645,143		2,974,015				5,619,158
(3) FPeriod + Perpetual Growth CFM	2,645,143			4,728,704			7,373,848
(4) FPeriod + Finite Growth CFM	2,645,143				3,947,852		6,592,996
(5) FPeriod + Terminal Value CFM	2,645,143					4,751,330	7,396,473

- Model (4), the finite growth model, yields a result that is an outlier. This is due to the growth rate used for the finite period selected or a combination of both. For example, had a 7% growth rate for 20 years been used, the value calculated by the model would have been $7,452,154, which would be almost identical to that calculated by the perpetual growth model (3).
- The perpetual growth and terminal value models yield higher post-forecast-period valuations primarily because of the higher perpetual growth rate and terminal value multipliers that were used.
- The value created by plan 2 is superior to plan 1 because it has the promise of a valuation of approximately $7,400,000 versus $6,300,000 – $6,700,000 for plan 1.

Valuation Number 2 of Company A's Plan 2

However, all was not well. One member of the management team felt there is little difference in the cash flows of the plans and that plan 2 was predestined to have a higher value than plan 1 because of the higher values used in the perpetual growth and terminal value models. Furthermore, since there was no certainty these assumptions were valid, he wanted to see the plans compared using the same assumption set. Others agreed that this was a point of view worthy of investigation. So, the perpetual growth rate, finite growth rate, and terminal value multiplier were reset to 3%, 5%, and 8 respectively and the models rerun. The results of plan 2's valuation under these conditions are shown in Table 4-14.

Once again management compared the results tabulated in Tables 4-10 and 4-14. As you would expect, the valuation of plan 2 decreased dramatically and was now almost the same as plan 1. In fact it could be argued that given the level of uncertainty, the values of the plans were the same. However, there was at least one major difference. If plan 2 could be achieved, the company would be entering the post-forecast

TABLE 4-14 Summary of Company A Plan 2 Valuation 2 $'s

Valuation Model Used to Value the Cash Flows of Company A	Discrete Cash Flow Model	Perpetual Fixed Cash Flow Model	Finite Fixed Cash Flow Model	Perpetual Growth Model	Finite Growth Model	Terminal Value Model	Company A, Plan 2 Value 2
(1) FPeriod + Perpetual Fixed CFM	2,645,143	3,167,553					5,812,696
(2) FPeriod + Finite Fixed CFM	2,645,143		2,974,015				5,619,158
(3) FPeriod + Perpetual Growth CFM	2,645,143			4,078,225			6,723,368
(4) FPeriod + Finite Growth CFM	2,645,143				3,714,289		6,359,432
(5) FPeriod + Terminal Value CFM	2,645,143					3,801,064	6,446,207

period at a higher growth rate and this in and of itself would have value because it would ultimately result in higher net incomes and cash flows. Everyone seemed to agree with this logic and didn't think valuation 2 added much and continued to favor valuation 1 of plan 2.

Valuation Number 3 of Company A's Plan 2

Just as they were about to reach a consensus, another member of the management team spoke up and questioned the logic of assuming that the risk in both plans was "about the same." She pointed out that plan 2 clearly had significant upside compared to plan 1 and experience had taught her that one seldom got something for nothing. Then she argued that while she was comfortable that the products and services contemplated in plan 2 would be completed and available as planned, she was concerned about market timing and rate of acceptance and therefore felt that the market risk in plan 2 was greater than plan 1. After some discussion the management team decided to add 1.5% points to the discount rate to account for market risk and rerun the numbers once again. The results are tabulated in Table 4-15.

With so many numbers on hand, some of the members of the management team were having trouble comparing the various scenarios, so the chief financial officer was asked to facilitate a discussion. While preparing for the discussion one of the first conclusions reached by the CFO was that the use of the perpetual fixed and finite fixed cash flow models wasn't appropriate because the management team wouldn't tolerate a business plan that didn't grow cash flow, let alone one that had cash flow dropping to zero after a fixed period. The next conclusion was that the finite growth model was difficult to use absent good data that would permit one to make reasonable estimates for the finite growth rate and finite period. Despite this caveat he decided to include it in the summary he was preparing (Table 4-16).

TABLE 4-15 Summary of Company A Plan 2 Valuation 3 $'s

Valuation Model Used to Value the Cash Flows of Company A	Discrete Cash Flow Model	Perpetual Fixed Cash Flow Model	Finite Fixed Cash Flow Model	Perpetual Growth Model	Finite Growth Model	Terminal Value Model	Company A, Plan 2 Value 3
(1) FPeriod + Perpetual Fixed CFM	2,548,573	2,698,925					5,247,498
(2) FPeriod + Finite Fixed CFM	2,548,573		2,571,671				5,120,243
(3) FPeriod + Perpetual Growth CFM	2,548,573			3,878,018			6,426,591
(4) FPeriod + Finite Growth CFM	2,548,573				3,405,477		5,954,050
(5) FPeriod + Terminal Value CFM	2,548,573					4,453,226	7,001,799

TABLE 4-16 Comparison of Valuations of Company A Plans 1 and 2 $'s

Plan	Table Number	Valuation Number	k	g_{FG}	TVM	g_{PG}	Implied Valuation Range FGM	TV	PGM	Average of TV & PGM
1	4-10	1	15.00%	5.00%	8	3.00%	6,300,000	6,400,000	6,700,000	6,550,000
2	4-13	1	15.00%	6.00%	10	4.50%	6,600,000	7,400,000	7,400,000	7,400,000
2	4-14	2	15.00%	5.00%	8	3.00%	6,400,000	6,400,000	6,700,000	6,550,000
2	4-15	3	16.50%	6.00%	10	4.50%	6,000,000	7,000,000	6,400,000	6,700,000

After studying Table 4-16 the CFO concluded the following:

- The analysis of plan 1, which relied on improved operations and investments as usual, resulted in a set of values that implied a range of $6,300,000 to $6,700,000 and an average of $6,550,000 based on an average of the terminal value and perpetual growth models.
- Plan 2, valuation 1 produced a different result, with the terminal value and perpetual growth models implying a value of $7,400,000. The finite growth model was an outlier largely due to the fact that a perpetual growth stream growing at 4.5% results in a larger post-forecast-period cash flow than one that grows at 6% for 15 years.
- Plan 2, valuation 2 brought the finite growth model much closer to the others and implied a value range of $6,400,000 to $6,700,000 as a result of the fact that both the terminal value multiplier and perpetual growth rates were much reduced. The CFO continued to feel that the relevance of this valuation was highly questionable since it was simply an attempt to value plan 2 with the same parameters as plan 1 and didn't ascribe any value to the higher cash flows that are expected at the end of the forecast period as a result of the investments contemplated in plan 2.
- Plan 2, valuation 3 once again cast the finite growth model into an outlier mode because the impact the post-forecast cash flows had on value were significantly reduced by the higher discount rate applied to the fixed growth period. The terminal value was similarly affected. The perpetual growth model fared better as a result of the higher growth rate. Averaging the terminal value and perpetual models implied a value of $6,700,000.
- The difference between plan 2 valuations 1 and 3 is the discount rate. Since plan 2 is considered to be inherently riskier this would seem to imply that the valuation with the higher discount rate (compared to plan 1) is more realistic.
- Even with the discount rate increased to 16.5%, plan 2 (valuation 3) still had significant upside compared to plan 1 and so it seemed that plan 2 was clearly superior to plan 1.

With this data at hand the CFO met with the management team and presented the results of his analysis. During the discussion that followed one slight problem emerged and that was that the low end of plan 2's third valuation was about $300,000 lower than plan 1. The chief financial officer explained that this value was determined by the growth rate used in the perpetual growth model and this difference would disappear very quickly with just a small change in either growth rate, and from a practical point of view the low ends of plan 1 and plan 2 (valuation 3) were not material. He went on to say that since there was a considerable difference in the upside of the two models, this upside shouldn't be ignored and therefore he was in favor of plan 2. The management group agreed.

VALUATION CONSIDERATIONS—LESSONS LEARNED

The examples used so far have involved multiple calculations. This was done in order to thoroughly familiarize the reader with valuing cash flow streams under various assumptions. However, as can be seen from the foregoing some of the valuation models aren't helpful when valuing post-forecast-period cash flows. The following is a summary of the lessons learned by virtue of working through the various examples.

Perpetual Fixed Model

This model assumes a fixed cash flow that continues forever. It's hard to think of a company's post-forecast-period cash flows that would suit this model and therefore it's seldom if ever used.

Finite Fixed Model

Unlike the perpetual fixed model this model values a fixed cash flow for a period of time. Again it's unlikely to be a realistic prototype for valuing post-forecast-period cash flows. However, it is useful for valuing a fixed annuity and perhaps finds its greatest use in this application.

Perpetual Growth Model

This model assumes that cash flow stream grows at some fixed rate forever and since companies generally strive to grow cash flow year over year it's a reasonable model to use for post-forecast-period cash flows. The fact that no company will continue to increase its cash flow forever doesn't invalidate the model because the outlying years don't contribute much to the present value. The rate to use can be difficult to establish. However, an examination of a company's historical performance will provide insight into an appropriate number that then needs to be tempered with judgment. There is no such thing as a typical number but one often sees growth rates in the 3–4% range when this model is used. In fact there are many mature companies that grow at a rate near and correlated to the Gross National Product, which in developed economies averages something like ±3%.

Finite Growth Model

Unlike the perpetual growth model this model assumes the cash flow grows at some constant rate for a fixed period of years. It can be used in place of the perpetual growth model when the number of years of growth is relatively high, say 25+ years. It is most frequently used in multi-stage models where a cash flow is expected to grow at one rate for a period of years and then followed by a series of cash flows that grow at another rate. This model yields the best results when there is sufficient data available to enable the user to make educated estimates of the finite growth rate and finite period.

Terminal Value Model

This is by far the most frequently used model when valuing post-forecast-period cash flows. As has been seen it simply requires an estimate of a suitable multiplier, which can be deduced from readily available industry data or obtained from professionals/organizations that have accumulated this type of data and developed valuation expertise.

MOST FREQUENTLY USED SINGLE-STAGE VALUATION MODELS

The following models are the most frequently used to value companies.

Forecast Period + Terminal Value Model

This model is defined by:

$$PV_{FP+TVM_N} = PV_{FP} + PV_{TVM_N} \qquad [4\text{-}50]$$

and is obtained by a combination of Equations [4-16] and [4-21].

$$PV_{FP+TVM_N} = \sum_{i=1}^{n} \frac{CFaIA_i}{(1+k)^i} + \frac{CFaIA_{TY}(TVM)}{(1+k)^N} \qquad [4\text{-}52]$$

Forecast Period + Perpetual Growth Model

This model is defined by:

$$PV_{FP+PGM_N} = PV_{FP} + PV_{PGM_N} \qquad [4\text{-}46]$$

and is obtained by combining Equations [4-16] and [4-19].

$$PV_{FP+PGM_N} = \sum_{i=1}^{n} \frac{CFaIA_i}{(1+k)^i} + \frac{CFaIA_{PG}}{(k-g_{PG})(1+k)^N} \qquad [4\text{-}53]$$

MULTI-STAGE VALUATIONS

Earlier it was mentioned that there are instances where the post-forecast-period cash flows are not adequately modeled by terminal value, perpetual growth, or for that matter any of the models. In instances such as these a multi-stage valuation may be appropriate.

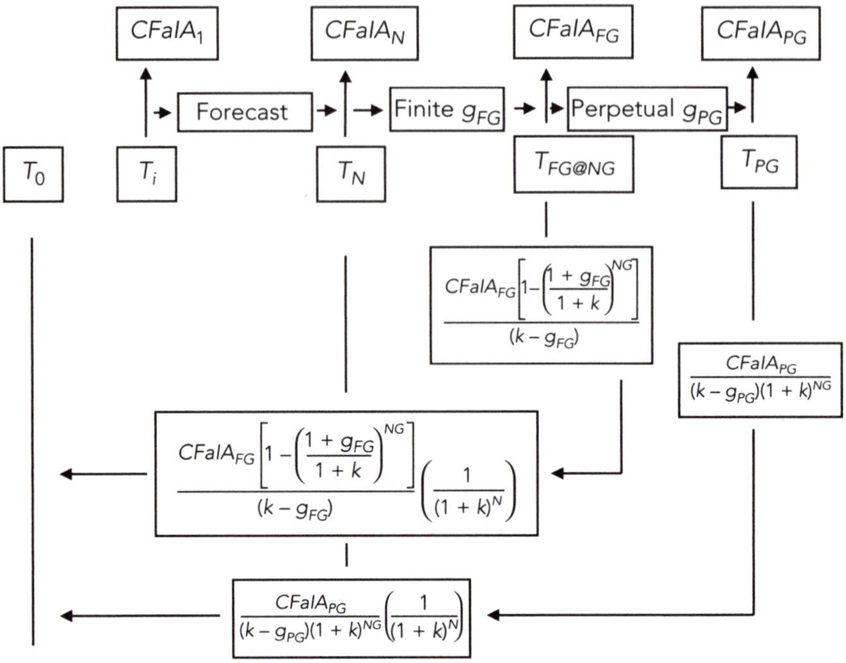

FIGURE 4-6 Multi-Stage Valuations

Figure 4-6 illustrates how a stream of cash flows can be valued when the post-forecast cash flows consist of a finite period of cash flow growth followed by a period of perpetual growth.

Mathematically this notion can be expressed by Equation [4-54].

$$PV_{FP+MS} = PV(Forecast\ Period\ CF) + PV\ (Finite\ Growth\ CF) + PV\ (Perpetual\ Growth\ CF) \quad [4\text{-}54]$$

where the Present Value of each term in Equation [4-54] is calculated with the use of Equations [4-16] (Forecast Period), [4-20] (Finite Growth), and [4-57] (Perpetual Growth).

$$PV(Forecast\ Period\ CF) = \sum_{i=1}^{n} \frac{CFaIA_i}{(1+k)^i} \quad [4\text{-}16]$$

$$PV(Finite\ Growth\ CF) = \frac{CFaIA_{FG}\left[1-\left(\frac{1+g_{FG}}{1+k}\right)^{NG}\right]}{(k-g_{FG})(1+k)^N} \quad [4\text{-}20]$$

$$PV(Perpetual\ Growth\ CF) = \frac{CFaIA_{PG}}{(k-g_{PG})(1+k)^{NG}(1+k)^N} \quad [4\text{-}57]$$

The Present Value of the Period of Perpetual Growth cannot be obtained by simply applying the Perpetual Growth Equation [4-19]. The reason for this is: The period of perpetual growth begins at the end of the period of finite growth, which takes place "NG" years after the period of forecasted cash flows. The expression that calculates the PV of *second stage perpetual growth* can be obtained as follows by starting with Equation [4-7].

$$PV_{PGM} = \frac{CFaIA_{PG}}{k - g_{PG}} \qquad [4\text{-}7]^{18}$$

Now since the period of perpetual growth starts after "NG" years of finite growth, Equation [4-7] needs to be present valued back to the end of the forecast period. This is done by multiplying Equation [4-7] by $1/(1 + k)^{NG}$. Hence the Present Value of the period of perpetual growth at time "N" is:

$$PV_{PGM_{T=NG}} = \frac{CFaIA_{PG}}{(k - g_{PG})}\left(\frac{1}{(1+k)^{NG}}\right) \qquad [4\text{-}55]$$

Next Equation [4-55] has to be present valued back to the beginning of the forecast period. This is done by multiplying Equation [4-55] by $1/(1 + k)^{N}$. Finally,

$$PV(Perpetual\ Growth\ CF) = \frac{CFaIA_{PG}}{(k - g_{PG})}\left(\frac{1}{(1+k)^{NG}}\right)\left(\frac{1}{(1+k)^{N}}\right) \qquad [4\text{-}56]$$

or

$$PV(Perpetual\ Growth\ CF) = \frac{CFaIA_{PG}}{(k - g_{PG})(1+k)^{NG}(1+k)^{N}} \qquad [4\text{-}57]$$

or

$$PV(Perpetual\ Growth\ CF) = \frac{CFaIA_{PG}}{(k - g_{PG})(1+k)^{NG+N}} \qquad [4\text{-}58]^{19}$$

Substituting in Equation [4-54] an expression for the Present Value of the Forecast Period cash flows followed by two stages of growth (finite and perpetual) is obtained.

$$PV_{FP+MS} = \sum_{i=1}^{n} \frac{CFaIA_i}{(1+k)^i} + \frac{CFaIA_{FG}\left[1 - \left(\frac{1+g_{FG}}{1+k}\right)^{NG}\right]}{(k - g_{FG})(1+k)^{N}} + \frac{CFaIA_{PG}}{(k - g_{PG})(1+k)^{NG}(1+k)^{N}} \qquad [4\text{-}59]$$

---

[18] E_{PG} has been replaced by $CFaIA_{PG}$.

[19] Equations [4-57] or [4-58] can be used. The author prefers Equation [4-57] because its derivation is somewhat more explicit.

EXAMPLE 4-4: MULTI-STAGE VALUATION OF COMPANY A'S PLAN 2

In Example 4-3 it was concluded that although plan 2[20] seemed to be the right answer and superior to plan 1, the fact that plan 2 was an investment plan suggests the difference between plan 1 and plan 2's valuations should have been more pronounced. This situation arises because none of the models used gave adequate consideration to the impact of plan 2's investments during the post-forecast period.

Recall that the valuation range that seemed to satisfy management for plan 1 was based on the terminal value model and the perpetual growth model. When it came to plan 2 the finite growth model didn't measure up against the perpetual growth model because 15 years of finite growth at 6% couldn't outpace 4.5% growth in perpetuity. One way of preparing a more realistic valuation of plan 2 would be to do a multi-stage valuation in which the period of forecasted cash flows is followed by a finite period of 6% growth for 15 years, which is then followed by 3% growth for perpetuity.

Also, if the multi-stage model is to yield a more accurate representation of plan 2's value, the discount rate has to be revisited. In Example 4-3, valuation 3 of plan 2 used a discount rate of 16.5% because the post-forecast-period cash flows were considered to involve more risk than those in plan 1. While this is correct for the period of finite growth it doesn't follow that the period of forecasted cash flows or the cash flows associated with the period of perpetual growth in plan 2 are any riskier than those in plan 1. Hence it would seem that the multi-stage valuation of plan 2 should use a discount rate (k_1) of 15% for the forecast period and 16.5% (k_2) and 15% (k_3) for the first-stage post-forecast and second-stage post-forecast cash flows respectively.

A depiction of the contemplated multi-stage valuation using the finite growth and perpetual growth models for plan 2 is shown in Figure 4-7.

By inspecting Figure 4-7 the Present Value of the Forecast Period and Multi-Stage Cash Flows (PV_{FP+MS}) can be represented by Equation [4-54].

$$\begin{aligned} PV_{FP+MS} &= PV(Forecast\ Period\ CF) + PV(Finite\ Growth\ CF) \\ &\quad + PV(Perpetual\ Growth\ CF) \end{aligned} \tag{4-54}$$

Previously the present value of Company A's plan 2, cash flows during the forecast period, was calculated by using Equation [4-16].

$$PV(Forecast\ Period\ CF) = PV_{FP} = \sum_{i=1}^{n} \frac{CFaIA_i}{(1+k)^i} \tag{4-16}$$

Expanding Equation [4-16] and substituting for $CFaIA_i$ from Table 4-12 and $k_1 = WACC = 15\%$,

$$\begin{aligned} PV(Forecast\ Period\ CF) &= \frac{690,000}{(1.15)} + \frac{734,808}{(1.15)^2} + \frac{788,873}{(1.15)^3} + \frac{866,971}{(1.15)^4} + \frac{955,662}{(1.15)^5} \\ &= \$2,645,143 \end{aligned}$$

[20] See Example 4-3.

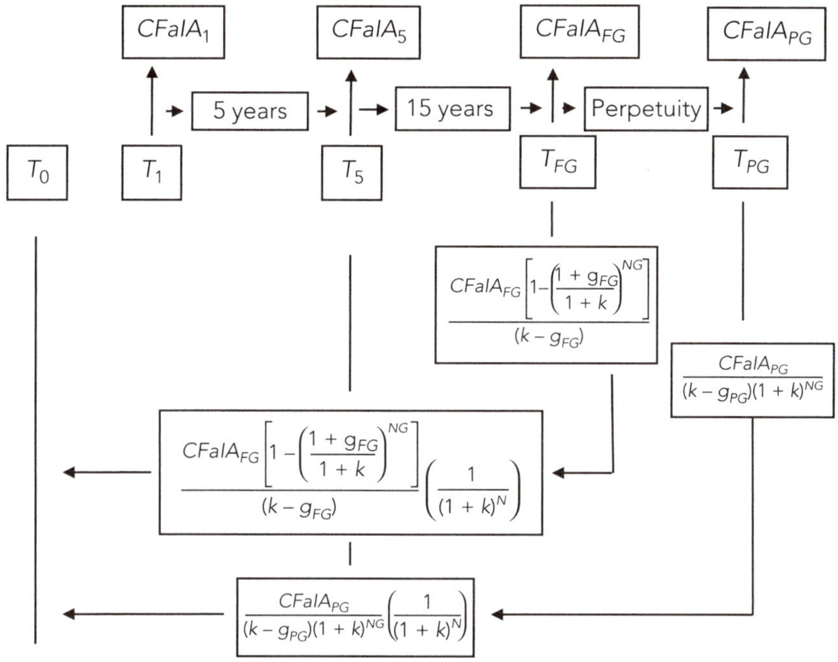

FIGURE 4-7 Multi-Stage Valuation of Company A Plan 2

Earlier the present value of a period of finite growth cash flows was calculated using Equation [4-20].

$$PV(Finite\ Growth\ CF) = PV_{FGM_N} = \frac{CFalA_{FG}\left[1-\left(\frac{1+g_{FG}}{1+k}\right)^{NG}\right]}{(k-g_{FG})(1+k)^N} \quad [4\text{-}20]$$

The value of the first cash flow in the finite growth model is:

$$CFalA_{FG} = (CFalA_5)(1+g_{FG}) = (955{,}662)(1.06) = \$1{,}013{,}002$$

Substituting $CFalA_{FG} = \$1{,}013{,}002$, $k_2 = 16.5\%$, $N = 5$ years, $NG = 15$ years, and $g_{FG} = 6\%$ in Equation [4-20], the *PV* for the first stage of post-forecast, the period of finite growth, is obtained.

$$PV(Finite\ Growth\ CF) = \frac{(1{,}013{,}002)\left[1-\left(\frac{1+0.06}{1+0.165}\right)^{15}\right]}{(0.165-0.06)(1+0.165)^5} = \$3{,}405{,}477$$

The present value of the second stage of growth is calculated by substituting in Equation [4-57]. However, before the present value of the second stage can be determined the value of the cash flow at the end of the period of finite growth ($CFalA_{EFG}$) must be calculated. As it turns out $CFalA_{EFG}$ is the final cash flow of the forecast period adjusted for 15 years of 6% growth and is obtained by substituting $CFalA_5 = 955{,}662$, $g_{FG} = 6\%$, and $NG = 15$ years in Equation [4-60].

$$CFalA_{EFG} = CFalA_5\,(1 + g_{FG})^{NG} \qquad [4\text{-}60]$$
$$CFalA_{EFG} = 955{,}662\,(1 + 0.06)^{15} = (955{,}662)(2.3966)$$
$$CFalA_{EFG} = \$2{,}290{,}300$$

Once again the first cash flow in the perpetual growth model has to be calculated by taking the cash flow at the end of the period of finite growth and adjusting it for the 3% growth in cash flow that takes place during the first period of perpetual growth.

$$CFalA_{PG} = CFalA_{EFG}\,(1 + g_{PG}) = (2{,}290{,}300)(1 + 0.03)$$
$$= (2{,}290{,}300)(1.03) = 2{,}359{,}009$$

Now recall that when the perpetual growth model was used to value plan 1 the discount rate used to value the perpetual earnings was $k = 15\%$. Earlier an argument was made that if plan 2's second stage earnings grow at the same rate as those in plan 1, they presumably involve the same risk and therefore there isn't any reason to penalize them by using the higher 16.5% discount rate. Hence the second-stage perpetual earnings are valued by substituting $CFalA_{PG} = \$2{,}359{,}000$, $k_1 = 15\%$, $N = 5$ years, $NG = 15$ years, and $g_{PG} = 3\%$ in Equation [4-57].

$$PV(Perpetual\ Growth\ CF) = \frac{CFalA_{PG}}{(k - g_{PG})(1+k)^{NG}(1+k)^{N}} \qquad [4\text{-}57]$$

$$PV(Perpetual\ Growth\ CF) = \frac{2{,}359{,}009}{(0.15-0.03)(1+0.15)^{15}(1+0.15)^{5}} = \frac{2{,}359{,}009}{(0.12)(1.15)^{15}(1.15)^{5}}$$

$$PV(Perpetual\ Growth\ CF) = \$1{,}201{,}134$$

Substituting in Equation [4-54] gives the present value of plan 2's cash flows when subjected to the multi-stage model.

$$PV_{FP+MS} = PV(Forecast\ Period\ CF) + PV(Finite\ Growth\ CF)$$
$$+\ PV(Perpetual\ Growth\ CF) \qquad [4\text{-}54]$$
$$PV_{FP+MS} = 2{,}645{,}143 + 3{,}405{,}477 + 1{,}201{,}134$$
$$PV_{FP+MS} = \$7{,}251{,}755$$

Comparisons of the present values of plans 1 and 2 are shown in Table 4-17. The reader will note that the value of plan 2 when subjected to a multi-stage valuation is notably higher than that obtained in any other valuation in which a perpetual growth rate of 3% was used in the previous examples. The fact that the multi-stage valuation

TABLE 4-17 Comparison of PVs of Plan 1 and Multi-Stage Valuation of Plan 2 $'s and %

Plan Number	*k*	g_{FG}	g_{PG}	PGM	MSM
Plan 1	15%	n/a	3.00%	6,700,000	
Plan 2 Multi-Stage	15%,16.5%,15%	6.00%	3.00%		7,250,000

is based on what can be argued as a more rational approach should increase one's confidence in the value obtained by this method. It should also augment the comfort level associated with plan 2 and lead one to conclude that plan 2 offers an opportunity to create more value and thus is superior to plan 1.

EXAMPLE 4-5: COMPANY C'S MULTI-STAGE VALUATIONS OF COMPANIES A AND B

In an earlier example, Company B,[21] a competitor of Company A, was introduced. Company B is very similar to A except that its NiROCE is 18.75% and as a result of an effort to grow as fast as Company A (7.5%), it had a Net Investment Rate (IR) of 40%. Like Company A, Company B has not made any forecasts beyond the five-year period but the business plan strongly suggests that cash flow growth will increase as a result of the investments made during the forecast periods. Company B's cash flows for the forecast period were calculated from the Company's Net Income and Investment Rate. The Cash Flow after Investing Activities is taken from Chapter 2 and repeated here in Table 4-18.

In addition to Company A, Company C is also considering the acquisition of Company B. Discussions with B's management team indicate that not only is Company B very similar to Company A but the post-forecast cash flows are also expected to consist of a five-year period of finite growth in the range of 4-to-8% (6% average) followed by perpetual growth of approximately 3%. After completing a multi-stage valuation of Company A's plan 2 the management of Company C decides that in order to compare the value of A's plan 2 to Company B it's necessary to do a multi-stage valuation of Company B as well. Also, since the level of uncertainty associated with B's post-forecast cash flows is similar

TABLE 4-18 Company B Forecasted CFaIA

	Year $'s				
	1	2	3	4	5
CF after Investing Activities	600,000	645,000	693,375	745,378	801,281

[21] See Chapter 2, Example 2-4.

to A's for plan 2 it is decided that identical discount and growth rates will be used in B's multi-stage evaluation. Hence, the valuation of B's cash flows incorporated the following parameters.

Forecast Period Cash Flows: $k_1 = 15\%$

Stage 1 Cash Flows (Finite Growth):

$$k_2 = 16.5\%,\ N = 5\ years,\ NG = 15\ years,\ g_{FG} = 6\%$$

Stage 2 Cash Flows (Perpetual Growth):

$$k_1 = 15\%,\ N = 5\ years,\ NG = 15\ years,\ g_{PG} = 3\%$$

The present value of Company B's Cash Flows during the forecast period is given by Equation [4-16].

$$PV_{FP} = \sum_{i=1}^{n} \frac{CFaIA_i}{(1+k)^i} \qquad [4\text{-}16]$$

Expanding and substituting for $CFaIA_i$ from Table 4-18 and $k = WACC = 15\%$,

$$PV_{FP} = \frac{600,000}{(1.15)} + \frac{645,000}{(1.15)^2} + \frac{693,375}{(1.15)^3} + \frac{745,378}{(1.15)^4} + \frac{801,281}{(1.15)^5} = \$2,289,908$$

The present value of B's Cash Flows during the post-forecast period is calculated by using the Finite Growth and Perpetual Growth Equations [4-20] and [4-57] respectively.

Stage 1 Cash Flows (Finite Growth)

$$PV(Finite\ Growth\ CF) = PV_{FGM_N} = \frac{CFaIA_{FG}\left[1 - \left(\frac{1+g_{FG}}{1+k}\right)^{NG}\right]}{(k - g_{FG})(1+k)^N} \qquad [4\text{-}20]$$

where:

$$CFaIA_{FG} = CFaIA_5\,(1 + g_{FG}) = (801,281)(1 + 0.06) = (801,281)(1.06) = \$849,358$$

Substituting $CFaIA_{FG} = 849,358$, $k = 16.5\%$, $N = 5$ years, $NG = 15$ years, $g_{FG} = 6\%$,

$$PV(Finite\ Growth\ CF) = \frac{(849,358)\left[1 - \left(\frac{1+0.06}{1+0.165}\right)^{15}\right]}{(0.165 - 0.06)(1+0.165)^5} = \$2,855,346$$

Stage 2 Cash Flows (Perpetual Growth)

$$PV(Perpetual\ Growth\ CF)PV_{PGM_N} = \frac{CFaIA_{PG}}{(k - g_{PG})(1+k)^{NG}(1+k)^N} \qquad [4\text{-}57]$$

The present value of the second stage of growth is obtained by substituting in Equation [4-57]. However, before this process can begin, the value of $CFaIA_{PG}$ needs to be calculated. This cash flow starts after 15 years of finite growth at 6%. Therefore, the cash flow at the end of the finite period is:

$$CFaIA_{EFG} = CFaIA_5\,(1 + g_{FG})^{NG} \qquad [4\text{-}60]$$

Substituting $CFaIA_{FG} = 801{,}281$, $g_{FG} = 6\%$, and $NG = 15$ years in Equation [4-60], we get the cash flow at the end of finite growth.

$$CFaIA_{EFG} = (801{,}281)(1 + 0.06)^{15} = (801{,}281)(2.3966) = \$1{,}920{,}317$$

Once again it is necessary to calculate the first cash flow that takes place during the period of perpetual growth.

$$\begin{aligned} CFaIA_{PG} &= CFaIA_{EFG}\,(1 + g_{PG}) = (1{,}920{,}317)(1 + 0.03) \\ &= (1{,}920{,}317)(1.03) = \$1{,}977{,}927 \end{aligned}$$

Substituting $CFaIA_{PG} = 1{,}977{,}927$, $k = 15\%$, $N = 5$, years, $NG = 15$ years, $g_{PG} = 3\%$ into Equation [4-57] gives the present value of the stage 2 cash flows.

$$PV(Perpetual\ Growth\ CF) = \frac{1{,}977{,}927}{(0.15-0.03)(1+0.15)^{15}(1+0.15)^{5}} = \$1{,}007{,}099$$

The results of the multi-stage valuations of Company A and Company B are summarized in Table 4-19.[22]

An inspection of Table 4-19 shows that in every period the present value of Company A's cash flows is greater than Company B's. This is because at a NiROCE = 18.75% (3/4 of A's), Company B has to invest 33.3% more than Company A in order to grow as fast as A. The result of this is Company B's Cash Flow after Investing Activities is considerably less than A's. And without information from the management of Company B that would

TABLE 4-19 Comparison of Multi-Stage Valuations of Company A Plan 2 and Company B $'s

	Multi-Stage Value of Company A Plan 2	Multi-Stage Value of Company B
PV (Forecast Period Cash Flows)	2,645,143	2,289,908
PV (Stage 1, Finite Growth Cash Flows)	3,405,477	2,855,346
PV (Stage 2, Perpetual Growth Cash Flows)	1,201,134	1,007,099
PV (FP + Stage 1 + Stage 2)	**7,251,755**	**6,152,353**

[22]The figures in Table 4-19 for Company A were calculated in Example 4-4.

support higher post-forecast growth it's hard to conclude anything other than Company B is not worth as much as Company A.

Clearly, Company C will have to pay more for Company A than Company B and in most instances (all other things being equal) Company C should probably prefer A to B. The implied reasoning is that A's superior NiROCE is probably the result of having a better management team, and in the final analysis access to management talent is often a key consideration.

However, this is not the whole story. It's also possible that Company B's performance could be improved and surpass A's if B's management and/or strategy or both were changed. For example, Company C may feel that:

- Company B's Net Income Return on Capital Employed could be quickly improved by downsizing the balance sheet and reducing the capital employed and increasing net income and cash flow by introducing world-class manufacturing techniques in B's facilities.
- Once Company B's NiROCE was improved, they could reduce the Investment Rate (and still maintain the growth rate) and thereby improve B's cash flow and value.

If Company C felt such a transition could be done with acceptable disruption and risk under its ownership, then it may well choose B over A. However, it is instructive to note that while Company B is not a turnaround situation, its cash flow and operating statistics are clearly inferior to Company A. Experienced management teams often favor quality over opportunity and are prepared to pay for it.

Up to this point, Company C's comparison of Companies A and B is based on what the management teams of the respective companies have provided. In real life and from a negotiating perspective, Company C would be arguing that the price for A should be based on plan 1. The management of Company A would be pushing Company C very hard to accept plan 2 as the basis for their valuation. If Company C's management was receptive to A's arguments, this would further enhance Company A's attractiveness. Company B would probably be trying to sell the management of Company C on the opportunity its company presents for improved financial performance.

EQUIVALENCE OF THE POST-FORECAST-PERIOD MODELS

Throughout the discussion and application of the post-forecast-period models, comments were often made on why one or more models might or might not be suitable or why some models gave similar results. Therefore, before this chapter comes to a close the relationships between the five post-forecast-period models will be examined.

Recall Equations [4-17]–[4-21].

(1) Perpetual Fixed Cash Flow Model:

$$PV_{PXM_N} = \frac{CFaIA_{PX}}{k(1+k)^N} \qquad [4\text{-}17]$$

(2) Finite Fixed Cash Flow Model:

$$PV_{FXM_N} = \frac{CFalA_{FX}\left[1-(1+k)^{-NX}\right]}{k(1+k)^N} \quad [4\text{-}18]$$

(3) Perpetual Growth Model:

$$PV_{PGM_N} = \frac{CFalA_{PG}}{(k-g_{PG})(1+k)^N} \quad [4\text{-}19]$$

(4) Finite Growth Model:

$$PV_{FGM_N} = \frac{CFalA_{FG}\left[1-\left(\frac{1+g_{FG}}{1+k}\right)^{NG}\right]}{(k-g_{FG})(1+k)^N} \quad [4\text{-}20]$$

(5) Terminal Value Model:

$$PV_{TVM_N} = \frac{CFalA_{TY}(TVM)}{(1+k)^N} \quad [4\text{-}21]$$

Perpetual Fixed = Finite Fixed Model

Earlier it was mentioned that the only fundamental difference between Equations [4-17] and [4-18] was the fact that one assumed a perpetual series of cash flows and the other a finite series. Letting Equation [4-17] equal Equation [4-18] and applying limits shows the condition under which they give the same results.

$$\frac{CFalA_{PX}}{k(1+k)^N} = \frac{CFalA_{FX}\left[1-(1+k)^{-NX}\right]}{k(1+k)^N} \quad [4\text{-}61]$$

Since $CFalA_{PX}$ and $CFalA_{FX}$ are both assumed to be equal to the last cash flow during the forecast period, then $CFalA_{PX} = CFalA_{FX}$. Canceling like terms in Equation [4-61] gives a much simplified expression.

$$1 = \left[1-(1+k)^{-NX}\right] \quad [4\text{-}62]$$

Now as NX, the number of years in the finite cash flow stream, increases, the term $(1+k)^{-NX}$ becomes smaller and in the $\underset{NC\to\infty}{\text{Limit}}(1+k)^{-NX} = 0$ and Equation [4-62] becomes $1 = 1$. Therefore, in conclusion, when NX is very large (∞), then the *Perpetual Fixed Cash Flow Model = Finite Fixed Cash Flow Model.*

Perpetual Fixed = Perpetual Growth Model

Now let Equation [4-17] = [4-19].

$$\frac{CFalA_{PX}}{k(1+k)^N} = \frac{CFalA_{PG}}{(k-g_{PG})(1+k)^N} \tag{4-63}$$

Again, since $CFalA_{PX}$ and $CFalA_{PG}$ are assumed to be equal to the last cash flow during the forecast period, then $CFalA_{PX} = CFalA_{PG}$. Cancel like terms and Equation [4-63] becomes:

$$\frac{1}{k} = \frac{1}{k-g_{PG}} \tag{4-64}$$

Hence, *when* $g_{PG} = 0$, $1/k = 1/k$ *and the Perpetual Fixed Cash Flow Model = Perpetual Growth Cash Flow Model.*

Perpetual Growth = Finite Growth Model

Earlier it was stated that the only difference between Equations [4-19] and [4-20] was the fact that one assumed a perpetual series and the other a finite series of growing cash flows. The condition under which they give the same result is obtained by letting Equation [4-19] equal [4-20] and examining the result:

$$\frac{CFalA_{PG}}{(k-g_{PG})(1+k)^N} = \frac{CFalA_{FG}\left[1-\left(\frac{1+g_{FG}}{1+k}\right)^{NG}\right]}{(k-g_{FG})(1+k)^N} \tag{4-65}$$

Setting $CFalA_{PG} = CFalA_{FG}$ and canceling like terms in Equation [4-65] yields:

$$\frac{1}{(k-g_{PG})} = \frac{1-\left(\frac{1+g_{FG}}{1+k}\right)^{NG}}{(k-g_{FG})} \tag{4-66}$$

Since k must be greater than g_{FG}, then the term $(1 + g_{FG})/(1 + k)$ must be less than 1 and as $NG \to \infty$ the term $(1 + g_{FG})/(1 + k) \to$ zero. Hence Equation [4-66] becomes

$$\frac{1}{(k-g_{PG})} = \frac{1-0}{(k-g_{FG})} \tag{4-67}$$

Simplifying,

$$(k - g_{FG}) = (k - g_{PG}) \tag{4-68}$$

or

$$g_{FG} = g_{PG} \qquad [4\text{-}69]$$

which says that *when* $NG \to \infty$ *and* $g_{FG} = g_{PG}$ *the perpetual and finite growth models give the same result.*

Perpetual Fixed = Terminal Value Model

Next let Equation [4-17] = [4-21].

$$\frac{CFaIA_{PX}}{k(1+k)^N} = \frac{CFaIA_{TY}(TVM)}{(1+k)^N} \qquad [4\text{-}70]$$

Setting $CFaIA_{PX} = CFaIA_{TY}$ and canceling like terms in Equation [4-70] yields:

$$\frac{1}{k} = TVM \qquad [4\text{-}71]$$

Therefore, *when* $TVM = 1/k$ *the perpetual fixed cash flow model = terminal value cash flow model.*

Perpetual Growth = Terminal Value Model

Finally let Equation [4-19] = [4-21].

$$\frac{CFaIA_{PG}}{(k - g_{PG})(1+k)^N} = \frac{CFaIA_{TY}(TVM)}{(1+k)^N} \qquad [4\text{-}72]$$

Once more letting $CFaIA_{PG} = CFaIA_{TY}$ and canceling like terms in Equation [4-72] the result is:

$$\frac{1}{(k - g_{PG})} = TVM \qquad [4\text{-}73]$$

Therefore, *when* $TVM = 1/(k - g_{PG})$, *the cash flow models defined by Equations* [4-19] *and* [4-21] *will yield the same result and under this condition: the perpentual growth model = the terminal value model.*

The reader is encouraged to work out the other possibilities. A summary of the various equivalence combinations is contained in Table 4-20.

TABLE 4-20 Summary of Post-Forecast Cash Flow Model Equivalence Equations

	Perpetual Fixed Cash Flow Model	Finite Fixed Cash Flow Model	Perpetual Growth Cash Flow Model	Finite Growth Cash Flow Model	Terminal Value Cash Flow Model
Perpetual Fixed Cash Flow Model	Not Applicable	$NX \to \infty$	$g_{PG} = 0$	$NG \to \infty$ $g_{FG} = 0$	$TVM = \frac{1}{k}$
Finite Fixed Cash Flow Model	$NX \to \infty$	Not Applicable	$NX \to \infty$ $g_{PG} = 0$	$NG \to \infty$ $NG \to \infty$ $g_{FG} = 0$	$NX \to \infty$ $TVM = \frac{1}{k}$
Perpetual Growth Model	$g_{PG} = 0$	$NX \to \infty$ $g_{PG} = 0$	Not Applicable	$NG \to \infty$ $g_{FG} = g_{PG}$ $g < k$	$TVM = \frac{1}{(k - g_{PG})}$
Finite Growth Model	$NG \to \infty$ $g_{FG} = 0$	$NX \to \infty$ $NG \to \infty$ $g_{FG} = 0$	$NG \to \infty$ $g_{FG} = g_{PG}$ $g < k$	Not Applicable	$NG \to \infty$ $g_{FG} < k$ $TVM = \frac{1}{(k - g_{FG})}$
Terminal Value Model	$TVM = \frac{1}{k}$	$NX \to \infty$ $TVM = \frac{1}{k}$	$TVM = \frac{1}{(k - g_{PG})}$	$NG \to \infty$ $g_{FG} < k$ $TVM = \frac{1}{(k - g_{FG})}$	Not Applicable

IMPACT OF 1/(*k* – *g*) ON THE PERPETUAL GROWTH MODEL

When Equation [4-19] was set equal to [4-21] the condition necessary for these models to yield the same result was:

$$\frac{1}{(k - g_{PG})} = TVM \qquad [4\text{-}73]$$

So in a sense and under the conditions assumed, $1/k - g_{PG}$ is equivalent to a terminal value multiplier, the relevance of which will be discussed in the following section. The real message here is that the expression $1/k - g_{PG}$ has an enormous impact on the value of the perpetual growth model when used to value post-forecast-period cash flow. Recall that when the perpetual growth model[23] as defined by Equation [4-19] was developed, it was based on the following.

- If $g_{PG} > k$, it will give a nonsensical result.
- If $g_{PG} = k$, the result is indeterminate.
- Equation [4-19] is a special case and based on a general equation developed in Appendix A. The constraint placed on this equation when it was developed was that $g_{PG} < k$.
- For any given level of cash flow, the value implied by the perpetual growth model is controlled by $k - g_{PG}$. When the difference is small, the impact is large and small changes in g_{PG} will have a big impact. As the difference increases, the effect that any given change in g_{PG} has diminishes.

The fact that small differences result in huge values for $1/k - g_{PG}$ can be seen by referring to Table 4-21. For example, when the difference in "$k - g_{PG}$" is 2%, the value of $1/k - g_{PG}$ is 50 and as the difference increases the value diminishes rapidly. Also after a $k - g_{PG}$ difference of 10 the impact for each increase in the difference is less than 10% and becomes less than 5% after a difference of 20%.

TABLE 4-21 Impact on Value that Various Values of $k - g_{PG}$ Have on the Perpetual Growth Model

$k - g_{PG}$	$\frac{1}{k - g_{PG}}$	% Change	$k - g_{PG}$	$\frac{1}{k - g_{PG}}$	% Change	$k - g_{PG}$	$\frac{1}{k - g_{PG}}$	% Change
—negative	nonsensical	n/a	10%	10.00	10.0%	21%	4.76	4.8%
0	indeterminate	n/a	11%	9.09	9.1%	22%	4.55	4.5%
1%	100.00	n/a	12%	8.33	8.3%	23%	4.35	4.3%
2%	50.00	50.0%	13%	7.69	7.7%	24%	4.17	4.2%
3%	33.33	33.3%	14%	7.14	7.1%	25%	4.00	4.0%
4%	25.00	25.0%	15%	6.67	6.7%	26%	3.85	3.8%
5%	20.00	20.0%	16%	6.25	6.3%	27%	3.70	3.7%
6%	16.67	16.7%	17%	5.88	5.9%	28%	3.57	3.6%
7%	14.29	14.3%	18%	5.56	5.6%	29%	3.45	3.4%
8%	12.50	12.5%	19%	5.26	5.3%	30%	3.33	3.3%
9%	11.11	11.11%	20%	5.00	5.0%	31%	3.23	3.2%

[23] And for that matter the finite growth model as well.

CONSIDERATIONS OF THE TERMINAL VALUE MULTIPLIER AS IMPLIED BY THE EQUIVALENCY EQUATIONS

Given there were several instances where the outcome of developing the Equivalency Equations resulted in simple expressions for the terminal value multiplier (TVM), one might be tempted to use one of these expressions to estimate a TVM in situations where a suitable TVM is not known. While there may be instances where using Equations [4-71] or [4-73] to estimate a TVM is appropriate it should be done with care as illustrated by the following. Refer to Tables 4-22 and 4-23.

$$\frac{1}{k} = TVM \qquad [4\text{-}71]$$

$$\frac{1}{(k - g_{PG})} = TVM \qquad [4\text{-}73]$$

As can be seen from Table 4-22, $k = 10\%$ and $g = 1\%$ gives the same Implied TVM as $k = 15\%$ and $g = 6\%$. This outcome presents a couple of problems. The first is that 11 would seem like a high TVM for a company that is only growing at 1% per year. The second is that even if 11 is an appropriate TVM for such a company it can be argued that it doesn't seem logical that it would be suitable for one growing at 6%. The difference of course is the higher discount rate k, which implies increased risk associated with the cash flow stream that offsets the impact of the higher growth. Table 4-23 supports the notion that higher cash flow discount rates have an impact on a particular company's TVM as evidenced by the TVM going from 10 to 6.7 as k goes from 10% to 15% respectively.

In conclusion, when using a TVM to value a cash flow at the end of a stream of forecasted cash flows it's really important to use a TVM established by market

TABLE 4-22 Using $k - g_{PG}$ to Estimate a TVM

k	g_{PG}	$k - g_{PG}$	$\frac{1}{k - g_{PG}}$	Implied TVM
10.0%	1.0%	9.0%	11.11	11
11.0%	2.0%	9.0%	11.11	11
12.0%	3.0%	9.0%	11.11	11
13.0%	4.0%	9.0%	11.11	11
14.0%	5.0%	9.0%	11.11	11
15.0%	6.0%	9.0%	11.11	11

TABLE 4-23 Using k to Estimate a TVM

k	$TVM = \frac{1}{k}$	Implied TVM
0.10	10.00	10.0
0.11	9.09	9.1
0.12	8.33	8.3
0.13	7.69	7.7
0.14	7.14	7.1
0.15	6.67	6.7

conditions. In instances where this isn't practical, Equation [4-71] or [4-73] may be used with care.

CASE STUDY: NEXGENSONICS AND THE POWER OF DISCIPLINE!

As part of Pharos Corporation's continuing education process for management teams of recently acquired companies, the CFO together with the corporate development team had just finished conducting a seminar on valuation models. As it turned out the corporate development team had just recently identified an acquisition candidate that they feel would form an excellent platform for building a large technology company. Given the timing of events, it was decided that the attendees break into groups and value NexgenSonics utilizing the models they had been shown and in the process of doing so prepare the following:

- Value NexgenSonics and explain the rationale.
- Summarize the valuation and discuss the results.
- Calculate the Enterprise Value.
- Discuss the EBITDA multiplier and demonstrate whether the one used is reasonable.
- Make a recommendation.

Historical Income Statements (Table CS 4-1), Forecasted Income Statements (Table CS 4-2), and a table containing statistics and financial data (CS 4-3) were provided.

TABLE CS 4-1 NexgenSonics Historical Income Statement $(000,000)'s

	CY – 4	CY – 3	CY – 2	CY – 1	CurYear
Revenue	186	214	261	312	483
Cost of Goods Sold	(112)	(100)	(119)	(138)	(201)
S,G & A	(56)	(52)	(63)	(76)	(115)
Research and Development	(19)	(18)	(23)	(28)	(43)
EBITDA	(1)	45	56	70	124
Depreciation	(10)	(8)	(6)	(6)	(15)
EBIT	(11)	37	50	64	109
Interest Expense	(12)	(9)	(2)	(5)	(8)
EBT	(23)	28	49	59	101
Taxes	(3)	(3)	(7)	(18)	(29)
Net Income	(26)	25	41	41	72

TABLE CS 4-2 NexgenSonics Forecasted Income Statement $(000,000)'s

	FY 1	FY 2	FY 3	FY 4	FY 5
Revenue	509	575	779	1,077	1,147
Cost of Goods Sold	(202)	(225)	(297)	(392)	(386)
S, G & A	(119)	(138)	(188)	(256)	(261)
Research and Development	(46)	(54)	(76)	(105)	(110)
EBITDA	142	158	218	324	390
Depreciation	(16)	(21)	(26)	(40)	(42)
EBIT	126	137	192	284	348
Interest Expense	(8)	(9)	(10)	(9)	(7)
EBT	118	128	182	275	341
Taxes	(30)	(31)	(52)	(85)	(110)
Net Income	88	98	130	190	230

TABLE CS 4-3 NexgenSonics Statistics and Financial Data

Historical Revenue CAGR	27%
Historical EBITDA CAGR	40%
Forecasted Revenue CAGR	23%
Forecasted EBITDA CAGR	29%
Weighted Average Cost of Capital	14%
Average EBITDA Multiplier	19
Long-Term Debt Current Year ($000,000)	58

Valuing NexgenSonics

Before the groups were turned loose on the project, the VP of Business Development conducted a brief review of valuation models and methodology.

He began by reminding all that the value of a company can be estimated by doing a present value analysis of the company's forecast and post-forecast-period cash flows and this notion is expressed by Equation [4-1], where PV_{FCF} is the present value of the future cash flows.

$$PV_{FCF} = PV(\textit{Cash Flows during the Forecast Period}) + PV(\textit{Post-Forecast-Period Cash Flows}) \quad [4\text{-}1]$$

And that as the participants will see, the first term in Equation [4-1] is common to most valuation models and the form the second term will take depends on how the post-forecast-period cash flows are characterized. He also pointed out that Equation [4-1] was somewhat unwieldy and can be shortened to:

$$PV_{FP+PFP_N} = PV_{FP} + PV_{PFP_N} \quad [4\text{-}74]$$

where:

PV_{FP+PFP} represents the PV of the sums of the forecast and post-forecast cash flows, PV_{FP} the PV of the forecast period cash flows, and PV_{PFP_N} the PV of the post-forecast cash flows

He then went on describe the model used to deal with the forecast period cash flows followed by several models that could be used to evaluate the post-forecast-period cash flows.

Forecast Period Model

When it came to the forecast period he explained that Equation [4-2][24] could be used to calculate the present value of any stream of discrete cash flows.

$$PV_{FP} = \frac{E_1}{(1+k)^1} + \frac{E_2}{(1+k)^2} + \frac{E_3}{(1+k)^3} + \ldots + \frac{E_N}{(1+k)^N} \quad [4\text{-}2]$$

Since the groups were very familiar with present value analysis the VP was able to move on quickly to the post-forecast-period models.

Post-Forecast-Period Models

He explained that there were five basic models that could be used for post-forecast-period PV calculations and went on to briefly describe each.

Perpetual Fixed Model

The first model described was a model that assumed some level of fixed cash flow continues for an infinite number of periods (very long time) and it takes the form of Equation [4-4].

$$PV_{PXM_N} = \frac{E_{PX}}{k(1+k)^N} \quad [4\text{-}4]$$

where:

E_{PX} is the fixed cash flow that continues for an infinite number of periods commencing after the final forecast cash flow E_N that takes place at the end of period N

[24] See Appendix A, Equation [A-2].

The VP pointed out that this model is suited for valuing a fixed stream of payments that are expected to go on for a very long time. Inspection of Tables CS 4-1 and CS 4-2 indicates that the historical and forecasted compound annual growth rates for NexgenSonics EBITDAs are 40% and 29% respectively, and while the forecasted growth rates won't continue at 29% forever there will be growth; therefore, this model is inappropriate for valuing the post-forecast-period cash flows for a company like NexgenSonics.

One of the participants who was somewhat familiar with calculating the value of a perpetual stream of cash flows said that Equation [4-4] looked a little more complicated than he recalled. The VP responded by saying the participant was right and actually Equation [4-4] consisted of two parts. The first was the classical PV Perpetual Cash Flow Equation E_{PX}/k but since this cash flow stream takes place after period N it needs to be present valued to the beginning of the discrete cash flow stream; hence the term $1/(1 + k)^N$. The VP went on to say that this was an important concept and the term $1/(1 + k)^N$ would show up often when considering post-forecast-period cash flows. After being convinced there was an adequate level of understanding he proceeded to quickly go through the other four post-forecast-period evaluation models.

Finite Fixed Model

$$PV_{FXM_N} = \frac{E_{FX}\left[1-(1+k)^{-NX}\right]}{k(1+k)^N} \qquad [4\text{-}6]$$

where:

E_{FX} is the fixed cash flow that continues for NX periods commencing after the final forecast cash flow E_N that takes place at the end of period N

When it came to this model the VP stated that Equation [4-6] provides a means of calculating the present value of a stream of cash flows fixed at some level for a finite period. Therefore, it's well suited to valuing annuities such as fixed pension payments, fixed royalties, and so on where the payment will continue for a period of time. However, since this model assumes the post-forecast cash flows remain at a fixed level for a finite period of time, an unlikely assumption to make in most business models, its use is seldom appropriate for the same reasons that the perpetual model was deemed unsuitable.

Perpetual Growth Model

$$PV_{PGM_N} = \frac{E_{PG}}{(k-g_{PG})(1+k)^N} \qquad [4\text{-}8]$$

where:

E_{PG} is the cash flow that grows at rate g_{PG} for an infinite number of periods (very long time) commencing after the final forecast cash flow E_N that takes place at the end of period N

The VP reminded everyone that management's task is to grow cash flow systematically period after period and that is the behavior modeled by this paradigm. Hence, when long periods of post-forecast cash flows are expected this model can be used with one caveat: g_{PG} must be less than k, otherwise a nonsensical result will be obtained.

He also reminded everyone that when this model is used it's important to get the value of E_{PG} correct, and that when this model was developed it was assumed that E_{PG} takes place one period after E_N has occurred. So, if E_N grows at rate g_{PG}, then:

$$E_{PG} = E_N(1 + g_{PG}) \qquad [4\text{-}9]$$

When Equation [4-9] represents the first cash flow that takes place in the perpetual growth model then Equation [4-10] becomes

$$PV_{PGM_N} = \frac{E_N(1+g_{PG})}{(k-g_{PG})(1+k)^N} \qquad [4\text{-}10]$$

Again like E_{PX} and E_{FX} there is no requirement that E_{PG} equal E_N. The only requirement is that whatever starting value E_N has, it grows at a fixed rate in perpetuity.

Finite Growth Model

$$PV_{FGM_N} = \frac{E_{FG}\left[1-\left(\frac{1+g_{FG}}{1+k}\right)^{NG}\right]}{(k-g_{FG})(1+k)^N} \qquad [4\text{-}12]$$

where:

E_{FG} is the cash flow that grows at rate g_{FG} for NG periods commencing after the final forecast cash flow E_N that takes place at the end of period N

And just as in the perpetual growth model, the right value for E_{PG} has to be used. If E_N grows at a rate g_{FG} for the first period after time T_N, then:

$$E_{FG} = E_N(1 + g_{FG}) \qquad [4\text{-}13]$$

and Equation [4-12] can be modified to become:

$$PV_{FGM_N} = \frac{E_N(1+g_{FG})\left[1-\left(\frac{1+g_{FG}}{1+k}\right)^{NG}\right]}{(k-g_{FG})(1+k)^N} \qquad [4\text{-}14]$$

In an attempt to preempt a question he went on to describe applications where the assumptions associated with the model were satisfied. For example, if a business's (or some subset of the business's) cash flow is dependent on royalties from intellectual property that are expected to start at some level and grow at a constant rate for a finite period of time, then this model can be used to present value the cash flows that are forecasted to eventuate. The same would be true for an annuity that was guaranteed to grow at some rate for a period of time.

Many in the group were uncomfortable with the concept of growth for an infinite period (perpetual growth model) and were more comfortable with this model because it provides a way of avoiding the notion of perpetual cash flows by limiting the periods of growth to some number of years *NG*. The VP of Business Development understood the point of view but pointed out that there are many businesses in mature industries and categories that grow year after year at about the same rate as Gross National Product (GNP), which on average is about 3%, and for these companies the infinite growth model works well.

Terminal Value Model

$$PV_{TVM_N} = \frac{E_{TY}(TVM)}{(1+k)^N} \qquad [4\text{-}15]$$

where:

$E_{TY} = E_N$, the final cash flow that takes place at the end of period *N*, and *TVM* is the terminal value multiplier

Since in the VP's experience this was one of the most widely used models for calculating the present value of the post-forecast-period cash flows when valuing a business, he reminded all of how it worked.

Typically, management prepared cash flow estimates based on pro-forma financial statements. This model assumes that the business is sold at the end of the forecast period for some multiple of the final year's (Year *n*'s) cash flow. This is known as the *terminal value*; hence the *terminal value multiplier* (TVM), which is usually obtained from industry statistics, comparable transactions, or expert advice.

He went on to say that it was not important that the business actually be sold or that the owners plan to sell it. Rather, the terminal value approach simply allows one to ascribe some value to the business by estimating what someone might pay for it at the end of the cash flow forecast period, assuming lots of things, including that all the value-added enhancements that management plans to put in place over the forecast period eventuate.

After the five post-discrete-cash-flow models had been presented, there was concern among the participants that they didn't have an adequate level of understanding to feel comfortable applying the models. The VP of Business Development acknowledged their concern and did a couple of things. The first was to assure them that there wasn't any need to understand how these equations were developed. The important thing was to get comfortable using them and this would come about once they started applying the various models, which they would do shortly when it was time for them to value NexgenSonics. Second, he handed out copies of "Appendix B: Business Valuation Models" and urged them to refer to the document frequently as they worked their way through the valuation.

Before he turned them loose he reminded the group of a few things.

- The expression contained in Equation [4-1] established the framework for the valuation exercise they were about to engage in.
- Three valuations were required and each one should consist of Equation [4-1] and one of the perpetual growth, finite growth, and terminal value cash flow models as defined by Equations [4-8] or [4-10], [4-12] or [4-14], and [4-15].
- Since the financial statements they were given for NexgenSonics didn't contain a cash flow statement, they would have to decide what to use in its place.

The issue of cash flow didn't remain a problem very long. Most in the group recalled from earlier training sessions that while cash flow per se was required to do a proper valuation a reasonable estimate could be made by using EBITDA.

The valuations done by the best group follow.

Valuing the Forecast Period Cash Flows

It was observed that according to Equation [4-74] all of the models included the present value of the cash flows during the forecast period. Hence, the cash flows during this period were the first for which a present value is calculated.

$$PV_{FP+PFP_N} = PV_{FP} + PV_{PFP_N} \quad [4\text{-}74]$$

Substituting EBITDA_i for E_i in Equation [4-2] and then substituting values for EBITDA and k from Tables 4-2 and 4-3, the Present Value of the Forecast Period Cash Flows PV_{FP} is obtained.

$$PV_{FP} = \frac{EBITDA_1}{(1+k)^1} + \frac{EBITDA_2}{(1+k)^2} + \frac{EBITDA_3}{(1+k)^3} + \frac{EBITDA_4}{(1+k)^4} + \frac{EBITDA_5}{(1+k)^5} \quad [4\text{-}2]$$

$$PV_{FP} = \frac{142{,}000{,}000}{(1+0.14)^1} + \frac{158{,}000{,}000}{(1+0.14)^2} + \frac{218{,}000{,}000}{(1+0.14)^3} + \frac{324{,}000{,}000}{(1+0.14)^4} + \frac{390{,}000{,}000}{(1+0.14)^5}$$

$$PV_{FP} = 125{,}000{,}000 + 122{,}000{,}000 + 147{,}000{,}000 + 192{,}000{,}000 + 203{,}000{,}000$$

$$PV_{FP} = \$788{,}000{,}000$$

Valuing the Post-Forecast-Period Cash Flows

With the PV of the Forecast Cash Flows at hand, the group proceeded to calculate the PVs of the Post-Forecast Cash Flows using the applicable post-forecast models.

Perpetual Growth Model

NexgenSonic's historical and forecast EBITDA growth rates are 40% and 29% respectively. While the growth rate is clearly going to decrease at some point there isn't any indication that modest single-digit growth will happen any time soon. Furthermore, the company is in an industry that is expected to grow at a double-digit rate for a long period of time. However, in the long run no company can grow at double digits forever, so while 29% may be credible for the forecast period, it certainly isn't for the post-forecast period. Given this information the group concluded a growth rate of something close to but less than 10% would seem to be a reasonable value for g_{PG}. An 8% growth rate is selected.

$$PV_{PGM_N} = \frac{E_{PG}}{(k - g_{PG})(1+k)^N} \qquad [4\text{-}8]$$

Recall that the last $EBITDA_5$ during the forecast period is \$390 million and the first post-forecast-period EBITDA is expected to be 8% greater than $EBITDA_5$. Therefore, the value of E_{PG}, the first post-forecast cash flow, is calculated to be:

$$E_{PG} = (390{,}000{,}000)(1.08) = 421{,}200{,}000$$

Substituting values for E_{PG} = 421,200,000, N = 5 years, g_{PG} = 8%, and k = 14% in Equation [4-8], a value for post-forecast-period cash flows can be calculated.

$$PV_{PGM_N} = \frac{421{,}200{,}000}{(0.14 - 0.08)(1+0.14)^5} = \frac{421{,}200{,}000}{(0.06)(1.14)^5} = \frac{421{,}200{,}000}{(0.06)(1.9254)}$$

$$PV_{PGM_N} = \$3{,}646{,}000{,}000$$

The present value of NexgenSonics according to this model is given by the expression:

$$PV_{FP+PGM_N} = PV_{FP} + PV_{PGM_N} \qquad [4\text{-}46]$$

Substituting,

$$PV_{FP+PGM_N} = 788{,}000{,}000 + 3{,}646{,}000{,}000$$

or

$$PV_{FP+PGM_N} = \$4{,}434{,}000{,}000$$

Finite Growth Model

The finite growth model provides a way of avoiding the notion of perpetual cash flows by limiting the periods of growth to some number NG. If the periods of growth are to be limited, it would seem that given this company's exceptional growth and the industry expectation of double-digit growth for a very long period of time, a double-digit growth rate could be used. After some discussion it was agreed that a

25-year run at 10% growth for a company like NexgenSonics would be a notable achievement but not without precedent. The next topic was: What happens after year 25? After some discussion it was concluded that the perpetual growth model could be used to value the post-finite growth cash flows, but since this was only an exercise they were engaged in, the group didn't think it was necessary to refine the model to that extent.[25]

$$PV_{FGM_N} = \frac{E_{FG}\left[1-\left(\frac{1+g_{FG}}{1+k}\right)^{NG}\right]}{(k-g_{FG})(1+k)^N} \quad [4\text{-}12]$$

Recall that the last $EBITDA_5$ during the forecast period is $390 million and the first post-forecast-period EBITDA is expected to be 10% greater than $EBITDA_5$. Therefore, the value of E_{FG}, the first post-forecast cash flow, is calculated to be:

$$E_{FG} = (390{,}000{,}000)(1.10) = 429{,}000{,}000$$

Substituting $429 million for E_{FG}, 10% for g_{FG}, $NG = 25$ years, $N = 5$ years, and $k = 14\%$ in Equation [4-12] produces a finite growth valuation for the post-forecast-period cash flows.

$$PV_{FGM_N} = \frac{(429{,}000{,}000)\left[1-\left(\frac{1+0.10}{1+0.14}\right)^{25}\right]}{(0.14-0.10)(1+0.14)^5} = \frac{(429{,}000{,}000)\left[1-\left(\frac{(1.10)}{(1.14)}\right)^{25}\right]}{(0.04)(1.14)^5}$$

$$PV_{FGM_N} = \frac{(429{,}000{,}000)[0.5906]}{(0.04)(1.9254)}$$

$$PV_{FGM_N} = \$3{,}290{,}000{,}000$$

NexgenSonics' value using the finite growth model for post-forecast cash flows is given by the expression:

$$PV_{FP+FGM_N} = PV_{FP} + PV_{FGM_N} \quad [4\text{-}48]$$

Substituting,

$$PV_{FP+FGM_N} = 788{,}000{,}000 + 3{,}290{,}000{,}000$$

or

$$PV_{FP+FGM_N} = \$4{,}077{,}000{,}000$$

---

[25] In the real world, the post-finite cash flows would not be ignored and they would be incorporated by doing a multi-stage valuation.

Terminal Value Model

This model is in widespread use because it avoids the need to make estimates of post-forecast cash flow growth rate and periods and relies on terminal value multipliers based on hard data. In Table CS 4-3 the value of the EBITDA multiplier is given as 19.

$$PV_{TVM_N} = \frac{E_{TY}(TVM)}{(1+k)^N} \qquad [4\text{-}15]$$

The terminal value of NexgenSonics is estimated by substituting 390,000,000 for E_{TY},[26] 19 for TVM, $N = 5$ years, and $k = 14\%$ in Equation [4-15]:

$$PV_{TVM_N} = \frac{(390{,}000{,}000)(19)}{(1+0.14)^5} = \frac{(390{,}000{,}000)(19)}{(1.14)^5} = \frac{7{,}410{,}000{,}000}{1.9254}$$

$$PV_{TVM_N} = \$3{,}849{,}000{,}000$$

The expression for NexgenSonics' value using the terminal value model for post-forecast cash flows is:

$$PV_{FP+TVM_N} = PV_{FP} + PV_{TVM_N} \qquad [4\text{-}50]$$

Substituting,

$$PV_{FP+TVM_N} = 788{,}000{,}000 + 3{,}849{,}000{,}000$$

or

$$PV_{FP+TVM_N} = \$4{,}636{,}000{,}000$$

Summary and Discussion of Valuation Results

The various valuations are summarized in Table CS 4-4. The finite growth model has the lowest value, which one might expect because it didn't take into account the post–finite period cash flows that take place after the 25-year period of finite growth and for this reason was not considered a suitable model for the valuation of NexgenSonics. The perpetual growth and terminal value models are in close agreement with the perpetual growth model, being approximately 4.6% lower. The valuation supported by the terminal value model was in their view based on a reasonable terminal value multiplier for a company of this kind. As for the valuation supported by the perpetual growth model, the group was surprised it was as close as it was to the terminal value–based model given the 8% rate they used in perpetuity. They recognized that a case can be made for using a range and averages in a valuation such as this and so they concluded the value of the Company was between \$4.4 and \$4.6 or \$4.5 billion.

[26]Note that in the terminal value model the cash flow in the final year of the forecast period is used, unlike the other models, which use the cash flow in the first year after the forecast period.

TABLE CS 4-4 Summary of NexgenSonics Valuations \$(000,000)'s

Valuation Model Used to Value the Cash Flows of NexgenSonics	Forecast Cash Flow Model	Perpetual Growth Model	Finite Growth Model	Terminal Value Model	Valuation of NexgenSonics
FPeriod + Perpetual Growth CFM	\$788	\$3,646			\$4,434
FPeriod + Finite Growth CFM	\$788		\$3,290		\$4,077
FPeriod + Terminal Value CFM	\$788			\$3,849	\$4,636

Enterprise Value

The Enterprise Value of a company is defined as:

$$EV = B + E_{FCF} \qquad [4\text{-}75]$$

where:

B = The market value of a company's debt, and E_{FCF} = the market value of a company's equity, and E_{FCF} is given by:

$$E_{FCF} = \textit{Present Value of the Company's Future Cash Flows} \qquad [4\text{-}76]$$

The debt level of NexgenSonics is expected to be \$58,000,000 (Table CS 4-3) at the end of the Current Year. Using the valuation based on the average of the perpetual and terminal value models and substituting in Equation [4-75] where B and E_{FCF} are \$58 and \$4,535 million respectively gives the Enterprise Value.

$$EV = \$58{,}000{,}000 + \$4{,}535{,}000{,}000 = \$4{,}593{,}000{,}000$$

or

$$EV = \$4.6 \text{ billion}$$

Discussion of EBITDA Multiplier

If the expressions for the terminal value and perpetual growth models (Equations [4-15] and [4-8]) are set up as equivalents,

$$\frac{E_{TY}(TVM)}{(1+k)^N} = \frac{E_{PG}}{(k - g_{PG})(1+k)^N}$$

and since $E_{TY} = E_{PG} = E$, then

$$\frac{E(TVM)}{(1+k)^N} = \frac{E}{(k - g_{PG})(1+k)^N}$$

Canceling like terms yields an expression that equates TVM with k and g_{PG},

$$TVM = \frac{1}{(k - g_{PG})} \qquad [4\text{-}73]$$

which says: Under these circumstances the expression $1/(k + g_{PG})$ is equivalent to the TVM.

TABLE CS 4-5 Enterprise Value Multiples

	Cur Year	FY 5
Multiple of Revenue	10	4
Multiple of EBITDA	38	12

When valuing NexgenSonics' post-forecast-period cash flows, the EBITDA multiplier used was really the TVM. Recalling $k = 0.14$, $g_{PG} = 0.09$, and substituting in Equation [4-73] estimates the terminal value multiplier to be 20.

$$TVM = \frac{1}{0.14 - 0.09} = \frac{1}{0.05} = 20$$

This is reasonably close to the 19 that was given and used in the case study.

Enterprise Value Multiples

When the group was asked what they thought about the valuation they produced Table CS 4-5 and said: "Revenue and EBITDA multiples of 10 and 38 respectively are big numbers and while they looked much better in FY 5 this assumes that the cash flow and growth forecasts are achieved which is by no means certain. Furthermore, if the forecasts were missed by significant amounts, management could be betting the Company if it proceeded to buy NexgenSonics for $4.5 billion."

The VP of Business Development then asked: "Should Pharos purchase the company?" The response was: "We would recommend against it at a price of $4.5 billion because the valuation depends on very high growth rates over a relatively long period of time."

The VP thanked them for their effort and went away and checked their numbers, compared them to the valuation done by the company's investment banker, and concluded their work product was a reasonable valuation. He then proceeded to meet with the CEO and the company's investment banker. The banker confirmed that in his opinion they would have to pay $4.5 billion and maybe as much as $5 billion if they wanted the company. After a long discussion the CEO decided he could not recommend a transaction to the board that had an uncomfortable level of probability of destroying shareholder value if everything didn't go as planned and instructed the banker to advise the seller that Pharos would not be submitting a bid.

Epilogue The company was sold to a huge conglomerate for approximately $5 billion in cash and stock. It didn't take management long to realize that being part of a giant corporation wasn't for them and they began to sell their shares and exit NexgenSonics shortly after their lockup period expired. Several years later the CEO of the conglomerate was replaced. The new CEO decided that since NexgenSonics wasn't doing well it didn't belong in the portfolio. The company was sold for $2.5 billion to a leveraged buyout group.

CHAPTER FIVE

ROCE and Cash Flow Analytics*

CHAPTER 5 TAKEAWAYS

- "We need to start making some serious money around here to improve the ROCE because anything we do to improve the balance sheet is 'one time,' whereas profits with momentum will continue to grow."
- EBIT/Rev is a definition of Return on Revenue and a measure of how effective the management of a company is in converting Net Revenues into Earnings before Interest and Taxes.
- Rev/CE is a definition of Capital Turnover and a measure of how well the managers of a company manage the capital employed in the company.
- ROCE is a measurement of value created and important because it compares what the management of a company is capable of delivering (Earnings before Interest and Taxes) to what has been invested in the business (Capital Employed). In practice the situation isn't quite that simple, because, in addition to the absolute value of ROCE a management team can deliver, investors are also concerned with the quality of earnings and risk. Therefore, even if a management team maximizes its ROCE, it may not be rewarded by the marketplace unless it has also taken actions to deal with some of the other issues that go into evaluating how good the ROCE really is.
- Simply because a company has a good Return on Capital Employed doesn't mean that investors will be looking to own the company's stock. Often high returns are correlated with high risk and, therefore, management must be able to convince investors that not only are the returns they talk about at investor conferences possible but they are also sustainable.
- Outside investors always have alternatives, so that while having the prospect of an attractive ROCE to offer to investors is necessary for a company to attract capital, it is not necessarily sufficient. It's also important to be attractive compared

(continued)

* The reader may notice minor discrepancies in the calculations in this chapter. When this occurs, it is the result of rounding.

to what else is out there in the same asset class. Furthermore, if the capital available to your asset class from investors familiar with your market segment is insufficient, then you have the additional task of creating interest from investors who don't normally invest in your industry.

- Companies with ROCEs that vary considerably from year to year are not appealing to many investors.
- There always is a group of investors who try to buy on the lows and sell on the highs, but a strategy that depends on market timing is not the first choice of the broad investor population. Most investors are looking for companies with management teams that can deliver predictable and consistent performance and returns over time.
- A company with high returns can be punished by the marketplace if investors feel that the company's earnings are highly susceptible to changes in the economy and the Balance Sheet is relatively inelastic. Everyone understands that if sales go down, Net Income will decrease. Investors like management teams that have not loaded their Balance Sheet with fixed costs so that in difficult times some cost relief can be given to the income statement and working capital can be reduced to pay off debt and thereby keep a relatively respectable ROCE.

INTRODUCTION

In Chapters 1 and 2 the foundation was laid for the notion that the drivers of cash flow are: Net Income (NI), Investment Rate (IR), and Net Income Return on Capital Employed (NiROCE). Furthermore, if the Investment Rate and Net Income Return on Capital Employed are constant from year to year, the Net Income growth rate (NIg) is given by Equation [2-44], which is renumbered here as Equation [5-1]:

$$NIg = (IR)(NiROCE) \qquad [5\text{-}1]$$

Also, groundwork was established for the case when the IR and NiROCE varied from year to year.[1] This, of course, is an important consideration because while many companies may have a fairly stable Net Income Return on Capital Employed over time, they may not have a fixed Investment Rate. However, whether the rates are fixed or variable, in the final analysis all companies depend on them for the creation of value.

All cash flow and, therefore, value starts with revenue. To increase value over time by driving revenue all companies have numerous strategies at their disposal, including:

1. Grow revenue organically or through acquisition.
2. Increase the investment rate and by doing so increase the growth rate of revenue, net income, and ultimately cash flow.
3. Increase profits and, therefore, cash flow from existing assets by making them more productive and efficient.

[1]See section in Chapter 2, "Estimating Growth Rates of Cash Flow after Investing Activities and Net Income."

4. Look for opportunities that are potentially more profitable and use a hurdle rate for new investments that adequately reflects the inherent risk.
5. Work the capital structure and strive to minimize the Weighted Average Cost of Capital, thus making more projects attractive.

Strategies (1) and (2) are dedicated to driving cash flow by increasing revenue. Strategy (3) is focused on improving the throughput of existing resources. Strategy (4) suggests the most profitable investment opportunities that should be pursued and that the hurdle rate used to evaluate new investment opportunities should reflect the risk inherent in the investment. And strategy (5) reminds us that a lower WACC allows management to consider a wider variety of opportunities.

One of the measures used to monitor the results of implementing strategies such as those previously listed is the impact they have on return on capital employed (a key driver of growth, cash flow and, therefore, value). The question that needs to be answered is: How should management work the Income Statement and Balance Sheet in order to maximize returns? This chapter and the one that follows are dedicated to answering this question.

BASIC DRIVERS OF ROCE

It all starts with what drives Net Income and that turns out to be the profit generated by the business. An examination of the Income Statement indicates there are several choices for profit measurement: specifically, EBITDA, EBIT, and EBT. EBITDA excludes depreciation and amortization, which are operational costs. EBT includes interest income and/or expense and these are not operational costs but rather a consequence of capital structure. This leaves EBIT as the best indicator of operational profit. For this reason ROCEs are calculated using tax-affected Earnings before Interest and Taxes.[2]

Earlier the Return on Capital Employed was defined as:

$$ROCE = \frac{NOPAT}{Capital\ Employed} = \frac{NOPAT}{CE} \qquad [5\text{-}2]$$

or since $NOPAT = (EBIT)(1 - TR)$, substituting in equation [5-2] gives an after-tax solution,

$$ROCE = \frac{(EBIT)(1 - TR)}{CE} \qquad [5\text{-}3]$$

where:

$EBIT$ = Earnings before Interest and Taxes, TR = Corporate Tax Rate, and
CE = Capital Employed in the business[3]

---

[2]The notion of NiROCE (a net income–based ROCE) was introduced in Chapter 2 in order to simplify the Envelope Equations. An ROCE using tax-affected EBIT is the definitionally correct measurement and will be used in this and all subsequent chapters. Also, when interest income or expense is zero (or negligible) NiROCE and ROCE are the same.

[3]Capital Employed may vary from one accounting period to the next due to changes in the Balance Sheet. In practice an Average of the Capital Employed during a year is employed when calculating the ROCE.

Equation [5-3] can also be rewritten as:

$$ROCE = \frac{EBIT}{CE}(1 - TR) \qquad [5\text{-}4]$$

Obviously, Equations [5-3] or [5-4] can be used to calculate ROCE under all circumstances. However, other than suggesting that the return on capital employed can be improved by increasing earnings before interest and taxes and decreasing capital employed, they don't provide much guidance on how to go about systematically improving ROCE. Therefore, the objective of the next section is to introduce the components of the Income Statement and Balance Sheet into Equation [5-4] and provide an analytical tool that will enable management to design, implement, and measure a program focused on maximizing the company's ROCE.

Return on Revenue and Capital Turnover

Earlier cases have been made for both Net Revenue (Rev) and Net Income (NI) as being drivers of cash flow and value. Equation [5-4] already incorporates the contribution of net income by virtue of EBIT. However revenue is absent and since all net income and recurring cash flow start with revenue, it needs to be introduced into the Equation. This can be done by dividing the top and bottom of the right-hand side of Equation [5-4] by the Net Revenue (Rev).

$$ROCE = \frac{\left(\frac{EBIT}{Rev}\right)}{\left(\frac{CE}{Rev}\right)}(1 - TR) \qquad [5\text{-}5]$$

Then, multiplying the top and bottom of Equation [5-5] by $\frac{Rev}{CE}$ creates an interesting expression:

$$ROCE = \left(\frac{EBIT}{Rev}\right)\left(\frac{Rev}{CE}\right)(1 - TR) \qquad [5\text{-}6]$$

where:

EBIT/Rev is a definition of Return on Revenue[4] and a measure of how effective the management of a company is in converting Net Revenues into Earnings before Taxes

Rev/CE is a definition of Capital Turnover and a measure of how well the managers of a company manage the capital employed in the company

Equation [5-6] says the ROCE is a function of the relationship between EBIT and Rev (Income Statement driven) and Rev and CE (Balance Sheet driven). Again, while this is helpful it only indicates the ROCE can be impacted by working the Income Statement and Balance Sheet. Fortunately, both of these expressions can be disaggregated into more

[4]Net Income and Operating Income are also used when measuring Return on Revenue.

TABLE 5-1 Mayfair Company Income Statement

Year Ending DD/MM//YYYY $(000)'s	
Revenues (Rev)	100,000
Cost of Goods Sold (COGS)	(40,000)
Gross Margin (GM)	60,000
Operating Expenses (OpExp)	(43,500)
Earnings before Interest, Taxes, Depreciation, and Amortization (EBITDA)	16,500
Depreciation and Amortization (D&A)	(5,000)
Earnings before Interest and Taxes (EBIT)	11,500
Interest Income/(Expense) (NetInt)	0
Earnings before Tax (EBT)	11,500
Taxes Paid (TaxesPaid) @ 40%	(4,600)
Net Income (NI)	6,900

tangible levers for management to work with. The starting point is to expand the EBIT/Rev term into its Income Statement components.

Introducing the Components of the Income Statement into ROCE[5]

To do this the Income Statement presented in Chapter 1 is used, which for convenience is reproduced here as Table 5-1, the Income Statement for the Mayfair Company.

Inspection of Table 5-1 suggests that EBIT can be expressed in terms of the Income Statement components:

$$EBIT = Rev - COGS - OpExp - D\&A \qquad [5\text{-}7]$$

As before, Net Revenue can be introduced into Equation [5-7] by dividing both sides of Equation [5-7] by the variable, Rev.

$$\frac{EBIT}{Rev} = \frac{Rev}{Rev} - \frac{COGS}{Rev} - \frac{OpExp}{Rev} - \frac{D\&A}{Rev} \qquad [5\text{-}8]$$

Simplifying and rearranging,

$$\frac{EBIT}{Rev} = 1 - \left(\frac{COGS}{Rev} + \frac{OpExp}{Rev} + \frac{D\&A}{Rev}\right) \qquad [5\text{-}9]$$

Equation [5-9] tells us the maximum value for EBIT/Rev is 1 and the extent to which it is approached depends on the degree to which the Cost of Goods Sold, Operating Expenses, Depreciation and Amortization, and Interest Expense per unit of Net Revenue can be minimized. Maximizing EBIT/Rev will maximize the contribution that the Return on Sales term makes in Equation [5-6].

---

[5]T. E. Copeland, T. Koller, and J. Murrin, *Valuation: Measuring and Managing the Value of Companies*, 2nd ed. (New York: John Wiley & Sons, 1995), 166, "ROIC Tree."

TABLE 5-2 Mayfair Company Balance Sheet

DD/MM/YYYY $(000)'s			
Current Assets		**Current Liabilities**	
Cash	750	Accounts Payable	2,500
Accounts Receivable	6,250	Taxes Payable	0
Inventory	5,000	Short-Term Debt (STD)	0
Total Current Assets (CA)	12,000	**Total Current Liabilities**	2,500
Fixed Assets (FA)			
At Cost	30,000	**Long-Term Debt (LTD)**	0
Less Depreciation	5,000		
Net Fixed Assets (NetFA)	25,000		
Intangible Assets (IA)		**Shareholders' Equity (TSHE)**	
Goodwill and Other Int Assets	0	Paid-in Capital	50,000
Less Amortization	0	Retained Earnings	(15,500)
Net Intangible Assets (NetIA)	0	**Total Shareholders' Equity**	34,500
Total Assets	37,000	**Total Liabilities**	37,000

Introducing the Components of the Balance Sheet into ROCE

Similarly the term Rev/CE (Capital Turnover) can be disaggregated into its Balance Sheet components. Table 5-2, the Balance Sheet of the Mayfair Company, is helpful in this regard.

Table 5-2 defines Total Liabilities and Shareholders' Equity as:

$$Total\ Liabilities + Total\ Shareholders'\ Equity = CL + LTD + TSHE \qquad [5\text{-}10]$$

where:

CL = Current Liabilities, LTD = Long-Term Debt, $TSHE$ = Total Shareholders' Equity

Now, Current Liabilities (CL) include Short-Term Debt (STD). The goal is to ultimately express Equation [5-10] with a Capital Employed (CE) term. Since STD is part of CE, to do so, STD needs to be subtracted from Current Liabilities and included with Long-Term Debt (LTD). This can be done by adding and subtracting STD from the right-hand side of Equation [5-10].

$$Total\ Liabilities + Total\ Shareholders'\ Equity = CL + LTD + TSHE - STD + STD \qquad [5\text{-}11]$$

Rearranging,

$$Total\ Liabilities + Total\ Shareholders'\ Equity = (CL - STD) + (STD + LTD) + TSHE \qquad [5\text{-}12]$$

In Chapter 1, STD + LTD was designated as Interest Bearing Debt (IBD) and IBD + TSHE as CE,[6] the Capital Employed in the business. Substituting, Equations [5-11] and [5-12] become:

$$\textit{Total Liabilities} + \textit{Total Shareholders' Equity} = (CL - STD) + IBD + TSHE \quad [5\text{-}13]$$

$$\textit{Total Liabilities} + \textit{Total Shareholders' Equity} = (CL - STD) + CE \quad [5\text{-}14]$$

Again, by referring to Table 5-2 it can be seen that:

$$\textit{Total Assets} = CA + NetFA + NetIA \quad [5\text{-}15]$$

where:

CA = Current Assets, $NetFA$ = Net Fixed Assets, $NetIA$ = Net Intangible Assets

$$\textit{Total Assets} = \textit{Total Liabilities} + \textit{Total Shareholders' Equity}$$

Now, since Equation [5-14] equals Equation [5-15] and

$$CA + NetFA + NetIA = (CL - STD) + CE \quad [5\text{-}16]$$

Rearranging,

$$CE = CA - (CL - STD) + NetFA + NetIA \quad [5\text{-}17]$$

Simplifying,

$$CE = (CA - CL + STD) + NetFA + NetIA \quad [5\text{-}18]$$

Now Working Capital is defined as (CA – CL). However, if a substitution for (CA – CL) is made, it's difficult to define what the term (WC + STD) would mean.[7] This problem can be solved with the assistance of Table 5-2, where it can be seen that Current Liabilities consists of Accounts Payable (AP), Taxes Payable (TP), and STD, which can be expressed as:

$$CL = AP + TP + STD \quad [5\text{-}19]$$

Substituting for "CL" (as defined by Equation [5-19]), the expression (CA – CL + STD) in Equation [5-18] becomes:

$$[CA - (AP + TP + STD) + STD]$$

Simplifying,

$$(CA - AP - TP - STD + STD)$$

The STD terms cancel, leaving (CA – AP – TP), which is essentially working capital excluding STD. Hence this expression can be defined as WC_{XSTD}, the Working Capital in a business excluding STD.

---

[6]See the section in Chapter 1, "Capital Employed."

[7]Recall that this problem is created by combining STD with LTD to get Interest Bearing Debt (IBD).

Substituting in Equation [5-18], it becomes

$$CE = WC_{XSTD} + NetFA + NetIA \qquad [5\text{-}20]$$

Once again, Net Revenues can be introduced by dividing both sides of Equation [5-20] by Rev.

$$\frac{CE}{Rev} = \frac{WC_{XSTD} + NetFA + NetIA}{Rev} \qquad [5\text{-}21]$$

Inverting,

$$\frac{Rev}{CE} = \frac{Rev}{WC_{XSTD} + NetFA + NetIA} \qquad [5\text{-}22]$$

Net Revenues can be introduced into each of the terms in the denominator of Equation [5-22] by dividing the top and bottom of the right-hand side of Equation [5-22] by the term Rev.

$$\frac{Rev}{CE} = \frac{\frac{Rev}{Rev}}{\left(\frac{WC_{XSTD}}{Rev} + \frac{NetFA}{Rev} + \frac{NetIA}{Rev}\right)} \qquad [5\text{-}23]$$

Simplifying,

$$\frac{Rev}{CE} = \frac{1}{\left(\frac{WC_{XSTD}}{Rev} + \frac{NetFA}{Rev} + \frac{NetIA}{Rev}\right)} \qquad [5\text{-}24]$$

Equation [5-24] states that minimizing Working Capital, Net Fixed Assets, and Net Intangible Assets per unit of Net Revenues maximizes the contribution the Capital Turnover Rev/CE makes in Equation [5-6] to increase the Return on Capital Employed.

The ROCE Driver Equation

Now that ROCE has been disaggregated into its Income Statement and Balance Sheet components, a general expression that brings all of these variables together is obtained by substituting the results of Equations [5-9] and [5-24] into Equation [5-6].

$$\frac{EBIT}{Rev} = 1 - \left(\frac{COGS}{Rev} + \frac{OpExp}{Rev} + \frac{D\&A}{Rev}\right) \qquad [5\text{-}9]$$

$$ROCE = \left(\frac{EBIT}{Rev}\right)\left(\frac{Rev}{CE}\right)(1 - TR) \qquad [5\text{-}6]$$

$$ROCE = \left[1 - \left(\frac{COGS}{Rev} + \frac{OpExp}{Rev} + \frac{D\&A}{Rev}\right)\right]\left[\frac{1}{\left(\frac{WC_{XSTD}}{Rev} + \frac{NetFA}{Rev} + \frac{NetIA}{Rev}\right)}\right](1 - TR) \qquad [5\text{-}25]$$

Simplifying,

$$ROCE = \left\{ \frac{\left[1 - \left(\frac{COGS}{Rev} + \frac{OpExp}{Rev} + \frac{D\&A}{Rev}\right)\right]}{\left(\frac{WC_{XSTD}}{Rev} + \frac{NetFA}{Rev} + \frac{NetIA}{Rev}\right)} \right\}(1 - TR) \qquad [5\text{-}26]$$

Equation [5-26] is very powerful. It says that *ROCE* is a function of key Income Statement variables and the corporate tax rate and an inverse function of key Balance Sheet variables. Furthermore, it specifically identifies all of the financial statement accounts that impact the Return on Capital Employed and arranges them so that the numerator and denominator are dedicated to the Income Statement and Balance Sheet respectively.

At this point it's worthwhile to summarize.

- If the only objective is to calculate a company's ROCE, it's simply done by applying Equation [5-4].
- Other than indicating that ROCE can be improved by increasing EBIT and decreasing CE, Equation [5-4] doesn't provide much insight into how to systematically increase ROCE.
- Another shortcoming of Equation [5-4] is that it doesn't incorporate net revenues, which are, of course, the ultimate driver of EBIT and cash flow.
- Equation [5-26] identifies the key Income Statement and Balance Sheet variables that drive ROCE and provides an opportunity to readily measure the impact that a change in all or any variables will have on ROCE.
- Equation [5-26] also provides management with an analytical tool to design and launch a program to increase ROCE in an organized and efficient way.

EXAMPLE 5-1: CALCULATING MAYFAIR COMPANY'S RETURN ON CAPITAL EMPLOYED

The Income Statement and Balance Sheet for the Mayfair Company, manufacturer of fine women's apparel, are shown in Tables 5-1 and 5-2 respectively. From this data, the ROCE will be calculated by first using the definitional equations for ROCE and then verifying the result by applying the ROCE Driver Equation.

Equation [5-4] defines the after-tax Return on Capital Employed as:

$$ROCE = \frac{EBIT}{CE}(1 - TR) \qquad [5\text{-}4]$$

EBIT is readily obtained from Table 5-1, where $EBIT = \$11{,}500{,}000$. Earlier, Capital Employed was defined as

$$CE = IBD + TSHE = (STD + LTD) + THSE \qquad [1\text{-}32]\ [1\text{-}33]$$

According to Mayfair's Balance Sheet (Table 5-2) the Mayfair Company doesn't have any Short-Term or Long-Term Debt. The Total Shareholders' Equity is $34,500,000. Therefore, the Capital Employed is:

$$CE = IBD + TSHE = (STD + LTD) + TSHE = (0 + 0) + 34{,}500{,}000$$
$$= \$34{,}500{,}000$$

The Company is paying taxes and has a Tax Rate (TR) of 40%; then substituting in Equation [5-4] gives the Return on Capital Employed.

$$ROCE = \frac{EBIT}{CE}(1 - TR) = \left(\frac{11{,}500{,}000}{34{,}500{,}000}\right)(1 - 0.40)$$
$$= (0.3333)(0.60) = 0.20$$
$$ROCE = 20\%$$

The ROCE can also be calculated by using the ROCE Driver Equation, Equation [5-26].

$$ROCE = \left\{ \frac{\left[1 - \left(\frac{COGS}{Rev} + \frac{OpExp}{Rev} + \frac{D\&A}{Rev}\right)\right]}{\left(\frac{WC_{XSTD}}{Rev} + \frac{NetFA}{Rev} + \frac{NetIA}{Rev}\right)} \right\}(1 - TR) \qquad [5\text{-}26]$$

The data in Table 5-3 was obtained from Tables 5-1 and 5-2, the Mayfair Income Statement and Balance Sheet respectively.

Tables 5-4 and 5-5 are obtained by dividing each of the statistics in Table 5-3 by Net Revenues.

TABLE 5-3 Mayfair Company Income Statement and Balance Sheet Statistics $(000)'s and %

Net Revenues	100,000
Cost of Goods Sold (COGS)	40,000
Operating Expenses (OpExp)	43,500
Depreciation and Amortization (D&A)	5,000
Net Interest (NetInt)	0
Tax Rate (TR)	40%
Working Capital Excluding STD (WC_{XSTD})	9,500
Net Fixed Assets (NetFA)	25,000
Net Intangible Assets (NetIA)	0

TABLE 5-4 Mayfair Income Statement Ratios

COGS/Rev	0.400
OpExp/Rev	0.435
D&A/Rev	0.050

TABLE 5-5 Mayfair Balance Sheet Ratios

WC_{XSTD}/Rev	0.095
NetFA/Rev	0.250
NetIA/Rev	0.000

Substituting in the ROCE Driver Equation [5-26] and solving, Mayfair's ROCE is obtained.

$$ROCE = \left\{ \frac{\left[1 - \left(\frac{COGS}{Rev} + \frac{OpExp}{Rev} + \frac{D\&A}{Rev} \right)\right]}{\left(\frac{WC_{XSTD}}{Rev} + \frac{NetFA}{Rev} + \frac{NetIA}{Rev} \right)} \right\} (1 - TR) \qquad [5\text{-}26]$$

$$ROCE = \left\{ \frac{[1-(0.40+0.435+0.05)]}{(0.095+0.25+0)} \right\} (0.60) = \left[\frac{(1-0.885)}{0.345} \right] (0.60) = 0.20$$

$$ROCE = 20\%$$

which, of course, agrees with the ROCE obtained using Equation [5-4].

EXAMPLE 5-2: ACHIEVING A TARGETED ROCE FOR THE RICHMOND COMPANY

The Richmond Company, a manufacturer of specialty hardware, has the Income Statement and Balance Sheet shown in Tables 5-6 and 5-7. The company has been recently taken over by a buyout group that has put in place its own management team.

TABLE 5-6 Richmond Company Income Statement

Year Ending DD/MM/YYYY $(000)'s		
Net Revenues		90,000
Cost of Goods Sold (COGS)		(40,000)
Gross Margin (GM)		50,000
Operating Expenses (OpExp)		(29,000)
Earnings before Interest, Taxes, Depreciation, and Amortization (EBITDA)		21,000
Depreciation and Amortization (D&A)		(4,000)
Earnings before Interest and Taxes (EBIT)		17,000
Interest Income/Expense (Int)		0
Earnings before Tax (EBT)		17,000
Taxes Paid (TaxesPaid) @	40%	(6,800)
Net Income (NI)		10,200

TABLE 5-7 Richmond Company Balance Sheet

DD/MM/YYYY $(000)'s			
Current Assets		**Current Liabilities**	
Cash	1,000	Accounts Payable	6,000
Accounts Receivable	14,000	Taxes Payable	0
Inventory	10,000	Short-Term Debt	0
Total Current Assets	25,000	**Total Current Liabilities**	6,000
Fixed Assets			
At Cost	35,000	**Long-Term Debt**	0
Less Depreciation	10,000		
Net Fixed Assets	25,000		
Intangible Assets		**Shareholders' Equity**	
Goodwill and Other Int Assets	0	Paid-in Capital	34,000
Less Amortization	0	Retained Earnings	10,000
Net Intangible Assets	0	**Total Shareholders' Equity**	44,000
Total Assets	50,000	**Total Liabilities**	50,000

The board of directors approved an incentive plan recommended by the compensation committee that pays a bonus based on financial performance with Return on Capital Employed being the key component. The target for ROCE was 30%, which was to be achieved within three years.

Job #1 as far as the CEO is concerned is to get a plan in place to achieve the targeted ROCE and by doing so increase the value of the Richmond Company and earn a bonus for the management team. The value issue is important because all members of management have an equity interest. The CEO is aware of the ROCE Driver model and has assigned the task of breaking the ROCE into its components to the CFO.

Using the ROCE Driver Equation [5-26] and Table 5-6 as a starting point, the CFO began by calculating Income Statement–related drivers.

$$ROCE = \left\{ \frac{\left[1 - \left(\frac{COGS}{NetRev} + \frac{OpExp}{NetRev} + \frac{D\&A}{NetRev}\right)\right]}{\left(\frac{WC_{XSTD}}{NetRev} + \frac{NetFA}{NetRev} + \frac{NetIA}{NetRev}\right)} \right\}(1 - TR) \qquad [5\text{-}26]$$

$$COGS/NetRev = \left(\frac{40,000,000}{90,000,000}\right)(100) = 44.4\%$$

$$OpExp/NetRev = \left(\frac{29,000,000}{90,000,000}\right)(100) = 32.2\%$$

$$D\&A/NetRev = \left(\frac{4,000,000}{90,000,000}\right)(100) = 4.44\%$$

TABLE 5-8 Richmond Income Statement Ratios

COGS/Rev	44.4%
OpExp/Rev	32.2%
D&A/Rev	4.4%

TABLE 5-9 Richmond Balance Sheet Ratios

WC_{XSTD}/Rev	21.1%
NetFA/Rev	27.8%
NetIA/Rev	0.0%

Next, by referring to Table 5-7, he proceeded to do the same for the Balance Sheet.

$$WC_{XSTD}/NetRev = \left(\frac{(25{,}000{,}000 - 6{,}000{,}000)}{90{,}000{,}000}\right)(100) = 21.1\%$$

$$NetFA/NetRev = \left(\frac{25{,}000{,}000}{90{,}000{,}000}\right)(100) = 27.8\%$$

$$OthA/NetRev = \left(\frac{0}{90{,}000{,}000}\right)(100) = 0\%$$

Using the *ROCE* Drivers summarized in Tables 5-8 and 5-9 and Equation [5-26], the CFO calculated the ROCE using the ROCE Driver model and then checked the result using the definitional equation for Return on Capital Employed, Equation [5-4],

$$ROCE = \left\{\frac{\left[1 - \left(\frac{COGS}{NetRev} + \frac{OpExp}{NetRev} + \frac{D\&A}{NetRev}\right)\right]}{\left(\frac{WC_{XSTD}}{NetRev} + \frac{NetFA}{NetRev} + \frac{NetIA}{NetRev}\right)}\right\}(1 - TR) \qquad [5\text{-}26]$$

$$ROCE = \left\{\frac{[1 - (0.444 + 0.322 + 0.0444)]}{(0.211 + 0.278 + 0)}\right\}(1 - .40) = \left(\frac{0.1889}{0.4889}\right)(0.60) = 0.2318$$

$$ROCE = 23.2\%$$

which is identical to the value obtained by using the definitional Equation[5-4].

$$ROCE = \frac{EBIT}{CE}(1 - TR) \qquad [5\text{-}4]$$

$$ROCE = \left(\frac{17{,}000{,}000}{44{,}000{,}000}\right)(1 - 0.40) = (0.3864)(0.60) = 0.2318$$ [8]

$$ROCE = 23.2\%$$

[8]The slight difference is due to rounding errors.

The data was summarized in an e-mail to the management team and a meeting was scheduled to discuss the results. During the course of the meeting the various functional managers gave their views on what could be done in their area of responsibility to cut costs and squeeze cash out of the Balance Sheet. Cost-reduction projects with significant savings were identified by manufacturing and R&D. Overhead and IT spending were examined closely and a long list of savings were identified and prioritized. Sales and Marketing cost-reduction discussions ended in a dilemma because no one wanted to see cuts that would impact revenue. This prompted a discussion on the question of revenue, the outcome of which was that it was only profitable revenue that should be protected and before unprofitable revenue was abandoned every effort should be made to increase price or reduce cost.

Finally, the VP of Marketing and Sales spoke up and stated that "between us we are responsible for millions of dollars of spending and there have to be ways to trim costs without endangering the Revenue line—we will find them." He went on to say, "When it comes to unprofitable revenue every effort will be made to address the cost and pricing issues but that will take time and our immediate focus must be on expense reduction."

Depreciation was an easy target because it could be brought down over time with careful attention to the capital spending budget (reduces D&A/Rev over time). As for the Balance Sheet, the CFO, who had liberated cash from many balance sheets during his career, had explained how he would form teams to collect cash (reduces WC/Rev), work with production on reducing inventory (reduces WC/Rev), and deal with reducing the net fixed assets (reduces NetFA/Rev).

Ultimately the goals tabulated in Tables 5-10 and 5-11 were agreed and the CFO proceeded to calculate the ROCE that would be achieved if the Income Statement and Balance Sheet goals were met.

$$ROCE = \left\{ \frac{\left[1 - \left(\frac{COGS}{NetRev} + \frac{OpExp}{NetRev} + \frac{D\&A}{NetRev}\right)\right]}{\left(\frac{WC_{XSTD}}{NetRev} + \frac{NetFA}{NetRev} + \frac{NetIA}{NetRev}\right)} \right\}(1 - TR) \tag{5-26}$$

$$ROCE = \left\{ \frac{[1-(0.429+0.312+0.0400)]}{(0.178+0.263+0)} \right\}(1-0.40) = \left(\frac{0.2190}{0.4410}\right)(0.60) = 0.2980$$

$$ROCE = 29.8\%$$

TABLE 5-10 Richmond Income Statement Goals

COGS/Rev	42.9%
OpExp/Rev	31.2%
D&A/Rev	4.0%

TABLE 5-11 Richmond Company Balance Sheet Goals

WC_{XSTD}/Rev	17.8%
NetFA/Rev	26.3%
NetIA/Rev	0.0%

Satisfied that a 30% ROCE was achievable within a three-year period, the management team proceeded to develop action plans to achieve the targeted goals.

SOME PRACTICAL ASPECTS OF MANAGING RETURN ON CAPITAL EMPLOYED

Managing the Return on Capital Employed is not only about numbers. In addition to performance, management teams of public companies are concerned with how the company is perceived by investors. In general, the management of private companies caters to a much smaller investor group and is focused on meeting the expectations of their investors. Should a private company have public debt, they also have to deal with some of the same issues that face public companies. The following are some practical aspects of managing ROCE as far as the market is concerned.

Investor Concerns

Earlier it was stated that ROCE is a measurement of value created and important because it compared what the management of a company is capable of delivering (Earnings before Interest and Taxes) to what has been invested in the business (Capital Employed). In practice the situation isn't quite that simple, because, in addition to the absolute value of ROCE a management team can deliver, investors are also concerned with the quality of earnings and risk. Therefore, even if a management team maximizes its ROCE, it may not be rewarded by the marketplace unless it has also taken actions to deal with some of the other issues that go into evaluating how good the ROCE really is.

Return versus Risk

Simply because a company has a good Return on Capital Employed doesn't mean that investors will be looking to own the company's stock. Often high returns are correlated with high risk and, therefore, management must be able to convince investors that not only are the returns they talk about at investor conferences possible but they are also sustainable.

Alternatives

Outside investors always have alternatives, so that while having the prospect of an attractive return to offer to investors is necessary for a company to attract capital, it is not necessarily sufficient. It's also important to be attractive compared to what else is out there in the same asset class. Furthermore, if the capital available to your asset class from investors familiar with your market segment is insufficient, then you have the additional task of creating interest from investors who don't normally invest in your industry.

Predictability and Consistency of Returns

Companies with ROCEs that vary considerably from year to year are not appealing to most investors. There always is a group of investors who try to buy on the lows and sell on the highs, but a strategy that depends on market timing is not the first choice of the broad investor population. Most investors are looking for companies with management teams that can deliver predictable and consistent performance and returns over time.

Fixed and Variable Costs

A company with high returns can be punished by the marketplace if investors feel that the company's earnings are highly susceptible to changes in the economy and the Balance Sheet is relatively inelastic and in this sense is "fixed"; hence making it very difficult to convert assets to cash during slowdowns in the economy. Everyone understands that if sales go down, Earnings before Interest and Taxes will decrease. What investors like are management teams that have not loaded their balance sheet with fixed costs so that in difficult times some cost relief can be given to the Income Statement and working capital can be reduced to pay off debt and thereby keep a relatively respectable ROCE.

In the following chapters strategies and best practices that will be helpful to management teams trying to maximize their company's ROCE will be discussed. The thrust of the effort will continue to be centered on the Drivers of ROCE and Cash Flow. In addition and where appropriate, material will be introduced that should be helpful to managers trying to develop strategies that deal with risk and return, predictability, and consistency of earnings and fixed and variable costs.

CASE STUDY: PHAROS CORPORATION—THE EARLY DAYS

After several days of meetings, much dialog, and learning, the new CEO and CFO of Pharos Corporation sat down to collect their thoughts on the Company that had been acquired prior to their arrival and whose performance was not satisfactory and had resulted in the dismissal of the president. A search for a new president was under way and it would take a couple of months to find the right person. The CEO couldn't leave the company without leadership, so he decided to step in and lead an initiative to improve the company's performance. The Company was profitable but had a bloated Balance Sheet, excess capacity, and plenty of spending everywhere. The CFO prepared the summary Balance Sheet and Income Statements shown in Tables CS 5-1 and CS 5-2, which was his best estimate of how the current year would turn out.

TABLE CS 5-1 Acquired Company Summary Balance Sheet $(000)'s

Current Assets	15,000	Current Liabilities$_{XSTD}$	2,000
Net Fixed Assets	34,000	Short-Term Debt	2,000
Net Intang Assets	4,000	Long-Term Debt	10,000
		Total SH Equity	39,000
Total Assets	53,000	Tot Liab + TSHE	53,000

TABLE CS 5-2 Acquired Company Summary Income Statement $(000)'s

Net Revenues (NetRev)	70,000	100.0%
Cost of Goods Sold (COGS)	(37,000)	–52.9%
Gross Margin (GM)	33,000	47.1%
Operating Expenses (OpExp)	(26,000)	–37.1%
EBITDA	7,000	10.0%
Depreciation and Amortization (D&A)	(3,500)	–5.0%
EBIT	3,500	5.0%
Interest Income (Expense)	(1,200)	–1.7%
EBT	2,300	3.3%
Taxes @ 40.0%	(920)	–1.3%
Net Income (NI)	1,380	2.0%

The Current ROCE

After receiving this data and looking for a place to start, the first thing the CEO did was to estimate the Company's ROCE by using data from Tables CS 5-1 and CS 5-2 and Equation [5-4].

$$ROCE = \frac{EBIT}{CE}(1 - TR) \qquad [5\text{-}4]$$

where:

$$CE = STD + LTD + TSHE$$

Substituting,

$$ROCE = \left(\frac{3{,}500}{(2{,}000 + 10{,}000 + 39{,}000)}\right)(1 - 0.4000) = \left(\frac{3{,}500}{51{,}000}\right)(0.6000) = 0.0412$$

$$ROCE = 4.12\%$$

An ROCE of 4.12%? A Company like this should produce something closer to 20–25%. At first he didn't believe it and decided to have the CFO check this result by using an analytical model that focused on the drivers of ROCE and Cash Flow and thereby gain some insight into the root causes of the problem. From Tables CS 5-1 and CS 5-2 the data shown in Table CS 5-3[9] was obtained.

[9] WC_{XSTD} and CL_{XSTD} are Working Capital excluding Short-Term Debt and Current Liabilities excluding Short-Term Debt, respectively. The reasoning is laid out in the theory presented earlier in this chapter.

TABLE CS 5-3 Acquired Company Data Obtained from Tables 5-1 and 5-2 $(000)'s

Revenue	70,000	Current Assets	15,000
Cost of Goods Sold	37,000	Current Liabilities Excluding STD	2,000
Operating Expenses	26,000	Short-Term Debt	2,000
Depreciation and Amortization	3,500	Working Capital Excluding STD	13,000
Earnings before Interest and Taxes	3,500	Net Fixed Assets	34,000
		Net Intangible Assets	4,000

With this data the CFO then prepared the Income Statement and Balance Sheet ratios as shown in Tables CS 5-4 and CS 5-5 and then substituted the ratios in Equation [5-26], which formed the basis of the analytical model he planned to use.

$$ROCE = \left\{ \frac{\left[1 - \left(\frac{COGS}{Rev} + \frac{OpExp}{Rev} + \frac{D\&A}{Rev}\right)\right]}{\left(\frac{WC_{XSTD}}{Rev} + \frac{NetFA}{Rev} + \frac{NetIA}{Rev}\right)} \right\}(1 - TR) \qquad [5\text{-}26]$$

Substituting into Equation [5-26] data from the tables, he verified his estimate of the current ROCE.

$$ROCE = \left\{ \frac{\left[1 - \left(\frac{COGS}{Rev} + \frac{OpExp}{Rev} + \frac{D\&A}{Rev}\right)\right]}{\left(\frac{WC_{XSTD}}{Rev} + \frac{NetFA}{Rev} + \frac{NetIA}{Rev}\right)} \right\}(1 - TR)$$

$$ROCE = \left\{ \frac{\left[1 - (0.5286 + 0.3714 + 0.0500)\right]}{(0.1857 + 0.4857 + 0.0571)} \right\}(1 - 0.4000)$$

$$ROCE = \left(\frac{0.0500}{0.7285}\right)(0.6000) = 0.0412$$

$$ROCE = 4.12\%$$

And then just to be sure he had his equation right he decided to calculate EBIT. To do this he rearranged Equation [5-4] into Equation [5-27], substituted STD + LTD + TSHE for the Capital Employed, and then proceeded to calculate the EBIT/Revenue ratio.

$$ROCE = \frac{EBIT}{CE}(1 - TR) \qquad [5\text{-}4]$$

TABLE CS 5-4 Current Year Income Statement Ratios

COGS/Rev	52.86%
OpExp/Rev	37.14%
D&A/Rev	5.00%

TABLE CS 5-5 Current Year Balance Sheet Ratios

WC_{XSTD}/Rev	18.57%
NetFA/Rev	48.57%
NetIA/Rev	5.71%

$$EBIT = \frac{(ROCE)(CE)}{(1 - TR)} \quad [5\text{-}27]$$

$$EBIT = \frac{(ROCE)(STD + LTD + TSHE)}{(1 - TR)}$$

$$EBIT = \frac{(0.0412)(2{,}000{,}000 + 10{,}000{,}000 + 39{,}000{,}000)}{(1 - .4000)}$$

$$EBIT = \frac{(0.0412)(51{,}000{,}000)}{0.6000} = \$3{,}500{,}000$$

$$EBIT/Rev = \frac{3{,}500{,}000}{70{,}000{,}000} = .0500 = 5.00\%$$

Summary of the Current Status of the Acquired Company

With this data in hand,[10] the CEO settled down and together with the CFO summarized what they learned from their study of the numbers, tours of the Company's facilities, and meetings with all of the function heads.

- **Revenue:** The Company's product line and markets were strong and well positioned for double-digit growth for the next several years. However, given the low level of profitability the product lines probably needed some culling. The CEO decided he could live with slightly lower growth if that's what it took to get the profit to a respectable level.
- **Cost of Goods Sold:** There were lots of production inefficiencies, and while this was a problem it also presented significant opportunities for cost reduction.
- **Operating Expenses:** At 37.1% they seemed to be very high—at least as judged by experience with companies like this. Past experience indicated that something closer to 32% would be more appropriate for this company.
- **Depreciation and Amortization:** A level of 5% seems excessive and this is borne out by data that indicates 3–4% of Revenue is more appropriate for companies in this industry. Going forward, investments need to be carefully controlled and scrutinized until the company reaches this range. Also, inefficient equipment and excess capacity need to be addressed.
- **Interest:** There was no need for the Company to borrow more money. In fact there is ample opportunity to squeeze cash out of the Balance Sheet and repay debt. Given the uncertainty of how quickly action plans can be put together, scrutinized, and implemented, it was decided it would be prudent to cap the debt at the existing level and let the cash build as the plan takes effect and repay the outstanding loans at some point in the future but not complicate matters by worrying about what to do with excess cash for the purpose of this exercise.[11]

---

[10] See Table 5-2.

[11] In fact it is desirable to have leverage on the Balance Sheet since it lowers the weighted average cost of capital.

- **Working Capital:** Again, based on experience, 18.6% of sales seems to be very high. Accounts Receivable and Inventory action plans directed at bringing the Receivables Days Outstanding down and Inventory Turns up should reduce the Working Capital Excluding STD to Revenue ratio to something in the range of 10–12%. In order to do this, the working capital excluding short-term debt would be set at 18.6% for the current year and systematically reduced to approximately 12% during the forecast years.
- **Net Fixed Assets:** The Company's manufacturing facility was vertically integrated and consisted of parts manufacturing, assembly, and test. None of the plant and equipment was fully utilized. Some was quite old. Production needed to be rationalized and future investments would be carefully vetted as part of an effort to reduce Depreciation over time.
- **Net Intangible Assets:** This asset class consists of goodwill and amortizable assets such as patents, non-competes, and so forth, which would decrease in value as the periodic amortization was run through the income statement. However, given the magnitude of other opportunities, this was assigned a low priority. Therefore, as far as the ROCE improvement plan being contemplated was concerned, this asset class was assumed to be flat at $4,000,000.
- **Tax Rate:** The Company was paying the maximum tax rate and not taking advantage of tax-avoidance opportunities. With expert assistance it was concluded that the average tax rate could be reduced at least a couple of percentage points.

Next, the CEO began to think about what performance level he should target. His experience told him that reasonable targets for EBIT/Rev and ROCE would be at least 15–20% and 20–25% respectively. However, he didn't want to appear to be arbitrary when he announced the goals to the management team and so he consulted the data provided by the company's industry association. The data indicated that the median EBIT/Rev and ROCE for peer companies was 16.2% and 22.1% respectively.

With this information in hand he prepared performance targets for each of the next three years as portrayed in Table CS 5-6. The next step was to call a special meeting of

TABLE CS 5-6 Performance Targets Set for Acquired Company $(000)'s and %

	Current	C + 1	C + 2	C + 3
NetRev (000)	70,000	80,000	95,000	110,000
COGS/NetRev	52.9%	51.5%	49.0%	48.0%
OpExp/NetRev	37.1%	35.0%	33.0%	32.0%
D&A/NetRev	5.0%	4.4%	3.7%	3.2%
Int/NetRev	1.7%	1.5%	1.3%	1.1%
WC_{XSTD}/NetRev	18.6%	16.3%	13.7%	11.8%
NetFA/NetRev	48.6%	42.5%	35.8%	30.9%
NetIA/NetRev	5.7%	5.0%	4.2%	3.6%
Tax Rate	40.0%	39.0%	38.0%	38.0%

the management team at which he and the CFO explained the reasoning behind the performance targets set and to solicit comments.

Presentation and Discussion of Performance Targets

The Vice President of Manufacturing was the first to speak and stated that the CEO's assumptions about production were indeed reasonable and that the Cost of Goods Sold could be reduced to meet the targets with some assistance from R&D. The new CEO was troubled by this and asked, "If these targets are achievable, presumably they have been possible all along. So, how will you and your team be able to do what you haven't managed to do up to now?"

The VP replied, "Before you came along our focus was on volume. The theory was that when the volume got high enough the margins would follow. According to your projections, our growth is going to be less than what is outlined in our current business plan. We have more than ample capacity to handle the growth indicated by your plan and so I feel that I can now devote my manufacturing engineering resources to cost reduction."

The CEO indicated that he was pleased to hear that much could be done and then proceeded to ask why the business was so asset intensive. The VP replied, "We weren't only focused on volume. The previous president was very much committed to vertical integration because it was felt by doing so we had better control of our processes, cost, and quality."

"And your view was what?" the CEO asked.

"I had my misgivings, but after numerous discussions, I decided that my choices were: insubordination, which would ultimately result in dismissal; resign; or get on board with the strategy. I chose to try and make it work."

"And now?"

The VP replied, "With your support we can focus on what we do best, outsource what is better and cheaper done by others, and reduce the asset intensiveness of our business."

"I take it, then, you are completely OK with the assumptions for Net Fixed Assets (New additions equal D&A) and that you and your team can meet the targets set at the Cost of Goods Sold line in the Income Statement?"

The answer was a brief *yes!*

The CEO countered, "That was a very quick response. How can you be so sure?"

The VP of Manufacturing replied that his staff had done many cost-reduction studies over the years but until now volume was the focus, so little came of them. "My team and I will commit to the goals you and the CFO have laid out."

The next area discussed was Operating Expenses. The VP of Research and Development stated that about 75% of the spending in his area is discretionary and that while he didn't recommend a cut he acknowledged that R&D spending could be easily reduced by several percentage points if that was deemed to be prudent. Furthermore, he agreed with the VP of Manufacturing regarding the opportunities for cost reduction driven by some redesign and was in favor of diverting effort but it would require that some of the resources be taken away from new product development, which as far as he was concerned, if done surgically, could be managed.

The VP of Sales and Marketing said that he didn't like the idea of cutting R&D spending on new products because the Company had a lot of good ideas that should be developed and brought to market sooner rather than later but he wasn't opposed to diverting a modest amount of the department's resources to cost reduction. Furthermore, if it was necessary to reduce the Sales and Marketing Expenses, he would try to make it work but thought it would place the revenue targets at risk.

At this point the CEO spoke up and said: "We can't live with a plan that places the proposed revenue targets at risk. Furthermore, I'm not talking about cutting operating expenses per se. I'm proposing we cut the rate of growth. Please take a look at this [Table CS 5-7]."

The VP of Sales and Marketing spent a few minutes studying the table and then said, "Look, we pride ourselves on making our numbers in my group and before I commit I would like to study the proposed changes more closely."

"Please do so and come to our next meeting with the facts as you see them," said the CEO.

The CFO of the Company spoke next. He said that based on the CEO's projections, he had run pro-forma cash flows for the Company and concluded that the Int/NetRev ratios assumed for Years C+2 and C+3 were very conservative, because the debt on the Company's Balance Sheet could be paid off by the end of Year C+2 or earlier. "As for the tax rate, we consulted a tax expert and I found his recommendations very compelling as did you. So after thinking about this further I'm very comfortable. In fact we may be able to do a little better."

At this point the CEO said, "The CFO's proposal is okay with me" and acknowledged what had been said about the debt. He then went on to clarify, "When the targets were set the CFO and I knew the company would be swimming in cash if the targets were met. However, given that we thought it would take a couple of meetings to reach agreement we didn't see any point in running pro-forma Balance Sheets. Furthermore, this company's problems won't be solved by paying off the debt. We need to start making some serious money around here to improve the ROCE because anything we do to improve the balance sheet is 'one time,' whereas solid profits have momentum and will continue to grow." (In other words, the CEO wants the emphasis on improving ROCE to be on focused on the

TABLE CS 5-7 Comparison of Acquired Company Operating Expenses $(000)'s and %

	Current	**C + 1**	**C + 2**	**C + 3**
OpExp—Existing Plan	26,000	29,000	34,000	39,000
Rate of Growth		11.5%	17.2%	14.7%
New Revenue Targets		80,000	95,000	110,000
Rate of Growth		12.5%	18.8%	15.8%
OpExp—CEO's Targets	26,000	28,000	31,350	35,200
Rate of Growth		7.7%	12.0%	12.3%

numerator in Equation [5-26].) Continuing, the CEO said, "Let's assume the debt stays in place and we continue to pay interest and as far as that aspect of the Balance Sheet is concerned we don't worry about it. If that bothers anyone, another way to think about all the cash we are talking about is to first generate the cash and then, after paying bonuses for achieving these targets and increasing our spending on new strategic investments, we pay the excess cash out in dividends, and that way the cash on the Balance sheet is irrelevant for our current purposes."

Performance Statistics for the Three-Year Plan

He then suggested that the CFO calculate the ROCE, EBIT, and EBIT/Rev for each of the years as proposed. The CFO proceeded as follows:

- Consulted Table CS 5-6 and prepared ratio tables for each Year: Year C + 1 (Tables CS 5-8 and CS 5-9), Year C + 2 (Tables CS 5-10 and CS 5-11), and Year C + 3 (CS 5-12 and CS5-13).
- Calculated the ROCE, EBIT, and EBIT/Rev using Equations [5-26] and [5-27] for each of the years, tabulated the results in Table CS 5-14, and presented them to the CEO.

Year C + 1

Applying Equation [5-26],

$$ROCE = \left\{ \frac{\left[1 - \left(\frac{COGS}{NetRev} + \frac{OpExp}{NetRev} + \frac{D\&A}{NetRev}\right)\right]}{\left(\frac{WC_{XSTD}}{NetRev} + \frac{NetFA}{NetRev} + \frac{NetIA}{NetRev}\right)} \right\} (1 - TR)$$

$$ROCE = \left\{ \frac{[1 - (0.5150 + 0.3500 + 0.0438)]}{(0.1625 + 0.4250 + 0.0500)} \right\} (1 - 0.3900)$$

$$ROCE = \left(\frac{0.0912}{0.6375}\right)(0.6100) = 0.0873$$

$$ROCE = 8.73\%$$

TABLE CS 5-8 Year C + 1 Income Statement Ratios

COGS / Rev	51.50%
OpExp / Rev	35.00%
D&A / Rev	4.38%

TABLE CS 5-9 Year C + 1 Balance Sheet Ratios

WC_{XSTD}/Rev	16.25%
NetFA/Rev	42.50%
NetIA/Rev	5.00%

Substituting in Equation [5-27],

$$EBIT = \frac{(ROCE)(CE)}{(1 - TR)} = \frac{(ROCE)(STD + LTD + TSE)}{(1 - TR)}$$

$$EBIT = \frac{(0.0873)(2{,}000{,}000 + 10{,}000000 + 39{,}000{,}000)}{(1 - 0.3900)}$$

$$EBIT = \frac{(0.0873)(51{,}000{,}000)}{0.6100} = \$7{,}300{,}000$$

and

$$EBIT/NetRev = \left(\frac{7{,}300{,}000}{80{,}000{,}000}\right)(100) = 9.13\%$$

Year C + 2

Applying Equation [5-26],

$$ROCE = \left\{\frac{\left[1 - \left(\frac{COGS}{NetRev} + \frac{OpExp}{NetRev} + \frac{D\&A}{NetRev}\right)\right]}{\left(\frac{WC_{XSTD}}{NetRev} + \frac{NetFA}{NetRev} + \frac{NetIA}{NetRev}\right)}\right\}(1 - TR)$$

$$ROCE = \left\{\frac{[1-(0.4900+0.3300+0.0368)]}{(0.1368+0.3579+0.0421)}\right\}(1-0.3800)$$

$$ROCE = \left(\frac{0.1432}{0.5368}\right)(0.6200) = 0.1654$$

$$ROCE = 16.54\%$$

Substituting in Equation [5-27],

$$EBIT = \frac{(ROCE)(CE)}{(1 - TR)} = \frac{(ROCE)(STD + LTD + TSE)}{(1 - TR)}$$

$$EBIT = \frac{(0.1654)(2{,}000{,}000 + 10{,}000{,}000 + 39{,}000{,}000)}{(1 - 0.3800)}$$

$$EBIT = \frac{(0.1654)(51{,}000{,}000)}{0.6200} = \$13{,}600{,}000$$

and

$$EBIT/NetRev = \left(\frac{13{,}600{,}000}{95{,}000{,}000}\right)(100) = 14.32\%$$

TABLE CS 5-10 Year C + 2 Income Statement Ratios

COGS/Rev	49.00%
OpExp/Rev	33.00%
D&A/Rev	3.68%

TABLE CS 5-11 Year C + 2 Balance Sheet Ratios

WC_{XSTD}/Rev	13.68%
NetFA/Rev	35.79%
NetIA/Rev	4.21%

Year C + 3

TABLE CS 5-12 Year C + 3 Income Statement Ratios

COGS/Rev	48.00%
OpExp/Rev	32.00%
D&A/Rev	3.18%

TABLE CS 5-13 Year C + 3 Balance Sheet Ratios

WC_{XSTD}/Rev	11.82%
NetFA/Rev	30.91%
NetIA/Rev	3.64%

Applying Equation [5-26],

$$ROCE = \left\{ \frac{\left[1 - \left(\frac{COGS}{NetRev} + \frac{OpExp}{NetRev} + \frac{(D\&A)}{NetRev} \right)\right]}{\left(\frac{WC_{XSTD}}{NetRev} + \frac{NetFA}{NetRev} + \frac{NetIA}{NetRev} \right)} \right\} (1 - TR)$$

$$ROCE = \left\{ \frac{[1 - (0.4800 + 0.3200 + 0.0318)]}{(0.1182 + 0.3091 + 0.0364)} \right\} (1 - 0.3800)$$

$$ROCE = \left(\frac{0.1682}{0.4637} \right) (0.6200) = 0.2249$$

$$ROCE = 22.49\%$$

Substituting in Equation [5-27],

$$EBIT = \frac{(ROCE)(CE)}{(1 - TR)} = \frac{(ROCE)(STD + LTD + TSE)}{(1 - TR)}$$

$$EBIT = \frac{(0.2249)(2{,}000{,}000 + 10{,}000{,}000 + 39{,}000{,}000)}{(1 - 0.3800)}$$

$$EBIT = \frac{(0.2148)(51{,}000{,}000)}{0.6200} = \$18{,}500{,}000$$

and

$$EBIT/NetRev = \left(\frac{18{,}500{,}000}{110{,}000{,}000} \right) (100) = 16.82\%$$

After thinking about the results presented in Table CS 5-14, the CEO was pleased that by Year 3 of the plan the company was projecting an EBIT expressed as percent of sales of 16.8%, which was above the industry median of 16.2%. The ROCE at 22.5% was also somewhat above the industry median. While these projected results represented a great improvement compared to the Company's current performance, the

TABLE CS 5-14 Forecasted Performance of Acquired Company $(000)'s and %

ROCE Driver	Current	C + 1	C + 2	C + 3
NetRev	70,000	80,000	95,000	110,000
COGS/NetRev	52.9%	51.5%	49.0%	48.0%
OpExp/NetRev	37.1%	35.0%	33.0%	32.0%
D&A/NetRev	5.0%	4.4%	3.7%	3.2%
Int/NetRev	1.7%	1.5%	1.3%	1.1%
WC_{XSTD}/NetRev	18.6%	16.3%	13.7%	11.8%
NetFA/NetRev	48.6%	42.5%	35.8%	30.9%
NetIA/NetRev	5.7%	5.0%	4.2%	3.6%
Tax Rate	40.0%	39.0%	38.0%	38.0%
ROCE	**4.1%**	**8.7%**	**16.5%**	**22.5%**
EBIT	3,500	7,300	13,600	18,500
%EBIT	**5.0%**	**9.1%**	**14.3%**	**16.8%**

Company wouldn't be in the upper quartile of its peers. He decided to call a meeting of his managers and discuss his reaction and what could be done to further escalate the forecasted performance.

Discussion of the Performance Statistics

The VP of Manufacturing stated that he wanted to have a thoroughly considered view on the proposed targets so he instructed the manufacturing engineers to get together with the R&D folks and study the targets. They confirmed that the assumptions were reasonable and suggested that if they formed a task force, they could probably achieve 48% and 47% at the Cost of Goods line in Years 2 and 3 respectively and are committed to delivering these.

The VP of Research and Development said he fully supported the creation of a task force as described. He went on to say that he and his team could live with the budgets implied by the reduction in operating expense. Furthermore, while the slower growth rate could cause some slippage in release dates, he didn't think the proposed reduction in the growth rate of the R&D budget would have significant impact in the long run as long as marketing and engineering made a point of taking the time up-front to establish firm design objectives and requirements and thereby avoiding costly rework delays.

The VP of Sales and Marketing was quick to chime in: "I want to cut to the chase. We have conducted a thorough review of our cost structure and sales plans. Our studies show that our organization is in need of change and the spending plans in the current business plan are excessive. In fact, our bottom-up approach shows we can deliver orders that will allow manufacturing not only to meet the target revenues but to exceed what is proposed by $2,000,000 and $5,000,000 in Years 2 and 3 respectively. Furthermore, with some reorganization and deployment of modern tools like CRM (Customer Resource Management) I think I can reduce my budget for Year 3 by 1% beyond what has been proposed. Also, since I'm roughly half of our operating expenses this would suggest operating expenses for Year 3 that are about 0.5% less than what are currently projected." He went on to say, "While this is a positive outcome in my view, it is embarrassing that it took an assignment like this to get to this point. I must take complete responsibility for this state of affairs and am prepared to offer my resignation."

The CEO thought for a moment and said, "Sometimes when an organization focuses on volume, costs become a secondary consideration. But in any case, I don't have time for resignations at the moment and I thank you for being so forthright."

The CFO of the Company spoke last, and said that "Finance and Administration can do what needs to be done at the reduced level of spending, including driving the working capital ratio down to the projected level by putting together a group focused on working capital. Also, even though the plan as reflected in the summary assumes no improvement in the Net Intangible Assets Ratio, I would put together a team to work that area as well. Finally, the additional work we had done on the tax issue indicated that a tax rate of 37.5% for Year 3 of the plan was doable."

The CEO was at first a little skeptical of all of this and asked many questions. In the end he agreed that what was being said made sense. The manufacturing plan, even at the lower COGS, seemed sound. He, like the rest of his team, was concerned about even modest cuts in R&D. When it was suggested that R&D's budget should not be impacted by the three-year plan, the VP of R&D objected and said that he was part of the team and had to do his share and managed to persuade everyone that a modest reduction in R&D was a risk worth taking. His concern about the Sales and Marketing leadership had evaporated when he saw a key executive admit the budgeting process he was responsible for was not as it should be, signed on for more revenue with fewer resources, and saw his way to reduce his budget for Year 3 by 1%. The news on the tax front was good as was the CFO's comment that the reduced finance and administration budget would not keep the finance group from making the goals implied by the targets and in fact they had plans to do more.

Performance Statistics for Revised Three-Year Plan

The CEO expressed his gratitude to all for the way they had chipped in and signed up for more than he originally asked. He then summarized what he heard.

- Revenues in years C + 2 and C + 3 should be increased to $97,000,000 and $115,000,000 respectively.
- Cost of Goods Sold for Year C + 2 would be set at 48% and in Year C + 3 would be reduced to 47%.

- Operating Expenses for Year C + 3 would be capped at 31.5%.
- The effective tax rate in Year C + 3 would be reduced to 37.5%.

The CFO was then asked to incorporate the new targets in his model.

Year C + 2 Revised

Refer to Tables CS 5-15 and CS 5-16.
Applying Equation [5-26],

$$ROCE=\left\{\frac{\left[1-\left(\frac{COGS}{NetRev}+\frac{OpExp}{NetRev}+\frac{D\&A}{NetRev}\right)\right]}{\left(\frac{WC_{XSTD}}{NetRev}+\frac{NetFA}{NetRev}+\frac{NetIA}{NetRev}\right)}\right\}(1-TR)$$

$$ROCE=\left\{\frac{[1-(0.4800+0.3300+0.0368)]}{(0.1368+0.3579+0.0421)}\right\}(1-0.3800)$$

$$ROCE=\left(\frac{0.1532}{0.5368}\right)(0.6200)=0.1769$$

$$ROCE=17.69\%$$

Substituting in Equation [5-27],

$$EBIT=\frac{(ROCE)(CE)}{(1-TR)}=\frac{(ROCE)*(STD+LTD+TSE)}{(1-TR)}$$

$$EBIT=\frac{(0.1769)(2{,}000{,}000+10{,}000{,}000+39{,}000{,}000)}{(1-0.3800)}$$

$$EBIT=\frac{(0.1769)(51{,}000{,}000)}{0.6200}=\$14{,}550{,}000$$

and

$$EBIT/NetRev=\left(\frac{14{,}550{,}000}{97{,}000{,}000}\right)(100)=15.00\%$$

TABLE CS 5-15 Year C + 2R Income Statement Ratios

COGS/Rev	48.00%
OpExp/Rev	33.00%
D&A/Rev	3.68%

TABLE CS 5-16 Year C + 2R Balance Sheet Ratios

WC_{XSTD}/Rev	13.68%
NetFA/Rev	35.79%
NetIA/Rev	4.21%

TABLE CS 5-17 Year C + 3R Income Statement Ratios

COGS/Rev	47.00%
OpExp/Rev	31.50%
D&A/Rev	3.20%

TABLE CS 5-18 Year C + 3R Balance Sheet Ratios

WC_{XSTD}/Rev	11.82%
NetFA/Rev	30.91%
NetIA/Rev	3.64%

Year C + 3 Revised

Refer to Tables CS 5-17 and CS 5-18.
Applying Equation [5-26],

$$ROCE = \left\{ \frac{\left[1 - \left(\frac{COGS}{NetRev} + \frac{OpExp}{NetRev} + \frac{D\&A}{NetRev}\right)\right]}{\left(\frac{WC_{XSTD}}{NetRev} + \frac{NetFA}{NetRev} + \frac{OthA}{NetRev}\right)} \right\}(1 - TR) \quad [5\text{-}26]$$

$$ROCE = \left\{ \frac{[1 - (0.4700 + 0.3150 + 0.0320)]}{(0.1182 + 0.3091 + 0.0364)} \right\}(1 - 0.3750)$$

$$ROCE = \left(\frac{0.1830}{0.4637}\right)(0.6250) = 0.2467$$

$$ROCE = 24.67\%$$

Substituting in Equation [5-27],

$$EBIT = \frac{(ROCE)(CE)}{(1 - TR)} = \frac{(ROCE)(STD + LTD + TSE)}{(1 - TR)} \quad [5\text{-}27]$$

$$EBIT = \frac{(0.2467)(2{,}000{,}000 + 10{,}000000 + 39{,}000{,}000)}{(1 - 0.3750)}$$

$$EBIT = \frac{(0.2467)(51{,}000{,}000)}{0.6250} = \$20{,}130{,}000$$

and

$$EBIT/NetRev = \left(\frac{20{,}130{,}000}{115{,}000{,}000}\right)(100) = 17.50\%$$

Revised Performance Statistics and Adoption of the Three-Year Plan

The CFO e-mailed the revised forecast performance tabulated in Table CS 5-19 to the CEO.

TABLE CS 5-19 Revised Forecasted Performance of Acquired Company $(000)'s and %

ROCE Driver	Current	C + 1	C + 2R	C + 3R
NetRev	70,000	80,000	97,000	115,000
COGS/NetRev	52.9%	51.5%	48.0%	47.0%
OpExp/NetRev	37.1%	35.0%	33.0%	31.5%
D&A/NetRev	5.0%	4.4%	3.7%	3.2%
Int/NetRev	1.7%	1.5%	1.3%	1.1%
WC/NetRev	18.6%	16.3%	13.7%	11.8%
NetFA/NetRev	48.6%	42.5%	35.8%	30.9%
OthA/NetRev	5.7%	5.0%	4.2%	3.6%
Tax Rate	40.0%	39.0%	38.0%	37.5%
ROCE	**4.1%**	**8.7%**	**17.7%**	**24.7%**
EBIT	3,500	7,300	14,550	20,150
%EBIT	**5.0%**	**9.1%**	**15.0%**	**17.5%**

After looking at it, the CEO concluded it was far from precise because of the requirements laid out at the beginning of the process. For example, the Net Intangible Assets could not stay fixed at $4,000,000 in a company growing like this and in reality while they could be trimmed during the first year or so they would grow in subsequent years. Also, in all likelihood the ROCEs that were projected were understated because, once the forecasted earnings and planned Balance Sheet programs were achieved, the cash flow would quickly pay off the debt and reduce the Capital Employed. And even though this debt-driven reduction in Capital Employed would be offset to some extent by the increase in Total Shareholders' Equity (resulting from improved earnings), the Capital Employed as a percentage of Revenue would decrease with a corresponding increase in ROCE—a high-class problem, he thought.

The CEO then called another meeting of his management team and presented Table CS 5-19. He began by thanking each and every one for the hard work they had done and announced that, in his view, this plan had considerable upside, and at the projected levels of ROCE and EBIT in Year C + 3R, the Company would be well on its way to achieving a level of performance in the upper quartile—an accomplishment of which they would all be justly proud when achieved.

At this point the VP of Manufacturing made a couple of statements followed by a question. He began by saying, "The management team wants you to know this has been a terrific learning process and everyone is totally committed, with one caveat. Earlier you informed us that a recruiter had been engaged to recruit a new president and there is some concern that this person may not have the commitment to what all of us think is an excellent plan and one we are all very excited about. So my question is: What's going to happen to our plan when the new person arrives?"

The CEO responded by saying he had been thinking about this and wanted to inform them that he had terminated the search. He then introduced them the new president of the Company, the former VP of Sales and Marketing.

CHAPTER SIX

Strategies and Best Practices for Managing ROCE and Cash Flow*

CHAPTER 6 TAKEAWAYS

- Manage for profit. Grow through innovation!
- Don't compete on the basis of price. BMW does not compete on price. Their objective is to provide the customer with a complete driving experience. This is of course what many drivers want. However, all drivers can't afford it. BMW knows this and has the discipline to only cater to those who can. This means they have to forgo some customer segments and, therefore, limit the market they serve and ultimately their growth. Your focus should be on maximizing profit and your share of your niche rather than expanding into a broad market if price is what it takes to do so.
- Never compromise your quality. Every product or service a company provides has the company's signature on it. Like a reputation, once sullied it is difficult to remove the blemish.
- You can be high-tech but don't forget how to be soft-touch. This applies to both employees and customers. There is some logic to the notion that in the final analysis, companies get the customers they deserve. If you treat your people well by showing day in and day out how much you value their contribution and train them so that they are able to deliver more value and then show them that you trust them by empowering them to make decisions, you will have a motivated and happy workforce. People who are all gassed up about their company go the extra mile to serve a customer and effuse enthusiasm and confidence that are contagious. Customers are very quick to sense a company's culture and are turned on or ultimately turned off by what they perceive. The outcome is that happy employees create happy customers who come back again and again.
- Don't forget the difference between arrogance and elegance. It can be wonderful to work for a company that is the best in the world at what is does.

(continued)

*The reader may notice minor discrepancies in the calculations in this chapter. When this occurs, it is the result of rounding.

Sometimes this leads to overconfidence and the company's culture evolves to one of not listening to the customer. The moment this happens, you have just turned the corner toward difficult times. One way to keep your perspective and stay humble is to remember the difference between arrogance and elegance.

Arrogance = Confidence out of Control

Elegance = Confidence + Warmth

- Competitors selling below cost? Don't believe it. You can't afford to take the risk of believing it, even if it's true. Making dire predictions about what may happen to your competitor if they don't change pricing behavior may be entertaining, but it isn't helpful. What is constructive is to focus on your costs and relentlessly drive them down. While there isn't any one way to go about cost reduction, it starts by having an understanding of the factors that contribute to cost.
- The day has passed for companies that are a mile wide and vertically deep. Even if you can get past the management and talent issues such a strategy presents, it's just too expensive. Today, survival depends on doing a few things and doing them extraordinarily well. What's more, once you have decided what your core activities are, you must be prepared to do two things. The first is to keep your technologies current. If not, your costs and ability to compete will get away from you. The second is to regularly review what's core and what's not and make changes when the day for one has passed and the time for another has come.
- If your assumptions have proven to be incorrect or your team has made an outright mistake and put the wrong resources in place, deal with it. For example, if the factory turns out to be too big, think long and hard before you put your company in the high-risk position of trying to fill it with strategies like pre-selling and marginal pricing. Sublet part of it as soon as possible. Or, if you have bought the wrong equipment, don't defocus the company's efforts by trying to sell the machine's capacity to others. Sell the machine and get what you need. This may sound like advice that is easy to give at a distance. However, as the saying goes, "been there and done that," and experience has taught that life doesn't get any better if you put off dealing with an issue once you know the right answer.
- Operating Expenses are poorly named. Managers shouldn't spend money on anything unless it is expected to provide a return. In this context, Operating Expenses are really investments. Business is stuck with this terminology. However, you will find it helpful when deciding where to spend money if you learn to think in terms of what any expenditure will return regardless of its accounting classification.
- Product differentiation is no longer a matter limited to what can be defined within a table of dimensions, functions, features, and benefits. A company must employ "thought leadership" and use media channels of all kinds, not the least of which is the Internet, to continuously put forward a unique concept or approach that outlines how its products deliver value, and the actual nature of the product must ultimately substantiate the claim.
- E-Commerce is producing a paradigm shift in the way business is done. Many companies see this technology as a tool that will enable them to reduce SG&A expenses, capture incremental business, improve inventory turns, improve cash flow, and increase the bottom line.

- Companies should have a thought-leadership vision when it comes to product planning that coalesces with the marketing thrust. In fact the vision must be the underpinning of the product itself since it is the genesis of all product ideas that would be formulated by R&D or marketing or product management. Without this, disjointed products will be spawned that don't fit the corporate message or vision and when this happens it usually ends badly.
- If you want your R&D, Marketing, Sales, and Manufacturing areas to be effective and efficient, focus on talent, not numbers of people. If you don't have a few of the best and brightest, it's going to be tough for you to compete. It's also important to recognize that in many situations it's not how much a company spends, but what it spends its money on and, for niche-oriented companies in particular, it's the only way they can compete with organizations that have more resources. Finally, because there is a tendency to want it yesterday, not enough time is spent doing investigations and experiments, identifying vendors, and so on before serious engineering gets under way.
- There is a school of thought that suggests it is always better to buy a good company. This is of course true. However, there is another school that suggests it's better to pay too much for a good company than to purchase a bad one. This assertion has been tried many times and it often turns out to be wrong. If you pay too much, it will probably take years to realize a return on the investment. In most cases it's better to walk away from an overpriced deal. Furthermore, it's too risky to get involved in a deal that isn't adequately supported by your Balance Sheet and Cash Flow because you may be betting the company.
- In general, you will end up ahead of the game if you pass along bad customers to your competitors and focus on keeping the good ones for yourself.

INTRODUCTION TO MAXIMIZING RETURN ON CAPITAL EMPLOYED AND CASH FLOW

Return on Capital Employed (ROCE) is important because it compares what the management of a company is capable of delivering (Net Income) to what has been invested in the business (Capital Employed). In practice, the situation isn't quite that simple. In Chapter 5, a framework was developed for quantifying the variables that impact ROCE and ultimately Cash Flow. The framework was based on the *ROCE Driver* model and its use was illustrated by way of examples and a case study. While Chapter 5 does identify the tools a management team has in its ROCE/Cash Flow tool kit, it doesn't discuss strategies and best practices that management can work with to achieve the desired result.

The thrust of this chapter is to systematically discuss "Strategies and Best Practices for Managing ROCE and Cash Flow." Because the ROCE Driver Equation is based on a combination of Income Statement and Balance Sheet variables, the chapter will begin with a line-by-line discussion of the issues associated with the various accounts where appropriate strategies and best practices will be suggested with the hope that, combined with the analytical framework of the ROCE Driver Equation, they will be helpful to management teams striving to maximize their company's ROCE.

BASIC PRICING-DRIVEN MODELS

None of the drivers of ROCE can have any impact without revenue. Furthermore, it is very difficult for any of them to make up for a low selling price. Therefore, in order for the system to produce the intended results, every company needs to find ways to get a fair price for the products and services that it offers. In this section, some of the issues this challenge presents will be discussed. The market would seem like a sensible place to start.

The market is really a combination of your customers, competitors, and your company. Contrary to what many people think, the market doesn't really establish a price. It establishes a range of prices for your technology, products, and services. Your task is to convince customers that your products and services add sufficient value to justify pricing them at the high end of the range. The following models are presented with the objective of stimulating your thoughts on ways of creating value added and how to get paid for it. The first to be discussed will be *demand-* and *cost-based* representations followed by *value-added* models.

Demand and Cost Models

Three demand and cost models are discussed in the next section. While each presents a framework for a business model, as will be seen, they all have shortcomings and lead one to be drawn to the value-added models that follow.

One of the pillars of microeconomics is the concept of *supply and demand*. The notion is that as the price of any product or service increases, producers are inclined to produce more and supply increases until it equals demand. In practice, supply often overshoots and the result is a downward shift of the price curve and lower prices until the balance is restored. Figure 6-1 portrays how the market works according to this model. The market-clearing price occurs at the intersection of the two curves and is the price that brings supply and demand into equilibrium.

The concept that the market-clearing price ultimately determines supply involves the notion that the market has some form of collective intelligence. While this may be

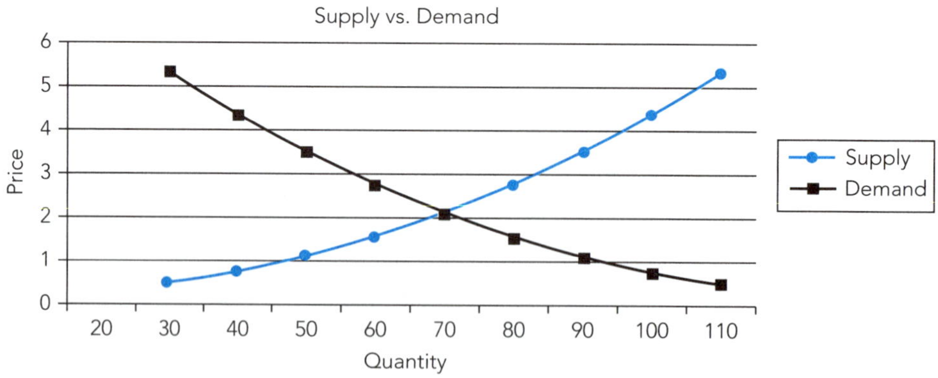

FIGURE 6-1 Supply-versus-Demand Model

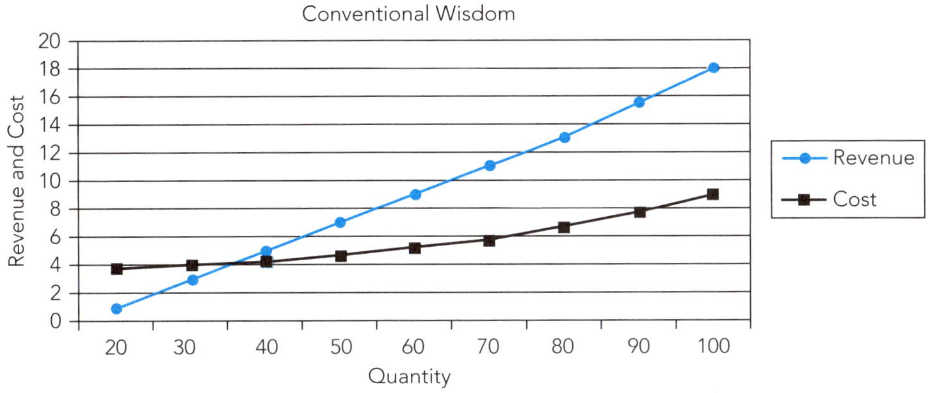

FIGURE 6-2 Conventional Wisdom Model

true, it doesn't mean that it is universally applicable. In fact, it's not. It's highly relevant when it comes to commodities. You don't have to live with it if you can differentiate your product. There are some other problems with the model that fly in the face of modern marketing. For example, the notion that others determine the price isn't necessarily true. Companies can and do influence pricing in a variety of ways. Furthermore, the model is relatively unattractive since it implies that the only thing a company can do to influence profit is control costs.

Conventional Wisdom

Unlike the supply and demand model, this model (Figure 6-2) provides for the supplier of a deliverable to exercise some control over the price. Revenue is, of course, the product of unit volume and price. Ideally, the company's management sets a price they think is fair and compelling enough to sell everything they plan to make. In practice, this rarely happens because everyone trying to sell something has to take into account their target market's ability and willingness to pay. In this model, management begins the process by setting the price at a level they consider to be fair and at the same time produces a satisfactory return for the shareholders and, then perhaps after some fine tuning, is prepared to live with the consequences even if this means that they won't be able to sell as much as they are capable of producing. In other words, at some point management arbitrarily decides that the price can't be lowered any further and caps production at that level. While an improvement over the pure supply and demand model, it has a few shortcomings: It does not maximize price or revenue-dependent profit and doesn't explicitly focus on the value received by the customer.

Gradation

This model is presented graphically in Figure 6-3 and is based on the premise that the higher the unit volume a customer signs up for, the lower the unit price. The logic associated with this model is sound. However, it often encounters difficulty during implementation.

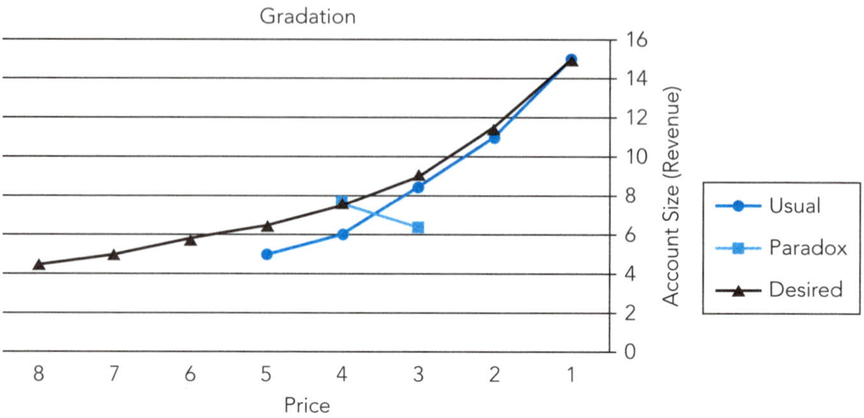

FIGURE 6-3 Gradation Model

In most manufacturing environments, the costs come down progressively with volume. The opportunities for cost reductions are highest at the start of a product life cycle and gradually diminish as volume increases over time. This suggests that the price volume-buyers pay should be controlled by a curve with a rather gradual slope (desired case). What often happens is that aggressive assumptions are made on how fast the costs will come down and, therefore, in reality the slope of the Account Size–Price curve is quite steep (usual case).[1] To further complicate matters, it's not unusual to encounter situations where the slope of the curve is reversed. This happens when an exuberant sales force decides to give very low prices to new low-volume accounts in order to establish a beachhead. This results in a situation were established customers with higher volume pay more for the product than new accounts with smaller volume (paradox case). It's a little difficult to graph this situation. The point is: The intersection of the desired case and paradox case is where the price should be given the volume discount. Instead, the paradox case customer is the beneficiary of a lower price than their volume would justify. While not widespread in well-run Original Equipment Manufacturers (OEM), it does happen. When it does, your longtime customers are subsidizing the accounts you are trying to capture.

To summarize, a well-executed gradation strategy would eliminate the paradox case and tilt the usual case so that it extracts high prices from low-volume accounts and offers attractive low prices to high-volume accounts. This would produce a curve that looks more like the gradual Account Size–Price relationship portrayed by the desired case.

VALUE-ADDED MODELS

The fact that all of the models discussed so far are in widespread use in one form or another speaks to the confidence that many management teams have placed in them. As

[1] Note the Usual curve suggests a price of 5 at Revenue 5 whereas the Desired curve would suggest a price of 7 for the same volume.

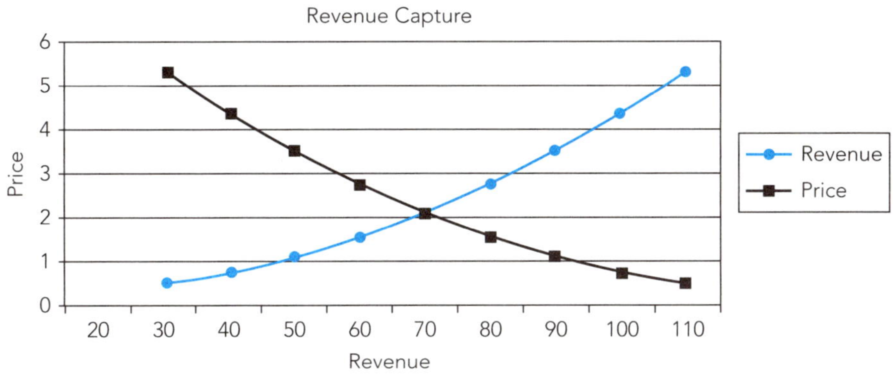

FIGURE 6-4 Revenue Capture Model

viable as they may be, they all have one important shortcoming: The prices they produce don't make any attempt to capture all of the value that is conveyed to the customer when they purchase the product or service. This leads us to a discussion of value-added models that can drive Net Revenue and profit.

Revenue Capture

Graphically, this model (Figure 6-4) looks a lot like the supply-and-demand model (Figure 6-1) but it is anything but that. It embodies the notion that at one end of the spectrum there are customers who are focused on having the latest technology as opposed to price and at the other end there are customers who really don't want to buy anything, but in the end succumb because the price is so attractive. The basic idea is: The supplier caters to all needs by introducing the product at a high price and then as manufacturing costs come down, reduces prices over time and gives all customers a chance to buy at their price.

The *revenue capture* model has been around for a long time. However, that doesn't mean that it's any less relevant or has lost its effectiveness. Companies like Intel continue to roll out generation after generation of microprocessors based on this model. Why has it had such longevity? The long answer is that it gives sellers an opportunity to maximize price during the early stage of the product life cycle when they are capacity constrained and the buyers an opportunity to purchase when the price is right for them. The short answer is that it discriminates and charges for the value perceived by each of the market segments.

Migration

Figure 6-5 is a graphical representation of the *migration* approach to pricing and revenue generation. In this model, features representing value to the customer are added when each updated or improved version of the product or service is rolled out and the price is increased accordingly. In this portrayal, when the product is released at time T1, the first customers who buy the product will pay $100. When the next version is available

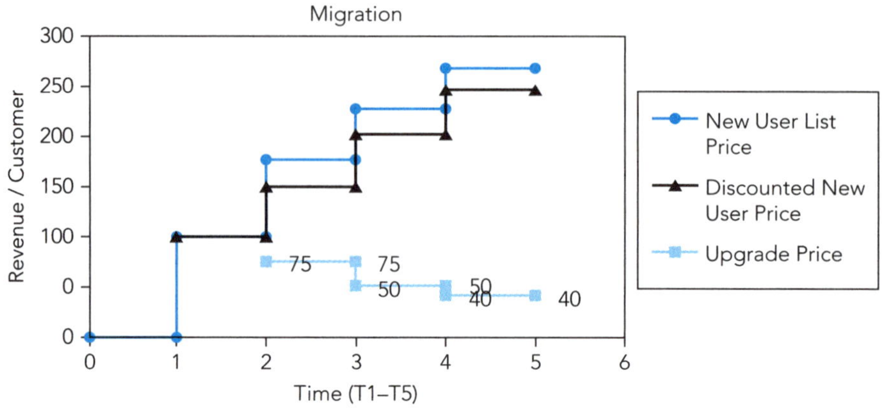

FIGURE 6-5 Migration Model

at time T2, existing customers will be able to upgrade for $75. The value conveyed at time T2 is $175 (New User List Price), based on the assumption that the value to the user has been enhanced by $75. New customers will probably be able to purchase for something less than $175, but more than $100, say $150 (Discounted New User Price), and so on. The customer who starts with the first release and buys all upgrades will pay more over the period T1–T5 than any other user. The argument for this is that the earlier one purchases, the more value they derive from the product or service. The migration model has one weakness: The value added by each upgrade is often less than its predecessor because the ability to add value generally diminishes over time. However, this doesn't have to be the case.

The key to using the migration model is product planning. Careful consideration must be given to product management, product design, and market development. Product management lays out a plan that defines the features and benefits that are to be incorporated into the product and released over time. Careful attention is paid to making sure that features aren't included before the customer appreciates the value. The design team has a couple of tasks. The most important is to make the product modular so that code (or hardware) can be reused from one generation to the next. Another is: New releases must integrate seamlessly with existing users' databases or installations. Third, the design must be flexible so that new ideas can be efficiently incorporated without resorting to massive rewrite of code or involving extensive redesign of hardware platforms. Market development's task is to focus on developing the customer's willingness to pay more.

The software industry has mastered this model. For example, when spreadsheets first came out they could have incorporated features like "undo" and "redo." They may have reasoned that first-time spreadsheet users would probably ascribe great value to the marvel of the spreadsheet per se and wouldn't have focused on much else. Only after using a spreadsheet and accidentally deleting or losing data does one really appreciate the value of the restore features. The product managers who waited to include advanced features until the market had developed to a point where the value they conveyed to the user was apparent have made fortunes for their company (and themselves).

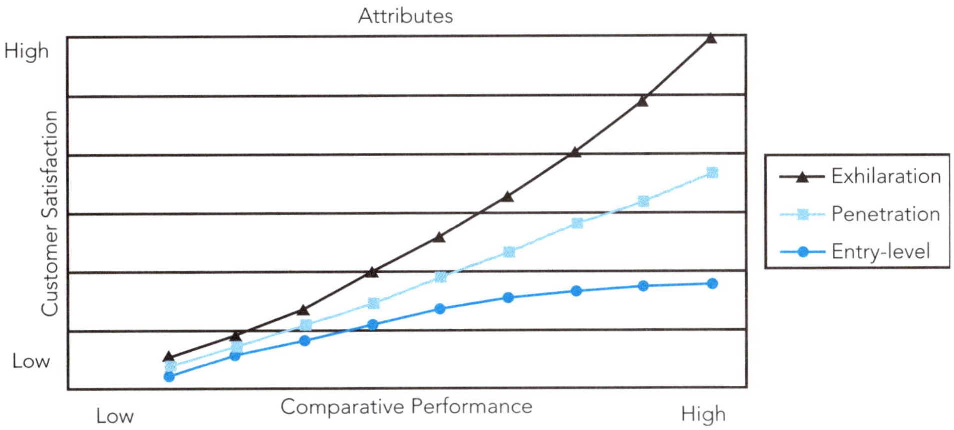

FIGURE 6-6 Attributes Model

Companies that build their marketing around the migration model recognize that cost is important but understand they are not in a business driven by cost. When their products are properly positioned and expertly rolled out over time, they are able to charge more and give more value over the product life cycle. Their profit is driven by value added.

Attributes

The attributes model (Figure 6-6) portrays a way of thinking about your performance relative to competitors (*comparative performance*) and the way your customer feels about the goods and services offered (*customer satisfaction*). The notion is that satisfaction, purchase orders, and better prices go hand in hand.

Entry-level attributes define what is required to get any business at all from a customer. They are characterized by the fact that the customer acknowledges a small and relatively insignificant increase in satisfaction for any given increase in performance relative to competitors. In other words, the customer sees your company as one of many supplying similar products and services with comparatively little significant differentiation.

If what you are offering evokes this kind of customer response, almost no amount of effort or dedication will get you more business unless a major competitor stumbles badly. Until then, you are in the price business and your company had better be focused on cost. It's almost like milling around the bottom of the ladder of success and no matter what you do, you can't seem to get on, or stay on, the first rung. At times it will appear that determination is your only strategy and this may well be true. It is always possible that persistently good service with an undifferentiated product or service will move you in the direction of account penetration. The problem is, even if you achieve some degree of success, you are still a fringe supplier in this category. When the market tightens or the customer can once again pick and choose, you will probably be relegated to entry-level status once more. Preferred entry level maybe, but entry level nevertheless. In summary, entry-level strategies guarantee your company a place at the table and not much more.

The *penetration attribute* is associated with account share and account retention. In this situation the supplier has something to which the customer ascribes sufficient value that they want more of in their facility—provided your company is competitive, or if more expensive, justifiably so. It can be brand name, differentiated product, safety in numbers (customer has lots of the product around, so more is probably okay), or a safe choice ("I can't be criticized for choosing this supplier").

This attribute is characterized by a medium increase in customer satisfaction for a given increase in comparative performance. While this may never have been one of IBM's strategies, it certainly plays well for the IBMs of this world. While IBM has had its share of breakthrough inventions and products, its legacy is not one of perpetual innovation. What they have is state-of-the-art products and services, the safety of the IBM name, and superb customer support. Because of this, customers have rewarded them with an ever-increasing stream of business for many years. The entry-level attribute allows a company to compete for a customer's business. A compelling penetration strategy is required to increase account share.

So far the discussion of this model has focused on getting a place at the table and then getting the largest piece of the pie. The *exhilaration attribute* introduces a third criterion: price. Referring to Figure 6-6, it should be apparent this attribute is characterized by a large increase in customer satisfaction for a given increase in comparative performance. The reason for this is the customer sees something that they think is really worth getting energized about. It doesn't have to be new or particularly clever. It simply has to be a product or service that redefines how they are able to add value to their customer offering or reduce their cost.

The automotive industry did this when they introduced the automatic transmission. The fractional horsepower motor revolutionized many industries and initiated an avalanche of products. Bell Labs did it when they invented the transistor. Texas Instruments laid the groundwork for the PC and a vast array of consumer products when they announced the integrated circuit. Volvo seemed to defy all logic when they built their product line around safety and went on to sell lots and lots of cars to families and safety-conscious buyers.[2] Intel redefined focus when they abandoned memory chips to concentrate on microprocessors that operate at speeds that defy comprehension and has gone on to deliver quarter after quarter of outstanding financial results. Apple changed operating systems forever when they introduced the first Mac and then again changed how we record and listen to music when they introduced the iPod. They have also revolutionized mobile communications and communications in general with the advent of the iPhone and iPad. Microsoft has repeatedly shown us how an industry can be dominated by a group of highly motivated people with vision and lots of money to pour into expanding their net. Dell Computer taught all of us how to sell high-technology products over the telephone and then over the Internet. Bell Labs did it once again when they demonstrated the first cellular telephone system, and while it took a little while to catch on, this technology has led to an unparalleled boom in the communications industry that

[2]Unfortunately over time other auto companies were able to make the same claims and Volvo lost its edge.

looks like it will continue for many years and has reached a point where the number of cell phones used as primary telephones exceeds installed landlines.

The discussion doesn't have to be limited to companies. Dr. W. Edwards Deming defied conventional wisdom and showed that quality actually reduces product cost. Germany has grown to be the strongest economy in Europe by being the hallmark of superb engineering and quality products for many years. Japanese industry has shown the world how to do things faster, better, and cheaper. And finally there is China and its policy of being the world's low-cost producer, which has allowed them to capture most of the manufacturing industry that once resided in the West.

Pages can be written on game-changers like these. However, it's important to stop here. Otherwise, readers may get the impression that exhilaration attributes require enormous resources and breakthrough strategies. This is not true or the point.

While the inventions mentioned may have required genius, the customer need they served did not. In fact, all of these seemingly breakthrough strategies were grounded on very basic customer needs. They provided or introduced: (1) ease of use (automotive industry's automatic transmission, Apple's Mac and iPod, Microsoft's integration of the operating system and applications), (2) technology platforms that others could build businesses upon (fractional horsepower motor, Bell Labs' transistor, Texas Instruments' integrated circuit, Microsoft's products, Intel's microprocessors), (3) redefined the sales and support model (Dell Computer), (4) reliability (Bell Labs' transistor, Texas Instruments integrated circuit), (5) reduced footprint (fractional horsepower motor, Bell Labs' transistor, TI's integrated circuit), (6) speed (Intel's microprocessors), (7) quality as a differentiator (Japan's and Germany's phenomenal postwar expansion), (8) productivity (inexpensive computers), (9) safety (Volvo), and (10) staying in touch (Bell Labs and all of the companies focused on mobile communications). All of these needs have been around for a very long time. In fact, only rarely does a new one emerge. What does materialize is new ways to serve them.

The main point is: If you don't want to compete on price or service, or you don't want price or service to be the deciding consideration in the purchase decision, you have to give the customer something to get wound up about. Your objective should be to "bring the child out in the customer" by presenting them with something that is so compelling that they want your product or service at almost any sensible price. If you are able to do this, you will have high account share and high customer retention, and your profits will flourish.

Premium

While the premium model (Figure 6-7) is similar to the attributes model in many ways, it's also different in several important aspects. To begin with, it provides a framework for thinking about relationships in a different way. It's built around the premise that "customer perception" is a deciding factor in account share (and therefore ultimate account profitability).

Like the attributes model, it starts by defining what it takes to have any account share. It states that the entry-level requirements are: (1) Satisfy basic performance and quality expectations (*basic needs*) and (2) consistently deliver an acceptable level of

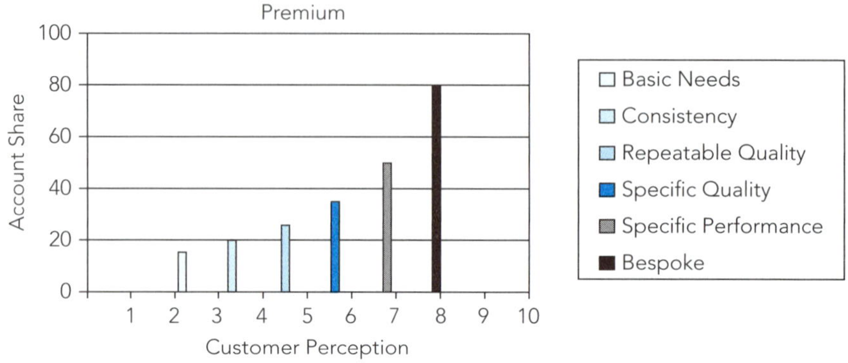

FIGURE 6-7 Premium Model

service (*consistency*). Premises like these are hard to argue with and are in fact what all of us expect from anyone or any company that we favor with our business.

When it comes to increasing account share, the model becomes a little more demanding. For starters, it requires that, in addition to satisfying basic performance and quality expectations, you must satisfy them repeatedly—so much so that the customer is able to eliminate any need for incoming inspection. In other words, the customer expects "repeatable quality"—confidence that when it goes into the product it will function as intended, assurance that when it is turned on it will perform as advertised, and the belief that the supplier will do their job with minimal supervision from the customer.

Beyond the general quality necessities are "specific quality" requirements. By satisfying a customer's specific quality requirements, suppliers can differentiate themselves from the competition and get more business at better margins. While different, the same is also true for "specific performance," which postulates that a supplier can increase account share at better prices by focusing on helping the customer add specific value to its product or services. Many companies make the mistake of waiting for their customer to bring the opportunity to their attention. By then it is too late, at least to get the business at a premium price. Once the customer has identified the specific quality or performance issues that are desired, the number of suppliers that can meet the requirements is usually significantly increased.

The crux of the model is the notion of "bespoke." By definition, *bespoke* means that something is made only for you and is, therefore, unique. If something is unique, it doesn't have anything that it can be compared to and value is completely subjective. This is a very powerful concept. Art has thrived on it for centuries. Companies have captured the essence of the concept by producing limited editions of such things as prints, mementos, books, and cars. (The interesting thing here is that many of these so-called limited editions aren't so limited at all but, even so, they command premium prices.) Architects and builders regularly plan large- and small-scale developments around one or a few basic plans. They entice customers with attractive entry-level models and then increase their margins by incentivizing their salespeople to sell options that customize the home for each buyer. Software companies are the current bespoke masters. SAP has built an enormous business by selling so-called standard modular software that ends up being customized for every installation. Consultants like Accenture Consulting and E&Y have ridden the bespoke bandwagon by putting together teams of people to help SAP customers reengineer (standardize) their process so that the SAP business system can function as intended. There are great examples in mature industries as well. For example, British Airways was the first to market seats that reclined to a flat position for sleeping and thereby fill their first-class cabins at premium prices. Some competitors are still trying to catch up 25 or more years later.

While these may not be earth-shattering concepts, they are of tremendous importance: (1) Sophisticated companies know that their customers are not inclined to pay them for non-value-added costs such as a supplier's quality problems. (2) Customers place great value on suppliers that do what they say they will do day after day without costly monitoring. (3) Innovative suppliers are a relatively rare phenomenon, especially those that are listening carefully to how they can help their customers add value to their products or reduce costs. (4) Everybody likes the idea that something may be made just for them and, when properly presented, they are prepared to pay for it. (5) Catering to basic needs in an innovative way changes the game (at least for a while) and creates an opportunity for suppliers to charge a premium with little associated marginal cost.

The pricing models just discussed are only part of the chronicle on how to compete. There are additional principles and guidelines that are important to observe. Here are a few:

- Manage for profit. Grow through innovation!
- Don't compete on the basis of price. BMW does not compete on price. Their objective is to provide the customer with a complete driving experience. This is of course what many drivers want. However, all drivers can't afford it. BMW knows this and has the discipline to only cater to those who can. This means they have to forgo some customer segments and, therefore, limit the market they serve and ultimately their growth. Your focus should be on maximizing profit and your share of your niche rather than expanding into a broad market if price is what it takes to do so.
- Never compromise your quality. Every product or service a company provides has the company's signature on it. Like a reputation, once sullied it is difficult to remove the blemish.
- You can be high-tech but don't forget how to be soft-touch. This applies to both employees and customers. There is some logic to the notion that in the final analysis, companies get the customers they deserve. If you treat your people well by showing day in and day out how much you value their contribution and train them so that they are able to deliver more value and then show them that you trust them by empowering them to make decisions, you will have a motivated and happy workforce. People who are all gassed up about their company go the extra mile to serve a customer and effuse enthusiasm and confidence that are contagious. Customers are very quick to sense a company's culture and are turned on or ultimately turned off by what they perceive. The outcome is that happy employees create happy customers who come back again and again.

- Don't forget the difference between arrogance and elegance. It can be wonderful to work for a company that is the best in the world at what is does. Sometimes this leads to overconfidence and the company's culture evolves to one of not listening to the customer. The moment this happens you have just turned the corner toward difficult times. One way to keep your perspective and stay humble is to remember the difference between arrogance and elegance.

$$Arrogance = Confidence\ out\ of\ Control$$

$$Elegance = Confidence + Warmth$$

INTRODUCTION TO FACTORS THAT IMPACT CORPORATE PERFORMANCE

There always seems to be a story in the press about one international company or another allegedly dumping in the U.S. or other markets. Occasionally these stories are true, but usually the case goes unproven. One story that comes to mind is of a major U.S. company that over a period of years lost its leadership position to a Far East competitor. Over time, the company became arrogant, lost their perspective, and began to manage by opinion and not by the facts. They believed that they were losing market share because their main competitor was selling below cost and so they focused on trying to get the U.S. government to solve their problem. The competitor got wind of their lobbying effort and invited the U.S. company to visit them. They sent over a team of accountants who came back and said that the U.S. company's costs were about the same as the Far East Company's selling price and the Far East Company was making a profit. U.S. management was skeptical. So, senior managers and union representatives made their own visit. They came back and admitted that their accounting team was right.

The moral to the story is: Competitors selling below cost? Don't believe it. You can't afford to take the risk of believing it, even if it's true. Making dire predictions about what may happen to your competitor if they don't change pricing behavior may be entertaining but it isn't helpful. What is constructive is to focus on your costs and relentlessly drive them down. While there isn't any one way to go about cost reduction, it starts by having an understanding of the factors that contribute to cost. Also, as will be seen in the discussions that follow, almost everything that happens in a company affects cost.

Research and Development

This subject is addressed later in this chapter. Therefore, there is no need to go into detail at this time. However, when you are thinking about cost, it's important to remember that it all starts here. Only products that are designed with cost as a target can achieve the targeted cost.

Manufacturing Technology

Manufacturing process efficiency is determined by the extent and nature of the technology utilized in the factory. In fact, your manufacturing technology establishes the base from which your Cost of Goods Sold is ultimately controlled. In general, the low-cost producer (in the niche being served) has the highest contribution from manufacturing process efficiency. "In the niche being served" are important words. It's not necessary to be the low-cost producer in all markets. The first requirement is to have a competitive cost structure in the market segments where you compete and where you ultimately want to grow. To be the low-cost producer in other markets as well is an additional benefit, but often a distraction if it involves significant resources.

When it comes to manufacturing technology the three most important aspects are the degree of vertical integration, the state of core technologies, and the manufacturing technology deployed.

Selective vertical integration and modern plant and equipment suited to the company's needs make a big difference to the Cost of Goods Sold. The downside of a high degree of vertical integration is a loss of flexibility and the cost of maintaining the overhead associated with the technology. Some people would argue with the flexibility statement because they think that you are more flexible when you can do things in-house. This is true, but this is not the kind of flexibility that is being discussed here. The concern is about being locked into a particular way of doing something. If you have the equipment, your inclination will be to use it even though there may be a better way.

Decide on core technologies and keep them current. When Henry Ford built his highly integrated Rouge River Facility, he was convinced that Ford could develop the technologies and components his car company needed faster and better than U.S. industry. None of us can know for sure if he was right because we weren't around at the time. However, what is clear today is that the situation has changed. Ford is no longer so highly integrated. Nor are most companies, for that matter. The day has passed for companies that are a mile wide and vertically deep. Even if you can get past the management and talent issues such a strategy presents, it's just too expensive. Today, survival depends on doing a few things and doing them extraordinarily well. What's more, once you have decided what your core activities are, you must be prepared to do two things. The first is keeping your technologies current. If not, your costs and ability to compete will get away from you. The second is to regularly review what's core and what's not and make changes when the day for one has passed and the time for another has come.

When it comes to manufacturing technology deployed, there are a wide variety of choices. At one extreme you have highly automated, capital-intensive plants and at the other you have labor-intensive custom facilities. The choice depends on the volume and cost objectives. Don't make the mistake of building today's factory for a highly uncertain future volume. If your manufacturing facility design and build lead-time is one to one and a half years, then it shouldn't be necessary to build out for more than two to four years.

Best Practices

Are your people aware of what's going on out there? Are they taking steps to keep your practices state of the art? You can learn a lot from what others are doing. In fact you will find that one of the things competitors are often willing to share are their best practices. This issue is so important that many companies have now assigned the task of keeping up to date and facilitating the implementation of best practices to a senior executive.

Manufacturing Mission and Strategy

Is your objective to be best in class, world class? Do you want to be a big fish in local waters or a fish that can hold its own in the world's oceans? Do you manufacture for a customer's order or for stock? Is your inventory management system just in time or just in case? Should your strategic objective be "continuous improvement"? And if it's continuous improvement, what should be continuously improved? Do you own or lease the facilities?

All of these are important questions but the first question should be based on a broader issue. Just like any other function, production needs to figure out what its mission is: How does it add value? The mission can be as simple as "Delivering what the customer wants, when they want it, and at the expected quality level." Once the mission statement has been defined, supporting strategies are very easy to define: build-to-order, reliable supplier network, statistical quality control, action teams, and so on. Once strategies are in place, the concept of "improving a little every day" has meaning and the relevance of such terms as *best in class* and *world class* starts to become apparent.

Whether a company's facilities should be owned or leased is an important issue and central to strategy formulation. The right answer depends on a number of considerations. The basic theory is that management should put the company's money to work where it can create the most value, and often this is not in bricks and mortar. In general, office facilities are leased unless they must be integral with a production facility that is owned. Furthermore, unless you can get an extremely favorable long-term lease, it's generally not a good idea to lease a manufacturing facility if your business is equipment intensive. All of this needs to be sorted out when the company's manufacturing strategies are being formulated. If you don't, you may place your company in the invidious position of one day having to choose between a big increase in leasing costs or an expensive and interruptive relocation. While it's impossible to cover all criteria, some general guidelines are summarized in Table 6-1.

Service Level

This is about giving meaning to a mission statement like "Delivering what the customer wants, when they want it, and at the expected quality level." For example, many people think it costs money to provide a high service level. This is true. However, experience has shown that it costs more if you aren't organized to deliver as promised. An enormous amount of non-value-added time goes into dealing with the consequences of not meeting your customer's expectations. It can range from the cost associated with making a phone call begging forgiveness to having to go out and get new customers. Furthermore, companies with high service levels are often the low-cost producers because they have

TABLE 6-1 Own or Lease Considerations

	Own	Lease
Capital intensiveness is	High	Low
Growth rate is	High	Low
Location in the long run is	Important	Unimportant
Relocation costs are	High	Low

designed and implemented the systems to provide what the customer is willing to pay for as efficiently as current technology permits and scale can justify.

Effectiveness of the Quality Program

The importance of quality is illustrated by the notion that if it costs 10 cents to fix something at the component level, it costs $1 to fix it at the subassembly level, $10 to fix it in final assembly l, and $100+ to fix it once it is in the customers' hands. While the absolute value of the various costs may be questioned, there are lots of examples that support the geometric expansion of the cost of poor quality.

Quality has been the subject of numerous texts and much literature and for good reason. Management has learned they can't survive without it and that it's one of the few ideas that cuts across all functions in an organization and is capable of delivering even more than first promised. The nature of quality is also changing. In a few short years it has gone from becoming a differentiator (Japanese cars) to being expected and often taken for granted. At one time, quality could play a decisive role in determining account share. Today it is necessary but not sufficient. In fact the quest for differentiating via quality has turned into something more. Quality has become a stepping-stone to creating additional value added.

Why has industry spent so much on quality and what are the results? Those who keep track of such things have produced formidable lists of what can be attributed to the introduction of quality programs in a company. A partial list includes increased profit, differentiation, a higher level of employee retention (people don't want to work in a company where customers yell at them), and a reduction in employee resistance to change. In fact, when it comes to culture, employee attitudes can move from one of being reactive to proactive where employees develop customer-oriented thinking and bureaucratic attitudes diminish. If the foregoing list isn't enough, here are a few more. Companies have found that when a culture is oriented around quality, two other things happen. The first is that it engages people in a process that regularly causes them to examine what they are doing and motivates them to eliminate non-value-added activities within their group or on their own. This reason alone is sufficient to justify a quality program. The second is that because you consistently deliver more than your customer expects, over time you increase your account and therefore market share, especially during tough times.

The message from the marketplace has been, "If you are not a quality company, you will be out of business." If this is so, why are there still companies out there that haven't got the message? The answer is human nature. If your management team hasn't implemented a quality program or your quality program isn't delivering as expected, the bad news is that time is running out. The good news is that you can learn from others.

Here are some lessons learned from companies with a quality culture.

- For a quality improvement program (QIP) to be effective, you have to have a cause. A cause or crisis creates the fever necessary to get real action. The cause can simply be, "If we don't do this, we will all be looking for jobs." Once you have a cause, it must be presented in such a way that it is believable and compelling.
- Implementing a QIP takes time, lots of time. As unattractive as that may be, it's better to face up to the need. Your company may go away but the need for a QIP won't.

- Every QIP involves a big culture change and all of the emotions that go with any change. You have to be in it for the long term.
- Despite an extraordinary plan and implementation, you will still make mistakes.
- QIPs fail when top management is not visibly committed.
- It is one of the hardest and most rewarding things a company can do.

When a company's quality program isn't measuring up, what does it do?

- Find yourself a teacher. There is no need to do this the hard way. There are plenty of people out there who have a verifiable track record and they can help you.
- Visit competitors and suppliers before you start.
- Get involved. Management must be committed and show the way. When leadership backs off, the process begins to wind down.
- Be the example. People will test your commitment every day. You have to say no when they ask you if they should ship a product or invoice for a service that is close but doesn't meet specification, especially if it's the end of the month or quarter.
- Keep score. Decide on the measurements and get them out there for everyone to see. This is one area in which more information is better than less.
- Encourage the people who know what the problems are to form quality action teams (QATs) that are focused on a particular issue. Help them define their charters, trust their judgment, give them the resources to implement their decisions—and stay out of their way.
- Go with those employees who embrace change, can lead, and aren't afraid to chart new ground. To the rest, you have to say "move over."
- Never give up. Perhaps more than anything else a QIP is a test of the will to succeed and do the seemingly impossible.

In summary, there probably isn't any other single program that can impact your Cost of Goods Sold as much as a solid quality improvement program. In fact, a QIP doesn't merely improve the Cost of Goods Sold; it can improve every aspect of a business. Furthermore, understand that quality is not a thing. It is a commitment to a way of managing. It's a management system.

Customer Support

This again comes back to the customer and design. There are situations where customers demand a lot of support. This shouldn't be a problem as long as you get them to pay for it upfront in the purchase price or afterward in a support service contract or on a demand basis. The problem occurs when a product is released that turns out to be support intensive and the customer doesn't want to pay for it. Then you are going to be stuck with support costs until something changes. Two possibilities exist. The first is to redesign the product or service. The second is to educate the customer. The latter isn't advisable in most circumstances. The customer will feel that you are unfairly passing the problem along to them, and while they may have to grin and bear it for now, they will be looking for an opportunity to right what they perceive to be a wrong.

Match

How well is what you are providing matched with what your customer wants? All of us open the mail every day and throw most of it out. This can become so irritating that one wishes there was some way to get the postal service to only deliver first-class mail and packages. While an extreme example, it does make the point. Are you delivering products to your customers that include things they don't use? If you want to keep costs under control, good management practice requires regular review of what is going into your deliverable and whether it should be there. For example, is there any need to include an instruction book or will a quick-start guide and a CD suffice? Furthermore, is there any need for a CD? Can the customers download what they need, when needed, from your website? A better example is packaging. Is your product both user and environmentally friendly? Unfortunately, theft and returns have caused so much havoc in the retail industry that products are packaged to prevent undesired possession and intrusion. An unintended consequence of this strategy is the customer having to literally struggle to get at the product that has been purchased and packaging that is not "green." A thorough and comprehensive design effort can result in the retailer's needs and environmental concerns being met and enhance the customer experience at the same time.

Difficult Decisions

If there is any place in a company that seems to frequently confront management with tough decisions, it's production. This area is no different from any other. Making tough decisions and making them prudently is vital. If your assumptions have proven to be incorrect or your team has made an outright mistake and put the wrong resources in place, deal with it. For example, if the factory turns out to be too big, think long and hard before you put your company in the high-risk position of trying to fill it with strategies like pre-selling and marginal pricing. Sublet part of it as soon as possible. Or, if you have bought the wrong equipment, don't defocus the company's efforts by trying to sell the machine's capacity to others. Sell the machine and get what you need. This may sound like advice that is easy to give at a distance. However, as the saying goes, "been there and done that," and experience has taught that life doesn't get any better if you put off dealing with an issue once you know the right answer.

Systems and Systemization

There are at least two places in most businesses that are highly amenable to systemization. Administration is one and production is the other. You can't have a cost-effective manufacturing operation without the right degree of systemization that permits the production people to work efficiently, and scorecards (control panel) that give employees the information needed. This is not to say that the production facility must have the latest system with all of the features that are proclaimed by some to be essential. In fact, often the opposite is true. The media are full of stories of major companies that have spent enormous amounts of money on business systems and still don't have what they need to run their businesses, let alone what they thought they were getting. In fact, some of these companies have virtually been brought to their knees for a period of time by systems that were too ambitious, and in some cases this caused them to aggressively seek damages.

While there is a long list of failures, the list of successes is much longer. In fact a manufacturing resource planning system (MRP) is essential if the company is to have cost-effective manufacturing or assembly plants, as are customer resource systems (CRS) and financial reporting systems vital to efficient Sales and Marketing and Administration, respectively. The bottom line based on experience is that systems that are friendly, easy to learn, and address 80–90% of the requirements are more effective and easier to implement than complicated systems that promise more and in fact are capable of delivering more but at a high price because they demand too much in the way of process reengineering and training.

Control

In some ways, control is a separate subject. And yet it is closely linked with the systematization issues. One way of looking at control is that it's what it takes to make a business operate efficiently and deliver products and services at the budgeted cost levels. Control can't do anything to lower the inherent cost of a product or service because the cost is built in when it is designed. What it can do is make sure that the art of the possible is achieved. Furthermore, it is invaluable when it comes to identifying problems and helpful when crafting solutions before things have escalated and management has a fire drill on their hands. There are numerous consultants out there who are ready to lend a hand when it comes to designing and implementing good control systems. The point is that unless you have good control and systems, you will not have predictable and cost-effective performance from the production facility, nor will you achieve your Cost of Goods Sold targets.

Operating Expenses

Operating Expenses are poorly named. Managers shouldn't spend money on anything unless it is expected to provide a return. In this context, Operating Expenses are really investments. Business is stuck with this terminology. However, you will find it helpful when deciding where to spend money if you learn to think in terms of what any expenditure will return regardless of its accounting classification.

The major components of a company's operating expenses are: Marketing, Research and Product Development, Sales, Service, and Administration. The attitude one takes to controlling the expenses associated with any of these is often driven by the need to

TABLE 6-2 Time Horizons for Operating Expenses

Function	Short Run	Long Run
Marketing		x
Research and Development		x
Sales	x	
Service		x
Administration		x

manage the bottom line. Over the years, Table 6-2 has been presented to various management teams by the author with the objective of having them complete the table by inserting a mark in either the "short run" or "long run" box, depending on which time horizon they thought was the correct one from a strategic perspective. In almost every case, the chart was completed as indicated. The only area that seemed to vacillate from one time domain to the other was Sales. On average, it came up as being "short run" and so it has been left that way even though there is a strong argument for saying that it, too, should be managed for the long run.

The interesting thing is that confronted with a chart that shows what they believed to be the right time perspective to take on these expenses, they didn't have a good answer to the question: "If you believe all of these should be managed for the long run, why do you use them as levers to control the short-run bottom line?" The best answer received was: "That's just the way the world is."

That of course is true, especially for public companies. But in well-managed companies, public or private, it's a matter of degree. Companies that are well managed do less chopping and changing of Operating Expenses than those management teams that can't seem to get it all together. One of the reasons for this is: They haven't worked out what the customer is paying for let alone how to efficiently provide it. One way of thinking about this issue is embedded in "The Expense Coverage Ratio," which is the subject of Chapter 8.

Marketing

Marketing in most well-managed companies is centered on brand building, identifying needs, and altering perceptions. When well spent, it represents one of the best investments a company can make.

Every manager believes marketing is important. However, human nature being what it is, people are more inclined to spend money on something they can see (like a machine or another salesperson) than something like marketing, where the consequences of the spending take time to emerge and, even when evident, what actually brought it about is subject to debate. The question isn't "Do you need to spend money on marketing?" but rather "How much and on what?" The *what* used to be relatively well understood (i.e., perception building, promotion, and product differentiation). The advent of the Internet has added a new dimension. The goal of marketing can be defined as branding, identifying needs, and altering perceptions. When the burdens of *marketing in tech markets* and the *Internet-driven information culture* are added, other aspects need to be considered. Here are some insights on how to deal with the marketing issues that confront manufacturers and channels alike.

The Internet: Issues for Marketing

Thought leadership Product differentiation is no longer a matter limited to what can be defined within a table of dimensions, functions, features, and benefits. A company must use media channels of all kinds, not the least of which is the Internet, to continuously put forward a unique concept or approach that outlines how its products deliver value, and the actual nature of the product must ultimately substantiate the claim. Much like a novel where the story has to have the cohesion afforded it by its theme, a vendor needs to set forth what is unique conceptually about the way it designs, delivers, or builds its offering and try to get the market to accept that concept as at least different from alternatives. Otherwise, the vendor becomes commoditized in a field of vendors attempting to differentiate at the feature/benefit level (or worse, by price), which often leaves customers frustrated and ends in unpredictable vendor selection behavior. For example: Steve Jobs's minimalist design obsession combined with "it just has to work" was the theme that eventually spawned the iPhone's thousands of unique design benefits upon its first release. Everyone wants to be considered *innovative* but the market is now tone-deaf to this overused term. Establishing one's company as the vendor that is innovating within the envelope of a unique vision still resonates, and becomes the foundation of the company's core articulated sales argument.

Supporting the ideal level of consumer self-education Marketing must support the consumer's demand for a great deal of information about products or services but needs to do so in a way that enables the customers to first educate themselves independently of interaction with sales personnel or the vendor directly. This means that Marketing must now walk a very delicate line between providing too much online product information and not enough. In the former scenario, customers may educate themselves to a very knowledgeable level without direct interaction with the company and exit their online exploration feeling no need to contact the vendor. When this happens, the opportunity to properly promote the solution directly and drive the sale forward in the traditional way via skilled sales personnel is missed. Or worse, if the marketing is misinterpreted, the customer could reject the vendor based on a flawed takeaway of the material that has been accessed. In the scenario of too little online information about the product, modern customers can become quickly frustrated with their inability to make an informed decision as to whether to consider the vendor for selection and exit the process before it begins. Today's consumer expects all manner of resources such as product videos, testimonials, typical applications, and product data to explore before they contact a salesperson.

Transactional speed and ease Here the focus must be on the delivery mechanism of the service or solution. This is due to the radical increase in consumer expectations for transactional speed and simplicity born of experiences such as video on demand, music and app purchases, streaming movie services, and so on. The experiences of these household and personal purchase processes are now becoming expected in business-to-business transactions. There is a simple foundational rule to creating an effective purchase experience in modern marketing: Make it easy for customers to part with their money. For reasons that are hard to fathom some venerable firms still do not understand this. For example, compare Apple's ecosystem to other competitors; Apple enables consumers to purchase movies, music, and apps instantly via only one username and password through either iTunes or the App Store—just two portals, which are usable through any of their content-delivery devices or even on competitors' devices and PCs. It's instant, simple, and always extracts money from the customer whenever they are willing to part with it. Compare this to a major competitor's implementation. Until recently and before the publishing of this book, one competitor required users to go to separate stores for movies, music, apps, and videos. Sometimes they use points, other times they use currency and a credit card. The points were related to actual currency but ran the risk of leaving the customer confused as to what they were actually paying. Consider the comparison of these two models. One requires considerable effort on how to part with your money to generate revenue and the other requires a single logon from any of your devices. This is a failure of marketing's ability to guide the engineers implementing the customer experience into building something that makes parting with money easy.

Human interface minimization In the not-so-long-run, consumers and businesses will favor vendors that make the transactions with the company as human-free as possible. There is a large and growing population of customers who believe the introduction of a human into any purchase or service transaction increases the risk of errors, failure, or aggravation. Perhaps 10 years ago, it was considered a positive differentiator if you had great customer service with real people on the phone. Now the paradigm has shifted; many consumers want the product to simply work and any service they might need should be delivered through online knowledge-bases. This shift has its genesis in the innumerable millions of bad service experiences with offshore support techs and unhelpful clerks. This drove a large number of consumers into the arms of the self-service support knowledge-base and online purchase transactions. It extends in particular to the expectation that the customer's entire interaction with a vendor be visible and accessible via an online "account" portal, further eliminating the need to contact a physical person for information.

Image and messaging uniformity The subconscious perception of the customer as to the professionalism of a vendor is impacted by the quality and uniformity of the image and message at each contact with that vendor. Some find the marketer's obsession with font and color uniformity amusing, but tight control over the entire image across literature, website, e-mails, e-mail signatures, PowerPoint presentations, shipping boxes, tradeshow booths, clothing, promotional items, office signage and colors, and business cards is like a fine business suit and conveys professionalism. Perhaps more important, a company with varied messaging across its mechanisms confuses their prospective customers and shows poorly.

Accountability While the impact of marketing has been and continues to be highly refined in consumer packaged goods companies like the Campbell's Soup Company, one of the great benefits of the new age of marketing is accountability for many for the first time. Gone are the days where the marketing director could really get away with substandard performance and hide under the veil of "It's hard to quantify results in marketing—trust me." Now, with online marketing, everything can be tracked: e-mail responses, clicks, even automatic mapping of visitors to the site back to their corporate ID and then auto-map to Hoovers data. The exact path through the website visitors take and the time they dwell on each page are all available. The depth of information available to a well-run marketing department is tremendous. The yield of every banner advertisement versus an e-mail campaign is instantly available. The actual return on investment can now be calculated and managers should demand that it is indeed assessed and that the information is used to continuously improve the marketing program by pruning the ineffective and augmenting the effective.

The Internet: Issues for Manufacturers and Channels

Take your marketing budget seriously Most companies budget some amount of expenditure on marketing. Then, in many companies, top management instructs the marketing group to go slowly and "see how the first quarter turns out" before they commit. In order for marketing to show results, it takes time and consistent strategies. When the marketing budget depends on the first quarter or some other milestone, then the company is not committed to marketing. A stop-and-go, up-and-down approach will not achieve very much, if anything. If your margins are thin and the mechanisms available to you to control the bottom line are minimal, you are better off agreeing on some level of marketing you can afford and challenging your people to be creative rather than building their expectations and then have them waiting around for management to fire the starting gun.

Commit and stay the course on marketing investments Unfortunately, this isn't always the case. Why is marketing spending often seen as the first thing that can be cut when budgets are under pressure? Here are three reasons:

1. Until the Internet and sophisticated CRM software systems became available, marketing return on investment was very difficult to calculate, so the natural inclination was to assume it wasn't really working.
2. Many marketing benefits, such as the uniformity and branding mentioned previously, continue to be nearly impossible to quantify in terms of return. If investments in marketing are to yield results, it is very important that corporate leadership accept and commit that at least some of these things are sacrosanct despite having no means of assessing their return. Essentially brand identity and maintaining uniformity and image are so important that the leadership team must send a strong message emphasizing that they are not disposable. By so doing, the value of these things will be better accepted by the organization, thus increasing adoption.
3. Since businesspeople are not very patient by nature, they often don't allow marketing programs to unfold as intended. It sometimes takes years of consistent messaging to become properly branded, and brand, like culture, is ultimately the foundation great companies are built upon.

Control of the customer The battle for control for the customer relationship is alive and well and seemingly without end. Distribution channels believe their role in the marketing equation has been undervalued. Sometimes manufacturers are of the view that the distributor is a necessary evil. In a manner of speaking, those that produce the product or service have been in a marriage of convenience with those that take it to the customer. The one thing that the Internet is doing is inadvertently bringing the producers and their distribution channels closer together. Historically, manufacturers have tried to control the customer relationship with the attributes of their product and service. The sales channel has historically focused on providing the human relationship. Both of these models are dated and need to be modified. The Internet is forcing manufacturers and distribution channels to redefine their roles. In fact, the new role for the distributor is one of having to build portals that eliminate the human intermediary in the buying process and replace the human with speed and information.

All of this perhaps really speaks to a larger and quite interesting question: What place in business does the skilled salesperson now occupy? Have online marketing, direct e-mail, online purchases and customer portals, and volumes of product videos and PDFs done away with the need for the art of selling person-to-person? In the Internet era, "Do we really need Willy Loman?" The answer to this has at least two aspects, depending on the nature of the product or service. First, consider commodities like media content, clothing, consumer goods—essentially almost anything that can be had via Amazon or eBay. In these areas, the skilled salesperson and rep/distributor is no longer of high value, if of any value at all. Many customers engaged in these transactions actually seek to avoid salespeople as it is a hindrance to the speed at which they expect to acquire the product. When it comes to higher value or highly complex products and services an online purchase transaction is not practical, and customers are more interested in attaining the feeling that they are certain they made the right selection via full awareness of product information and value than they are in transactional speed. It is in these types of solution sales where marketing (as mentioned previously) must strive to provide enough initial data to the online consumer, but then create a natural inclination for that consumer to then contact the skilled salesperson, because only through a thorough sales process will they get the information they need to make an informed selection. In these sales, the sales skill and possibly the relationships involved are critical to driving the sale forward.

Look at the Internet as a tool In some ways, the fuss that is being made over the Internet is comical. One would almost think that nothing like it had existed before. Primitive Internets have been around for some time, for example, the African Internet (drums) and the Aboriginal Internet (smoke signals). More recently, other Internets have emerged. For example: the Victorian Internet (telegraph and teletype) and the transmission Internet (facsimile machine). In their day, they all had an impact and, in the context of the technology that was around at the time, represented remarkable advancements. In the case of the teletype and facsimile machines, they revolutionized how business was done. Like its predecessors, the Internet is a tool and nothing more. It will only deliver lasting benefits for those who take time to think through the issues, form a view on the impact the Internet will have on their business, and develop strategies that will build new customer relationships and loyalty.

In a sense the drama over the Internet is overblown, as it is just a new mechanism. However, there is one major difference between it and any mechanism before it. The difference is related to the prior section. In certain cases the Internet can literally dispose of the salesforce. It becomes the salesperson and can take the transaction completely autonomously from curiosity, customer education, promotion, to completing the financial transaction. Perhaps the uniqueness of this bears noting.

The online marketplace The fact that everyone can go online has changed the playing field. It has also brought a new participant to the game, the online (OL) marketplace. At first, the prognosis was that the online marketplace would render the "middleman" obsolete. Anyone who believes this will happen anytime soon needs to take a look at what's happening. Building a portal can be expensive—$50 million-plus. This has made OL marketers (like Amazon and Alibaba) recognize that unless they are very large, a business model based on a fee for processing transactions may not be viable for the long run and that they, like everyone else, have to find ways to offer other services that add margin, such as advertising.

Now that the majority of the hype is past, the OL marketers are facing a reality check and are increasingly seeing manufacturers and distributors as providers of logistical services, sources for brand-name products, and in fact potential customers. One of the online marketplace's pitches to manufacturers is: "Give me access to your brand and let me show you what I can do with it." Another is: "In return for access to your brand, we will give you a chance to become an equity partner." Some are trying to charge fees for virtual shelf-space. The reality is that many manufacturers have the financial wherewithal to go it alone. This and the fact that the online marketplace can offer distributors access to information technology services that few could afford on their own, may drive the traditional distribution channels and the OL marketers closer together. What will be the outcome of all of this? Only time will tell. In some instances, it will bring manufacturers and distributors closer together. In others, it will drive them apart and cause OL marketers and distributors to work together. One thing is for sure: There is plenty of opportunity and all models are evolving. No one-size-fits-all model is anywhere near being dominant and manufacturers, distributors, and OL marketers alike will only end up at the right place if they are in there working the opportunity.

The online marketer (OLM) The advantage an OLM (like a niche player such as Best Buy and their strong commercial site) has over a manufacturer building their own portal is the very fact that an OLM can promote many brands whereas the manufacturer cannot. And this limitation negates the "collateral" or information requirements that buyers have come to expect. An example is Samsung, which hosts its own first-class commerce site. This site and others like it are outstanding for learning about what the company offers, but better prices are available at other sites such as Buy.com or Amazon or Best Buy, which sell all of the brands. Special cases do exist where the OLM is bypassed, instances where the product is esoteric and has little competition. An example is replacement high-end filters for furnaces that local HVAC (heating, ventilation, and air conditioning) companies charge premiums for but an online vendor sells at a lower price. No need for an OLM layer there.

Supply chain and customer relationships are changing. The dynamics of the manufacturer–distribution channel–customer relationship are changing but the distribution channel as we know it will be around for some time. While the use of the Internet continues to evolve, the one thing that seems certain is that the OLMs will have an impact on customer relationships. Direct salesforces, distributors, and so on have already figured out that their role has changed and are moving away from selling product to redefining themselves as more of an extension of the customer than as part of the manufacturer's marketing efforts. In a sense, they are moving toward a business model of providing outsourcing services to customers. The manufacturers' response is twofold. One is they accept that their product is a commodity and focus on finding new ways to motivate the distribution channel. The other is to develop strategies that will provide new and innovative ways to satisfy end user needs and use the Internet to further their quest for control of the customer relationship.

E-Commerce Considerations

E-commerce is producing a paradigm shift in the way business is done. Many companies see this technology as a tool that will enable them to reduce SG&A expenses, capture incremental business, improve inventory turns, improve cash flow, and increase the bottom line. Recognizing the promise is one thing; delivering results is another. Like any other business tool, applying it effectively requires a clear objective.

Much of its economic promise has been difficult to capture and as a result goals and strategies vary all over the map. Some see e-commerce as a way to take a more direct control of the customer relationship. Others see the objective as being one of changing the game and thereby capturing business that is currently going to competitors. However, those taking this approach should be wary that Internet marketing is actually making product differentiation based on "controlling the relationship" or perhaps "salesmanship" largely obsolete because buyer self-education has been made easy to access and simple. Another group views this as an epiphany. They are focused on the experience factor and are determined to learn how to leverage the opportunities presented by the Internet and in the long run position their company for the new marketing paradigm. Companies that have successfully gone down the E-commerce path have come to grips with a few basic issues:

Who buys products and services over the Internet? A better question would be: Who doesn't? Before getting into the question of who buys on the Internet, it is important to recognize that product availability is also often a strong motivation for Internet purchases. The Internet offers a much broader scope of products and brands than you are likely to have access to within reasonable driving distance of your home. This effect is even more dramatic for consumers in less urban areas.

There is considerable support for the notion that a growing group of consumers would rather not involve a salesperson and that this results in a motivator for online transactions. Evidence of this is the advent of "buy online, pick up at store." Home Depot, Best Buy, Lowe's, and Wal-Mart all offer this convenience now. Consider the interesting buyer motivation that underlies this model. They are obviously able and willing to drive to the store, but then they add the online process at home to actually complete the transaction. Why would someone do this? Expediency, perhaps, in that they don't have to walk the showroom, but that is really a minor benefit. Another and perhaps more credible explanation for the growth of these models is consumer disappointment with salespeople as a result of years of having sales personnel give poor and in some cases misleading information to consumers, who are often better educated about the products than they are. A third reason may be that consumers are so pressed for time that they place value on searching for the items they need after-hours at home online, and then having these items queued up for them the next day and by doing so eliminating such things as the time involved in aisle-hunting.

The instant gratification factor is also in play here. The consumer benefits from the online transaction, but gets the product in 30 minutes or less if it can be downloaded. However, it should be noted that Google and others are testing services to actually cut delivery times of physical products to same-day delivery in select markets. This could usher in another paradigm shift and possibly have major ramifications for companies like UPS and FedEx as well.

This notion of a desire to eliminate contact with people, whether point of sale (POS) clerks or salespeople, is a major motivator in the shifts in consumer buying patterns as exemplified by the Wawa experience. Wawa has introduced kiosks for ordering a deli sandwich just in front of the POS clerk to whom one formerly gave one's order verbally. Shortly after the installation of those kiosks, almost no one ordered from the attendants anymore. The kiosk eliminates order-taking risk, presents options much better, does a much better job of upselling, and enables the consumer to pay while the sandwich is being made rather than waiting until it is finished. If and when Wawa extends that kiosk to online, they could introduce an efficient drive-through window and increase their turnover by double or more. Restaurants have already begun to move in the Wawa direction with the introduction of menus and wine lists on iPads. Given this development, terminals to eliminate the order-taker cannot be far behind. In fact the original Microsoft "Surface" was a very interesting interactive glass surface. The original design was in part intended for restaurant tables. The thought was menus, wine lists, and ordering would be via the table surface and at the end of the meal the credit card would be scanned by simply putting it down on the table. Unfortunately it was complicated and expensive and one of those great ideas whose time had not come.

"Configure to order" has become a major driver of online transactions and consumers love it. Dell and others allow incredible depth of product configuration completely online. Consumers value this tremendously. They not only are able to customize their order but can also adjust the cost of the product to their liking. However, on the manufacturing side, it is extremely difficult to operate a factory in which each product is essentially a unique permutation. The consumer could not care less, of course, but this does have tremendous impact on manufacturing systems.

There are several kinds of E-commerce customers. Six of the more common are:

1. Customers who need something immediately such as downloadable media or software that can be obtained within moments of credit card approval are attracted to the web. No other distribution channel equals or surpasses that service.
2. People who feel comfortable with their underlying knowledge base and can find sites that offer a full range of complex, option-heavy products with shopping comparisons

that have great analysis value and an ordering system that has dynamic order tracking and e-mail notification.

3. The convenience buyer who simply finds an Internet purchase easier than driving 10 minutes to a store even if there is a shipping charge. Or they are legitimately so busy that they buy things online at 11 p.m. when stores are not an option.
4. Buyers like the high-end replacement filter buyer mentioned earlier. Commodity items may have been traditionally only sold through local service outlets at great markups but now are available online and there is no need to research or compare.
5. Purchasers of products that don't require any evaluation of quality or function and buyers who don't need to touch and feel the product to determine what they want to purchase.
6. Then there are those who know exactly what they want and madly search the various sites for the lowest price.

What kind of products and services should be offered? There are three broad categories that have so far shown that they are amenable to Internet commerce:

1. An immediate gratification product such as software, music, or video downloads.
2. Option-heavy, brand-proven products like Dell, Sony, and Lenovo that require a lot of option comparisons, price tallying, and so on and where order tracking is important.
3. Products that have become commodities and don't require function or quality analysis prior to purchase are prime candidates. Consumable contact lenses, maintenance and office supplies, and other branded consumables are prime candidates for web ordering.

None of this should suggest that the in-store experience is passé. If it were, how would one account for the Apple stores and manufacturers' kiosks at Best Buy? The point is: While there will always be consumers who want the in-store experience, this will only be one market segment, which more than likely will shrink over time.

Is the targeted customer group ready for e-commerce? Just placing the order may be more trouble than it's worth for a company that has effective systems in place for ordering industrial components with International Standards Organization (ISO) procedures stacked to the ceiling that are based on processing paper purchase orders with paper order tracking, and so forth. If orders for a broad product or service category can't be placed efficiently, purchasing agents may regard the benefits of Internet purchasing as terribly minor given the bigger picture and their stack of orders that they have to process every day.

Credit cards Payment by credit card has become standard Internet protocol. This means buyers will have to pay for their purchase on 30-day terms or less. This is inconsistent with the objectives of the finance department in a company that wants to hold on to as much money as possible for as long as possible and negotiates terms of 60 days and longer.

Even if a broad product offering and credit cards aren't an issue, companies will balance the cost of altering internal procedures and so on with the benefits they receive through web ordering. To be sure, there is a transition under way but it's driven by investment and payback considerations, not what's in vogue at the moment.

What will the impact be on your existing distribution channel? This is a very important question for manufacturers. While Internet marketing is no longer speculative, the list of disappointments is much longer than the compendium of successes. The win-win scenario occurs when everyone benefits. This can't always be the case and so manufacturers still have to worry about undercutting their distribution network and what the network may do to survive, because, like manufacturers, distributors are determined to add value and play a role in future customer relationships.

Developing E-Commerce Strategies

Assuming your company gets comfortable with these and other fundamental issues, the following are some of the things successful companies think about when developing e-commerce strategies.

Decide on the Targeted Customers Often there is a temptation to keep the site simple and only offer certain products or features for purchase on the web. Buyers in general expect to be able to view and purchase a fully optioned product or service. Companies that have taken this limited approach have often found it backfired because buyers were put off by the fact they were only able to purchase certain elements of a company's offering online and not others. So the message here is your site should offer the targeted customers a complete buying experience and not give them any reason to go elsewhere and run the risk of having them purchase from a competitor.

Define Ways to Get Customers to Visit the Website *Driving traffic to the site* must come first and foremost. All media mechanisms such as press releases, executive interviews, videos, articles, case studies, webinars, blogging, and so on should strive to drive traffic to the website as well. To accomplish this, the website must be broadly focused or offer a truly unique product or service. Narrowly focused websites are inconsistent with one of the objectives of web marketing, which is to give full accessibility and visibility to the company's entire line. It is very frustrating for users when they cannot compare all of the products and services the company offers on one site and have to go from site to site to figure out what's going on.

The "web experience" must be meaningful, positive, and memorable. The availability of an online knowledge base forms the backbone of the experience. There would be no need for this if consumers could dial a number and talk to someone who could answer their questions. However, this is not the real world. Customers are increasingly growing to appreciate what a knowledge base can deliver because, again, it isolates them from what most often turns out to be inefficient human interaction. They can find out answers to service questions and are increasingly making use of knowledge bases when it comes to higher value industrial products and software as well.

Driving Internet traffic is a complex subject in and of itself and it is beyond the scope of this book to adequately deal with it. However, a few key mechanisms are perhaps worth noting:

- Pay-per-click search advertising
- Banner advertising on industry-related sites
- "Swarming" by supporting blog and other site activity around your offering to drive your search rankings organically
- Linking of noncompetitive sites into your site
- E-Direct marketing via e-mail advertisement driven by internal marketing lists and purchased lists

Ecosystems In certain businesses, the concept of ecosystems is becoming a tremendously powerful marketing mechanism. Locking customers into a platform in such a way that the pain of leaving it is too great in terms of infrastructure investments or software or content investment is an excellent marketing strategy. For example: Once someone goes down the Apple road buying video content and music along with some of their devices, it is very difficult to move away. Much like production robots with feeders in a manufacturing site, once a company has purchased a certain brand of feeder and robot, it's hard to migrate, not because of the robot but because of the feeder investment.

The current battle going on is for the media ecosystems, and it's a complicated affair of having the consumption devices, the media itself, and the software delivery systems. Google, Amazon, Microsoft, and Apple all want to own that ecosystem. The problem is that no one vendor can deliver everything, at least for now. It's possible that such systems can embed a vendor and their products into customers unlike any other mechanism. Vendors should strive to develop some form of *entrenchment ecosystem* that has three goals: (1) It must actually deliver real value to the customers through their adoption of it by designing the ecosystem to offer something individual point solutions cannot. (2) It should be structured so that it organically compels customers to further entrench themselves in the ecosystem. (3) Exiting it is so costly in terms of money, time, or aggravation that the customer simply is disinclined to even contemplate it.

Make the Buyer Feel Comfortable with E-Commerce Changing customers' buying habits is really the objective. Some of the issues that your strategies must deal with are:

- **Credit:** Breaking through the credit card barrier, if there is one, is first and foremost. When another company is the customer, take time to get them comfortable with this practice. In some cases you may have to offer inducements. In other cases you will need to be prepared to deal with the unexpected. Remember, consumers have been conditioned to accept a level of shoddy credit card etiquette. A company won't take kindly to being told their request has been turned down.
- **Overlap:** Manage any overlap between current customers and the market segment at which the website is targeted. If you don't take the time to think this through and put an effective plan in place in the beginning, your salesforce is going to find itself very busy trying to sort out the inevitable confusion that will follow.

- **Differentiation:** Unless everything you have is on the web, you need to have the discipline and skills to differentiate web and non-web products and services in a manner that is comprehensible and intuitively compelling to the customer.
- **Commitment:** The Company must commit to keeping the site fresh and ever changing. A static site over time is off-putting to customers, but keeping it dynamic requires continuous investment and dedication.

The Web Experience Must Be Completely Integrated and Automated It should provide real-time order status and e-mail notification. Customers must be able to track their shipments if they wish to do so, 24 hours per day, 7 days per week, and able to talk or chat with support personnel 24/7. If this isn't possible, it must be available throughout the working day, taking customer time zones into account. Delivery promises must be met. Instances where there are problems must be flagged by the system and result in an e-mail to the customer detailing the issues, actions taken, and choices available to the customer before the customer finds out that there is a problem on their own.

Maintain Website Content at a Level That Keeps Customers Coming Back For example, if the site is automated and loaded with product option comparisons, competitive product and price comparisons, dynamic applets that change coloring, and other content that will bring the buyers back, then the site will have value and people will use it.

Examine Your Cost Structure Those companies that examine their cost structure in the context of the power and capabilities of the Internet will realize the promise of e-commerce. Remember, Internet companies are focused on controlling the customer relationship and they are going to have an impact on distribution costs. More important, perhaps, the opportunities presented by e-commerce may turn out to be the most viable strategy for manufacturers and distributors alike to take steps that assure they will continue to be in charge of the customer relationship. E-commerce has the potential of: providing customers and distributors with up-to-date product specifications and data in real time as opposed to depending on the mail or salespeople; reducing order processing costs and minimizing errors with expert systems; giving customers access to order status and details associated with shipping; reducing the cost of serving small customers and at the same time increasing the service level; providing competent technical support in real time on a cost-effective basis; gathering input and data that are helpful in product design and the design of programs focused on responding to changing customer needs, and so forth.

There are benefits to be captured by functions outside of sales and marketing as well. These opportunities include permitting manufacturers to schedule production based on point-of-sale demand as opposed to forecast and thereby achieve a higher on-time delivery performance with less inventory, and the ability to optimize inventory and shipping costs by checking all warehousing and manufacturing sites before deciding where to place the order.

Research and Development

Earlier the concept of thought leadership was introduced as was the importance of same when planning and executing websites. Companies should have a thought-leadership vision when it comes to product planning that coalesces with the marketing thrust. In fact the vision must be the underpinning of the product itself, since it is the genesis of all product ideas that would be formulated by R&D or marketing or product management. Without this, disjointed products will be spawned that don't fit the corporate message or vision. When this happens it usually ends badly.

While this function is called R&D in most companies it is really *product development*. This is because in practice most companies do very little basic research.

If one of marketing's tasks is to identify customer needs, then the product development group's prime responsibility is to find solutions to customers' needs that have been identified.

Types of R&D

The objectives of any R&D investment plan should be: Grow the business; maintain a core of key technologies; advance the state of the art in those technologies that give the company a sustainable competitive advantage; achieve or maintain a number-1 or number-2 position in the major markets served; achieve a balance between the development cycle and the product life cycle, and thereby position the product to provide an adequate return on investment for the company. To accomplish this, companies engage in different types of R&D that can be described as follows:

- **Defensive:** This is where the competition is ahead and the company is losing market share.
- **Offensive or innovation:** This consists of new and hopefully big ideas that will create a leading concept. It is concerned with developing next-generation products, advancing the state of the art, and developing new technologies.
- **Renovation:** This consists of product line maintenance (PLM[3]) and product line extensions (PLE).

The mistake many companies make is spending too much money on renovation and not doing innovation particularly well. Programs like cost reduction (PLM), component substitution (PLM), and new options and features (PLE) are important, but the fact is that renovation spending is tantamount to spending money on yesterday's deliverable and technology. Most company management teams know this and yet find it difficult to resist renovation (or *continuation* as it is sometimes called) projects. Why? It may be because, relatively speaking, it is perceived to be an incremental approach and thereby inherently involving less risk. While this may be true early in the life cycle of a product or technology, it certainly isn't if a technology shift is on the horizon.

---

[3] *PLM* is also used to designate "product lifecycle management," which is used by many companies to manage the R&D cycle and all of the software subsystems involved.

Getting It Right

Ideally, marketing should tell the R&D people what they want—end of story. This generally works very well in consumer product companies in food or cosmetic businesses. However, things seldom work that way in technology companies, because marketing usually has great difficulty specifying in sufficient detail what they require. This is not necessarily because they are incompetent. In fact, they can be skilled and still fail because, unless the department has an unusual cadre of people with a flair for vision and an understanding of both the application and technologies involved, the folks in R&D will always know more. Another reason is that marketing can formulate unfounded assumptions about what a technology can deliver and, therefore, makes unrealistic demands, at least unrealistic in the time frame available. If you want your R&D, Marketing, Sales, and Manufacturing areas to be effective and efficient, focus on talent, not numbers of people. If you don't have a few of the best and brightest, it's going to be tough for you to compete. It's also important to recognize that in many situations it's not how much a company spends but what it spends its money on. For niche-oriented companies in particular, it's the only way they can compete with organizations that have more resources. Finally, because there is a tendency to want it yesterday, not enough time is spent doing investigations and experiments, identifying vendors, and so on before serious engineering gets under way.

Technology

Technology cannot be turned on and off like a water tap. Investment must be continuous and aligned with long-term objectives. If you want to be a technology leader in your niche, then you need to take a measured view of the long term and put suitable strategies in place. An effective long-term technology strategy should require the company to make explicit outsourcing and licensing choices. You don't need to do everything yourself.

It's smart to purchase technology when it is readily available or prohibitively expensive to develop and precludes an adequate return on investment. In addition, work your patent portfolio and license and be licensed. But keep in mind: Purchasing or licensing technology can only go so far. Management must ensure that the company always has a sufficient stream of proprietary technology and core skills and competencies to maintain its desired competitive position. This involves developing and keeping core technology in-house and the manufacture/assembly of strategy-critical components and products in-house as well.

Technology shifts do happen. When a new technology emerges remember you have choices. You can walk away. Sometimes this is the only possible course when the technology shift is too great and it takes great leadership to recognize such threats and accept the pain. However, if you have a strong position, it may be worth defending. There may be time to reinvigorate. It may be possible to buy and bury the competitor. Or a position can be built by internal development, licensing, or the purchase of suitable technologies. Whatever you do, keep your nerve. Run the business as usual but look forward and outward at other industries, potential partners, joint ventures, and academia. Place side bets on longshot technologies that just might work out and become big threats. Learn how to build an organization that can innovate and create the capacity for growth. One final thought on this subject: Be careful of the consequences of bringing radically new technologies into factories or organizations designed and trained in other ways of working.

Innovation

Managing spending on innovation is extremely challenging and the results are often disappointing. Reasons why spending on innovative projects often yields little are poor market research and a lack of understanding of the art of the possible.

There are four concepts traditionally associated with innovation. While all of them are useful, they do have some downsides. *Creativity* can lead to a warehouse of unexploited ideas. *Entrepreneurship* can lead to fragmented efforts. *Champions* can become prima donnas who are impossible to manage. And a *can-do climate* can lead to barely controlled chaos. Before a project is started, subject it to *roadmapping*. This will lead to the creation of an integrated map of required technologies, competencies, products, and market position. It will also bring structure to the process of creating breakthrough product plans and increase the probability that the objective will be achieved. The principles of strategic planning are also valuable when it comes to innovation because "the project becomes a process" whereby the entire organization becomes involved in defining a complete chain of activities from translating market intelligence and insights into customers' future needs, to creating a product and technology vision, to formulating a strategy for producing and marketing those products and technologies.

The discipline engendered by strategic planning will help the people in the organization learn how to develop key competencies, that is, discovering potential customers' unarticulated needs, systematically screening for and managing the really valuable ideas, venturing to take ideas to market rapidly and in a lean fashion, testing new concepts very quickly and inexpensively, and learning how to identify mechanisms that will make the whole process repeatable and therefore continuously improvable.

Here are a few guidelines for launching an innovation program for R&D projects.

- View it as an ideal vehicle for a mind-set change.
- Appoint an experienced and successful manager who is keen to pioneer "the new way" to lead the program.
- In the beginning get a coach, someone who can help the project team identify and employ tools and techniques that support the learning processes.
- It must cut across key functional roles. The entire organization needs to learn how to play a role.
- The project must be bounded and of a manageable size.
- A fixed constraint (such as a launch date) should be set.

Software

When it comes to software there are also unique challenges that are consistently encountered. First, unlike a hardware device or a service, software cannot be fully designed up front and turn out well. This is particularly true when it comes to the user interface experience. Next, customers, no matter how insightful or helpful or smart, seem unable to define what they actually want in software at any depth beyond the top-level capabilities. In a sense, this is an unusual burden for software architects as opposed to other product designers to create something that actually meets the customer requirements without the customer being able to properly articulate what those requirements are. Finally, there is the issue of latency and experience.

The product must operate quickly and not make the user wait or respond in a non-intuitive manner to latency and the experience must look slick. It can be argued that Apple's fortune rests on their understanding of the value people place on these things. In fact the capability of a software interface or product is actually secondary to these critical issues. Many things in Apple's iOS are limited compared to other platforms. However, Apple understood that people will embrace a limited scope of features in exchange for something that responds instantly to input. They have set a bar now and nothing infuriates users more than waiting for an interface to respond—and this does not mean results must come instantly—it merely means the interface has to do something when they interact with it, just as physical entities in the world do. This is a seemingly simple concept but one that seems to be lost on many other companies entirely.

Thoughts on how to engineer a software product:

- First the functional capabilities must be defined, with the underlying architecture, and serious choices about what technical generation of underlying software technologies are to be used must be made. Bleeding-edge development tools are risky. Safe current technology usually results in an outdated product at release. Experience has shown that selecting a tool that is one generation back from the bleeding edge typically becomes mature and stable by the time the product is released and tends to be ideal.
- A few capabilities must be utterly new and not shared by any competitor. It is even better if they are obvious, tangible, and indisputable to even an untrained person. Something truly new must exist in order to have a few key points to press when faced with the basic question: "What's different about your product versus the competitor's product?" It could be a style of interface or a whole product extension not done by any competitor, but above all it must be something different and of value when presented to the customer. The ideal situation is one in which the differentiators are utterly unique and obviously different and the value they represent for the customer crystal clear.
- An iterative design cycle is required that involves service personnel, marketing, sales, applications engineering, QA, finance, and R&D. These disciplines are involved for four reasons. (1) The people in the service organization are closest to the customers in terms of understanding how they react to interfaces and what they like least about current capabilities in the offering. In addition, these people will instinctively object to designs that will cause them nightmares in supporting the product once released. They have no desire to be on the phone explaining the operation of a bad GUI (graphical user interface) to myriad customers in the future. (2) The sales and applications people know what customers say they want during sales processes, which is often unrelated to what they really want. However, without this input, nothing can be sold because it's the first line of interaction with the customer, and features and interface must align with what sells in those early demonstrations. (3) The quality

assurance team must be able to demonstrate that the release is bulletproof. Without their input along the way the likelihood of achieving this becomes increasingly difficult. (4) Finance involvement ensures the team has access to cost information and financial models and provides a reality check when it comes to assumptions. (5) In the final analysis the R&D people have to build the solution, but experience has shown they tend to be terrible with user interfaces and confuse the customer's value perception with how hard something was to engineer. Having the other disciplines present brings them back to understanding that just because something is difficult to engineer does not mean the customer will value it or accept latency in its operation.

- While the design can be challenging, the cycle that is encountered in designing user interfaces is repeatable. It starts by engineering building a barely functional interface for a given application—enough for members of the team to see and use the interface. Next a collaborative meeting of all parties is held to try it out and be guided through it. This spawns feedback that is normally rather brutal and engineering goes back and creates a new iteration and the cycle repeats. At some point the VP of Engineering must be the voice of reason. That occurs once the system reaches an asymptote of improvement. At that point the specification is then locked and actually built out to completion. When this cycle is religiously followed, the process yields a system that never looks anything like the original concepts, but one that actually has very high first-pass appeal at release to the customers and is easy to support.

Lessons Learned

This can be an endless list so no effort will be made here to make it thorough and exhaustive. Here are some highlights.

- A "thought leadership vision" must be the underpinning of any product since it is the genesis of all product ideas that are to be developed. Without this, disjointed products will be spawned that don't fit the corporate message or vision and when this happens it usually ends badly.
- Pick your niches carefully. Plan to dominate and be prepared to defend them vigorously.
- Your only objective should be to be the best. Your core technologies must be world class. If you want to be viewed as *responsive*, you have to be among best in class for design cycle time.
- Stay on top of the sales and marketing strategies and rollout plans. Product rollouts conducted in a fire-drill environment rarely achieve the intended results. Make the first sales to long-term and local customers. When it comes to new technology, it's cheaper to monitor performance and implement fixes in a close-by and friendly environment.
- Keep the time associated with what you are trying to do in perspective! Product or process generation shift = ±10 years. Getting a new customer for life = 5 years. Product line modernization = 3 years. Manufacturing rationalization = 10 months. Change in the market = 10 days. Losing a customer = 10 minutes.

- Foster a culture that encourages and welcomes new ideas from any source. Studies have shown that sources of new ideas for high-technology companies come from: analysis and experiments (30%), customers (20%), outside suppliers (15%), and other sources (35%).
- Payback period should not be the key criterion for strategic investments. Look for opportunities to make strategic investments that will give you a (sustainable) competitive advantage.
- Vertical integration projects should be carefully monitored and justified on aggressive payback criteria and all technology-sensitive investments should be written off as fast as possible.
- Minimize the time and effort spent on product line maintenance. Focus on new and next-generation products and services. Make fast, complete steps.
- Spend 10% of the project cost on investigation and applied research.
- Don't release products for sale prematurely. This is tantamount to finishing product development on the customers' site. If you do, it will come back to haunt you and often at the most inappropriate time. The cost of making fixes in the field is often 100 or more times more expensive than catching the problem during the manufacturing process.
- R&D cost cutting can be very shortsighted and often doesn't make financial sense. Experience has repeatedly shown that enhancing the efficiency of R&D, speeding up the R&D process to reduce time to market, and making better strategy choices early in the cycle results in bigger savings than you can generate through cost cutting.
- Time is more important than money. Studies have shown that, for the same amount of money spent on comparable projects, the ROCEs were 65% if completed in three years, 115% if completed in two, and 145% if completed in one year.
- Size (scale) can be important. Some projects are just too big and risky to be taken on for a given size company. Asea (Swedish company) and Brown Boveri (Swiss company) were multibillion-dollar businesses that were about the same size before they merged. Asea spent US$750 million on R&D, made little profit, but was very innovative. Brown Boveri spent US$230 million, but was profitable. Asea needed the scale Brown Boveri offered. Brown Boveri needed Asea's innovative products. Both needed to merge to stay alive.
- Watch inventory. There is a long list of companies that have gone out of business because a new generation made the inventory of their existing product line (which they had lots of) obsolete.[4]
- When it comes to software, experience has shown that a tool that is one generation back from the bleeding edge typically becomes mature and stable by the time the product is released and tends to be ideal.
- A few capabilities must be utterly new and not shared by any competitor, otherwise you won't have anything to say when asked: "What is different about your product and how does it convey value?"

---

[4]Osborne Computer, one of the early computer companies, made this mistake and ended up declaring bankruptcy.

- An iterative design cycle is required that involves services personnel, marketing, sales, applications engineering, QA, finance, and R&D. Having these disciplines involved assures that R&D is regularly reminded that just because something is difficult to engineer doesn't mean the customer will value it or accept latency in its operation.
- At some point, all projects reach an asymptote of improvement. At that point, lock down the requirements and build out to completion.
- If the final product doesn't look anything like the original concept, it probably means the process you have followed religiously has yielded a product that actually has very high first-pass appeal at release to the customers and is easy to support.

How Much Is Enough?

The amount of money a company spends on R&D will have a dramatic impact on growth and profit. Too little and profitable life will be shortened. Too much and returns will be mediocre. While it's difficult to strike a balance, experience has shown that it's better to spend a little too much than a lot too little. Over time strategies tend to shift from the top line to the bottom line. When a company focuses on the bottom line, its strategies shift from long run to short run and cost reduction becomes a central theme. If (profit) growth slows down or doesn't eventuate as planned, R&D spending is often curtailed to maintain profitability. Regardless of how successfully a company has grown profits, at some point all companies focused on cost end up in the same place and are faced once again with the challenge of growing the top line. A key element of every growth strategy will be an innovative and productive R&D program.

One of the challenges of deciding on appropriate amounts of R&D spending is estimating how the cost of developing the next generation interacts with revenue that must be achieved to provide an adequate return. The R&D Growth and Investment Equation (Equation [E-23], renumbered here as [6-1]), developed in Appendix E provides a simple way to quickly estimate the investment required for the next-generation product or service.

$$I_{Next} = \frac{(g)(F)(I_{Current})(LTRev_{CurGen})}{\left[(1+g)^{(PLC+1)} - (1+g)\right](Rev_{LYCurGen})} \qquad \text{[E-23] [6-1]}$$

The variables for Equation [6-1] and those used in Example 6-1 are defined in Table 6-3.

TABLE 6-3 Terminology of R&D Growth and Investment Equation

Generational cost factor	F
Cost of current generation R&D as percent of lifetime revenues	$I_{Current}$
Cost of next generation R&D as percent of lifetime revenues	I_{Next}
Growth rate of next generation	g
Product life cycle of next generation	PLC
Lifetime revenue of current generation	Rev_{CurGen}
Revenue for the last year of current generation	$Rev_{NextGen}$

The use of Equation [6-1] and meaning of the variables in Table 6-3 are best illustrated in the following example.

EXAMPLE 6-1: ESTIMATING THE R&D COST OF NEW TECH INC.'S NEXT GENERATION PRODUCT

New Tech Inc. has just completed its twentieth year of operations. While it struggled during the early years, it has achieved critical mass in several of its product lines, one of which is expected to achieve lifetime sales of $170 million for the current generation with $31 million of this generated during the final year. On the assumption that these estimates are accurate, the CFO calculated the R&D costs for the current generation to equate to 7% of the current generation's lifetime revenues.

The company has a policy of having all significant investment projects vetted by the Finance Committee before being presented to the board of directors. The responsibility for preparing estimates for new projects associated with product lines rests jointly with the vice presidents of Research and Development and Marketing.

Management has decided it would like to launch an R&D project for the next generation of the product under consideration. During the investigatory phase of the project, Marketing, together with Finance and Engineering, determined that the fully burdened cost of R&D expense has increased by 35% since the current generation was developed. Allowing for inflation, 40% was deemed to be a reasonable estimate of the generational cost factor for the next generation. Marketing estimated the compound annual growth rate and product life cycle of the next generation at 12% and five years, respectively. The Finance Committee only requires a ballpark figure in order to decide if the project should proceed to the next phase, which is the preparation of a detailed estimate that would ultimately be presented to the board.

Since only a rough estimate is required at this stage of the process, the VPs of R&D and Marketing decide they can get the cost estimates required by applying Equation [6-1] and substituting data from Table 6-4.

TABLE 6-4 Parameters for Calculating the Cost of the Next Generation

Cost of next generation as % of lifetime revenue	I_{Next}
Expected CAGR for next generation	12.00%
Generational cost factor	1.4
Cost of current generation as % of lifetime revenue	7.00%
Lifetime revenue of current generation $'s	170,000,000
Expected product life cycle for next generation (Years)	5
Revenue for the last year of the current generation $'s	31,000,000

$$I_{Next} = \frac{(g)(F)(I_{Current})(LTRev_{CurGen})}{\left[(1+g)^{(PLC+1)} - (1+g)\right](Rev_{LYCurGen})} = \frac{(0.12)((1.4)(0.07)(170,000,000))}{\left[(1+0.12)^{(5+1)} - (1+0.12)\right](31,000,000)}$$

$$I_{Next} = \frac{1,999,200}{26,468,503} = 0.0755$$

$$I_{Next} = 7.55\%$$

While expressing the cost of the next generation's R&D cost as a percentage of the next generation's lifetime sales is helpful, it doesn't monetize the cost. In order to monetize this percentage the VP of Marketing consulted Table 6-5, which gives the *lifetime revenue factors* (LTRFs) for various growth rates and product life cycles (see Table E-1, Appendix E).[5]

In this case a Growth Rate of 12% and Product Life Cycle of five years correspond to an LTRF of 7.115. Since the last year of revenue for the current generation is expected to be $31,000,000, the lifetime revenue of the next generation is:

$$LTRev_{NextGen} = (Rev_{LYCurGen})(LTRF) = (31,000,000)(7.115)$$

$$LTRev_{NextGen} = \$220,565,000$$

And the lifetime R&D cost of the next generation is estimated to be:

$$\$I_{Next} = (LTRev_{NextGen})(I_{Next}) = (220,565,000)(0.0755)$$

$$\$I_{Next} = \$16,653,000$$

After thinking about these results, the VP of Marketing wondered what it would take in terms of compound annual growth rates and product life cycles for the current and next generations to have the same percentage cost.

$$(I_{Next}) = \frac{(g)(F)(I_{Current})(LTRev_{CurGen})}{\left[(1+g)^{(PLC+1)} - (1+g)\right](Rev_{LYCurGen})} \quad [6\text{-}1]$$

To answer this question he took Equation [6-1] and set $I_{Current}$ equal to I_{Next}.

$$(I_{Next}) = \frac{(g)(F)(I_{Next})(LTRev_{CurGen})}{\left[(1+g)^{(PLC+1)} - (1+g)\right](Rev_{LYCurGen})}$$

---

[5] To calculate the lifetime revenue factor of a product or service with a known average compound annual growth rate and product life cycle, simply note the intersection of the two. For example: if g = 10% and PLC = 5, then the lifetime revenue factor is 6.716 and the lifetime revenue for the product or service is 6.716 times the revenue that immediately preceded this revenue stream.

TABLE 6-5 Lifetime Revenue Factors for Various Growth Rates and Product Life Cycles

	Growth Rates *g*														
PLC	**1%**	**2%**	**3%**	**4%**	**5%**	**6%**	**7%**	**8%**	**9%**	**10%**	11%	12%	13%	14%	15%
1	1.010	1.020	1.030	1.040	1.050	1.060	1.070	1.080	1.090	1.100	1.110	1.120	1.130	1.140	1.150
2	2.030	2.060	2.091	2.122	2.153	2.184	2.215	2.246	2.278	2.310	2.342	2.374	2.407	2.440	2.473
3	3.060	3.122	3.184	3.246	3.310	3.375	3.440	3.506	3.573	3.641	3.710	3.779	3.850	3.921	3.993
4	4.101	4.204	4.309	4.416	4.526	4.637	4.751	4.867	4.985	5.105	5.228	5.353	5.480	5.610	5.742
5	5.152	5.308	5.468	5.633	5.802	5.975	6.153	6.336	6.523	6.716	6.913	7.115	7.323	7.536	7.754
6	6.214	6.434	6.662	6.898	7.142	7.394	7.654	7.923	8.200	8.487	8.783	9.089	9.405	9.730	10.067
7	7.286	7.583	7.892	8.214	8.549	8.897	9.260	9.637	10.028	10.436	10.859	11.300	11.757	12.233	12.727
8	8.369	8.755	9.159	9.583	10.027	10.491	10.978	11.488	12.021	12.579	13.164	13.776	14.416	15.085	15.786
9	9.462	9.950	10.464	11.006	11.578	12.181	12.816	13.487	14.193	14.937	15.722	16.549	17.420	18.337	19.304
10	10.567	11.169	11.808	12.486	13.207	13.972	14.784	15.645	16.560	17.531	18.561	19.655	20.814	22.045	23.349
11	11.683	12.412	13.192	14.026	14.917	15.870	16.888	17.977	19.141	20.384	21.713	23.133	24.650	26.271	28.002
12	12.809	13.680	14.618	15.627	16.713	17.882	19.141	20.495	21.953	23.523	25.212	27.029	28.985	31.089	33.352
13	13.947	14.974	16.086	17.292	18.599	20.015	21.550	23.215	25.019	26.975	29.095	31.393	33.883	36.581	39.505
14	15.097	16.293	17.599	19.024	20.579	22.276	24.129	26.152	28.361	30.772	33.405	36.280	39.417	42.842	46.580
15	16.258	17.639	19.157	20.825	22.657	24.673	26.888	29.324	32.003	34.950	38.190	41.753	45.672	49.980	54.717

And then by canceling like terms and transposing obtained Equation [E-27] (renumbered here as [6-2]), which dealt with exactly the same assumption,

$$\frac{\left[(1+g)^{(PLC+1)}-(1+g)\right]}{g}=\frac{(F)(LTRev_{CurGen})}{(Rev_{LYCurGen})} \qquad \text{[E-27] [6-2]}$$

Substituting,

$$\frac{\left[(1+g)^{(PLC+1)}-(1+g)\right]}{g}=\frac{(F)(LTRev_{CurGen})}{(Rev_{LYCurGen})}=\frac{(1.4)(170,000,000)}{31,000,000}$$

$$=\frac{238,000,000}{31,000,000}=7.667$$

By consulting Table 6-5 he noted that 7.667 corresponded to a growth rate g of approximately 14.5% and *PLC* of five years. The implication of this was, of course, if he could grow the business faster than 12% for five years, the lifetime sales would be larger and the R&D investment as a percentage of lifetime sales would decrease.

He then proceeded to check the result by substituting 14.5% and five years for g and *PLC* respectively in Equation [6-1].

$$I_{Next}=\frac{(g)(F)(I_{Next})(LTRev_{CurGen})}{\left[(1+g)^{(PLC+1)}-(1+g)\right](Rev_{LYCurGen})}=\frac{(0.145)(1.4)(0.070)(170,000,000)}{\left[(1+0.145)^{(5+1)}-(1+0.145)\right](31,000,000)}$$

$$I_{Next}=\frac{2,415,700}{34,359,536}=0.0703$$

$$I_{Next}=7.03\%$$

Sure enough, growing at 14.5% for five years brought the percentage cost of the next generation to roughly 7% and the same as the current generation. The VP of Marketing thought 12% was a tough but achievable goal but 14.5% was unrealistic: He took no comfort from this solution and once again consulted Table 6-5 where he noticed that a *g* and *PLC* of 7% and six years respectively gave a lifetime revenue factor of 7.654, which was very close to 7.667, the lifetime revenue factor that makes the percentage cost of the next and current generations the same. While he recognized that growing slower for longer can get one to the same place, he wanted to be sure he was interpreting the data correctly, so once again he checked the result by substituting in Equation [E-23].

$$I_{Next}=\frac{(g)(F)(I_{Next})(LTRev_{CurGen})}{\left[(1+g)^{(PLC+1)}-(1+g)\right](Rev_{LYCurGen})}=\frac{(0.07)(1.4)(0.70)(170,000,000)}{\left[(1+0.07)^{(6+1)}-(1+0.07)\right](31,000,000)}$$

$$I_{Next}=\frac{1,166,200}{16,609,226}=0.0702$$

$$I_{Next}=7.02\%$$

After mulling over what he had discovered, the VP of Marketing considered going back and discussing this result with Engineering, Product Marketing, and Sales and see if the next-generation specification could be altered in some way to get another year out of the product life cycle, even if it reduced the growth rate somewhat, thereby increasing the probability of achieving the product's lifetime sales. However, after giving the matter further thought and recalling that the present value of any future number reduces with time, he concluded that a better lifetime ROCE would be achieved by sticking with the current plan.

Sales

Sales' prime challenge is to consistently influence the customer's purchasing behavior. Here are a few lessons learned that should be helpful in managing your selling expenses.

Regularly review account coverage and make sure you are not over- or under-servicing. The key indicators are growth and profitability. The relationship between the two is very telling. If your growth and profitability are good, you may be able to divert some of your resources. On the other hand, if growth is slow and profitability is good, consider targeting additional effort to getting growth going. A situation where growth is good but profitability is poor also demands action. Sales effort, like anything else, is a valuable resource. If you can't get price up, then you should find a way to cut the cost of servicing the customer without measurably impacting the deliverable. If the account is unprofitable, redirect the selling effort.

If you have to cut costs, cut where it will do the least damage. Unlike marketing, the effects of cutting selling expenses will be experienced relatively quickly. Instances where every sale is dependent on a specialized effort or where a customer has standardized on a particular supplier are prime candidates. The temptation in this case would obviously be to reduce the selling effort at the standardized customer. Do so thoughtfully and you will probably still have a happy customer. If you approach the problem in an arbitrary fashion, you may regret it. In the long run, there is no such thing as a locked-in account. As for the customer that requires a specialized effort, the decision here should be based on profitability.

Set aside some of the sales budget for new account development. Of course, it is prudent to make sure that existing customers are served well and you have to be prepared to spend money to make sure this happens. However, you can only grow one of two ways. The first is to sell more to existing customers. The other is to sell to new customers. In order to keep the growth engine going, you have to do both. New customers can be found in your category, adjacent categories, and completely new categories. Successful sales managers have learned how to direct a meaningful amount of the selling effort at scouring the market for new customers.

Use all of the channels at your disposal. Your choices are manifold (direct, distributors, dealers, agents, media, etc.) and you are not necessarily limited to any particular set or subset. The reason you have to consider all possibilities and get the right answer for your company is that some channels can get a better price for your product than you can. For example, a good representative can often get a higher price for a product than a company's direct sales force. If you don't believe it, look at the facts. Discounts to representatives are often less than a company's cost of selling direct. If this is true, how does a representative survive? One possibility is that they have lower selling costs. A better answer is that they are closer to the customer and the customer is prepared to pay for the higher service level.

Training is part of learning and like learning must be a lifelong commitment. Customers see their time as being worth something. Salespeople who say, "I will get back to you on that," often don't get the opportunity. Top sales professionals try hard to never put themselves in a position where they can be embarrassed by not being able to respond to questions that customers legitimately expect them to be able to answer. In this day and age of information being available instantly at a click, there is seldom a reason for a salesperson to leave an account with unanswered questions. Furthermore, salespeople sell what they feel comfortable with and understand. They value product knowledge and will go to greener pastures if they don't get regular infusions. If you don't have a sales training schedule that provides for at least one day of training per month, you are probably not getting good value for your selling expenses.

Incentive systems can make a huge difference. Every top salesperson has at least two unwritten rules. Rule number one is: They sell what they feel comfortable with and this of course is part of the training issue. Rule number two is: Given a choice they will sell what makes them the most money. Once you have decided on your sales targets, finish the job and make sure that you have incentive plan alignment. Differentiation in your incentive system is also important. If new customer development is a priority for your company, then new business should have a higher incentive than repeat business. Caps are usually not a good idea. It's probably okay to have some provision that limits an incentive payment in the case of a windfall, but otherwise stay clear of this temptation. The message you want to send to your salespeople is, "Bring in as much profitable business as you can." Finally, incentive systems should not be a static thing. They should change as the company's needs change. If designing schemes is not your company's strong suit, get help. There is lots of good advice out there.

Don't promote sales professionals into positions for which they aren't suited or qualified. Great salespeople often don't make great managers. We have all seen examples of this and yet one hears over and over again stories about failed attempts. This is not to say that great salespeople can't be successful managers. In fact, there are numerous success stories. However, like great engineers, great salespeople are not a dime a dozen, so when you have a rainmaker, take extra steps to make sure that a move into management is good for the individual and the company.

One of the reasons mistakes are made is rooted in the notion of the power of persuasion. Very successful salespeople have mastered the power of the spoken word and presentation and thereby demonstrated an ability to make things happen. It's tempting to believe that these skills will have the same impact in a management role. Often they don't. Why? There is a saying that goes something like this: "Happy families are alike. Unhappy families are unhappy in their own way." This means that in order for a family to be happy all of the ingredients that go into creating a happy family must be there. If one or more is missing, then the family is unhappy in its own unique way. In the context of a management environment, a management role requires a different set and priority of skills and unless all are there, it is unlikely that success will follow.

Service and Customer Support

A service department's mission statement has to be "complete customer satisfaction." Some of the issues are:

Organize to provide what your customer expects. Just as form follows function, the service you must provide to fulfill this requirement depends on your product and how it's used by the customer. The first step in designing a service program is to make sure you understand what the customer expects. Does your customer expect on-site support, telephone support, Internet support (or all three), and is it required during working hours or 24/7? Furthermore, if your product is used in a critical application, then you probably will have to provide support 24/7 and maybe provide it on-site. There is nothing more frustrating to customers than not being able to get the assistance they require when they need it. They won't take much comfort from the fact that support is not available on Wednesday mornings even if the support staff is attending a training program.

Charge for what you provide. In general, there is no reason why you should give away service and customer support. Even very demanding customers are prepared to pay for help. The charge can be included in the cost of a product, service agreement, or on a user pay basis. If a customer is not prepared to pay, there is a reason such as poor quality or late delivery. If you are faced with a situation where the customer's representative is a bully, blindly following some cost reduction command from above, or simply wants something for nothing, you are probably better off without this customer. It's also possible that the customer has become comfortable with the technology and doesn't want to pay for support he no longer requires. In this case, you should contemplate eliminating the support component from your price and cut your support costs. Your objective should be to provide a service level that exceeds your customer's expectations. If you do this, you will find that you can charge plenty.

Don't train your service and customer support people at your customer's expense. There is nothing more exasperating for customers than to be confronted with a situation where they know more than the people trying to help them. For example, you won't have satisfied customers, let alone an efficient service department, if you have a high callback frequency. Your goal should be to have the service and customer support people in the required numbers in place and trained as part of the product launch. If you can't do this or have underestimated the demand, you are far better off to make your customers wait a little to get quality support than to simply provide them someone to hold their hand. Providing substandard support over the telephone is one thing because you can always try to convince your customers to wait until a more experienced person is available. Placing unqualified people in the field is unforgivable. Right or wrong, your customers expect the people who represent your company to be among your best. If you disappoint them, future business will be at risk.

Compete on the basis of excellent service and support, not price. Your customers are well aware of how most games are played. They are experts at "Fool me once, shame on you; fool me twice, shame on me." The kinds of customers you want to cultivate are those who recognize that the initial purchase price is only part of the total consideration. Your intent should be to charge more because you provide more and avoid participating in the price game. Your marketing and sales programs should be designed around several key notions. One of them is: By buying your product, your customer also buys a place at the table of "outstanding support."

Service and support should be a profit center. Gone is the day where the multitude of skills provided by the service and support organization has to be thrown in to close the sale. If you are still doing any of this, you are living in another time. Some of America's most admired companies consider themselves to be doing well to cover their costs on the equipment sale and make "their money" on service and support. While not advocating this particular business model, it's hard to deny it works.

When you disappoint, make sure you exceed expectations when corrective action is taken. Unless someone is having a bad day, they probably won't make a point of letting you know how they really feel about your failure to do something they expected you to do. The safe assumption to make is that they are trying to be civilized about the incident. Your corrective action should not just fix the problem. It should also do something about dealing with any lingering feelings of disappointment. For example, if you missed a next-day shipping promise by a day, an offer to pick up the shipping charges will show that you recognize that expectations have value and not meeting them has a price. If you shipped an order incomplete, consider sending a small gift along with the part(s) that complete the order. If you sense the customer is seriously troubled, have someone in your damage control group make personal contact.

An example may help to underscore the importance of this point.

EXAMPLE 6-2: EXCEEDING CUSTOMER EXPECTATIONS

In early August an order was placed for 15 pieces of outdoor furniture with a local leisure furniture store (dealer). The promised delivery was three weeks.

Sequence of events: At the end of September, the furniture still hadn't arrived and when questioned, the dealer literally had no idea when it would be delivered. The choices offered to the customer by the dealer were, cancel or wait. The customer didn't like either and decided to contact the manufacturer. After a few calls, the buyer got through to the Company's president, explained the situation, and stated that it was outrageous that no one could tell him when a product promised for three-weeks' delivery would be delivered eight weeks into the cycle. The president agreed and then explained they were having difficulties with their supplier and acknowledged that this wasn't the customer's problem. He offered substitutes at the Company's expense and if this wasn't acceptable, he would do everything he could to right a wrong. The customer's spouse really liked the design so a decision was made to let the order stand. For the next few weeks, the president called the customer every Monday and updated him on the status of the order. After several weeks the furniture arrived. When it was delivered, the president followed up to make sure that delivery had been made and "unexpectedly" reduced the price by $1,000.00 (10%). The product was delivered 10 weeks late to a "satisfied customer" who then placed a follow-on order for several more pieces. How is it that the details of this experience came to light? The author was the customer!

Administration

This function determines the basic infrastructure of the company. Its objective has to be efficiency and facilitation of quality decisions. Those who have to absorb administrative costs in their P&L do not always appreciate the important role a good administrative function fills. This attitude is not entirely without foundation. In many companies, the effort to match what users want with what providers provide is not well managed. Here are some things to reflect on if you want to get the most out of your administrative spending.

Keep the corporate staff small. The biggest risk associated with corporate staff is its propensity to create work at the business unit level. In general, if expertise is to be effective, the need must be recognized and it should be as close as possible to the user of the service. While the Internet has changed much of this, it is often still hard to be effective at a distance. From an execution point of view, you will get a better return on your investment in staff at the business unit level than if they are located in the corporate group.

Refrain from parking people in staff positions unless it's for a very short transitional period. Also, be careful about who you let loose at the corporate level. An exuberant manager of strategic planning can bring the key managers in your business units to a standstill with seemingly unending requests. The rule of thumb for CEOs is: Surround yourself with the people you need to do your job, not with those who are necessary to help others do theirs.

Be a minimalist. Think hard before you go beyond providing accounting, finance, human resources, legal, risk management, and information technology at the corporate level. Your objective should be to only centralize tasks where you add value and that are absolutely necessary to maintain control or too expensive to locate in multiple sites.

If you have a corporate staff, don't let them have a staff. Other than Finance, Accounting, and Human Resources, the other members of your staff should be individual contributors. The exception to this is where they can clearly demonstrate that it's significantly cheaper to do it in-house. Why *significantly*? The reason is that workloads vary and you are better to keep as much of your corporate costs variable as you can. History shows that managers are quick to staff-up but slow to voluntarily staff-down. They are more inclined to go looking for things to keep their people busy.

Measure the corporate functions by the value they add as perceived by the business units. If your business unit managers don't want to pay for a particular service, there may be a message there. When the noise level is high, give serious consideration to eliminating the function in the corporate group and move it to the business unit. Let them decide how much, if any, they need and whether to do it in-house or outsource.

Take into account what all of your customers expect. Most companies have two kinds of customers: internal and external. Don't put programs or resources in place that your internal customers don't support. If you are convinced that you really do know what is good for them, go a little slower and build support for what you propose to provide before implementation.

One way of measuring the degree of internal support is to ask them to carry their share of the development cost on their budget. If you can't generate interest for what is proposed, you should probably abandon it.

Your outside customers are also important. For example, if electronic funds transfer is increasingly on your outside customer's mind and not of immediate concern to your internal customers, then this is an area in which you may have to act unilaterally. Decisions like this help define the value of central staff leadership.

It's all about adding value. Remember, at the end of the day, it's your outside customer who buys your company's product. Collectively customers make judgments about what adds value and what doesn't. You can only pass along those costs that your customer perceives as value added. If the perception isn't there, you will absorb the cost or lose the sale because your price is too high.

DEPRECIATION AND AMORTIZATION

Depreciation and amortization are not like other expenses. They involve assets that were purchased (and presumably paid for) in the past and represent non-cash charges to the Income Statement that are intended to depreciate or amortize the asset over its useful life.

Depreciation is associated with hard assets such as buildings, machine tools, computers, and so on. There are numerous methods of depreciation that are used depending on the circumstances. A partial list would include:[6]

- Straight line method
- Declining balance method
- Sum of the years digits method
- Units of production method

Amortization is not as straightforward as depreciation and is associated with Intangible Assets. These assets fall into two categories: those with identifiable lives (e.g., patents, copyright, non-compete agreements) and those with unidentifiable useful lives (primarily trademarks and goodwill). As will be seen, the assets in the first category are amortized over their useful lives whereas assets with unidentifiable lives remain on the books indefinitely unless impaired.

EXAMPLE 6-3: DEPRECIATION OF ASSETS[7]

A company purchases a computer system for $110,000. It is estimated to have a useful life of five years and a residual value of $10,000. The day it is purchased,[8] it would go on the Balance Sheet at $110,000. This is the book value at the time of purchase and will decline by the annual depreciation until it reaches the residual value. The depreciation

[6] Financial Accounting Standards Board, Accounting Standards Codification.
[7] All values are end-of-year values in this and subsequent tables in this example.
[8] In the interest of simplicity, it's assumed the asset is purchased at the beginning of the year.

for each year of the computer's useful life for the various methods of depreciation is calculated as follows.

Straight Line Method

The *straight line* method, because of its inherent simplicity, is widely used. It is calculated by using Equation [6-3].

$$\textit{Annual Depreciation Expense} = \frac{\textit{Cost of Fixed Asset} - \textit{Residual Value}}{\textit{Useful Life of Fixed Asset}} \qquad [6\text{-}3]$$

The amount to be depreciated over the life of the asset is $100,000 ($110,000 – $10,000). The depreciation expense charged to the Income Statement per year until fully depreciated would be $20,000 ($100,000/5), as shown in Table 6-6. The corresponding entry for each charge to the Income Statement would be an identical reduction in the value of the asset on the Balance Sheet.[9] At the end of Year 5, the computer system would no longer be depreciated and the "book value ($10,000)" would remain on the books at its residual value until the computer system is disposed of.

Declining Balance Method

This is an accelerated depreciation method that provides for higher depreciation during the first few years and has merit due to the fact that assets are often more useful during the early years. It is calculated by using Equation [6-4].

$$\textit{Annual Depreciation Expense} = (\textit{Book Value of Asset at the Beginning of the Year})(\textit{Depreciation Rate}) \qquad [6\text{-}4]$$

The depreciation rate is normally double the straight line rate (as implied by the straight line calculation). The salvage or residual value is not used in calculating the depreciation expense and the book value is never brought below the salvage value.

TABLE 6-6 Straight Line Depreciation $'s

Year	Depreciation	Accumulated Depreciation	Remaining Depreciation	Book Value
1	20,000	20,000	80,000	90,000
2	20,000	40,000	60,000	70,000
3	20,000	60,000	40,000	50,000
4	20,000	80,000	20,000	30,000
5	20,000	100,000	0	10,000
6	0	100,000	0	10,000

[9] The concept of offsetting entries is further explained in Chapter 10, "Understanding Financial Statements."

TABLE 6-7 Declining Balance or Residual Balance Depreciation $'s

Year	Depreciation	Accumulated Depreciation	Remaining Depreciation	Book Value
1	44,000	44,000	56,000	66,000
2	26,400	70,400	29,600	39,600
3	15,840	86,240	13,760	23,760
4	9,504	95,744	4,245	14,256
5	4,256	100,000	0	10,000
6	0	100,000	0	10,000

As can be seen from Table 6-6, the annual depreciation is 20% (20,000/100,000*100). Doubling the straight line rate would result in a depreciation rate of 40%. If this method was used to depreciate the computer system, the annual depreciation would be as shown in Table 6-7. Note that when this method is used, the remaining depreciation is written off during the last year of the asset's estimated useful life, which in this case is Year 5.

Sum of the Years Digits Method

This is another accelerated depreciation method that gives a result that is less than the declining balance but more than the straight line method. It is calculated by multiplying the depreciable cost by a schedule of fractions. The depreciation for each year is given by:

$$Depreciation = (Acquired\ Value\ of\ Asset\ to\ be\ Depreciated)(Depreciation\ Rate) \quad [6\text{-}5]$$

The depreciation rate is a fraction (*DepRate*), the denominator of which is the sum of a series of integers (Sum of the Years Digits, Sum of YD) and is denoted by:

$$Sum\ of\ YD = \frac{n(n+1)}{2} \quad [6\text{-}6]$$

Where n is the number of years over which the asset is to be depreciated

The numerator for each Depreciation Rate Fraction is the integer in the series for which the depreciation is being calculated. Hence:

$$Numerator_{Year\ 1} = n,\ Numerator_{Year\ 2} = (n-1),\ Numerator_{Year\ 3} = (n-2), \ldots \quad [6\text{-}7]$$

And the Depreciation Rate Fractions for Years 1, 2, 3... are:

$$DepRate_{Year\ 1} = \frac{n}{Sum\ of\ YD},\ DepRate_{Year\ 2} = \frac{(n-1)}{Sum\ of\ YD},\ DepRate_{Year\ 3} = \frac{(n-2)}{Sum\ of\ YD} \quad [6\text{-}8]$$

TABLE 6-8 Depreciation Rate and Depreciation Percentage

Year	Depreciation Rate	Depreciation %
1	5/15	33.33%
2	4/15	26.67%
3	3/15	20.00%
4	2/15	13.33%
5	1/15	6.67%
6	0	0.00%

For example, if the life of the asset is four years, then by substituting into Equation [6-6] the denominator is calculated to be:

$$Sum of\ YD_4 = \frac{n(n+1)}{2} = \frac{(4)(4+1)}{2} = \frac{20}{2} = 10$$

or simply the sum of the four digits in the series, $4 + 3 + 2 + 1 = 10$.

The depreciation rates for each of the years are obtained with the aid of Equation [6-8].

$$DepRate_{Year\ 1} = \frac{4}{10} = 0.40,\ DepRate_{Year\ 2} = \frac{3}{10} = 0.30,$$

$$DepRate_{Year\ 3} = \frac{2}{10} = 0.20,\ DepRate_{Year\ 4} = \frac{1}{10} = 0.10$$

In this example, the computer system has a useful life of five years. Hence the sum of the years digits is 15,

$$Sum\ of\ YD_5 = \frac{n(n+1)}{2} = \frac{(5)(5+1)}{2} = \frac{30}{2} = 15$$

and the depreciation rate and percentage for each year would be as depicted in Table 6-8.

Applying this method and these percentages to a $110,000 computer system with a residual value of $10,000 would result in the annual depreciations shown in Table 6-9.

TABLE 6-9 Sum of the Years Digits Depreciation $'s

Year	Depreciation	Accumulated Depreciation	Remaining Depreciation	Book Value
1	33,333	33,333	66,667	76,667
2	26,667	60,000	40,000	50,000
3	20,000	80,000	20,000	30,000
4	13,333	93,333	6,667	16,667
5	6,667	100,000	0	10,000
6	0	100,000	0	10,000

Units of Production Method

In this method, the asset is determined to have a useful life that is measured by the units of production it supports. It's calculated with the use of Equation [6-9].

$$\text{Annual Depreciation Expense} = \left(\frac{\text{Cost of Fixed Asset} - \text{Residual Value}}{\text{Estimated Total Units}}\right)(\text{Actual Units Produced}) \quad [6\text{-}9]$$

According to the manufacturer, if the computer is to be used in a production environment, it should be upgraded to an industrial version with an extended life at an additional cost of $25,000. Assuming the computer system is to be dedicated to a line that produces widgets and is expected to have a residual value of $5,000 after producing 150,000 widgets, the annual depreciation percentage can be calculated based on the estimated annual production as shown in Table 6-10.

Since the computer's cost is $135,000 ($110,000 + $25,000) with a residual value of $5,000, the depreciation that must be written off is $130,000 ($135,000 – $5,000). Applying the depreciation percentages shown in Table 6-10, the annual depreciation can be calculated and is shown in Table 6-11. It's important to note that, in the Units of Production Method, the computer system isn't fully depreciated until the end of Year 8. While this may seem a little odd when the life of the asset (computer) is estimated to be "extended" beyond five years, in practice it's not unusual for an asset to be used well beyond its depreciable life. For example, machine tools can have a life of ±20 years with periodic updates to the key components and control systems. This can also happen when the asset is not used 24/7. In addition, it's not unusual for management to want to depreciate assets as fast as possible because of the impact on cash flow.

TABLE 6-10 Unit Production Data

Year	Estimated Annual Production	Fraction of Life Time Production	Percent Depreciation	Remaining Units to Be Produced
1	5,000	5/150	3.33%	145,000
2	10,000	10/150	6.67%	135,000
3	15,000	15/150	10.00%	120,000
4	25,000	25/150	16.67%	95,000
5	40,000	40/150	26.67%	55,000
6	30,000	30/150	20.00%	25,000
7	15,000	15/150	10.00%	10,000
8	10,000	10/150	6.67%	0

TABLE 6-11 Units of Production Depreciation $'s

Year	Depreciation	Accumulated Depreciation	Remaining Depreciation	Book Value
1	4,333	4,333	125,667	130,667
2	8,667	13,000	117,000	122,000
3	13,000	26,000	104,000	109,000
4	21,667	47,667	82,333	87,333
5	34,667	82,333	47,667	52,667
6	26,000	108,333	21,667	26,667
7	13,000	121,333	8,667	13,667
8	8,667	130,000	0	5,000

Impact of Taxes on Depreciation

Once taxes are introduced the matter of depreciation can become more complex. For example, Generally Accepted Accounting Principles (GAAP) accounting requires that an asset be depreciated over its useful life. When it comes to calculating the taxes that a company may have to pay, GAAP may not apply. For example, in order to encourage investment, governments will often allow companies (and individuals, for that matter) to write off the entire cost of an asset or some substantial portion thereof during the first year. This is one of the reasons that companies have two sets of books (so to speak), one for GAAP and another for tax purposes.

Sale of Depreciated Assets and Depreciation Recapture

When an asset that has been depreciated is sold, it will require accounting treatment. For example, if the computer with a residual value of $10,000 is sold for $12,000, then the gain on the sale is $2,000 ($12,000 – $10,000). Because the company received depreciation deductions, it would be required to include the $2,000 gain in its income and this gain would be taxed as ordinary income. This is known as *depreciation recapture*. If the sales price is less than the book (residual) value, the resulting loss is tax deductible. If the sales price is in excess of the original book value, this excess is recognized as a capital gain.

Amortization

Amortization is similar to depreciation except it is associated with soft assets and categorized as having either an identifiable or indefinite life.

Intangible assets with an identifiable life are amortized on a straight line basis over their economic life. Examples are intellectual property, patents, copyrights, and non-compete agreements. The annual amortization of these assets is treated just like depreciation in the sense that it is a cost included when preparing the periodic income statements.

Assets with an indefinite life are not amortized but instead are subject to annual impairment tests. Impairment occurs when the asset's fair market value is less than the book value contained in the company's financial records. Examples of assets with indefinite useful lives are goodwill and trademarks. When (as a result of a test) it has been determined that an asset has been impaired, the difference between the book value and the fair value is recognized as a loss in the Income Statement. If the fair value is greater, nothing is done to the book value.

Goodwill (the difference between what is paid for an asset, like a company, and the estimated fair value of the identifiable assets and liabilities) is also considered a soft asset but is not amortized under GAAP for public entities. For private entities there is an alternative available that permits companies to amortize goodwill on a straight-line basis over 10 years, or less than 10 years if the entity can demonstrate another useful life is more appropriate.

Impairment Testing for Goodwill

The procedure for testing for impairment of goodwill is as follows.

Step 0: The Company has the ability to attempt to qualify for a qualitative test to be able to represent that they meet the guidance that requires them to be able to assert that they are confident that it is more likely than not that the fair value exceeds the carrying value of the segment being tested. From a practical perspective, this would only come into play in a small number of instances where, for example, there is significant cushion in the prior year's assessments of the impairment of the asset.

Step 1: If the Company is not able to meet the qualitative test, then it is necessary to move to Step 1, which requires that an estimate of the fair value of the segment be made, which is typically done by calculating the present value of the future cash flows. If the fair value exceeds the carrying value of that segment (including all of its assets and liabilities), then there is no impairment.

Step 2: If the fair value is less than the carrying value of that segment, the Company would need to perform a pro-forma purchase price allocation, basically assuming that the acquisition closed as of the date of the impairment test, and determine estimated fair values for each of the assets (including intangibles other than goodwill) and liabilities, and the difference between the goodwill calculated from this assessment and carrying value would be the impairment charge.

Tax Treatment of Impairment

The tax treatment of impairment depends on whether the acquisition was a stock or asset acquisition. A thorough treatment is well beyond the scope of this book. The following is a brief explanation.

If the acquisition was a stock acquisition, the tax basis in the assets and liabilities carries over to the new owner. As a result there would be no tax basis in the goodwill and it would not be deductible for tax purposes. So any impairment would not be deductible for tax purposes. Therefore, an impairment charge would have no impact for tax purposes and the charge would get added back for income tax return purposes. That would mean that there would be a significant impact on the effective tax rate as there would not be any tax benefit recorded related to the impairment.

If the acquisition was an asset acquisition, then there would be a tax basis in the goodwill and it is amortized over a 15-year period for income tax purposes. Any impairment charge would be run through the Income Statement, but not result in an additional tax deduction. However, the goodwill for tax purposes would continue to be amortized over the 15-year amortization period.

For example, if an asset acquisition resulted in $15 million of goodwill for tax purposes, that goodwill would be amortized for income tax purposes over 15 years or $1 million per year. If after 5 years there was a full impairment of the asset for book purposes, the remaining $10 million of goodwill would be written off via the Income Statement, but, for tax purposes, the $1 million amortization per year would continue through the remaining 10 years.

EXAMPLE 6-4: AMORTIZATION OF ASSETS

A company acquires a competitor for $15,000,000 and the estimated fair value of identifiable assets (before intangibles) and liabilities is $3,000,000. As part of the process, the acquirer's accountants determine that the assets with an identifiable life are: patents ($1,200,000), copyrights ($500,000), and non-compete agreements negotiated with management ($2,400,000). This results in $7,900,000 of assets with an unidentifiable life ($15,000,000 – $3,000,000 – $1,200,000 – $500,000 – $2,400,000). The amortization associated with the assets with an identifiable life would be as shown in Table 6-12. It is worthwhile to note that there is no residual or salvage value ascribed and, over time, the assets with an identifiable life are completely amortized.

The assets with an unidentifiable life are called *goodwill*, which in this case is $7,900,000. This amount is the book value or carrying cost of the asset and for public entities remains on the Company's books indefinitely unless at some point it turns out to be impaired. Under the accounting rules, the acquirer would be obliged to carry out an impairment test at least annually on the goodwill. This is usually done by calculating the present value of the acquired company's future cash flows. If it turned out that as a

TABLE 6-12 Amortization of Assets with an Identifiable Life $'s

Asset Purchased	Ascribed Value	Estimated Useful Life in Years	Annual Amortization
Patents	1,200,000	15	80,000
Copyrights	500,000	5	100,000
Non-compete agreements	2,400,000	2	1,200,000

result of this calculation, the present value of the cash flows was an amount less than the net book value of the Company's investment in the acquired business, then an additional assessment would be required to evaluate if an impairment loss is required.

Non-Cash Charges

As explained earlier, depreciation and amortization are non-cash charges and, therefore, earnings that exclude depreciation and amortization is a good indicator of a company's cash flow. EBITDA is the Earnings before Depreciation and Amortization (as well as before Interest and Taxes) and it's for this reason that EBITDA is so widely used as an indicator of cash flow and therefore of value. In Chapter 5, it was seen that EBITDA could be expressed as:

$$EBITDA = Gross\ Margin - Operating\ Expenses \quad [6\text{-}10]$$

and

$$EBIT = EBITDA - (Depreciation\ \&\ Amortization) \quad [6\text{-}11]$$

As can be seen, Equation [6-10] involves current cash-related revenue and expenses. Equation [6-11], on the other hand, introduces non-cash charges. Most companies are valued on the basis of their "cash flows." The fact that EBITDA doesn't involve non-cash charges is the reason it is more indicative of cash flow than EBIT and why it is used as a surrogate for the cash flow a company is capable of generating.[10]

The drivers of depreciation and amortization are, of course, what you pay for assets in the first place. While it's possible to pay too much for a depreciable asset, this isn't where most mistakes are made because purchases are usually made at market prices that are easy to compare. Problems arise when the wrong asset has been purchased.

As discussed earlier, amortization is a little different. When it comes to patents, it's difficult to value them based on hard market-driven information, so their value is usually estimated. Goodwill is a good example of another soft asset. It results when the purchase price exceeds the net worth of the company being purchased less the value of any assets with an identifiable life. There is a school of thought that suggests it's always better to buy a good company. This is of course true. However, there is another school that suggests it's better to pay too much for a good company than to purchase a bad one. This assertion has been tried many times and it can turn out to be wrong. Why? If you pay too much, it will probably take years to realize a return on the investment. In most cases it's better to walk away from an overpriced deal. Furthermore, it's too risky to get involved in a deal that isn't adequately supported by your Balance Sheet and Cash Flow because you may be betting the company.

Manufacturing companies have most of their productive assets tied up in Accounts Receivable, Inventory, and Fixed and Soft Assets. Service companies rarely have inventory,

[10] Strictly speaking this is only true when there are no net changes in working capital, interest, and debt and when capital expenditures are zero. EBIT would be indicative of the cash a company can generate if Capital Expenditures = Depreciation and Amortization.

but since they are people intensive they will have equipment, facilities, and improvements to depreciate or capital leases to write off. Any company that has been acquisitive will have a good dose of goodwill[11] as well. In most manufacturing or service companies, assets that have to be depreciated or amortized account for a significant portion of the capital employed and, therefore, impact the ROCE. Management teams that are focused on maximizing ROCE have learned that it pays to take the job of procuring assets that result in depreciation or amortization seriously. They have put in place disciplines that subject all proposals to rigorous pre-purchase analysis and, if purchased, regular post-purchase follow-up to see if returns are in line with expectations and, if not, take action.

Balance Sheet Drivers of ROCE

Return on Capital Employed is a function of EBIT and the Capital Employed in the business. Capital Employed is defined as the sum of interest-bearing debt and Total Shareholders' Equity. Therefore anything that impacts debt or TSHE is a driver of ROCE. The following is a discussion of items that can directly or indirectly impact cash and therefore affect the debt component of Capital Employed.

Working Capital

Working Capital is defined as *Current Assets – Current Liabilities*. The usual measure is illustrated by Equation [6-12].

$$\%WC = \left(\frac{Working\ Capital}{Annual\ Net\ Revenues}\right)(100) \qquad [6\text{-}12]$$

The Working Capital Ratio is an aggregate measure of how well the management team manages the liquid assets of the business. The objective is to keep this ratio (percentage) as low as possible. World-class companies regularly achieve ratios of 10–15% and lower. This ratio is managed by having good Accounts Receivable, Inventory, and Accounts Payable practices.

Accounts Receivable

The usual measurements are:

$$\%Receivables/Net\ Revenues = \left(\frac{Accounts\ Receivable}{Annual\ Net\ Revenues}\right)(100) \qquad [6\text{-}13]$$

and

$$ARDOS = \left(\frac{Accounts\ Receivable}{Annual\ Net\ Revenue}\right)(360) \qquad [6\text{-}14]$$

[11] This is true if the accounting is done in accordance with U.S. GAAP. In other parts of the world, the United Kingdom, for example, any goodwill that results from the purchase of a company is written off at the time of closing against the acquiring company's equity account.

Equation [6-13] expresses the receivables as a percent of Net Revenues whereas Equation [6-14] defines them in days of a 360-day year. While both methods are in use, Accounts Receivable Days Outstanding (ARDOS) or simply Receivables Days Outstanding is the most common. As far as your customer is concerned, your Accounts Receivable from him (his Accounts Payable to you) is like an interest-free loan. His objective will often be to pay as slowly as possible.

In general, there are three kinds of problem customers: customers who can't pay, won't pay, or shouldn't pay.

If your customer can't pay, your only choice is to work with him on a pay-down program and be careful about extending future credit. If your exposure is large, try to get some form of security or preferred position. Customers who continually throw up reasons not to pay are playing the interest game. In this case, you need to be aggressive in collecting your money and take a disciplined approach. The last category is a shame-on-you situation. When a customer thinks she has a legitimate dispute, don't waste time trying to convince her otherwise. Unless she is being totally unreasonable, fix the problem and collect your money.

Before getting into the specifics of Accounts Receivable management, it may be helpful to highlight some basic issues that set the stage for the success or otherwise of a receivables program.

Product quality: Most people will pay promptly if they are satisfied with the product or service they have purchased. Accounts Receivable patterns and trends can be an indicator of deeper and, in some cases, serious issues. If you have a good collection team in place and feel you are spending too much effort collecting from your customers, then maybe all is not well on the product quality front.

Customer quality: In the end, companies get the customers they deserve. While it can be very hard to turn down a request for credit and thereby run the risk of losing a sale, sometimes that is exactly what is required. There are customers out there who don't care a whole lot about relationships (let alone long-lasting ones) and try to maximize the benefit they can derive from each and every transaction. They reason that if they can maximize their return at your expense, they have just won another round in the great game of business. In general, you will end up ahead of the game if you pass along bad customers to your competitors and focus on keeping the good ones for yourself.

Customer profitability: This is really a subset of customer quality. It is identified as a separate issue because of its importance. People with money are more inclined to pay their bills than those without. In the long run, the only source of cash to pay bills is profit. If you don't want to get caught with a bad debt, you should regularly run profitability analyses on customers who are slow payers.

Shipping and invoicing patterns: Just like you, your customer has some sort of cycle in which invoices are processed for payment. If your factory shipments are heavily skewed to the end of a month and your invoicing department doesn't invoice promptly, you may have just added 30 days (or more) to some of your receivables. Furthermore, even if the shipments from a factory are more or less level and invoices are allowed to pile up and sent out in batches, you end up in the same place.

Interest-free loan: When you provide your customers credit, it is like giving them an interest-free loan. Loaning money interest free is seldom a good idea. It's a worse idea to make an interest-free loan to someone who may not be creditworthy. An interest-free loan has value, so don't view it as merely a cost of doing business and give it away. Make your "interest-free loans" only to creditworthy customers. Better still, try to get something (price) for it.

Investment: Receivables are generated by delivery of a product or service to a customer. To deliver a product, a company has to buy parts and materials and then, using labor, convert these items into what the customer wants. As long as they remain on the books, Receivables represent money you have spent to conduct business and therefore, an investment in the business. Like any other investment, it needs to be managed to achieve the intended result.

The essence of Accounts Receivable management is discipline and good credit control. Here is a list of do's and don'ts:

- Do thorough credit checks before you extend credit and regularly review credit ratings of existing customers. Remember, an order is only good news when you get paid.
- Try and get high-risk customers to pay with a credit card.
- If you are paying your salesforce or distributor a commission, pay them when you get paid. It also helps if you design the collection program so that it involves participation by the sales and marketing people in those instances where the customer is being difficult.
- Spell your credit terms out clearly on all proposals and invoices.
- Agree on credit limits with your customers before accepting an order. Giving unlimited credit is dangerous. Liberal credit arrangements will usually ultimately result in a write-off.
- Take the time necessary to make sure that the payment terms and all paperwork associated with a transaction or ongoing arrangement are in order before you make any deliveries. Thereafter, make sure the invoices are accurate, relate to the goods or services delivered, clearly include all details that will allow the customers to tie their paperwork to yours, and sent out promptly to the right address.
- If your customers require you to sign contracts involving significant money or risk, form a contract review board. Define its authority in a charter that delineates the kinds of contracts the board can recommend the company enter into, the signatures required to approve the recommendation, and the procedure that the board must follow before recommending something that conflicts with the charter.
- Make sure your people are getting the reports they need. The sales ledger must be accurate, real time, and contain records of all sales, receipts, and credit notes issued. Payments should be matched against invoices with a separate record of unpaid invoices. Furthermore, don't make the mistake of assuming that because the data is available it is well understood. Regular training is an important component of a well-managed receivables program.
- Consider bringing in specialists to train your people on how to ask for money. If you don't believe this is an acquired skill, think back to the days when your children were at home.

- Age your receivables (at least monthly) and go after any amounts that are outstanding beyond your normal terms. Remember, the older a receivable gets, the less likely it is to be collected.
  - Get in the habit of issuing monthly statements on time and don't hesitate to send out reminder letters.
  - Check that the customer has received the invoice and that it has been approved for payment.
  - Before you get on the telephone, take a moment and plan the call. The objectives should include obtaining payment and retaining the goodwill of the customer. Always ask to speak to the same person and during the course of the conversation make sure you confirm which invoices are being paid, how much is being paid, when payment will be made, and how payment will be made.
  - Get in the habit of confirming in writing what was agreed to during the telephone call.
  - If you say you will do something, do it promptly!
- Put an escalation procedure in place and implement it consistently when some milestone is breached.
- Consider having some degree of "high-level executive" participation on the top 20% of slow-paying customers.
- Insist on a practice of requesting face-to-face meetings when conventional methods haven't produced results.
- If all else fails, don't hesitate to consider legal proceedings. Experience has shown that often a threat is enough and payment is forthcoming after receipt of a lawyer's letter.
- If your receivables are in a big mess, put together a task force to deal with the problem that reports to the CFO and, when appropriate, includes outside expertise.
- Periodically have some third party audit your credit control program and practices.

Inventory

The usual measurement for Inventory is Inventory Turns as defined by Equation [6-15].

$$\textit{Inventory Turns} = \frac{\textit{Annualized Cost of Goods Sold}}{\textit{Inventory}} \qquad [6\text{-}15]$$

In general, there are two distinct management philosophies in widespread use today: *just in time* or *just in case*.

For many years, management felt that the best way to service customers' needs was to deliver product quickly at a price that reflected the value inherent in the product or service. This, of course, was and still is true. However, the way they went about it was suspect at best. In order to get the cost down they ordered or manufactured parts in large quantities. Usually the quantities were not balanced, so much of the inventory was unusable at any given time. Then they built up subassemblies and placed these in stock and often ended up with the same out-of-balance situation. When an order was received, the subassemblies were pulled from some central location and with a little luck all of the required parts were there and the customers got what they ordered. The outcome of this approach was huge inventories, excess parts, frequent shortages, and obsolescence write-offs.

To solve the problems inherent in this approach, *material requirements planning* (MRP) systems were introduced. Basically what these systems did was start with a sales forecast at the finished product level and then using the power of the computer, work through the various levels of the bills of material to generate component and subassembly requirements and then after comparing these requirements to shelf counts and order points, generate the required shop and purchase orders. While better, this approach had two fundamental flaws. The first was that the sales forecast was more often wrong than right. The second was that the quantities for the shop and purchase orders were usually generated using something called an *Economic Order Quantity* (EOQ).

Economic Order Quantity[12] In general, Carrying Costs increase and Procurement Costs decrease as the level of average inventory increases. The quantity at which the cost of inventory for a particular part is minimized is calculated by something called the Economic Order Quantity (EOQ). Equation [F-21] (renumbered here as [6-16]) defines the relationship and the parameters that go into calculating the Economic Order Quantity for any part.

$$\mathrm{EOQ} = \sqrt{\frac{2(FixPCost)(U)}{(\%CCost)(UCost)}} \qquad \text{[F-21] [6-16]}$$

where:

EOQ = The Economic Ordering Quantity of the inventory item under consideration

FixPCost = The Fixed Procurement (ordering and handling) Costs per order

U = The Annual Usage of the inventory item under consideration

%CCost = The Carrying Cost of inventory as a percentage of the total investment in inventory

UCost = The Unit Cost (cost per unit) of the inventory item under consideration

Obviously the smaller the EOQ, the lower the average inventory will be. Equation [6-16] tells us the way to get the EOQ down is to minimize Fixed Procurement Costs per order and the Annual Usage and to maximize the Carrying and Unit Costs. No sensible manager would think it prudent to minimize inventory by selling less (reduce Annual Usage) or by increasing the Carrying or Unit Costs. This leaves Fixed Procurement Costs as the one mechanism by which inventory costs can be minimized in this model.

Fixed Procurement Costs are the fixed costs associated with ordering and receiving parts. These costs include the infrastructure required to generate orders and receive the parts and the setup times required to prepare the machinery and jigs to manufacture the parts. Infrastructure tends to be lumpy and difficult to minimize because a company

---

[12] See Appendix F for a more complete and rigorous discussion of the Economic Order Quantity.

needs some basic ordering and receiving function in order to deal with one or a thousand parts. While it is always possible to reduce these costs, at some time the point of diminishing returns is reached and further effort yields very little because they can never be zero. Setup time is different. Numerous companies have shown that the key to minimizing Fixed Procurement Costs is to minimize setup times. Obviously, and in an extreme case, if the setup time for manufacturing a part is zero, then it is economically feasible (as far as the manufacturing unit is concerned) to manufacture the part in quantities of one.

In real life, even if all of the costs that go into calculating the EOQ are optimized, the Economic Order Quantity for each part is usually different. Therefore, even in a well-managed company, if order quantities are driven by the EOQ formula, the result will be unbalanced inventories and at some point the inevitable write-offs that go with excess parts when the quantity of a part on hand represents years of usage or a part is superseded or a product is phased out of production.

While no system is perfect, the best answer (so far) for managing inventory has come from Japanese industry. Manufacturing managers in Japan reasoned that there was no point in making parts that weren't required and that rather than trying to anticipate what the customer wanted and build for stock, it was better to shorten the manufacturing cycle so that finished product could be manufactured on demand. In other words, the factory and the suppliers that feed it were organized to respond to a demand-pull system. Basically the system works like this:

- The manufacturing processes are reengineered and setup times for the manufacture of parts and subassemblies are minimized.
- The factory is organized into cells that (wherever possible) flow logically from near receiving (input) to shipping (output). All of the cells have relatively small amounts of inventory on hand to build some quantity of a particular product(s), subassembly(ies), or part(s).
- When an order is received from a customer, product is assembled and tested in a "final product" cell and sent to shipping.
- If the quantity of any parts or subassemblies on hand in the "final product" cell falls below some small minimum, one of the people in the cell triggers a replacement by delivering a simple card to some adjacent cell with its own inventory. This cell then proceeds to manufacture the part or subassembly in a small quantity and refills the bin of the cell creating the demand. This process is repeated sequentially in a demand-pull fashion through the rest of the factory.
- Suppliers are organized to work in the same way.
- The result is that just-in-time replenishments are made within hours from internal manufacturing cells and the next day or days from outside vendors.

What started out as a just-in-time movement to deal with inventory problems has evolved into practices that integrate quality management and productivity enhancement into what is now called *world class* or *lean manufacturing*. The demonstrated results of this system are improved quality, better on-time delivery relative to promise, and lower inventory and manufacturing costs.

From a manager's perspective the inventory issues are:

- **Responsiveness versus obsolescence.** Every company wants their factory to deliver what the customer wants, when they want it, and meet or exceed the customer's quality expectations. As demonstrated in this short history of inventory management, this is rarely achieved by equating shelf count of parts with responsiveness and the ability to deliver product on demand. For example, if a product consists of 100 parts and the probability of each part being in stock is 99%, the probability that all 100 parts will be available when needed is 37% (0.99^{100}). One way around the part shortage problem is to carry excess stock. Experience demonstrates that this rarely helps and when it does it sets the stage for another problem: Write-off of excess parts when a part or product is superseded or made obsolete. A better answer is an integrated manufacturing system that is based on short lead times and designed to meet the customer's needs without creating excess inventories.
- **Product design and process design.** It is extremely difficult to take significant cost out of a product once it has been designed. Furthermore, quality isn't a thing. It's an outcome. The expected quality level will only be achieved if the product design is done with the manufacturing process in mind. Therefore, if a manufacturing unit is to meet its objectives, the product design team and manufacturing engineers have to work together as a seamless unit right from the outset of any project.
- **Visibility and space.** One of the fundamental flaws of centralized inventory schemes was that no one who used the inventory had any visible access to what and how much was in the cage. If you can't see it, how do you know how much is there? Experience has shown that if you get the inventory out on the floor where the people who use it control it, you will find that you need less inventory and free up space that can be used for other needs.
- **Administrative costs.** Large centralized inventories require staff to administer them. If you can eliminate (minimize) inventory, you will reduce your indirect administrative costs.
- **Inventory investment.** At times, inventory is viewed as a necessary evil and, therefore, the less one has of it the better off they are. While it is true that less inventory is usually better than more, this isn't the right way to look at it. Inventory is an investment in the business just like any other investment except that it is replenished more often than most. Like any investment it will provide better returns if subjected to rigorous planning and sensibly managed.
- **Cash flow.** It is fairly obvious that one has to ultimately pay for everything they purchase and, therefore, inventory is a user of cash. However, there is a flip side to this and that is that those companies that religiously focus on improving inventory turns by continuously striving to reduce cycle times and increase factory throughput reduce the inventory on hand for any given level of sales and thereby liberate cash. Therefore, inventory management is a potential onetime source of cash flow and essential to minimizing inventory cash flow needs.
- **Profit.** Good inventory managers can actually help the bottom line. Not only will the cost of financing and managing an inventory decline as inventory levels are reduced,

but doing so will also create opportunities to take advantage of cost reductions taking place at your suppliers. For example, for many years the cost of personal computer components had been decreasing at about 30% per year. When Dell was the largest supplier of PCs, some of Dell Computer's competitors carried about 70 days more inventory than Dell, which builds PCs on demand. The outcome of this was that because Dell could avail themselves of the lower-cost parts, at any given time the parts Dell used cost about 6% less.[13] It's hard to think of any other simple act that will add a comparable amount to a company's Gross Margin.

Accounts Payable

The usual measurement for Accounts Payable is:

$$APDOS = \left(\frac{Accounts\ Payable}{Annual\ Cost\ of\ Goods\ Sold} \right)(360) \qquad [6\text{-}17]^{14}$$

Equation [6-17] expresses the Accounts Payable in terms of a 360-day year. While other methods are in use, Accounts Payable Days Outstanding (APDOS) or simply Payable Days Outstanding is the most common.

Before getting into what constitutes good Accounts Payable practices, highlights of some of the issues that underlie and therefore impact payables management are in order.

Financing As far as your company is concerned, your Accounts Payable to any supplier is like an interest-free loan. Your supplier will know that you realize that you are borrowing money for free and that your objective will be to pay no sooner than necessary and sometimes as slowly as possible. To see how this works, assume that a company's Accounts Payable averages $1,000,000 over a year. If the Accounts Payable Days Outstanding average 60 days, this means that every 60 days the company will pay down the $1,000,000 debt and replace it with another $1,000,000 of debt without paying any interest. So in a sense, the company will be borrowing $1,000,000 interest free forever and use this money to help finance the business. If your suppliers are thinking properly, they will view the extension of credit as an investment in your business and should only provide it if they feel the money is well placed.

Relationships While it is perfectly understandable for a company to want to delay payment of a bill as long as possible, this should not be done at the expense of a relationship. Apart from any ethical question, remember that you will want to do business with this company again in the future and you don't want them to have been preconditioned by

[13]The 70 days represents about 19% of a year. Thus Dell was able to take advantage of the lower-priced parts for that period and save 30% or nearly 6% on an annual basis.

[14]Once again the reader is reminded this is a simplified definition. First, it is only true for manufacturing companies, since all of the other kinds of companies in the world don't have COGS per se. Second, most manufacturing companies would use COGS + OpExp + CapEx in the denominator when calculating APDOS.

virtue of your past payment practices and put your requirements at the end of a queue. Furthermore, don't run the risk of sullying your company's reputation by breaking payment promises. If you have a problem, contact your supplier and work out an arrangement. You may be surprised at how cooperative people will be when you treat them as you like to be treated.

Quality A company's suppliers play a key role in determining the quality level of what they ship to their customers. To properly fulfill this function, the supplier has to be motivated. Just as you wouldn't do anything to demotivate an employee, don't lord over your suppliers and continually demand more for less. If you do this, you will ultimately force your supplier to take shortcuts that are unknown to you and quality may suffer. Work cooperatively on cost reduction programs and be fair about sharing the savings.

Technology Just as there isn't any such thing as a car made (assembled—yes; made from American parts—no) in America anymore, there aren't many vertically integrated companies left in this world. Most every company now specializes in a small number of core technologies. The benefit, of course, is that the focus results in better quality and the economies of scale result in lower prices. The downside is that virtually every company is dependent on other entities for key technologies. So, in a sense, every company has entered into informal partnerships with each of its key suppliers. So much so that some companies have gone to great lengths to formalize these partnerships through joint ventures, technology sharing arrangements, cross-licensing of patents, and so on. Partnerships only work when both parties get what they bargained for. Protect your company's interest by all means, but take a balanced approach especially on issues that are important to the other side. Remember, if you can't work openly and forthrightly with a key supplier, the technology you are counting on is at risk and your company is headed for troubled times unless you do something about it.

Preferred Customer Pay as and when you have agreed to pay. By all means go after the best payment terms that you can. But remember, if you want to protect your reputation, the time to bargain for extended credit is before you place an order. Often you will get concessions with little effort. Don't hide from your supplier when it comes time to meet your obligations. Nothing infuriates a supplier more than getting the impression that you are only available when you need something from them. If you want to be a preferred customer, don't play the "payables game." If you do, the word will get out and your company's standing and creditworthiness will ultimately suffer.

Paying Early Terms like "2% 10 days, net 30" are often seen on invoices. These terms mean that the full amount of the invoice is due 30 days after the date of the invoice and that if you pay within 10 days of the invoice date, you can take a 2% discount. A simple calculation is helpful in deciding when to pay.

- Assume that the invoice is for $1,000. Also, every day you delay payment you are earning interest on money in the bank or avoiding paying interest on money you would have to borrow. If you pay on the tenth day, you can take a deduction of $20 and pay $980. If you pay on the 30th day, you pay $1,000 instead of $980 on the tenth. This is like borrowing $980 at 2% interest for a 20-day period. The effective interest rate is:

$$\textit{Effective Interest Rate} = (0.02)\left(\frac{360}{20}\right) = (0.02)(18) = 0.36$$

$$\textit{Effective Interest Rate} = 36\%$$

- Another way of looking at this is: If you pay on the thirtieth day, you are paying $20 in interest for a 20-day loan. There are 18 ($^{360}/_{20}$) 20-day periods in a year. Therefore, the annual interest would be $360 ($20*18) or an effective interest rate of 36%. $\left(\left(^{\$360}/_{\$1000}\right) * 100\right)$.

Unless you are borrowing money at a rate greater than 36%, you should take the discount and pay on the tenth day.

Paying Late If a supplier's terms are "2% interest/month on all overdue amounts," this is equivalent to 24% interest per annum. Again, unless your borrowing cost is > 24%, you should pay on time. In practice, this is often not enforced since the company is usually satisfied to collect the receivable and not engage in a discussion on collecting the interest.

Deciding When to Pay If a supplier offers you a discount for paying early, your accounting people should make their decision on when to pay after comparing the cost of forgoing the discount with the return available on short-term money.

Accounts Payable is like free money coming into the business. The general rules and issues associated with managing Payables are:

- Hold on to money that comes into the business as long as possible.
- Make sure your suppliers are aware of your policies, delivery and invoice requirements, and payment cycle. Take time where necessary to educate them on how to do business effortlessly with your company. Remember you are the customer and most suppliers want to please.
- Faithfully check the terms of your purchase order against the supplier's acknowledgment, especially when significant money is involved. If there is a discrepancy, deal with it. Simply because a situation isn't expected to occur doesn't eliminate the need for all parties to understand what they have agreed to, including the remedies if there is a problem. It is true that the time spent clarifying a discrepancy often proves to be unnecessary because the situation envisaged doesn't come to fruition. However, where possible, business shouldn't be conducted as a game of chance. Deal with material, remote issues up front and, should they occur, your company will be protected.

- Your supplier wants its money but doesn't expect to be paid for at least 30 days. Therefore, unless there is an exceptionally early payment discount or unless you are interested in establishing extraordinary goodwill from your suppliers, don't pay your bills early. You don't have any moral obligation to do so. Your suppliers will be satisfied if you pay your bills on time.
- Suppliers are a valuable resource. Treat them accordingly.

EXAMPLE 6-5: CALCULATING BALANCE SHEET STATISTICS

The object of this example is to use the Income Statement and Balance Sheet shown in Tables 6-13 and 6-14 respectively of the Richmond Company to calculate the Working Capital as a % of Net Revenue, Accounts Receivable as a % of Net Revenue, Accounts Receivable Days Outstanding, Inventory as % of Net Revenue, Inventory Turns, and Accounts Payable Days Outstanding.

The Richmond Company's Working Capital as percentage of Revenues is calculated by substituting values from the Income Statement and Balance Sheet into Equation [6-12].

$$\%WC = \left(\frac{Working\ Capital}{Annual\ Net\ Revenues}\right)(100) \qquad [6\text{-}12]$$

$$\%WC = \left(\frac{CurrentAssets - CurrentLiabilities}{Annual\ Net\ Revenues}\right)(100) = \left(\frac{25{,}000{,}000 - 6{,}000{,}000}{90{,}000{,}000}\right)(100)$$

$$\%WC = \left(\frac{19{,}000{,}000}{90{,}000{,}000}\right)(100) = 21.1\%$$

TABLE 6-13 Richmond Company Income Statement

Period Ending DD/MM/YY $(000)'s	
Net Revenues	90,000
Cost of Goods Sold (COGS)	(40,000)
Gross Margin (GM)	50,000
Operating Expenses (OpExp)	(29,000)
Earnings before Interest, Taxes, Depreciation & Amortization (EBITDA)	21,000
Depreciation & Amortization (D & A)	(4,000)
Earnings before Interest & Taxes (EBIT)	17,000
Interest Income/Expense (Int)	0
Earnings before Tax (EBT)	17,000
Taxes Paid (TaxesPaid) @ 40%	(6,800)
Net Income (NI)	10,200

TABLE 6-14 Richmond Company Balance Sheet

DD/MM/YYYY $(000)'s			
Current Assets		**Current Liabilities**	
Cash	1,000	Accounts Payable	6,000
Accounts Receivable	14,000	Taxes Payable	0
Inventory	10,000	Short-Term Debt	0
Total Current Assets	25,000	**Total Current Liabilities**	6,000
Fixed Assets			
At Cost	35,000	**Long-Term Debt**	0
Less Depreciation	10,000		
Net Fixed Assets	25,000		
		Shareholders' Equity	
Intangible Assets		Paid-in Capital	34,000
Goodwill & Oth Intang Assets	0	Retained Earnings	10,000
Net Intangible Assets	0	**Total Shareholders' Equity**	44,000
Total Assets	50,000	**Total Liabilities and TSHE**	50,000

The Receivables as a percentage of Annual Revenues and the Accounts Receivable Days Outstanding can be calculated using Equations [6-13] and [6-14] respectively.

$$\%Receivables/Net\ Revenues = \left(\frac{Accounts\ Receivable}{Annual\ Net\ Revenue}\right)(100) \qquad [6\text{-}13]$$

$$\%Receivables = \left(\frac{14,000,000}{90,000,000}\right)(100) = 0.1556 = 15.6\%$$

$$ARDOS = \left(\frac{Accounts\ Receivable}{Annual\ Net\ Revenue}\right)(360) \qquad [6\text{-}14]$$

$$ARDOS = \left(\frac{14,000,000}{90,000,000}\right)(360) = 56\ Days$$

Similarly, applying Equation [6-15] calculates the Inventory Turns.

$$InventoryTurns = \frac{Annual\ Cost\ of\ Goods\ Sold}{Inventory} \qquad [6\text{-}15]$$

$$InventoryTurns = \frac{40,000,000}{10,000,000} = 4\ \text{Times}$$

TABLE 6-15 Richmond Company Statistics

Working Capital/Revenue	21.1%
Accounts Receivable/Revenue	15.6%
ARDOS	56
Inventory Turns	4.0
APDOS	54

Finally the Accounts Payable Days Outstanding is obtained by applying Equation [6-17].

$$APDOS = \left(\frac{Accounts\ Payable}{Annual\ Cost\ of\ Goods\ Sold}\right)(360) \qquad [6\text{-}17]$$

$$APDOS = \left(\frac{6{,}000{,}000}{40{,}000{,}000}\right)(360) = 54 \text{ Days}$$

The results are summarized in Table 6-15.

Fixed Assets

In order to understand how to manage fixed assets and the costs associated therewith, it's helpful to be aware of how Revenue, Profit, and Costs interact.

The data represented by Cases A and B in Figures 6-8 and 6-9, respectively, are essentially break-even curves. Assume that a company in a period of high growth has just reached $90 million in sales and has a Profit-versus-Revenue curve depicted by Case A.

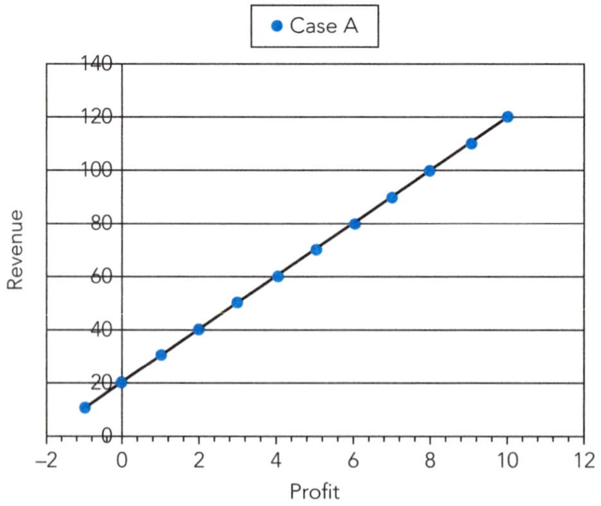

FIGURE 6-8 Break-Even Curve for Case A

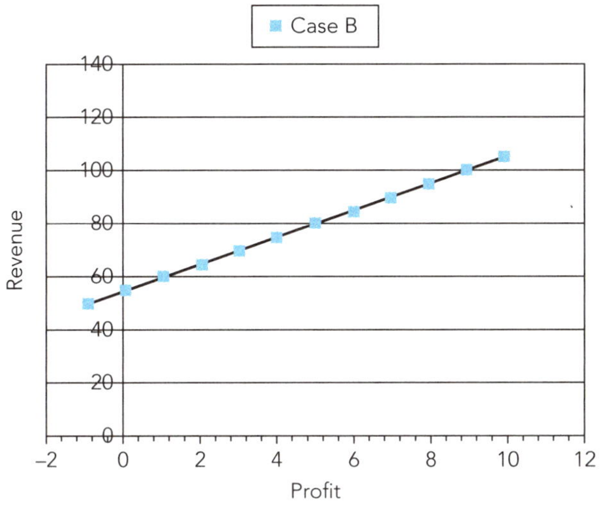

FIGURE 6-9 Break-Even Curve for Case B

The management of the company determines they can add automation that is breakeven at their current level of sales but will lower the cost per unit of production by more than what they are currently paying for the labor the automation will replace. Since they are confident that Revenue will continue to increase, they decide to make the investment. When management does this, the company's profit per unit will increase with volume. The price it pays for this is an increase in its fixed cost base and the break-even point. The net effect of this is the slope of curve A will decrease and the new Profit-versus-Revenue curve for the company will look like curve B. An overlay of the curves is shown in Figure 6-10.

Table 6-16 contains the data used to prepare Figure 6-10. As can be seen from this table, once the equipment is up and running, at Revenue of $95 million, the profit will be $8 million versus $7.5 million. If the business continues to grow according to plan, they will

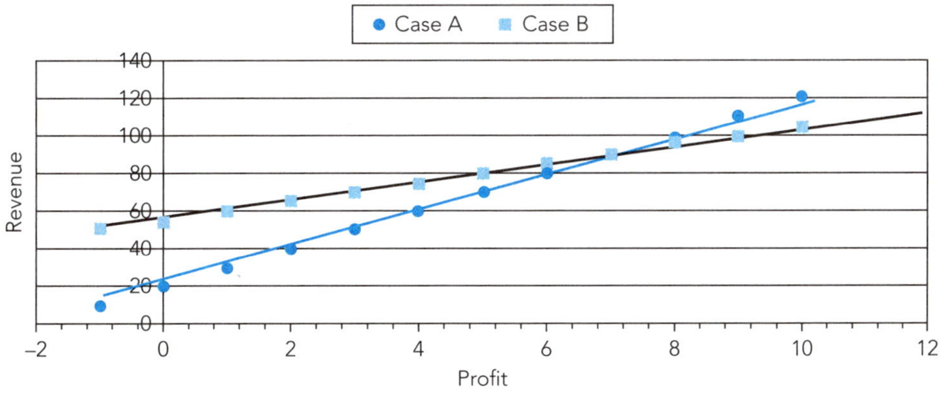

FIGURE 6-10 Comparison of Break-Even Curves for Case A and Case B

TABLE 6-16 Data for Comparison of Case A and Case B Break-Even Curves $(000,000)'s

Revenue	55	60	65	70	75	80	85	90	95	100	105	110	115
Profit Case A	3.5	4	4.5	5	5.5	6	6.5	7	7.5	8	8.5	9	9.5
Profit Case B	0	1	2	3	4	5	6	7	8	9	10	11	12

further leverage their investment and at $110 million will create $11 million in Profit versus the $9 million they would have achieved without the automation. The price the company pays for this upside is the increased downside risk. For example, if a recession comes along and Revenue was to drop to $80 million, their profitability would be $5 million, which is $1 million lower than it would have been prior to making the investment.

Does this increased risk mean that management shouldn't have made the investment? Certainly not; taking risk goes hand in hand with making investments and that is one of management's prime responsibilities. The real question is: How should management think about adding fixed costs and what do they do when they have added too much? Here are a few guidelines.

Make Focused Investments

Once made, relentlessly pursue meaningful productivity gains. Companies now find themselves in a world where they are forced to be world class in whatever they do. To achieve this, it's necessary to limit the number of things that a company engages in if the intent is be the best at what it does. It's unrealistic to believe that you can be the most innovative, fastest moving, and lowest-cost producer in a wide range of products and services. Just putting all of this together for a few products and services is a challenging task that demands the utmost effort from the best team the management of the company can put together.

Take Make-versus-Buy Decisions Seriously

The importance of having a rigorous process cannot be overstated. If the item under consideration can be manufactured in-house but competitive bids from outside suppliers are lower cost, then a thorough review of your manufacturing processes is in order because you clearly aren't a low-cost supplier. For example, if you are in the twenty-fifth percentile compared to your competitors when it comes to manufacturing cost, outsourcing manufacturing may be the right answer. However, it's not hard to find someone who can produce cheaper if you are that inefficient. A better answer might be to fix your production problems and then revisit the outsourcing question when you have achieved the seventy-fifth percentile. On the other hand, if you don't have the equipment to manufacture the item in-house, then it's probably better to source it outside, unless of course it has a strategic aspect.

Strategic Investments

Focus on investments that will give you a competitive advantage. Increasing your fixed cost base simply because you think you can do it better and cheaper in-house at the moment may not make sense in the long run. Also, be prepared to make a commitment to putting in place the infrastructure that is required to maintain the underlying technology and the resultant cost advantage. Otherwise, you probably won't have a cost advantage for very long.

Vertical Integration

This is a blessing and a curse. It's good, because it can give you control over your own destiny. It's bad, because it commits you to using technology because it's there and to the infrastructure required to keep it current. There are two good reasons to vertically integrate. The first is when a technology gives you a sustainable competitive advantage. The second is that it isn't available from any other supplier. Because it's cheaper to make versus buy is necessary but is usually an insufficient reason. This could simply mean you haven't tried hard enough to find competitive suppliers. In this age of intense global competition, survival requires focus and being the best (or among the best) at what you do. It's dangerous to think your company can be the best at everything that goes into your products. In most cases, a strategy that embraces a high degree of vertical integration will make it very hard for your company to be a leading player in the world markets.

Outsourcing

This is the flip side of vertical integration and what all companies must excel at if they want to deliver superior performance. A sound outsourcing strategy is critical to every company. Stated simply, it means that one of your core competencies has to be a highly proficient procurement function that can find very competent, high-quality suppliers for all of your non-core requirements.

Simply because your company doesn't make a particular part doesn't mean that the performance criteria for the part have to be relaxed. Most companies can procure non-core parts, products, and services at better price-performance levels than they could produce them in-house. This is because, just like you, when your suppliers specialize in something, they become very good at it and better than you could ever hope to be even with the same effort because you probably wouldn't have the same passion. Outsourcing has another great advantage: You only buy what you need and, in this sense, you convert what would otherwise be fixed into variable costs. Table 6-17 contains a summary of the attributes of outsourcing.

TABLE 6-17 Outsourcing and Implications

Why Do Companies Outsource?	Negatives Associated with Outsourcing
Focus on core activities.	Skill sets and technology are lost.
Gain access to world-class capabilities and skills.	Loss of control.
Convert fixed costs into variable costs.	Impact on security, loyalty, and morale.
Skills or resources are not available internally.	
Free up capital for other purposes.	
A particular function is difficult to manage.	
Reduce/share risk on a demanding undertaking.	
Generate cash, assets owned and managed by others.	

Investments Should Make a Difference

Making investments pay off is hard work. In most cases, you and your team will work just as hard to make a marginal investment pay off as you will those that have the potential of providing superior returns. If the investment doesn't make a real difference to the future of your company, you should probably walk away from it and focus your resources on something that will.

Cost Reduction

The road to product and service cost reduction is paved with success and failure. The successes come about when you design a product or service for a specific cost and performance level and carefully and expertly make the right investments in people, equipment, and manufacturing process. While new products can miss their cost goals, most of the failures come about when companies try to reduce the cost of existing products. Unless a product or service has an unusually long life, it's usually a bad idea to make major investments except when the potential payoffs are very attractive. For example, if a product is in Year 2 of a five-year life cycle, you should think long and hard about making any significant investment in plant and equipment to reduce cost unless the cost can be reduced substantially (say 25%) and you can get the cost reduced product into production very quickly. Unless you have this kind of margin, you run the risk of your savings being completely eaten up by delays, changing market conditions, and excess and obsolete inventories when you try to phase out more expensive parts for the new and more cost-effective version. Furthermore, if you encounter delays, you will run out of time to recover your investment even if the cost reduction is right on target.

When Fixed Costs Have Become Too High or Obsolete

When this occurs, the right decision is obvious. It's implementing the action plan that takes courage. The first hurdle is relatively easy. You have to identify all of the fixed assets that have become nonproductive or inefficient and find a way to get rid of them. The second is how to account for the dispositions and write-offs, and this is where courage is required on the part of operating management. Experienced management teams seldom encounter situations where any purpose is served by delay. The lesson learned by those who procrastinate is: If you delay, you are only putting off the inevitable and ratcheting up the total cost of ultimately dealing with the fixed cost problem.

In general terms, when it comes to tactics for fixed cost reduction your choices are: Reduce vertical integration, downsize your facilities, increase outsourcing of services and people, rationalize your product and service offerings and focus on those opportunities where you can add the most value and offer the best growth and profit potential.

Overhead

Overhead is another name for fixed costs. It's normally associated with manufacturing and administrative infrastructure and the people who are necessary to oversee and support some function, be it the factory, service area, or Finance. The usual question associated with overhead is: How much is enough? There really isn't a right answer here. Obviously, if a company has too much overhead, then profits suffer. And if a company has too little overhead, then profits can still suffer because the business may not be running efficiently. Figure 6-11 hypothetically portrays how overhead costs can vary over time.

When Overhead is charted over time, it can be expressed as a percentage of Revenue or Direct Costs.[15]

Either method will give a similar result and show that Overhead is lumpy. The usual model is that Overhead comes down as a percent of Revenue as Revenue increases. In Figure 6-11, excess capacity in the Overhead is used up as Revenues increase. When Revenues hit $60, $70, $95, $105, and $115 million, overhead is increased by the addition of people or infrastructure or both and the cycle repeats.

The amount of Overhead that a company will require is a function of the business. Some of the business factors that impact Overhead are: number of product lines or services offered, product or service complexity, degree of vertical integration, diversity of the customer base, and geographical coverage.

Indicators that the business may need more or less overhead are:

- Noise level in the organization
- Difficulty of task execution

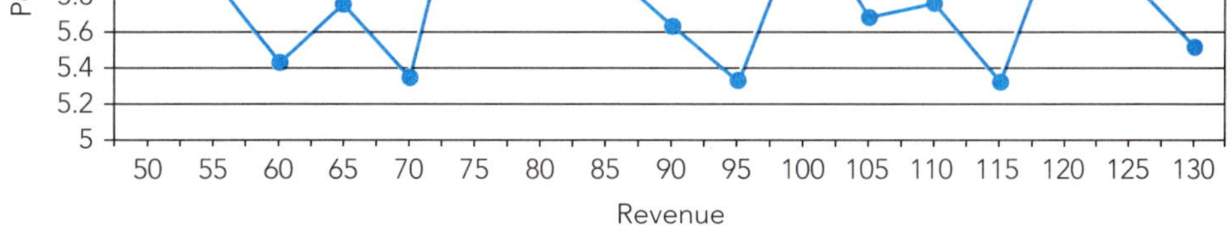

FIGURE 6-11 Illustrative Portrayal of Overhead as a Percent of Revenue versus Revenue

[15]Overhead as a percentage of Direct Costs is probably better since it eliminates the impact of pricing and double counting of Overhead. However, Revenue is easier to visualize, hence its use in Figure 6-11.

Too little noise and/or things seem to be going along effortlessly can indicate that Overhead is on the high side or that the company is running as intended. Excessive clamor and/or a perpetual state in which it is seemingly hard to get things done can indicate that more resources are required or the resources are misplaced.

Intangibles and Other Assets[16]

As the name implies, this asset category normally consists of intangibles and other assets. Examples of intangibles are patents, non-competes, customer lists, and goodwill. These are usually a consequence of an acquisition. In the case of patents, it's usual to ascribe some value to patents because the value ascribed to patents is deductible for tax purposes.[17] Non-competes are also a consequence of an acquisition and like patents are deductible for tax purposes in an asset deal. In this case, the owners or key employees of the business being acquired are paid to not compete with the new owner for some period of time after they leave the company. Like non-competes (and patents), customer lists are also valued and amortized. All of these are expensed through the Income Statement over their useful life. For example, if $1,000,000 is ascribed to a patent with 10 years of protection remaining, then it will be written off at a rate of $100,000 per year. Non-competes seldom go beyond three years. But whatever the period, the method of expensing the value ascribed to it is the same as for patents. The same is true for customer lists. After portions of the purchase price have been allocated to assets with identifiable lives (patents, non-competes, and customer lists) and if the remainder exceeds the estimated fair value of identifiable assets and liabilities of the company being acquired, the remaining difference is allocated to goodwill.

Goodwill, according to the GAAP[18] rules for public companies, is not amortized except when impaired. Companies are required to do impairment tests annually on their goodwill. When the test shows that the current value of the goodwill (i.e., the business purchased isn't performing as originally planned) is less than what is on the books, the difference is written off. How matters such as this and the tax treatment are handled is briefly discussed in the sections on depreciation and amortization and those that followed earlier in this chapter. For private entities there is an accounting alternative available that permits companies to amortize goodwill on a straight-line basis over 10 years or less if the entity can demonstrate that another useful life is more appropriate. However, this is not a book on taxes and, as emphasized in a brief discussion of taxes at the end of this chapter, a thorough discussion of the tax treatment of Intangible Assets and taxes in general is left to others.

Prepaid expenses include such things as insurance and rent. It's customary to pay a 12-month premium for insurance at the beginning of the policy year. When this happens, cash is credited and prepaid insurance is debited in the "Other Assets" account. As the year progresses, the prepaid insurance account is credited monthly with the cost flowing through the Income Statement until the account is cleared and then the process starts over again with the arrival of another premium

[16] See Example 6-4 for a discussion of amortization of identifiable and unidentifiable asset lives and impairment.
[17] Only if the Intangible Assets were acquired in an asset deal.
[18] Generally Accepted Accounting Principles.

for another year. Prepaid rent is rent paid for future use of land, buildings, or equipment. Like insurance, it is written off monthly for the period that has been paid in advance.

Like most individuals, many companies and partnerships keep their books on a cash basis (as opposed to accrual). In order to minimize the tax obligation that will flow to their owners, it is common for these companies and partnerships to prepay expenses to suppliers at year-end for goods and services to be provided in the future. When this occurs, these prepayments will be recorded as prepaid assets in the "Other Assets" section of the balance sheet.

Taxes

Taxes are right up there with one of humankind's greatest inventions.

Throughout recorded history, nations, governments, and people have been struggling with the consequences of the advent of taxes. Nowhere is this struggle more prevalent than in modern business. On one side, you have hordes of accountants, lawyers, and businesspeople devoting enormous resources to tax planning, avoidance, and filing tax returns. On the other hand, there is an army of government bureaucrats clawing every tax dollar they can out of the system to feed the massive spending machines that have been put in place. So intense is this battle that countries, states, provinces, and so forth have used the prospect of low or no taxes as a strategy to attract industry and the employment that it brings. However, when all is said and done on this subject, societies require money to function and so taxes aren't going to go away anytime soon. It's simply a matter of where the money comes from: business, individuals, or both?

Since value is based on Cash Flow, which in turn is heavily impacted by taxes, it would seem that no discussion on value could possibly be complete without a comprehensive dialogue on the subject. For this reason, in this and other chapters some space has been devoted to this topic in order to assist the reader in grasping some of the fundamental issues and provide insights into the importance and impact taxes can have on value. However, once you get beyond the fundamentals, taxes and tax strategies are a subject that is beyond the scope of this undertaking.

CASE STUDY: INNOVATIVE ENGINEERING CORPORATION

Innovative Engineering hasn't been so innovative lately. At least that is the conclusion Graydon Lawrence and his partner Stephen Thomas had come to after looking at the most recent financial report (Table CS 6-1). The partners started the business right out of engineering school and founded it on the principle of only taking on projects that created lots of value for their customers, and this of course was reflected in the pricing. Their startup money was modest and came mostly from family and friends, who have long since been bought out at a nice profit for all concerned. The first five years were a struggle, as they are for most startups, but finally the company achieved double-digit growth and started to make some real money.

The problems in the business started to show up several years ago when the growth rate slowed and margins began to gradually contract. Graydon and Stephen's reaction to this was typical of most management teams who had built a successful business, and that was to work harder and get a "bigger hammer," so to speak. In other words, they continued to do more of the same with renewed effort, expecting a different outcome. Today neither Graydon nor Stephen is active in the day-to-day management of the company; they currently serve on the Board as Co-Chairs.

After studying the results displayed in Table CS 6-1, Graydon was struck by the fact that despite the assurances given by management that their strategies were sound and just required more time to show results, and the company was on the right track, the fact of the matter was that the company's Net Income was now barely $5,000,000. Perhaps more disturbing was the fact that it was down considerably from prior years even though Revenues had grown to $67,000,000. After consulting with his partner and co-founder Stephen, they decided to become more active and as a first step asked the CFO to produce a comparative income statement contrasting the performance of the company five years ago to the current year. The result of that effort is presented in Table CS 6-2.

The partners were astonished by the message Table CS 6-2 sent. It was clear that management's strategies had not been working for some time. In fact, given the trend, they were driving the business in the wrong direction, and breakeven or worse was not far ahead. Rather than confront management, the partners decided that the place to start was with an executive session with the independent directors.

TABLE CS 6-1 Income Statement for the Current Year

Year Ending 12/31/20XX $(000)'s		
	Current Year	**Percent of Revenue**
Revenues (Rev)	67,000	100.0
Cost of Goods Sold (COGS)	(43,550)	(65.0)
Gross Margin (GM)	23,450	35.0
Operating Expenses (OpExp)	(13,400)	(20.0)
EBITDA	10,050	15.0
Depreciation & Amortization (D&A)	(1,139)	(1.7)
Earnings Before Interest & Taxes (EBIT)	8,911	13.3
Interest Income/(Expense) (NetInt)	0	0.0
Earnings Before Tax (EBT)	8,911	13.3
Taxes Paid (TaxesPaid) @ 40%	(3,564)	(5.3)
Net Income (NI)	5,347	8.0

TABLE CS 6-2 Comparative Income Statements

Year Ending 12/31/20XX $(000)'s	Percent of Revenue	Current Year – 5	Current Year	Percent of Revenue	% CAGR
Revenues (Rev)	100.0	51,000	67,000	100.0	5.6
Cost of Goods Sold (COGS)	(53.0)	(27,030)	(43,550)	(65.0)	10.0
Gross Margin (GM)	47.0	23,970	23,450	35.0	(0.4)
Operating Expenses (OpExp)	(19.0)	(9,690)	(13,400)	(20.0)	6.7
EBITDA	28.0	14,280	10,050	15.0	(6.8)
Depreciation & Amortization (D&A)	(1.2)	(612)	(1,139)	(1.7)	13.2
Earnings Before Interest & Taxes (EBIT)	26.8	13,668	8,911	13.3	(8.2)
Interest Income/(Expense) (NetInt)	0.0	0	0	0.0	0.0
Earnings Before Tax (EBT)	26.8	13,668	8,911	13.3	(8.2)
Taxes Paid (TaxesPaid) @ 40%	(10.7)	(5,467)	(3,564)	(5.3)	(8.2)
Net Income (NI)	16.1	8,201	5,347	8.0	(8.2)

Table CS 6-2 was presented with a commentary that went as follows.

- The five-year compound annual growth rate was now 5.6%, which was well below the double-digit growth the company had experienced for many years.
- The Cost of Goods Sold was a big problem. Not only was it trending in the wrong direction, but at 10% (almost twice the Revenues growth rate) it had driven the Gross Margin down from 47% to 35% over the past five years.
- Operating Expenses had grown from 19% to 20% of Revenues, and, while it is always desirable to reduce costs, it was clear that the issues the company currently faced weren't going to be solved by cuts in this area.
- EBITDA performance was a disaster. Given that companies like Innovative Engineering have a market value of roughly 7.5 times EBITDA, the value of the enterprise had gone from $107,100,000 ($14,280,000 * 7.5) to $75,400,000 ($10,050,000 * 7.5), a systematic reduction in value of 6.8% per year.
- D&A's impact on financial performance was de minimis. If there was a problem here, it probably would have more to do with the kind of investments that had been made rather than their magnitude.
- When it came to Net Income, the numbers spoke for themselves. It wouldn't improve until the problems implied by performance further up the Income Statement were solved.

A discussion followed, which resulted in a broad consensus that boiled down to a simple statement: Given the dramatic reduction in Gross Margin, they were either not pricing projects correctly or had significantly departed from the long-standing strategy of delivering high value-added solutions that customers confirmed by their willingness to pay.

This performance analysis was of course the easy part of the bigger question, "What to do?" Graydon Lawrence was the first to speak: "It seems to me that the Board can no longer wait for management's strategy to pay off. We need to appoint someone to meet with management and convey our concern over the Revenue growth and Gross Margin trends, and come up with a recommended course of action." The Board agreed and asked Graydon or Stephen to take on that task. They responded by saying they appreciated the confidence the Board apparently had in them but declined because "a fresh approach" was required to get to the right answer, and neither of them met that requirement. During the pause that followed, the youngest Board member, Michael Henry, asked for permission to speak, which of course was granted. "As you know, I have extensive experience in 'fixing businesses' and have been on this Board for three years," Michael said. "Whether or not I want to admit it, I have watched our performance continue to deteriorate, and, while I did comment, as many of you also did on many occasions, it was to no avail. It's not in my nature to take Board fees for this kind of performance, so I'm prepared to step up and take on this challenge. Give me this assignment and 30 days to come back with a plan. . . . I promise not to disappoint."

Graydon thanked Michael for his offer and inquired as to how he expected to be compensated for the work he was about to undertake. His reply: "I don't want any salary. If it's necessary that I take something in order to be part of the management team, pay me $10.00 per year. What I do want is 5% of the value that is created after three years." Stephen then asked, "How will we measure that?" Michael responded by saying: "It could be some multiple of a weighted average of earnings that the company's investment banker could be tapped to propose. But in any case the value created would be very clear, and to make matters simple I would leave it up to the Board to decide what was fair if there were any complications or disputes." The Board quickly agreed.

Michael's first meeting was with the management team, during which he reviewed what had been discussed at the Board meeting and told the team that the degradation in performance had to come to a stop and be followed by rapid improvement. The CEO asked what he meant by this. Michael's answer was: "We have 30 days to come up with a plan and quarterly improvement in performance as it is implemented." The CEO responded, "All of this happened when I was in charge; I feel I should offer my resignation." Michael responded by saying, "It may come to that, but right now I'm more concerned about getting on with the task I have been assigned and coming up with a plan. If you are not comfortable with the plan that will be developed or I think you are not the right person to execute it, then we will work something out." The CEO agreed, and assignments were handed out to each member of the task force Michael had formed. The task of developing a plan was completed on schedule, and a special Board meeting was called to consider what was to be proposed.

Michael began his address to the Board by reminding all that the growth rate had slowed considerably and profitability was not what it once was. In order to address this, he had formed a task force consisting of the top talent from all parts of the company and asked them to stretch themselves and come up with some scenarios that were both imaginative and unique, and that could launch the company on a new growth trajectory. He told the Board, "After numerous iterations and some truly matchless thought leadership, the task force has developed a proposal that I would like to present to you today.

"As you know, our current strategic thrust is centered around an 'Attributes Model' where for years we have targeted our customers and focused on delivering a high level of customer satisfaction for a given level of comparative performance. Over the years we have become very good at this and have managed to get premium pricing for our deliverables because we have consistently shown our customers that we always do what we say we will do, when we say we will do it and at the expected quality level. In other words, our objective in every contract we take on is to exceed the customers' expectations. Unfortunately, the competition has figured much of this out, and since the management team hasn't strategically reacted to this development, our pricing and our growth rate now reflect this. Before I get to the result of the task force's work I would like to make a few comments.

"It seems that our sales and business development team have drifted away from our pricing model and been inclined to discount as opposed to selling the company's value proposition. This is somewhat understandable given that the company has been driving the same strategy for many years with little, if any, update to current market conditions. Stated differently, they forgot 'The Power of No!' and have been taking the price reduction route as opposed to politely saying no to a request for a price concession and explaining why in a compelling way. Fortunately, the task force has developed a solution to this state of affairs, which I will get to shortly.

"Our CEO and CFO are certainly qualified and experienced leaders. However, the decline in the company's fortunes has occurred on their watch and this cannot be ignored. I can't quite put my finger on why they have let the performance of the company drift. However, in my view there is little to be gained by studying what has happened. Therefore, while it's not a task force recommendation, it is my recommendation that both of these executives be replaced. My proposal is to negotiate a separation agreement with our CEO and begin a search for a new leader. I'm prepared to fill in if that is the Board's wish while a search for a new CEO is conducted. As for the CFO, my recommendation is to leave the decision of what to do up to the new CEO."

Michael continued, "Those of you who know me know that my DNA is such that I always try to say what I think needs to be said, even if it results in a level of discomfort or more. As I just said, our CEO has not been doing his job. Unfortunately, the same is also true of our Board of Directors. The decline in the company's fortunes has also taken place on our watch. After thinking about what happened at the Board level, it seems to me that the Board needs to examine our governance model. My suggestion is that a special committee of the Board be established to identify shortfalls in our current Board practices and chart a way forward."

At this point Graydon Lawrence interjected a comment: "I think all of us here agree with your recommendations. The Board has had offsite discussions on what to do about management and therefore your suggested course of action is fine with us. As for what to do in the interim, we unanimously accept your proposal and thank you for your willingness to step in and lead the company. I have been authorized to negotiate a compensation agreement with you and would like to do so at the earliest opportunity." Michael replied, "We have already done that. I simply want to be paid for the value created, and with the Board's permission would like to get on with the results of the task force's work and the proposed course of action.

"First: We have studied the projects we have taken on and successfully executed over the past five years and have concluded that nearly 80% of them consisted of common building blocks starting with the specification and design and finishing with the handover at the conclusion of the project. The team then looked at each building block in detail and concluded that we could cut the time from start to finish by 30% and in some cases by as much as 50% if we reengineered the way we do things into a 'Concurrent Model.' These charts illustrate the point I'm trying to make." He presented Tables CS 6-3 and CS 6-4.

"Activities '1' and 'A' are of course project management," Michael explained. "Activities '6' and 'J' the handover phase. Other than these activities, the two models don't have anything else in common. Activities '2' through '5' are quite different from Activities 'B through 'I.' Furthermore, while the models are quite different, our investigation strongly supports the fact that the amount of work required to complete an undertaking is about the same or less depending on the project.

TABLE CS 6-3 Sequential Project Model

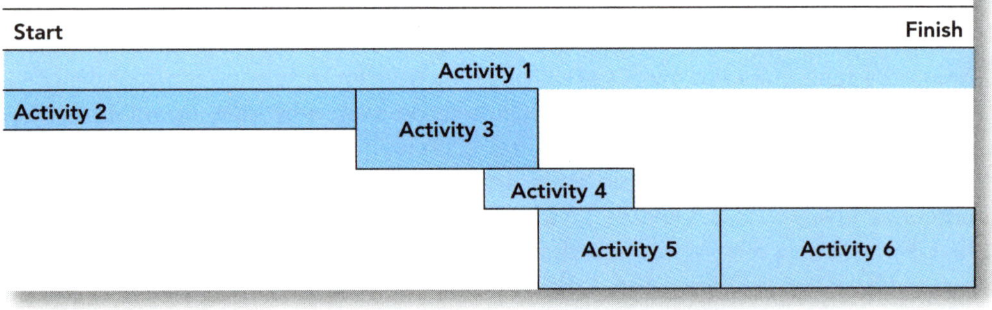

TABLE CS 6-4 Concurrent Project Model

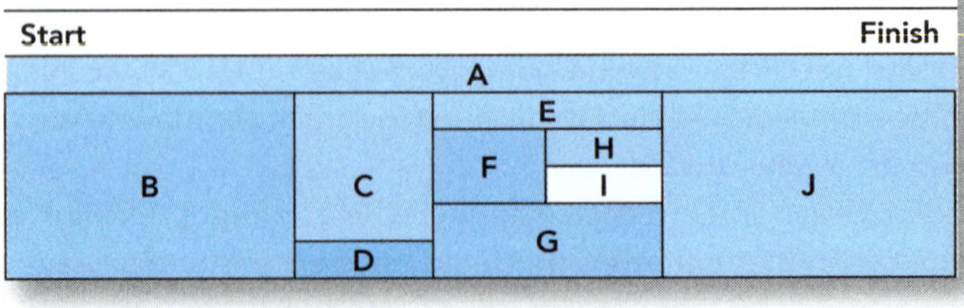

"This dramatic reduction in time to complete is of great strategic importance because time is money. But it doesn't stop there. When the task force was doing the investigation, they were struck by the dramatic difference in time to complete and consulted the literature to determine what this could mean financially. They found studies that showed for the same amount of money spent on comparable projects, the Returns on Capital Employed (ROCEs) were 65% if completed in three years, 115% if completed in two years, and 145% if completed in one year. At first the team was puzzled by this finding, but then they realized that completing a project one or two years ahead of schedule amounted to extending the life cycle of the investment by that amount of time.

"Not content to simply stop there, the task force continued to refine what they had discovered. They returned to our project database and reworked the data that accounted for the vast majority of our projects. They discovered that within this set, there where unique combinations of work and work flow, and with the aid of our IT department and top engineers they were able to define about a dozen variations of the Concurrent Model that literally amounted to customized engineering. For example, depending on the customer's needs, the Operator Interface could be provided at the outset for value engineering and evaluation by the customer, followed by a customer-prioritized rollout of the constituents of the system. This latter capability would enable customers to, should they wish to do so, time phase the release of their product, reduce the time to market, and capture more value as subsequent releases were made available. Also, remarkably enough, most of our projects are of three years' duration, so the implication of all this is that we have an opportunity to improve the ROCE for our customers by completing a project one year ahead of schedule. Our CFO and his team ran the numbers for the kind of work that we do, and while none of our projects had a three-year 65% ROCE, they did cluster around 40% for a three-year completion and 75% if completed in two years.

"So, in summary, the Concurrent Model will enable us to:

- "Cut the completion time for our projects with no increase in engineering hours, thereby increasing our infrastructure capacity to take on additional projects at little incremental expense.
- "Offer customers a solution that can be customized to suit their needs at a level of detail that will be unique.
- "Reduce the time to completion for a vast majority of our projects from three to two years, thereby handing over our deliverable one year ahead of schedule and improve the ROCE for the customer from 40% to 75%."

Continuing, Michael went on to say, "When our Marketing and Business Development team members were confronted with the findings, they went away and reworked our strategy to be more in line with a 'Premium' value-added model than our current 'Attributes' approach."

At this point a Board member interrupted, saying, "This is all quite remarkable, and I compliment you and your team on the work product, but I don't understand how the 'Premium Model' you propose takes advantage of these findings."

"Great question, and thank you for the segue," Michael replied. "While the Premium Model is similar to the Attributes Model in many ways, it's also different in several important aspects. To begin with, it provides a framework for thinking about relationships in a different way.

"Like the Attributes Model, the Premium Model starts by defining what it takes to have any account share. It states that the entry-level requirements are: (1) satisfy basic performance and quality expectations (Basic Needs) and (2) consistently deliver an acceptable level of service (Consistency). Premises like these are hard to argue with and are, in fact, what all of us expect from anyone or any company that we favor with our business.

"Beyond the general quality necessities are (3) supplying 'Specific Quality' requirements. By satisfying a customer's Specific Quality requirements, suppliers can differentiate themselves from the competition and get more business at better margins. While different, the same is also true for the Attributes Model, which postulates that a supplier can increase account share at better prices by focusing on helping the customer add specific value to its products or services. As some of you may recall, we have occasionally made the mistake of waiting for our customers to bring the opportunity to our attention, and by then it was too late to get the business at a premium price. The reason for this is that once the customer has identified the Specific Quality or performance issues that are desired, the number of competitors that can meet the requirements is usually much increased.

"Now to the crux of the Premium Model, which is the notion of 'Bespoke.' As many of you know, by definition, *bespoke* means that something is made only for you and is therefore unique. If something is unique, it doesn't have anything that it can be compared to, and value is completely subjective. This is a very powerful concept. Art and other limited (and not so limited) editions of products and services have thrived on this concept for centuries. In our case we are going to go to our customers with a 'Bespoke Model' based on offering them a customized solution that better suits their business model but will also give them an opportunity to approximately double the expected Return on Capital Employed.

"While these may not be earth-shattering concepts, they are of tremendous importance, because:

- "Innovative suppliers are a relatively rare phenomenon, especially those that are listening carefully to how they can help their customers add value and improve the returns on their investments.
- "Taking an innovative approach to our customers creates an opportunity for us to uniquely differentiate our company from the competition with little associated marginal cost.
- "Everybody likes the idea that something may be made just for them and, when properly presented, they are prepared to pay for it.

- "Because we can significantly cut the time to completion, we get an increase in capacity with no significant investment in infrastructure or engineering staff.

"Now to what all this means. The task force has modeled the implications of going to a 'Premium' value-added strategy. The results are shown in this Income Statement." Michael presented Table CS 6-5.

"As can be seen from the table:

- The first year of the three-year forecast is relatively flat and expected to grow at the same rate the business has grown for the past five years.
- Over the three years, Revenues are expected to grow at a CAGR of 16.2%.
- Gross Margin improvement is factored into each year of the plan and reaches a level more consistent with our historical rate. This is driven by the premium pricing we expect to start getting beginning in Year 2 (accelerating in Year 3) and the improvement in COGS driven by the reduction in project completion times.
- Year 1 is a year of investment in reengineering our process in order to reduce our project completion time by 30%.
- The investment in reengineering continues into Year 2 and will be completed by the end of the year.
- Operating expenses grow in line with Revenues and if anything will come in lower than projected.
- The valuation of the company on a comparable basis grows to $297,315,000 ($39,642,000 * 7.5) as a consequence of the dramatic improvement in EBITDA. This represents an increase in value of approximately $222,000,000 ($297,300,000 – $75,400,000).

TABLE CS 6-5 Projected Three-Year Income Statement

Years Ending 12/31/20XX $(000)'s						
	Current Year	**Year C + 1**	**Year C + 2**	**Year C + 3**	**Year 3 % Revenue**	**% CAGR**
Revenues (Rev)	67,000	70,350	80,903	105,173	100	16.2
Cost of Goods Sold (COGS)	(43,550)	(42,880)	(42,210)	(44,496)	(42)	0.7
Gross Margin (GM)	23,450	27,470	38,693	60,677	58	37.3
Operating Expenses (OpExp)	(13,400)	(14,070)	(16,181)	(21,035)	(20)	16.2
Reengineering	0	(5,000)	(5,000)	0	0	
EBITDA	10,050	8,400	17,512	39,642	38	58.0
Depreciation & Amortization (D&A)	(1,139)	(2,111)	(2,832)	(4,207)	(4)	54.6
EBIT	8,911	6,290	14,680	35,435	34	58.4
Interest Income/(Expense) (NetInt)	0	0	0	0	0	
Earnings Before Tax (EBT)	8,911	6,290	14,680	35,435	34	58.4
TaxesPaid (TaxesPaid) @ 40%	(3,564)	(2,516)	(5,872)	(14,174)	(13)	
Net Income (NI)	5,347	3,774	8,808	21,261	20	58.4

- Depreciation increases significantly due to investments made in workstations, laptops, iPads, smartphones, and 3-D CAD (Computer-Aided Design) systems and other software.
- Net Income once again will be about 20%, which approximates what the company achieved when it was growing rapidly."

At this point a Board member asked: "This is clearly a very aggressive plan and, if accomplished, will result in a very different company. What is your confidence in achieving the plan, and how will we finance it?" To which Michael replied: "My confidence is very high, and I will stake my reputation on it. I realize this sounds like 'Trust me' but the fact that we will be able to offer bespoke solutions to our customers that reduce the time to completion by at least a year and the accompanying doubling of their return on their investment is a story that all of our competitors would love to have but won't have at least within the time frame of this plan. Year 3 is a year of 30% growth, which I agree is high but, given what we have, is very achievable—at least in my view. However, I take your point, and let's assume the growth is only 10%, which records show is at the low end of the range of 10% to 20% the company achieved in prior periods when it had a unique solution. Should this be the outcome, the EBITDA would be approximately $26,000,000 or valued at roughly $200,000,000 ($26,000,000 * 7.5), which represents an increase in value of $125,000,000 ($200,000,000 – $75,000,000).

"Now to the second part of your question: The first year of the plan will be partially financed by a $5,946,000 reduction in working capital. As can be seen in this table, this comes about by collecting the company's Accounts Receivable (AR) and extending the Accounts Payable (AP) from their current 72 and 33 days sales outstanding (DOS), respectively, to 45 days, which is very much in line with the industry practices." Michael presented Table CS 6-6.

"As for the remainder of the financing for the first year of the plan, it will come from operations, as the Pro Forma Cash Flow Statement shows," Michael continued, referring to Table CS 6-7. "According to the plan, the Cash Balance hits a low point of $3,529,000, which is a little more than 4% of Revenues and on the light side. However, this assumes a dividend of $4,000,000, which could be delayed or reduced if need be."

The Board then entered into a lengthy debate discussing the pros and cons of the plan. Convinced that the plan could be financed and the risk was acceptable, they unanimously approved the plan.

TABLE CS 6-6 Innovative Engineering Working Capital Statistics

Statistic	**AR**	**AP**
AR/AP at End of Current Year	13,400	4,020
DOS at end of Current Year	72	33
DOS at End of Year C + 1	45	45
AR/AP at End if Year C + 1	8,794	5,360
Change in AR/AP	4,606	1,340

TABLE CS 6-7 Projected Three-Year Cash Flow Statement

Years Ending 12/31/20XX $(000)'s			
Operating Activities			
Operations	C +1	C + 2	C + 3
Net Income (Loss)	3,774	8,808	21,261
Depreciation and Amortization	2,111	2,832	4,207
Net Cash Flow from Operations (CFfO)	5,884	11,640	25,468
Working Capital Accounts			
(Increase)/Decrease Accounts Receivable	4,606	(1,319)	(3,034)
Increase/(Decrease) Accounts Payable	1,340	804	1,849
Increase/(Decrease) Taxes Payable	0	0	0
Net Change in Working Capital (NetΔWC)	5,946	(515)	(1,185)
Cash Flow from Operating Activities (CFfOA)	11,830	11,125	24,283
Investing Activities			
Fixed Asset Additions	4,858	3,605	6,877
Reengineer Processes	5,000	5,000	0
Cash Flow After Investing Activities (CFaIA)	1,973	2,519	17,407
Financing Activities			
Increase/(Decrease) Short-Term Debt	0	0	0
Increase/Decrease Long-Term Debt	0	0	0
Proceeds (Purchase) of Common Stock	0	0	0
Dividends Paid	2,800	3,200	4,000
Cash Generated/(Used)	(827)	(681)	13,407
Cash Flow Proof			
Beginning Cash Balance	5,037	4,210	3,529
Cash Generated/(Used)	(827)	(681)	13,407
Ending Cash Balance	4,210	3,529	16,936

PROLOGUE

Late during Year 1, Michael brought on board Pat Letterle as Chief Operating Officer, whose performance in subsequent years exceeded expectations. When the audited results for Year 3 were available, Michael was paid $10,000,000 as his share of the value created over the three-year period. An additional $10,000,000 was set aside to top up the bonuses that had been earned by the management team in recognition of their outstanding performance. The company negotiated a $10,000,000 line of credit with its bank to cover the bonus payments and provide adequate working capital. Pat was promoted to President and CEO. Michael was elected Chair of the Board of Directors.

7

CHAPTER SEVEN

Productivity and Operating Margin*

CHAPTER 7 **TAKEAWAYS**

- Economic history has shown that in the long run and on average, a company will not be able to increase prices in the international market by more than 2–3% per year. As interesting as this statistic may be, it's not very helpful in the short run. The point is: If the costs of a company's inputs are increasing by 5% and these costs cannot be passed along to the customer, then the minimum annual increase in productivity must be the difference between the cost increase and price increase that is achievable; otherwise, financial performance will deteriorate.
- Any measure of productivity should include the concepts of *manufactured value added, operating value added,* and *premium value added.*
- If a reduction in force (RIF) is to have any impact on cost, the management team has to go after the highly paid people and refrain from the temptation of laying off clerks and secretaries.
- Customers will only pay for value added and will not pay for inefficiencies.
- A company can't save its way into prosperity.
- Without an effective productivity program focused on value added, any benefit achieved via cost reduction will be quickly erased. Cost creep is relentless. Your efforts have to be without end in order to keep them under control and you need imaginative strategies to continuously bring them down.
- While it is seemingly very compelling to be the low-cost producer, the concept may be flawed. You are probably better off if you are the low-cost producer of the value added that your customer is purchasing.
- If your customers buy on price, despite what you may think, you are in the cost business. But even if your customers don't buy on price, you still need a cost reduction strategy.
- *Cycle time reduction* is a technique that permits management to improve productivity, reduce cost, and increase value-added time and customer service, all at the same time.

---

*The reader may notice minor discrepancies in the calculations in this chapter. When this occurs, it is the result of rounding.

PRODUCTIVITY

Other than the Internet, it's hard to find a modern-day business activity that exceeds the time and attention that has been devoted to *productivity*. In some ways the need for it is ubiquitous—here, there, and everywhere. A mistake that many managers make is to relentlessly pursue productivity improvements before they have a clear understanding of exactly what productivity is, how to go about measuring it, and how to design and manage a program. Furthermore, once they have achieved satisfactory measurement of productivity, they fail to take the next step, which is to quantify what improvements in productivity mean in terms of EBIT or Operating Margin (OpMargin). The objective in this chapter is to do four things:

1. State the case for focusing on productivity.
2. Establish a framework that provides a structured way of how to think about and measure productivity.
3. Expand the productivity framework to quantify the impact productivity improvements can have on the financial performance of the company, specifically Operating Margin.
4. Provide practical advice on how to employ the model and work the issues a company is confronted with when it's continuously faced with the challenge of doing more with less.

The Case for Focusing on Productivity

There are many ways to deal with costs. However, in the long run there is only one way and that is by systematically improving productivity. The general rule is, if the annual cost increase is *X*%, then to stay where you are:

$$\textit{Minimum Annual Productivity Increase} = X - \textit{Price Increase} \qquad [7\text{-}1]$$[1]

Economic history has shown that in the long run and on average, a company will not be able to increase prices in the international market by more than 2–3% per year. As interesting as this statistic may be, it's not very helpful in the short run. The point is: If the costs of a company's inputs are increasing by 5% and all of these costs cannot be passed along to the customer (competition will not increase prices to offset input costs), then the minimum annual increase in productivity must be the difference between the cost increase and price increase that is achievable; otherwise, financial performance will deteriorate.

---

[1] Actually a company doesn't have to increase prices by as much as costs go up since hopefully it is making money. If this factor is taken into account, the right-hand side of Equation [7-1] would be rewritten as: (*X* – *Price Increase*)(1 – *Operating Margin*). Since the point being made is the need to increase productivity the simplified version of Equation [7-1] is adequate.

This means that, if the costs of a company's inputs are increasing by 5% and only 2% of it can be passed along to the customer, then the minimum annual increase in productivity must be 3%; otherwise, the company's products will become uncompetitive.

$$\textit{Minimum Annual Productivity Increase} = 5 - 2 = 3\% \quad [7\text{-}2]$$

And to increase profits:

$$\textit{The Sustainable Productivity Increase} > 5 - 2 > 3\% \quad [7\text{-}3]$$

In the real world things usually aren't this simple. Competitors may not be satisfied with the status quo. A far more likely scenario is one in which they relentlessly pursue market share. Often they do this by offering lower prices. When this happens, the new benchmarks become more challenging.

Example 7-1: Productivity and Price Erosion

Companies A and B are competitors with relatively undifferentiated product lines. Company A has been working hard on improving productivity for several years. They now believe they are the low-cost producer in the niche they serve and in fact have identified opportunities to further reduce costs. Management feels it's now time to go for market share and adopts a strategy of systematically decreasing price by 5% per year for each of the next three years. Company B has the highest market share and is currently enjoying good profits and Return on Capital Employed. Both companies expect costs to increase about 3% per year. The question is: How much will Company B have to increase its productivity if profitability is to be maintained when it defends its market position by matching Company A's price cuts?

Now if for each of the next three years Company B is faced with Annual Cost Increase = X = 3% and Annual Price Increase = –5%, then the minimum annual productivity increases that Company B must achieve in order to maintain its current performance are:

Year 1:
$\textit{The Minimum Annual Productivity Increase} = X - \textit{Price Increase} = 3 - (-5) = 8\%$

Year 2:
$\textit{The Minimum Annual Productivity Increase} = X - \textit{Price Increase} = 3 - (-5) = 8\%$

Year 3:
$\textit{The Minimum Annual Productivity Increase} = X - \textit{Price Increase} = 3 - (-5) = 8\%$

This is not a trivial matter for Company B. What this means is that B must increase its productivity by 26% (1.08^3) in three years, not an easy task under the best of circumstances. It's even tougher if they don't have a productivity program in place.

If Company B can't do this, they will have to choose between losing market share or lower profits and ROCE or both.

Basics of a Productivity Model[2]

Without a doubt productivity is one of the most discussed topics in all industries and all businesses. As with most things, a manager can be more effective if he or she can objectively measure the outcomes of an improvement program or action plan. In a company there are several ways to make measurements and in most cases there isn't any one right way. This is also true of productivity. As will be seen, most productivity models have serious flaws. The model that is developed in the next section is designed to eliminate the shortcomings of other models and yet retain the essence of simplicity.

Steps Involved in Developing the Model

Productivity is a simple concept. In the end, trying to quantify it and the impact it can have on financial performance is also straightforward. However, the process of getting there can be a little laborious and so it may be instructive to begin by outlining the seven steps involved in developing the Productivity and Operating Margin models.

Step 1: Define *productivity* in terms of value added and number of employees.
Step 2: Develop expressions for manufacturing, operating, and premium value added.
Step 3: Deal with the issues presented by using "Number of Employees" in the measurement.
Step 4: Bring all of the material together and state the expression for the productivity model.
Step 5: Incorporate EBIT and Operating Margin into the productivity model.
Step 6: Introduce the concepts of *correlation* and *integration coefficients*.
Step 7: Express Operating Margin in terms of the integration coefficient and productivity.

Productivity Defined

Historically, productivity models have focused on manufacturing enterprises. While the reasons for this are clearly understandable, the rise and importance of service companies require that a broader perspective be taken. In this regard the manufacturing model is developed first and then generalized to encompass a broader array of businesses. When it comes to defining productivity there isn't any common convention let alone one right answer. A simple and broadly accepted definition is:

$$Productivity = \frac{Value\ Added}{Number\ of\ Employees} \qquad [7\text{-}4]$$

[2]The productivity model developed in this chapter was outlined in a meeting of the board of directors of ABB Robotics Inc., on which I served as a director for many years.

Value Added

In the final analysis, value added is what a customer purchases. A buyer won't pay much, if any, premium for something she can buy direct from the source. What she will pay for is what you actually do to efficiently transform the various inputs (labor, materials, parts, supplies, etc.) in the value-added process that converts them into a product, plus a fair return on the investments the company has made adjusted for risk.

Manufactured Value Added By now, Table 7-1 should be familiar. It has been used repeatedly since its introduction in Chapter 1. A close look at the table indicates that the difference between Revenue and Gross Margin is the Cost of Goods Sold. The Cost of Goods Sold represents all of the inputs required to actually physically produce the product that will ultimately be offered for sale. It consists of:

- **Direct material.** Parts and materials used to make the finished product. The materials are usually outsourced as are parts the company chooses to purchase from others rather than produce in-house. The outsourcing of material is easy to understand. Parts are outsourced for myriad reasons. Among them are cost and proprietary technology possessed by a vendor.
- **Direct and indirect labor and benefits.** This is the cost of the direct labor that produces the parts and subassemblies manufactured in-house, assembles and tests the final product before it is shipped to the customer, plus the indirect labor, which purchases the materials and parts that are outsourced, plans, supervises, and otherwise supports the direct labor effort, or more simply stated, the cost of direct and indirect labor and the benefits associated therewith.
- **Other production costs.** Supplies, heating, electricity, water, and so on for the production facility.

TABLE 7-1 Basic Income Statement

Year Ending DD/MM/YYYY $(000)'s		
Net Revenues		100,000
Cost of Goods Sold (COGS)		(40,000)
Gross Margin (GM)		60,000
Operating Expenses (OpExp)		(43,500)
Earnings before Interest, Taxes, Depreciation, and Amortization (EBITDA)		16,500
Depreciation and Amortization (D&A)		(5,000)
Earnings before Interest and Taxes (EBIT)		11,500
Interest Income (Expense)		0
Earnings Before Tax (EBT)		11,500
Taxes Paid (TaxesPaid) @	40%	0
Net Income (NI)		11,500

- **Change in work in progress and finished goods.** Revenue: The revenue generated by the company in any period is a function of what is shipped and invoiced to customers. *Manufactured revenue* is a little different. It is a function of what is produced and shipped to customers plus added to work in progress and finished goods inventory (Δ Inventory). This point can be a little subtle. During any period (consider a month), the revenue the company generates could be produced and shipped during the period and, if this was the case, the revenue and manufactured revenue would be the same. If the month's shipments are a combination of product produced during the month plus product from inventory, then:

  $$\textit{Manufactured Revenue} < \textit{Revenue Invoiced to Customers}$$

  If the month's shipments to customers are all made from product produced during the month and in addition product is manufactured for inventory, then:

  $$\textit{Manufactured Revenue} > \textit{Revenue Invoiced to Customers}$$

  A more likely scenario is one in which product shipped to customers is a combination of what's produced during the month plus some from inventory and some manufactured product added to inventory. In this case the difference between additions and subtractions to inventory determines which is larger (more on this later).

The Cost of Goods Sold broken into its constituents is shown in Table 7-2.

The direct materials in Table 7-2 are purchased from some outside supplier. The direct and indirect labor (including the benefits associated therewith) together with the production support costs transform the direct materials into parts, higher level subassemblies, and finished product. However, as indicated earlier, buyers won't pay any premium for materials or other production costs. *Premium* is the operative word here. Customers are prepared to pay for the cost of the purchased materials and the other production costs, including such costs as purchasing and material handling, but not a premium for them because they don't add value per se. Hence the first attempt at defining value added can be represented as:

$$\textit{Value Added 1} = \textit{COGS} - \textit{Direct Materials} - \textit{Other Production Costs} \qquad [7\text{-}5]$$

or

$$\textit{Value Added 1} = \textit{COGS} - \textit{DM} - \textit{OthPC} \qquad [7\text{-}6]$$

TABLE 7-2 Breakdown of Cost of Goods Sold $(000)'s and %

Direct Materials (DM)	50%	20,000
Direct and Indirect Labor (DL&IL)	30%	12,000
Other Production Costs (OthPC)	18%	7,200
Change in Work in Progress and Finished Goods (ΔInv)	2%	800
Cost of Goods Sold (COGS)	100%	40,000

By referring to Table 7-2 it can be seen that the Cost of Goods Sold can be expressed algebraically as:

$$COGS = Direct\ Materials + Cost\ of\ Direct\ Labor + Cost\ of\ Indirect\ Labor \\ + Other\ Production\ Costs \pm \Delta Inventory \qquad [7\text{-}7]$$

or

$$COGS = DM + DL + IL + OthPC \pm \Delta Inv \qquad [7\text{-}8]$$

Substituting Equation [7-8] for the COGS in Equation [7-6],

$$Value\ Added\ 1 = DM + DL + IL + OthPC \pm \Delta Inv - DM - OthPC \qquad [7\text{-}9]$$

Now ΔInv represents parts or product that were either manufactured for inventory or sourced from inventory. (Note: an increase in inventory would reduce the cost of goods sold and a decrease in inventory would increase the cost of goods sold.) So, it also consists of direct materials (DM_{Inv}), direct labor (DL_{Inv}), and indirect labor (IL_{Inv}), the benefits associated with the DL and IL, and other production costs ($OthPC_{Inv}$). Hence Equation [7-9] can be rewritten as:

$$Value\ Added\ 1 = DM + DL + IL + OthPC \pm (DM_{Inv} + DL_{Inv} + IL_{Inv} + OthPC_{Inv}) \\ - DM - OthPC \qquad [7\text{-}10]$$

Grouping like terms:

$$Value\ Added\ 1 = (DM - DM \pm DM_{Inv}) + (DL \pm DL_{Inv}) + (IL \pm IL_{Inv}) \\ + (OthPC - OthPC \pm OthPC_{Inv}) \qquad [7\text{-}11]$$

Eliminating the direct material and other production costs leaves direct labor and indirect labor and the inventory terms for direct material and other production costs:

$$Value\ Added\ 1 = \pm DM_{Inv} + (DL \pm DL_{Inv}) + (IL \pm IL_{Inv}) \pm OthPC_{Inv} \qquad [7\text{-}12]$$

As far as the customer is concerned, the terms $\pm DM_{Inv}$ and $\pm\ OthPC_{Inv}$ don't add value. Hence:

$$Value\ Added\ 1 = (DL \pm DL_{Inv}) + (IL \pm IL_{Inv}) \qquad [7\text{-}13]$$

Now the inclusion of the inventory components of DL and IL (DL_{Inv} and IL_{Inv}) in Equation [7-13] alters the meaning of Value Added 1, which is now better described as *manufactured* value added. Furthermore, the DLs and ILs can be added together and called the *production personnel costs*. Finally the first element of value added is:

$$Manufactured\ Value\ Added = Production\ Personnel\ Costs \qquad [7\text{-}14]$$

TABLE 7-3 Breakdown of Operating Expenses $(000)'s and %

Salaries and Benefits (OpExpS&B)	80%	34,800
Other Operating Expense–Related Costs (OthOpExp)	20%	8,700
Operating Expense (OpExp)	100%	43,500

Operating Value Added Continuing with the analysis of Table 7-1 it is apparent that the Earnings before Interest, Taxes and Depreciation and Amortization (EBITDA) is the difference between Gross Margin and Operating Expenses. Operating Expenses represent the cost of managing the business, sales and marketing costs, research and development, service and support costs, and other operating expense–related costs. All of these costs are required to run the business. But, as will be seen, only some are perceived as adding value from a buyer's perspective. Continuing with the practice of breaking costs into their components, it can be seen that Operating Expenses consists of salaries and benefits and other expense-related costs as depicted in Table 7-3,

where:

Operating Expense Salaries and Benefits
The cost of salaries and benefits of the people who do the Research and Development, Marketing, Sales, Service, and Support and provide the Administration and Finance functions for the company.

Other Operating Expense–Related Costs
These are the supplies, heating, electricity, water, and so forth that are consumed by the Operating Expense Functions.

Algebraically,

$$OpExp = Operating\ Expense\ Salaries\ \&\ Benefits + Other\ Operating\ Expense\ Related\ Costs \quad [7\text{-}15]$$

or

$$OpExp = OpExpS\&B + OthOpExp \quad [7\text{-}16]$$

Just as in manufactured value added where the customer didn't count $\pm DM_{Inv}$ and $\pm OthPC_{Inv}$ as value added, other operating expenses are also considered as not adding value. Hence *operating value added* can be described as:

$$Operating\ Value\ Added = OpExp - OthOpExp \quad [7\text{-}17]$$

Substituting the results of Equation [7-16] in [7-17] yields the equation for operating value added,

$$\text{Operating Value Added} = OpExpS\&B + OthOpExp - OthOpExp \quad [7\text{-}18]$$

or

$$\text{Operating Value Added} = OpExpS\&B \quad [7\text{-}19]$$

The Operating Expense Salaries and Benefits can also be described as Operating Personnel Costs. Using this terminology, Equation [7-19] becomes:

$$\text{Operating Value Added} = \text{Operating Personnel Costs} \quad [7\text{-}20]$$

Produced Value Added Since manufactured value added and operating value added are related, their sum can be referred to as *produced value added.*

$$\text{Produced Value Added} = \text{Manufactured Value Added} + \text{Operating Value Added} \quad [7\text{-}21]$$

Premium Value Added So far, two areas in which a company adds value to its products have been identified. The third kind of value added can be called *premium value added.* It is acknowledged when a buyer will pay a price for the product that is greater than anything that can be justified by the manufactured and operating value added. Cosmetics, Starbucks coffee, pharmaceutical products, electronic devices such as the iPod and iPad, software, collector's items, and anything that is in short supply are examples of products that fall into this category. In order to quantify premium value added, the Income Statement is the point of reference, but this time the required form is one that reflects the terminology developed so far in the discussion of value added. So once again the Income Statement is restructured.

Reconstructing the Income Statement

From Table 7-1 it can be seen that:

$$EBITDA = \text{Net Revenue} - COGS - OpExp \quad [7\text{-}22]$$

Substituting for COGS (Equation [7-8]) and OpExp (Equation[7-16]) in Equation [7-22],

$$EBITDA = Rev - (DM + DL + IL + OthPC \pm \Delta Inv) - (OpExpS\&B + OthOpExp) \quad [7\text{-}23]$$

where:

Rev = Net Revenues

Now, the Cost of Direct and Indirect Labor, including the associated benefits and Operating Expense Salaries and Benefits, can be broadly described as *personnel costs*

(Personnel Costs). Also, Other Production Expenses and Other Operating Expense–Related Costs can be combined into Other Production and Operating Expenses (OthProd&OpExp). By doing so Equation [7-23] becomes

$$EBITDA = Rev - DM - Personnel\ Costs - OthProd\&OpExp \pm \Delta Inv \qquad [7\text{-}24]$$

And since

$$EBIT = EBITDA - D\&A \qquad [7\text{-}25]$$

Substituting Equation [7-24] for EBITDA in Equation [7-25] creates an expression that can be used as a model.

$$EBIT = (Rev - DM - Personnel\ Costs - OthProd\&OpExp \pm \Delta Inv) - D\&A \qquad [7\text{-}26]$$

Utilizing Equation [7-26] and the data contained in Tables 7-2 and 7-3, the Income Statement shown in Table 7-1 can be reconstructed into a form that is better suited to the purpose. The reconstructed Income Statement is tabulated in Table 7-4.

An inspection of Table 7-4 indicates that the earlier treatment of manufactured value added and operating value added has accounted for all lines in the reconstructed Income Statement except Depreciation and Amortization (D&A) and Earnings before Interest and Taxes (EBIT). D&A is considered to be part of the risk–reward equation and represents the use of the tools and resources (i.e., property, plant, and equipment) that are provided by the company so that manufacturing and operating personnel can do their job.

The one thing that hasn't been accounted for is premium value added. Premium value added comes about as a result of management teams that have vision, operate highly efficient facilities, procure the correct hard and soft assets, and so on, and are able to put all of this together in such a way that creates perceived value added beyond manufactured and operating value added and results in premium selling prices. Premium

TABLE 7-4 Reconstructed Income Statement

		Year Ending DD/MM/YYYY $(000)'s
Net Revenues (Rev)		100,000
Less:	Direct Materials (DM)	20,000
	Personnel Costs (PersonnelCosts)	46,800
	Other Expenses (OthProd&OpExp)	15,900
	Change in Inventory (Δ Inv)	800
EBITDA		16,500
Less:	Depreciation and Amortization	5,000
EBIT		11,500

value added is captured in EBIT, since if there isn't any price premium, the EBIT is simply reflective of the value placed by customers on manufactured value added and operating value added, which in turn often reflects a fair return to investors. Hence, for our purposes EBIT is a measurement of premium value added, and our third kind of value added can be quantified as:

$$\textit{Premium Value Added} = \textit{EBIT} \tag{7-27}$$

Value Added Quantified

In summary, three kinds of value added have been identified and they are quantified by Equations [7-14], [7-20], and [7-27].

$$\textit{Manufactured Value Added} = \textit{Production Personnel Costs} \tag{7-14}$$

$$\textit{Operating Value Added} = \textit{Operating Personnel Costs} \tag{7-20}$$

$$\textit{Premium Value Added} = \textit{EBIT} \tag{7-27}$$

Therefore, according to this model, value added is simply the sum of the three types of value added:

$$\textit{Value Added} = \textit{Manufactured Value Added} + \textit{Operating Value Added} + \textit{Premium Value Added} \tag{7-28}$$

or

$$\textit{Value Added} = \textit{Production Personnel Costs} + \textit{Operating Personnel Costs} + \textit{EBIT} \tag{7-29}$$

Production personnel costs and operating personnel costs are simply people costs and can be combined into "Personnel Costs." Hence:

$$\textit{Value Added} = \textit{Personnel Costs} + \textit{EBIT} \tag{7-30}$$

Number of Employees

In the previous sections a fairly rigorous definition of value added was developed. However, the denominator of the Productivity Equation [7-4] presents a number of problems.

$$\textit{Productivity} = \frac{\textit{Value Added}}{\textit{Number of Employees}} \tag{7-4}$$

First it requires one to actually know the number of employees and to define what constitutes an employee. For example, how do you count part-time help and contractors? Furthermore, is it simply a matter of headcount or is the number of hours worked divided by the hours in a workweek that is the right measurement?

What do you do about people who are absent due to sickness or away on vacation? Also, how do you account for the different compensation levels? Presumably people are paid for the value they add, so does this mean that those who are paid twice or three times the lowest level of compensation in your company should count as two or three people respectively?

Other Considerations

Even if you can get by the "Number of Employees" issues, what do you do about the fact that value added as defined by Equation [7-30] is affected by inflation and the number of employees is not? If this is not bad enough, how do you compare productivity in different countries when different currencies are involved?

The Productivity Model

Fortunately, there is a way around all of this. It requires that you focus on personnel expenses instead of the number of employees. "Personnel Costs" goes a long way toward dealing with the issues that are raised by defining what constitutes an employee, absenteeism and vacations, compensation levels, inflation, and currency because it monetizes the issues that the "Number of Employees" raises and over time cancels out the impact of local economic performance and currency considerations.

Substituting the results of Equation [7-30] for value added and "Personnel Costs" for the "Number of Employees" in Equation [7-4] provides a better expression for productivity.

$$Productivity = \frac{Personnel\ Costs + EBIT}{Personnel\ Costs} \qquad [7\text{-}31]$$

Basics of an Operating Margin Model

Having quantified productivity, the next step is to decide to what end this or any productivity model should be used. Recall that the genesis of value is cash flow and that cash flow is driven by Net Income. Referring to Table 7-1 reminds us that Net Income is driven by EBIT, which in turn is driven by Net Revenues. Therefore, it would seem that in order for any productivity model to be useful to management it must somehow not only deal with personnel costs and EBIT but, in addition, incorporates Net Revenues. One way of doing this is to introduce Operating Income and Operating Margin into the discussion of productivity.

Operating Margin Defined

EBIT (as defined in Tables 7-1 and 7-4) is often referred to as Operating Income and the ratio of EBIT to Net Revenues as Operating Margin.

$$Operating\ Margin = \frac{EBIT}{Net\ Revenues} \qquad [7\text{-}32]$$

Operating Margin Redefined

Just as there proved to be some issues associated with a generalized approach to defining productivity, there are also some problems with the definition of Operating Margin as defined by Equation [7-32].

If a measurement of productivity is to be meaningful, it should be compared to something. Since EBIT is what management is ultimately interested in, it would seem sensible to incorporate the EBIT produced in a period with the revenue that produced it.

Revenues describe what has been invoiced to the customer. It doesn't necessarily represent what the factory produced. As you may recall, when the equation for value added was developed the concept of manufactured value added was introduced. The message was, at one extreme it's possible that a company filled all customer orders from inventory produced in a prior period. At the other extreme is that everything that was shipped to customers during a period was manufactured during the period in question. The most likely case is somewhere in between and this means that the denominator of Equation [7-32] should be adjusted for what was produced for inventory and what inventory was shipped to customers that was manufactured during a prior period, or simply the *changes in work in process and finished goods*. To do this a new term called *manufactured revenues* needs to be introduced into the discussion and it is defined as:

$$Manufactured\ Revenues = Rev \pm \Delta\ in\ Work\ In\ Progress\ \&\ Finished\ Goods \qquad [7\text{-}33]$$

And the equation for Operating Margin, adjusted for changes in inventory, becomes

$$OpMargin = \frac{EBIT}{ManRev} \qquad [7\text{-}34]$$

where:

$OpMargin$ = Operating Margin based on Manufactured Revenue
$ManRev$ = Manufactured Revenues

Incorporating Operating Margin into the Productivity Model

As mentioned in the preceding, if the productivity model is to be of practical value, it should provide management with the ability to predict the impact that improvements in productivity will have on the company's Operating Margin and thereby its financial performance. Therefore, in order to do this, it would seem that it is necessary to derive a relationship between productivity and Operating Margin.

As will be seen, this is a rather lengthy process and begins by recalling the expressions for productivity (Equation [7-31]) and Operating Margin ([7-34]).[3]

$$Productivity = \frac{Personnel\ Costs + EBIT}{Personnel\ Costs} \qquad [7\text{-}31]$$

[3]Readers interested only in the final equation can skip the next few pages and proceed to Equation [7-49].

$$OpMargin = \frac{EBIT}{ManRev} \quad [7\text{-}34]$$

If both sides of productivity (Equation [7-31]) are multiplied by Personnel Costs, it becomes:

$$(Productivity)(Personnel\ Costs) = \left(\frac{Personnel\ Costs + EBIT}{Personnel\ Costs}\right)(Personnel\ Costs) \quad [7\text{-}35]$$

or

$$(Productivity)(Personnel\ Costs) = Personnel\ Costs + EBIT \quad [7\text{-}36]$$

Rearranging,

$$EBIT = (Productivity)(Personnel\ Costs) - Personnel\ Costs \quad [7\text{-}37]$$

or

$$EBIT = (Personnel\ Costs)\ (Productivity - 1) \quad [7\text{-}38]$$

The next step in introducing OpMargin into the model is to express manufacturing revenue in terms of value added. This can be done by dividing the term Value Added by the expression $\frac{Value\ Added}{ManRev}$. If the right-hand side of Equation [7-39] is simplified, the result is manufactured revenue.

$$ManRev = \frac{Value\ Added}{\left(\frac{Value\ Added}{ManRev}\right)} \quad [7\text{-}39]$$

Correlation Coefficient

The term $\frac{Value\ Added}{ManRev}$ is interesting (and as will be seen, special) because it is the ratio of Value Added and Manufactured Revenue. In effect it is a ratio between what all companies try to do (add value) and the driving force behind Operating Margin (manufactured revenue). Therefore, the ratio of Value Added to Manufactured Revenue will be defined as the Correlation Coefficient C_C. Hence:

$$C_C = \frac{Value\ Added}{ManRev} \quad [7\text{-}40]$$

Substituting the results of Equation [7-30] into Equation [7-40],

$$Value\ Added = Personnel\ Costs + EBIT \quad [7\text{-}30]$$

$$C_C = \frac{Personnel\ Costs + EBIT}{ManRev} \quad [7\text{-}41]$$

Rearranging, an expression for manufacturing revenue in terms of Personnel Costs, EBIT, and the Correlation Coefficient is obtained.

$$ManRev = \frac{Personnel\ Costs + EBIT}{C_C} \qquad [7\text{-}42]$$

But from Equation [7-38] it was determined that EBIT = (Personnel Costs)(Productivity – 1). Substituting for EBIT in Equation [7-42],

$$ManRev = \frac{Personnel\ Costs + (Personnel\ Costs)(Productivity - 1)}{C_C} \qquad [7\text{-}43]$$

Factoring,

$$ManRev = \frac{(Personnel\ Costs)(1 + Productivity - 1)}{C_C} \qquad [7\text{-}44]$$

Canceling the 1's,

$$ManRev = \frac{(Personnel\ Costs)(Productivity)}{C_C} \qquad [7\text{-}45]$$

Rearranging,

$$ManRev = \left(\frac{Productivity}{C_C}\right)(Personnel\ Costs) \qquad [7\text{-}46]$$

Recall that Operating Margin is defined as:

$$OpMargin = \frac{EBIT}{ManRev} \qquad [7\text{-}34]$$

and substituting the results of Equations [7-38] and [7-46] for EBIT and ManRev respectively in Equation [7-34],

$$OpMargin = \frac{(Personnel\ Costs)(Productivity - 1)}{\left(\frac{Productivity}{C_C}\right)(Personnel\ Costs)} \qquad [7\text{-}47]$$

Canceling like terms,

$$OpMargin = \frac{Productivity - 1}{\frac{Productivity}{C_C}} \qquad [7\text{-}48]$$

Finally, rearranging, an expression that defines OpMargin in terms of the Correlation Coefficient C_C and Productivity is obtained.

$$OpMargin = C_C\left(\frac{Productivity - 1}{Productivity}\right) \qquad [7\text{-}49]$$

At this point the objective of expressing Operating Margin in terms of productivity has been accomplished. However, the process by which this was brought about introduced the Correlation Coefficient. In order to appreciate the power of Equation [7-49] the Correlation Coefficient needs to be described in the context of a company and how adjusting it impacts Operating Margin.

Figure 7-1 is a family of curves obtained by solving Equation [7-49] for various values of the Correlation Coefficient C_C. As can be seen, the Operating Margin for any given level of productivity depends on the magnitude of the Correlation Coefficient.

$$C_C = \frac{Value\ Added}{Manufactured\ Revenue} = \frac{Value\ Added}{ManRev} = \frac{Personnel\ Costs + EBIT}{ManRev} \qquad [7\text{-}41]$$

Integration Coefficient

By referring to an expanded version of Equation [7-40] it can be reasoned that the Correlation Coefficient represents the complexity of the operations required to create the manufactured revenue. For example, if the so-called manufactured revenue consists of products purchased and resold by a Sales division of a company, you would expect the value added and personnel costs incurred in selling, ordering, and delivering product to the customer to be relatively low and this would result in a low value for C_C. Similarly, if a highly integrated manufacturing company generated the manufactured revenue,

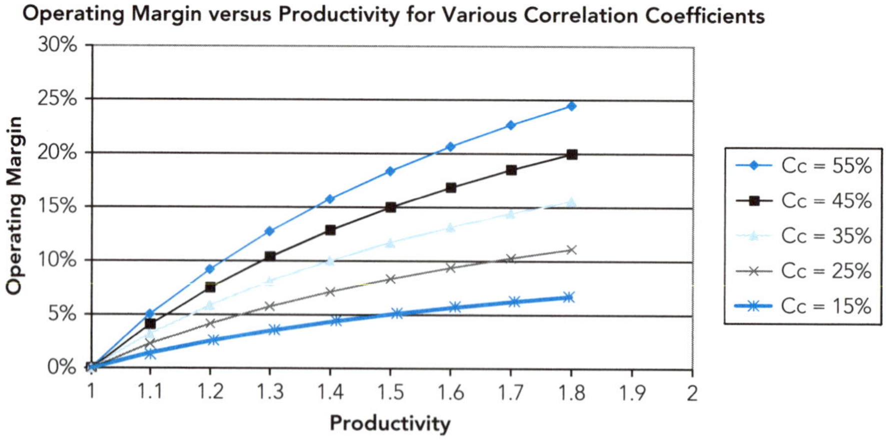

FIGURE 7-1 Correlation Coefficients

then you would expect a relatively large value for C_C because the value added and personnel costs would also be high. Therefore, the term C_C can be considered to be a measure of the degree of vertical integration involved in the company or business unit being measured and therefore more appropriately called the Integration Coefficient I_C:

$$I_C = \frac{\text{Value Added}}{\text{Manufactured Revenue}} = \frac{\text{Value Added}}{\text{ManRev}} = \frac{\text{Personnel Costs} + \text{EBIT}}{\text{ManRev}} \quad [7\text{-}50]$$

Operating Margin Model

Having defined the Integration Coefficient it can now be used to finalize an expression for the Operating Margin model. Using the nomenclature developed in the preceding section and substituting I_C for C_C in Equation [7-49], an equation for Operating Margin expressed in terms of productivity and the Integration Coefficient is obtained.

$$OpMargin = I_C\left(\frac{Productivity - 1}{Productivity}\right) \quad [7\text{-}51]$$

It's important to note that Equation [7-51] takes the measurement of productivity an additional step and allows management to estimate the impact that improvements in productivity can have on their company's financial performance.

The Integration Coefficient in Practical Terms

If one was to try to create descriptions that capture the essence of what most companies, their subsidiaries, or divisions do, the list might consist of Sales, Sales and Service/Engineering, Assembly and Test, Light Manufacturing, Integrated Manufacturing, and Highly Integrated Manufacturing. Furthermore, if these categories are combined with the coefficients used to generate the family of curves in Figure 7-1, the result would be Table 7-5.

Finally, combining the family of curves in Figure 7-1 with the categories and Integration Coefficients tabulated in Table 7-5, a picture of a productivity model for a manufacturing company (Figure 7-2) emerges.

TABLE 7-5 Integration Coefficients for Various Service and Manufacturing Models

Type of Operation	**Integration Coefficient**
Sales	$Ic < 0.15$
Sales and Service/Engineering	$0.15 < Ic < 0.25$
Assembly and Testing	$0.25 < Ic < 0.35$
Light Manufacturing	$0.35 < Ic < 0.45$
Vertically Integrated Manufacturing	$0.45 < Ic < 0.55$
Highly Vertically Integrated Manufacturing	$Ic > 0.55$

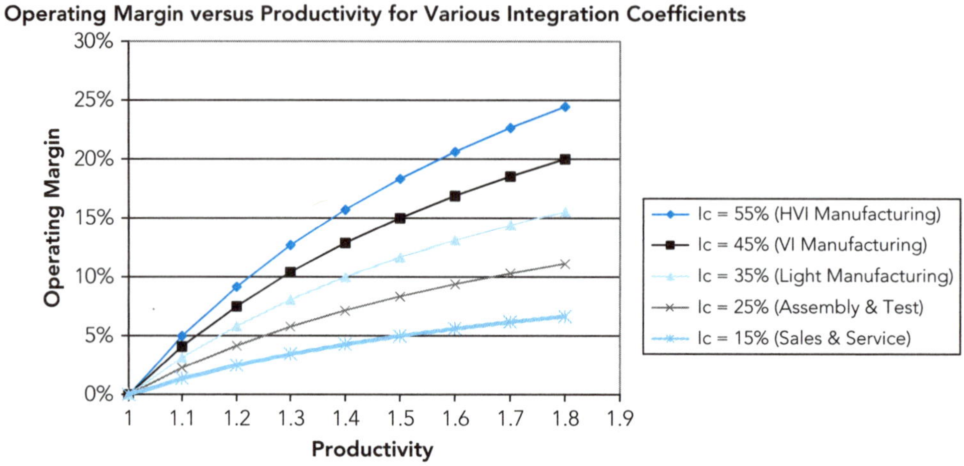

FIGURE 7-2 Operating Margin versus Productivity for Various Service and Manufacturing Models

Non-Manufacturing Models

So far the productivity discussion has focused on a manufacturing enterprise. The model outlined is equally applicable to service companies. The definitions of productivity, value added, and operating margin remain unchanged. Since service companies don't normally have any inventory to speak of, the concept of manufactured revenue is not relevant. However, they often have "unbilled" or "deferred revenue" that occurs when they do work for a customer but don't invoice for the work during that period. To accommodate this difference, Equations [7-33], [7-34], and [7-50] need to be modified and become [7-52], [7-53], and [7-54] respectively. Equations [7-30], [7-31], and [7-51] remain unchanged.

$$Produced\ Revenues = Rev \pm \Delta\ in\ Unbilled\ or\ Deferred\ Revenue \quad [7\text{-}52]$$

$$OpMargin = \frac{EBIT}{ProdRev} \quad [7\text{-}53]$$

$$I_C = \frac{Value\ Added}{Produced\ Revenue} = \frac{Value\ Added}{ProdRev} = \frac{Personnel\ Costs + EBIT}{ProdRev} \quad [7\text{-}54]$$

$$Value\ Added = Personnel\ Costs + EBIT \quad [7\text{-}30]$$

$$Productivity = \frac{Personnel\ Costs + EBIT}{Personnel\ Costs} \quad [7\text{-}31]$$

$$OpMargin = I_C\left(\frac{Productivity - 1}{Productivity}\right) \quad [7\text{-}51]$$

TABLE 7-6 Integration Coefficients for Various Service and Non-Manufacturing Models

Type of Operation	**Integration Coefficient**
Sales	Ic < 0.15
Sales and Software Support	0.15 < Ic < 0.25
System Integration	0.25 < Ic < 0.35
Complex Software	0.35 < Ic < 0.5
Integrated Business Systems	0.5 < Ic < 0.6
Integrated Highly Complex Systems	Ic > 0.6

The concept of an Integration Coefficient still has meaning but the categories ascribed to various coefficients change. Table 7-6 suggests some definitions and ranges for Integration Coefficients that may be suitable for companies engaged in software-intensive industries.

Example 7-2: JM Maher Corporation

JM Maher is a developer and producer of specialty compounds for a wide variety of industries. Its products can be found in numerous products, including pharmaceuticals, food, cosmetics, electronic components, and specialty metals. The company's performance as portrayed in Table 7-7 has been lackluster and deteriorating.

The stock has fallen out of favor and the board is under pressure from shareholders to take action. It ultimately acts and recruits a new CEO. The company is debt free and has cash, so, while the new CEO is well aware of the fact he can't spend his way into prosperity, he is prepared to spend money to turn the company's performance around. While touring the facilities, he increasingly sensed a lack of urgency among the workforce and when he compared it to the spirited environment from which he just came this was one of slow motion. Upon returning to his office, he met with the CFO and VP of

TABLE 7-7 JM Maher Corporation's Income Statement

Year Ending DD/MM/YYYY $(000)'s and %		
Net Revenues	458,000	
Cost of Goods Sold (COGS)	(251,900)	–55.00%
Gross Margin (GM)	206,100	45.00%
Operating Expenses (OpExp)	(146,560)	–32.00%
Earnings before Interest, Taxes, Depreciation, and Amortization (EBITDA)	59,540	13.00%
Depreciation and Amortization (D & A)	(22,900)	–5.00%
Earnings before Interest and Taxes (EBIT)	36,640	8.00%
Interest Income (Expense)	0	
Earnings before Tax (EBT)	36,640	8.00%
Taxes Paid (TaxesPaid) @ 35%	(12,824)	–2.80%
Net Income (NI)	23,816	5.20%

TABLE 7-8 Breakdown of JM Maher Corporation's Cost of Goods Sold $(000)'s and %

Direct Materials (DM)	31%	78,089
Direct and Indirect Labor (DL&IL)	42%	105,798
Other Production Costs (OthPC)	29%	73,051
Change in Work in Progress and Finished Goods (ΔInv)	–2%	(5,038)
Cost of Goods Sold (COGS)	100%	251,900

TABLE 7-9 Breakdown of JM Maher Corporation's Operating Expenses $(000)'s and %

Salaries and Benefits (OpExpS&B)	77%	112,851
Other Operating Expenses (OthOpExp)	23%	33,709
Operating Expense (OpExp)	100%	146,560

Manufacturing and asked them to describe the essence and results of their productivity plan. The response was simple and to the point. The company did not have one. The CEO outlined the basics of the productivity measurement model he had in mind and tasked them to go away and calculate the company's current productivity index.

The first step in this model involves breaking the Income Statement into its constituents. For the Cost of Goods Sold and Operating Expenses the CFO and VP of Manufacturing came up with Tables 7-8 and 7-9 respectively.

With this data, they proceeded to prepare the restructured Income Statement shown in Table 7-10.

TABLE 7-10 JM Maher Corporation's Reconstructed Income Statement

Year Ending DD/MM/YYYY $(000)'s and %				
Net Revenues (Rev)			458,000	
Less:	Direct Materials (DM)		78,089	17.05%
	Personnel Costs (PersonnelCosts)			
	Direct and Indirect Labor (DL&IL)	105,798		
	Salaries and Benefits (OpExpS&B)	112,851	218,649	47.74%
	Other Expenses (OthProd&OpExp)			
	Other Production Costs (OthPC)	73,051		
	Other Operating Expenses (OthOpExp)	33,709	106,760	23.31%
	Change in Inventory (ΔInv)		(5,038)	–1.10%
EBITDA			59,540	13.00%
Less:	Depreciation and Amortization		22,900	5.00%
EBIT			36,640	8.00%
Taxes Paid (TaxesPaid) @	35%		(12,824)	–0.028
Net Income (NI)			23,816	5.20%

Using the definitional equation for the *productivity index*, Equation [7-31], and the data in the restructured Income Statement they proceeded to calculate the company's productivity index:

$$Productivity = \frac{Personnel\ Costs + EBIT}{Personnel\ Costs} \quad [7\text{-}31]$$

$$Productivity = \frac{218{,}649{,}000 + 36{,}640{,}000}{218{,}649{,}000} = 1.17$$

Since they didn't have any experience with this productivity model, when they met with the CEO and presented the results, they inquired as to whether this was a good or bad number. The CEO explained: "If the productivity index is equal to one, that means the company is not producing any EBIT. In our case we are producing some EBIT but as you can see compared to the personnel expenses, not very much." He continued by saying there was little to be gained by debating how good or bad 1.17 was but rather treat it as a starting point and move on from there. He then drew their attention to Table 7-11, which he had prepared, that laid out what effect a 5% per annum compounded improvement in productivity would have over a five-year period.

After a brief discussion it wasn't clear that these targets were reasonable or what the impact on the company's Operating Margin would be if achieved. So rather than debate the appropriateness of the numbers in the Productivity Improvement Table the CEO suggested this topic be tabled for the moment and asked the management team to prepare an estimate of what the Operating Margin would be in Year "C + 5" at a productivity of 1.49.

Using the CEO's productivity model they proceeded to calculate the Integration Coefficient. Since personnel costs and current level of EBIT were known, the first step in the process according to Equation [7-50] was to calculate the company's manufactured revenue using Equation [7-33].

$$Manufactured\ Revenues = Rev \pm \Delta in\ Work\ In\ Progress\ \&\ Finished\ Goods \quad [7\text{-}33]$$

According to the work done in preparing the restructured Income Statement the change in "Work in Progress and Finished Goods" was –$5,038,000, which meant that $5,038,000 of the $458,000,000 of revenue for the year came from goods manufactured in a prior period. Hence the manufactured revenues for the year are:

$$Manufactured\ Revenues = 458{,}000{,}000 - 5{,}038{,}000 = \$452{,}962{,}000$$

TABLE 7-11 JM Maher Corporation's Productivity Improvement Table

	Current	**C + 1**	**C + 2**	**C + 3**	**C + 4**	**C + 5**
Prod Increase = 5%	–	1.0500	1.1025	1.1576	1.2155	1.2763
Productivity =	1.17	1.23	1.29	1.35	1.42	1.49

and the Integration Coefficient is:

$$I_C = \frac{(Personnel\ Costs + EBIT)}{ManRev} \quad [7\text{-}50]$$

$$I_C = \frac{218{,}649{,}000 + 36{,}640{,}000}{452{,}962{,}000} = 0.56$$

Next, the CFO and VP of Manufacturing referred to the CEO's Productivity Improvement Table and noted that if productivity were improved 5% for five years in a row the productivity index would be 1.49. Substituting in Equation [7-51] they estimated the Operating Margin in Year 5 to be 18.5%:

$$OpMargin = I_C\left(\frac{Productivity - 1}{Productivity}\right) \quad [7\text{-}51]$$

$$OpMargin = \left[(0.56)\left(\frac{1.49 - 1}{1.49}\right)\right](100) = 18.54\%$$

When they presented their results to the CEO he produced a chart (Figure 7-3) he had used many times before.

The CFO and VP of Manufacturing were struck by the close agreement and wondered why the CEO hadn't saved them a lot of time and allowed them to use the graphical solution. His reply was: "To begin with I couldn't save you all the work you did because to use the graph you need to know the Integration Coefficient. However, my main reason was I wanted to be sure both of you understood that a prime driver of productivity is personnel costs and that EBIT (Operating Margin) moves up in unison with productivity.

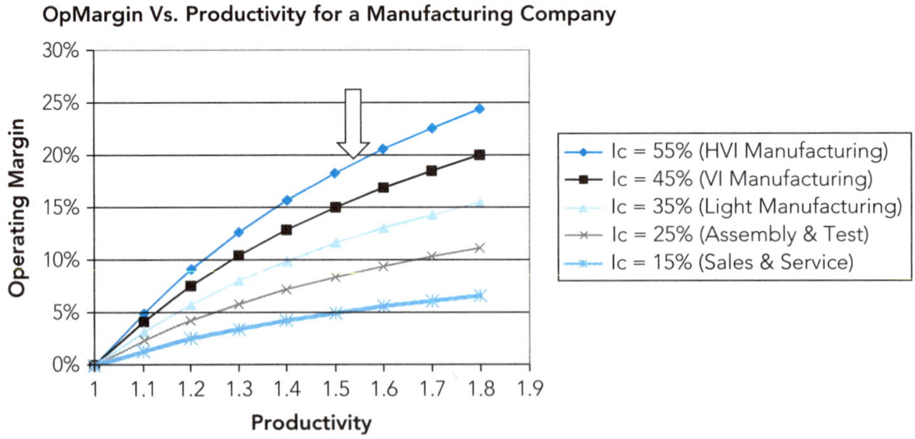

FIGURE 7-3 Operating Margin versus Productivity for a Manufacturing Company

"Also, I realize that I haven't convinced either of you that the numbers in my Productivity Improvement Table are achievable. However, you folks haven't convinced me they are not. Based on my experience I can tell both of you I have seen other companies achieve comparable results. So now that we have a starting point and goals, I want both of you to gather the management team together and map out a program that will systematically take our EBIT from 8% to 18% in five years or less."

A Qualitative Perspective on Productivity

One of the dangers of trying to be quantitative is that things that should be or are relatively straightforward can be made to appear more complicated than they really are. A model for quantifying productivity and its impact on Operating Margin has been presented in this chapter. It may be that some people find it a little too demanding. While it's a sound methodology and a powerful tool, it may not be suitable for some companies. Therefore, in order to do the subject justice, it's important that a more general picture of productivity be described and the issues associated with productivity be discussed in a broader context. Here are some things to think about.

The two dimensions of productivity. For starters, there are many ways to define productivity. However, in the final analysis, productivity only has two dimensions: people and property, plant, and equipment (PP&E).

Sustainable results. In order for a productivity program to justify the effort that it takes, the results it produces must be sustainable and deliver the desired outcome year after year. Otherwise, cost creep will come into play and the company will incrementally give up what has been achieved, let alone prosper as intended.

Nonproductive resources. Never accumulate nonproductive resources. Be thoughtful before adding people, buildings, or equipment, extending credit,[4] and so on. When you have made a mistake or market conditions render resources or assets unnecessary or obsolete, get rid of them and put what is required in place.

Be specific. Productivity programs must be highly explicit. Programs that don't have precise, identifiable, and executable tasks probably won't happen, let alone achieve the intended results.

Non-value-added activities. Customers recognize value when they see it. Sometimes it is a consequence of education. In other instances it is driven by intuition. They also recognize waste when it comes their way. Management's job is to eliminate all waste. Your customer won't pay for it, so why should you?

It's a management system that requires commitment. Productivity is not a thing or a number of things. It's a management system. Until the entire management team understands how productivity increases are to come about and is committed to making them happen, nothing lasting will come to pass.

Implement customer-focused versus aggregate measurements. The productivity model developed in this chapter could be called a *customer-focused* model.

---

[4] Recall that credit is a resource; it takes the form of capital and capital should be productive.

Specifically it looks at productivity from a customer's value-added perspective. This has to be a legitimate and correct point of view because, in the end, it's the customer who decides what constitutes value. Some management teams may not consider this model to be appropriate to their circumstances. There are numerous instances where other and seemingly distant metrics have provided a basis for measuring successful productivity programs. These measurements can be called *aggregate* approaches because the units of measurement are not refined and exactly what to do to improve productivity is not clear.

Generally speaking, experience indicates that a customer-centric approach to measuring productivity is preferable to an aggregate method and that implementing an aggregate model is better than doing nothing at all. In either case the important thing is to consistently apply the chosen methodology and refine it over time. For example: If the entire company is focused on revenue and interested in how the company is doing as a whole, then "Sales/Employee" may be appropriate. Similarly, if Gross Margin is of prime concern, then "Gross Margin/Employee" may be suitable. Another measurement that may be suitable could be "(Cost of Goods Sold – Purchases)/Number of Employees." However, be mindful of the shortfalls. Aggregate measurements involving people would be improved if "Personnel Costs" were used in place of "Number of Employees."

Trends. Other than for peer comparisons, absolute measurements of productivity usually aren't very helpful. The important thing is the trend. In order to know where you are going it's helpful to know where you have been and where you are currently. Therefore, once productivity measures have been chosen, develop curves by plotting data for the last five years, current period, and next three years and make regular comparisons against the plan. Why make the past part of the plan? It provides a reality check. If you haven't been able to show historical progress in what you are trying to measure, it may be appropriate to ask the question: Why would the future be different from the past?

Goals should make a difference. Good measurements of productivity can be difficult to make. For example, defining who should be counted as an "Employee" in an aggregate model can be a challenging process. Therefore, if the magnitudes of the prospective productivity increases are not relatively easy to measure with adequate precision or of a size that makes a difference, then rework your productivity plan. Whatever you do, don't implement a plan that you know is flawed, thinking that you can fix it as you go. You can fix as you go but you will lose credibility and support along the way.

Fixed costs. When it comes to productivity, there are no such things as fixed costs. Remember, with time and money, everything is variable. You have to be creative.

Cost reduction. Productivity and cost reduction go hand in hand and often are one and the same. Cost reduction is like religion. You have to believe in it, live by it, practice it, and do missionary work. Otherwise, it soon loses its followers and impact on the bottom line. Some of the world's most successful companies have cost reduction as a key strategy and focus on it day-in and day-out.

Accordion syndrome. Be aware of the accordion syndrome. During periods of high growth, costs usually grow slower than sales revenue.[5] Once growth slows down,

[5]An obvious exception to this is a "start-up" company. Start-ups by their very nature are destined to have expenses grow faster than revenue.

costs, if unchecked, will have achieved momentum and continue to grow. This can be fatal for a productivity plan. The plan can only survive if the brakes are put on costs the moment revenue growth begins to weaken. Otherwise, all that has been achieved may be lost in a couple of accounting periods. Unfortunately, this is easier said than done because the costs that are put in place are often fixed in the short term and therefore by their nature difficult to deal with quickly. The subject of *fixed assets* and how to deal with them is dealt with elsewhere in this book.[6]

CYCLE TIME

Cycle time reduction is a technique that permits management to improve productivity, reduce cost, and increase value added time and customer service, all at the same time. Like lean manufacturing, it is a production practice that considers the expenditure of resources for any goal other than the creation of value for the end customer to be wasteful and thus a target for elimination.[7] Cycle time is defined as the total time taken from the receipt of an order to delivery of all of the goods and/or services to the customer. The theory of cycle time is based on the notion that time is money and that a shorter cycle time will result in a lower cost and better customer service, even if it isn't valued by the customer. It presumes that in general, things that impact cycle time cost money. It focuses on getting it right early because the cost of fixes increases exponentially downstream of the component level. A key metric of cycle time is:

$$\text{Cycle Time Efficiency} = \frac{\text{Value Added Time}}{\text{Cycle Time}} \quad [7\text{-}55]$$

Companies that haven't taken steps to reduce cycle time often have *cycle time efficiency* of 20% or less. This means that 80% or more of the time spent from when an order is received until it is delivered to the customer adds no value.[8]

If you asked customers if they thought they should pay for your company to move material from A to B, you would probably get confused looks because they wouldn't immediately understand the question. If you then asked customers if they should pay for your company to then move the material back from B to A, you probably would get a resounding *no*. The reason is that your customer doesn't perceive any value associated with moving materials around your facility. Attacking activities like this is the essence of cycle time reduction.

The idea is to focus on identifying and removing in a systematic way all of the constraints in the proposal, order entry, and manufacturing cycle that slow things down (laborious proposal and order entry systems, inspection, materials handling,

---

[6] See Chapter 5.

[7] The author was introduced to the concept of cycle time by the Leverage Group Inc.

[8] The first time the author saw this statistic he was astounded. Subsequent experience indicates it to be true.

moving paper, entering data, etc.) and don't add value to the customer. Basically it is a methodology that is targeted at getting rid of as many non-value-added activities as possible.

Cycle time reduction is a fertile area and there are many consultants out there who can help your company implement a program. Here are a few things you should think about when considering such a program.

- **Potential for significant reduction.** Don't start unless there is the potential to make a significant reduction in cycle time. Without a big opportunity (and big potential cost savings) you won't be able to keep the organization's interest.
- **Be prepared for major changes.** Nor should you initiate a program unless your company is prepared to make major changes in the way it will operate in the future. Management must be willing to support a big change in culture. Otherwise, you won't have the commitment to focus the organization and its resources on the task.
- **Company-wide commitment.** Initiating a program without a company-wide commitment to continuous improvement will prove to be a mistake. The systematization that goes into cycle time reduction is like any other system and it's subject to entropy. This means that unless you continuously maintain and try to improve cycle time efficiency, it will tend to become less orderly and before long much of the benefit will be lost.

Once you have decided to implement a program:

- **Time is important.** Move quickly to reduce the risk of being overtaken by changing business priorities.
- **Capture benefits quickly.** Insist that the program be designed to quickly capture incremental benefits (low-hanging fruit).
- **Chain of command.** Realign reporting and management relationships. Otherwise, you will find yourself fighting both the past and the future.
- **Metrics.** Put new metrics in place as promptly as possible.
- **Be systematic.** Move systematically through the process. Avoid deploying scarce resources across too many fronts. Remember, higher efficiency is usually achieved by a series of short, focused, incremental efforts.
- **Know when to stop.** Stop trying to reduce cycle time when you have achieved ±80% of the expected reduction. Trying to get at the remaining 20% is usually not worth the effort.
- **Institutionalization.** You are not finished until you have put in place the organizational and methodical frameworks needed to carry out future improvement cycles. In other words, this methodology needs to become part of everyday activities in the organization.
- **Is it worthwhile?** One of the first questions asked is: Can a cycle time reduction project really pay off? The answer is yes. It's not easy, but significant non-value-added costs are eliminated in well-executed programs. It's not unusual for

a company to cut its cycle time by 50% or more. Furthermore, experience has shown that a big cut in cycle time equals a large reduction in cost. An added benefit is the culture of the company can become one of can-do, can-do-quickly, and can-do-it-right the first time.

CLOSING COMMENTS ON VALUE ADDED AND COST

Without an effective productivity program focused on value added any benefit achieved via cost reduction will be quickly erased. Cost creep is relentless. Your efforts have to be without end in order to keep them under control and you need imaginative strategies to continuously bring them down. While it is seemingly very compelling to be the low-cost producer, the concept may be flawed. You are probably better off if you are the low-cost producer of the value added that your customer is purchasing. Finally, if your customers buy on price, despite what you may think, you are in the cost business. But even if your customers don't buy on price, you still need a cost reduction strategy.

CASE STUDY

In the following case study a management team gets serious about tackling operational improvements and uses the productivity and Operating Margin models introduced in this chapter to develop a cost reduction/operating margin improvement plan.

Laser Technology Inc. Develops Its Productivity Strategy

The CEO has decided that now that they are in the fifth year of operations and growth has slowed somewhat, it is time to get serious about operational improvements that are not simply volume (revenue) driven. After much thought, he called his management team together and challenged them to come up with a plan to improve the Operating Margin. Being a young and relatively inexperienced team, they struggled for a while trying to decide on an approach. After much investigation and discussion, they concluded the first thing they need to do is figure out where they are. Being familiar with the productivity and operating models for Operating Margin improvement, the VP of Manufacturing was tasked with the job of defining the starting point. His first step involved soliciting the CFO's assistance in preparing Income and restructured Income Statements for the last twelve months (LTM) and then using this data to estimate the current level of productivity and Operating Margin.

Part 1: Defining Metrics and Possible Courses of Action

After preparing the LTM Income Statement shown in Table CS 7-1 the CFO proceeded to break down the Cost of Goods Sold and Operating Expenses into their constituents (Tables CS 7-2 and CS 7-3).

TABLE CS 7-1 Laser Technology LTM Income Statement

Last Twelve Months Income Statement $(000)'s and %		
Net Revenues	200,000	100.0%
Cost of Goods Sold (COGS)	(80,000)	40.0%
Gross Margin (GM)	120,000	60.0%
Operating Expenses (OpExp)	(87,000)	43.5%
Earnings before Interest, Taxes, Depreciation, and Amortization (EBITDA)	33,000	16.5%
Depreciation and Amortization (D & A)	(10,000)	5.0%
Earnings before Interest and Taxes (EBIT)	23,000	11.5%
Interest Income (Expense)	0	
Earnings before Tax (EBT)	23,000	11.5%
Taxes Paid (TaxesPaid) @ 40%	0	
Net Income (NI)	23,000	11.5%

Then, using the data in Tables CS 7-2 and CS 7-3 she prepared the restructured Income Statement shown in Table CS 7-4.

TABLE CS 7-2 Laser Technology LTM Cost of Goods Sold

	$ (000)'s	%COGS	%Rev
Direct Materials (DM)	40,000	50%	20.0%
Direct and Indirect Labor (DL&IL)	24,000	30%	12.0%
Other Production Costs (OthPC)	14,400	18%	7.2%
Change in Work in Progress and Finished Goods (ΔInv)	1,600	2%	0.8%
Cost of Goods Sold (COGS)	80,000	100%	40.0%

TABLE CS 7-3 Laser Technology LTM Operating Expenses

	$ (000)'s	%OpExp	%Rev
Salaries and Benefits (OpExpS&B)	69,600	80%	34.8%
Other Operating Expense–Related Costs (OthOpExp)	17,400	20%	8.7%
Operating Expense (OpExp)	87,000	100%	43.5%

TABLE CS 7-4 Laser Technology LTM Restructured Income Statement

Restructured LTM Income Statement $(000)'s and %			
Net Revenues (Rev)		200,000	100.0%
Less:	Direct Materials (DM)	40,000	20.0%
	Personnel Costs (PersonnelCosts)	93,600	46.8%
	Other Expenses (OthProd&OpExp)	31,800	15.9%
	Change in Inventory (ΔInv)	1,600	0.8%
EBITDA		33,000	16.5%
Less:	Depreciation and Amortization	10,000	5.0%
EBIT		23,000	11.5%

Using the data in Table CS 7-4 and Equations [7-31], [7-33], [7-50], [7-51], and [7-53] with the assistance of the CFO, the VP of Manufacturing calculated the Productivity, Manufactured Revenue, Integration Coefficient, and Operating Margin for Laser Technology based on the LTM of operations.

$$Productivity = \frac{Personnel\ Costs + EBIT}{Personnel\ Costs} \qquad [7\text{-}31]$$

$$Productivity = \frac{93{,}600 + 23{,}000}{93{,}600} = 1.2457 \ = 1.25$$

$$Manufactured\ Revenues = Rev \pm \Delta\ in\ Work\ In\ Progress\ \&\ Finished\ Goods \qquad [7\text{-}33]$$

$$Manufactured\ Revenues = 200{,}000 + 1{,}600 = \$201{,}600$$

$$I_C = \frac{(Personnel\ Costs + EBIT)}{ManRev} \qquad [7\text{-}50]$$

$$I_C = \frac{93{,}600 + 23{,}000}{201{,}600} = 0.5784 \ = 0.58$$

$$OpMargin = I_C\left(\frac{Productivity - 1}{Productivity}\right) \qquad [7\text{-}51]$$

$$\%OpMargin = \left[(0.5784)\left(\frac{1.2457 - 1}{1.2457}\right)\right](100) = 11.4\%$$

which agrees well with the definitional expression for Operating Margin:

$$OpMargin = \frac{EBIT}{ManRev} \qquad [7\text{-}34]$$

$$\%OpMargin = \left(\frac{23{,}000}{201{,}600}\right)(100) = 11.4\%$$

The results of these calculations were then summarized in Table CS 7-5 and plotted in the chart in Figure CS 7-1.

TABLE CS 7-5 Results of Productivity and Operating Margin Calculations

Productivity	1.25
Manufactured Revenues	$201,600,000
Operating Margin	11.41%

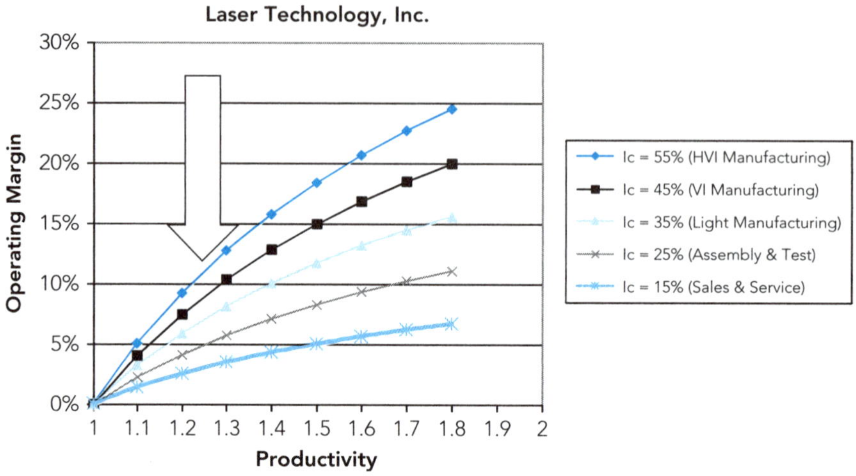

FIGURE CS 7-1 Laser Technology's Integration Coefficient

After presenting the results of their calculations to the management team, the VP of Manufacturing found himself embroiled in a partisan discussion involving the various functional managers. The good news was: Everyone agreed that with an Integration Coefficient greater than 55%,[9] a productivity improvement program would result in a substantial improvement in Operating Margin, cash flow, and value of the business. Unfortunately, the executives couldn't agree on a course of action. The VP of Marketing was pitching for a Cost of Goods Sold cost reduction program focused on direct materials and labor. In response, the VP of Procurement argued that they have pushed their suppliers very hard and, while they could always do better, he thought the company might get better results by considering a price increase and/or pursuing a headcount reduction.

This brought the VP of Human Resources into the discussion and he pointed out that while he was not opposed to a reduction in force (RIF), he thought that if the program was to have any impact they would have to go after the highly paid people and refrain from the temptation of laying off clerks and secretaries. The VP of R&D, who had been listening carefully to all of this finally spoke up and said that he thought all of the issues raised were valid and should be considered in a systematic manner.

Realizing that the meeting had probably run its productive course, the CEO interrupted the discussion. He began by thanking everyone for his or her candid input and then proceeded to summarize what he had heard. He said, "It seems to me there are several courses of action: (1) Reduce the number of employees, (2) reduce personnel related and other expenses, (3) increase volume, (4) increase prices, (5) reduce the cost of direct materials and associated labor, or (6) all or some combination of the above." He went on to say: "While I have listened carefully to all your

[9]This is what the VP expected given the manufacturing facilities were highly vertically integrated.

views, I'm not persuaded that any course of action is superior or inferior to another but I have concluded that the VP of R&D is right and we need to go about this in a systematic way."

He continued: "Before any more work is done on this, I think we need to remind ourselves of what we are trying to do here and that is improve our Operating Margin. As our VP of Manufacturing has pointed out, one way of doing this is by being guided by the productivity and Operating Margin models. In my view our goal should be to come up with a plan that increases our Operating Margin from 11.4% to 15%."

The CEO, who was very familiar with the model, wanted to be sure everyone understood how it worked and the process it suggested, so he decided to take the team through it step by step. "If you refer to Figure CS 7-1, you will note that a 15% Operating Margin can be obtained by about a12% increase in productivity from our LTM level of 1.25 to something approximating 1.4. Therefore, I suggest that if we are going to follow the models our VP of Manufacturing has suggested, the team needs to work with expressions for Value Added [7-30], Productivity [7-31], Manufactured Revenue [7-33], and Operating Margin [7-53] and let them point us in the right direction.

"It all starts with value added, which is defined as:

$$Value\ Added = Personnel\ Costs + EBIT \qquad [7\text{-}30]$$

"Equation [7-30] tells us is that our customers will only pay for things that add value, which consist of manufacturing value added, operating value added, and premium value added, all of which according to this model turn out to be the cost of our skilled personnel plus the value they perceive our product brings as reflected by our EBIT. Hence, as a starting point, our focus should be on reducing personnel costs and adding value that enhances EBIT. Currently our value added stands at \$116,600,000 (93,600,000 + 23,000,000).

"It may be obvious, but in the interest of completeness it's important to note that we can't increase value added by increasing our personnel costs. If our personnel costs are excessive, our EBIT will be reduced accordingly and value added remains the same. The point is our customers won't pay for inefficiencies.

"How productive a company is in delivering its value added can be measured by Equation [7-31], which in our case is currently about 1.25 as calculated by our CFO and VP of Manufacturing.

$$Productivity = \frac{Personnel\ Costs + EBIT}{Personnel\ Costs} \qquad [7\text{-}31]$$

"Again you will notice the key drivers are personnel costs and EBIT.

"Our expression for Operating Margin requires that EBIT be referenced to revenues, which in this case needs to be manufactured revenues (Equation [7-33]) because not everything manufactured during a period is necessarily shipped to our customers during that period. Some of manufacturing's output could go into inventory and some of the period shipments could come from inventory manufactured during a prior period. In this case our manufacturing facilities shipped $200,000,000 to customers and increased work in progress and finished goods by $1,600,000, giving us a manufactured revenue of $201,600,000.

$$\textit{Manufactured Revenues} = \textit{Rev} \pm \Delta \textit{ in Work In Progress \& Finished Goods} \quad [7\text{-}33]$$

"Then with the manufactured revenue at hand the Operating Margin is simply the ratio of EBIT to manufactured revenue, which for the LTM is 11.4%, which of course I would like to see at 15%.

$$OpMargin = \frac{EBIT}{ManRev} \quad [7\text{-}34]$$

"In summary, it seems to me that if we follow the productivity and Operating Margin models just discussed, we should be focused on the following:

- Personnel costs associated with the Cost of Goods Sold and Operating Expenses
- Anything that drives EBIT, including direct material costs, other costs, revenue increases, and price increases

"Therefore, I think the next step is for our CFO and VP of Manufacturing to lead a workgroup that investigates the possible strategies and come back with a report that tabulates the impact of the various scenarios. Once we have this information, we can decide on next steps."

Part 2: Scenarios for Improving Productivity

At the next regular meeting of the Management Committee, the VP of Manufacturing presented his report, pointing out that Case C (Current) was the Income Statement for the LTM (last twelve months) and represented where the company was now, and then proceeded to make the following points with respect to the data presented in Table CS 7-6.

Case 1

"It took a while for all of us in manufacturing to realize that while Case C was an accurate representation of our LTM performance, it was not the place to start. We reasoned that while inflation was still under control, the reality was that it was there, and, furthermore, an examination of the records in personnel revealed that wage and salary increases were consistently greater than inflation. To place this in perspective, we concluded that when inflation was running at 3%, direct materials costs and other operating expense would increase at 3% on average. However, a review of past wage and salary increases indicated we could expect personnel costs to increase at about twice that rate (6%). Therefore, if we did nothing and had a year of flat sales, one year from now the Operating Margin and productivity would be 7.55% and 1.15 respectively, as indicated by Case 1."

TABLE CS 7-6 Scenarios for Improving Productivity and Operating Margin

Scenarios	Case C	Case 1		Case 2		Case 1 + 2		Case 3		Case 1 + 3	
1, 2, 1 + 2, 3, 1 + 3	LTM	3% Inflation		5% RIF, –6% Personnel Costs		3% Inf, 5% RIF, –6% Personnel Costs		–8% DM&OE, –3% Personnel Costs		3% Inf, –8% DM&OE, –3% Personnel Costs	
Net Revenues	200,000	0.0%	200,000	0.0%	200,000	0.0%	200,000	0.0%	200,000	0.0%	200,000
Direct Materials	(40,000)	3.0%	(41,200)	0.0%		3.0%	(41,200)	–8.0%		–5.0%	(38,000)
Personnel Costs	(93,600)	6.0%	(99,216)	–11.0%		–5.0%	(88,920)	–3.0%		3.0%	(96,408)
Other Prod&Op Expenses	(31,800)	3.0%	(32,754)	0.0%		3.0%	(32,754)	–8.0%		–5.0%	(30,210)
Change in Inventory	(1,600)	0.0%	(1,600)	0.0%		0.0%	(1,600)	0.0%		0.0%	(1,600)
EBITDA	33,000		25,230				35,526				33,782
D&A	(10,000)	0.0%	(10,000)			0.0%	(10,000)			0.0%	(10,000)
EBIT	23,000		15,230				25,526				23,782
Operating Margin	11.41%		7.55%				12.66%				11.80%
Productivity	1.25		1.15				1.29				1.25

Case 2 and Case 1 + 2

"Once we got into the data, one of the first things that struck us was the rate at which personnel costs were increasing, so we asked ourselves: What would happen if the Company had an across-the-board wage and salary freeze and a reduction in force (RIF) (Case 2), and would it deal with the impact of increases in direct materials and other production and operating expense, which were increasing at a rate of 3% per year (Case 1 + 2)? After much discussion the largest RIF we considered feasible was 5% and so we ran the numbers. The outcome was that a wage and salary freeze (personnel costs frozen at LTM level) and a 5% reduction in personnel expenses as a result of a RIF would yield Operating Margin and Productivity of 12.66% and 1.29 (net of inflation) respectively—a notable improvement compared to current performance and where we could be headed. Ultimately this was considered to be a risky strategy at this stage of the Company's development and even if this scenario were possible it would have a short life (1 year at best) and for this reason it was not given any additional consideration. However, it did make the point that personnel costs had to be brought under control."

Case 3 and Case 1 + 3

"The next thing considered was direct material and other expenses. A careful examination showed that while direct materials were completely variable, other expenses were not. In fact about half of other expenses are revenue dependent with the rest semi-variable, and taking costs out of the semi-variable component would take more time and effort. This means that if we were to target an 8% across-the-board cost reduction program on direct materials, we would net 5% after inflation (3% – 8%) and the most we could hope to get in other expenses would be a 2.5% reduction (3% – 8%)*(0.50). Just as we were about to introduce this refinement we realized that we were concerning ourselves with an unnecessary refinement at this stage and there was little to be gained by worrying about the impact of treating the semi-variable as a variable and so we assumed the 8% cost reduction and 3% inflation applied to both the variable and semi-variable costs. As you can see from Table CS 7-6, this program (Case 3) in combination with the inflation scenario (Case 1) continues to yield an unsatisfactory result with Operating Margin increasing modestly to 11.8% and productivity remaining steady at 1.25. By this point we were all a little surprised at how difficult it was to deal with the enervating effects of inflation and our compensation policy and simply hold on to where we were, let alone make some progress.

"At this point we concluded the following:

- A reduction in force with or without a wage and salary freeze was not an attractive option.
- Personnel costs have to be brought under control.
- Cost reduction alone does not allow us to achieve the desired results.
- Volume and/or price increases had to be part of the ultimate strategy."

Case 4 and Case 1 + 4

The VP of Manufacturing continued: "As you know we have been growing rapidly and the event that triggered all of this was the fact that our growth rate appeared to be slowing from 10%-plus to 6–8% and so while we were hesitant to introduce volume growth it was clear from the cases considered so far that without it we would have to propose drastic reductions in personnel costs. So for this case we decided to include revenue growth in our model.

"Next we looked at throughput and concluded that capacity was not a problem insofar as our productive assets were concerned and speculated that our workforce was capable of at least 10% and possibly more volume. This number presented a problem. We had one group that felt our people were exhausted and "on the ropes" at the end of the day. Others felt we can always do better and it was simply a matter of mind-set and organizing ourselves to do "more with the same." It didn't seem like a good use of time to decide which group was right, so we focused on the things we could agree on: (1) We should not ignore the revenue option and (2) if revenue growth was to be included, it should be at the low end of the range. At the end of a very long day, we also agreed that personnel costs played such a dominant role in our models and even with revenue growth we couldn't continue to increase wages and salaries at the historical rate and decided on 3% to basically offset the effects of inflation.

"As for direct materials and other production and operating expenses there was a feeling that the 8% used in the previous scenario may have been a little too aggressive and it was suggested we should consider a 5% decrease or 2% per year after inflation. As you can see from the data presented in Table CS 7-7, this didn't get us very far since this scenario only offered the promise of 11.6% and 1.23 Operating Margin and Productivity respectively versus the LTM of 11.4% and 1.25. Clearly 6% volume, modest reductions in direct materials and other expense, and personnel costs keeping up with inflation weren't the answer."

Case 5 and Case 1 + 5

"At this point we went back to basics and reviewed the available options. Then the light went on. The one thing we hadn't considered was a price increase and after consultation with Sales and Marketing it was concluded that a price increase was realistic. While we were thinking about this, our CFO reminded us that historically companies have only been able to increase prices by approximately 3% per year on average. Our VP of Marketing responded by saying he was comfortable with a price increase of 3% per annum, which just happened to be the same as the expected rate of inflation. So we modified Case 4 + 1 to include a 3% increase in price in addition to the increase in volume and direct material and other expense reductions.

"After running the numbers, we were embarrassed by the result because it reminded all of us of what should have been obvious: The best way to deal with cost increases is to pass them along to the customer—if you can. Be that as it may, we finally had a simple strategy that was moving the pointer in the right direction with Operating Margin increasing to 13.5%, very near the target set by the CEO. In addition, it left room for considering other strategies we had discussed but not modeled."

TABLE CS 7-7 Modified Scenarios for Improving Productivity and Operating Margin $(000)'s and %

Scenarios 1, 4, 1 + 4, 5, 1 + 5	Case C LTM	Case 1 3% Inflation		Case 4 6%Vol, –5% DM&OE, –3%PC		Case 1 + 4 3% Inf, 6%Vol, –5%DM&OE, –3%PC		Case 5 3% Price, 6%Vol –5%DM&OE –3%PC		Case 1 + 5 3% Inf, 3% P, 6% V –5%DM&OE –3%PC	
Net Revenues	200,000	0.0%	200,000	6.0%	212,000	6.0%	212,000	9.0%	218,000	9.0%	218,000
Direct Materials	(40,000)	3.0%	(41,200)	–5.0%		–2.0%	(41,552)	–5.0%		–2.0%	(41,552)
Personnel Costs	(93,600)	6.0%	(99,216)	–3.0%		3.0%	(102,192)	–3.0%		3.0%	(102,192)
Other Prod&Op Expenses	(31,800)	3.0%	(32,754)	–5.0%		–2.0%	(33,034)	–5.0%		–2.0%	(33,034)
Change in Inventory	(1,600)	0.0%	(1,600)			0.0%	(1,600)			0.0%	(1,600)
EBITDA	33,000		25,230				33,622				39,622
D&A	(10,000)	0.0%	(10,000)			0.0%	(10,000)			0.0%	(10,000)
EBIT	23,000		15,230				23,622				29,622
Operating Margin	11.41%		7.55%				11.06%				13.49%
Productivity	1.25		1.15				1.23				1.29

Part 3: Viable Alternatives

The VP of Manufacturing continued his report: "Having looked at all of these scenarios, we concluded that the next step was to share them with an expanded workgroup and solicit their comments on the viability of the strategies we had examined. The result of these discussions culminated in three clear alternatives and these are contained in Table CS 7-8."

Case LTM + Price

"In order to remind ourselves of the Power of Price, we adjusted the LTM case to reflect a 3% price increase."

Alternative 1 "With 'Price' in our tool kit we took a fresh look at our assumptions and decided we would systematically adjust them to illustrate three alternatives. For Alternative 1 we set: Price Increase = 3%, Volume Increase = 6%, Direct Materials and Other Production and Operating Expenses = –3% (so net of inflation the increase was 0%), and Personnel Costs = 3% (in line with inflation). The result was Operating Margin = 12.8% and Productivity = 1.27, and in line with what we expected because we hadn't been aggressive in bringing down the cost of direct materials and other production and operating expenses and had failed to adequately deal with our biggest problem, which was personnel costs."

TABLE CS 7-8 Alternatives for Improving Productivity and Operating Margin $(000)'s and %

	Case C	Case LTM + Price		Alternative 1		Alternative 2		Alternative 3	
Alternatives 1, 2, and 3	**LTM**	**Case LTM + 3% Price Increase**		**3% price 6% Vol DM&OE –3% PC 3%**		**3% price 6% Vol DM&OE –5% PC 3%**		**3% price 6% Vol DM&OE –5% PC 0%**	
Net Revenues	200,000	3.0%	206,000	9.0%	218,000	9.0%	218,000	9.0%	218,000
Direct Materials	(40,000)	0.0%	(40,000)	0.0%	(42,400)	–2.0%	(41,552)	–2.0%	(41,552)
Personnel Costs	(93,600)	0.0%	(93,600)	3.0%	(102,192)	3.0%	(102,192)	0.0%	(93,600)
Other Prod&Op Expenses	(31,800)	0.0%	(31,800)	0.0%	(33,708)	–2.0%	(33,034)	–2.0%	(33,034)
Change in Inventory	(1,600)	0.0%	(1,600)	0.0%	(1,600)	0.0%	(1,600)	0.0%	(1,600)
EBITDA	33,000	0.0%	39,000		38,100		39,622		48,214
D&A	(10,000)	0.0%	(10,000)	0.0%	(10,000)	0.0%	(10,000)	0.0%	(10,000)
EBIT	23,000	0.0%	29,000		28,100		29,622		38,214
Operating Margin	11.41%		13.97%		12.80%		13.49%		17.40%
Productivity	1.25		1.31		1.27		1.29		1.41

Alternative 2 "For Alternative 2 we modified the assumption set and factored in more aggressive direct material and other expenses. This changed the assumption set to: Price Increase = 3%, Volume Increase = 6%, Direct Materials and Other Production and Operating Expenses = –5% (so net of inflation the decrease was 2%), and Personnel Costs = 3% (in line with inflation). The result was a notable improvement to 13.5% and 1.29 for Operating Margin and Productivity respectively, and as you would expect after taking a bigger cut at the second largest cost, Direct Materials (20%) + Other Production and Operating Expenses (15.9%). All of us believe that this alternative was achievable and relatively low risk."

Alternative 3 "The sense of the workgroup at this point was we had the making of a plan that spread the pain. Sales and Marketing and Manufacturing were on board with 3% price and 6% volume increases respectively. Our supply chain people had signed up for a 2% reduction in direct materials and other production and operating expenses in real terms (3% inflation minus 5% cost reduction). The one thing that still had not been addressed was personnel costs. Despite our reluctance to go there we finally concluded that the only way we could meet the 15% Operating Margin goal was to deal with the fact that our personnel costs had been exceeding inflation by 3% for some time. We all believe that people are our most valuable resource and so we were very concerned about recommending anything that sent a contrary signal. On the other hand, we felt we weren't doing our people any favor by allowing our personnel costs to get out of line and make us noncompetitive. It took some time but finally we agreed that the right answer here was to develop an alternative that had no wage or salary increase.

The result was Alternative 3, which is based on: Price Increase = 3%, Volume Increase = 6%, Direct Materials and Other Production and Operating Expenses = –5% (–2% net of inflation), and Personnel Costs = 0% (no increase for 12 months). When we ran the numbers our anticipated outcome was confirmed. Operating Margin = 17.4% and Productivity = 1.41, reasonably in agreement with the Productivity and Operating Margin models we used and with the potential of exceeding the goal set by our CEO."

Part 4: Reaching Agreement

The president thanked everyone for the excellent work they had done and then opened the meeting for discussion. As you might expect, the first question came from the CEO. He asked, "Why did you settle on 6% increase in volume and a 3% increase in price?"

The VP of Manufacturing: "Our reasoning was, first and foremost, our VPs of Sales and Marketing were very comfortable with the numbers. Second, after an investigation Manufacturing Engineering confirmed there was adequate capacity to handle the additional volume for at least three years at the 6% growth rate and possibly longer. They also stated that with rather minor investments labor efficiency could be improved. In addition there were many in Sales and Marketing comfortable with an 8% growth rate. We thought it prudent to start at the low end of the expected growth range because at that level Alternative 3 is more conservative. And, finally, we don't want to overpromise. We are committed to 6% in the first year with our existing labor force and our belief is that we will achieve 6%+ in the succeeding years with lower labor per unit of output, thereby positioning us for further improvements in productivity and operating margin."

The CEO then asked the CFO for her opinion. She responded: "All of this is very compelling; however, since I missed the last meeting when Manufacturing Engineering presented their report I need to know what they mean by a "relatively minor investment" before I can have an informed view on the various strategies that have been proposed."

VP of Manufacturing: "We are not talking about a new building. What we will need are some additional workstations, minor jigs, fixtures, and tooling, so the additional investment that would form part of our capital expenditure plan could be as much as $3,000,000."

To this the CFO replied: "That shouldn't be a problem. I don't have to run the numbers to know that an investment of that magnitude that results in higher throughput and productivity will show an attractive return."

The CEO continued and asked the Sales and Marketing people how they felt about what was being proposed. After a rather lengthy interchange and discussion the VP summed it up by saying: "All of us in Sales and Marketing believe in the numbers proposed and probably will do better."

Turning to the VP of Procurement, the CEO said, "I know you folks have been working hard to deal with our growth and control costs but as you can see, we will find it difficult to continue growing profits as we have in the past unless we can implement this or some comparable program. Furthermore, we can't implement this program without your help."

In response, the VP said: "It is true that we have been working hard with our suppliers and some of them are stressed, but it's not only because we have been pushing them on price. Given our growth rate, our top priority was on-time delivery to meet production schedules and at the same time continue to improve inventory turns. Frankly, I think we now have most of the delivery issues worked out and so while I do it with some reservation, we will accept the challenge of reducing expenses by 5% (–2% net of inflation) for next year and after that we will set a new goal. Furthermore, since we have several months before our next fiscal year begins we will target to have 80% of the cost reductions done and in place so that most of the projected savings fall to the bottom line next year."

"Excellent," said the CEO. "So, it seems that we have Sales and Marketing signed up for 3% price and 6% volume increases and our supply chain folks on board for a net –2% direct material and other expense reduction. The open issue for me is the volume question. My own feeling on this is our factory can accommodate a 6% compound revenue increase for a period of several years for a lot less than $3,000,000. However, given what's at stake I must say that I'm attracted by the opportunity to reach our targeted Operating Margin of 15% within one year, so let's go forward on the assumption that the $3,000,000 investment will prove to be attractive when the CFO does her formal analysis and in the meantime get on with implementing Alternative 3, with one caveat: Once the actions associated by Alternative 3 are under way, I will ask you folks to revisit the productivity question but this time from a premium-value-added perspective. Also, since this is essentially a one-year plan all of this will have to be revisited a year from now. Before we break up, are there any questions?"

The VP of R&D broke his silence and asked: "It's clear to me we could have got to Alternative 3 by simply working the LTM Income Statement. Why did you push us in the direction of the Productivity and Operating Margin models and all the work associated with it? Also, what do you mean by revisiting productivity from a premium-value-added perspective?"

The CEO responded: "Great questions. You are correct; the models we used are the 'long solution.' I suggested that path because I wanted to emphasize the importance of our mission, which is to add value in everything we do. It's hard to make that clear by simply massaging our GAAP financial statements. If you are to add value, you need to measure it. Once you have measured value added, one needs to have some index that incorporates the definition of value added and that is done by measuring productivity.

Once you have this benchmark and an estimate of your degree of vertical integration and an understanding of the relationship between Productivity and Operating Margin, the model points you in a very unambiguous direction. It's all about personnel costs and anything else that improves EBIT. I'm not sure your team would have reached the same conclusion by simply doing what-if analyses with the Income Statement. In fact, many of the scenarios you looked at were a form of what-if analysis and it wasn't until you folks decided to deal with the personnel costs and the cost of direct materials and combined these with a price increase that the way forward became clear.

What I mean by "anything else that improves EBIT" may not be clear. Remember our customers will only pay us for value added. It's reflected in our EBIT. They will pay us for manufacturing, operational, and premium value added. Hopefully you recognize that Alternative 3 does a great job of improving manufacturing and operational value added. It doesn't address the premium question, which is achieved when a customer will pay a price for the product that is greater than anything that can be justified by the manufactured and operating value added. So I see Alternative 3 as a step that improves our manufacturing and operating efficiency and delivers 15%+ Operating Margin. If we are to move the Operating Margin needle forward beyond 15%, it is going to have to be with premium value added." The VP of R&D thanked the CEO for the response.

The CEO continued: "In conclusion and before we break up the meeting, I want to thank all of you for the excellent work that has been done, the spirit in which this task was addressed, and the rigorous approach that has been taken. All of you have confirmed once again that I'm very fortunate to be part of such a talented management team."

CHAPTER EIGHT

The Expense Coverage Ratio*

CHAPTER 8 TAKEAWAYS

Disciplines of a healthy company: The management of a healthy company will have the courage to subject itself to the following:

- Get the match right between what the customer is willing to pay for (as reflected in the Gross Margin) and how the company is spending money (Operating Expenses).
- Invest in Sales, Marketing, Service and Customer Support, R&D, and Administration while keeping in mind the customer won't pay for inefficient or indulgent expenditures.
- Design the investment programs so they have low-cost exit strategies. Fixed costs or high termination costs should be avoided wherever possible—at least until the viability of the investment has been demonstrated. Extraordinary efforts should be made to minimize long-term commitments and to look for opportunities to outsource even if they are more expensive.
- Constantly and critically review changing customer needs and market conditions.
- Judiciously monitor the progress and continuing relevance of all investment projects, including sanity checks on the match between the objectives of an investment program and the needs to be served.
- Step back and take actions to restore the relationship between Gross Margin and Operating Expenses, especially when an investment has failed to produce the intended result or market conditions have changed.
- If your management team can't quantify what constitutes excellent performance, ask your customers.
- Judgment often turns out to be the most important factor in making a decision. Good judgment comes from experience. Experience comes from making bad decisions.

(continued)

*The reader may notice minor discrepancies in the calculations in this chapter. When this occurs, it is the result of rounding.

- It's important to keep in mind that you are engaged in a process of trying to do things and learning from the outcomes. Stay close to what is going on, focus on getting the most out of what's working, fix or cut your losses on what's not, learn a lesson, and get on with something else.
- Things are often not what they seem. You have to be vigilant and make sure you understand what's really happening in your business.
- The important question to ask is: Is this a business that you would get into today? If it isn't, plan to sell, rejuvenate, or operate as a cash cow.
- Don't take on high-risk projects unless: (1) the company is financially positioned to do so or (2) everyone clearly understands that you may be betting the business and wants to make the bet.
- It takes time to do things right. It takes longer when you shortchange the process.

THE EXPENSE COVERAGE RATIO

Throughout this book, Cash Flow and its surrogate, EBITDA (both of which are driven by revenue), have been a central theme. In Chapter 7, the case was made that EBIT is a measurement of value added, and in particular premium value added, and that the productivity and operating margin models were tools that can be used by management to improve profitability. In this chapter, another model that can be used to improve a company's profitability is introduced: the Expense Coverage Ratio.

Introduction

The Expense Coverage Ratio (ExpCR) model focuses on maximizing Gross Margin (GM) (and thereby EBITDA) by making sure there is alignment between the GM and Operating Expenses (OpExp).

As has been the case in other chapters, the starting point for the development of the ExpCR is the Income Statement first introduced in Chapter 1. In the interest of convenience, it has been designated here as Table 8-1.

TABLE 8-1 Basic Income Statement

Year Ending DD/MM/YYYY $(000)'s		
Revenues (Rev)		100,000
Cost of Goods Sold (COGS)		(40,000)
Gross Margin (GM)		60,000
Operating Expenses (OpExp)		(43,500)
Earnings before Interest, Taxes, Depreciation, and Amortization (EBITDA)		16,500
Depreciation and Amortization (D & A)		(5,000)
Earnings before Interest and Taxes (EBIT)		11,500
Interest Income/(Expense) (NetInt)		0
Earnings before Tax (EBT)		11,500
Taxes Paid (TaxesPaid) @	40%	(4,600)
Net Income (NI)		6,900

In Chapter 5, the issues associated with improving EBITDA and the impact it has on the Return on Capital Employed were discussed. The key drivers were maximizing price (Net Revenues) and minimizing the Cost of Goods Sold and Operating Expenses. In the discussion that follows a different approach is taken in that the central theme will be the ratio of Gross Margin to Operating Expenses and the implications this ratio has on management's strategies and a company's performance.

Reference to Table 8-1 once again enables a definition of Gross Margin (GM):

$$Gross\ Margin = Net\ Revenues - Cost\ of\ Goods\ Sold \qquad [8\text{-}1]$$

And Earnings before Interest, Taxes, Depreciation, and Amortization is defined as

$$EBITDA = Gross\ Margin - Operating\ Expenses \qquad [8\text{-}2]$$

The relationship defined by Equation [8-2] says that the drivers of EBITDA and therefore of ROCE are Gross Margin and Operating Expenses.

In practice, EBITDA and therefore ROCE are not improved if improvements in gross margin are offset by increased operating expenses. Therefore, it is not the absolute level of gross margin or operating expenses that is important but rather the relationship between the two. One way to derive benefits from improvements in one or both of these ROCE drivers is to understand how they interact and manage their relationship with the aid of the Expense Coverage Ratio.

Basics

A company's gross margin and operating expenses can be combined into a single metric called the Expense Coverage Ratio (ExpCR). It is defined as:

$$ExpCR = \frac{Gross\ Margin}{Operating\ Expenses} \qquad [8\text{-}3]$$ [1]

where:

$$Operating\ Expenses = Marketing + R\&D + Sales + Service\ \&\ Customer\ Support + Administrative\ Costs \qquad [8\text{-}4]$$

[1] In order to facilitate cash flow analysis, the Income Statement format chosen here identifies Depreciation and Amortization (D&A) as a separate line item. In this method of presentation, Gross Margin is defined by the price the company obtains from the customer and the Cost of Goods Sold and doesn't include D&A. Strictly speaking; D&A is an expense that should be taken into account to present a true picture. To keep things simple, D&A is ignored when calculating and discussing the Expense Coverage Ratio. Experience has shown that as long as Manufacturing D&A is relatively small (less than 5% or Revenue) or insignificant when compared to Gross Margin, it can be safely ignored. Otherwise, it should be subtracted from Gross Margin when calculating this ratio. It should also be noted that some portion of a company's Depreciation and Amortization applies to Operating Expenses. To the extent this is true, it offsets to some extent any D&A that is not included in Gross Margin since if prorated and included, D&A would be subtracted from both the numerator and denominator of Equation [8-3].

The logic behind this ratio is based on the notion that customers understand they have to pay for the products and services they require and they expect their suppliers to make a profit. In other words, if your customers need to be informed on what's out there (Marketing), want leading-edge products (R&D), require assistance during the purchase cycle (Sales), need after-sales support (Service and Customer Support), and desire a well-run company behind all of this (Administration), then they expect to pay for this cadre of expenses and infrastructure and this will be reflected in the price a company can charge for their deliverable. Assuming the company's production costs are under control, this translates directly into gross margin. Management's job is to make sure that what the company is spending its operating expense on is matched to the gross margin the company is receiving—ideally no more and no less.

Matching is an important word. The reason is: If you don't match what the customer is paying (gross margin) with the operating expenses you incur to service the customer, you run the risk of sub-optimizing profit! It sounds rather fundamental, doesn't it? Unfortunately, many management teams miss this very subtle point.

Equation [8-1] stated that gross margin is the money a company has left after deducting the cost of producing the product or service. Or, stated differently, the gross margin depends on two things: (1) the price the customer has been persuaded to pay and (2) the cost of providing the deliverable (Cost of Goods Sold). The customer usually views a supplier's Cost of Goods Sold as an internal matter. The price the customer will pay is a different issue and depends on such factors as:

- **Marketing and sales:** The success your company achieves creating value in the customer's mind by devising and implementing value-added strategies (like those inherent in the Revenue Capture, Migration, Attributes, and Premium models) will have a significant impact on the price a company charges for its deliverable.
- **Risk sharing:** Price will be influenced by the technologies involved in the product or service, complexity, and the customer's competence. In the case of mature technologies, the customers will usually be comfortable with their in-house capability and therefore prepared to assume the implementation risk. When technology is new or fast moving, the customer is willing to pay the supplier to share (if not assume) the risk.
- **Support:** This is another aspect of the customer's internal resource capability and deliverable complexity. If a company is expected to support their products and services with 7-day, 24-hour on-site service, the customer understands this costs money and will pay for it.
- **Permanence:** The question raised by this factor is whether the customer cares if the company is around in the future. If the customers view the deliverable as a commodity, then they are not likely to be concerned about your profitability, but will only be willing to pay the minimum required for a supplier to keep its long-term infrastructure in place.
- **Technology advancement:** This is the R&D question. Customers understand that great ideas, products, and services are culled from a long list of possibilities and investigations. If the technologies you are developing are important to them, they

will be prepared to support high R&D costs. If not, they will expect you to spend at a more modest level or for the company to pay for speculative programs out of its profits.

- **Availability:** If your product is expected to be on the shelf and available upon demand, customers understand they have to pay for this convenience. In fact, in this age of telephone and Internet purchasing, they are primed to pay for next-day availability as evidenced by their willingness to pick up the express delivery charges.
- **Financing:** The management of most companies recognizes that credit (extended terms) has a cost. Unfortunately too few have incorporated this fact into their pricing model. This is really a shame-on-me situation because the psychological stage has been set for charging for credit as evidenced by the fact that customers often expect a discount for paying early.

In summary, the case that is being made is that customers are prepared to pay for value added, risk sharing, supplier permanence, technology advancement, availability, and financing when they are perceived as being suitable for their business model.

The challenge for suppliers is to provide what the customer is prepared to pay for—nothing more and nothing less.[2] If your company is spending money on marketing that is repetitive and without impact because customers already have the message; is maintaining resources intended to hold the customer's hand when he is quite comfortable to go it alone; has technology that your customers don't see as promising as you do; and is carrying large inventories of completed products because your manufacturing process is inefficient and cycle times long, you are welcome to do so but don't expect your customer to pay for any of this. On the other hand, if your value added is demonstratively compelling and your technology shows great promise, you are in a position to charge accordingly.

Hopefully, the following examples will drive home the points just made. The first example portrays the company's lack of profitability at one end of the spectrum: not charging enough. The second example illustrates the thinking that needs to take place when unsatisfactory profitability is driven by operating expenses being no longer matched to the value the customers perceive and what they are prepared to pay.

Example 8-1: A Company Learns How to Price Their Product

A late-stage start-up is losing money (ExpCR < 1) but is cash flow positive because D&A is greater than spending on PP&E. The management team is led by the two founders who developed the technology that has enabled the Company to achieve critical mass in a relatively short period of time. The venture capital groups (VCs) that provided the funding the business required are frustrated by the fact that management doesn't have any credible plan to cross the break-even threshold and move into the realm of sustained profitability.

---

[2] In practice this state of affairs is very hard to achieve, let alone maintain. Therefore, prudent suppliers will try to err on the side of providing a little more and pride themselves on exceeding customer expectations.

TABLE 8-2 A Company Learns How to Price Their Product

	Stage 1	Stage 2	Stage 3	Stage 4	Stage 5
Gross Margin	37.0%	42.0%	47.0%	52.0%	57.0%
Operating Expenses	40.0%	40.0%	40.0%	40.0%	40.0%
EBITDA	–3.0%	2.0%	7.0%	12.0%	17.0%
Expense Coverage Ratio	0.93	1.05	1.18	1.30	1.43

Stage 1 The current state of affairs is reflected in Stage 1 of Table 8-2.[3]

Stage 2 The VCs decide to act and meet with the founders to discuss the state of affairs and find they are in agreement that the company has reached a stage that requires new leadership, and they were prepared to step aside and focus on advancing the technology. A new CEO is recruited and the first thing he does is look at the company's performance. The production facilities appear to be efficient so he doesn't think the problem lies in the Cost of Goods Sold. After a careful study of the product lines, customers, and competitors, his intuition tells him the EBITDA problem is driven by the way the Company prices its deliverable, and if operating expenses are out of line, they are a second-order effect.

After an unproductive meeting with the VPs of Sales and Marketing, both of whom impressed him as being competent, he concluded they need a starting point and instructed them to initiate a competitive pricing study. The VPs thought the pricing was fine but since they had been working hard on driving revenue for the past several periods they ended up concluding that a study couldn't hurt and might even be instructive. The result was stunningly clear! The Company was underpricing. The data was so compelling that there wasn't any opposition to a price increase. The market accepted the price increase with little resistance. Discussions with customers indicated they perceive great value in the company's products and some even suggested obliquely that they occasionally wondered why such superb products were priced below market. The result is for the first time the company becomes profitable.

Stage 3 The management team was now very much motivated by the fact that the price increase turned out to be a non-event and they were at long last profitable. The CEO didn't want to let the momentum lapse so he decided to lead a discussion on value added—a subject in which he had considerable experience. The consequence was forming a group to make estimates of the probable value added of their deliverables. Everyone except possibly the CEO was surprised by what the study suggested and quickly agreed there was more room on the price front. The question was how to present it to the customer. As it turned out, new versions of several major products were imminent and so

[3]The figures in this table and some of those that follow are quoted as a percentage of Total Sales or Revenues except for the ExpCRs, which are the ratios of the respective Gross Margins to Operating Expenses.

rather than follow their normal pricing models they also factored in their estimates of value added. So price was increased once again with little or no reaction from the market. However, there was a reaction in the company's financial statement. The ExpCR increased to 1.18, which corresponded to an EBITDA of 7%.

Stage 4 During the next regular business review meeting that the new CEO introduced after his arrival, the CFO comments on the fact that the Company's R&D expenses continued to advance at a rapid clip and that product life cycles were shortening. After a careful review, they conclude they must continue to invest at this rate and the time available for them to recover investments is more likely to shorten than lengthen. The VPs of Marketing and Sales agree that they need to get a more rapid payback but urged restraint. Ultimately, the management team decides to factor the escalating R&D costs into the next generation of products and to encourage customers to purchase the latest release. They also decide to announce that support for some of the older versions would be discontinued. There is some customer resistance but in the end the customers move on to the new release and live with the higher prices because of the value inherent in the deliverable. The financial statements quickly show the impact of the change in strategy with an ExpCR and EBITDA of 1.30 and 12%.

Stage 5 After being hounded by the CFO for escalating expenses, the VPs of Sales and Marketing finally decide to analyze spending and they quickly realize that the sales support their customers require has been increasing over time and exceeds what was originally priced into the products and agree to tackle the problem. Their first thoughts are along the lines of more of the same with a marketing and sales campaign promoting (among other things) "unlimited after sales support" to cushion the impact on the market of another price increase. The CEO isn't enthusiastic about the approach and thinks the customers won't be so easily taken in. He believes unlimited anything ultimately leads to abuse and being upfront with customers is good business practice and suggests a different approach—a *user-pay* model whereby rather than increase prices, new customers would get free support for the first 90 days and thereafter be offered a menu of plans that varied from pay per call to 24/7 support. Existing customers would be grandfathered for one year but after that time they would be offered the same choices.

After much discussion it was decided that this could be much better for the company in the long run and so plans were prepared to implement the change in strategy. One of the major action items involved face to face meetings with all customers explaining the rationale, which was very simple: The Company's support costs had grown over the years to a point where in order to sustain them another price increase would be necessary, but rather than pass the cost along to all customers the Company felt the user-pay model was fairer to all concerned. It took some time but ultimately the strategy prevailed with an increase in Revenue, ExpCR (1.43) and EBITDA (17%) to levels the new CEO felt were more appropriate for a company in this space.

Conclusion While Stages 1 through 5 are hypothetical and arbitrary, the message is not. The customer base has been willing to pay for the value offered by the deliverable all along. The problem has been the Company's reluctance to charge for it in a way the customers didn't find offensive. By systematically increasing the prices in a logical manner, the Company was able to increase the Expense Coverage Ratio from 0.93, a loss of 3% (37 – 40), to 1.43, or an operating profit of 17% (57 – 40).[4]

Example 8-2: Responding to Changes in Market Conditions

Years passed, the Company grew rapidly, and during this period was acquired by a conglomerate, and like many acquisitions, this one didn't work out as originally envisaged. Management left after their contracts expired, and the team installed by the conglomerate didn't understand the business, and after an analysis, incorrectly decided that the problem was the gross margin, which had deteriorated significantly. What they didn't realize was that the market for the deliverable had matured, competition had increased, and customers no longer perceived the "incremental" value added claimed by the Company for recent generations of products to be what they once were and had grown very comfortable with the technology. The new team correctly determined the production facilities were efficient but unfortunately concluded the gross margin problem could be fixed by addressing the Revenue line. They soon discovered that price increases were difficult to make stick and for some product lines they began to erode further despite Herculean efforts to play the price card with intensified marketing and a flurry of new product releases. Furthermore, there weren't any quick solutions available that could increase volume. The Company soon found itself in the loss situation. The conglomerate had little patience for a loss-making company and sold it to a buyout group.

Stage A When the ownership of the company was transferred to the new owner, the company was still not profitable at the EBITDA line. The performance of the Company is summarized in Table 8-3, Stage A.

Stage B The leveraged buyout group quickly changed out the management team with seasoned professionals who understood the leverage the Company had taken

TABLE 8-3 Responding to Changes in Market Conditions

	Stage A	Stage B	Stage C	Stage D	Stage E
Gross Margin	37.0%	37.0%	37.0%	37.0%	37.0%
Operating Expenses	40.0%	35.0%	30.0%	25.0%	22.5%
EBITDA	–3.0%	2.0%	7.0%	12.0%	14.5%
Expense Coverage Ratio	0.93	1.06	1.23	1.48	1.64

[4] It's important to note that the improvement in operating profit was achieved by getting the pricing right. Another array of opportunities to improve profit may exist in the Cost of Goods Sold.

on, required that the debt be serviced, and therefore very quickly began to explore options to increase profitability and cash flow. Like the management team before them, they quickly concluded that the COGS, which can always be improved, was not the low-hanging fruit and the opportunities to increase profitability were in the operating expenses. Their first conclusion was that selling expenses were high given their experience in past similar situations. The new VP of Sales and Marketing decided to do an analysis of the customer base and observed a couple of things. First, the Company had over 5,000 customers but a vast majority of the business came from about 1,000 accounts. Second, when the customers were allocated to A, B, and C categories, 80% of the revenue came from the customers in the A and B categories, which accounted for roughly 2,500 or half of their customers.

Not knowing what this meant in terms of sales effort, the next step was to quantify how much was being spent on the customers in the C category. The answer was approximately 35% of the sales budget. The 20% of the revenue these customers represented was important to the Company so they couldn't walk away from it. After much strategizing, the management team arrived at an innovative idea. Why not service the category C customers with a well-trained inside salesforce supported by a revamped user-friendly website? The idea was tested with a statistically significant sample. The results were better than they hoped. A vast majority of the customers felt that given the sporadic nature and volume of their purchases, their needs could be adequately met by the redesigned website and inside salespeople dedicated to their account, who would call on a regular schedule. With this data in hand, the management team moved to trim the outside salesforce and replace them with lower cost inside salespeople. While not a game-changing step, it did move the pointer to an ExpCR and EBITA of 1.06 and 2% respectively.

Stage C Customer Service and Support, Marketing, and Promotional expenses also quickly emerged as candidates for cuts because of their magnitude. Customer Service and Support was almost a no-brainer. It had been struggling to break even for some time due to the fact that over time customers had acquired sufficient experience with the products that they no longer relied on the Company for support as they once did. Notable exceptions were new accounts and the complex high-end systems. No one tried to make a case for continuing to spend money on something the customer didn't want, but the team was reminded that the Company's reputation in this area was second to none and the budget should be reviewed in this context. It would be a big mistake to dismember something that had taken years to build and would play a role in the future when new technology was introduced. This was acknowledged and agreement was reached on the actions to take to restore profitability to this area.

Another study showed that the marketing story wasn't getting the response it once did. However, management was hesitant to make deep cuts. There was a strong feeling that while the marketing budget should be surgically trimmed, the right answer was to redesign it to focus on an adjacent market segment that was underserved.

As for promotional spending, this was another matter. The consensus view of those who had dealt with problems like this in previous assignments was that this spending should be cut back because all it was doing was getting tomorrow's sale today at a lower price.

The team concluded its review of marketing expenses by looking at the mail order business. All evidence pointed to the fact there was no longer a high correlation between the money spent on direct mail and orders garnered. What they did find was the responses to their Internet initiatives had grown nicely and that it appeared their customers were increasingly comfortable with purchasing through this channel.

During the wrap-up session, it was agreed that the Customer Service and Support department would be downsized, the marketing budget would be trimmed and refocused, and promotional spending would be severely cut as would the direct mail budget, with one caveat: Some of the savings would be used to supplement the Internet effort. Net-net these decisions involved serious money, so the improvement in the ExpCR and EBITDA was significant.

Stage D The management team spent some time looking at administrative expenses. Their conclusion was that this area functioned well and they weren't able to identify any significant savings.

R&D had a huge budget and the spending and activities received plenty of scrutiny. It no longer had a large backlog of ideas and was increasingly spending more on product line maintenance and product enhancements. It was marketing's view that there was way too much effort directed at the existing product and service offering and it was clear customers were skipping releases because the enhancements and features didn't add sufficient value to justify the historical frequency of purchase. So here again the Company was spending money on things the customer considered to have marginal value at best. Marketing also suggested the backlog of projects should be culled and only the most promising ideas be funded. No management team likes to cut R&D, but after much procrastination and wringing of hands, management finally decides marketing is right and systematically goes through the product and service offerings, cuts expenditure on product line maintenance and enhancements, and funds the promising projects. The outcome is a significant reduction in R&D expense and a corresponding improvement in the Company's profitability.

Stage E The VP of R&D was on board with the decisions that had been taken and in fact continued to give the matter some thought. Working with product marketing and the CFO, he was able to identify additional savings and discussed them with the CEO, who was impressed by his candor and agreed there was further room for budget cuts. He reflected on the fact that the actions they had taken had returned the Company to profitability and it was now financially stable. He was tempted by the prospect of the proposal because, if implemented, it would increase the ExpCR and EBITDA to 1.64 and 14.5% respectively. However, he was hesitant to take this step because he was concerned that by doing so they might be "cutting the core out of the apple." Instead he opted for another approach.

He called his management team together and brought them up to date on what the VP of R&D had proposed, and his reaction, and said, "What has been proposed is very attractive but upon reflection I'm very concerned that while our actions taken to date were necessary, we are not spending much if anything on investigations and projects that could drive future growth. So my preference is to let the R&D folks make the adjustments they propose but not cut their budget further. Instead, I want them to take the money and work with marketing to identify investments that can drive our top line. Furthermore, the actions we have taken to improve profitability have impacted morale so I think we need to get something positive out there and hopefully news of this decision will be a welcome first step and help us build credibility among our employees of our intention to once again make this a growth company." It didn't take long for what had been proposed to sink in and be enthusiastically approved.

The outcome of this progression of events just described is that by concentrating on what the customer wants (as represented by the price the customers are prepared to pay, frequency of purchase, and what services they require), and facing up to the fact that customer service and support were no longer required as they once were and the marketing spend was not having the desired impact, promotional spending had the effect of reducing the selling price, redirecting money spent on mail order to the Internet effort, and fixing an R&D program that had lost its way to some extent, management was able to take the company from a loss situation of –3% (ExpCR = 0.93) to an operating profit of 12% (ExpCR = 1.48) with the possibility of going to 14.5% (ExpCR = 1.64), which they opted not to do.

While no management team relishes the thought of cutting back or undoing something they have successfully implemented, sometimes it must be done because markets and customer expectations change. It's better if it's part of an ongoing process as opposed to a survival program. But either way it accomplishes the goal of positioning the company to fight another day.

The Dynamic Model

The sole purpose of the foregoing discussion on the Expense Coverage Ratio was to make the point that the gross margin you are able to generate is a reflection of what your customers are willing to pay for your deliverable.

Management needs to clearly understand what customers are paying for and match costs accordingly if the company is to remain profitable. Stated differently, play the price card, fortified by marketing, as hard and best you can to keep prices up there. But don't lose sight of the fact that your strategy should also focus on matching the money you are spending on operating expense with the gross margin you are able to generate and thereby maintain an Expense Coverage Ratio that contributes handsomely to EBITDA and the Return on Capital Employed.

Hopefully, Examples 8-1 and 8-2 have been helpful in gaining an understanding of the notion of adjusting the operating expenses to reflect the customer's message suggested by the gross margin. However, they are not illustrative or demonstrative of how to use the Expense Coverage Ratio in the day-to-day management of the business. Example 8-3 is intended to meet this objective.

Example 8-3: Day-to-Day Management of the Expense Coverage Ratio

Prior to Time 2 in Figure 8-1, the company had gone through an extended period of growth. Management has not hesitated to invest for the future. Revenue and gross margin have consistently grown faster than operating expenses. The outcome of this strategy has

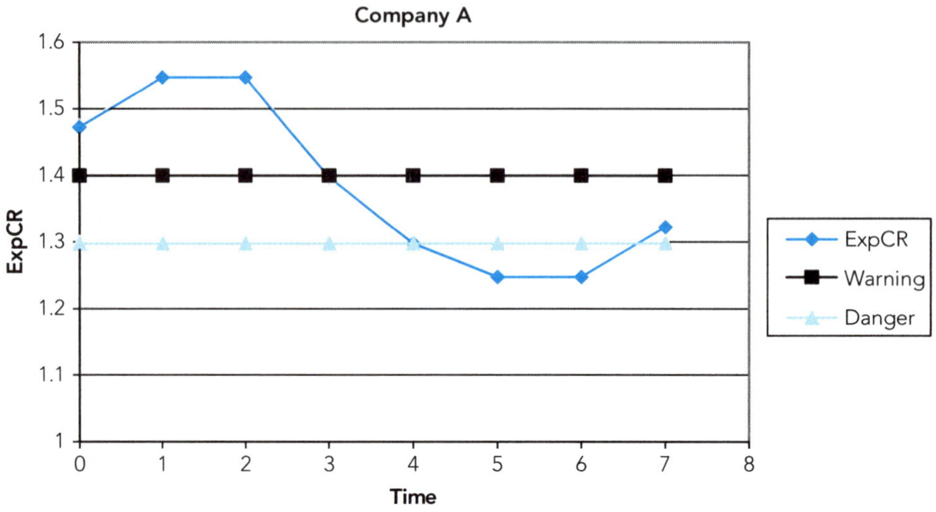

FIGURE 8-1 Expense Coverage Ratio Trend for Company A

been that the company's Expense Coverage Ratio has hovered at or above 1.5; management's track record has been world class and the envy of peers. Investments have varied over time and profits have dipped periodically more or less as planned, only to turn up once again as the investments have begun to pay off.

Time 1 While much remains the same, one thing has changed: The company's product lines are in the process of maturing with the usual consequences, and management, with the support of the board, decide they need to venture into a new but adjacent area in order to fuel future growth.

Time 2 The consequence of product maturity is slower profit growth and this adds additional urgency to the need to develop products in an adjacent product area. While management understand that different strategies may require different models, they believe their past investment model has proven itself over time and now is no time to change course and decide to launch their investment for the new products with their usual enthusiasm and expectations. As expected, this results in a decrease in profits and a corresponding decline in the ExpCR as the spending takes effect.

Time 3 Investment spending continues to be on plan but product releases are behind schedule and revenue has weakened substantially. The outcome is the ExpCR has dipped a little lower than it has in the past and profits have followed. Management believe they understand the reasons for this and are not overly concerned because the Sales and Marketing people confidently assert that they can still make plan if Engineering can meet the revised product release schedule and, even though the ExpCR has hit the floor management previously set for themselves (ExpCR = 1.4), they carry on with their spending plans on all fronts.

Time 4 Profits have clearly declined and haven't turned up as "they always did." In fact the Expense Coverage Ratio (and profits) has hit a new low of 1.3. Strategies are reviewed. The management team persuades themselves that their plan is still viable; the programs simply need more time and the investments they are making will pay off, just as they always have. The board of directors is getting a little nervous. Questions are asked. Management reminds everyone of their track record. Their pitch is: "Trust us." Minor adjustments are made but spending continues more or less as before.

Time 5 The new products have been released and the factory can deliver but revenues have still not turned up. Profits have reached a dangerously low and unprecedented level. The Expense Coverage Ratio has plunged below 1.3 and the operating environment is clearly uncomfortable. During times of uncertainty, the natural tendency is to latch onto every positive sign. (In fact, people are amazingly capable of sometimes finding them even when they don't exist.) The management team looks hard for good news but is pressed to find any. The problem is that by deferring decisions and counting on revenue to come bouncing back they have placed themselves in a tough position. After much agonizing and discussion, they realize that they have two options: (1) Take the hard decisions now and cut back on spending, or (2) fine tune their strategies, make minor adjustments to spending, and hope they are right.

Option 1 requires that management revise their business model and adjust sooner as opposed to later to the new environment. Option 2 offers hope and therefore is very tempting. The problem is that if they are wrong, they will have further depleted the company's resources and be faced with tougher decisions that have serious consequences. The bottom line is that imprudent management has taken the Company into troubled waters and it is now faced with numerous serious issues.

Time 6 and Onward Regardless of the choice, it will take time for the Company's fortunes to recover. The best that can be hoped for is that actions taken after Time 5 will be sufficient to reverse the adverse trend and things will begin to turn around and profits be restored.

Working your way out of a misery zone is at least a quadruple-whammy! First, you don't have the luxury of throwing money at the top line. Second, you have to cut deep to make sure that costs are sufficiently curtailed to commence the beginning of the turnaround. Third, you have a demoralized workforce on your hands who seriously question management's ability to lead them out of the mess. Fourth, you are now focused on survival instead of value added and have set the stage for your competitors to have a field day at your expense.

How Could Things Have Been Different?

Please refer to Figure 8-2.

Time 3 When the Expense Coverage Ratio hit a new low, prudent management could have faced up to the fact that something was wrong. Perhaps they had failed to recognize

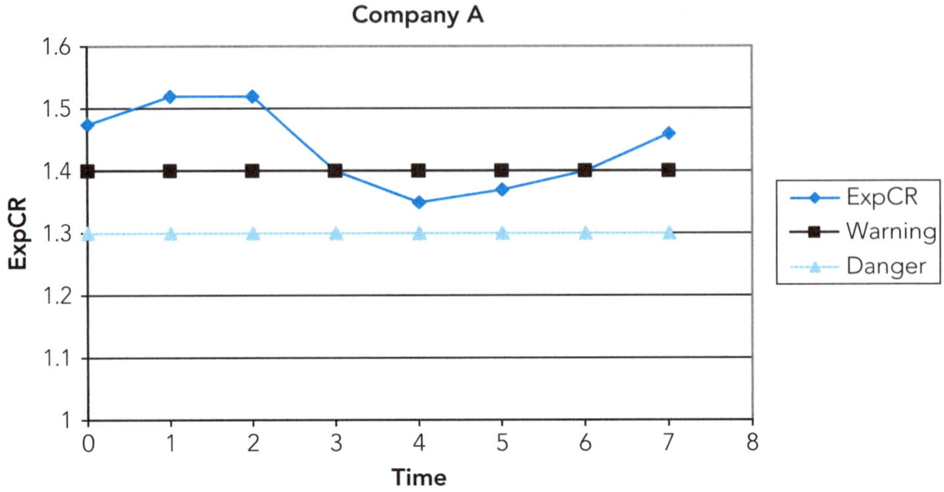

FIGURE 8-2 Different Expense Coverage Ratio Trend for Company A

that developing products in an adjacent market required a different strategy and more effort than originally planned. They could have reminded themselves that despite good implementation, when things aren't proceeding according to plan, either the assumptions are wrong or the environment has changed. Either way, they should have conceded that the risk/reward profile for the current rate of investment had become adverse and worked hard identifying what had changed and prepared a menu of actions they could take under the circumstances.

What actions could they have taken? For starters, they could have made a careful review of what was happening in the marketplace and how it compared to what they were doing. Were they managing by the facts, emotion, or worse yet, arrogance based on past successes? With this information and resolve, management could have identified why the business model they were following was failing and identify the changes they need to make in strategy as well as make a review of the state of the company's controls, systematization, and cost structure and ultimately focus on abolishing non-value-added activities. This would restore profitability by once again having a match between what they were spending their money on and what the customer was willing to pay for.

Time 4 and Afterward Had management had the courage to act sooner they would have been able to leave more resources in place, the Expense Coverage Ratio and profits would have turned around earlier, and the company's employees would have been able to get on with the task of capturing market share in the adjacent product area as opposed to living to fight another day. Thus, they could once again resume the mission of creating value for their customers and a better future for the company and all of its stakeholders.

Some Practical Aspects

While the material just covered is somewhat hypothetical, it is based on the author's experience in managing niche-oriented technology companies. The so-called ExpCR thresholds ("warning" and "danger zones") were largely applicable to these companies but may not be for other companies in other industries. For example, a reseller with a gross margin of 30% and OpExp of 15% (ExpCR = 2) would not consider letting the ExpCR deteriorate to 1.4 let alone 1.3 before taking action. The point is: The ExpCR thresholds described as warning and danger zones are different for every industry and may be for every management team. The important thing is for management to know when enough is enough and take actions to correct a decline in the ExpCR.

There is no literature that I'm aware of that is helpful in establishing the ExpCR thresholds. One approach I have found useful is to measure your company's ExpCR versus the competition. For example, the warning threshold could be the median or fiftieth percentile and the danger zone the twenty-fifth percentile.

Expense Coverage Ratio and EBITDA

Hopefully, Examples 8-1 through 8-3 have been helpful in making the case for the value of the thinking behind the Expense Coverage Ratio and the model as a supplemental tool for managing a company. One of the assertions that has been made is that by managing the ratio, you are also managing the company's profitability. The following is intended to present the basis for the close correlation between ExpCR and EBITDA.

Earlier, the ExpCR was defined as

$$ExpCR = \frac{Gross\ Margin}{Operating\ Expenses} \qquad [8\text{-}3]$$

Recalling Equation [8-2],

$$EBITDA = Gross\ Margin - Operating\ Expenses \qquad [8\text{-}2]$$

Equation [8-3] can be rearranged so that

$$Gross\ Margin = (ExpCR)(Operating\ Expenses) \qquad [8\text{-}5]$$

Substituting the results of Equation [8-5] into Equation [8-2], an expression for EBITDA in terms of the ExpCR and Operating Expenses (OpExp) is obtained.

$$EBITDA = (ExpCR)\ (Operating\ Expenses) - (Operating\ Expenses) \qquad [8\text{-}6]$$

Factoring,

$$EBITDA = (Operating\ Expenses)\ (ExpCR - 1) \qquad [8\text{-}7]$$

Similarly, an expression for EBITDA in terms of the ExpCR and Gross Margin can be derived by once more rearranging Equation [8-3]

$$Operating\ Expenses = \frac{Gross\ Margin}{ExpCR} \tag{8-8}$$

and substituting the result in Equation [8-2].

$$EBITDA = Gross\ Margin - \frac{Gross\ Margin}{ExpCR} \tag{8-9}$$

Factoring,

$$EBITDA = (Gross\ Margin)\left(1 - \frac{1}{ExpCR}\right) \tag{8-10}$$

Equation [8-10] describes the relationship between Earnings before Interest, Taxes, Depreciation and Amortization (EBITDA) and the Expense Coverage Ratio for any level of gross margin. Figure 8-3 is a plot of a family of curves for gross margins from 30% to 65% and EBITDA. While curves could be plotted for any GM, this range encompasses actual gross margins achieved by a wide variety of businesses. Figure 8-4 permits one to estimate EBITDA for a business if you know the gross margin and ExpCR.

Example 8-4: Calculating EBITDA from Gross Margin and the ExpCR

Company X has a Gross Margin of 40% and ExpCR = 1.6. Company Y has a GM and ExpCR of 60% and 1.5, respectively. Company Z, which is in a more difficult business and isn't especially well positioned, has a GM = 30% and an ExpCR = 1.2. What are the estimated EBITDAs for these companies? The answer to this question can be obtained by referring to Figure 8-3.

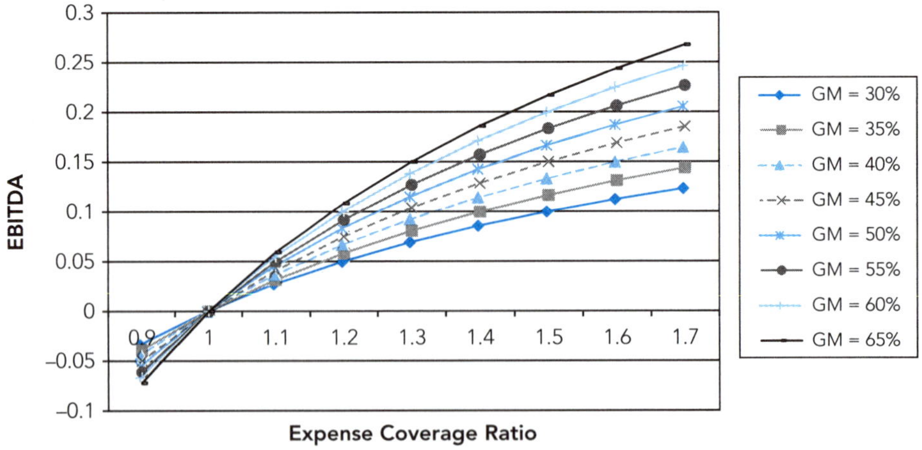

FIGURE 8-3 EBITDA versus Expense Coverage Ratio for Various GMs

Starting at ExpCR = 1.6 on the *x*-axis and moving up until it intersects with the curve for GM = 40% and then reading across to the *y*-axis, the EBITDA for Company X is found to be 15%. Similarly, Company Y's EBITDA is 20%, and Company Z is struggling at the 5% level.

Likewise, Equation [8-7] describes the relationship between EBITDA and the Expense Coverage Ratio for any level of operating expenses. Figure 8-4 is a plot of a family of curves for operating expenses from 10% to 45%. The operating expenses for many companies would fall within this range. Having said that, it's important to realize that OpExp = 10% may be too low to qualify for this kind of statement but is included to make a particular point that is illustrated in Example 8-5.

Example 8-5: Calculating EBITDA from Operating Expenses and the ExpCR

A private investor has been looking for a company that doesn't have a lot of overhead or expenses. His rationale is that if costs are inherently low, "I can simply price to market and make money." A business broker brings to his attention a company that he knows of that is profitable. He doesn't know the exact level of profitability but is certain that the operating expenses are in the range of 10%. With only this information, how does the investor decide if this company's gross margin is attractive and if this company is worth spending any time investigating?

Fortunately, the investor has Figures 8-3 and 8-4 at his disposal. First he refers to Figure 8-4 and notices that at Expense Coverage Ratios of 1.3, 1.4, 1.5, and 1.6, the EBITDA is 3, 4, 5, and 6% respectively. Next he refers to Figure 8-3 and finds there isn't any gross margin curve that covers EBITDAs in the range of 3–6% with ExpCRs of 1.3 to 1.6 respectively and that if he were to plot such a curve, the gross margin would be considerably less than 30%. This confirms his fear that this may be a very-low-gross-margin business.

The private investor recalls that

$$EBITDA = Gross\ Margin - Operating\ Expenses \qquad [8\text{-}2]$$

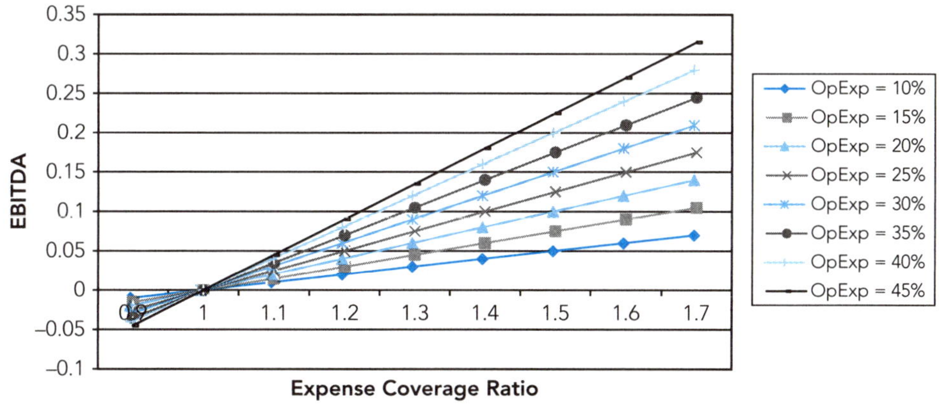

FIGURE 8-4 EBITDA versus Expense Coverage Ratio for Various OpExp

which he promptly rearranges in the form of Equation [8-11],

$$Gross\ Margin = EBITDA + Operating\ Expenses \quad [8\text{-}11]$$

and calculates that if operating expenses are 10% and EBITDA is in the range of 3–6%, then the gross margin for this company is most likely in the range of 13–16%.

The expression "most likely" is important because it presumes that the range for the Expense Coverage Ratio he used was reasonable. His view is that an ExpCR = 1.6 is the very best a company like this could achieve and he doesn't want to get involved in a business with an ExpCR ≤ 1.3. This process leads him to conclude that the margin in this business is just too thin and there isn't any room for error and he decides not to pursue the opportunity further.

From this example, it can be seen that with only one number (Operating Expenses = 10%) and some business experience, the Expense Coverage Ratio model is a powerful tool.

Managing ExpCR Is Also Managing EBITDA

Now that it has been demonstrated that the ExpCR, GM, OpExp, and EBITDA are all tied inextricably together, the next step is to proceed and demonstrate that if a company manages its ExpCR, it is also managing its EBITDA.

Figure 8-5 was created by first using Equation [8-3] to determine the values of the ExpCR for various gross margins with the operating expenses fixed at an arbitrarily chosen level of 40% (Equation [8-12]),

$$ExpCR = \frac{Gross\ Margin}{Operating\ Expenses} \quad [8\text{-}3]$$

$$ExpCR = \frac{Gross\ Margin}{40\%} \quad [8\text{-}12]$$

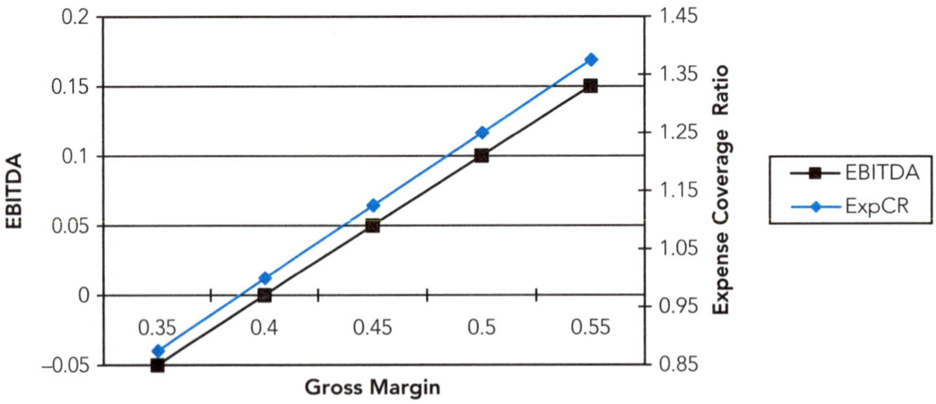

FIGURE 8-5 EBITDA and ExpCr versus GM (Operating Expenses = 40%)

and then using Equation [8-2] to calculate values of EBITDA for the same range of values of gross margin with the operating expenses also fixed at 40% ([8-13]).

$$EBITDA = Gross\ Margin - Operating\ Expenses \quad [8\text{-}2]$$

$$EBITDA = Gross\ Margin - 40\% \quad [8\text{-}13]$$

The important thing to observe is that as the Expense Coverage Ratio increases, so does the EBITDA. The fact that the two curves almost fall on each other is simply a consequence of the value chosen for the EBITDA axis on the left and the ExpCR axis on the right. Any notion that the slopes of the two curves are congruent is dispelled by reference to Figure 8-6, where it can be seen that the slope of the ExpCR curve is 2.5, versus 1.0 for EBITDA.

Furthermore, anyone who takes the time to plot another set of curves can show that the result is the same for other levels of operating expenses.

Figure 8-7 is more of the same except that Equations [8-3] and [8-2] were used to obtain values for the ExpCR and EBITDA for a range of values of operating expenses with the gross margin fixed at 40%. Or specifically,

$$ExpCR = \frac{40\%}{Operating\ Expenses} \quad [8\text{-}14]$$

$$EBITDA = 40\% - Operating\ Expenses \quad [8\text{-}15]$$

Again, Figure 8-7 shows that EBITDA closely tracks the Expense Coverage Ratio.

In summary, if management understands the rationale behind the Expense Coverage Ratio model and manages the ratio, they are also managing the company's EBITDA and therefore ultimately the company's Net Income and Cash Flow.

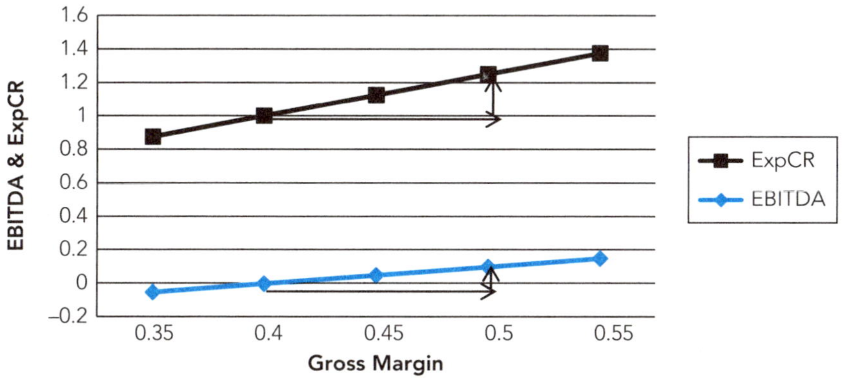

FIGURE 8-6 EBITDA and ExpCR versus Gross Margin (Operating Expenses = 40%)

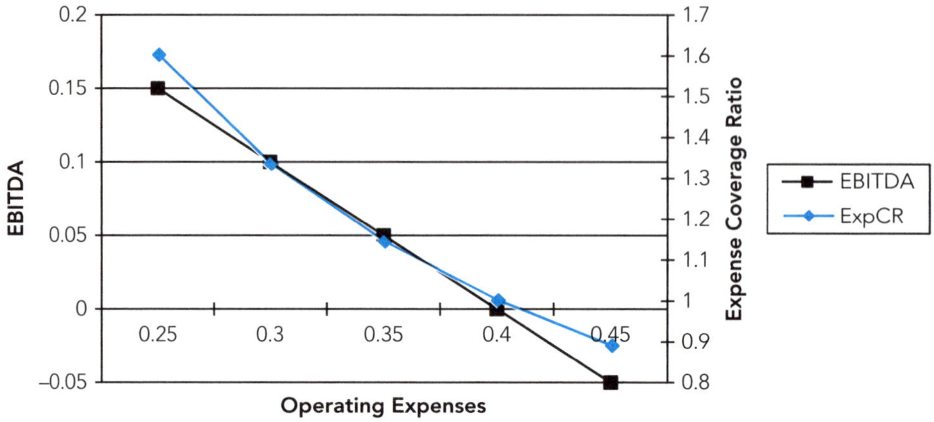

FIGURE 8-7 EBITDA and ExpCR versus OpExp (Gross Margin = 40%)

Development of the ExpCR over Time

Management's overall objective should be to conduct the business in such a way that the ExpCR is on a relatively smooth upward trend in growth companies as illustrated in Figure 8-8 and at least level in more mature businesses. While Figure 8-8 is highly idealistic, it illustrates the point that while every company is different, the ExpCR can move around and this is not necessarily a bad thing because the important issue is the trend. Also, history shows that when performance like this is achieved, the Company will consistently deliver great profits and performance during good times and satisfactory profits and cash flow during the difficult periods in the business cycle.

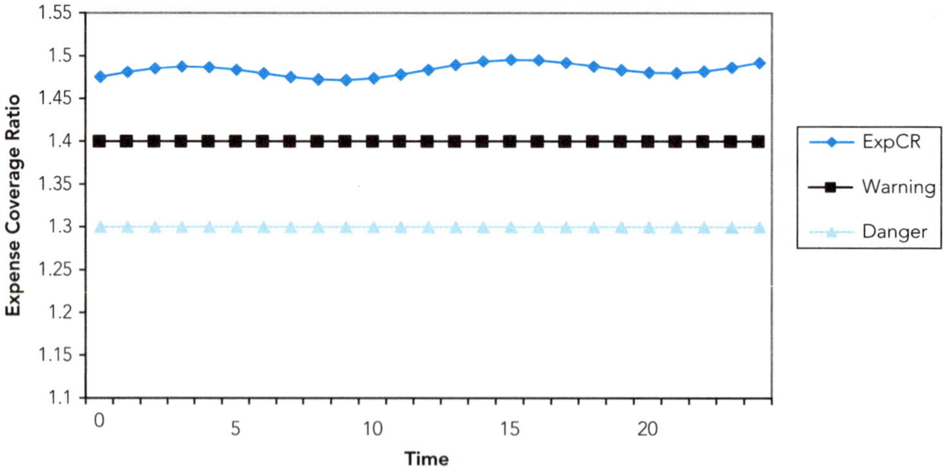

FIGURE 8-8 Expense Coverage Ratio Variation Over Time

Good Management Practices and the ExpCR Model

The beauty of the Expense Coverage Ratio model is that it forces management to continually focus on price, investments, and expenses simultaneously as opposed to a common scenario where attention moves sequentially from one area to another. The following guidelines are intended to help management teams derive maximum benefit from the model.

Disciplines of a Healthy Company

The management of a healthy company will have the courage to subject itself to the following:

- Get the match right between what the customer is willing to pay (as reflected in the gross margin) and how the company is spending money (operating expenses).
- Invest in Sales, Marketing, Service and Customer Support, R&D, and Administration while keeping in mind the customer won't pay for inefficient or indulgent expenditures.
- Design the investment programs so they have low-cost exit strategies. Fixed costs or high termination costs should be avoided wherever possible, at least until the viability of the investment has been demonstrated. Extraordinary efforts should be made to minimize long-term commitments and to look for opportunities to outsource even if they are more expensive.
- Constantly and critically review changing customer needs and market conditions.
- Judiciously monitor the progress and continuing relevance of all investment projects, including sanity checks on the match between the objectives of an investment program and the needs to be served.
- Step back and take actions to restore the relationship between gross margin and operating expenses, especially when an investment has failed to produce the intended result or market conditions have changed.
- If your management team can't quantify what constitutes excellent performance, ask your customers.

Learn as you go

While much of what goes on in business is highly quantifiable, the outcomes associated with most ventures are highly qualitative and uncertain. Therefore, judgment often turns out to be the most important factor in making a decision. Good judgment comes from experience. Experience comes from making bad decisions. Consequently it's important to keep in mind that you are engaged in a process of trying to do things and learning from the outcomes. Stay close to what is going on, focus on getting the most out of what's working, fix or cut your losses on what's not, learn a lesson, and get on with something else.

Beware of Expense Coverage Ratio Drift

Things are often not what they seem. You have to be vigilant and make sure you understand what's really happening in your business. It's easy to think all is well with the business when you have a high ExpCR. A company with a ratio of 1.6 or 1.5 will

TABLE 8-4 Expense Coverage Ratio Drift

1.60	Good profits, good times.
1.55	Profits have weakened but still healthy.
1.50	Something is happening! Strategy may not be working? Wakeup call.
1.40	Something is terribly wrong given the 20-point decline!
1.30	Company is in trouble. Difficult times ahead.
1.20	Heading for losses and management changes.

certainly be delivering good profits; 1.4 will also probably be satisfactory. However, if you have consistently been in the range of 1.6 or 1.55 and you dip to 1.5, this should send a strong wakeup call. Table 8-4 is intended to illustrate this point.

Frequently Reevaluate the Businesses You Are In

In this context, a business can be a product line, service, or stand-alone unit. The important question to ask is: "Is this a business that you would get into today"? If it isn't, plan to sell, rejuvenate, or operate as a cash cow.

- If "sell" is the decision, then obviously a strategic buyer is your first choice (i.e., a company that has a high need for the business and the synergy opportunities it presents that will induce the company to pay an attractive price). Second choice should probably be a financial buyer, preferably a group that is trying to build a platform involving the space your business occupies. If you can't find arm's-length buyers prepared to pay an acceptable price, then consider selling to management.
- If "rejuvenation" is the course of action, then you have to be prepared to invest and give this business careful attention and loads of management time. If you are not prepared to do both of these things, reconsider this decision.
- If "cash cow" ends up being the most sensible path to follow, manage for cash and be prepared to live with the consequences. Don't take half-measures. You are either managing for cash or you are not. This doesn't mean the business is headed for the scrap-heap. You can still invest in the business but from a different perspective. In this mode you are trying to maximize cash flow, and top-line growth while still important will probably ultimately slow down as investments taper off.
- Revenue and profits don't have to taper off when operating a company for cash flow. One strategy that has worked well for many companies is acquiring bolt-on companies or product lines. This model has the corporate development folks searching the marketplace for companies with complementary product lines serving the same space. The object is to fold the acquired company or product line into the acquirer's operations and eliminate duplicative manufacturing and operating expenses.

Alignment

It's okay to be out of alignment—a mismatch between what your customers are willing to pay for and how you are spending money on servicing this need—as long as you know why you choose to be in this state of affairs. For example, it's entirely possible that you could want to keep a high service level capability in the Customer Service department pending the release of a new product.

High-Risk Projects

The management team needs to consider high-risk ventures at times if it wants to target higher returns and/or growth rates. Don't take on high-risk projects unless: (1) the company is financially positioned to do so or (2) everyone clearly understands that you may be betting the business and wants to make the bet. You can be sure that things won't go as planned and at some point your bottom line will likely take a licking. At such times some people have memory loss and you may find yourself alone and out on a limb. The better answer is to have a strong Balance Sheet and cash flow so that management can pursue these opportunities when they arise with adequate runway to see them through to success or abandonment. To do this you need both a high ExpCR and a team that knows how to manage the process. Otherwise, absent a betting mentality, the impact on the bottom line will scare you off or result in funding that doesn't really give the project a chance and ultimately results in premature abandonment.

Strategy, Board Support, and Financing

Strategies that don't have the support of the board of directors and the necessary financial resources to support them are bound to fail. Put differently, you need to have board support and the project financing they control if you want to be sure you can stay the course and give your strategy a chance to prove itself one way or the other. Board backing is built on credibility. Credibility develops when you do what you say you will do and consistently produce good results and few surprises.

Infrastructure

Try as you may, you won't get everything right—especially in a high-growth situation. Continuing to overload the systems or forcing them to do things they were never intended to do will ultimately result in a loss of control and when that happens you are in real trouble. Investments in infrastructure are like any other investment and need to be done at the right time by competent people with clear and executable objectives. There will be instances when infrastructure investments compete with product investments. A very human response is either "do both," or "infrastructure will have to wait." It isn't necessarily a bad thing to do both if you have both the money and management talent. If you only have the money, you are going to waste it if you go ahead. It's something like climbing a mountain without first getting in top physical condition. At some point you will wish you never started, but by then everyone will be aware of your failure if you turn back and so you put yourself in a position of being compelled to press on.

When you don't have the systems, procedures, and people necessary to keep the business running efficiently, you should change pace until you can get the infrastructure in place. As difficult as making such a decision may seem to be at the time, your employees will thank you and the marketplace will reward you if you have the courage to do the right thing.

It takes time to do things right. It takes longer when you shortchange the process.

CONCLUSION

The material in this chapter emphasizes the need to price the deliverable properly and manage the operating expenses so there is a match between what the customer is paying for (gross margin) and how the company is spending money. In addition to proper pricing and in real life, the gross margin is also highly dependent on the Cost of Goods Sold, volume, and changes in mix. The case study that follows incorporates all the factors that impact gross margin and operating expenses and builds on the concepts presented in this chapter.

CASE STUDY: SAFETY SOLUTIONS CORPORATION

Safety Solutions Corporation (SSC) is a supplier of safety equipment and solutions to a wide variety of industries. At one end of the spectrum, they service the auto industry and their special-purpose vehicles and at the other end they provide high-tech solutions to manufacturers in the construction equipment, aerospace, and rolling stock industries.

Corporate governance has been part of the Company's culture for many years, resulting in a professionally managed business with a non-executive chairman presiding over the board and a CEO running the business. SSC is a family-owned business that takes its role as custodians of an iconic business very seriously and for some time has been more concerned about preservation than profit. The outcome of this passive approach has been a gradual decrease in operating margin. The Company has been professionally managed for many years and very few family members have worked in the business. The family has not been satisfied with the performance of the business for several years and so they encouraged family members to broaden their horizons and work in different industries with the hope that a family member with the prerequisite smarts, business experience, and acumen would eventually take a leadership role in the business. Ultimately, the strategy paid off when the board recognized the contribution Steve Gradson was making and appointed him lead director.

The Company Installs a New Chairman

For some time, Steve had been concerned that the chair and CEO were not working well together. The chairman was a retired high-profile executive who had views on everything and almost always considered them to be right. While he didn't use a gavel, his style was rigid and confrontational. The CEO, on the other hand, was a seasoned executive at the prime of his career with great experience and leadership qualities. Given this talent, Steve was determined to find out why the Company wasn't better managed.

As a first step in his new role, he decided to sit down with each of the directors and get their candid views on why the Company wasn't performing up to expectations. Without exception the board members felt the root of the problem started with the chair, who they all felt was overbearing and inclined to meddle in the business, and this was exacerbated by a very talented CEO who wouldn't push back. After thinking about what he had learned, Steve called a family meeting and presented his findings and recommendation. After much discussion the family bought into his plan and gave him their complete support.

Step one was to bring the board up to date on his thinking. Step two was to meet with the chairman and inform him that the board would not support his reelection at the end of his current term. The chair took this as a vote of no-confidence and offered to resign immediately. Steve stated that he didn't want the chair to depart under a cloud and suggested that he announce his retirement, work with him during the transition, and exit at the end of the current term as chairman emeritus. Steve went on to say that he would ask the board to pass a resolution confirming the designation.

The third step was to have a frank discussion with the CEO. Steve explained that the chairman would be retiring and that he would assume that position and as chair he would focus on managing the board and expected the CEO to run the business and dramatically improve its performance. He went on to explain that time was of the essence and that if the CEO was to continue running the company, he would have to demonstrate very quickly that he was able to improve the company's financial performance. The CEO was elated by the news and a new partnership was formed.

LTM Income Statement

At their first meeting, Steve made it very clear that managing the company was the responsibility of the CEO. The board of directors were there to monitor the performance of the company as compared to the strategic plan and peer companies, participate in the development of strategy, oversee risk management, and make sure talent development is getting adequate attention. As chair, his role was to make sure that both constituencies did their jobs. Also, he pointed out that at his request the CFO prepared a last-twelve-month (LTM) Income Statement (Table CS 8-1) and suggested that it would be very helpful if the CEO would explain what was behind the numbers.

The CEO began by saying that Net Revenues had never been a problem since they had grown at a double-digit rate for many years. He went on to explain that the real problem was the thin gross margin and operating expenses required to support the Net Revenue. The chairman asked, "If it's as simple as this, why haven't you and your management team fixed the problems?"

The CEO responded, "I have to take responsibility for that because I allowed myself to be overly influenced by our previous chair, who incidentally had the support of the board and was completely focused on growth. In response to this thrust we greatly

TABLE CS 8-1 Safety Solutions LTM Income Statement

Last Twelve Months Income Statement $(000)'s and %		
Net Revenues	460,250	100.0%
Cost of Goods Sold (COGS)	(311,129)	–67.6%
Gross Margin (GM)	149,121	32.4%
Sales, Marketing and Service (S,M & S)	44,644	9.7%
Research & Development (R & D)	27,615	6.0%
Administration (Admin)	45,105	9.8%
Total Operating Expenses (OpExp)	(117,364)	–25.5%
Earnings Before Interest, Taxes & D&A (EBITDA)	31,757	6.9%
Depreciation and Amortization (D&A)	(9,205)	–2.0%
Earnings Before Interest and Taxes (EBIT)	22,552	4.9%
Interest	0	0.0%
Earnings Before Taxes (EBT)	22,552	4.9%
Taxes Paid (TaxesPaid) @ 40%	(9,021)	–2.0%
Net Income (NI)	13,531	2.9%

expanded the number of SKUs,[5] and the expenses required to support them, and engaged in marginal costing to keep the Net Revenues growing."

Steve asked the CEO to explain what was meant by "marginal costing." The CEO said: "The concept is very simple. It assumes that the overhead in the company is carried by the existing products and services and that any new products or services only have to carry their incremental costs."

"Ah," said Steve, "now I'm starting to get it. What you are really saying is that we have a mismatch between our gross margin and operating expenses, and if this is so, we need to understand the drivers of the mismatch."

The Expense Coverage Ratio and an EBITDA Improvement Plan

The CEO concurred so the question was where to start. After thinking about the problem for some time, he concluded that since gross margin and operating expenses were the problem they both had to be addressed, but the classical way of arbitrarily increasing prices and slashing costs was at best a short-run solution. He wanted a more rational approach. He reasoned that customers were prepared to pay for value and expected the company to make a profit. So the customers weren't the problem. In fact, looking at the gross margin and operating expenses from the customer's

[5]*Stock keeping unit* (SKU) is a distinct item with a unique number such as a product or service that distinguishes it from all others.

perspective could well provide insight into how to address the problem in a logical way and equip him to present his plan to the chair and the management team in a compelling fashion that would result in enthusiastic execution. As he was pondering this thought, he recalled a paper he has seen on something called the Expense Coverage Ratio, which his administrative assistant promptly found. After rereading the business article he decided to approach his problem using the theory underlying this model.

He began by calculating the current Expense Coverage Ratio (Equation [8-3]) using the data in Table CS 8-1.

$$ExpCR = \frac{Gross\ Margin}{Operating\ Expenses} \qquad [8\text{-}3]$$

$$ExpCR = \frac{Gross\ Margin}{Operating\ Expenses} = \frac{149{,}121{,}000}{117{,}364{,}000} = 1.27$$

Since the CEO was having trouble understanding the significance of an ExpCR = 1.27 he decided to see if the chair could shed any light on the subject.

The Company had never really paid much attention to the ExpCR and so it took a few moments for the new chair to recognize the significance of the number. He said, "As you may be aware, in my previous life I worked in a number of businesses. Now that I think about the kind of gross margins and operating expenses they had I don't recall one that had an ExpCR below 1.5 and so I just have to believe that 1.27 is unusually low."

The CEO's response was: "While we haven't used the ExpCR as a measure of the health of our business I can tell you that managing a business with an ExpCR of 1.27 is a real struggle and if where you are headed is for SSC to develop a strategy and action plan to get us to 1.5 or better, I can tell you our management team is on board." He concluded by saying, "Give us two weeks and we will come back to you with a plan."

EBITDA Improvement Plan

As promised, two weeks later the CEO and his team presented Tables CS 8-2, CS 8-3 , and CS 8-4 to the chairman.

The CEO began by saying, "As you can see from Tables CS 8-2 and CS 8-3, the management team has come up with a plan to increase the Company's EBITDA from 6.9% to 16.9% by increasing the ExpCR from 1.27 to 1.6." The chair was very impressed but before he could give the plan his blessing he needed to understand the reasoning behind the various scenarios and asked the CEO to elaborate.

Discussion of the Plan

"I would be glad to," he replied. "But before we get into an explanation of the various scenarios, I need to say a few words about Tables CS 8-2 and

TABLE CS 8-2 Safety Solutions Income Statement for Various Scenarios $(000)'s and %

Scenario	1		2		3		4		5	
	LTM		DS DecSKU's 10%		DS & IP IncPrice 5%		DS, IP, IncD&A CutAdm 20%		DS, IP, IDA, CA, RedCOGS IncR&D 50%	
Net Rev	460,250	100.0%	414,225	100.0%	434,936	100.0%	434,936	100.0%	434,936	100.0%
COGS	311,129	67.6%	259,305	62.6%	272,270	62.6%	272,270	62.6%	239,215	55.0%
GM	149,121	32.4%	154,920	37.4%	162,666	37.4%	162,666	37.4%	195,721	45.0%
S,M & S	44,644	9.7%	44,644	10.8%	44,644	10.3%	44,644	10.3%	44,644	10.3%
R & D	27,615	6.0%	27,615	6.7%	27,615	6.3%	27,615	6.3%	41,423	9.5%
Admin	45,105	9.8%	45,105	10.9%	45,105	10.4%	36,084	8.3%	36,084	8.3%
OpExp	117,364	25.5%	117,364	28.3%	117,364	27.0%	108,343	24.9%	122,150	28.1%
EBITDA	31,757	6.9%	37,556	9.1%	45,302	10.4%	54,323	12.5%	73,571	16.9%
D & A	9,205	2.0%	9,205	2.2%	9,205	2.1%	11,205	2.6%	11,205	2.6%
EBIT	22,552	4.9%	28,351	6.8%	36,097	8.3%	43,118	9.9%	62,366	14.3%
Interest	0	0.0%	0	0.0%	0	0.0%	0	0.0%	0	0.0%
EBT	22,552	4.9%	28,351	6.8%	36,097	8.3%	43,118	9.9%	62,366	14.3%
Taxes	9,021	2.0%	11,341	2.7%	14,439	3.3%	17,247	4.0%	24,946	5.7%
NI	13,531	2.9%	17,011	4.1%	21,658	5.0%	25,871	5.9%	37,420	8.6%

TABLE CS 8-3 Safety Solutions Expense Coverage Ratio for Various Scenarios

Scenario	LTM	Eliminate 10% SKUs	Increase Price +5%	Cut Admin –20%	Inc R & D +50%
ExpCR	1.27	1.32	1.39	1.50	1.60

CS 8-4. If you look carefully at these tables, you will note that each scenario builds on the previous one. For example, Scenario 3 incorporates the benefit of decreasing the number of SKUs by 10% and increasing prices by 5%, hence the notation 'DS & IP.' Similarly, Scenario 4 includes the benefits of decreasing the number of SKUs by 10%, increasing price by 5%, as well as allowing for the increase in Depreciation and Amortization (IDA) and cutting administration expenses by 20% (DS, IP, IDA, & CA). Finally, Scenario 5 (DS, IP, IDA, CA, RedCOGS, & IR&D) incorporates all of the activities contemplated in Scenario 4 plus a focus on increasing gross margin by a 50% increase in R&D expenses, which results in a 12.6 percentage point improvement (62.6% – 55%) in the Cost of Goods Sold. Finally, none of the scenarios contemplate any revenue growth."

TABLE CS 8-4 Income Statement Scenarios for Safety Solutions

Scenario	Acronym	Comment/Assumptions
1	LTM	Last 12 months
2	DS	Decrease SKUs 10%
3	DS and IP	Decrease SKUs 10% Increase Prices 5%
4	DS, IP, IDA, and CA	Decrease SKUs 10% Increase Prices 5% Increase D & A Cut Admin Costs 20%
5	DS, IP, IDA, CA, RedCOGS, and IncR&D	Decrease SKUs 10% Increase Prices 5% Increase D & A Cut Admin Costs 20% Reduce COGS 12.6% Increase R & D 50%

SKUs, Scenario 2

Continuing, the CEO said, "Let's start with the SKU scenario. During our first meetings I mentioned that our explosion in SKUs came about as part of our strategy to drive the top line. I was always a little uncomfortable with this strategy because, while I was certain the direct costing was correct, I wasn't convinced that the marginal pricing model we were using included all of the incremental expenses."

The chair asked, "What does that mean?"

"It means that every product represented by an SKU requires some support from R&D, manufacturing engineering, quality engineering, sales, marketing, admin, and often service. The problem was that the market for these SKUs seemed to have a price cap and so every time we tried to pass the support costs along, our volume decreased notably. So as part of this exercise, I had a taskforce look at all of our SKUs and compare the selling price to fully burdened costs and what they found was that about 30% of our products lost money according to this analysis. These SKUs were further dissected and what we found was over half were priced below market and the remainder represented about 10% of our Net Revenues. The message seemed to be that our customers placed little if any value on the products that constituted 10% of our revenue, so we decided to run a scenario without these SKUs. The result was a decrease in Net Revenue, an increase in GM percentage, an ExpCR of 1.32, and a first step toward focusing on those products to which our customers ascribed value."

$$ExpCR = \frac{Gross\ Margin}{Operating\ Expenses} = \frac{154{,}920{,}000}{117{,}364{,}000} = 1.32$$

Pricing, Scenario 3

"Next we systematically took a look at the pricing of the products that constituted 80% of our Net Revenue. Once again the results were illuminating. We found that these were high-value-added products, some of which were underpriced relative to market, and our prices didn't support the OpExp that we need to keep in place to meet the customer's needs. The outcome of these exercises was that numerous products were underpriced by as much as 25%. After taking a weighted average of the contemplated price increases we concluded playing the price card would have a net impact of +5 to +7% on Net Revenue with negligible impact on unit volume. To be conservative we decided to settle on 5%. When we ran the numbers the result was another increase in gross margin and an increase in the ExpCR to 1.39."

$$ExpCR = \frac{Gross\ Margin}{Operating\ Expenses} = \frac{162{,}666{,}000}{117{,}364{,}000} = 1.39$$

Cut Sales Marketing and Service Expenses

"We began this exercise by looking at all operating expenses. Frankly, there was and is room to trim the Sales, Marketing, and Service expenses by a point or two, but our products are sophisticated, require consultative selling, and involve a lengthy sales cycle. It's true that our products add great value to our customers. However, it's also true that our customers demand among other things 24/7 support, which incidentally is priced into the selling price, and where it hasn't been it will be when we put through the price increases we talked about earlier. While on the subject of support costs, I'm not a fan of including them in the selling price. I much prefer a user-pay approach. We talked about changing but in the end, since this would involve a major effort, it was decided to stay with what we had and consider going over to the user-pay model with our next major product launch. So our decision on this front was not to trim these expenses."

Research and Development

"Next, we looked at R&D. Here the results were rather startling. What we discovered was that our capable but passive VP of R&D had been very responsive to requests for product modifications and enhancements and was now almost totally focused on product line maintenance with little or no effort being expended in cost reduction and perhaps more importantly new products. It didn't take us long to conclude that this was no place to cut cost. If anything, there was a strong case to be made for increased R&D spending—more on this later."

Administrative Expenses

"Administrative expenses were another matter. The task force that looked at these costs was astounded by what they found. Stated simply, they concluded that our systems are not up to date and involve considerable manual effort. In addition, they couldn't find any significant areas where best practices were evident. When the report was presented at our management meeting, the CFO offered to resign. Initially, I was not inclined to accept his offer, but after thinking about it I concluded this area needed new leadership and so our VP of Human Resources is working on an exit plan, which I will present to the CFO in a few days. What the taskforce found among numerous other things was multiple general ledgers, no common database, numerous spreadsheets supporting the manual closing process, and an outdated standard costing system. Obviously, we can run our administration area as we see fit but we can't expect our customers to pay for gross inefficiencies. The bottom line is our administrative processes and financial reporting systems need to be completely reengineered and while the final figures aren't available, the first-pass indication is at least a 20% reduction can be achieved with an investment of less than \$10 million. Obviously this will have an impact on our D&A (in this model an increase of \$10,000,000/5 = \$2,000,000 per year) but frankly on a comparative basis our current D&A is about half the industry average and, as you can see, it is showing. The message is we have been under-investing here and in the Company as a whole. If we ignore the impact of additional D&A for the moment, you can see from the tables we have presented that cutting administration costs by 20% has considerable impact on our EBITDA and improves the ExpCR to 1.5, which is consistent with your experience."

$$ExpCR = \frac{Gross\ Margin}{Operating\ Expenses} = \frac{162{,}666{,}000}{108{,}343{,}000} = 1.50$$

Research and Development

"Earlier I stated that R&D was under-spending. Let me explain what I mean by that. The report presented by the team that looked into R&D costs made a number of points. First, 55% was being spent on product line maintenance. This is way too high. A more reasonable number would be 20–25%. Our customers don't expect us to be supporting releases of our products forever. In fact it turned out we were supporting products that a large number of customers were no longer using as they had migrated to later versions.

"Second, minimal effort was expended on cost reduction. This is fine for low-volume products and those that have limited life cycles but we do have some workhorses that are manufactured in sizable quantities that would justify a cost reduction effort. Third, our foray into marginal costing has resulted in considerable engineering effort being devoted to products that aren't likely to be much more than fringe players in a commodity niche of the market.

"Finally, we have a long list of product ideas that aren't getting high-priority attention. Fortunately, all of this is easily fixed, but it will take some discipline and money. And so while increasing R&D spending in the short run will adversely affect EBITDA and the ExpCR, it is absolutely essential. In this model we have assumed a

50% increase. However, this is only the beginning. We not only need to get to the 15% level but in addition keep spending at that level of Net Revenues. In the long run it will contribute to revenue, reduce the Cost of Goods Sold, increase gross margin and EBITDA, and according to our estimates will ultimately drive the gross margin to 55% and the ExpCR to 1.6."

$$ExpCR = \frac{Gross\ Margin}{Operating\ Expenses} = \frac{195{,}721{,}000}{122{,}150{,}000} = 1.60$$

The chairman needed a few moments to consider the consequences of what had just been presented. In order to buy some time, he said, "Each scenario you have presented systematically improves EBITDA and the ExpCR, and while the rationale you have provided is very clear, you haven't given any indication of the time required to do all this and what the Company's Income Statement will look like at that time."

Year 3 Income Statement

The CEO said, "We anticipated your question and would now like to draw your attention to Table CS 8-5."

TABLE CS 8-5 Safety Solutions Corporation Year 3 Income Statement $(000)'s and %

	Eliminate 10% of SKU's		Year 3		CAGR
Net Revenues	414,225	100.0%	551,333	100.0%	10.0%
Cost of Goods Sold (COGS)	(259,305)	62.6%	(248,100)	45.0%	–1.5%
Gross Margin (GM)	154,920	37.4%	303,233	55.0%	25.1%
Sales, Marketing & Service (S,M & S)	44,644	10.8%	66,160	12.0%	14.0%
Research & Development (R&D)	27,615	6.7%	77,187	14.0%	40.9%
Administration (Admin)	45,105	10.9%	44,107	8.0%	–0.7%
Total Operating Expneses (OpExp)	(117,364)	28.3%	(187,453)	34.0%	16.9%
Earnings Before Interest, Taxes & D & A (EBITDA)	37,556	9.1%	115,780	21.0%	45.5%
Depreciation and Amortization (D & A)	(9,205)	2.2%	(22,053)	4.0%	33.8%
Earnings Before Interest and Taxes (EBIT)	28,351	6.8%	93,727	17.0%	49.0%
Interest	0	0.0%	0	0.0%	
Earnings Before Taxes (EBT)	28,351	6.8%	93,727	17.0%	49.0%
Taxes Paid (TaxesPaid) @ 40.0%	(11,341)		(37,491)		
Net Income (NI)	17,011	4.1%	56,236	10.2%	49.0%
Expense Coverage Ratio	1.32		1.62		

After studying the table, Steve said: "If I understand what the table is saying, the first column is simply the last twelve months' Income Statement recast to reflect the elimination of 10% of our SKUs. The Year 3 column incorporates the impact of pricing to market to better align the support costs with the value delivered to the customer, a focused effort in R&D to cut the costs of our high-volume products with considerable life ahead of them, increased sales, marketing, and service expenditure to make sure we are delivering the support our customers expect, a big increase in R&D spending to accelerate new product development so that as our customers' needs expand we are ready to serve them with an attractive value proposition, a big reduction in administrative expenses as a percent of sales brought about by modernizing our systems and electronically eliminating manual operations wherever possible, and a near-doubling of Depreciation and Amortization as a percent of sales as a result of increased capital spending."

The CEO's response was: "Correct, but there are a couple of other notable aspects. First, our revenue will grow at a compound annual rate of 10%, which is very near our historical rate. Second, our gross margin increases from 37.4% to 55%. Third, R&D spending has been increased and administration expenses decreased to levels more consistent with our peer group. Fourth, our EBIT will more than double to 17%, which will be in the upper quartile of our peer group. Finally, once a healthy ExpCR of 1.62 is achieved, it will give us leeway to explore new opportunities without an unacceptable impact on the bottom line."

Shaking his head, Steve said: "I can't help saying what I'm thinking. Why didn't you start a program like this when you first joined us a couple of years ago?"

The CEO responded: "I tried to. I prepared a gross margin and expense reduction plan shortly after my arrival and presented it to our chairman. The response was negative. He didn't want me and the management team to be distracted from growing revenue. His comment was: 'Top-line growth is what creates value for the shareholders and when the bottom line becomes important we can get to where we need to be by cutting costs at that time.' What he said is true, but I knew that a strategy of relentlessly driving the top line with little or no regard for profit would ultimately have consequences and my day would come. So I decided to focus on our sales and marketing effort until the board took action or the strategy changed. Frankly, before you came to me I was at the point of going around my chairman to the board and, if that failed, follow up on the calls I have been getting from executive search firms. Having said that, I do understand that you may be skeptical, and if this is the case, I'm prepared to resign. In anticipation of your question, my resignation is in this envelope. However, I'm not one to walk away from a challenge and right now fixing this company is the right thing to do for the shareholders and my reputation. The choice is yours."

The next sound heard was the tearing up of paper and a comment from the chair: "You are not going anywhere; let's get to work."

PROLOGUE

Dear Steve:

While the management team was working its way through our Expense Coverage Ratio improvement plan we noticed a couple of things that we have subsequently found very useful and I thought I would pass them along to you.

First and foremost, the ExpCR turns out to be an excellent tool to use when one has a need to estimate EBITDA. All you need is the ExpCR and either the Operating Expenses or the Gross Margin. Second, the relationships that predict EBITDA by using the Expense Coverage Ratio and either Operating Expenses or Gross Margin are easy to develop. The methodology goes like this.

One starts with the definitional relationship of the Expense Coverage Ratio:

$$ExpCR = \frac{Gross\ Margin}{Operating\ Expenses} \qquad [8\text{-}3]$$

This can be rearranged as:

$$Gross\ Margin = (ExpCR)(Operating\ Expenses) \qquad [8\text{-}5]$$

Recall the widely used Income Statement definition of EBITDA:

$$EBITDA = Gross\ Margin - Operating\ Expenses \qquad [8\text{-}2]$$

Then, substituting the result of the rearranged version of the definitional equation of the Expense Coverage Ratio (Equation [8-5]) into Equation [8-2] and factoring, one gets an expression (Equation [8-6]) for EBITDA in terms of the Operating Expenses and the ExpCR.

$$EBITDA = (ExpCR)\ (Operating\ Expenses) - (Operating\ Expenses) \qquad [8\text{-}6]$$

Factoring gives a very simple expression.

$$EBITDA = (Operating\ Expenses)\ (ExpCR - 1) \qquad [8\text{-}7]$$

Similarly, an expression for *EBITDA* in terms of the *ExpCR* and *Gross Margin* is obtained by once more rearranging Equation [8-3].

$$Operating\ Expenses = \frac{Gross\ Margin}{ExpCR} \qquad [8\text{-}8]$$

Substituting the result of Equation [8-8] in Equation [8-6], canceling like terms, and factoring an expression in terms of Gross Margin and the ExpCR, Equation [8-9] is obtained,

$$EBITDA = Gross\ Margin\ - \frac{Gross\ Margin}{ExpCR} \qquad [8\text{-}9]$$

or

$$EBITDA = (Gross\ Margin)\left(1 - \frac{1}{ExpCR}\right) \qquad [8\text{-}10]$$

The simplicity and utility of Equations [8-7] and [8-10] is easily demonstrated by applying them to the LTM scenario you had prepared some time ago and summarized in Table CS 8-1. From this table, the ExpCR is calculated to be 1.27 and the Operating Expenses are noted as being \$117,364,000.

Substituting these values in Equation [8-7], the EBITDA is calculated to be:

$$EBITDA = (Operating\ Expenses)(ExpCR - 1) = (117{,}364{,}000)(1.27 - 1) = \$31{,}757{,}000$$

The same result is obtained by substituting 1.27 for the ExpCR and $149,121,000 for the Gross Margin in Equation [8-10].

$$EBITDA = (Gross\ Margin)\left(1 - \frac{1}{ExpCR}\right) = (149{,}121{,}000)\left(1 - \frac{1}{1.27}\right) = \$31{,}757{,}000$$

In addition, graphical solutions of Equations [8-7] and [8-10] turn out to be useful for predictive purposes. These are provided as attachments CS 8-1 and CS 8-2.

We hope that you will find all of this helpful.

Sincerely,
Your Management Team

PS: Thought you might like to know we are ahead of schedule and expect to be delivering the EBITDA we agreed to for Year 3 at the end of Year 2.

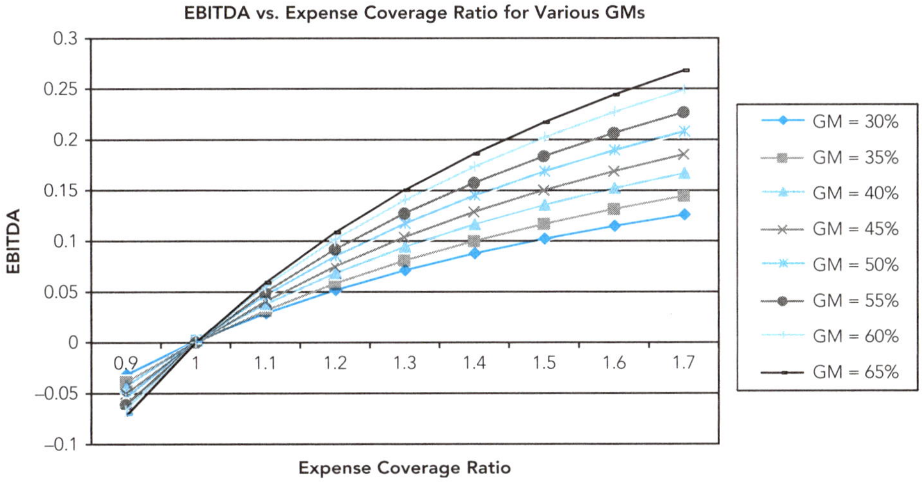

FIGURE CS 8-1 Attachment 1

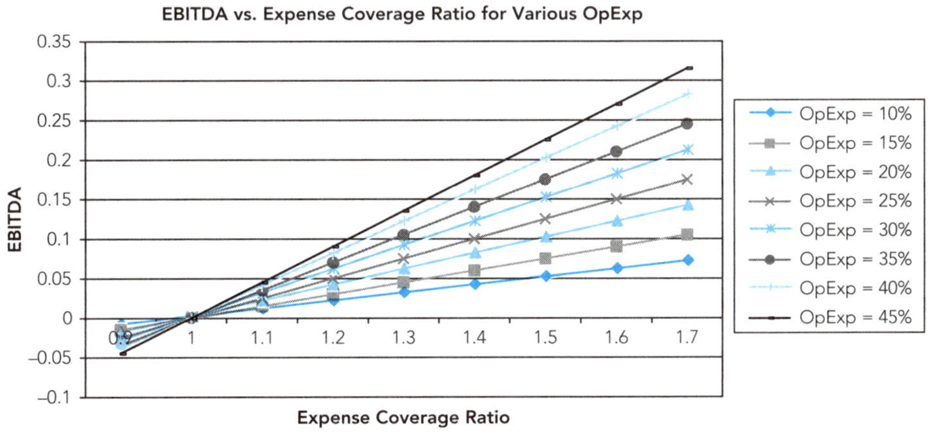

FIGURE CS 8-2 Attachment 2

CHAPTER NINE

Debt and Leverage*

CHAPTER 9 TAKEAWAYS

- Companies have essentially two sources of capital. One is equity, which it gets from shareholders, and the other is loans from lenders.
- Companies with no debt on their Balance Sheet have an *unlevered* Balance Sheet and have obtained their capital from the equity markets.
- A company that borrows money and puts debt on its Balance Sheet now has a *levered* Balance Sheet. Once a company borrows money (leveraging up the Balance Sheet) it places the company at risk of not being able to meet its obligations.
- Unlike dividends, interest payments have to be made, so taking on debt not only increases the company's risk of meeting obligations but in addition allocates a portion of its cash flow to making interest payments and repaying the debt, thus reducing the cash flow available for other purposes.
- Debt is generally less expensive than equity and is attractive because it reduces the company's weighted average cost of capital (WACC). By doing so, it reduces the hurdle rate and increases the opportunity set of investments management can consider.
- The purpose of borrowing money and leveraging the Balance Sheet is to increase the return to shareholders or the Return on Equity (ROE). It accomplishes this at the expense of the Return on Capital Employed (ROCE).
- *LIBOR* is an acronym for "London Inter-Bank Offered Rate" and it is the interest rate that banks charge each other for interbank loans.
- When the terms of a loan are negotiated, one of the most important is the interest rate the borrower will pay to the lender. Typically, the rate is LIBOR plus a number

(continued)

*The reader may notice minor discrepancies in the calculations in this chapter. When this occurs, it is the result of rounding.

of *basis points*.[1] The number of basis points the borrower pays in addition to the LIBOR rate depends on several criteria, including the creditworthiness of the company desiring to borrow the money, the security pledged (if any), the covenants and agreed-upon financial performance ratios, tenor, and priority.

- Debt financing is available in many forms, including bank revolvers and term loans, asset-based lending, private placements, institutional term loans, high-yield bonds, and mezzanine financing.
- Commercial bank financing is usually the most convenient source of debt for creditworthy lenders.
- Credit ratings are opinions about relative credit risk. They are not guarantees of credit quality or of future credit risk. In addition, they are not absolute measures of default probability because there are future events and developments that cannot be foreseen. For these and other reasons, establishing a credit rating is not an exact science.
- Credit ratings express relative opinions about the creditworthiness of an issuer or credit quality of an individual debt issue from strongest to weakest within a universe of credit risk.
- A corporate bond that is rated AA is viewed by the rating agency as having a higher credit quality than a corporate or governmental bond with a BBB rating.
- The AA rating isn't a guarantee that the issuer will not default. It is only that, in the rating agency's opinion, the AA issuer is less likely to default than the company or agency going to the capital markets with a BBB bond.
- As a general rule, the more creditworthy an issuer or an issue of debt is, the lower the interest rate the issuer would typically have to pay to attract investors. The reverse is also true: An issuer with lower creditworthiness will typically pay a higher interest rate to offset the greater credit risk assumed by investors.
- A company's creditworthiness primarily depends on the borrower's ability to generate cash flow.
- In Standard & Poor's long-term rating scale, issuers and debt issues that receive a rating of BBB– or above are generally considered by regulators and market participants to be "investment grade," while those that receive a rating lower than BBB– are generally considered to be "speculative grade."
- Lenders are essentially only concerned about two things. The first is receiving interest payments as scheduled, and the second is having the loan repaid when due. To a large extent, this depends on the borrower's ability to generate cash flow. For this reason, at least one of the covenants or financial performance ratios will involve cash flow.
- *Financial covenants:* When lenders negotiate loans with borrowers, they want to be sure the borrower's ability to meet financial obligations does not deteriorate to a level that adds undue interest or principal collection risk. To protect themselves, they require that certain financial ratios be met. They also want to know how the money they lend will be used and, therefore, may place limits on such things as dividends, capital expenditures, and acquisitions.
- Loans that meet the requirements of the covenants are considered to be "performing." Those that don't are categorized as "nonperforming." When that happens, the level of attention lenders pay to the business moves up several notches and, if bad enough, the lender will assign the loan to their "troubled asset" or "workout team."

[1] One percentage point is the equivalent of 100 basis points.

INTRODUCTION

Companies have essentially two sources of capital. One is equity, which they get from shareholders, and the other is loans from lenders. Companies with no debt on their balance sheet have an *unlevered* balance sheet and have obtained their capital from the equity markets. As you would expect, once a company borrows money and puts debt on its balance sheet it has a *levered* balance sheet. The purpose of borrowing money and leveraging the balance sheet is to increase the return to shareholders or the Return on Equity (ROE). It accomplishes this at the expense of the Return on Capital Employed (ROCE).

On one occasion, the author walked into a board meeting and encountered a spirited debate on the merits of measuring performance with ROE versus ROCE. The ROE camp maintained that shareholders were primarily concerned with the return on their investment. The ROCE people argued that management should be judged based on the returns provided on all sources of capital at their disposal. Ultimately the matter was settled when someone pointed out they both were right and that the appropriate metric to use to measure performance depends on the perspective of the interested party.

Investors are primarily interested in what is done with the capital they provide, but that doesn't mean they are disinterested in what management does with money they borrow from the bank or bondholders. Furthermore, they are very interested in how much debt a company takes on because all of this debt has priority over their investment in the event of a liquidation, and it doesn't do an investor much good to have management enhance the return on equity by borrowing so much money (leveraging up the Balance Sheet) that it places the company at risk of not being able to meet its obligations.

Stated differently, unlike dividends, interest payments have to be made, so taking on debt not only increases the company's risk of meeting obligations but in addition allocates a portion of its cash flow to making interest payments and repaying the debt and thus reducing the cash flow available for other purposes.

DEBT AND LEVERAGE

As you may recall, debt is generally less expensive than equity and is attractive because it reduces the company's weighted average cost of capital (WACC). By doing so it reduces the hurdle rate and increases the opportunity set of investments management can consider. As suggested in the Introduction, it also has an impact on the return on capital employed (ROCE) and return on equity (ROE). This chapter addresses the kinds of debt available to a company, some of the attributes of each, and the impact various capital structures have on ROCE and ROE. However, before delving into this subject matter, a discussion of LIBOR and how loans are priced is necessary.

LIBOR AND PRICING LOANS

This is an acronym for "London Inter-Bank Offered Rate." It is the interest rate that banks charge each other for interbank loans. When the terms of a loan are negotiated, one of the most important is the interest rate the borrower will pay to the lender. Typically the rate is LIBOR plus a number of *basis points*.[2] The number of basis points the borrower pays in addition to the LIBOR rate depends on several criteria, including the creditworthiness of the company desiring to borrow the money, the security pledged (if any), the covenants and agreed-upon financial performance ratios, tenor, and priority.

Pricing

If at the time the loan is negotiated, LIBOR is 1.0% and the lender requires 350 basis points to take on the risk associated with the loan, then the cost to the borrower would be 1.0% + 3.5% or 4.5%. LIBOR rates fluctuate daily but loan rates are usually fixed for periods from one month to one year.

Creditworthiness

Essentially the company's credit profile must meet standards or criteria the lender has set. These requirements can cover a wide variety of considerations ranging from attractiveness of the industry at one end of the spectrum to the borrower's track record at the other end. Once all the boxes have been checked, lenders are essentially only concerned about two things. The first is receiving interest payments as scheduled, and the second is having the loan repaid when due. To a large extent, this depends on the borrower's ability to generate cash flow. For this reason, at least one of the covenants or financial performance ratios will involve cash flow.

Security

If the borrower doesn't meet the credit standard set by the lender, then the lender may insist on the loan being secured by some asset or assets that make the lender comfortable that in the event of a default the loan will be repaid. Also, the parties in the transaction may agree to securitize the loan in return for a lower interest rate.

Covenants and Financial Performance

When a loan is negotiated, various measurements of the company's performance (in addition to making the interest payments) are agreed upon. The objective is to monitor the company's ability to continue to make interest payments and repay the loan when it becomes due. Typical financial covenants can include *debt to equity, senior leverage, total leverage, fixed charges and interest coverage ratios*, and *net-worth requirements*.[3]

Tenor

This is the length of time the borrower has before being required to repay or renew the loan and can vary from as little as 1 year to 10 years or more.

---

[2] One percentage point is the equivalent of 100 basis points.

[3] Definitions and calculating financial covenants are covered later in this chapter.

Priority

In the event of a default (the company can't make interest payments or repay its loans), the people at the bottom of the ladder are the shareholders, and they are often wiped out. Standing above them would be the mezzanine financing, and so on up to the senior lenders (usually banks and private placements), which would be repaid first from the proceeds of liquidation.

DEBT FINANCING ALTERNATIVES

Companies, private and public, have many sources of financing available to them. As will be seen, private companies tend to use bank and institutional loans to finance their operations and growth. This of course changes when their borrowing gets to a level[4] that banks and institutions aren't prepared to finance and then they go to the public market with its disclosure requirements. Public companies have access to numerous sources of financing, both equity and debt, in the public capital markets. In the following section the various debt financing alternatives are discussed.

Bank Revolver

This is the simplest type of loan. A *bank revolver* takes its name from the practice of being able to borrow when needed, then repay, and the amount repaid is available again for future borrowing. It is obtained from a bank and can be of any size with a maturity of up to five years.[5] It's only made to creditworthy companies and depending on the circumstances secured or unsecured. Major advantages include attractive interest rates, no rating by a credit agency, no amortization, and it can be repaid without penalty.

Bank Term Loan

A bank term loan may be part of the total bank lending facility, including the bank revolver. The *term loan* portion of the facility is funded to the borrower immediately and principal payments are made periodically based on an amortization schedule and the scheduled principal amount when paid to the bank is no longer available for future borrowing. Like the revolver, it's only made to creditworthy companies and depending on the circumstances secured or unsecured. Major advantages include attractive interest rates and no rating by a credit agency.

Asset-Based Lending

This type of loan is also available from banks and finance companies, but, in this case, the loan is secured by the assets that are pledged. Hence, the term *ABL* (*asset-based lending*) is used to designate this type of loan. Typical assets that are pledged are accounts

---

[4]The tipping point is in the vicinity of $1 billion.

[5]The term of this or any loan can be longer or shorter. At the time this book was written, the years quoted are typical of what lenders were offering.

receivable and inventory. Like the revolver, the loan can be of any size with a maturity of up to five years, there is no requirement for credit agency rating, and it can be repaid at any time without penalty. Portions of the loan must be repaid should assets securing the loan fall below certain required levels.

Private Placement

The lenders in this case are typically insurance companies. Typical sizes and tenors are $50–$500 million or more and between 5 and 15 years. The loan can be secured or unsecured depending on the borrower and interest rate. A rating from a credit agency is usually not required because the insurance companies have their own credit rating system. However, the borrower usually has to be of *investment grade* as determined by the lender's rating system. Usually no amortization of principal is required. Standard practice is to repay the loan in full at the end of the tenor or to renew it at market rates for another period of time. Insurance companies like to make loans and then put the documents on the shelf and collect interest. Therefore, covenant waiver is often difficult and prepayment comes with a penalty. When it comes to pricing, private placement loans are usually priced on the yield on Treasuries as opposed to LIBOR.

Institutional Term Loan

Lenders in this category are typically hedge funds or mutual funds. The minimum amount is $150–$200 million. The tenor is typically 5–7 years and the loan is generally secured with some form of collateral. Prepayments usually involve a penalty. A rating is required from a credit agency such as Standard & Poor's or Moody's. These loans are for non-investment-grade borrowers. There is usually a modest amortization schedule during the term of the loan with a significant principal payment at maturity. An advantage of this type of loan is the access the borrower has to a deep and liquid lender base. While these loans can be LIBOR based there is usually a minimum threshold.

High-Yield Bonds

As the name implies, access to this market involves higher interest rates. Lenders are typically mutual funds, insurance companies, and pension funds. Like institutional term loans, the minimum amount that can be borrowed is in the range of $150–$200 million and depending on the creditworthiness of the borrower is secured or unsecured. Ratings from a recognized rating agency are required. However, just as in the case of the institutional term loan, these loans are for non-investment-grade borrowers. Tenor is typically 7–10 years and non-callable for a period of time and, if called, usually subject to penalty. Amortization is not required. The coupon (interest rate) is higher than any of the other sources of financing discussed so far. However, even though the interest cost is higher, bonds are highly attractive because no amortization is required and they represent a source of highly flexible long-term capital. The bond markets in most countries are regulated by a government agency[6] and, therefore, require public disclosure and a registration statement.

[6]In the United States, the bond markets are regulated by the Securities and Exchange Commission (SEC).

Mezzanine Financing

This is a very expensive form of financing because, for starters, its priority is below any other form of financing and sits just above the equity holders.[7] Loan amounts can be of any size and the lenders are typically institutional investors, hedge funds, and asset managers. Tenor is typically 7–10 years and the loans are not secured. Ratings from a credit agency are not required, nor are any public disclosures. They are subject to a non-call period and, if called after the non-call period, often involve a penalty. Their advantage is that they represent a source of equity-like capital. A major disadvantage is they usually involve warrants that when exercised result in equity dilution.

High-Investment-Grade Bond Market

The discussion so far has been about debt financing that is available to both private and public companies. However, there is another very important source of debt financing and that is the *high-investment-grade bond* market. This is a huge and highly liquid source of flexible long-term capital. To access this market a company needs scale, which roughly translates into revenues in excess of $5,000,000,000 and EBITDA in the range of $1,000,000,000. Because of these requirements, this market is usually accessed by large public corporations.[8] The interest rate will depend on the rating secured from one of the credit rating agencies. The interest rate difference between AAA-rated credit and BBB can be several hundred basis points. For top-rated credits, the coupon (interest rate) can be highly attractive. Tenor is typically 10 years or more. The bonds can be callable but if so will usually involve a penalty. Amortization is generally not a requirement, although the borrower can be required to set aside funds on a periodic basis to assure the bonds will be repaid when due. This market is highly regulated by government agencies and therefore requires public disclosure and a registration statement.

CREDIT RATINGS[9]

In the discussion on the various forms of debt financing, the need for credit ratings was mentioned several times. Credit ratings are one of several tools that investors can use when making decisions about purchasing bonds and other fixed-income investments from corporations and government agencies. The purpose of this section is to give the reader some insight into what credit ratings are, and are not, who uses them, and how they may be useful to the capital markets.

---

[7] The implication of this is: In the event of a bankruptcy, banks, institutions, and bondholders are paid off before mezzanine lenders.

[8] It is also accessed by large private companies, but when doing so, the company is required to disclose financial information that hitherto may not have been public.

[9] This section is based in part on public material made available by Wells Fargo Advisors and Standard and Poor's.

What Credit Ratings Are and Are Not

Credit ratings are opinions about *relative credit risk*. They are not investment advice or buy, hold, or sell recommendations. In fact they are just one factor investors may consider in making investment decisions. Credit ratings are not indications of the market liquidity of a debt security or its price in the secondary market. Most important, they are not guarantees of credit quality or of future credit risk. In addition, they are not absolute measures of default probability because there are future events and developments that cannot be foreseen. For these and other reasons, establishing a credit rating is not an exact science.

Instead, credit ratings express relative opinions about the creditworthiness of an issuer or credit quality of an individual debt issue from strongest to weakest within a universe of credit risk. For example, a corporate bond that is rated AA is viewed by the rating agency as having a higher credit quality than a corporate or governmental bond with a BBB rating. But the AA rating isn't a guarantee that the issuer will not default. It is only that in the rating agency's opinion the AA issuer is less likely to default than the company or agency going to the capital markets with a BBB bond.

Who Uses Credit Ratings?

Companies borrow money to fund acquisitions, expansion, and/or research and development. In addition, they use debt as a means to lower their weighted average cost of capital and, as will be seen, increase their return on equity. States, cities, and other municipalities borrow money to fund public projects. Generally speaking, there are two groups of users of credit rating information: *investors* and *intermediaries*.

Investors most often use credit ratings to help assess credit risk and to compare different issuers and debt issues when making investment decisions and managing their portfolios. Individual investors, for example, may use credit ratings in evaluating the purchase of a municipal or corporate bond from a risk tolerance perspective. Institutional investors, including mutual funds, pension funds, banks, and insurance companies, often use credit ratings to supplement their own credit analysis of specific debt issues. Institutional investors may use credit ratings to establish thresholds for credit risk and investment guidelines.

Intermediaries such as investment bankers and other entities help to facilitate the flow of capital from investors to issuers of debt. They use credit ratings to benchmark the relative credit risk of different debt issues, as well as to set the initial pricing for individual debt issues they structure and to help determine the interest rate the debt issuers will pay. They may also use the credit information when making their own decisions about how to configure debt issues or different tiers of debt.

Impact of the Credit Rating on the Interest Rate

As a general rule, the more creditworthy an issuer or an issue of debt is, the lower the interest rate the issuer would typically have to pay to attract investors. The reverse is also true: An issuer with lower creditworthiness will typically pay a higher interest rate to

TABLE 9-1 General Summary of the Opinions Reflected by Standard & Poor's Ratings

Grade	Rating	Description
Investment	AAA	Extremely strong capacity to meet financial commitments; highest rating.
	AA	Very strong capacity to meet financial commitments.
	A	Strong capacity to meet financial commitments, but somewhat susceptible to adverse economic conditions and changes in circumstance.
	BBB	Adequate capacity to meet financial commitments, but more subject to adverse market conditions.
	BBB–	Considered to be the lowest investment grade by market participants.
Speculative	BB+	Considered to be the highest speculative grade by market participants.
	BB	Less vulnerable in the near term but faces major ongoing uncertainties to adverse business, financial, and economic conditions.
	B	More vulnerable to adverse business, financial, and economic conditions, but currently has the capacity to meet financial commitments.
	CCC	Currently vulnerable and dependent on favorable business, financial, and economic conditions to meet financial commitments.
	CC	Currently highly vulnerable.
	C	A bankruptcy petition has been filed or similar action taken but payments of financial commitments are continued.
	D	Payment default on financial commitments.
	NR	Insufficient information on which to base a rating, that no rating has been requested or S&P does not rate a particular obligation.

offset the greater credit risk assumed by investors. For this reason, treasurers of companies or government agencies need to be aware of what it takes to have the best possible rating. Table 9-1 is a general summary of the opinions reflected by Standard and Poor's Ratings.[10]

Investment- and Speculative-Grade Debt

The term *investment grade* has historically referred to bonds and other debt securities that bank regulators and market participants viewed as suitable investments for financial institutions. The reason for this was to prevent banks from speculating in risky securities that could undermine their capital base. Now the term is broadly used to describe issuers

[10]Ratings from AA to CCC may be modified by the addition of a plus (+) or minus (–) sign to show relative standing within the major rating categories.

and issues with relatively high levels of creditworthiness and credit quality. In contrast, the term *non-investment grade*, or *speculative grade*, generally refers to debt securities where the issuer currently has the ability to repay but faces significant uncertainties, such as adverse business or financial circumstances that could affect credit risk. In Standard & Poor's long-term rating scale, issuers and debt issues that receive a rating of BBB– or above are generally considered by regulators and market participants to be investment grade while those that receive a rating lower than BBB– are generally considered to be speculative grade.

RELATIVE COST OF DEBT FINANCING

Before moving on to the impact of debt on a company's capital structure, return on capital employed, and return on equity, it is instructive to look at the cost of the various forms of debt financing.

The least expensive and most convenient source of debt for creditworthy lenders is usually commercial banks. Since interest rates vary, any interest rate selected for comparison purposes quickly becomes dated. The relative cost of the various forms of debt financing just discussed can be shown by taking typical interest rates charged for the various types of loans and normalizing them by dividing each by the *bank revolver/term loan* interest rate. The result of this calculation is shown in Table 9-2.

As can be seen, the normalized interest rate for a bank revolver is 1 and the cost of an asset-based loan is 15% higher. This may at first be counterintuitive. However, ABLs are usually made to borrowers whose creditworthiness doesn't meet the standards required of a revolver. Hence, security is required and the interest rate reflects the benefit of the security, but, at the same time, the additional risk. The private placement rate is 85% higher and it reflects the risk and longer tenor of the loan. The institutional term loan and high-yield bonds have a lower priority and possibly less creditworthy borrowers, which is reflected in the interest rates. As mentioned previously, mezzanine financing stands just above the equity holders and below private placement, institutional term loans, and high-yield bonds, and in order for mezzanine lenders to be induced to make a loan they require a huge premium, in this case, 404% or 4.04 times the rate for a bank revolver/term loan.

TABLE 9-2 Relative Cost of Financing Alternatives

Debt Financing Source	Normalized Interest Rate
Bank Revolver/Term Loan	1.00
Bank Asset-Based Lending	1.15
Private Placement	1.85
Institutional Term Loan	2.32
High-Yield Bonds	3.23
Mezzanine Financing	4.04

TABLE 9-3 Cost of Financing Alternatives

Debt Financing Source	Interest Rate
Bank Revolver/Term Loan	2.48
Bank Asset-Based Lending	2.85
Private Placement	4.58
Institutional Term Loan	5.75
High-Yield Bonds	8.00
Mezzanine Financing	10.00

At the time this chapter was written, LIBOR was 0.35% and creditworthy companies could borrow at LIBOR plus 200 to 225 basis points for a five-year term.[11] If one assumes the rate in the middle of the range for illustration purposes, the all-in borrowing cost becomes 2.48% (0.35% + 2.13%). Table 9-3 shows the cost of the other kinds of financing based on the normalized premiums shown in Table 9-2. As can be seen from Table 9-3, the high-yield bond and mezzanine lenders are well compensated for the risk they take. Borrowers are well advised to maintain strong operating results and balance sheets so that they have access to attractive lower-cost financing from the banks and private placement lenders and when not large enough to access the high-investment-grade bond markets.

IMPACT OF DEBT ON RETURN ON CAPITAL EMPLOYED AND RETURN ON EQUITY

In Chapter 5, considerable time and effort was spent quantifying the impact various Balance Sheet and Income Statement accounts had on the return on capital employed (ROCE). In this chapter, the impact that debt has on both ROCE and the return on equity (ROE) is analyzed. To see how leveraging up the Balance Sheet works and the impact it has on both the ROCE and ROE, the discussion begins once again with the definition of ROCE and the ROCE Driver Equation.

Equation [9-1] is a modified form of the definitional equation for ROCE used in Chapter 5, where EBIT is the Earnings before Interest and Taxes and CE is the Capital Employed in the business and equal to the sum of short-term debt, long-term debt, and shareholders' equity (STD + LTD + TSHE).

$$ROCE = \frac{EBIT}{CE}(1-TR) = \frac{(EBIT)(1-TR)}{STD+LTD=TSHE} \qquad [9\text{-}1]$$

[11]The term of a loan does impact the interest rate. For example, the rate for a 1-year loan is typically lower than that for a 5-year loan, which in turn is lower than the rate for some longer terms, such as 10 years.

Then, from this an expression for the ROCE Driver Equation was developed in Chapter 5.

$$ROCE = \left\{ \frac{\left[1 - \left(\frac{COGS}{Rev} + \frac{OpExp}{Rev} + \frac{D\&A}{Rev} \right) \right]}{\left(\frac{WC_{XSTD}}{Rev} + \frac{NetFA}{Rev} + \frac{NetIA}{Rev} \right)} \right\} (1 - TR) \qquad [9\text{-}2]$$

Obviously there is a big difference in the effort that goes into utilizing Equation [9-1] versus Equation [9-2]. So the reader may ask: Why would one utilize Equation [9-2] when the same answer can be obtained with Equation [9-1]? The reason is: [9-1] only gives a number where as [9-2] not only gives a number but in addition shows what is driving the ROCE and therefore what to work on to improve it and estimate the impact changes in any of the variables will have on the ratio. It is left to the reader to decide which equation should be used. Also, as will be seen, the same rationale will apply to the two equations that can be used to calculate the return on equity.

Developing the ROE Driver Equation[12]

To quantify the impact that leverage (debt) has on the return on equity, an expression needs to be derived that defines the impact the various Income Statement and Balance Sheet accounts have on ROE. The financial statements used in this process are the Income Statement and Balance Sheet for the Mayfair Company, first encountered in Chapter 5 and designated here as Tables 9-4 and 9-5 respectively.

TABLE 9-4 Mayfair Company Income Statement

Year Ending DD/MM/YYYY $(000)'s		
Revenues (Rev)		100,000
Cost of Goods Sold (COGS)		(40,000)
Gross Margin (GM)		60,000
Operating Expenses (OpExp)		(43,500)
Earnings before Interest, Taxes, Depreciation, and Amortization (EBITDA)		16,500
Depreciation and Amortization (D&A)		(5,000)
Earnings Before Interest and Taxes (EBIT)		11,500
Interest Income/(Expense) (NetInt)		0
Earnings before Tax (EBT)		11,500
Taxes Paid (TaxesPaid) @	40%	(4,600)
Net Income (NI)		6,900

[12]T. E. Copeland, T. Koller, and J. Murrin, *Valuation, Measuring and Managing the Value of Companies*, 2nd ed. (New York: John Wiley & Sons, 1995), 166, "ROIC Tree" (model modified to apply to ROE).

TABLE 9-5 Mayfair Company Balance Sheet

As at DD/MM/YYYY $(000)'s			
Current Assets		**Current Liabilities**	
Cash	750	Accounts Payable	2,500
Accounts Receivable	6,250	Taxes Payable	0
Inventory	5,000	Short-Term Debt (STD)	0
Total Current Assets (CA)	12,000	**Total Current Liabilities**	2,500
Fixed Assets (FA)			
At Cost	30,000	**Long-Term Debt (LTD)**	0
Less Depreciation	5,000		
Net Fixed Assets (NetFA)	25,000		
		Shareholders' Equity (TSHE)	
Intangible Assets		Paid-in Capital	50,000
Goodwill and Other Intangible Assets	0	Retained Earnings	(15,500)
Net Intangible Assets (NetIA)	0	**Total Shareholders' Equity**	34,500
Total Assets	37,000	**Total Liabilities + TSHE**	37,000

The first step is to start with the definitional equation for ROE (Equation [9-3]).

$$ROE = \frac{Net\ Income}{Total\ Shareholders'\ Equity} \qquad [9\text{-}3]$$

By referring to Table 9-4, the following expressions can be written.

$$Net\ Income = EBT - Taxes\ Paid \qquad [9\text{-}4]$$

$$Taxes\ Paid = (EBT)(TR) \qquad [9\text{-}5]$$

Substituting [9-5] into [9-4],

$$Net\ Income = EBT - (EBT)(TR) = (EBT)(1 - TR) \qquad [9\text{-}6]$$

Then substituting Equation [9-6] for Net Income in Equation [9-3] gives Equation [9-7].

$$ROE = \frac{EBT}{TSHE}(1 - TR) \qquad [9\text{-}7]$$

Proceeding as in the development of the ROCE Driver Equation, revenue can be introduced into Equation [9-7] by dividing the top and bottom of the right-hand side of the equation by the Revenue term (Rev).

$$ROE = \frac{\left(\frac{EBT}{Rev}\right)}{\left(\frac{TSHE}{Rev}\right)}(1 - TR) \qquad [9\text{-}8]$$

Multiplying the top and bottom of Equation [9-8] by $\left(\frac{Rev}{TSHE}\right)$,

$$ROE = \frac{\left(\frac{EBT}{Rev}\right)\left(\frac{Rev}{TSHE}\right)}{\left(\frac{TSHE}{Rev}\right)\left(\frac{Rev}{TSHE}\right)}(1-TR) \qquad [9\text{-}9]$$

Equation [9-9] can be simplified by canceling like terms in the denominator:

$$ROE = \left(\frac{EBT}{Rev}\right)\left(\frac{Rev}{TSHE}\right)(1-TR) \qquad [9\text{-}10]$$

Where in Equation [9-10]:

$\left(\frac{EBT}{Rev}\right)$ = Return on Revenue[13] and a measure of how effective the management of a company is in converting Net Revenues into Earnings before Taxes

$\left(\frac{Rev}{TSHE}\right)$ = Capital Turnover and a measure of how well the managers of a company manage the money provided by shareholders

Both of these terms can be further disaggregated. This process is started by reducing the term $\left(\frac{Rev}{TSHE}\right)$ into its balance sheet components.

By referring to Table 9-5, it is noted that

$$Total\ Liabilities + TSHE = CL + LTD + TSHE \qquad [9\text{-}11]$$

where:

CL = Current Liabilities, LTD = Long-Term Debt, and
TSE = Total Shareholders' Equity

Now recall that Current Liabilities includes short-term debt (STD). To exclude STD from Current Liabilities, Equation [9-11] can be rewritten as

$$Total\ Liabilities + TSHE = (CL - STD) + (STD + LTD) + TSHE \qquad [9\text{-}12]$$

Earlier, Interest-Bearing Debt[14] was defined as IBD = STD + LTD. Substituting this expression in Equation [9-12],

$$Total\ Liabilities + TSHE = (CL - STD) + IBD + TSHE \qquad [9\text{-}13]$$

Next the asset side of the Balance Sheet is examined and, again by referring to Table 9-5, it is noted that

$$Total\ Assets = CA + NetFA + NetIA \qquad [9\text{-}14]$$

where:

CA = Current Assets, $NetFA$ = Net Fixed Assets, and
$NetIA$ = Net Intangible Assets

[13] Net income and operating income are also used when measuring return on revenue.
[14] See Chapter 1, "Capital Employed."

Now, since Total Assets = Total Liabilities + TSHE, Equation [9-14] = Equation [9-13] and

$$CA + NetFA + NetIA = (CL - STD) + IBD + TSHE \quad [9\text{-}15]$$

Rearranging Equation [9-15] creates an expression for Total Shareholder Equity in terms of the balance sheet accounts.

$$TSHE = CA - (CL - STD) + NetFA + NetIA - IBD \quad [9\text{-}16]$$

Now, CA – (CL – STD) is an expression that defines the working capital in a business excluding short-term debt or WC_{XSTD}. Hence,

$$TSHE = WC_{XSTD} + NetFA + NetIA - IBD \quad [9\text{-}17]$$

Once again, net revenues can be introduced into the expression for Total Shareholders' Equity by dividing both sides of Equation [9-17] by the Revenue term (Rev).

$$\frac{TSHE}{Rev} = \frac{WC_{XSTD} + NetFA + NetIA - IBD}{Rev} \quad [9\text{-}18]$$

Inverting [9-18] yields an expression for $\frac{Rev}{TSHE}$ or capital turnover:

$$\frac{Rev}{TSHE} = \frac{Rev}{WC_{XSTD} + NetFA + NetIA - IBD} \quad [9\text{-}19]$$

To introduce revenues into each of the terms in the denominator of Equation [9-19], the top and bottom of the right-hand side are divided by Rev,

$$\frac{Rev}{TSHE} = \frac{\frac{Rev}{Rev}}{\left(\frac{WC_{XSTD}}{Rev} + \frac{NetFA}{Rev} + \frac{NetIA}{Rev} - \frac{IBD}{Rev}\right)} \quad [9\text{-}20]$$

or

$$\frac{Rev}{TSHE} = \frac{1}{\left(\frac{WC_{XSTD}}{Rev} + \frac{NetFA}{Rev} + \frac{NetIA}{Rev} - \frac{IBD}{Rev}\right)} \quad [9\text{-}21]$$

Equation [9-21] says: When working capital (excluding STD), net fixed assets, and intangible assets per unit of net revenues are minimized and interest-bearing debt per unit of net revenues is maximized, the contribution the Capital Turnover term $\left(\frac{Rev}{TSHE}\right)$ makes in Equation [9-10] to the ROE is maximized.

Recall that the other term in Equation [9-10] that impacts the ROE is $\left(\frac{EBT}{Rev}\right)$. This term deals with EBT as a function of revenues. Using a similar procedure, the term $\left(\frac{EBT}{Rev}\right)$ can be broken down into its Income Statement components. By referring to Mayfair's Income Statement (Table 9-4) an expression for EBT can be written as

$$EBT = Rev - COGS - OpExp - D\,\&\,A - NetInt \quad [9\text{-}22]$$

As before, revenue can be introduced into Equation [9-22] by dividing the top and bottom of the right-hand side of the equation by Rev.

$$\frac{EBT}{Rev} = 1 - \frac{COGS}{Rev} - \frac{OpExp}{Rev} - \frac{D\,\&\,A}{Rev} - \frac{NetInt}{Rev} \quad [9\text{-}23]$$

Rearranging,

$$\frac{EBT}{Rev} = 1 - \left(\frac{COGS}{Rev} + \frac{OpExp}{Rev} + \frac{D\,\&\,A}{Rev} + \frac{NetInt}{Rev}\right) \quad [9\text{-}24]$$

The story Equation [9-24] tells is: By minimizing the cost of goods sold, operating expenses, depreciation and amortization, and interest per unit of revenues, the contribution that the Return on Sales term $\left(\frac{EBT}{NetRev}\right)$ makes in Equation [9-10] to the return on equity is maximized.

The ROE Driver Equation

With ROE disaggregated into its Balance Sheet and Income Statement components, a general equation that brings all of these variables together is obtained by substituting the results of Equations [9-24] and [9-21] into Equation [9-10].

$$ROE = \left[1 - \left(\frac{COGS}{Rev} + \frac{OpExp}{Rev} + \frac{D\,\&\,A}{Rev} + \frac{NetInt}{Rev}\right)\right] \times \left[\frac{1}{\left(\frac{WC_{XSTD}}{Rev} + \frac{NetFA}{Rev} + \frac{NetIA}{Rev} - \frac{IBD}{Rev}\right)}\right](1 - TR) \quad [9\text{-}25]$$

Or by simplifying,

$$ROE = \left\{\frac{\left[1 - \left(\frac{COGS}{Rev} + \frac{OpExp}{Rev} + \frac{D\,\&\,A}{Rev} + \frac{NetInt}{Rev}\right)\right]}{\left(\frac{WC_{XSTD}}{Rev} + \frac{NetFA}{Rev} + \frac{NetIA}{Rev} - \frac{IBD}{Rev}\right)}\right\}(1 - TR) \quad [9\text{-}26]$$

Like its *ROCE* equivalent, Equation [9-26] is a very powerful expression. It specifically identifies all of the financial statement variables that impact the return on equity.[15]

Now, in the ROE version of the ROCE Driver Equation, the impact that substituting debt for shareholders' equity has on the two metrics can be demonstrated. However, before doing so, it's instructive to take some time to comment on what each of these terms mean.

Income Statement–Related Terms

COGS/Net Rev: This is a measure of the material and labor required to produce a dollar of revenue. Obviously, the lower the ratio is, the higher the gross margin and potentially EBITDA.

OpExp/Net Rev: Operating expenses consist of sales and marketing, service, administrative, research and development, and other general expenses. These are the expenses necessary to bring the company's products and services to market and satisfy customer needs. The lower the amount spent on operating expenses, the higher the contribution to EBITDA and ultimately profitability.

D&A/Net Rev: Here is a measure of how quickly the assets the company has on its balance sheet are depreciated or amortized per unit of revenue. Once again, the lower this ratio, the greater the contribution to the Earnings before Interest and Tax (EBIT) and the company's overall profitability.

Interest/Net Rev: Interest is the cost of borrowing money. The lower the interest per dollar of net revenue, the higher the earnings before tax (EBT).

In summary, all of the terms just discussed constitute the numerator of the Driver Equation and since the sum of these is subtracted from 1 (which is essentially the Net Revenue term), the lower the sum, the higher the Company's EBT. Also, at this point, one may ask why there isn't a term for taxes? Well, the answer is, it's there. It's the term (1–TR). Obviously, the higher the tax rate (TR) is, the lower the net income and vice versa.

Balance Sheet–Related Terms

WC_{XSTD}/Net Rev: Recall that working capital consists of such items as cash, accounts receivable, accounts payable, inventory, and other current obligations but not short-term debt. WC_{XSTD} and everything else on the balance sheet is supported by shareholders' equity and short- and long-term debt. Hence, if the amount of working capital required per unit of net revenue is reduced, this will impact cash and make cash available for growing the company and reduce the immediate need for further debt or equity. Alternatively, the cash could be used to reduce debt and hence interest payments. Also the

[15]The effort associated with memorizing the ROE and ROCE Driver Equations is facilitated by noting the Drivers are arranged so that the numerator and denominator are dedicated to the Income Statement and Balance Sheet respectively and that Equation [9-26] (ROE Driver Equation) is identical to Equation [9-2] (ROCE Driver Equation) except for the addition of the terms $\left(\frac{NetInt}{Rev}\right)$ and $\left(\frac{IBD}{NetRev}\right)$ in the numerator and denominator respectively.

company can increase its dividend and reduce its shareholders' equity, all of which will contribute to an increase in ROE.

NetFA/Net Rev: Fixed assets consist of property, plant, and equipment net of accumulated depreciation. Similar to the WC_{XSTD}/Net Rev, if management takes actions to lower this ratio by selling assets, replacing them more slowly, or better yet, making them more productive, there is an impact on cash and, hence, an opportunity to operate with a smaller balance sheet.

NetIA/Net Rev: Assets in this category consist of non-competes, patents, and goodwill net of accumulated amortization. Minimizing this ratio has the same impact on the company as minimizing WC_{XSTD}/Net Rev and NetFA/Net Rev.

IBD/Net Rev: This is a measure of the interest-bearing debt the company has per unit of revenue. Obviously, a company can minimize the amount of equity it needs by borrowing money in place of issuing more stock. This is the reason that a company's ROE will increase if it borrows money to support its growth. Also, since capital employed is the sum of all interest-bearing debt and equity, increasing debt will reduce a company's ROCE unless there is a corresponding reduction in shareholders' equity.

EXAMPLE 9-1: IMPACT OF LEVERAGE ON CAPITAL STRUCTURE, ROCE, AND ROE

Nobel Electronics Inc., a manufacturer of control systems, has the condensed Balance Sheet and Income Statement shown in Tables 9-6 and 9-7 respectively. The Company has just finished beta testing a breakthrough innovative control system that is expected to launch the company on a growth trajectory. The Company doesn't have any debt and the challenge for the treasurer is to advise the CFO and CEO on the best way to finance the growth: with debt or equity?

The treasurer is very much aware the financing he will ultimately decide to recommend will have an impact on ROCE and ROE. For this reason, he starts by taking the Company's existing Balance Sheet and most recent Income Statement and calculating what the Company's ROCE and ROE would look like for various hypothetical financial structures. The scenarios he works with are identified as Capital Structures (1)–(4).[16] As for the period of growth that is expected to commence when the new control system is launched, he turns to the forecasted Income Statement, Balance Sheet, and Cash Flow[17] and concludes that $20,000,000 of financing will be required. He then runs Capital Structure scenarios (5) and (6) to quantify the impact each will have.

Capital Structure (1)

No interest-bearing debt on the Balance Sheet (unlevered Balance Sheet).

Capital Structure (2)

$10,000,000 of long-term debt at 10% in place of $10,000,000 of total shareholders' equity (TSHE).

Capital Structure (3)

$10,000,000 of short-term debt at 8% in place of $10,000,000 TSHE.

Capital Structure (4)

$3,000,000 of 8% STD and $7,000,000 of 10% LTD in place of $10,000,000 of TSHE.

Capital Structure (5)

Future growth financed with $20,000,000 of additional equity.

Capital Structure (6)

Future growth financed with $20,000,000 of LTD at 10%. Equity remains unchanged.

Capital Structure (1): Unlevered Balance Sheet (No Interest-Bearing Debt)

TABLE 9-6 Nobel Electronics Inc. Balance Sheet for Capital Structure (1) $(000)'s

Total Current Assets	25,000	Other Current Liabilities	6,000
		Short-Term Debt	0
Net Fixed Assets	25,000	Long-Term Debt	0
Net Intang Assets	0	Shareholders' Equity	44,000
Total Assets	50,000	Total Liabilities + TSHE	50,000

TABLE 9-7 Nobel Electronics Inc. Income Statement for Capital Structure (1) $(000)'s

Net Revenues		90,000
Cost of Goods Sold (COGS)		(40,000)
Operating Expenses (OpExp)		(29,000)
EBITDA		21,000
Depreciation and Amortization (D&A)		(4,000)
EBIT		17,000
Interest Income/Expense (NetInt)		0
Earnings before Tax (EBT)		17,000
Taxes Paid (TaxesPaid) @	40%	(6,800)
Net Income (NI)		10,200

The procedure is to begin by referring to Tables 9-6 and 9-7 and using this data to develop Table 9-8.

The ROCE can be calculated by applying Equation [9-1]. Applying Equation [9-1],

$$ROCE = \frac{EBIT}{CE}(1-TR) = \frac{(EBIT)(1-TR)}{STD+LTD+TSE} \qquad [9\text{-}1]$$

$$ROCE = \frac{EBIT(1-TR)}{STD+LTD+TSE} = \frac{(17{,}000{,}000)(1-0.40)}{0+0+44{,}000{,}000} = \frac{(17{,}000{,}000)(0.60)}{44{,}000{,}000} = 23.2\%$$

[16] In each and every case, the reader will note it is simpler to use the definitional equations for ROCE and ROE than the expanded equations that take into account the key elements of the Income Statement and Balance Sheet. In this example, the calculations are done both ways to illustrate how the various components of the financial statements interact to impact the returns and, perhaps more important, to do what-if scenarios and their impact on ROCE and ROE.

[17] Not shown.

TABLE 9-8 Capital Structure (1) Data for ROCE and ROE Calculations $(000)'s and %

Income Statement				
EBIT	=	17,000,000	=	17,000,000
EBT	=	17,000,000	=	17,000,000
COGS/Rev	=	40,000,000/90,000,000	=	44.44%
OpExp/Rev	=	29,000,000/90,000,000	=	32.22%
D&A/ Rev	=	4,000,000/90,000,000	=	4.44%
NetInt/Rev	=	0/90,000,000	=	0.00%
Tax Rate (TR)	=	0.4	=	40.00%
Balance Sheet				
Cap Employed (CE)	=	0 + 0 + 44,000,000	=	44,000,000
Total SHE (TSHE)	=	44,000,000		44,000,000
WC_{XSTD}/Rev	=	(25,000,000 – 6,000,000)/90,000,000		
	=	19,000,000/90,000,000	=	21.11%
NetFA/Rev	=	25,000,000/90,000,000	=	27.78%
NetIA/Rev	=	0/90,000,000	=	0.00%
IBD/Rev	=	(0 + 0)/90,000,000	=	0.00%

Applying Equation [9-2] and using the data in Table 9-8 gives the same result.

$$ROCE = \left\{ \frac{\left[1 - \left(\frac{COGS}{NetRev} + \frac{OpExp}{NetRev} + \frac{D\&A}{NetRev}\right)\right]}{\left(\frac{WC_{XSTD}}{NetRev} + \frac{NetFA}{NetRev} + \frac{NetIA}{NetRev}\right)} \right\}(1 - TR) \qquad [9\text{-}2]$$

$$ROCE = \left\{ \frac{[1 - (0.4444 + 0.3222 + 0.0444)]}{(0.2111 + 0.2778 + 0)} \right\}(1 - 0.40) = 23.2\%$$

The ROE for the unlevered case is calculated by applying Equations [9-7] or [9-26]. Applying Equation [9-7],

$$ROE = \frac{EBT}{TSHE}(1 - TR) = \frac{(17{,}000{,}000)(1 - 0.40)}{44{,}000{,}000} = \frac{(17{,}000{,}000)(0.60)}{44{,}000{,}000} = 23.2\%$$

Applying Equation [9-26] and using the data in Table 9-8 once again gives the same result.

$$ROE = \left\{ \frac{\left[1 - \left(\frac{COGS}{NetRev} + \frac{OpExp}{NetRev} + \frac{D\&A}{NetRev} + \frac{Int}{NetRev}\right)\right]}{\left(\frac{WC_{XSTD}}{NetRev} + \frac{NetFA}{NetRev} + \frac{NetIA}{NetRev} - \frac{IBD}{NetRev}\right)} \right\}(1 - TR) \qquad [9\text{-}26]$$

$$ROE = \left\{ \frac{[1 - (0.4444 + 0.3222 + 0.0444 + 0)]}{(0.2111 + 0.2778 + 0 - 0)} \right\}(1 - 0.40) = 23.2\%$$

It's worthwhile to note that when a company has an unlevered balance sheet ROCE and ROE are identical.

Capital Structure (2): $10 Million of Long-Term Debt at 10% in Place of $10 Million of TSHE

The financial statements for Nobel Electronics with $10,000,000 of LTD bearing interest at 10% in place of an equal amount of equity are shown in Tables 9-9 and 9-10, and from which the data in Table 9-11 was calculated.

Following the same procedure as the unlevered case, the ROCE and ROE for Capital Structure (2) are obtained. Applying Equation [9-1],

$$ROE = \frac{EBIT(1-TR)}{STD+LTD+TSHE} = \frac{(17{,}000{,}000)(1-0.40)}{0+10{,}000{,}000+34{,}000{,}000}$$
$$= \frac{(17{,}000{,}000)(0.60)}{44{,}000{,}000} = 23.2\%$$

Applying Equation [9-2] and using the data in Table 9-11 gives the same result.

$$ROCE = \left\{ \frac{\left[1-\left(\frac{COGS}{NetRev}+\frac{OpExp}{NetRev}+\frac{D\&A}{NetRev}\right)\right]}{\left(\frac{WC_{XSTD}}{NetRev}+\frac{NetFA}{NetRev}+\frac{OthA}{NetRev}\right)} \right\}(1-TR) \qquad [9\text{-}2]$$

$$ROCE = \left\{ \frac{[1-(0.4444+0.3222+0.0444)]}{(0.2111+0.2778+0)} \right\}(1-0.40) = 23.2\%$$

The ROE for Capital Structure (2) is calculated by applying Equations [9-7] or [9-26]. Applying Equation [9-7],

$$ROE = \frac{EBIT}{TSHE}(1-TR) = \frac{(16{,}000{,}000)(1-0.40)}{34{,}000{,}000} = \frac{(16{,}000{,}000)(0.60)}{34{,}000{,}000} = 28.2\%$$

TABLE 9-9 Nobel Electronics Inc. Balance Sheet for Capital Structure (2) $(000)'s

Total Current Assets	25,000	Other Current Liabilities	6,000
		Short-Term Debt	0
Net Fixed Assets	25,000	Long-Term Debt	10,000
Net Intang Assets	0	Shareholders' Equity	34,000
Total Assets	50,000	Total Liabilities + TSHE	50,000

TABLE 9-10 Nobel Electronics Inc. Income Statement for Capital Structure (2) $(000)'s

Net Revenues		90,000
Cost of Goods Sold (COGS)		(40,000)
Operating Expenses (OpExp)		(29,000)
EBITDA		21,000
Depreciation and Amortization (D&A)		(4,000)
EBIT		17,000
Interest Income/Expense (NetInt)		(1,000)
Earnings before Tax (EBT)		16,000
Taxes Paid (TaxesPaid) @	40%	(6,400)
Net Income (NI)		9,600

TABLE 9-11 Capital Structure (2) Data for ROCE and ROE Calculations $(000)'s and %

Income Statement				
EBIT	=	17,000,000	=	17,000,000
EBT	=	16,000,000	=	16,000,000
COGS/Rev	=	40,000,000/90,000,000	=	44.44%
OpExp/Rev	=	29,000,000/90,000,000	=	32.22%
D&A/Rev	=	4,000,000/90,000,000	=	4.44%
NetInt/Rev	=	1,000,000/90,000,000	=	1.11%
Tax Rate (TR)	=	0.4	=	40.00%
Balance Sheet				
Cap Employed (CE)	=	0 + 10,000,000 + 34,000,000	=	44,000,000
Total SHE (TSHE)	=	34,000,000		34,000,000
WC_{XSTD}/Rev	=	(25,000,000 – 6,000,000)/90,000,000		
	=	19,000,000/90,000,000	=	21.11%
NetFA/Rev	=	25,000,000/90,000,000	=	27.78%
NetIA/Rev	=	0/90,000,000	=	0.00%
IBD/Rev	=	10,000,000/90,000,000	=	11.11%

Applying Equation [9-26] and again using the data in Table 9-11 gives the same result.

$$ROE = \left\{ \frac{\left[1 - \left(\frac{COGS}{NetRev} + \frac{OpExp}{NetRev} + \frac{D\&A}{NetRev} + \frac{NetInt}{NetRev} \right) \right]}{\left(\frac{WC_{XSTD}}{NetRev} + \frac{NetFA}{NetRev} + \frac{NetIA}{NetRev} - \frac{IBD}{NetRev} \right)} \right\} (1 - TR) \qquad [9\text{-}26]$$

$$ROE = \left\{ \frac{[1 - (0.4444 + 0.3222 + 0.0444 + 0.0111)]}{(0.2111 + 0.2778 + 0 - 0.1111)} \right\} (1 - 0.40) = 28.2\%$$

Capital Structure (3): $10 Million of Short-Term Debt at 8% in Place of $10 Million of TSHE

The financial statements for Nobel Electronics with $10,000,000 of STD in place of an equivalent amount of equity and no LTD are shown in Tables 9-25 and 9-26.

The data necessary to calculate the ROCE and ROE for Capital Structure (3) is taken from Tables 9-12 and 9-13. The data required for the calculations is summarized in Table 9-14.

The *ROCE* can be calculated by applying Equations [9-1]:

$$ROCE = \frac{(EBIT)(1-TR)}{STD + LTD + TSHE} = \frac{(17,000,000)(1-0.40)}{10,000,000 + 0 + 34,000,000}$$

$$= \frac{(17,000,000)(0.60)}{34,000,000} = 23.2\%$$

TABLE 9-12 Nobel Electronics Inc. Balance Sheet for Capital Structure (3) $(000)'s

Total Current Assets	25,000	Other Current Liabilities	6,000
		Short-Term Debt	10,000
Net Fixed Assets	25,000	Long-Term Debt	0
Net Intang Assets	0	Shareholders' Equity	34,000
Total Assets	50,000	Total Liabilities + (TSHE	50,000

TABLE 9-13 Nobel Electronics Inc. Income Statement for Capital Structure (3) $(000)'s

Net Revenues		90,000
Cost of Goods Sold (COGS)		(40,000)
Operating Expenses (OpExp)		(29,000)
EBITDA		21,000
Depreciation and Amortization (D&A)		(4,000)
EBIT		17,000
Interest Income/Expense (NetInt)		(800)
Earnings before Tax (EBT)		16,200
Taxes Paid (TaxesPaid) @	40%	(6,480)
Net Income (NI)		9,720

Applying Equation [9-2] and using the data in Table 9-14, the result is repeated.

$$ROCE = \left\{ \frac{\left[1 - \left(\frac{COGS}{NetRev} + \frac{OpExp}{NetRev} + \frac{D\&A}{NetRev}\right)\right]}{\left(\frac{WC_{XSTD}}{NetRev} + \frac{NetFA}{NetRev} + \frac{NetIA}{NetRev}\right)} \right\}(1 - TR) \qquad [9\text{-}2]$$

$$ROCE = \left\{ \frac{[1-(0.4444+0.3222+0.0444)]}{(0.2111+0.2778+0)} \right\}(1-0.40) = 23.2\%$$

TABLE 9-14 Capital Structure (3) Data for ROCE and ROE Calculations $(000)'s and %

Income Statement				
EBIT	=	17,000,000	=	17,000,000
EBT	=	16,200,000	=	16,200,000
COGS/Rev	=	40,000,000/90,000,000	=	44.44%
OpExp/Rev	=	29,000,000/90,000,000	=	32.22%
D&A/Rev	=	4,000,000/90,000,000	=	4.44%
NetInt/Rev	=	800,000/90,000,000	=	0.89%
Tax Rate (TR)	=	0.4	=	40.00%
Balance Sheet				
Cap Employed (CE)	=	10,000,000 + 0 + 34,000,000	=	44,000,000
Total SHE (TSHE)	=	34,000,000		34,000,000
WC_{XSTD}/Rev	=	(25,000,000 – 6,000,000)/90,000,000		
	=	19,000,000/90,000,000	=	21.11%
NetFA/Rev	=	25,000,000/90,000,000	=	27.78%
NetIA/Rev	=	0/90,000,000	=	0.00%
IBD/Rev	=	10,000,000/90,000,000	=	11.11%

The ROE for Capital Structure (3) is calculated by applying Equations [9-7] or [9-26]. Applying Equation [9-7],

$$ROE = \frac{EBIT}{TSHE}(1-TR) = \frac{(16,200,000)(1-0.40)}{34,000,000} = \frac{(16,200,000)(0.60)}{34,000,000} = 28.6\%$$

Once again using data in Table 9-14 and Applying Equation [9-26] the result is repeated for the ROE.

$$ROE = \left\{ \frac{\left[1 - \left(\frac{COGS}{NetRev} + \frac{OpExp}{NetRev} + \frac{D\&A}{NetRev} + \frac{NetInt}{NetRev}\right)\right]}{\left(\frac{WC_{XSTD}}{NetRev} + \frac{NetFA}{NetRev} + \frac{NetIA}{NetRev} - \frac{IBD}{NetRev}\right)} \right\}(1-TR) \qquad [9\text{-}26]$$

$$ROE = \left\{ \frac{[1-(0.4444+0.3222+0.0444+0.0089)]}{(0.2111+0.2778+0-0.1111)} \right\}(1-0.40) = 28.6\%$$

Capital Structure (4): \$3 Million 8% STD and \$7 Million 10% LTD Replacing \$10 Million TSHE

The financial statements for Nobel Electronics with \$3,000,000 of STD and \$7,000,000 of LTD in place of \$10,000,000 of equity are shown in Tables 9-15 and 9-16 and from these tables the data in Table 9-17 was calculated.

Applying Equation [9-1],

$$ROCE = \frac{(EBIT)(1-TR)}{STD+LTD+TSHE} = \frac{(17,000,000)(1-0.40)}{3,000,000+7,000,000+34,000,000}$$

$$= \frac{(17,000,000)(0.60)}{44,000,000} = 23.2\%$$

TABLE 9-15 Nobel Electronics Inc. Balance Sheet for Capital Structure (4) \$(000)'s

Total Current Assets	25,000	Other Current Liabilities	6,000
		Short-Term Debt	3,000
Net Fixed Assets	25,000	Long-Term Debt	7,000
Net Intang Assets	0	Shareholders' Equity	34,000
Total Assets	50,000	Total Liabilities + TSHE	50,000

TABLE 9-16 Nobel Electronics Inc. Income Statement for Capital Structure (4) \$(000)'s

Net Revenues		90,000
Cost of Goods Sold (COGS)		(40,000)
Operating Expenses (OpExp)		(29,000)
EBITDA		21,000
Depreciation and Amortization (D&A)		(4,000)
EBIT		17,000
Interest Income/Expense (NetInt)		(940)
Earnings before Tax (EBT)		16,060
Taxes Paid (TaxesPaid) @	40%	(6,424)
Net Income (NI)		9,636

TABLE 9-17 Capital Structure (4) Data for ROCE and ROE Calculations $(000)'s and %

Income Statement				
EBIT	=	17,000,000	=	17,000,000
EBT	=	16,060,000	=	16,060,000
COGS/Rev	=	40,000,000/90,000,000	=	44.44%
OpExp/Rev	=	29,000,000/90,000,000	=	32.22%
D&A/Rev	=	4,000,000/90,000,000	=	4.44%
NetInt/Rev	=	940,000/90,000,000	=	1.04%
Tax Rate (TR)	=	0.4	=	40.00%
Balance Sheet				
Cap Employed (CE)	=	3,000,000 + 10,000,000 + 34,000,000	=	44,000,000
Total SHE (TSHE)	=	34,000,000	=	34,000,000
WC_{XSTD}/Rev	=	(25,000,000 – 6,000,000)/90,000,000		
	=	19,000,000/90,000,000	=	21.11%
NetFA/Rev	=	25,000,000/90,000,000	=	27.78%
NetIA/Rev	=	0/90,000,000	=	0.00%
IBD/Rev	=	(3,000,000 + 7,000,000)/90,000,000	=	11.11%

Applying Equation [9-2] and using the data in Table 9-17 confirms the ROCE just calculated.

$$ROCE = \left\{ \frac{\left[1 - \left(\frac{COGS}{NetRev} + \frac{OpExp}{NetRev} + \frac{D\&A}{NetRev}\right)\right]}{\left(\frac{WC_{XSTD}}{NetRev} + \frac{NetFA}{NetRev} + \frac{NetIA}{NetRev}\right)} \right\} (1 - TR) \qquad [9\text{-}2]$$

$$ROCE = \left\{ \frac{[1 - (0.4444 + 0.3222 + 0.0444)]}{(0.2111 + 0.2778 + 0)} \right\} (1 - 0.40) = 23.2\%$$

Applying Equation [9-7], the ROE is calculated to be

$$ROE = \frac{EBIT}{TSHE}(1 - TR) = \frac{(16{,}060{,}000)(1 - 0.40)}{34{,}000{,}000} = \frac{(16{,}060{,}000)(0.60)}{34{,}000{,}000} = 28.3\%$$

which is duplicated by applying Equation [9-26] and using the data in Table 9-17.

$$ROE = \left\{ \frac{\left[1 - \left(\frac{COGS}{NetRev} + \frac{OpExp}{NetRev} + \frac{D\&A}{NetRev} + \frac{NetInt}{NetRev}\right)\right]}{\left(\frac{WC_{XSTD}}{NetRev} + \frac{NetFA}{NetRev} + \frac{NetIA}{NetRev} - \frac{IBD}{NetRev}\right)} \right\} (1 - TR) \qquad [9\text{-}26]$$

$$ROE = \left\{ \frac{[1 - (0.4444 + 0.3222 + 0.0444 + 0.0104)]}{(0.2111 + 0.2778 + 0 - 0.1111)} \right\} (1 - 0.40) = 28.3\%$$

Capital Structure (5): $20 Million of Additional Equity to Fund Future Growth

The financial statements for the Company with $20,000,000 of additional TSHE are shown in Tables 9-18 and 9-19.

As before the data necessary to calculate the ROCE and ROE for Capital Structure (5) is taken from Nobel's financial statements and summarized in Table 9-20.

The ROCE is calculated by applying Equation [9-1],

$$ROCE = \frac{(EBIT)(1-TR)}{STD+LTD+TSHE} = \frac{(17,000,000)(1-0.40)}{0+0+64,000,000} = \frac{(17,000,000)(0.60)}{64,000,000} = 15.9\%$$

or by applying Equation [9-2] and using the data in Table 9-20:

$$ROCE = \left\{ \frac{\left[1-\left(\frac{COGS}{NetRev}+\frac{OpExp}{NetRev}+\frac{D\&A}{NetRev}\right)\right]}{\left(\frac{WC_{XSTD}}{NetRev}+\frac{NetFA}{NetRev}+\frac{NetIA}{NetRev}\right)} \right\}(1-TR) \qquad [9\text{-}2]$$

$$ROCE = \left\{ \frac{[1-(0.4444+0.3222+0.0444)]}{(0.4333+0.2778+0)} \right\}(1-0.40) = 15.9\%$$

The ROE for Capital Structure (5) is calculated by applying Equations [9-7] or [9-26]. Applying Equation [9-7], the ROE is calculated to be

$$ROE = \frac{EBT}{TSHE}(1-TR) = \frac{(17,000,000)(1-0.40)}{64,000,000} = \frac{(17,000,000)(0.60)}{64,000,000} = 15.9\%$$

TABLE 9-18 Nobel Electronics Inc. Balance Sheet for Capital Structure (5) $(000)'s

Total Current Assets	45,000	Other Current Liabilities	6,000
		Short-Term Debt	0
Net Fixed Assets	25,000	Long-Term Debt	0
Net Intang Assets	0	Shareholders' Equity	64,000
Total Assets	70,000	Total Liabilities + TSHE	70,000

TABLE 9-19 Nobel Electronics Inc. Income Statement for Capital Structure (5) $(000)'s

Net Revenues		90,000
Cost of Goods Sold (COGS)		(40,000)
Operating Expenses (OpExp)		(29,000)
EBITDA		21,000
Depreciation and Amortization (D&A)		(4,000)
EBIT		17,000
Interest Income/Expense (NetInt)		0
Earnings before Tax (EBT)		17,000
Taxes Paid (TaxesPaid) @	40%	(6,800)
Net Income (NI)		10,200

TABLE 9-20 Capital Structure (5) Data for ROCE and ROE Calculations $(000)'s and %

Income Statement				
EBIT	=	17,000,000	=	17,000,000
EBT	=	17,000,000	=	17,000,000
COGS/Rev	=	40,000,000/90,000,000	=	44.44%
OpExp/Rev	=	29,000,000/90,000,000	=	32.22%
D&A/Rev	=	4,000,000/90,000,000	=	4.44%
NetInt/Rev	=	0/90,000,000	=	0.00%
Tax Rate (TR)	=	0.4	=	40.00%
Balance Sheet				
Cap Employed (CE)	=	0 + 0 + 64,000,000	=	64,000,000
Total SHE (TSHE)	=	64,000,000		64,000,000
WC_{XSTD}/Rev	=	(45,000,000 – 6,000,000)/90,000,000		
	=	39,000,000/90,000,000	=	43.33%
NetFA/Rev	=	25,000,000/90,000,000	=	27.78%
NetIA/Rev	=	0/90,000,000	=	0.00%
IBD/Rev	=	(0 + 0)/90,000,000	=	0.00%

The result just calculated is confirmed using Equation [9-26] and the data in Table 9-20.

$$ROE = \left\{ \frac{\left[1 - \left(\frac{COGS}{NetRev} + \frac{OpExp}{NetRev} + \frac{D\&A}{NetRev} + \frac{NetInt}{NetRev} \right)\right]}{\left(\frac{WC_{XSTD}}{NetRev} + \frac{NetFA}{NetRev} + \frac{NetIA}{NetRev} - \frac{IBD}{NetRev} \right)} \right\}(1 - TR) \qquad [9\text{-}26]$$

$$ROE = \left\{ \frac{[1 - (0.4444 + 0.3222 + 0.0444 + 0)]}{(0.2111 + 0.2778 + 0 - 0)} \right\}(1 - 0.40) = 15.9\%$$

Capital Structure (6): $20 Million of LTD at 10% in Place of an Equal Amount of TSHE

The financial statements for the Company with $20,000,000 of LTD at a 10% interest rate are shown in Tables 9-21 and 9-22.

As before, the data necessary to calculate the ROCE and ROE for Capital Structure (6) is taken from Tables 9-21 and 9-22 and summarized in Table 9-23.

Using the data and Equation [9-1], the ROCE for Capital Structure (6) is calculated.

$$ROCE = \frac{(EBIT)(1 - TR)}{STD + LTD + TSHE} = \frac{(17,000,000)(1 - 0.40)}{0 + 20,000,000 + 44,000,000}$$

$$= \frac{(17,000,000)(0.60)}{64,000,000} = 15.9\%$$

TABLE 9-21 Nobel Electronics Inc. Balance Sheet for Capital Structure (6) $(000)'s

Total Current Assets	45,000	Other Current Liabilities	6,000
		Short-Term Debt	0
Net Fixed Assets	25,000	Long-Term Debt	20,000
Net Intang Assets	0	Shareholders' Equity	44,000
Total Assets	70,000	Total Liabilities + TSHE	70,000

TABLE 9-22 Nobel Electronics Inc. Income Statement for Capital Structure (6) $(000)'s

Net Revenues		90,000
Cost of Goods Sold (COGS)		(40,000)
Operating Expenses (OpExp)		(29,000)
EBITDA		21,000
Depreciation and Amortization (D&A)		(4,000)
EBIT		17,000
Interest Income/Expense (NetInt)		(2,000)
Earnings before Tax (EBT)		15,000
Taxes Paid (TaxesPaid)s @	40%	(6,000)
Net Income (NI)		9,000

Once again applying Equation [9-2], but this time using the data in Table 9-23, gives the same result.

$$ROCE = \left\{ \frac{\left[1 - \left(\frac{COGS}{NetRev} + \frac{OpExp}{NetRev} + \frac{D\&A}{NetRev}\right)\right]}{\left(\frac{WC_{XSTD}}{NetRev} + \frac{NetFA}{NetRev} + \frac{NetIA}{NetRev}\right)} \right\}(1 - TR) \qquad [9\text{-}2]$$

$$ROCE = \left\{ \frac{[1 - (0.4444 + 0.3222 + 0.0444)]}{(0.4333 + 0.2778 + 0)} \right\}(1 - 0.40) = 15.9\%$$

TABLE 9-23 Capital Structure (6) Data for ROCE and ROE Calculations $(000)'s and %

Income Statement				
EBIT	=	17,000,000	=	17,000,000
EBT	=	15,000,000	=	15,000,000
COGS/Rev	=	40,000,000/90,000,000	=	44.44%
OpExp/Rev	=	29,000,000/90,000,000	=	32.22%
D&A/Rev	=	4,000,000/90,000,000	=	4.44%
NetInt/Rev	=	2,000,000/90,000,000	=	2.22%
Tax Rate (TR)	=	0.4	=	40.00%
Balance Sheet				
Cap Employed (CE)	=	0 + 20,000,000 + 44,000,000	=	64,000,000
Total SHE (TSHE)	=	44,000,000		44,000,000
WC_{XSTD}/Rev	=	(45,000,000 – 6,000,000)/90,000,000		
	=	39,000,000/90,000,000	=	43.33%
NetFA/Rev	=	25,000,000/90,000,000	=	27.78%
NeIA/Rev	=	0/90,000,000	=	0.00%
IBD/Rev	=	(0 + 20,000,000)/90,000,000	=	22.22%

The ROE for Capital Structure (6) is calculated by utilizing the data in Table 9-23 and Equation [9-7]:

$$ROE = \frac{EBT}{TSHE}(1-TR) = \frac{(15{,}000{,}000)(1-0.40)}{44{,}000{,}000} = \frac{(15{,}000{,}000)(0.60)}{44{,}000{,}000} = 20.5\%$$

Applying Equation [9-26] and once again using the data in Table 9-23 confirms the result.

$$ROE = \left\{ \frac{\left[1-\left(\frac{COGS}{NetRev}+\frac{OpExp}{NetRev}+\frac{D\&A}{NetRev}+\frac{NetInt}{NetRev}\right)\right]}{\left(\frac{WC_{XSTD}}{NetRev}+\frac{NetFA}{NetRev}+\frac{NetIA}{NetRev}-\frac{IBD}{NetRev}\right)} \right\}(1-TR) \qquad [9\text{-}26]$$

$$ROE = \left\{ \frac{[1-(0.4444+0.3222+0.0444+0.0222)]}{(0.4333+0.2778+0-0.2222)} \right\}(1-0.40) = 20.5\%$$

Discussion

When the exercise is complete, the treasurer prepares a summary of the results of the various capital structures and returns as shown in Table 9-24 and proceeds to prepare notes on each case.

Capital Structure (1), the return on capital employed and return on equity, are identical at 23.2%. This is consistent with what one would expect since the Company has no debt and the capital employed consists solely of shareholders' equity.

Capital Structure (2) shows the impact of levering up the Balance Sheet by substituting $10,000,000 of LTD at 10% for an equivalent amount of total shareholders' equity. EBT is $1,000,000 less than the unlevered case due to interest on the debt. Since EBIT

TABLE 9-24 Leverage Summary for Capital Structures (1)–(6) $(000)'s and %

Capital Structure, ROCE and ROE	CS (1) No Leverage	CS (2) LTD @ 10%	CS (3) STD @ 8%	CS (4) LTD @ 10% STD @ 8%	CS (5) Equity Financed Growth	CS (6) LTD Financed Growth
Short-Term Debt (STD)	0	0	10,000	3,000	0	0
Long-Term Debt (LTD)	0	10,000	0	7,000	0	20,000
Total Shareholder Equity (TSHE)	44,000	34,000	34,000	34,000	64,000	44,000
Interest-Bearing Debt (IBD)	0	10,000	10,000	10,000	0	20,000
Return on Capital Employed (ROCE)	23.2%	23.2%	23.2%	23.2%	15.9%	15.9%
Return on Equity (ROE)	23.2%	28.2%	28.6%	28.3%	15.9%	20.5%

and capital employed are unchanged, ROCE remains at 23.2%. The ROE, on the other hand, is enhanced dramatically due to the large reduction in TSHE and increases from 23.2% to 28.2%.

In Capital Structure (3), the ROCE is unaffected since the EBIT and capital employed remain unchanged. The ROE is modestly enhanced as a result of higher net income facilitated by the substitution of $10,000,000 of 10% LTD with an equal amount of 8% STD.

The ROE in Capital Structure (4) is largely unchanged and falls in between Capital Structures (2) and (3) because of a blend of 8% STD and 10% LTD and their impact on EBT. ROCE remains at 23.2% due to the fact that the blend of STD and LTD did not change the capital employed.

In Capital Structure (5), the company raises $20,000,000 of equity to finance growth, thus increasing the TSHE and capital employed to $64,000,000. Since EBIT remains unchanged at $17,000,000, ROCE is dramatically reduced to 15.9%. With no debt, the EBT is the same as EBIT. But since the TSHE has increased, the ROE takes a corresponding decrease and once again equals the ROCE.

Capital Structure (6) finances growth with $20,000,000 of LTD and by doing so results in capital employed of $64,000,000, which is identical to Capital Structure (5), producing an ROCE of 15.9%. The EBT decreases to $15,000,000 as a result of the interest expense. But this is more than offset by the reduction in TSHE to $44,000,000 and produces a ROE of 20.5%.

While the case for debt is made by Capital Structure (6), the treasurer feels that this scenario isn't comparable to any other because while (6) includes the impact of debt financing it doesn't reflect the income that is expected to result from the growth. He returns to the forecasted financials and sees that over the life of the plan, the EBT systematically increases significantly as a percentage of revenue due to the higher volume and lower cost of goods sold. The OpExp and D&A ratios remain relatively constant as do the Balance Sheet statistics. Also, as one would expect, interest expense as a percentage of revenue decreased. The treasurer runs some quick calculations and sees that, based on the plan, the ROCE and ROE will be in the mid-twenties and mid thirties respectively by Year 5. With this information in hand he proceeds to draft his financing recommendation to the management team and board of directors.

Something for Nothing?

Perhaps the most dramatic messages from Table 9-24 are: Every time debt is used in place of equity (CS (2), CS (3), CS (4), and CS (6)) the ROE improves and is greater than ROCE. Does this mean that shareholders get something for nothing? The answer is no. Shareholders have an opportunity for higher returns at the expense of increased risk by virtue of the debt obligations the company has taken on its Balance Sheet. Also, the debt has implications for cash flow and stands above the equity holders in the event of a default that results in a reorganization or liquidation.

FINANCIAL COVENANTS

When lenders negotiate loans with borrowers, they want to be sure the borrower's ability to meet financial obligations does not deteriorate to a level that adds undue interest or principal collection risk. To protect themselves, they require that certain financial ratios be met. They also want to know how the money they lend will be used and, therefore, may place limits on such things as dividends, capital expenditures, and acquisitions. Usually the borrower is required to calculate the performance of the company against the covenants quarterly and certify at least annually that the calculations are an accurate and true representation of the performance of the business. Loans that meet the requirements are considered to be *performing*. Those that don't are categorized as *nonperforming*. When that happens, the level of attention lenders pay to the business moves up several notches and, if bad enough, the lender will assign the loan to their "troubled asset" or "workout" team.

There isn't any standard set of covenants. They vary from loan to loan and are arrived at after a process whereby the lender (who may want the tightest possible performance covenants to minimize risk) and the borrower (who wants maximum flexibility when using the proceeds of the loan) arrive at a middle ground that both parties consider to be "market." It may seem to the reader that the process is unfairly biased in favor of the lender because, after all, they have the money. This can be true especially if a borrower has a weak balance sheet and a non-stellar Income Statement. However, lenders are in the business of lending money and there are lots of good companies with solid performance out there; in order to gain leverage, the company's treasurer will outline the borrowing requirements and ask several institutions to prepare term sheets. Once the term sheets are in, the treasurer will pick two or three of the most attractive offers and begin the negotiating process.

Some of the more common covenants are as follows.

$$Debt\ to\ Equity\ Ratio = \frac{Total\ Debt}{Total\ Shareholders'\ Equity} = \frac{Total\ Debt}{TSHE} \qquad [9\text{-}27]$$

In practice a company can have several levels of debt and each secured party will have their own definition of Equation [9-27]. For example, if a bank or insurance company is the senior lender, they will be primarily concerned with the equity that stands below them. If the company has other kinds of debt (mezzanine), then the senior lender will probably insist on a couple of definitions of *debt-to-equity*: one with only their debt and the other that includes all debt. This ratio is seldom seen in loan agreements and, if present, will be of a magnitude that other covenants are tripped before the debt-to-equity covenant is breached. The reason for this is that interest and loans are paid with cash flow and hence EBITDA usually becomes the critical consideration.

$$Senior\ Leverage\ Ratio = \frac{Senior\ Debt}{EBITDA} \qquad [9\text{-}28]$$

The *Senior Leverage Ratio* is a measure of the ability of the company's cash flow (as represented by EBITDA) to service and repay the loan. This ratio is very important to holders of the senior debt (senior to other debt and the shareholders' equity), which is often banks.

$$\text{Total Leverage Ratio} = \frac{\text{Total Debt}}{\text{EBITDA}} \quad [9\text{-}29]$$

Like the Senior Leverage Ratio, the *Total Leverage Ratio* is a measure of the company's ability to service debt but, in this case, all of the debt. Like all ratios, this one is also of interest to senior lenders but it is especially important to lenders that stand below the senior debt.

When it comes to the *Fixed Charge Ratio*, there are at least two in common usage. The difference, of course, is whether the Taxes Paid is deducted from EBITDA. Equation [9-31] may appear to be more stringent than Equation [9-30], but it need not be so. It all depends on the number negotiated for the covenant.

$$\text{Fixed Charge Ratio} = \frac{\text{EBITDA}}{\text{Fixed Charges}} = \frac{\text{EBITDA}}{\text{Interest} + \text{Principal Repayment} + \text{Capital Expenditures}} \quad [9\text{-}30]$$

And

$$\text{Fixed Charge Ratio} = \frac{\text{EBITDA} - \text{Taxes Paid}}{\text{Fixed Charges}} = \frac{\text{EBITDA} - \text{Taxes Paid}}{\text{Interest} + \text{Principal Repayment} + \text{Capital Expenditures}} \quad [9\text{-}31]$$

This ratio measures the number of times the company's after-tax cash flow can service the debt as well as meet the needs of the capital expenditure budget. If dividends are material or a concern to the lenders, dividends paid may also be subtracted from the EBITDA in the numerator. At first glance, one might wonder why the lenders would be concerned about anything except interest payments and loan repayments. The reason is that to stay healthy a company needs to reinvest cash flow in the business and the lenders want to be sure they have the wherewithal to do so. In addition, they don't want the company's capital expenditures to reach a point that ratchets up the risk associated with the interest and principal repayment.

The *Interest Coverage Ratio* is another measure of the company's cash flow (as measured by EBITDA) to service the debt.

$$\text{Interest Coverage Ratio} = \frac{\text{EBITDA}}{\text{Interest}} \quad [9\text{-}32]$$

The net worth of a company is the sum of the shareholders' capital and retained earnings. The retained earnings are the aggregate earnings of the business less any dividends paid. It is usually intended to make sure dividend payments do not reach a level that adversely affects the company's capital base.

$$\text{Net Worth Covenant} = \text{Net Worth Always} > \text{Some Specified \$ Value} \quad [9\text{-}33]$$

EXAMPLE 9-2: FINANCIAL PERFORMANCE COVENANTS

Paradigm Corporation, as its name implies, has entered a niche of the smart-chip industry with game-changing technology. The original investors wanted to limit the capital they had at risk, so rather than raise another round of equity, they went to the debt markets to obtain working and growth capital for the business. Under the terms of the loan agreements, the CFO of Paradigm is obliged to calculate the company's performance against the financial covenants at the end of every quarter and certify annually that the data presented to the lenders is an accurate and a true representation of the performance of the company. Tables 9-25 and 9-26 are the year-end Income and Balance Sheet Statements for Paradigm.

Table 9-27 is a summary of the financial covenants contained in the loan agreements. According to the terms of the agreements, Paradigm is not obliged to make any principal payments during the life of the loans.

Using the data in Tables 9-25 and 9-26 the CFO proceeds to calculate the company's performance against the covenants as follows.

TABLE 9-25 Paradigm Corporation Income Statement

Year Ending December 31, 20XX $(000)'s		
Net Revenues		153,000
Cost of Goods Sold (COGS)		(79,900)
Gross Margin (GM)		73,100
Operating Expenses (OpExp)		(45,900)
Earnings before Interest, Depreciation, and Amortization (EBITDA)		27,200
Depreciation and Amortization (D&A)		(5,100)
Earnings before Interest and Taxes (EBIT)		22,100
Interest Income/Expense (Int)		(2,953)
Earnings before Tax (EBT)		19,147
Taxes Paid (TaxesPaid) @	40%	(7,659)
Net Income (NI)		11,488

TABLE 9-26 Paradigm Corporation Balance Sheet ($000's)

As at December 31, 20XX $(000)'s			
Current Assets		**Current Liabilities**	
Cash	1,500	Accounts Payable	9,000
Accounts Receivable	21,000	Taxes Payable	0
Inventory	37,500	Short-Term Debt	0
Total Current Assets	60,000	**Total Current Liabilities**	9,000
Fixed Assets		**Long-Term Debt**	
At Cost	105,000	Bank Revolver (3.5%)	12,000
Less Depreciation	45,000	Institutional Term Loan	22,500
Net Fixed Assets	60,000	**Total Debt**	34,500
		Shareholders' Equity	
Intangible Assets		Paid-in Capital	54,750
Goodwill and Other Int Assets	19,500	Retained Earnings	41,250
Net Intangible Assets	19,500	**Total Shareholders' Equity**	96,000
Total Assets	139,500	**Total Liabilities + TSHE**	139,500

TABLE 9-27 Paradigm Corporation Financial Performance Covenants

Total Debt-to-Equity Ratio	Not to exceed	0.45
Senior Leverage Ratio	Less than	2.5
Total Leverage Ratio	Less than	3.5
Fixed Charge Ratio	Greater than	1.5
Interest Coverage Ratio	Greater than	3.5
Net Worth Covenant $(000)'s	Greater than	65,000

While the covenants don't require the Senior and Institutional Debt-to-Equity Ratios to be certified, it is the CFO's practice to track these ratios as well as the total debt-to-equity ratio and he proceeds to calculate them using Equation [9-27].[18]

$$\textit{Senior Debt to Equity Ratio} = \frac{\textit{Senior Debt}}{\textit{Total Shareholders' Equity}} = \frac{12{,}000{,}000}{96{,}000{,}000} = 0.13$$

$$\textit{Institutional Debt to Equity Ratio} = \frac{\textit{Institutional Debt}}{\textit{Total Shareholders' Equity}} = \frac{22{,}500{,}000}{96{,}000{,}000} = 0.23$$

$$\textit{Total Debt to Equity Ratio} = \frac{\textit{Total Debt}}{\textit{Total Shareholders' Equity}} = \frac{34{,}500{,}000}{96{,}000{,}000} = 0.36$$

Next the Senior and Total Leverage Ratios are calculated using equations [9-28] and [9-29] respectively. Once again, note that while the covenants don't call for the Institutional Leverage Ratio, the CFO calculates it here as well since this is another financial statistic he has chosen to track.

$$\textit{Senior Leverage Ratio} = \frac{\textit{Senior Debt}}{\textit{EBITDA}} = \frac{12{,}000{,}000}{27{,}200{,}000} = 0.44$$

$$\textit{Institutional Leverage Ratio} = \frac{\textit{Institutional Debt}}{\textit{EBITDA}} = \frac{22{,}500{,}000}{27{,}200{,}000} = 0.83$$

$$\textit{Total Leverage Ratio} = \frac{\textit{Total Debt}}{\textit{EBITDA}} = \frac{34{,}500{,}000}{27{,}200{,}000} = 1.27$$

Next on the list is the Fixed Charge Ratio. Like the other ratios, Paradigm's Income and Balance Sheets contain most of the required information. The exception is the amount of capital expenditures that took place during the year. To get this data the CFO

[18]Note that the Total Debt-to-Equity Ratio is the sum of the Senior and Institutional Debt to Equity Ratios. Hence, if any two are known, the other is easily calculated. The same is also true for the Leverage Ratios.

accesses the Cash Flow Statement and notes that they were $6,120,000 for the year. The ratio is then calculated with the use of Equation [9-31].

$$Fixed\ Charge\ Ratio = \frac{EBITDA - Taxes\ Paid}{Interest + Principal\ Repayment + Capital\ Expenditures} \quad [9\text{-}31]$$

$$Fixed\ Charge\ Ratio = \frac{27{,}200{,}000 - 7{,}659{,}000}{2{,}953{,}000 + 0 + 6{,}120{,}000} = 2.15$$

Paradigm's Interest Coverage Ratio is calculated by substituting values for EBITDA and interest in Equation [9-32].

$$Interest\ Coverage\ Ratio = \frac{EBITDA}{Interest} = \frac{27{,}200{,}000}{2{,}953{,}000} = 9.21$$

Finally the *net-worth covenant* is obtained using Equation [9-33] and data from the Balance Sheet.

$$Net\ Worth\ Covenant = Net\ Worth\ Always > Some\ Specified\ \$\ Value$$
$$= 96{,}000{,}000 > 65{,}000{,}000$$

To complete the analysis, the CFO prepares Table 9-28, which compares Paradigm's financial ratios with the performance covenants specified in the loan documents.

The CFO notes that Paradigm's ratios exceed the lenders' requirements by a wide margin. The one area that may appear to him to be a little tight is the Debt-to-Equity Ratio. A simple calculation shows that even this ratio has a considerable safety margin.

For example, in order to reach a ratio of 0.45 the total debt would have to climb to $43,200,000 ($96,000,000)* 0.45), which is 25% higher than the current level, a healthy margin and an unlikely situation given the company's cash flow and the fact that the debt it takes on is largely under its control.

$$Maximum\ Debt\ at\ Current\ Net\ Worth = (96{,}000{,}000)(0.45) = \$43{,}200{,}000$$

Similarly the company's net worth would have to fall to $76,700,000 or 20% less than the current net worth for the Company to be in violation of this covenant. Again an unlikely situation, given the company's profitability, unless they decided to pay a healthy dividend, but that would be unusual for a fast-growing high-technology company.

$$Minimum\ Net\ Worth\ at\ Current\ Level\ of\ Debt = 34{,}500{,}000/0.45 = \$76{,}700{,}000$$

TABLE 9-28 Paradigm Corporation Performance versus Financial Covenants

Covenant	**Requirement**	**Actual**
Total Debt-to-Equity Ratio	<0.45	0.36
Senior Leverage Ratio	<2.5	0.44
Total Leverage Ratio	<3.5	1.27
Fixed Charge Ratio	>1.5	2.15
Interest Coverage Ratio	>3.5	9.21
Net-Worth Covenant $(000)'s	>65,000	96,000

In conclusion, the CFO is very comfortable presenting the certification and financial statements of a well-managed company that is not in danger of breaching its covenants with a balance sheet and Income Statement that is attractive to lenders.

CASE STUDY: EDSSON CORPORATION

Edsson Corporation has just completed its first pass at a five-year plan and, among other things, concluded it needs additional capital to support the forecasted organic growth and opportunistic acquisitions and decides to access the debt markets rather than raise another round of equity. The treasurer, who is relatively new to the company, is assigned the task of investigating possible sources of funding by the CFO. The treasurer considers various forms of financing including: bank revolver, bank term loan, asset-based lending, private placement, institutional term loan, high-yield bonds, mezzanine financing, and high-investment-grade bonds. While he was confident an asset-based loan could be obtained at attractive rates, he was reluctant to go there because of the complexity involved in the administration of such a loan. After giving the matter further thought, he concluded that high-yield bonds weren't attractive because of the interest rate they would command. Mezzanine financing was ruled out because the company has a very strong Balance Sheet and cash flow and, therefore, could borrow at much more attractive rates than what mezzanine lenders would demand. Finally, he eliminated high-investment-grade bonds for two reasons. First, the company is not large enough as measured by revenue and EBITDA. Second, Edsson is a private company and does not wish to get involved in public disclosure. That left bank, private placement, or institutional financing as possible sources for financing.

Condensed Financial Statements

The next thing the treasurer did was prepare a set of condensed financial statements for the most recent year (Tables CS 9-1 and CS 9-2).

TABLE CS 9-1 Edsson Corporation Income Statement

Year Ending December 31, 20XX $(000)'s and %			
Net Revenues		568,700	100.0%
Cost of Goods Sold		(238,854)	42.0%
Gross Margin		329,846	58.0%
Operating Expenses		(132,446)	–23.3%
EBITDA		197,400	34.7%
Depreciation and Amortization		(21,400)	–3.8%
EBIT		176,000	30.9%
Interest		(15,700)	–2.8%
EBT		160,300	28.2%
TaxesPaid (TaxesPaid) @	38%	(60,914)	–10.7%
Net Income		99,386	17.5%

TABLE CS 9-2 Edsson Corporation Balance Sheet

As at December 31, 20XX $(000)'s			
Total Current Assets	197,700	Other Current Liabilities	57,900
		Short-Term Debt	0
Net Fixed Assets	327,600	Long-Term Debt	215,600
Net Intangible Assets	31,200	Total Shareholders' Equity	283,000
Total Assets	556,500	Total Liabilities +TSHE	556,500

TABLE CS 9-3 Edsson Financial Ratios and Bank Loan Covenants

Financial Ratios		**Existing Loan Covenants**	
Debt-to-Equity Ratio	0.76	Not to exceed	1.2
Senior Leverage Ratio	1.09	Less than	3.5
Total Leverage Ratio	1.09	Less than	4.5
Fixed Charge Ratio	5.21	Greater than	1.5
Interest Coverage Ratio	12.57	Greater than	3
Net Worth $(000)'s	283,000	Not less than	121,500

And then, using the data contained in the financial statements and noting the long-term debt was all bank debt, the company's capital expenditures were running at a rate of $22,200,000, and there weren't any loan amortization payments, the treasurer proceeded to compute a set of financial ratios for the company using definitional Equations [9-27]–[9-32], comparing them to the financial covenants contained in their bank loan agreement and tabulating the results in Table CS 9-3.

Current Financial Ratios and Bank Loan Covenants

$$Debt\ to\ Equity\ Ratio = \frac{Debt}{TSHE} \quad [9\text{-}27]$$

$$Senior\ Leverage\ Ratio = \frac{Senior\ Debt}{EBITDA} \quad [9\text{-}28]$$

$$Total\ Leverage\ Ratio = \frac{Total\ Debt}{EBITDA} \quad [9\text{-}29]$$

$$Fixed\ Charge\ Ratio = \frac{EBITDA}{Interest + Loan\ Amortization + Capital\ Expenditures} \quad [9\text{-}30]$$

$$Interest\ Coverage\ Ratio = \frac{EBITDA}{Interest} \quad [9\text{-}32]$$

$$Total\ Debt\ to\ Equity\ Ratio = \frac{Total\ Debt}{TSHE} = \frac{STD + LTD}{TSHE} = \frac{0 + 215,600,000}{283,000,000} = 0.76$$

$$Senior\ Leverage\ Ratio = \frac{Senior\ Debt}{EBITDA} = \frac{Bank\ Debt}{EBITDA} = \frac{LTD}{EBITDA} = \frac{215,600,000}{197,400,000} = 1.09$$

$$Total\ Leverage\ Ratio = \frac{Total\ Debt}{EBITDA} = \frac{STD + LTD}{EBITDA} = \frac{0 + 215,600,000}{197,400,000} = 1.09$$

$$Fixed\ Charge\ Ratio = \frac{EBITDA}{Interest + Loan\ Amortization + Capital\ Expenditures}$$
$$= \frac{197,400,000}{15,700,000 + 0 + 22,200,000} = 5.21$$

$$Interest\ Coverage\ Ratio = \frac{EBITDA}{Interest} = \frac{197,400,000}{15,700,000} = 12.57$$

After studying the ratios, it was clear the company was well within the requirements of the bank covenants and the treasurer wondered why they weren't more restrictive. After doing some research, the answer was clear. The existing bank loan was negotiated nearly three years ago when the company had less than half of the current revenue and a much smaller EBITDA. Furthermore, at the time the bank loan was negotiated, these covenants were typical of what a company that wanted to maintain an investment grade rating of BBB– or better would have to live with.

Comparative Term Sheets

The next step was to invite several lenders to submit term sheets for a loan of $400,000,000 and no amortization. Included with the request was the company's five-year plan. The plan provoked many questions by the lenders, which the treasurer responded to by arranging several meetings with management. Two areas of the five-year pro-forma statements prompted questions from all potential lenders. They were the forecasted gross margin and operating expenses. The GM-related questions were relatively easy to deal with because Edsson was the low-cost producer and competition was increasing and so when the plan was put together it was decided to be conservative and show some deterioration. However, if the past was any indication of future events, previous five-year plans made the same assumption but the deterioration never came to pass. The increased operating expenses were explained by pointing out that the budget included a significant increase in research and development to fund a new and very promising breakthrough project. When this process was complete, the lenders presented their preliminary term sheets.[19] The results are tabulated in Table CS 9-4.

[19] Private placement lenders are also categorized as senior debt and pari passu with bank debt. For the purpose of this exercise the private placement lender is not categorized as senior debt.

TABLE CS 9-4 Comparison of Term Sheets Submitted to Edsson

Terms/Lender	Bank Revolver Loan	Private Placement	Institutional
Loan Amount	$400,000,000	$400,000,000	$400,000,000
Interest Rate	LIBOR + 300–400 bp	Treasuries + 425–525 bp	LIBOR + 550–675 bp
Tenor	5 years	10 Years	7 Years
Senior Debt Ratio	<3.8	n/a	n/a
Total Leverage Ratio	<4.9	<4.8	<4.5
Fixed Charge Ratio	>1.5	>1.8	>1.9
Interest Coverage Ratio	>3.5	>4.1	>4.3
Net Worth (000's)	225,000	225,000	250,000
Unused Commitment Fee	35 bp	n/a	n/a

Analyzing the Comparative Term Sheets

The treasurer's inclination was to rule out the loan offered by the banks[20] because of the tenor and the company's practice of not financing long-term assets with short-term money. However, after thinking about it for a time, he realized that the existing bank term loans had to be rolled over in about one-and-one-half years and, since the rates offered by the banks were attractive, he should consider renegotiating the loan at that time. Furthermore, he liked the idea of replacing the term loan with a revolver.

He also considered going back to the banks to see what the interest rate would be if the company was prepared to secure the loan with assets. He exchanged e-mails on this subject with the CFO, who ruled out asset-based lending due to the complications associated with pledging assets such as customer receivables and inventory and because the loan agreement would involve strict compliance requirements and reduce the company's flexibility. The next step was to share Table CS 9-4 with the CFO.

The CFO liked the idea of replacing the current $300 million bank loan with a revolver because not only were the spreads over LIBOR attractive for a $400 million revolver but, in addition, the market is very competitive at this time and in his view spreads over LIBOR were more likely than not to increase in the future.[21] He was also inclined to go with the private placement because he had a long-standing relationship with the insurance company offering the loan that started many years ago when he was treasurer of another company.

When asked how he felt by the CFO, the treasurer said he was fine with where they were headed for the reasons stated. Continuing, he said, "While the tenor of the institutional term sheet is in line with market, the interest rate that goes along with the seven-year tenor is high given they had a minimum of 1.5% on LIBOR and would involve

[20] Banks like to diversify their risk. Hence, revolvers and term loans are usually negotiated by one lead bank and once in place funded by a group of banks that have each agreed to take an amount they are comfortable with based on how they view the credit, their exposure to the borrower's market, and their loan portfolio as a whole.
[21] LIBOR is a floating rate, so if rates go up, so will the company's cost. The basis points the company pays in addition to the LIBOR rate are fixed.

putting the company through one or more of the rating agency processes. In addition, the loan would have to be secured."

A discussion followed, during which they concluded they wouldn't rule out an institutional loan but their focus would be on the private placement, at which time the treasurer floated the idea of increasing the amount of the loan to $450 million.

After thinking about it, the CFO stated, "If we can arrange a loan at attractive rates, I'm all in favor of it. It would mean that we wouldn't use the revolver to the limit in the short run but given the way the company is growing, it sure would be nice to have the additional borrowing capacity. While we are on the subject of borrowing capacity, I hope we agree that we only top up the bank loan to $400 million providing the unused commitment fee, if any, is less than 20 basis points."

The meeting concluded with agreement that the treasurer should go back to the private placement folks and negotiate the terms for a 10-year $450 million loan and talk to the banks about a revolver with a 5-year tenor and a total line of credit of $400 million.

Discussions with Lenders

The treasurer's first call was to the lead bank. During the call, he stated the company would like to renegotiate the bank loan in the amount of $400 million for a five-year period. He also explained that, in addition, they would be doing a $450 million private placement and, in order for them to do so, the company would require a much higher Total Leverage Ratio. The treasurer then stated that he was pleased to see the banks were looking at this as a cash flow loan and were no longer requiring a debt-to-equity covenant but that he thought given the company's performance, the net-worth covenant was somewhat on the high side. Finally, he reinforced the importance of the banks coming back with a much lower unused commitment fee.[22]

The next call was to the insurance company (private placement). During this call the treasurer explained the company was now looking at a $450 million private placement and was considering two sources of long-term financing: the 10-year tenor the insurance company had offered and another that had an acceptable tenor of 7 years. He also indicated that the CFO had a preference for doing the loan with the insurance company because of the long history, but he, as the treasurer, had to get the best deal for the company and asked them to go back and reconsider their terms, especially the interest rate, Total Leverage Ratio, and the net-worth requirement. The insurance company questioned the need for a Total Leverage Ratio given that typically they were considered as senior debt.

The treasurer responded by saying, "Our current thinking is we only want one senior lender (banks), so you should price your loan and calculate your covenants accordingly." A week later the treasurer had the results, which he tabulated in Table CS 9-5.

Revised Term Sheets

After studying the revised term sheets summarized in Table CS 9-5, the treasurer concluded that as far as the banks were concerned the interest rate they proposed was "at market,"

[22]Once banks have agreed to fund a loan that can be drawn down to some amount they are obliged keep the funds that are not drawn down available to lender when required. This impacts their ability to make other loans. Therefore, there usually is an unused commitment fee applied to any unused amount.

TABLE CS 9-5 Comparison of Revised Term Sheets Submitted to Edsson

Terms/Lender	Bank Revolver Loan	Private Placement
Loan Amount	$400,000,000	$450,000,000
Interest Rate	LIBOR + 340 bp	Treasuries + 485 bp
Tenor	5 years	10 Years
Senior Leverage Ratio	<3.8	n/a
Total Leverage Ratio	<5.2	<5.3
Fixed Charge Ratio	>1.5	>1.8
Interest Coverage Ratio	>3.5	>4.1
Net Worth (000's)	215,000	215,000
Unused Commitment Fee	35 bp	n/a

the net-worth requirement was not excessive, and the Senior and Total Leverage Ratios were acceptable, but the unused commitment fee was still out of line. As for the insurance company, he felt their interest rate was above market, but otherwise the terms were okay.

His first call was to the lead bank. He informed them he had a big problem with the unused commitment fee and unless they proposed something more reasonable, he was going to shop the loan. The discussion with the insurance company was equally direct and focused on the interest rate being above market and, if they wanted the loan, they need to come back with a rate that reflected the quality of the Company's balance sheet and earnings. The responses are shown in Table CS 9-6.

Final Term Sheets

At this point, the treasurer felt he was close to a deal but, before he discussed it with the CFO, he needed to look at what the ratios would look like in Year 5 of the business plan.

The first step would be to update the Year 5 Income Statement to reflect the interest the Company would pay during that year. After looking at the LIBOR trend for several months, it appeared that it was fairly constant at 1.25% and more than likely this would be the rate in effect when lender documents were signed. Also, 10-year Treasuries had been stable at 2.30% for some time.

TABLE CS 9-6 Comparison of Final Term Sheets Submitted to Edsson

Terms/Lender	Bank Revolver Loan	Private Placement
Loan Amount	$400,000,000	$450,000,000
Interest Rate	LIBOR + 340 bp	Treasuries + 460 bp
Tenor	5 years	10 Years
Senior Leverage Ratio	<3.8	n/a
Total Leverage Ratio	<5.2	<5.3
Fixed Charge Ratio	>1.5	>1.8
Interest Coverage Ratio	>3.5	>4.1
Net Worth $(000)'s	215,000	215,000
Unused Commitment Fee	25 bp	n/a

Calculating Interest Costs

Using the basis points the lenders had quoted, the interest rates on the bank and private placement loans were calculated as follows:

$$\textit{Bank Loan Interest Rate} = 1.25 + 3.40 = 4.65\%$$

$$\textit{Private Placement Loan Interest Rate} = 2.30 + 4.60 = 6.90\%$$

Referring to Edsson's pro-forma balance sheet for Year 5 (Table CS 9-8), he noted that the amount drawn down on the bank loan would be $290,500,000 and the private placement loan would be fully utilized at $450,000,000. With this information, he calculated the interest charges as follows.

$$\textit{Bank Interest} = (290{,}500{,}000)(0.0465) = \$13{,}508{,}000$$

$$\textit{Unused Commitment Fee} = (400{,}000{,}000 - 290{,}500{,}000)(0.0025)$$
$$= (109{,}500{,}000)(0.0025) = \$274{,}000$$

$$\textit{Total Bank Charges} = 13{,}508{,}000 + 274{,}000 = \$13{,}782{,}000$$

$$\textit{Private Placement Interest} = (450{,}000{,}000)(0.069) = \$31{,}050{,}000$$

$$\textit{Total Interest Expense Year } 5 = 13{,}782{,}000 + 31{,}050{,}000 = \$44{,}832{,}000$$

Business Plan Year 5 Pro-Forma Financial Statements Adjusted to Reflect Interest Costs

The adjusted Income Statement and Balance Sheet for Year 5 of the business plan are shown in Tables CS 9-7 and CS 9-8. With this information in hand, he proceeded to calculate the Senior Leverage [9-28], Total Leverage [9-29], Interest Coverage [9-32], and Fixed Charge [9-31] ratios.

TABLE CS 9-7 Edsson Corporation Income Statement for Year 5 of the Business Plan ($000's and %)

Net Revenues		1,421,750	100.0%
Cost of Goods Sold		(639,788)	45.0%
Gross Margin		781,963	55.0%
Operating Expenses		(426,525)	30.0%
EBITDA		355,438	25.0%
Depreciation and Amortization		(56,870)	4.0%
EBIT		298,568	21.0%
Interest		(44,832)	3.2%
EBT		253,736	17.8%
Taxes Paid (TaxesPaid) @	38%	(96,419)	6.8%
Net Income		157,316	11.1%

TABLE CS 9-8 Edsson Corporation Balance Sheet for Year 5 of the Business Plan ($000's and %)

Total Current Assets	344,250	Other Current Liabilities	144,750
		Short-Term Debt	0
Net Fixed Assets	801,000	Senior Bank Debt	290,500
		Private Placement Debt	450,000
Net Intangible Assets	106,000		
		Total Shareholders' Equity	366,000
Total Assets	1,251,250	Total Liabilities + TSHE	1,251,250

Year 5 Financial Ratios and Headroom versus Lenders Covenant Requirements

$$\textit{Senior Leverage Ratio} = \frac{\textit{Senior Debt}}{\textit{EBITDA}} = \frac{290{,}500{,}000}{355{,}438{,}000} = 0.82$$

$$\textit{Total Leverage Ratio} = \frac{\textit{Total Debt}}{\textit{EBITDA}} = \frac{\textit{Senior Debt} + \textit{LTD}}{\textit{EBITDA}}$$

$$= \frac{290{,}500{,}000 + 450{,}000{,}000}{355{,}438{,}000} = 2.08$$

$$\textit{Interest Coverage Ratio} = \frac{\textit{EBITDA}}{\textit{Interest}} = \frac{355{,}438{,}000}{44{,}832{,}000} = 7.93$$

While perusing the business plan, the treasurer noted that capital expenditures during Year 5 are expected to amount to $60,000,000. Also, since there isn't any loan amortization and total interest charges were previously estimated to be $44,832,000, the treasurer was able to quickly compute the expected Fixed Charge Ratio and prepare Table CS 9-9.

$$\textit{Fixed Charge Ratio} = \frac{\textit{EBITDA}}{\textit{Interest} + \textit{LoanAmort} + \textit{CapitalEx}}$$

$$= \frac{355{,}438{,}000}{44{,}832{,}000 + 0 + 60{,}000{,}000} = 3.39$$

TABLE CS 9-9 Year 5 Ratios versus Bank and Private Placement Requirements

Terms/Lender	Year 5 Ratios	Bank Term Loan	Private Placement
Senior Leverage Ratio	0.82	<3.8	n/a
Total Leverage Ratio	2.08	<5.2	<5.3
Fixed Charge Ratio	3.39	>1.5	>1.8
Interest Coverage Ratio	7.93	>3.5	>4.1
Net Worth $(000)'s	366,000	>215,000	>215,000

TABLE CS 9-10 Year 5 Ratios as Percentage of Lender Covenant Requirements

Terms/Lender	Year 5 Ratio	% Bank Covenant	% Private Covenant
Senior Leverage Ratio	0.82	22%	n/a
Total Leverage Ratio	2.08	40%	39%
Fixed Charge Ratio	3.39	226%	188%
Interest Coverage Ratio	7.93	227%	193%
Net Worth $(000)'s	366,000	170%	170%

Finally, he estimated the "covenant headroom" the company would have by expressing each of Year 5's ratios as a percentage of the bank's and private placement covenant requirements and summarized them in Table CS 9-10.

The treasurer was now ready to present the results of his effort to the CFO.

The CFO was on the whole very satisfied with what he saw but thought the unused commitment fee was still too high. The treasurer agreed it was higher than what they had set as a goal but pointed out the interest rate was attractive and given his druthers he would rather pay a little more for money the company didn't draw down than a higher fee on the money the company borrowed. The CFO resisted this line of reasoning briefly but quickly came to the conclusion the treasurer was right. The discussion then proceeded to the Year 5 financial ratios and the covenants. At first, the CFO was sure there was something wrong with the calculations because in his former life as a treasurer he had never seen such headroom. The treasurer assured him the calculations had been checked and were correct.

The CFO then proceeded to ask why the lenders were so generous. The treasurer pointed out that covenants were "market" and the reason there was so much room for unforeseen business conditions or adverse financial events was that the Company was best in class, growing rapidly, hugely profitable, and threw off lots of cash. The CFO congratulated him on a job well done and asked him to go ahead and begin negotiations with the lenders, but before the agreements were finalized, he would like to see the impact that the new debt would have on the company's return on equity and return on capital employed. The treasurer responded by saying he had already done that and handed the CFO a copy of Table CS 9-11 and the supporting calculations. (See definitional Equations [9-3] and [9-1].)

TABLE CS 9-11 Edsson Current and Forecasted Year 5 ROE and ROCE

	Current	Year 5
Return on Equity	35.1%	43.0%
Return on Capital Employed	21.9%	16.7%

Impact of Leverage on ROE and ROCE

$$ROE = \frac{Net\ Income}{Total\ Shareholders'\ Equity} \quad [9\text{-}3]$$

$$ROCE = \frac{EBIT}{CE}(1-TR) = \frac{(EBIT)(1-TR)}{STD+LTD+TSHE} \quad [9\text{-}1]$$

$$Current\ ROE = \frac{99,386,000}{283,000,000} = 35.1\%$$

$$Current\ ROCE = \frac{EBIT}{CE}(1-TR) = \frac{(176,000,000)(1-0.38)}{215,600,000+283,000,000}$$
$$= \frac{(176,000,000)(0.62)}{498,600,000} = 21.9\%$$

$$Year\ 5\ ROE = \frac{157,316,000}{366,000,000} = 43.0\%$$

$$Year\ 5\ ROCE = \frac{EBIT}{CE}(1-TR) = \frac{(298,568,000)(1-0.38)}{290,500,000+450,000,000+366,000,000} = 16.7\%$$

While the CFO was scanning the material he had just received, the treasurer pointed out that while the additional debt will result in a 5.2-point decrease in ROCE, the ROE will increase from 35.1% to 43.0%, or 7.9 points. The CFO's response was: "The reduced ROCE is not a problem because the increased ROE is good for shareholders." He was, however, concerned about the magnitude of the changes and asked the treasurer to come up with a more detailed explanation of what exactly is driving the changes in ROE and ROCE.

The treasurer returned to his office, reviewed the literature, and identified a couple of expressions that broke down ROE and ROCE in terms of Balance Sheet and Income Statement components (ROE and ROCE Driver Equations, [9-26] and [9-2] respectively).

$$ROE\ (Driver\ Equation) = \left\{ \frac{\left[1-\left(\frac{COGS}{NetRev}+\frac{OpExp}{NetRev}+\frac{D\&A}{NetRev}+\frac{Int}{NetRev}\right)\right]}{\left(\frac{WC_{XSTD}}{NetRev}+\frac{NetFA}{NetRev}+\frac{NetIA}{NetRev}-\frac{IBD}{NetRev}\right)} \right\}(1-TR) \quad [9\text{-}26]$$

$$ROCE\ (Driver\ Equation) = \left\{ \frac{\left[1-\left(\frac{COGS}{NetRev}+\frac{OpExp}{NetRev}+\frac{D\&A}{NetRev}\right)\right]}{\left(\frac{WC_{XSTD}}{NetRev}+\frac{NetFA}{NetRev}+\frac{NetIA}{NetRev}\right)} \right\}(1-TR) \quad [9\text{-}2]$$

Then, substituting data from Tables CS 9-1 and CS 9-2 in Equation [9-26] (ROE Driver Equation), the ROE for the current year was obtained in terms of the Income Statement and Balance Sheet components.

$$\text{Current ROE} = \left\{ \frac{\left[1 - \left(\frac{238,854}{568,700} + \frac{132,446}{568,700} + \frac{21,400}{568,700} + \frac{15,700}{568,700}\right)\right]}{\left(\frac{197,700 - 57,900}{568,700} + \frac{327,600}{568,700} + \frac{31,200}{568,700} - \frac{215,600}{568,700}\right)} \right\}(1 - 0.38)$$

$$\text{Current ROE} = \left\{ \frac{[1 - (0.420 + 0.233 + 0.038 + 0.028)]}{(0.246 + 0.576 + 0.055 - 0.379)} \right\}(0.62) = 35.1\%$$

Similarly, using data from Tables CS 9-7 and CS 9-8, the ROE for Year 5 of the business plan was obtained.

$$\text{Year 5 ROE} = \left\{ \frac{\left[1 - \left(\frac{639,788}{1,421,750} + \frac{426,525}{1,421,750} + \frac{56,870}{1,421,750} + \frac{44,832}{1,421,750}\right)\right]}{\left(\frac{344,250 - 144,750}{1,421,750} + \frac{801,000}{1,421,750} + \frac{106,000}{1,421,750} - \frac{290,500 + 450,000}{1,421,750}\right)} \right\}(1 - 0.38)$$

$$\text{Year5 ROE} = \left\{ \frac{[1 - (0.450 + 0.300 + 0.0400 + 0.0316)]}{(0.140 + 0.563 + 0.0746 - 0.521)} \right\}(0.62) = 43.0\%$$

Next he proceeded to apply the Income Statement and Balance Sheet data to the ROCE Driver Equation.

$$\text{Current ROCE} = \left\{ \frac{\left[1 - \left(\frac{238,854}{568,700} + \frac{132,446}{568,700} + \frac{21,400}{568,700}\right)\right]}{\left(\frac{197,700 - 57,900}{568,700} + \frac{327,600}{568,700} + \frac{31,200}{568,700}\right)} \right\}(1 - 0.38)$$

$$\text{Current ROCE} = \left\{ \frac{[1 - (0.420 + 0.233 + 0.038)]}{(0.246 + 0.576 + 0.055)} \right\}(0.62) = 21.9\%$$

$$\text{Year 5 ROCE} = \left\{ \frac{\left[1 - \left(\frac{639,788}{1,421,750} + \frac{426,525}{1,421,750} + \frac{56,870}{1,421,750}\right)\right]}{\left(\frac{344,250 - 144,750}{1,421,750} + \frac{801,000}{1,421,750} + \frac{106,000}{1,421,750}\right)} \right\}(1 - 0.38)$$

$$\text{Year 5 ROCE} = \left\{ \frac{[1 - (0.450 + 0.300 + 0.0400)]}{(0.140 + 0.563 + 0.0746)} \right\}(0.62) = 16.7\%$$

After studying the results of the calculations, the treasurer first noted that the results were identical to the ROE and ROCE obtained using the traditional method and summarized in Table CS 9-11. Then he decided the meaning of the terms in the Driver Equations

TABLE CS 9-12 Summary of ROE Drivers

	Year 5	Current	Δ
COGS/Net Rev	45.00%	42.00%	–3.00%
OpExp/Net Rev	30.00%	23.29%	–6.71%
D&A/Net Rev	4.00%	3.76%	–0.24%
Interest/Net Rev	3.15%	2.76%	–0.39%
WC_{XSTD}/Net Rev	14.03%	24.58%	10.55%
NetFA/Net Rev	56.34%	57.61%	1.27%
NetIA/Net Rev	7.46%	5.49%	–1.97%
IBD/Net Rev	–52.08%	–37.91%	14.17%

were more easily understood when expressed as percentages and tabulated. He then proceeded to make some notes on what he saw in Tables CS 9-12 and CS 9-13.

$$Current\ ROE = \left\{ \frac{[1-(42.0\% + 23.3\% + 3.8\% + 2.8\%)]}{(24.6\% + 57.6\% + 5.50\% - 37.9\%)} \right\} (0.62) = 35.1\%$$

$$Year\ 5\ ROE = \left\{ \frac{[1-(45.0\% + 30.0\% + 4.00\% + 3.15\%)]}{(14.0\% + 56.3\% + 7.46 - 52.1\%)} \right\} (0.62) = 43.0\%$$

$$Current\ ROCE = \left\{ \frac{[1-(42.0\% + 23.3\% + 3.8\%)]}{(24.6\% + 57.6\% + 5.50\%)} \right\} (0.62) = 21.9\%$$

$$Year\ \ 5\ ROCE = \left\{ \frac{[1-(45.0\% + 30.0\% + 4.00\%)]}{(14.0\% + 56.3\% + 7.46\%)} \right\} (0.62) = 16.7\%$$

Clearly the earnings before tax (as represented by the numerator in the ROE Driver Equation) were adversely affected by a 3-point and 6.71-point increase in the COGS and

TABLE CS 9-13 Summary of ROCE Drivers

	Year 5	Current	Δ
COGS/Net Rev	45.00%	42.00%	–3.00%
OpExp/Net Rev	30.00%	23.29%	–6.71%
D&A/Net Rev	4.00%	3.76%	–0.24%
Interest/Net Rev	NA	NA	NA
WC_{XSTD}/Net Rev	14.03%	24.58%	10.55%
NetFA/Net Rev	56.34%	57.61%	1.27%
NetIA/Net Rev	7.46%	5.49%	–1.97%
IBD/Net Rev	NA	NA	NA

OpExp ratios and to a much lesser extent by a decrease in the D&A and interest ratios. The capital employed in the business was favorably impacted by a 10.55-point reduction in the WC_{XSTD} ratio and a 14.17-point increase in the IBD (interest-bearing debt) ratio, whereas the increase in the NetFA ratio was largely offset by a decrease in the NetIA ratio.

In summary, the drivers of the increase in ROE were the increases in the cost of goods sold and operating expenses per revenue dollar, which were more than offset by the reduction in working capital and the increase in interest-bearing debt per revenue dollar. The combination was an increase in ROE from 35.1% to 43.0%.

The ROCE story is very similar. The 3-point increase in the cost of goods sold ratio and 6.71-point increase in the operating expenses per revenue dollar ratio had a significant adverse impact on the EBIT (numerator). However, this was offset somewhat by the improvement in the WC_{XSTD}/Net Rev ratio. The capital employed per unit of revenue in the business was increased significantly by the additional debt that was taken on. Hence the balance sheet (as represented by the denominator) had grown considerably, further reducing the ROCE.

Conclusion

The treasurer arranged a meeting with the CFO and presented his work product. After a lengthy discussion, the pair concluded the improvement in working capital suggested in the plan would be a significant accomplishment and that it was achievable. That left the COGS and OpExp. It was clear from the data that the forecasted ROEs and ROCEs could be further improved if the current COGS could be maintained and the OpExp plan curtailed. However, the planned increase in R&D was the driver of the step-up in OpExp and other than point out the impact this kind of spending had on the ROE and ROCE there wasn't much they could do since this was a decision for the management team as a whole.

CHAPTER TEN

Understanding Financial Statements*

CHAPTER 10 **TAKEAWAYS**

Financial Statements

There are three basic financial statements that define the financial performance of an enterprise: the Income Statement, Balance Sheet, and Cash Flow Statement. The relationships between all of the accounts in these statements can be derived by inspection.

Income Statement

- The purpose of the Income Statement is to quantify the financial consequences of the activities that take place in a company when it serves customers' needs during a particular *period* of time. The various accounts follow a logical process, starting with revenues and ending with net income. All of the line items in the statement are important, but one in particular, EBIT, deserves special mention.
- Technically, *earnings before interest and taxes* (EBIT) is an indicator of profitability after accounting for depreciation and amortization but before the impact of interest and taxes. In practice, it is much more. It is a measurement of "value added" in the sense that higher EBITs are associated with higher value added as perceived by the customers and their willingness to recognize the value by the price they are prepared to pay.
- The following equations define the Income Statement.

$$\textit{Revenue} = \textit{Value of all Goods and Services Invoiced to Customers}$$

$$\textit{Net Revenues} = \textit{Revenues} - (\textit{Discounts, Allowances and Like Items})$$

$$\textit{Gross Margin} = \textit{Net Revenue} - \textit{Cost of Goods Sold}$$

$$\textit{Operating Expenses} = \textit{Research \& Development} + \textit{Sales \& Marketing} + \textit{General \& Administrative}$$

(continued)

*The reader may notice minor discrepancies in the calculations in this chapter. When this occurs, it is the result of rounding.

$$EBITDA = Gross\ Margin - Operating\ Expenses$$

$$EBIT = EBITDA - (Depreciation\ \&\ Amortization) = EBITDA - D\ \&\ A$$

$$EBT = EBIT \pm Interest\ Income/Expense$$

$$Net\ Income = EBT - Taxes\ Paid$$

Balance Sheet

- The Balance Sheet portrays the status of what the company "owns" and what the company "owes + shareholders' equity" as of some date. Therefore, compared to the Income Statement, which deals with a period of time, the Balance Sheet is focused on a *point* in time. The key to understanding the Balance Sheet is the premise the Balance Sheet is based on, which is: The Balance Sheet must *balance*.
- The following equations define the Balance Sheet:

$$Total\ Assets = Total\ Liabilities + Total\ Shareholders'\ Equity$$

$$Current\ Assets = Cash + Accounts\ Receivable + Inventory$$

$$Property\ Plant\ \&\ Equipment\ at\ Cost_{(End\ Year\ n)} = PP\&E@Cost_{(End\ Year\ n-1)} + \Delta PP\&E@Cost_{(Year\ n)}$$

$$Accumulated\ Depreciation_{(End\ Year\ n)} = Accumulated\ Depreciation_{(End\ Year\ n-1)} + Depreciation_{(Year\ n)}$$

$$Net\ Fixed\ Assets = Property\ Plant\ \&\ Equipment\ at\ Cost - Accumulated\ Depreciation$$

$$Intangible\ Assets\ at\ Cost_{(End\ Year\ n)} = Intangible\ Assets\ at\ Cost_{(End\ Year\ n-1)} + \Delta Intangible\ Assets\ at\ ar\ Cost_{(Year\ n)}$$

$$Accumulated\ Amortization_{(End\ Year\ n)} = Accumulated\ Amortization_{(End\ Year\ n-1)} + Amortization_{(Year\ n)}$$

$$Net\ Intangible\ Assets = Intangible\ Assets\ at\ Cost - Accumulated\ Amortization$$

$$Total\ Assets = Current\ Assets + Net\ Fixed\ Assets + Net\ Intangible\ Assets$$

$$Total\ Current\ Liabilities = Accounts\ Payable + Wages\ \&\ Salaries\ Payable + Accrued\ Expense + Taxes\ Payable + Short\text{-}Term\ Debt$$

$$Total\ Liabilities = Current\ Liabilities + Long\text{-}Term\ Debt$$

$$Total\ Shareholders'\ Equity = Paid - in\ Capital + Retained\ Earnings$$

$$Retained\ Earnings_{(End\ Year\ n)} = RetainedEarnings_{(End\ Year\ n-1)} + NI_{(Year\ n)} - Dividends\ Paid_{(Year\ n)}$$

$$Total\ Liabilities + TSHE = Current\ Liabilities + Long\text{-}Term\ Debt + Total\ Shareholders'\ Equtiy$$

Cash Flow Statement

- The Cash Flow Statement consists solely of line items (accounts) from the Income Statement and Balance Sheet, and like the Income Statement, the Cash Flow Statement covers a period of time. One of the most important objectives of an enterprise is to produce cash, and this statement accounts for all of the transactions that impact cash and helps managers understand where a company's cash came from (sources) and where it went (uses).

- The following equations define the Cash Flow Statement.

$$\textit{Net Cash Flow from Operations (CFfO)} = \textit{Net Income} + D\,\&\,A$$

$$\textit{Net Change in WC (Net}\Delta\textit{WC)} = \pm\Delta AR \pm \Delta INV \pm \Delta AP \pm \Delta TP$$

$$\textit{Cash Flow from Operating Activities (CFfOA)} = \textit{Cash Flow from Operations} \pm \textit{Net }\Delta WC$$

$$\textit{Cash Flow after Investing Activities (CFaIA)} = \textit{CFfOA} - \textit{Additions to Fixed Assets}$$

$$\textit{Cash Flow after Financing Activities (CFaFA)} = \textit{CFaIA} \pm \Delta STD + \Delta LTD \pm \Delta \textit{Paid-in Capital}$$

$$\textit{Cash Generated / (Used)} = \textit{Cash Flow after Financing Activities} - \textit{Dividends Paid}$$

$$\textit{Ending Cash Balance}_{(Year\ n)} = \textit{Beginning Cash Balance}_{(Year\ n)} \pm \textit{Cash Generated or Used}_{(Year\ n)}$$

INTRODUCTION

Most managers have taken one or more accounting courses during the course of their career and yet, for various reasons, many still feel uncomfortable with their grasp of their company's financial statements. This is a serious handicap. Financial statements are a snapshot of a company's performance and like a picture they are literally "worth a thousand words." The intent of this chapter is not to focus on the accounting aspects of financial statements because accounting is merely a methodology that is used to prepare the statements. Our objective is to provide a framework from which managers with a limited knowledge of accounting can understand and work with the numbers that are crucial to helping them manage their business.

Throughout this book, the reader has been exposed to the three important financial statements, the Income Statement, Balance Sheet, and Cash Flow Statement, in various forms. Of the three, the Income Statement followed by the Balance Sheet are usually the most intuitive and easiest to understand. The Cash Flow Statement is for many the most difficult. Therefore, considerable time will be spent on the nuances of the Cash Flow Statement, how it comes about, and how it is intricately tied to the Income Statement and Balance Sheet. The groundwork for understanding financial statements was laid out in Chapter 1 and subsequent chapters. Therefore, the material in this chapter is intended to give the reader an overview and review. The discussion begins with the Income Statement.

TABLE 10-1 Typical Income Statement

			Month of January, 20XX $(000)'s
Net Revenues (NetRev)			
Cost of Goods Sold (COGS)			
Gross Margin (GM)			
Operating Expenses (OpExp):	Research and Development (R&D)		
	Sales and Marketing (S&M)		
	General and Administrative (G&A)		
Total Operating Expenses			
Earnings Before Interest, Taxes, Depreciation, and Amortization (EBITDA)			
Depreciation and Amortization (D&A)			
Earnings Before Interest and Taxes (EBIT)			
Interest Income/Expense (NetInt)			
Earnings Before Tax (EBT)			
Taxes Paid (TaxesPaid) @ 40%			
Net Income (NI)			

THE INCOME STATEMENT

The accounts for a typical Income Statement are shown in Table 10-1. All of the Income Statement–related equations that follow are derived by inspection of this table.

The first thing that is important to note is that the purpose of the Income Statement is to quantify the financial consequences of the activities that take place in a company when it serves customers' needs during a particular period of time. Typically, it reads "Income Statement for the Month of January, 20XX," "Quarter Ending March 31, 20XX," or "Year Ending December 31, 20XX." Second, it is designed to capture all of the costs (cost of goods sold [COGS]) and expenses (operating expenses [OpExp]) that are associated with the sales that have been made during the period in question plus any depreciation, amortization, interest (income or expense), and taxes incurred or accrued during that period.

Revenue or Net Revenue (NetRev): This is always the first line item in an Income Statement. It is the aggregate value of all goods and services invoiced to customers during a particular period. When there are discounts and like items associated with the period's invoices, they can be netted against revenues, resulting in "net revenues."

Cost of Goods Sold (COGS): This is the cost of all materials and labor as well as associated overhead that was incurred to generate the revenue for the period in question. "Associated overhead" is an important concept and worthy of explanation.

Overhead: This is everything it takes to operate a production facility except direct labor, which is the cost of the labor that actually produces the deliverable, and direct materials, which are the parts, components, subassemblies, and so on required to manufacture the deliverable. The cost of the benefits that direct labor enjoys plus indirect labor (which are all the folks who support and manage the production facility) and all of their benefits plus the cost of electricity, heating, maintenance, taxes, and so on all fall into the overhead category described by *associated overhead*. It is also referred to as *manufacturing overhead* or *factory burden*.

Example 10-1: Manufacturing Overhead

Scenario A: If manufacturing overhead is estimated to be $20,000,000 for a year, the total of all direct labor (DL) hours for the year is 500,000, and the average hourly cost of direct labor is $25.50, what is the fully burdened rate?

The overhead rate per hour of direct labor is $40.00:

$$Overhead/Hour\ of\ DL = 20{,}000{,}000 / 500{,}000 = \$40.00$$

Adding the burden per hour to the average hourly cost of direct labor gives a fully burdened cost of DL of $65.50.

$$Fully\ Burdened\ Cost\ of\ DL/Hour = 40.00 + 25.50 = \$65.50$$

This would be the amount charged to the cost of goods sold or inventory, whichever is the case for each hour spent.

Scenario B: If 100 widgets were produced by a direct labor employee in one week that had a material cost of $500 per widget, what would be the total cost of each widget?

$$Widget\ Unit\ Cost = 500 + (40)(65.50) / 100 = 500 + 26.20 = \$526.20$$

This would be the amount charged to the COGS every time the widget was shipped to a customer.

In practice, the accounting is a little more complicated because the estimates are almost never accurate. So, as the year goes on, the costs are tracked and if during an accounting period the overhead was less than budgeted or the DL was more efficient and spent less time than budgeted, this would result in a favorable variance that would be reflected in the COGS in the Income Statement. Conversely, if the overhead was higher than budgeted or more DL was used than budgeted or both, the variance would be negative and this, too, would be charged against the Income Statement in the cost of goods sold.[1]

Gross Margin (GM): This is the difference between net revenues and the cost of goods sold and is a measure of the effectiveness of a company's pricing policy and its efficiency in producing the deliverable.

$$Gross\ Margin = Net\ Revenue - Cost\ of\ Goods\ Sold \qquad [10\text{-}1]$$

[1] Anyone wishing to explore this subject in more detail can consult any basic book on accounting.

Operating Expenses (OpExp): These are the sum of research and development, sales and marketing, and general and administrative expenses that were incurred during the period.

$$Operating\ Expenses = Research\ \&\ Development + Sales\ \&\ Marketing + General\ \&\ Administrative \quad [10\text{-}2]$$

Earnings before Depreciation, Amortization, Interest, and Taxes (EBITDA): This is the difference between the gross margin and operating expenses. It is also an indication of how well the company matches what the customer deems as value as measured by gross margin and the money the company spends creating and servicing the deliverable for which the company has invoiced the customer. In addition (as seen in earlier chapters) it is a rough measure of cash flow.

$$EBITDA = Gross\ Margin - Operating\ Expenses \quad [10\text{-}3]$$

Earnings before Interest and Taxes (EBIT): This is an indicator of profitability after accounting for depreciation and amortization but before the impact of financing activities such as interest and taxes.

Deprecation (D): This is the result of an effort to match the depletion of resources, such as plant and equipment and software, with the revenue they produce. For example, if a piece of equipment costing $5 million is estimated to have a useful life of five years, then one fifth of the cost of that equipment would be charged against each year's Income Statement until the asset was written off (completely depreciated). Similarly, software costing $3,000,000 with a useful life of three years would be depreciated and charged to the Income Statement at a rate of $1,000,000 per year for three years. (Note: In the interests of simplicity, assets subject to depreciation are assumed to have no residual value.)

$$Depreciation = \frac{Total\ Cost\ of\ Asset}{Useful\ Life} \quad [10\text{-}4]$$

Amortization (A): This is similar to depreciation except that it deals with "soft" assets such as goodwill and intangibles.

Goodwill is created when an income-creating asset is purchased at a price in excess of either its *book value* or the *present value of future cash flows*. For example, if a company with $50 million of shareholders' equity is purchased for $90 million, then the $40 million difference between the purchase price and shareholders' equity would be accounted for as goodwill, and barring an *impairment*, would stay on the purchasing company's books at that level forever. On the other hand, if the present value of future cash flows were $100 million, the goodwill would be $60 million.

Intangible assets are other soft assets. They consist of such things as trademarks, patents, and non-compete agreements with sellers that have a finite life and are amortized over their remaining life. For example, if the sellers of the business signed a non-compete agreement for three years that was deemed to have a value of $3,600,000, then the value associated with the agreement would be identified in the Balance Sheet as an intangible asset and the non-compete would be amortized and charged through the Income Statement at $1,200,000 per year.

$$Amortization = \frac{Total\ Cost\ of\ Intangible\ Asset}{Useful\ Life} \qquad [10\text{-}5]$$

Normally depreciation and amortization (D&A) are combined into one line in the Income Statement.

$$EBIT = EBITDA - (Depreciation\ \&\ Amortization) = EBITDA - D\ \&\ A \qquad [10\text{-}6]$$

Earnings before Taxes (EBT): This is a measure of the company's profitability after accounting for all financing costs (but before income taxes) and reflects the interest income from cash the company has invested or on deposit in an interest-bearing account, and/or the interest cost associated with bank loans, commercial paper, bonds, or other debt instruments the company has undertaken. When interest has to be calculated, Equations [10-7] and [10-8] can be used.

$$Interest\ Income = (Deposit)\left(\frac{Interest\ Rate}{100}\right) \qquad [10\text{-}7]$$

$$Interest\ Expense = (Debt)\left(\frac{Interest\ Rate}{100}\right) \qquad [10\text{-}8]$$

Once the interest income or expense is known, the EBT is given by Equation [10-9].

$$EBT = EBIT \pm Interest\ Income/Expense \qquad [10\text{-}9]$$

Net Income (NI): This is the profit a company generates after taking into account all the federal, state, and local income taxes (*IncTaxes*) the company is required to pay.[2] It's worthwhile to note that these are taxes the company owes based on its income and will only be paid when due. Until then, they give rise to an account called "Taxes Payable," which is discussed in the next section.

$$Net\ Income = EBT - Taxes\ Paid \qquad [10\text{-}10]$$

THE BALANCE SHEET

The Balance Sheet portrays the status of what the company "owns" and what the company "owes + shareholders' equity" as of some date. Typically, it reads "Balance Sheet as of "January 31, 20XX," as of "March 31, 20XX" for a quarter, or as of "December 31, 20XX" for a year. Therefore, compared to the Income Statement, which deals with a *period* of time, the Balance Sheet is focused on a *point* in time. In other words, a Company's Balance Sheet

[2] All other taxes, such as property taxes, use taxes, license fees, and so forth, are included in the appropriate COGS or OpExp category.

TABLE 10-2 Typical Balance Sheet

March 31, 20XX $(000)'s			
Current Assets		**Current Liabilities**	
Cash		Accounts Payable	
Accounts Receivable		Accrued Payroll	
Inventory		Accrued Expenses	
Total Current Assets		Taxes Payable	
		Short-Term Debt	
Fixed Assets		**Total Current Liabilities**	
Property, Plant, and Equipment at Cost			
Less Accumulated Depreciation		**Long-Term Debt**	
Net Fixed Assets			
Intangible Assets		**Shareholders' Equity**	
Goodwill and Other Intangible Assets		Paid-in Capital	
Less Accumulated Amortization		Retained Earnings	
Net Intangible Assets		**Total Shareholders' Equity**	
Total Assets		**Total Liabilities + TSHE**	

is only accurate on the date it is prepared. A day later things have changed because of the ongoing nature of an enterprise as it receives supplies, parts, and materials, pays employees and suppliers, and collects cash. Stated differently, the Balance Sheet is designed to be an *inventory* of all of the company's assets and liabilities plus total shareholders' equity (Table 10-2).

The key to understanding the Balance Sheet is the premise on which it is based:

$$\textit{Total Assets} = \textit{Total Liabilities} + \textit{Total Shareholders' Equity} \qquad [10\text{-}11]$$

The accounts that constitute a typical Balance Sheet as shown in Table 10-2 are discussed in the material that follows together with the equations that define the relationships between the various accounts. As was the case with the Income Statement, all equations that describe the Balance Sheet are obtained by inspection.

Current Assets

Cash (Cash): This is the most liquid asset on the Balance Sheet and represents money (or money-like instruments) on deposit with the company's bank and is the money the company uses to pay suppliers, employees, interest, and dividends.

Accounts Receivable (AR): This asset represents the aggregate monetary value of revenues that were invoiced to customers on credit terms and have not been paid.

Inventory (Inv): This is a more complicated asset than any discussed so far. It consists of parts, subassemblies, finished goods, and so forth that a company has purchased or produced and the labor and overhead that have gone into creating the deliverable, which has not been delivered to any customer. This, of course, only applies to a manufacturing company. A service company would have an account for "work in progress" or may not have any corresponding account depending on the nature of its business. It can also include supplies[3] that have been purchased but not used.

Other Current Assets (OCA): This account captures assets that are not included in the Cash, Accounts Receivable, or Inventory accounts.[4]

As can be seen from Table CS 10-2, total current assets are:

$$\textit{Current Assets} = \textit{Cash} + \textit{Accounts Receivable} + \textit{Inventory} \qquad [10\text{-}12]$$

If total current assets, accounts receivable, and inventory are known, the cash on the Balance Sheet can be obtained by rearranging Equation [10-12].

$$\textit{Cash} = \textit{Current Assets} - \textit{Accounts Receivable} - \textit{Inventory} \qquad [10\text{-}13]$$

Fixed Assets

Property, Plant, and Equipment (PP&E): When a company purchases land, buys or builds a building, or purchases machine tools, computers, office furniture, and so on, these factors of production are expected to have benefits over several years and are therefore captured as assets and depreciated (expensed through the Income Statement).

Depreciation (D): Buildings,[5] machine tools, computers, office furniture, and so on have finite lives and in order to match the use of an asset with the inventory or revenue they produce, these assets are depreciated (expensed) over their useful lives. Depreciation is accumulated, so the difference between PP&E at cost less any accumulated depreciation is *net fixed assets*.

$$\begin{aligned}\textit{Net Fixed Assets} = \ & \textit{Property Plant and Equipment at Cost} \\ & - \textit{Accumulated Depreciation}\end{aligned} \qquad [10\text{-}14]$$

The value of property, plant, and equipment at cost is simply the sum of the PP&E at the beginning of a period plus what was added during the period:

$$\begin{aligned}\textit{Property Plant \& Equipment at Cost}_{(EndYear\ n)} = \ & PP\&E@Cost_{(EndYear\ n-1)} \\ & + \Delta PP\&E@Cost_{(Year\ n)}\end{aligned} \qquad [10\text{-}15]$$

---

[3] In practice, supplies below some threshold amount would be expensed through the Income Statement during the period in which they were purchased because the magnitude of the purchase doesn't warrant the effort required to keep track of usage even if they are used over several accounting periods.

[4] In the interest of simplicity, this account is not included in the equations or discussions that follow.

[5] Land is not considered to have a finite life and therefore it is not depreciated. It remains on the Balance Sheet at cost as long as the company owns it.

The amount of accumulated depreciation at the end of a period is the sum of the accumulated depreciation at the beginning of the period plus the depreciation during the period.

$$\textit{Accumulated Depreciation}_{(\text{End Year } n)} = \textit{Accumulated Depreciation}_{(\text{End Year } n-1)} + \textit{Depreciaton}_{(\text{Year } n)} \quad [10\text{-}16]$$

Intangible Assets

Goodwill: Goodwill can result when a company purchases assets and can be measured in two ways.

$$\textit{Goodwill} = \textit{Present Value of Future Cash Flows} - \textit{Book Value of Net Tangible Assets} \quad [10\text{-}17]$$

$$\textit{Goodwill} = \textit{Present Value of Future Cash Flows} - \textit{Appraised Value of Net Tangible Assets} \quad [10\text{-}18]$$

In practice, when there is a need to estimate goodwill, the preferred method is to use the appraised value as opposed to the book value. For example, if a company is buying land from a company that purchased it 20 years ago and had it on the books at $100 an acre, it is unrealistic to think this represents the current market value.

Also, when assets are purchased (i.e., a company or the assets of the company), the assets' earning power can also be ascribed in part to such intangible assets as trademarks, patents, intellectual property, and non-compete agreements. When intangible assets are involved they are usually identified in the "Other Intangible Assets" account and written off (amortized) over their estimated useful life. Goodwill per se is not written off.[6]

Amortization (A): Like depreciation, amortization is also accumulated. *Net intangible assets* is the difference between goodwill and the accumulated amortization:

$$\textit{Net Intangible Assets} = \textit{Goodwill\&Other Intangible Assets} - \textit{Accumulated Amortization} \quad [10\text{-}19]$$

where:

$$\textit{Goodwill \& Other IA at Cost}_{(\text{End Year } n)} = \textit{GW\&OIA@Cost}_{(\text{End Year } n-1)} + \Delta \textit{GW\&OIA@Cost}_{(\text{Year } n)} \quad [10\text{-}20]$$

and

$$\textit{Accumulated Amortization}_{(\text{End Year } n)} = \textit{Accumulated Amortization}_{(\text{End Year } n-1)} + \textit{Amortizaion}_{(\text{Year } n)} \quad [10\text{-}21]$$

---

[6]Technically this is correct. However, goodwill can be "impaired." This happens when an event occurs whereby the present value of cash flows is less than the goodwill on the company's books. When this occurs the difference is written off. The accounting rules in the United States require that goodwill be tested for impairment once a year.

Total Assets

Finally, on the asset side of the Balance Sheet, total assets are defined by adding up all of the assets just discussed.

$$\textit{Total Assets} = \textit{Current Assets} + \textit{Net Fixed Assets} + \textit{Net Intangible Assets} \qquad [10\text{-}22]$$

There is another form of Equation [10-22] that will prove to be useful in the case study at the end of this chapter. If the total assets and the net fixed and intangible assets are known, it can be rearranged to solve for *current assets.*

$$\textit{Current Assets} = \textit{Total Assets} - \textit{Net Intangible Assets} - \textit{Net Fixed Assets} \qquad [10\text{-}23]$$

Current Liabilities

Accounts Payable (AP): This is a liability and represents the money the company owes to suppliers that have provided goods and services.

Wages and Salaries Payable (W&SP): These are also a liability and represent wages and salaries that have been earned and expensed through the Income Statement or put into inventory but not paid to the employees.

Accrued Expense (AccExp): These are liabilities that management knows are out there and represent costs that have been incurred during an accounting period but have not been invoiced by the suppliers and therefore not included in the "Accounts Payable" liability account.

Short-Term Debt (STD): All debt is a liability. Short-term debt is that portion of a company's debt that is due for repayment to the lenders within one year. So, when some portion of long-term debt becomes payable within a year, the amount that has to be repaid is reclassified as short-term debt.

Taxes Payable (TaxPayable): Companies pay taxes periodically. In order to match the taxes due with the profit that was earned during a particular period, the tax due on the profit is calculated and accrued as a liability until paid.

Other Current Liabilities (OCL): Like "Other Current Assets," this account captures liabilities that are not included in the liability accounts just discussed. As was the case with other current assets, and in the interest of simplicity, the expression for other current liabilities will be omitted from the Total Current Liabilities account.

$$\begin{aligned}\textit{Total Current Liabilities} = {} & \textit{Accounts Payable} + \textit{Wages \& Salaries Payable}\\ & + \textit{Accrued Expense} + \textit{Taxes Payable}\\ & + \textit{Short-Term Debt} \qquad [10\text{-}24]\end{aligned}$$

Equation [10-24] can be further simplified for use in the case study by eliminating wages and salaries payable and accrued expenses. It is assumed that both of these accounts are paid in full at the end of the accounting period.

$$\begin{aligned}\textit{Current Liabilities} = {} & \textit{Accounts Payable} + \textit{Taxes Payable}\\ & + \textit{Short-Term Debt} \qquad [10\text{-}25]\end{aligned}$$

Long-Term Debt (LTD)

This is debt that is due for repayment to the debt holders beyond one year and is shown on the Balance Sheet as a liability.

Total Liabilities

Total liabilities are defined as current liabilities plus long-term debt:

$$\text{Total Liabilities} = \text{Current Liabilities} + \text{Long-Term Debt} \tag{10-26}$$

Total Shareholders' Equity (TSHE)

This is money owed to shareholders that they have no right to collect or demand from the company. It consists of the money provided by shareholders (in exchange for an ownership position in the company), called *paid-in capital* and *retained earnings*. Shareholders' equity is calculated by Equation [10-27]:

$$\begin{aligned}\text{Total Shareholders' Equity}_{(\text{End Year } n)} = {} & \text{Paid-in Capital}_{(\text{End Year } n)} \\ & + \text{Retained Earnings}_{(\text{End Year } n)}\end{aligned} \tag{10-27}$$

where:

$$\begin{aligned}\text{Paid-in Capital} = {} & \text{Aggregate price paid by shareholders} \\ & \text{for shares in the company}\end{aligned} \tag{10-28}$$

After the initial capital infusion, any additional capital that is raised is additive to the initial tranche as defined in Equation [10-29].

$$\text{Paid-in Capital}_{(\text{End Year } n)} = \text{Paid-in Capital}_{(\text{End Year } n-1)} + \Delta\text{Paid-in Capital}_{(\text{Year } n)} \tag{10-29}$$

Like paid-in capital, retained earnings (RetEarnings) are an ongoing accounting of all of the earnings of the company less any dividends paid since its inception.[7]

$$\begin{aligned}\text{RetEarnings}_{(\text{End Year } n)} = {} & \text{RetEarnings}_{(\text{End Year } n-1)} \pm NI_{(\text{Year } n)} \\ & - \text{Dividends Paid}_{(\text{Year } n)}\end{aligned} \tag{10-30}$$

And, if no dividends are paid, Equation[10-30] becomes:

$$\text{RetEarnings}_{(\text{End Year } n)} = \text{RetEarnings}_{(\text{End Year } n-1)} \pm NI_{(\text{Year } n)} \tag{10-31}$$

[7]When dividends are paid they constitute a distribution of the retained earnings of the company and can be shown as a separate line item in Total Shareholders' Equity or accounted for by subtracting the dividend from the Retained Earnings account.

Total Liabilities + Total Shareholders' Equity (TSHE)

The total liabilities and total shareholders' equity is given by Equation [10-32].

$$\begin{aligned} \textit{Total Liabilities} + \textit{TSHE} = &\ \textit{Current Liabilities} + \textit{Long-Term Debt} \\ &+ \textit{Total Shareholders' Equity} \end{aligned} \qquad [10\text{-}32]$$

Or, by substituting Equation [10-26] for current liabilities + long-term debt,

$$\textit{Total Liabilities} + \textit{TSHE} = \textit{Total Liabilities} + \textit{Total Shareholders' Equtiy} \qquad [10\text{-}33]$$

And finally, since a Balance Sheet must balance,

$$\textit{Total Assets} = \textit{Total Liabilities} + \textit{Total Shareholders' Equity} \qquad [10\text{-}11]$$

Other Balance Sheet Relationships

There are other Balance Sheet relationships that were covered in earlier chapters and are worthwhile to recall.[8]

Accounts receivable is measured in terms of *days outstanding*. For the purpose of this measurement, the year is assumed to have 360 days and is measured against the *annualized revenues* since the receivables are created by the revenue associated with the deliverable that hasn't been paid.

$$\textit{Accounts Receivable Days Outstanding (ARDOS)} = \frac{\textit{Accounts Receivable}}{\textit{Annualized Net Revenues}}(360) \qquad [10\text{-}34]$$

When the ARDOS is known, the value of the accounts receivable can be calculated by rearranging Equation [10-34] into the form of Equation [10-35].

$$\textit{Accounts Receivable (AR)} = (\textit{Annualized Net Revenues})\left(\frac{\textit{ARDOS}}{360}\right) \qquad [10\text{-}35]$$

Inventory is measured in terms of *inventory turns* (IT). This is measurement of the amount of inventory on hand relative to the annualized cost of goods sold.

$$\textit{Inventory Turns (IT)} = \frac{\textit{Annualized Cost of Goods Sold}}{\textit{Inventory}} \qquad [10\text{-}36]$$

When the inventory turns are known, the value of the inventory can be calculated by rearranging Equation [10-36] into Equation [10-37]:

$$\textit{Inventory} = \frac{\textit{Annualized Cost of Goods Sold}}{\textit{Inventory Turns}} \qquad [10\text{-}37]$$

---

[8] Also see Chapter 1.

Like accounts receivable, accounts payable are measured in days outstanding. Again, for the purpose of this measurement, the year is assumed to have 360 days and involves annualized cost of goods sold for accounts payable since payables are the main liability generated by inputs to the COGS.

$$Accounts\ Payable\ Days\ Outstanding\ (APDOS) = \left(\frac{Accounts\ Payable}{Annualized\ Cost\ of\ Goods\ Sold}\right)(360) \quad [10\text{-}38]^{9}$$

When the APDOS is known the value of the accounts payable can be calculated by rearranging Equation [10-38] into the form of Equation [10-39]:

$$Accounts\ Payable\ (AP) = (Annualized\ Cost\ of\ Goods\ Sold)\left(\frac{APDOS}{360}\right) \quad [10\text{-}39]$$

Working capital is defined as current assets less current liabilities and is a measure of a company's ability to meet its day-to-day obligations.

$$Working\ Capital\ (WC) = Current\ Assets - Current\ Liabilities \quad [10\text{-}40]$$

SOME COMPLICATIONS

As is so often the case, things aren't as simple as they seem. In this section, some of the subtleties associated with the workings of accounts receivable, cost of goods sold, inventory, and operating expenses are discussed.

Accounts Receivable

One of the first things that managers often ask is: "If the income statement says we earned $100,000, why hasn't our bank account gone up by a commensurate amount?" The answer is simple to state but sometimes difficult to understand: "Because the Income Statement is a combination of current-period cash and non-cash items." For starters, the Income Statement can give one the impression that all of the sales made during the period are paid for by customers during that period. This is rarely the case and is only the case when all sales to customers are paid for with cash. The business practice of providing a company's deliverable to customers on credit terms gives rise to an asset account that has been discussed, called "Accounts Receivable"—money that is owed to the company by its customers and that only shows up in the company's "Cash" account when the company receives the money.

[9] In practice, accountants will generally use more than the cost of goods sold in the denominator when calculating accounts payable days outstanding (i.e., capital expenditures and operating expenses). However, in manufacturing companies, the cost of goods sold is usually the largest factor and therefore used here as a simplifying assumption. This is not the case for service companies, so when calculating the APDOS for a service company capital expenditure and operating expenses will be appropriately annualized and also included in the denominator.

Cost of Goods Sold and Inventory

Furthermore, the Income Statement only accounts for the cost of what was shipped to customers in the "Cost of Goods Sold" line. It takes no notice of any inventory[10] the company may have bought or produced during the period in question and did not ship to customers. Nor does it account for goods that have been received by the company and not delivered to customers during this period. Again, and as discussed earlier, this practice creates an asset account called "Inventory," which is material on hand in the company's storage facilities. This inventory consists of parts and materials purchased by the company and the labor and overhead that was used to transform the purchased components into the company's deliverable, which will ultimately be shipped to customers when a purchase order is received.

Most of the parts and materials are purchased on terms (credit) granted by the company's suppliers. Therefore, the company will have shipped or have in its inventory parts and materials that it hasn't paid for. This gives rise to a Balance Sheet liability account called "Accounts Payable."[11]

Operating Expenses

There are also costs in operating expenses that suffer the same fate: used but not paid for or purchased but not used. For example, suppose a company purchased $1,000,000 of marketing material representing a multi-period supply that was only partially used and not paid for during the period in question. Like manufacturing parts and materials, any marketing material that was not used would be listed as an asset in some account on the Balance Sheet and the liability recognizing the obligation to pay for what has been purchased would also be accounted for in the Accounts Payable account in the Balance Sheet.

In addition, there are expenses that management knows will have been incurred during an accounting period that have not been paid, or for that matter, not invoiced to the company by suppliers. For example, a consulting or legal firm that is doing some work for the company may have a practice of invoicing quarterly for their services. Rather than hit one month with three months of expense, the company will usually make some estimate of the quarterly expense and charge one third of the estimate to each month during the period. Accruals such as these result in the creation of another liability account on the Balance Sheet, called "Accrued Expenses." Once the actual invoice is received, it will be matched against the accruals with any excess or under-expense accounted for in the current-period Income Statement.

All of the foregoing lays the groundwork for the statement that deals with all of this: the Cash Flow Statement.

THE CASH FLOW STATEMENT

One of the most important objectives of an enterprise is to produce cash. As shall be seen, the Cash Flow Statement consists of line items (accounts) from the Income Statement and Balance Sheet and, therefore, there is no need to define any new accounts.

---

[10] Inventory accounts are usually only associated with manufacturing companies, distributors, retailers, and so forth. Service companies rarely have any inventory.

[11] Similarly, any wages that have been earned but not paid would be accounted for as a liability in another Balance Sheet account called "Wages Payable."

Like the Income Statement, the Cash Flow Statement covers a period of time. Typically it reads: "Cash Flow Statement for the Month of January 20XX," "Quarter ending March 31, 20XX," or "Year Ending December 31, 20XX." A typical Cash Flow Statement is shown in Table 10-3.

TABLE 10-3 Typical Cash Flow Statement

Quarter Ending March 31, 20XX $(000)'s	
Operating Activities	
Operations	
Net Income (Loss)	
Depreciation and Amortization	
Other Adjustments	
Net Cash Flow from Operations (CFfO)	
Working Capital Accounts	
(Increase)/Decrease Accounts Receivable	
(Increase)/Decrease Inventory	
(Increase)/Decrease Other Current Assets	
Increase/(Decrease) Accounts Payable	
Increase/(Decrease) Wages Payable	
Increase/(Decrease) Taxes Payable	
Increase/(Decrease) Other Current Liabilities	
Net Change in Working Capital (NetΔWC)	
Cash Flow from Operating Activities (CFfOA)	
Investing Activities	
Fixed Asset Additions	
Other Investments	
Cash Flow after Investing Activities (CFaIA)	
Financing Activities	
Increase/(Decrease) Short-Term Debt	
Increase/(Decrease) Long-Term Debt	
Proceeds (Purchase) of Common Stock	
Increase/(Decrease) Other Financing	
Dividends Paid	
Cash Generated/(Used)	
Cash Flow Proof	
Beginning Cash Balance	
Cash Generated/(Used)	
Ending Cash Balance	

To help better appreciate why a Cash Flow Statement is necessary, consider this. It was just demonstrated that the Income Statement is a mixture of cash (e.g., payroll) and non-cash items (e.g., depreciation of assets that were paid for during a previous period but are being expensed over their useful lives in order to match a company's revenues with the assets that produce them). In addition, every day there are changes in Balance Sheet accounts like Accounts Receivable, Inventory, and Accounts Payable as and when a company receives payments from customers, makes shipments, buys inventory, and pays suppliers. All of these transactions impact cash and, therefore, to help managers understand where a company's cash came from (*sources*) and where it went (*uses*), Cash Flow Statements are prepared. The relationships between the various accounts that constitute the Cash Flow Statement are as follows.

Operating Activities

The purpose of the Operations section of the Cash Flow Statement is to adjust net income for non-cash charges that were incurred when preparing the Income Statement so that it is reflective of the cash flow generated by the operations for the period. The typical adjustment is to add back depreciation and amortization since they reflect the write-off of assets over their useful lives that in the main were purchased during a previous period.

The depreciation of assets that were purchased during the current period is also included here even if the supplier hasn't been paid because the obligation to pay for the asset will be included in accounts payable, and since the invoice for the asset hasn't been paid, the company still has the cash. Therefore the *cash flow from operations* (CFfO) is:

$$Net\ Cash\ Flow\ from\ Operations\ CFfO = Net\ Income + Depreciation + Amortization \pm Other\ Adjustments \qquad [10\text{-}41]$$ [12]

Working Capital Accounts

The next step in adjusting net income to a cash basis is to adjust net cash flow from operations to reflect changes in the Balance Sheet Working Capital accounts.

For example, if accounts receivable decreased from the prior period, this represents an inflow of cash. Similarly, if inventory increased from the prior period, this represents a use of cash and the change would be subtracted from cash flow from operations.

The Liabilities accounts have the opposite impact. An increase in accounts payable from one period to the next means the company received products and services it didn't pay for and the magnitude of the change would be added to net cash flow from operations. If wages payable increase from one period to the next, this means that while they have been accounted

[12] As mentioned previously, other accounts can be included here and elsewhere when appropriate or to facilitate understanding. To avoid getting lost in the details, the introduction of other accounts is avoided in order to simplify matters in the examples and case studies throughout this text.

for in cost of goods sold, inventory, or operating expenses, they haven't been paid and the difference is added to net cash flow from operations. When it comes to taxes payable, the Income Statement assumes that taxes were paid since they are deducted from earnings before taxes when computing net income. Hence, if taxes payable increase from a prior period, this means that some of the taxes weren't paid and the increase would be added to net cash flow from operations.

Changes in other current assets and other current liabilities would be treated similarly and added to or subtracted from net cash flow from operations, depending on the impact the change had on cash.

The *net change in working capital* (NetΔWC) is calculated using the following equations:

$$\begin{aligned} Net\ \Delta\ in\ Working\ Capital\ =\ & \pm\Delta\ in\ Accounts\ Receivable\ \pm\Delta\ in\ Inventory \\ & \pm\Delta\ in\ Other\ Current\ Assets\ \pm\Delta\ in\ Accounts\ Payable \\ & \pm\Delta\ in\ Wages\ Payable \pm\Delta\ in\ Taxes\ Payable \\ & \pm\Delta\ in\ Other\ Current\ Liabilities \end{aligned} \qquad [10\text{-}42]$$

or

$$\begin{aligned} Net\Delta WC = & \pm\Delta AR \pm \Delta INV \pm \Delta OtherCA \pm \Delta AP \pm \Delta WP \\ & \pm \Delta TP \pm \Delta OtherCL \end{aligned} \qquad [10\text{-}43]$$

where:

$$\begin{aligned} \Delta Accounts\ Receivable = & Accounts\ Receivable_{(Year\ n-1)} \\ & - Accounts\ Receivable_{(Year\ n)} \end{aligned} \qquad [10\text{-}44]$$

$$\Delta Inventory = Inventory_{(Year\ n-1)} - Inventory_{(Year\ n)} \qquad [10\text{-}45]$$

$$\begin{aligned} \Delta Other\ Current\ Assets = & Other\ Current\ Assets_{(Year\ n-1)} \\ & - Other\ Current\ Assets_{(Year\ n)} \end{aligned} \qquad [10\text{-}46]$$

$$\begin{aligned} \Delta Accounts\ Payable = & Accounts\ Payable_{(Year\ n)} \\ & - Accounts\ Payable_{(Year\ n-1)} \end{aligned} \qquad [10\text{-}47]$$

$$\Delta Wages\ Payable = Wages\ Payable_{(Year\ n)} - Wages\ Payable_{(Year\ n-1)} \qquad [10\text{-}48]$$

$$\Delta Taxes\ Payable = Taxes\ Payable_{(Year\ n)} - Taxes\ Payable_{(Year\ n-1)} \qquad [10\text{-}49]$$

$$\begin{aligned} \Delta Other\ Current\ Liabilities = & Other\ Current\ Liabilities_{(Year\ n)} \\ & - Other\ Current\ Liabilities_{(Year\ n-1)} \end{aligned} \qquad [10\text{-}50]$$

Sources and Uses of Cash

This terminology sometimes causes confusion. As the names imply, they are used to identify whether a Cash Flow Statement–related activity is a *source* or a *use* of cash. If accounts receivable increases from one period to another, this constitutes a use of cash. Similarly if accounts payable increases from one period to another, this is a source of cash. To get the cash impact of all of the changes in the Working Capital accounts it's necessary to add them up. For example, if the changes in the Working Capital accounts from one period to another are: ΔAccounts Receivable (ΔAR) = increase of $1,500 (Use of Cash), ΔInventory (ΔINV) = increase of $2,000 (Use of Cash), ΔAccounts Payable (ΔAP) = Increase of $3,000 (Source of Cash), and Δ Taxes Payable (ΔTP) = reduced by $1,000 (Use of Cash), then the actual cash impact of changes in the Working Capital accounts is a $1,500 reduction in the company's cash.

$$\begin{aligned} \textit{Cash Impact of Sources and Uses of Cash} &= \Delta AR + \Delta INV + \Delta AP + \Delta TP \\ &= -1{,}500 - 2{,}000 + 3{,}000 - 1{,}000 \\ &= -\$1{,}500 \end{aligned}$$

As will be seen in the sections that follow, when it comes to such things as capital expenditures and bank loans, the reasoning is exactly the same (i.e., the purchase of a $10,000 piece of equipment is a use of cash). A $100,000 loan from a bank is a source of cash, and so on. The point is: The terms *sources* and *uses of cash* are like a vector in that they have a magnitude (dollar amount) and direction (source or use), and only after one adds up all the sources and uses does one get the actual impact all of the changes in the Cash Flow Statement have on the company's cash.

Cash Flow from Operating Activities

The cash flow from operating activities is obtained by adding or subtracting (as the case may be) the net change in working capital from the cash flow from operations.

$$\begin{aligned} \textit{Cash Flow from Operating Activities (CFfOA)} = \textit{Cash Flow from Operations} \\ \pm \textit{Net } \Delta WC \end{aligned} \qquad [10\text{-}51]$$

Investing Activities

Typical fixed asset additions that constitute an investing activity are investments made in property, plant, and equipment. Other investments would include the purchase of stock in another company and bonds or other financial instruments. Additions of assets are a use of cash. When an asset is sold, any gain or loss on the sale is run through the Income Statement. While the disposition of assets is always a source of cash, any gain or loss is a non-cash amount that adjusts the net book value to realized value. This difference is reflected in the Cash Flow Statement as an adjustment to the Cash Flow from Operations and the Change in Fixed Assets sections of the Cash Flow Statement, since it isn't an operating item. The result is that the entire cash impact of the sale of an asset is reflected in the Fixed Assets section of the Cash Flow Statement.[13]

Cash Flow after Investing Activities

Cash flow after investing activities is arrived at by taking the cash flow from operating activities and subtracting from it fixed asset additions and other investments. Asset dispositions, depending on whether there was a gain or loss, would be added or subtracted respectively.

$$\text{Cash Flow after Investing Activities (CFaIA)} = \text{CFfOA} - \text{Additions to Fixed Assets} - \text{Other Investments} \quad [10\text{-}52]$$

Financing Activities

Entries that are made in this category of the Cash Flow Statement are the increases/(decreases) in short-term debt and/or long-term debt. Share repurchases as well as any proceeds from the issue of the company's stock also constitute a financing activity. Other financing activities would include such transactions as the purchase of the company's bonds by the company. Equation [10-53] defines the *cash flow after financing activities* (CFaFA).

$$\text{Cash Flow after Financing Activities (CFaFA)} = \text{CFaIA} \pm \Delta\text{Financing Activities} \quad [10\text{-}53]$$

Dividends Paid

Dividends are monies that the company is returning to the owners of the business. Normally companies that pay dividends are those that have cash flow in excess of their needs. Start-ups never pay dividends because in the early years there is little income if any and their net cash flow is negative. Growth companies have ample opportunities to reinvest their cash so unless they are hugely profitable it is very unusual for them to pay a dividend during the early years. The *cash flow after the payment of dividends* (CFaDP) is given by Equation [10-54].

$$\text{CFaDP} = \text{CFaFA} - \text{Dividends Paid} \quad [10\text{-}54]$$

[13]Since the sale of fixed assets is not a normal part of the operations of most companies, making provision for such an eventuality would introduce additional complexity into the financial statements used in this book and have no relevant take-home value. For this reason, all of the case studies that involve assets assume that no assets are sold.

Cash Generated/(Used)

This line item reflects the net result of all of the cash flows. It is obtained by subtracting any dividends paid to shareholders from the cash flow after financing activities.[14]

$$Cash\,Generated/(Used) = Cash\,Flow\ after\ Financing\ Activities - Dividends\,Paid \quad [10\text{-}55]$$

It is also the result of adjusting cash flow after investing activities for changes in short-term debt, long-term debt, paid-in capital, and any dividends paid:

$$CGU = CFaIA \pm \Delta STD \pm \Delta LTD \pm \Delta PinC - DP \quad [10\text{-}56]$$

or

$$Cash\,G/(U) = CFfO \pm \Delta NetWC \pm NetInvst\ Activities \pm NetFinActivities - Dividends\,Paid \quad [10\text{-}57]$$

Cash Flow Proof

This calculation is very useful because it starts with the cash on hand at the beginning of the period, adds or subtracts the cash generated/(used), and obtains the cash on hand at the end of the period, which will reconcile with the bank statement.

$$Ending\,Cash\,Balance_{(Year\ n)} = Beginning\,Cash\,Balance_{(Year\ n)} \pm Cash\,Generated\ or\ Used_{(Year\ n)} \quad [10\text{-}58]$$

CASH FLOW STATEMENT REVISITED

The Cash Flow Statement just discussed was intentionally designed to be representative of what one would encounter. However, it is complicated by the fact that in doing so, accounts like Other Adjustments, Other Current Assets, Other Current Liabilities, Other Investments, and Other Financing are included. As far as this book is concerned, these accounts don't serve a purpose because they make the Cash Flow Statement appear to be more complicated than it needs to be (although in reality less complicated than most companies' Cash Flow Statements). Therefore, throughout this book, the Cash Flow Statement format depicted in Table 10-4 is used. In fact, the format used in some instances goes one step further and eliminates the "Dividends Paid to Shareholders" when it is irrelevant in the example or case study.

The following equations have been modified to reflect the simplified Cash Flow Statement format presented in Table 10-4.

---

[14] Cash generated/(used) is often abbreviated as *CGU*.

TABLE 10-4 Simplified Cash Flow Statement

Quarter Ending March 31, 20XX $(000)'s	
Operating Activities	
Operations	
Net Income (Loss)	
Depreciation and Amortization	
Net Cash Flow from Operations (CFfO)	
Working Capital Accounts	
(Increase)/Decrease Accounts Receivable	
(Increase)/Decrease Inventory	
Increase/(Decrease) Accounts Payable	
Increase/(Decrease) Taxes Payable	
Net Change in Working Capital (NetΔWC)	
Cash Flow from Operating Activities (CFfOA)	
Investing Activities	
Fixed Asset Additions	
Cash Flow after Investing Activities (CFaIA)	
Financing Activities	
Increase/(Decrease) Short-Term Debt	
Increase/(Decrease) Long-Term Debt	
Proceeds (Purchase) of Common Stock	
Dividends Paid	
Cash Generated/(Used)	
Cash Flow Proof	
Beginning Cash Balance	
Cash Generated/(Used)	
Ending Cash Balance	

Operating Activities

Net Cash Flow from Operations:

$$\begin{aligned} \textit{Net Cash Flow from Operations (CFfO)} &= \textit{Net Income} + \textit{Depreciation} \\ &\quad + \textit{Amortization} \end{aligned} \qquad [10\text{-}59]$$

Working Capital Accounts

Net Change in Working Capital:

$$\begin{aligned} \textit{Net } \Delta \textit{ in Working Capital} &= \pm\Delta \textit{ in Accounts Receivable} \pm \Delta \textit{ in Inventory} \\ &\quad \pm\Delta \textit{ in Accounts Payable} \pm \Delta \textit{ in Taxes Payable} \end{aligned} \qquad [10\text{-}60]$$

or

$$\textit{Net } \Delta WC = \pm\Delta AR \pm \Delta INV \pm \Delta AP \pm \Delta TP \qquad [10\text{-}61]$$

where:

$$\Delta Accounts\ Receivable = Accounts\ Receivable_{(Year\ n-1)} - Accounts\ Receivable_{(Year\ n)} \quad [10\text{-}44]$$

$$\Delta Inventory = Inventory_{(Year\ n-1)} - Inventory_{(Year\ n)} \quad [10\text{-}45]$$

$$\Delta Accounts\ Payable = Accounts\ Payable_{(Year\ n)} - Accounts\ Payable_{(Year\ n-1)} \quad [10\text{-}47]$$

$$\Delta Taxes\ Payable = Taxes\ Payable_{(Year\ n)} - Taxes\ Payable_{(Year\ n-1)} \quad [10\text{-}49]$$

Cash Flow from Operating Activities

$$Cash\ Flow\ from\ Operating\ Activities\ (CFfOA) = Cash\ Flow\ from\ Operations \pm Net\ \Delta WC \quad [10\text{-}51]$$

Cash Flow after Investing Activities

$$Cash\ Flow\ after\ Investing\ Activities\ (CFaIA) = CFfOA - Additions\ to\ Fixed\ Assets \quad [10\text{-}62]$$

Cash Flow after Financing Activities

$$Cash\ Flow\ after\ Financing\ Activities\ (CFaFA) = CFaIA \pm \Delta Financing\ Activities \quad [10\text{-}53]$$

or

$$CFaFA = CFaIA \pm \Delta STD \pm \Delta LTD \pm (Sale/Purchase\ of\ Common\ Stock) \quad [10\text{-}63]$$

Cash Flow after Payment of Dividends

$$CFaDP = CFaFA - Dividends\ Paid \quad [10\text{-}54]$$

Cash Generated/(Used)

$$Cash\ Generated/(Used) = Cash\ Flow\ after\ Financing\ Activities - Dividends\ Paid \quad [10\text{-}55]$$

or

$$CGU = CFaIA \pm \Delta STD \pm \Delta LTD \pm \Delta PinC - DP \quad [10\text{-}56]$$

where:

$$\Delta PinC = Change\ in\ Paid\text{-}in\ Capital$$

or

$$CGU = CFfO \pm \Delta NetWC \pm NetInvstActivities \\ \pm NetFinActivities - Dividends\ Paid \qquad [10\text{-}57]$$

Cash Flow Proof

$$Ending\ Cash\ Balance_{(Year\ n)} = Beginning\ Cash\ Balance_{(Year\ n)} \\ \pm Cash\ Generated\ or\ Used_{(Year\ n)} \qquad [10\text{-}58]$$

Closing Comments

By now some readers may feel that despite the pledge to make understanding financial statements crystal clear, the pace has been too rapid and insufficient time has been spent discussing the relationships implied by the various equations and definitions that have been cited. While this may be true for some readers, it is not a reason for concern. As mentioned earlier, this is not an accounting approach to preparing pro-forma financial statements. The objective is to present a methodology for managers that does not hinge on a solid accounting background but rather relies on a commonsense approach to understanding the essential issues that need to be grasped and applying the underlying principles. Hopefully, this is adequately done in the case study that follows. You are now well prepared to work your way through it and you will find it beneficial.

CASE STUDY: LIGHT TECHNOLOGIES INC.

This case study is designed to assist the reader in bringing together all of the material that has been covered in understanding financial statements and what it takes to prepare them. It takes the reader through the thinking associated with questioning financial data presented in an investment prospectus and then in an orderly fashion proceeds to prepare revised financial statements that reflect the new set of assumptions. It concludes by valuing the investment opportunity.

Description of the Investment Opportunity

Light Technologies Inc. (LTI) is a start-up that plans to develop, manufacture, and sell semiconductor lasers and subsystems incorporating its technology to a broad range of customers in the graphic arts, semiconductor, medical, and communications markets. Two of the founders are highly inventive and, on their own time and using their own money, have built prototypes of high-value-added systems for printing, marking, medical, and telecommunications applications. One of their inventions, a device that will increase the capacity of fiber-optic cable by at least an order of magnitude, is especially interesting. The management team of LTI is very highly regarded by the investment community.

This combined with the uniqueness of their inventions and the high growth prospects of the telecom market enabled them to convince an investment banker to underwrite the $50 million in capital (net of fees) their business plan required. One very knowledgeable investor, Ms. Debson, was skeptical about the bullishness of the financial projections in the offering memorandum and so she decided that she would prepare a set of pro-forma financial statements as an aid to help her decide on whether to invest in LTI.

Defining the Issues and Redefining the Assumptions

Ms. Debson began by studying the Balance Sheet Assumptions made by the LTI management team. She concluded that management's assumption that they would get paid in 40 days was optimistic in light of the fact that the average for their industrial peer group was closer to 45 days. Also, by adjusting the ARDOS in this way, it would match the 45-day accounts payable assumption that LTI had made and was consistent with the notion, "You get paid when I get paid." Furthermore, inventory turns of five for a company that was planning to grow as fast as LTI would take at least several years to achieve and an average of four turns over the life of the plan was probably more realistic. A comparison of Ms. Debson's and LTI's Balance Sheet Assumptions is summarized in Table CS 10-1.

Next she looked at LTI's Operating Assumptions and concluded that some of them were also too aggressive. For starters, reaching $25 million in sales the second year in operation and doubling every year thereafter was at the high end of the probable range. In her view, even $20 million for Year 2 would be tough if the telecom companies cut back their investment programs significantly, but at a $20 million starting point, she was prepared to give them the benefit of the doubt on doubling sales every year thereafter. Also, the cost of goods sold assumption was difficult to understand since it would take time for manufacturing to reach an efficient level of operations and so she increased the COGS projections for the first years of the plan.

The proposed spending on operating expenses also troubled her. The economy was booming and competition for the kind of talent they needed would be fierce. Therefore, despite the best of intentions and effort, it was highly unlikely that LTI would be able to staff up as quickly as they assumed, and, furthermore, once at critical mass, management would realize that spending at the planned rates was not necessary to keep their technology and marketing at the leading edge. This would ultimately cause LTI management to focus on becoming a little more efficient and lead to an increase in internally

TABLE CS 10-1 Balance Sheet Assumptions

	Investor	LTI's
Shareholders' Investment $(000)'s	50,000	50,000
Average Useful Life of Fixed Assets in Years	10	10
Days in an Accounting Year	360	360
Accounts Receivable Days Outstanding (ARDOS)	45	40
Inventory Turns (IT)	4	5
Accounts Payable Days Outstanding (APDOS)	45	45

TABLE CS 10-2 Operating Assumptions $(000)'s and %

	Investor	LTI	Investor	LTI	Investor	LTI	Investor	LTI	Investor	LTI
Operating Assumptions	**Year 1**	**Year 1**	**Year 2**	**Year 2**	**Year 3**	**Year 3**	**Year 4**	**Year 4**	**Year 5**	**Year 5**
Net Revenues $(000)'s	na	na	0	0	20,000	25,000	40,000	50,000	80,000	100,000
% Cost of Goods Sold	na	na	0.00%	0.00%	45.00%	37.50%	42.50%	37.50%	40.00%	37.50%
% Gross Margin	na	na	0.00%	0.00%	55.00%	62.50%	57.50%	62.50%	60.00%	62.50%
Research and Development	na	na	6,000	8,000	7,000	8,000	9,000	10,000	13,000	15,000
Sales and Marketing	na	na	3,000	4,000	6,000	7,000	8,000	9,000	13,000	16,000
General and Administrative	na	na	2,000	2,000	2,500	2,500	3,000	3,000	5,000	5,000
Fixed Asset Additions	na	na	10,000	10,000	10,000	10,000	20,000	20,000	10,000	10,000
Additional Long-Term Debt	na	na	0	0	0	0	12,000	0	0	10,000
LTD Interest Rate	na	na	na	na	na	na	10.00%	na	na	10.00%
Additional Short-Term Debt	na	na	0	0	0	0	0	0	2,000	0
STD Interest Rate	na	na	na	na	na	na	na	na	8.00%	na

generated cash flow. Such a scenario would be attractive to management since it would permit them to finance some of their growth with their own cash flow and not find it necessary to borrow excessively from the banks and forestall or eliminate the need to go back to the capital market for more equity money. Based on this thinking, she made adjustments to their operating expenses. She didn't have a problem with their fixed asset investment plan but thought that they may need to borrow a year sooner than they were currently projecting. A summary of Ms. Debson's and LTI's Operating Assumptions are shown in Table CS 10-2.

In addition, Ms. Debson assumed that investments in PP&E would be made at the beginning of the year, all loans drawn down at the beginning of the year, and any cash on hand would not earn any interest.

Preparation of Pro-Forma Financial Statements for LTI

Ms. Debson began her task of preparing pro-forma financial statements by first laying out what the financial statements would look like. The Income Statement, Balance Sheet, and Cash Flow Statement formats she decided to use are shown in Tables CS 10-3, CS 10-6, and CS 10-9. Then referring to the assumptions tabulated in Tables CS 10-1 and CS 10-2 she proceeded to systematically work her way through each year covered by the business plan.

Year 1 Income Statement

Since it was already late in the year, Ms. Debson assumed that the remainder of the year would be focused on raising the $50,000,000 (net of underwriting fees). This activity would not result in any significant costs to LTI and so she assumed that the Income Statement for Year 1 would not result in any revenue or expenses, as shown in Table CS 10-3.

TABLE CS 10-3 Light Technologies Income Statement for Year 1 $(000)'s

Net Revenues			0
Cost of Goods Sold (COGS)			0
Gross Margin (GM)			0
Operating Expenses (OpExp):	Research and Development (R&D)	0	
	Sales and Marketing (S&M)	0	
	General and Administrative (G&A)	0	
Total Operating Expenses			0
Earnings before Interest, Taxes, Depreciation, and Amortization (EBITDA)			0
Depreciation and Amortization (D&A)			0
Earnings before Interest and Taxes (EBIT)			0
Interest Income/Expense (Int)			0
Earnings before Tax (EBT)			0
Taxes Paid(TaxesPaid) @ 40%			0
Net Income (NI)			0

Year 1 Balance Sheet Once the financing was completed, the company would have raised $50,000,000 in cash, as shown in Table CS 10-4. This would also result in total shareholders' equity of $50,000,000 (Table CS 10-5).

TABLE CS 10-4 Asset Entry $(000)'s

Current Assets	
Cash	50,000
Accounts Receivable	0
Inventory	0
Total Current Assets	**50,000**

TABLE CS 10-5 Liability Entry $(000)'s

Shareholders' Equity	
Paid-in Capital	50,000
Retained Earnings	0
Total Shareholders' Equity	**50,000**

By definition, total assets must equal total liabilities plus total shareholders' equity (Equation [10-11]):

$$\textit{Total Assets} = \textit{Total Liabilities} + \textit{Total Shareholders' Equity} \qquad [10\text{-}11]$$

Since LTI did not spend any money on assets or incur any liabilities, the Balance Sheet, as of December 31 of Year 1, would be as shown in Table CS 10-6. The $50,000,000 of cash and $50,000,000 of total shareholders' equity would be the only entries that LTI had on their Balance Sheet.

Year 1 Cash Flow Statement During Year 1, LTI did not conduct any operating activities so there is no cash flow from operating activities. Similarly, since no assets were purchased, the cash flow after investing activities is also zero. Therefore, the cash flow for Year 1 is the result of the proceeds from the sale of the company's common stock and the section on Financing Activities in the Cash Flow Statement for Year 1 would be as shown in Table CS 10-7.

TABLE CS 10-6 Light Technologies Balance Sheet for Year 1 $(000)'s

Current Assets		**Current Liabilities**	
Cash	50,000	Accounts Payable	0
Accounts Receivable	0	Taxes Payable	0
Inventory	0	Short-Term Debt	0
Total Current Assets	50,000	**Total Current Liabilities**	0
Fixed Assets		**Long-Term Debt**	0
Property, Plant, and Equipment at Cost	0		
Less Accumulated Depreciation	0	**Total Liabilities**	0
Net Fixed Assets	0		
Intangible Assets		**Shareholders' Equity**	
Goodwill and Other Intangible Assets	0	Paid-in Capital	50,000
Less Accumulated Amortization	0	Retained Earnings	0
Net Intangible Assets	0	**Total Shareholders' Equity**	50,000
Total Assets	50,000	**Total Liabilities + TSHE**	50,000

TABLE CS 10-7 Financing Activities $(000)'s

Increase/(Decrease) Short-Term Debt	0
Net Proceeds (Payments) Long-Term Debt	0
Proceeds (Purchase) of Common Stock	50,000

The balance in the Cash account (on deposit in the Company's bank) is reconciled by performing a calculation called "Cash Flow Proof." The beginning cash balance is $0. The cash generated during Year 1 was $50,000,000. Therefore, the ending cash balance is $50,000,000 (See Table CS 10-8).

TABLE CS 10-8 Cash Flow Proof $(000)s

Beginning Cash Balance	0
Cash Generated/(Used)	50,000
Ending Cash Balance	50,000

With this information at hand, Ms. Debson worked her way down the Cash Flow Statement format she had designed and made the following entries shown in Figure CS 10-1 in Table CS 10-9.

Net Cash Flow from Operations	0
Net Change in Working Capital Accounts	0
Cash Flow from Operating Activities	0
Investments in Fixed Asset Additions	0
Increase in Short-Term and Long-Term Debt	0
Proceeds from Sale of Common Stock	50,000,000
Cash Generated / (Used)	50,000,000
Beginning Cash Balance	0
Cash Generated / (Used)	50,000,000
Ending Cash Balance	50,000,000

FIGURE CS 10-1 Cash Flow Statement Entries $'s

TABLE CS 10-9 Light Technologies Cash Flow Statement for Year 1 $(000)'s

Operating Activities	
Operations	
Net Income (Loss)	0
Depreciation	0
Amortization	0
Net Cash Flow from Operations	0
Working Capital Accounts	
(Increase)/Decrease Accounts Receivable	0
(Increase)/Decrease Inventory	0
Increase/(Decrease) Accounts Payable	0
Increase/(Decrease) Taxes Payable	0
Net Change in Working Capital	0
Cash Flow from Operating Activities	0
Investing Activities	
Fixed Asset Additions	0
Cash Flow after Investing Activities	0
Financing Activities	
Increase/(Decrease) Short-Term Debt	0
Net Proceeds (Payments) Long-Term Debt	0
Proceeds (Purchase) of Common Stock	50,000
Dividends Paid	0
Cash Generated/(Used)	50,000
Cash Flow Proof	
Beginning Cash Balance	0
Cash Generated/(Used)	50,000
Ending Cash Balance	50,000

Year 2 Income Statement

According to Tables CS 10-1 and CS 10-2, Year 2 is the first year of LTI's operations. Management focus is on developing their products (research and development) and sales and marketing, and putting infrastructure in place (general and administrative). There are no sales during Year 1 and therefore the net revenues and cost of goods sold are zero dollars, as is the gross margin, as calculated by Equation [10-1].

$$Gross\ Margin = Net\ Revenue - Cost\ of\ Goods\ Sold \qquad [10\text{-}1]^{15}$$

$$Gross\ Margin = 0 - 0 = \$0$$

Because LTI is spending money on research and development ($6,000,000), sales and marketing ($3,000,000), and general and administrative ($2,000,000), significant operating expenses are incurred during Year 2. They are calculated using Equation [10-2] and summarized in Table CS 10-10.

$$Operating\ Expenses = Research\ \&\ Development + Sales\ \&\ Marketing + General\ \&\ Administrative \qquad [10\text{-}2]$$

$$Operating\ Expenses = 6{,}000{,}000 + 3{,}000{,}000 + 2{,}000{,}000 = \$11{,}000{,}000$$

TABLE CS 10-10 Operating Expenses $(000)'s

Operating Expenses (OpExp):	Research and Development (R&D)	6,000
	Sales & Marketing (S&M)	3,000
	General and Administrative (G&A)	2,000
Total Operating Expenses		**11,000**

Substituting the gross margin ($0) and total operating expenses ($11,000,000) in Equation [10-3], the earnings before interest, taxes, depreciation and amortization (EBITDA) are calculated to be:

$$EBITDA = Gross\ Margin - Total\ Operating\ Expenses \qquad [10\text{-}3]$$

$$EBITDA = 0 - 11{,}000{,}000 = -\$11{,}000{,}000$$

[15] This and all equations pertaining to the Income Statement can be logically derived by inspection. This is also true for all equations pertaining to the Balance Sheet and Cash Flow Statement.

At the beginning of Year 2, LTI purchases $10,000,000 of fixed assets. These assets are deemed to have a useful life of 10 years. Therefore, the depreciation in Year 2 is calculated with the assistance of Equation [10-4].

$$Depreciation = \frac{Total\ Cost\ of\ Asset}{Useful\ Life} \qquad [10\text{-}4]$$

$$Depreciation = \frac{10,000,000}{10} = \$1,000,000\ per\ year$$

There are no intangible assets to amortize and so the earnings before interest and taxes (EBIT) are calculated by substituting values for EBITDA and depreciation into Equation [10-6], which results in a loss of $12,000,000.

$$EBIT = EBITDA - Depreciation - Amortization \qquad [10\text{-}6]$$

$$EBIT = -\ 11{,}000{,}000 - 1{,}000{,}000 - 0 = -\$12{,}000{,}000$$

Since LTI doesn't have any interest-bearing debt and doesn't receive any interest on its cash,[16] the interest income/expense is $0 and the company's EBT is the same as its EBIT (Equation [10-9]).

$$EBT = EBIT \pm Interest\ Income/Expense \qquad [10\text{-}9]$$

$$EBT = 12{,}000{,}000 \pm 0 = -\$12{,}000{,}000$$

Also, since the company isn't making money, it doesn't have any income tax obligations.[17] Therefore, the net income (NI) as per Equation [10-10] is:

$$NI = EBT - Taxes\ Paid \qquad [10\text{-}10]$$

$$NI = -12{,}000{,}0000 - 0 = -\$12{,}000{,}000$$

Ms. Debson then uses the results of the calculations she has just completed to prepare Light Technologies Inc.'s Income Statement for Year 2 (Table CS 10-11).

---

[16] This is a simplifying assumption. In practice, the company would receive interest. For example, if the cash balance at the beginning and end of a year was $10 million and $5 million, respectively, the average cash balance would be $7.5 million. If the interest rate on cash deposits was 5%, then the company would have $375,000 ($7,500,000 * .05) of interest income.

[17] While this assumption is generally true when it comes to federal corporate taxes, it does not necessarily apply to state or local taxes.

TABLE CS 10-11 Laser Technologies Inc. Income Statement for Year 2 $(000)'s

Net Revenues			0
Cost of Goods Sold (COGS)			0
Gross Margin (GM)			0
Operating Expenses (OpExp):	Research and Development (R&D)	6,000	
	Sales and Marketing (S&M)	3,000	
	General and Administrative (G&A)	2,000	
Total Operating Expenses			(11,000)
Earnings before Interest, Taxes, Depreciation, and Amortization (EBITDA)			(11,000)
Depreciation and Amortization (D&A)			(1,000)
Earnings before Interest and Taxes (EBIT)			(12,000)
Interest Income/Expense (Int)			0
Earnings before Tax (EBT)			(12,000)
Taxes Paid (TaxesPaid) @ 40%			0
Net Income (NI)			(12,000)

Year 2 Balance Sheet There are several places Ms. Debson could have started to prepare LTI's Balance Sheet for Year 2. She chose to start with the Equity section of the Balance Sheet.

The total shareholders' equity (Equation [10-27]) is the sum of paid-in capital ([10-29]) and retained earnings ([10-30]).

$$\textit{Total Shareholders' Equity}_{(\textit{End Year } 2)} = \textit{Paid-in Capital}_{(\textit{End Year } 2)} + \textit{Retained Earnings}_{(\textit{End Year } 2)} \qquad [10\text{-}27]$$

There wasn't any additional capital raised during the year. Therefore, the paid-in capital at the end of Year 2 is given by Equation [10-29] and "is" the same as it was at the end of Year 1.

$$\textit{Paid-in Capital}_{(\textit{End Year } 2)} = \textit{Paid-in Capital}_{(\textit{End Year } 1)} + \Delta \textit{Paid-in Capital}_{(\textit{Year } 2)} \qquad [10\text{-}29]$$

$$\textit{Paid-in Capital} = 50{,}000{,}000 + 0 = \$50{,}000{,}000$$

Net income for the year was a loss of $12,000,000. No dividends were paid. The retained earnings (RetEarnings) at the end of Year 2 are calculated using Equation [10-30].

$$RetEarnings_{(End\ Year\ 2)} = RetEarnings_{(End\ Year\ 1)} \pm NI_{(Year\ 2)} - Dividends\ Paid_{(Year\ 2)} \quad [10\text{-}30]$$

$$Retained\ Earnings = 0 - 12{,}000{,}000 - 0 = -\$12{,}000{,}000$$

The total shareholders' equity is the sum of paid-in capital and retained earnings. Hence the total shareholders' equity is arrived at by applying Equation [10-27]. See Table CS 10-12.

TABLE CS 10-12 Shareholders' Equity $(000)'s

Paid-in Capital	50,000
Retained Earnings	(12,000)
Total Shareholders' Equity	**38,000**

$$Total\ Shareholders'\ Equity = 50{,}000{,}000 - 12{,}000{,}000 = \$38{,}000{,}000$$

Since Year 2's expenses are payroll and the consumable supplies required to support the payroll expenses, she assumed that LTI will be current on these obligations and not have any accounts payable at the end of Year 2. Furthermore, since the company will lose money during the first year and didn't borrow any money, the taxes payable, short-term debt, and long-term debt will all be zero. Therefore, the Current Liabilities and Long-Term Debt sections of the Balance Sheet will be as shown in Tables CS 10-13 and CS 10-14.

$$Current\ Liabilities = Accounts\ Payable + Taxes\ Payable + Short\text{-}Term\ Debt \quad [10\text{-}25]$$ [18]

$$Current\ Liabilities = 0 + 0 + 0 = \$0$$

TABLE CS 10-13 Current Liabilities $(000)'s

Accounts Payable	0
Taxes Payable	0
Short-Term Debt	0
Total Current Liabilities	**0**

[18] As mentioned earlier in the chapter, Equation [10-25] was obtained by modifying Equation [10-24] to exclude "Accrued Payroll" and "Accrued Expenses" because throughout the case study it is assumed that both of these accounts are paid in full at the end of the accounting period.

TABLE CS 10-14 Long-Term Debt $(000)'s

Long-Term Debt	**0**

Since Tables CS 10-12, 13, and 14 account for all of LTI's liabilities, the total liabilities and TSHE side of the Year 2 Balance Sheet is as shown in Table CS 10-15.

$$Total\ Liabilities + TSHE = Current\ Liabilities + Long\text{-}Term\ Debt \\ + Total\ Shareholders'\ Equtiy \quad [10\text{-}32]$$

$$Total\ Liabilities + TSHE = 0 + 0 + 38{,}000{,}000 = \$38{,}000{,}000$$

TABLE CS 10-15 Liabilities and Total Shareholders' Equity $(000)'s

Current Liabilities	
Accounts Payable	0
Taxes Payable	0
Short-Term Debt	0
Total Current Liabilities	0
Long-Term Debt	0
Total Liabilities	0
Shareholders' Equity	
Paid-in Capital	50,000
Retained Earnings	(12,000)
Total Shareholders' Equity	38,000
Total Liabilities + TSHE	38,000

With the Balance Sheet liabilities for Year 2 defined, Ms. Debson turned her attention to the Company's assets, and this process begins with the use of Equation [10-11].

$$Total\ Assets = Total\ Liabilities + Total\ Shareholders'\ Equity \quad [10\text{-}11]$$

where:

$$Total\ Assets = 0 + 38{,}000{,}000 = \$38{,}000{,}000$$

Starting with what she knew, she worked her way from the bottom up to define the asset side of the Balance Sheet. The first asset class encountered is Intangible Assets. The company does not have any goodwill or other intangible assets such as intellectual property to amortize and therefore the "Net Intangible Assets" are $0 and tabulated as such in Table CS 10-16.

TABLE CS 10-16 Intangible Assets $(000)'s

Goodwill and Other Intangible Assets	0
Less Accumulated Amortization	0
Net Intangible Assets	**0**

According to Table CS 10-2, LTI purchased plant and equipment during Year 2 in the amount of $10,000,000. The mix of purchases was such that the average life of the mix is deemed to be 10 years with Year 2's depreciation equal to $1,000,000.[19,20] Furthermore, to simplify the model, Ms. Debson assumed the $10,000,000 of plant and equipment was in place for the entirety of Year 2.[21] Therefore, the net fixed assets are as shown in Table CS 10-17. The calculation is shown in Equation [10-14].

$$\begin{aligned} \textit{Net Fixed Assets} &= \textit{Property, Plant \& Equipment at Cost} \\ &\quad - \textit{Accumulated Depreciation} \end{aligned} \qquad [10\text{-}14]$$

$$\textit{Net Fixed Assets} = 10{,}000{,}000 - 1{,}000{,}000 = \$9{,}000{,}000$$

TABLE CS 10-17 Fixed Assets $(000)'s

Property, Plant, and Equipment at Cost	10,000
Less Accumulated Depreciation	(1,000)
Net Fixed Assets	**9,000**

To complete the Balance Sheet Ms. Debson turned her attention to "Current Assets." By looking at the asset side of the Balance Sheet in its entirety, she sees that it consists of: intangible assets, fixed assets, and current assets. The relationship between these three asset classes is defined by Equation [10-22].

$$\textit{Total Assets} = \textit{Current Assets} + \textit{Net Fixed Assets} + \textit{Net Intangible Assets} \qquad [10\text{-}22]$$

[19] This is a simplifying assumption. In reality the spending would probably include land (which is not depreciated), buildings (normally assumed to have a 40-year life), and equipment such as test equipment (3–5 years), manufacturing jigs and tooling (3 years more or less depending on the expected life of the product), and computers (3- to 5-year useful life). Throughout this example, the weighted average of all fixed asset purchases is 10 years.

[20] See the section on the Year 1 Income Statement for details of the depreciation calculation.

[21] This is another simplifying assumption. In practice the plant and equipment would have been purchased throughout the year and the first year's depreciation for each fixed asset would be calculated on a pro-rata basis. For example, if a $1,000,000 asset with a useful life of 10 years was put in service July 1, then the first and subsequent years' depreciation would be $50,000 and $100,000, respectively, with the exception of year 10, which would be $50,000.

She knows the total assets, net intangible assets, and net fixed assets are $38,000,000, $0, and $9,000,000 respectively. Rearranging Equation [10-22] and plugging in these values gives her the value for current assets.

$$\textit{Current Assets} = \textit{Total Assets} - \textit{Net Intangible Assets} - \textit{Net Fixed Assets} \quad [10\text{-}23]$$

$$\textit{Current Assets} = 38{,}000{,}000 - 0 - 9{,}000{,}000 = \$29{,}000{,}000$$

As can be seen from Equation [10-12] and the Balance Sheet from Year 1, current assets consist of cash, accounts receivable, and inventory.

$$\textit{Current Assets} = \textit{Cash} + \textit{Accounts Receivable} + \textit{Inventory} \quad [10\text{-}12]$$

LTI has no revenue during Year 2. Furthermore, purchasing of components and supplies for manufacturing has not commenced. Hence, there are no accounts receivable or inventory and they both equal zero. Therefore, LTI's current assets must consist entirely of cash, as shown in Table CS 10-18.

Rearranging Equation [10-12],

$$\textit{Cash} = \textit{Current Assets} - \textit{Accounts Receivable} - \textit{Inventory} \quad [10\text{-}13]$$

$$\textit{Cash} = 29{,}000{,}000 - 0 - 0 = \$29{,}000{,}000$$

TABLE CS 10-18 Current Assets $(000)'s

Cash	29,000
Accounts Receivable	0
Inventory	0
Total Current Assets	**29,000**

By combining these asset classes with the result of Equation [10-22] Ms. Debson obtained the asset side of the Balance sheet (Table CS 10-19).

$$\textit{Total Assets} = \textit{Current Assets} + \textit{Net Fixed Assets} + \textit{Net Intangible Assets} \quad [10\text{-}22]$$

$$\textit{Total Assets} = 29{,}000{,}000 + 9{,}000{,}000 + 0 = \$38{,}000{,}000$$

Finally, by combining the assets tabulated in Table CS 10-19 with the liabilities + total shareholders' equity shown in Table CS 10-15, Ms. Debson created the pro-forma Balance Sheet for Year 2 (Table CS 10-20).

[22] As mentioned earlier, of the three key financial statements, the Cash Flow Statement is considered by many to be the most difficult to understand. Every manager who shares this view does so for his or her own reasons. In practice the Cash Flow Statement is actually quite simple, because as will be seen, the statement converts net income from the Income Statement to a cash basis and accounts for the cash implications of changes in the Balance Sheet. Hopefully, the approach taken in this case study drives this point home and facilitates comprehension.

TABLE CS 10-19 Total Assets $(000)'s

Current Assets	
Cash	29,000
Accounts Receivable	0
Inventory	0
Total Current Assets	29,000
Fixed Assets	
Property, Plant, and Equipment at Cost	10,000
Less Accumulated Depreciation	(1,000)
Net Fixed Assets	9,000
Intangible Assets	
Goodwill and Other Intangible Assets	0
Less Accumulated Amortization	0
Net Intangible Assets	0
Total Assets	38,000

TABLE CS 10-20 Light Technologies Balance Sheet for Year 2 $(000)'s

Current Assets		**Current Liabilities**	
Cash	29,000	Accounts Payable	0
Accounts Receivable	0	Taxes Payable	0
Inventory	0	Short-Term Debt	0
Total Current Assets	29,000	**Total Current Liabilities**	0
Fixed Assets		**Long-Term Debt**	0
Property, Plant, and Equipment at Cost	10,000		
Less Accumulated Depreciation	(1,000)		
Net Fixed Assets	9,000		
Intangible Assets		**Shareholders' Equity**	
Goodwill and Other Intangible Assets	0	Paid-in Capital	50,000
Less Accumulated Amortization	0	Retained Earnings	(12,000)
Net Intangible Assets	0	**Total Shareholders' Equity**	38,000
Total Assets	38,000	**Total Liabilities + TSHE**	38,000

Year 2 Cash Flow Statement[22] Having completed the Income Statement and Balance Sheet for Year 2, Ms. Debson proceeded to prepare the Cash Flow Statement.

Operations Recalling the early days of preparing pro-forma Cash Flow Statements and the difficulties first encountered, she decided to proceed systematically and started at the top by adjusting "Net Income" as shown in the Income Statement for non-cash charges. She recalled that "depreciation" is simply an accounting technique used to match revenue with the depletion of assets that produce or are used to generate the revenue. In this case, there are $10,000,000 of assets that are purchased at the beginning of Year 2 with an average useful life of 10 years. The depreciation is a non-cash charge and therefore is added back to net income.[23,24] Since there isn't any amortization, the net cash flow from operations is easily calculated using Equation [10-59] and shown in Table CS 10-21.

$$\textit{Net Cash Flow from Operations (CFfO)} = \textit{Net Income} + \textit{Depreciation} + \textit{Amortization} \qquad [10\text{-}59]^{25}$$

$$\text{CFfO} = -12{,}000{,}000 + 1{,}000{,}000 + 0 = -\$11{,}000{,}000$$

TABLE CS 10-21 Operations $(000)'s

Net Income (Loss)	(12,000)
Depreciation	1,000
Amortization	0
Net Cash Flow from Operations	**(11,000)**

Working Capital Accounts Having adjusted net income for non-cash charges, Ms. Debson proceeded to deal with the cash implications of changes in the Working Capital accounts in the Balance Sheet. Since there weren't any sales during Year 2, no revenue was generated and the Accounts Receivable account would show a zero balance. Similarly, since no inventory has been purchased and all supplies were paid for on a cash basis, the balances in the Inventory and Accounts Payable accounts are also zero. Net income for the year was a loss and, therefore, there are no taxes payable. The result of all of this, Ms. Debson reasoned, was "zero" cash-related activity in the Working Capital accounts and so she proceeded to tabulate the Working Capital accounts in Table CS 10-22.

[23] Depreciation is a non-cash charge because it simply represents the depletion of assets. The cash associated with purchasing these assets is accounted for in the Cash Flow Statement section titled "Investing Activities." In subsequent years, there will be depreciation of $1,000,000 per year (due to this asset purchase) but no cash implications in the "Investing Activities" section of the Cash Flow Statement because the cash was paid out during Year 1.

[24] At this point there isn't any amortization to account for. However, if there were some, it would be treated in exactly the same way. For example, if LTI had purchased a patent at the beginning of Year 1 for $2,000,000 with a remaining useful life of say 20 years, then the amortization per accounting period would be $2,000,000/20 or $100,000 per year. Again the cash associated with the actual purchase would be accounted for in the section of the Cash Flow Statement titled "Investing Activities." In subsequent years there would not be any cash flow impact because the patent was paid for during Year 1.

[25] Since there aren't any "Other Adjustments," the term has been dropped from the Equation.

TABLE CS 10-22 Working Capital Accounts $(000)'s

(Increase)/Decrease Accounts Receivable	0
(Increase)/Decrease Inventory	0
Increase/(Decrease) Accounts Payable	0
Increase/(Decrease) Taxes Payable	0
Net Change in Working Capital	**0**

Cash Flow from Operating Activities Cash flow from operating activities is defined as the sum of net cash flow from operations and change in the working capital (Equation [10-51]). Since the net change in working capital is zero, the CFfOA is equal to the cash flow from operations (Table CS 10-23).

$$\textit{Cash Flow from Operating Activities (CFfOA)} = \textit{Cash Flow from Operations} \pm \textit{Net } \Delta WC \qquad [10\text{-}51]$$

$$CFfOA = -11{,}000{,}000 \pm 0 = -\$11{,}000{,}000$$

TABLE CS 10-23 Cash Flow from Operating Activities $(000)'s

Cash Flow from Operating Activities	(11,000)

Investing Activities In Year 2, $10,000,000 of fixed assets was purchased. Therefore, Ms. Debson concludes that the cash outlay for investing activities is $10,000,000 (Table CS 10-24).

TABLE CS 10-24 Investing Activities $(000)'s

Fixed Asset Additions	10,000

Cash Flow after Investing Activities By definition CFaIA is the sum of cash flow from operating activities less any fixed asset additions (Equation [10-62]). The CFfOA is a negative $11,000,000. Earlier, the fixed asset additions were stated to be $10,000,000. Hence, Ms. Debson concluded the CFaIA to be a negative $21,000,000 (Table CS 10-25).

$$\textit{Cash Flow after Investing Activities (CFaIA)} = \textit{CFfOA} - \textit{Additions to Fixed Assets} \qquad [10\text{-}62]$$

$$CFaIA = -11{,}000{,}000 - 10{,}000{,}000 \pm 0 = -\$21{,}000{,}000$$

TABLE CS 10-25 Cash Flow after Investing Activities $(000)'s

Cash Flow after Investing Activities	(21,000)

Financing Activities Being well aware of the ways a company can be financed (equity, short-term bank debt, long-term bank debt, bonds,[26] or some combination thereof[27]), Ms. Debson was able to quickly work her way through this part of the Cash Flow Statement. According to the Balance Sheet, LTI does not have any debt. LTI raised $50,000,000 of equity during Year 1 and since then there hasn't been any need for additional financing. Therefore, the net impact of financing activities on Year 2's operations is zero and the cash flow after financing activities is the same as the cash flow after investing activities (Table CS 10-26).

$$CFaFA = CFaIA \pm \Delta STD \pm \Delta LTD \pm (Sale/Purchase\ of\ Common\ Stock) \qquad [10\text{-}63]$$

$$CFaFA = -\,21{,}000{,}000 \pm 0 \pm 0 \pm 0 = -\$21{,}000{,}000$$

TABLE CS 10-26 Financing Activities $(000)'s

Increase/(Decrease) Short-Term Debt	0
Net Proceeds (Payments) Long-Term Debt	0
Proceeds (Purchase) of Common Stock	0

Cash Generated/(Used) The cash generated or used (CGU) by LTI during Year 2 is simply the sum of the cash flow after investing activities and any cash generated or used as a result of financing activities and any dividends paid (Equation [10-56]).

$$CGU = CFaIA \pm \Delta STD \pm \Delta LTD \pm \Delta TSHE - DP \qquad [10\text{-}56]$$

In this case, there isn't any cash generated or used by financing activities nor are there any dividends paid and so the cash generated/(used) is equal to the cash flow after investing activities (Table CS 10-27).

$$CGU = -21{,}000{,}000 \pm 0 \pm 0 \pm 0 - 0 = -\$21{,}000{,}000$$

TABLE CS 10-27 Cash Generated/(Used) $(000)'s

Cash Generated/(Used)	(21,000)

[26] In this example, long-term bank debt and bonds with a maturity of more than one year would be classified as long-term debt. Any debt due for repayment in one year or less would be short-term debt.
[27] See Chapter 9 for a discussion of financing alternatives.

Cash Flow Proof[28] The cash on hand at the end of Year 1 and the beginning of Year 2 ("Beginning Cash Balance") was $50,000,000. During Year 2, $21,000,000 of cash was used. Therefore, the cash on hand at the end of Year 2 ("Ending Cash Balance") is calculated to be $29,000,000 using Equation [10-58] and substituting "Year 2" for *n*. From this data Ms. Debson prepared the Cash Flow Proof section of the Cash Flow Statement (Table CS 10-28).

$$Ending\,Cash\,Balance_{(Year\ 2)} = Beginning\,Cash\,Balance_{(Year\ 2)} \pm Cash\,Generated\ or\ Used_{(Year\ 2)} \qquad [10\text{-}58]$$

$$Ending\ Cash\ Balance_{(Year\ 2)} = 50{,}000{,}000 - 21{,}000{,}000 = \$29{,}000{,}000$$

TABLE CS 10-28 Cash Flow Proof $(000)'s

Beginning Cash Balance	50,000
Cash Generated/(Used)	(21,000)
Ending Cash Balance	29,000

LTI's Cash Flow Statement for Year 2 is obtained by combining Tables CS 10-21–CS 10-28 and is shown in Table CS 10-29.

Year 3 Income Statement

Having completed the pro-forma statements for the first two years, Ms. Debson proceeded to do the same for Year 3. Again, referring to the assumptions in Tables CS 10-1 and CS 10-2, Ms. Debson notes that Year 3 is the first year that LTI generates any revenue. The revenue and cost of goods sold during Year 3 are $20 million and $9 million ($20,000,000 * 0.45) respectively. Therefore, gross margin is calculated using Equation [10-1] and the result is tabulated in Table CS 10-30.

$$Gross\ Margin = Net\ Revenue - Cost\ of\ Goods\ Sold \qquad [10\text{-}1]$$

$$Gross\ Margin = 20{,}000{,}000 - 9{,}000{,}000 = \$11{,}000{,}000$$

[28] It is customary to append at the bottom of the Cash Flow Statement a section titled "Cash Flow Proof." It provides a reconciliation of the cash flow for the period with the cash on hand (bank balance) at the beginning of the period plus or minus any cash generated/(used) to give the end-of-period cash. The "Cash Flow Proof" section is actually quite comforting to most managers since it provides a link between the cash shown on the asset side of the Balance Sheet and the cash generated or used during the period the Cash Flow Statement covers. In fact $29,000,000 will be the cash balance shown in the Balance Sheet and is the "real" cash flow proof.

TABLE CS 10-29 Light Technologies Inc. Cash Flow Statement for Year 2 $(000)'s

Operating Activities	
Operations	
Net Income (Loss)	(12,000)
Depreciation	1,000
Amortization	0
Net Cash Flow from Operations	(11,000)
Working Capital Accounts	
(Increase)/Decrease Accounts Receivable	0
(Increase)/Decrease Inventory	0
Increase/(Decrease) Accounts Payable	0
Increase/(Decrease) Taxes Payable	0
Net Change in Working Capital	0
Cash Flow from Operating Activities	(11,000)
Investing Activities	
Fixed Asset Additions	(10,000)
Cash Flow after Investing Activities	(21,000)
Financing Activities	
Increase/(Decrease) Short-Term Debt	0
Net Proceeds (Payments) Long-Term Debt	0
Proceeds (Purchase) of Common Stock	0
Dividends Paid	0
Cash Generated/(Used)	(21,000)
Cash Flow Proof	
Beginning Cash Balance	50,000
Cash Generated/(Used)	(21,000)
Ending Cash Balance	29,000

TABLE CS 10-30 Gross Margin $(000)'s

Net Revenues	20,000
Cost of Goods Sold (COGS)	(9,000)
Gross Margin (GM)	**11,000**

Expenditures on research and development (R&D), sales and marketing (S&M), and general and administrative (G&A) keep on increasing as LTI continues to invest in new products, compete for customers, and build infrastructure for growth. R&D, S&M, and G&A increase to $7, $6, and $2.5 million respectively. The total operating expenses increase to $15,500,000 as calculated by Equation [10-2].

$$\begin{aligned} \textit{Operating Expenses} &= \textit{Research \& Development} + \textit{Sales \& Marketing} \\ &\quad + \textit{General \& Administrative} \end{aligned} \qquad [10\text{-}2]$$

$$\textit{Operating Expenses} = 7{,}000{,}000 + 6{,}000{,}000 + 2{,}500{,}000 = \$15{,}500{,}000$$

The total operating expenses as they would appear in the Income Statement are shown in Table CS 10-31.

TABLE CS 10-31 Operating Expenses $(000)'s

Operating Expenses (OpExp):	Research and Development (R&D)	7,000
	Sales and Marketing (S&M)	6,000
	General and Administrative (G&A)	2,500
Total Operating Expenses		**15,500**

Earnings before interest, taxes, depreciation and amortization (EBITDA) are defined by Equation [10-3]. For Year 3, the gross margin and total operating expenses are $11 and $15.5 million respectively. Hence:

$$\textit{EBITDA} = \textit{Gross Margin} - \textit{Operating Expenses} \qquad [10\text{-}3]$$

$$\textit{EBITDA} = 11{,}000{,}000 - 15{,}500{,}000 = -\$4{,}500{,}000$$

LTI continues to invest during Year 3 and purchases another $10 million of fixed assets, which Ms. Debson assumes takes place at the beginning of Year 3. These assets also have a useful life of 10 years. Therefore the depreciation of the assets purchased at the beginning of Year 3, during Year 3, is expressed by Equation [10-4].

$$\textit{Depreciation} = \frac{\textit{Total Cost of Asset}}{\textit{Useful Life}} \qquad [10\text{-}4]$$

$$\textit{Depreciation} = \frac{10{,}000{,}000}{10} = \$1{,}000{,}000 \textit{ per year}$$

However, this is not the end of the depreciation story for Year 3. Recall that $10 million of fixed assets were also purchased at the beginning of Year 2. These assets are only in the second year of their useful life and so they will depreciate by an additional $1 million during the current year. Therefore, the total depreciation for Year 3 will be the sum of the depreciations, as shown in Table CS 10-32.

TABLE CS 10-32 Depreciation and Amortization $(000)'s

	Year 2	Year 3	Total Yr 3
Fixed Asset Additions	10,000	10,000	20,000
Avg Useful Life in Years	10	10	
Year of Assets Depreciation	2nd	1st	
Depreciation	1,000	1,000	2,000
Amortization	0	0	0

Again, since there is no goodwill or other intangible assets such as intellectual property, amortization is once again zero, and earnings before interest and taxes (EBIT) are determined by the use of Equation [10-6].

$$EBIT = EBITDA - Depreciation - Amortization \quad [10\text{-}6]$$

$$EBIT = -4{,}500{,}000 - 2{,}000{,}000 - 0 = -\$6{,}500{,}000$$

LTI doesn't have any interest-bearing debt and since it doesn't receive any interest on its cash, the interest expense and income are zero and the company's EBT is the same as its EBIT (Equation [10-9]).

$$EBT = EBIT \pm Interest\ Income/Expense \quad [10\text{-}9]$$

$$EBT = -6{,}500{,}000 \pm 0 = -\$6{,}500{,}000$$

Also, since LTI still isn't making money, it doesn't have any income tax obligations. Therefore, net income (NI) per Equation [10-10] is:

$$NI = EBT - Taxes\ Paid \quad [10\text{-}10]$$

$$NI = -6{,}500{,}000 - 0 = -\$6{,}500{,}000$$

Ms. Debson then prepared the Income Statement for Year 3 by entering the results of her calculations into the Income Statement format she has used for Years 1 and 2 (Table CS 10-33).

Year 3 Balance Sheet

Net income for the year was a loss of $6,500,000 and no capital was raised during the year, nor were any dividends paid. Once again Ms. Debson begins her preparation of the Balance Sheet by calculating total shareholders' equity using Equations [10-27], [10-29], and [10-30]. The results of the calculations are shown in Table CS 10-34.

$$Total\ Shareholders'\ Equity_{(End\ Year\ 3)} = Paid\text{-}in\ Capital_{(End\ Year\ 3)} + Retained\ Earnings_{(End\ Year\ 3)} \quad [10\text{-}27]$$

TABLE CS 10-33 Light Technologies Inc. Income Statement for Year 3 $(000)'s

Net Revenues			20,000
Cost of Goods Sold (COGS)			(9,000)
Gross Margin (GM)			11,000
Operating Expenses (OpExp):	Research and Development (R&D)	7,000	
	Sales and Marketing (S&M)	6,000	
	General and Administrative (G&A)	2,500	
Total Operating Expenses			(15,500)
Earnings before Interest, Taxes, Depreciation, and Amortization (EBITDA)			(4,500)
Depreciation and Amortization (D&A)			(2,000)
Earnings before Interest and Taxes (EBIT)			(6,500)
Interest Income/Expense (Int)			0
Earnings before Tax (EBT)			(6,500)
Taxes Paid (TaxesPaid) @ 40%			0
Net Income (NI)			(6,500)

$$Paid\text{-}in\ Capital_{(End\ Year\ 3)} = Paid\text{-}in\ Capital_{(End\ Year\ 2)} + \Delta Paid\text{-}in\ Capital_{(Year\ 3)} \qquad [10\text{-}29]$$

$$Paid\text{-}in\ Capital = 50{,}000{,}000 + 0 = 50{,}000{,}000$$

and

$$Ret\ Earnings_{(End\ Year\ 3)} = Ret\ Earnings_{(End\ Year\ 2)} + NI_{(Year\ 3)} - Dividends\ Paid_{(Year\ 3)} \qquad [10\text{-}30]$$

$$Ret\ Earnings_{(End\ Year\ 3)} = -12{,}000{,}000 - 6{,}500{,}000 - 0 = -\$18{,}500{,}000$$

Substituting these values in Equation [10-27], the total shareholders' equity is calculated to be:

$$Total\ Shareholders'\ Equity = 50{,}000{,}000 - 18{,}500{,}000 = \$31{,}500{,}000$$

TABLE CS 10-34 Shareholders' Equity $(000)'s

Paid-in Capital	50,000
Retained Earnings	(18,500)
Total Shareholders' Equity	**31,500**

Ms. Debson now turns her attention to current liabilities. Since LTI is shipping product and is well financed, the Company is able to arrange credit terms with its suppliers. The first account is Accounts Payable. To estimate what these may be at the end of Year 3 she assumes 45 days as spelled out in Table CS 10-2 for the accounts payable days outstanding (APDOS). Then with the use of Equation [10-39] and the cost of goods sold (COGS) from the Year 3 Income Statement she calculates the year-end accounts payable for her LTI model.[29]

$$\textit{Accounts Payable (AP)} = (\textit{Annualized Cost of Goods Sold})\left(\frac{\textit{APDOS}}{360}\right) \qquad [10\text{-}39]$$

$$\textit{Accounts Payable} = (9{,}000{,}000)\left(\frac{45}{360}\right) = \$1{,}125{,}000$$

LTI continues to lose money during Year 3 and therefore doesn't have any tax obligations. Also, given its strong cash position there isn't any need for short-term debt. Therefore, both of the year-end balances in these accounts are zero and the Current Liabilities section of the Balance Sheet for Year 3 will be as shown in Table CS 10-35.

$$\textit{Current Liabilities} = \textit{Accounts Payable} + \textit{Taxes Payable} + \textit{Short-Term Debt} \qquad [10\text{-}25]$$

$$\textit{Current Liabilities} = 1{,}125{,}000 + 0 + 0 = \$1{,}125{,}000$$

TABLE CS 10-35 Current Liabilities $(000)'s

Accounts Payable	1,125
Taxes Payable	0
Short-Term Debt	0
Total Current Liabilities	**1,125**

Ms. Debson observes that LTI is still highly liquid and doesn't have a need to borrow money during Year 3. Therefore, the long-term debt on the Company's Balance Sheet would be as shown in Table CS 10-36.

[29]The Accounts Payable Ledger is a record of what a company owes its suppliers. Most companies monitor and express the magnitude of their accounts payable in *accounts payable days outstanding* (APDOS). In this book, the accounts payable are converted to APDOS by using the *annualized cost of goods sold.* In practice, accountants will generally use more than the cost of goods sold when calculating accounts payable days outstanding. However, in manufacturing companies, cost of goods sold is by far the largest factor and therefore used as a simplifying assumption. When this simplifying assumption is used, year-end statements are prepared using COGS for the year. When periodic statements are prepared, COGS for the period is annualized. For example, COGS for a month would be multiplied by 12, by 4 for a quarter, and so on to get the annualized figure.

TABLE CS 10-36 Long-Term Debt $(000)'s

Long-Term Debt	0

Tables CS 10-34, CS 10-35, and CS 10-36 account for all of LTI's liabilities. By combining these tables the liability + total shareholders' equity side of LTI's Year 3 Balance Sheet is created (Table CS 10-37).

$$\begin{aligned} \textit{Total Liabilities} + \textit{TSHE} = \textit{Current Liabilities} + \textit{Long-Term Debt} \\ + \textit{Total Shareholders' Equity} \end{aligned} \quad [10\text{-}32]$$

$$\textit{Total Liabilities} + \textit{TSHE} = 1{,}125{,}000 + 0 + 31{,}500{,}000 = \$32{,}625{,}000$$

TABLE CS 10-37 Liabilities and Total Shareholders' Equity $(000)'s

Current Liabilities	
Accounts Payable	1,125
Taxes Payable	0
Short-Term Debt	0
Total Current Liabilities	1,125
Long-Term Debt	0
Total Liabilities	1,125
Shareholders' Equity	
Paid-in Capital	50,000
Retained Earnings	(18,500)
Total Shareholders' Equity	31,500
Total Liabilities + TSHE	32,625

Having defined the Balance Sheet Liabilities and TSHE, she now turns her attention to the asset side of the Balance Sheet and begins the process with the aid of Equation [10-11].

$$\textit{Total Assets} = \textit{Total Liabilities} + \textit{Total Shareholders' Equity} \quad [10\text{-}11]$$

where:

$$\textit{Total Assets} = 1{,}125{,}000 + 31{,}500{,}000 = \$32{,}625{,}000$$

Once again working from the bottom up, the first account she encounters is Intangible Assets. Since the company still does not have any goodwill or other intangible assets to amortize, both of these are zero and the net intangible assets are as shown in Table CS 10-38.

TABLE CS 10-38 Intangible Assets $(000)'s

Goodwill and Other Intangible Assets	0
Less Accumulated Amortization	0
Net Intangible Assets	**0**

LTI further expanded its production facilities during Year 3 at a cost of $10,000,000. As Equation [10-15] indicates, the property, plant and equipment at the end of Year 3 is the sum of the PP&E at the end of Year 2 plus the purchases during Year 3.

$$Property\ Plant\ \&\ Equipment\ at\ Cost_{(End\ Year\ 3)} = PP\&E@Cost_{(End\ Year\ 2)} + \Delta PP\&E@Cost_{(Year\ 3)} \quad [10\text{-}15]$$

$$Property\ Plant\ \&\ Equipment\ at\ Cost = 10{,}000{,}000 + 10{,}000{,}000 = \$20{,}000{,}000$$

When Ms. Debson prepared the Income Statement for Year 3, she assumed once again the average life of Year 3's additions to PP&E to be 10 years,[30] and the depreciation during Year 3 was the sum of the depreciation resulting from Year 2's PP&E purchases ($1,000,000) plus the depreciation associated with Year 3's additions to PP&E ($1,000,000). (Refer to Table CS 10-32.) Hence, the *accumulated depreciation* at the end of Year 2 is as calculated by Equation [10-16].

$$Accumulated\ Depreciation_{(End\ Year\ 3)} = Accumulated\ Depreciation_{(End\ Year\ 2)} + Depreciaton_{(Year\ 3)} \quad [10\text{-}16]$$

$$Accumulated\ Depreciation = 1{,}000{,}000 + 2{,}000{,}000 = \$3{,}000{,}000$$

And the net fixed assets are calculated with the use of Equation [10-14] and displayed in Table CS 10-39).

$$Net\ Fixed\ Assets = Property\ Plant\ \&\ Equipment\ at\ Cost - Accumulated\ Depreciation \quad [10\text{-}14]$$

$$Net\ Fixed\ Assets = 20{,}000{,}000 - 3{,}000{,}000 = \$17{,}000{,}000$$

TABLE CS 10-39 Fixed Assets $(000)'s

Property, Plant, and Equipment at Cost	20,000
Less Accumulated Depreciation	(3,000)
Net Fixed Assets	**17,000**

[30] Again it is assumed that the fixed assets were added at the beginning of the year.

In order to complete the Balance Sheet Ms. Debson rearranges Equation [10-22] to solve for current assets and then applies the resulting Equation ([10-23]).

$$\text{Total Assets} = \text{Current Assets} + \text{Net Fixed Assets} + \text{Net Intangible Assets} \qquad [10\text{-}22]$$

$$\text{Current Assets} = \text{Total Assets} - \text{Net Intangible Assets} - \text{Net Fixed Assets} \qquad [10\text{-}23]$$

The values for total assets, net intangible assets, and net fixed assets are $32,625,000, $0, and $17,000,000 respectively. Plugging in these values yields the value for current assets.

$$\text{Current Assets} = 32{,}625{,}000 - 0 - 17{,}000{,}000 = \$15{,}625{,}000$$

LTI's current assets consist of cash, accounts receivable, and inventory as expressed by Equation [10-12].

$$\text{Current Assets} = \text{Cash} + \text{Accounts Receivable} + \text{Inventory} \qquad [10\text{-}12]$$

Knowing the value of the current assets and wanting to determine the Year 3 ending cash balance she rearranged Equation [10-12] to solve for cash and proceeded to calculate year-end accounts receivable and inventory.

$$\text{Cash} = \text{Current Assets} - \text{Accounts Receivable} - \text{Inventory} \qquad [10\text{-}13]$$

Since LTI was shipping product on credit to customers, Ms. Debson needed to make some assumption about what the accounts receivable days outstanding (ARDOS) would be at the end of Year 3. After referring to Table CS 10-2 she concluded 45 days was still a reasonable assumption so with the aid of Equation [10-35] she proceeded to calculate the year-end value of the accounts receivable.[31]

$$\text{Accounts Receivable (AR)} = (\text{Annualized Net Revenues})\left(\frac{ARDOS}{360}\right) \qquad [10\text{-}35]$$

$$\text{Accounts Receivable} = (20{,}000{,}000)\left(\frac{45}{360}\right) = \$2{,}500{,}000$$

Inventory is forecasted to turn at four times per year. The dollar value of the inventory can be calculated by using Equation [10-37].

$$\text{Inventory} = \frac{\text{Annualized Cost of Goods Sold}}{\text{Inventory Turns}} \qquad [10\text{-}37]$$

$$\text{Inventory} = \frac{9{,}000{,}000}{4} = \$2{,}250{,}000$$

[31] Like accounts payable, the accounting year is assumed to be 360 days. Since revenue generates the accounts receivable, *annualized* revenue is used as the reference point.

TABLE CS 10-40 Current Assets $(000)'s

Cash	10,875
Accounts Receivable	2,500
Inventory	2,250
Total Current Assets	**15,625**

Having determined the year-end current assets, accounts receivable, and inventory she substituted the values for each in Equation [10-13] and calculated the year-end cash and summarized the results in Table CS 10-40.

$$Cash = Current\ Assets - Accounts\ Receivable - Inventory \quad [10\text{-}13]$$

$$Cash = 15{,}625{,}000 - 2{,}500{,}000 - 2{,}250{,}000 = \$10{,}875{,}000$$

Then by combining Tables CS 10-38, CS 10-39, and CS 10-40 and the result of Equation [10-22] she was able to produce the asset side of the Year 3 Balance Sheet (Table CS 10-41).

$$Total\ Assets = Current\ Assets + Net\ Fixed\ Assets + Net\ Intangible\ Assets \quad [10\text{-}22]$$

$$Total\ Assets = 15{,}625{,}000 + 17{,}000{,}000 + 0 = \$32{,}625{,}000$$

TABLE CS 10-41 Total Assets

Current Assets	
Cash	10,875
Accounts Receivable	2,500
Inventory	2,250
Total Current Assets	15,625
Fixed Assets	
Property, Plant, and Equipment at Cost	20,000
Less Accumulated Depreciation	(3,000)
Net Fixed Assets	17,000
Intangible Assets	
Goodwill and Other Intangible Assets	0
Less Accumulated Amortization	0
Net Intangible Assets	0
Total Assets	32,625

The Balance Sheet for Year 3 is the combination of total assets (Table CS 10-41) and total liabilities + total shareholders' equity (Table CS 10-37) and is shown in Table CS 10-42.

TABLE CS 10-42 Light Technologies Balance Sheet for Year 3 $(000)'s

Current Assets		**Current Liabilities**	
Cash	10,875	Accounts Payable	1,125
Accounts Receivable	2,500	Taxes Payable	0
Inventory	2,250	Short-Term Debt	0
Total Current Assets	15,625	**Total Current Liabilities**	1,125
Fixed Assets		**Long-Term Debt**	0
Property, Plant, and Equipment at Cost	20,000		
Less Accumulated Depreciation	(3,000)	**Total Liabilities**	1,125
Net Fixed Assets	17,000		
Intangible Assets		**Shareholders' Equity**	
Goodwill and Other Intangible Assets	0	Paid-in Capital	50,000
Less Accumulated Amortization	0	Retained Earnings	(18,500)
Net Intangible Assets	0	**Total Shareholders' Equity**	31,500
Total Assets	32,625	**Total Liabilities + TSHE**	32,625

Year 3 Cash Flow Statement

Having completed the Income Statement and Balance Sheet for the third year of operations, Ms. Debson was now in a position to gather together the data she would require to complete the Cash Flow Statement for Year 3.

Operations Once again Ms. Debson followed the procedure used for preparing previous Cash Flow Statements and began preparing the Year 3 Cash Flow Statement by adjusting the Year 3 net income for non-cash charges such as depreciation and amortization, which were calculated to be $2,000,000 and $0 respectively, when preparing the Year 3 Income Statement. Then using Equation [10-59], the Year 3 net cash flow from operations was determined to be a negative $4,500,000. The results are summarized in Table CS 10-43.

$$\text{Net Cash Flow from Operations (CFfO)} = \text{Net Income} + \text{Depreciation} + \text{Amortization}$$

$$CFfO = -6{,}500{,}000 + 2{,}000{,}000 + 0 = -\$4{,}500{,}000 \qquad [10\text{-}59]$$

TABLE CS 10-43 Operations $(000)'s

Net Income (Loss)	(6,500)
Depreciation	2,000
Amortization	0
Net Cash Flow from Operations	**(4,500)**

Working Capital Accounts As was the case in Year 2, Ms. Debson then proceeded to deal with the cash implications of changes in the Working Capital accounts in the Balance Sheet.

At the end of Year 2, LTI's accounts receivable was \$0. At the end of Year 3, they were \$2,500,000. Therefore, the increase in accounts receivable is \$2,500,000 (Equation [10-44]).

$$\Delta Accounts\ Receivable = Accounts\ Receivable_{(Year\ 2)} - Accounts\ Receivable_{(Year\ 3)}$$

$$\Delta Accounts\ Receivable = 0 - 2{,}500{,}000 = -\ \$2{,}500{,}000 \qquad [10\text{-}44]$$

At this point she stopped to think about whether this represented a use or a source of cash. She ultimately concluded the increase in the accounts receivable represented a use of cash. To arrive at this conclusion, her thinking went something like this. She assumed for a moment that if everything shipped during Year 3 was on a COD basis and LTI collected cash upon delivery to the customer, LTI's accounts receivable would be \$0 at year-end. However, LTI ships product to its customers on net-30-days, and customer behavior being what it is, on average, gets paid on a 45-day basis. This means that at the end of Year 3, there is the equivalent of 45 days of sales that remain uncollected (use of cash) and so net income adjusted for non-cash charges for Year 3 has to be adjusted to reflect the 45 days of sales that remain uncollected at the end of the year.

Similarly, inventories at the end of Year 2 and Year 3 are \$0 and \$2,250,000 respectively. If LTI had no Inventory at the end of Year 3, the Company's investment in inventory would have been zero. However, it ended up the year with \$2,250,000 and thereby increased its inventory by this amount; this represents a use of cash as shown by the results of Equation [10-45].[32]

$$\Delta Inventory = Inventory_{(Year\ 2)} - Inventory_{(Year\ 3)} \qquad [10\text{-}45]$$

$$\Delta Inventory = 0 - 2{,}250{,}000 = -\$2{,}250{,}000$$

Since LTI had established financial credibility and creditworthiness with its suppliers, the Company is able to purchase on a net-30-day basis. Like its customers, it takes liberties with the terms and pays when it gets paid, which on average is 45 days. Once again the Income Statement assumes that everything else (supplies, etc.) purchased was paid for during the period in question and reflected in the COGS. Hence, at the end of Year 3, LTI has \$1,125,000 of accounts payable on its Balance Sheet compared to \$0 at the end of Year 2. This means that LTI's suppliers are helping

[32] As it turns out, LTI didn't pay for this entire inventory and has accounts payable of \$1,125,000 on its Balance Sheet at the end of this period, which partially offsets the cash flow implications of the inventory purchases by this amount.

to finance their business and by doing so provided a source of cash and allowed the Company to conserve $1,125,000 (Equation [10-47]).

$$\Delta Accounts\ Payable = Accounts\ Payable_{(Year\ 3)} - Accounts\ Payable_{(Year\ 2)} \qquad [10\text{-}47]$$

$$\Delta Accounts\ Payable = 1{,}125{,}000 - 0 = \$1{,}125{,}000$$

Despite LTI's progress, Year 3 was another loss year. Therefore, the Company did not incur any tax obligations. This is exactly the same situation the Company found itself in at the end of Year 2. Therefore, the change in the "Taxes Payable" account is zero and thereby represents neither a use nor a source of cash. This conclusion is supported by Equation [10-49].

$$\Delta Taxes\ Payable = Taxes\ Payable_{(Year\ 3)} - Taxes\ Payable_{(Year\ 2)} \qquad [10\text{-}49]$$

$$\Delta Taxes\ Payable = 0 - 0 = \$0$$

Ms. Debson then pulled together the result of all of the calculations associated with changes in the Working Capital accounts with the use of Equation [10-61] and Table CS 10-44 and noted that the Working Capital accounts in aggregate used $3,625,000 of cash in Year 2 with the uses in accounts receivable and inventory somewhat offset by the source in accounts payable.

$$Net\ \Delta WC = \pm\ \Delta AR \pm \Delta INV \pm \Delta AP \pm \Delta TP \qquad [10\text{-}61]$$

$$Net\ \Delta WC = -\ 2{,}500{,}000 - 2{,}250{,}000 + 1{,}125{,}000 + 0 = -\$3{,}625{,}000$$

TABLE CS 10-44 Working Capital Accounts $(000)'s

	Year 2	Year 3	Change
(Increase)/Decrease Accounts Receivable	0	2,500	(2,500)
(Increase)/Decrease Inventory	0	2,250	(2,250)
Increase/(Decrease) Accounts Payable	0	1,125	1,125
Increase/(Decrease) Taxes Payable	0	0	0
Net Change in Working Capital			**(3,625)**

Cash Flow from Operating Activities Cash flow from operating activities is defined as the sum of net cash flow from operations and the change in working capital as expressed by Equation [10-51]. Since cash flow from operations is negative $4,500,000 and the net change in working capital is negative $3,625,000, the CFfOA is equal to the sum of the two or a use of $8,125,000 of cash (Table CS 10-45).

$$\textit{Cash Flow from Operating Activities (CFfOA)} = \textit{Cash Flow from Operations} \pm \textit{Net } \Delta WC \qquad [10\text{-}51]$$

$$CFfOA = -4{,}500{,}000 - 3{,}625{,}000 = -\$8{,}125{,}000$$

TABLE CS 10-45 Cash Flow from Operating Activities $(000)'s

Cash Flow from Operating Activities	(8,125)

Investing Activities During Year 3 another $10,000,000 of fixed assets are purchased. Since no assets are sold, the cash outlay for investing activities is $10,000,000 and Ms. Debson easily prepared Table CS 10-46.

TABLE CS 10-46 Investing Activities $(000)'s

Fixed Asset Additions	10,000

Cash Flow after Investing Activities Cash flow after investing activities (CFaIA) is defined as the sum of cash flow from operating activities (CFfOA) and fixed asset additions. During Year 3 the CFfOA was a negative $8,125,000 and the fixed asset additions were $10,000,000. With the use of Equation [10-62] the CFaIA was calculated to be a negative $18,125,000 (Table CS 10-47).

$$\textit{Cash Flow after Investing Activities (CFaIA)} = CFfOA - \textit{Additions to Fixed Assets} \qquad [10\text{-}62]$$

$$CFaIA = -8{,}125{,}000 - 10{,}000{,}000 = -\$18{,}125{,}000$$

TABLE CS 10-47 Cash Flow after Investing Activities $(000)'s

Cash Flow after Investing Activities	(18,125)

Financing Activities LTI raised $50,000,000 of equity during Year 1. Since then there hasn't been any additional equity financing. Nor has there been any short- or long-term debt put on the Balance Sheet. Therefore, the net impact of financing activities on Year 3's operations is zero (Table CS 10-48) and the Cash Flow after Financing Activities is –$18,125,000.

$$CFaFA = CFaIA \pm \Delta STD \pm \Delta LTD \pm (Sale/Purchase\ of\ Common\ Stock) \quad [10\text{-}63]$$

$$CFaFA = -18{,}125{,}000 \pm 0 \pm 0 \pm 0 = -\$18{,}125{,}000$$

TABLE CS 10-48 Financing Activities $(000)'s

	Year 2	Year 3	Change
Increase/(Decrease) Short-Term Debt	0	0	0
Net Proceeds (Payments) Long-Term Debt	0	0	0
Proceeds (Purchase) of Common Stock	0	0	0

Cash Generated (Used) As was the case in Year 2, the cash generated or used by LTI during Year 3 is simply the sum of the cash flow after investing activities, any cash generated or used as a result of financing activities, and any dividends paid, as displayed by Equation [10-56]. During Year 3, there isn't any cash generated or used by financing activities, nor are any dividends paid, and so the cash generated (used) for the year is equal to the cash flow after investing activities and summarized in Table CS 10-49.

$$CGU = CFaIA \pm \Delta STD \pm \Delta LTD \pm \Delta PinC - Dividends\ Paid \quad [10\text{-}56]$$

$$Cash\ Generated\ (Used) = -18{,}125{,}000 \pm 0 \pm 0 \pm 0 - 0 = -\$18{,}125{,}000$$

TABLE CS 10-49 Cash Generated/(Used) $(000)'s

Cash Generated/(Used)	(18,125)

Cash Flow Proof To complete the Year 3 Cash Flow Statement, Ms. Debson proceeded to reconcile the $18,125,000 of cash used during Year 3 with the cash on hand (bank balance) at the end of Year 2 and beginning of Year 3. The cash on hand at the beginning of Year 3 ("Beginning Cash Balance") was $29,000,000. During Year 3, $18,125,000 of cash was used. Therefore, the cash on hand at the end of the year ("Ending Cash Balance") is $10,875,000, as shown with the use of Equation [10-58], and agrees with the cash balance calculated earlier for the Balance Sheet. The cash flow proof is shown in Table CS 10-50.

$$Ending\ Cash\ Balance_{(Year\ 3)} = Beginning\ Cash\ Balance_{(Year\ 3)} \pm Cash\ Generated\ or\ Used_{(Year\ 3)} \quad [10\text{-}58]$$

$$Ending\ Cash\ Balance = 29{,}000{,}000 - 18{,}125{,}000 = \$10{,}875{,}000$$

Finally Ms. Debson produced LTI's Cash Flow Statement for Year 3 by combining Tables CS 10-43–CS 10-50, and this is shown in Table CS 10-51.

TABLE CS 10-50 Cash Flow Proof $(000)'s

Beginning Cash Balance	29,000
Cash Generated/(Used)	(18,125)
Ending Cash Balance	10,875

TABLE CS 10-51 Light Technologies Inc. Cash Flow Statement for Year 3 $(000)'s

Operating Activities	
Operations	
Net Income (Loss)	(6,500)
Depreciation	2,000
Amortization	0
Net Cash Flow from Operations	(4,500)
Working Capital Accounts	
(Increase)/Decrease Accounts Receivable	(2,500)
(Increase)/Decrease Inventory	(2,250)
Increase/(Decrease) Accounts Payable	1,125
Increase/(Decrease) Taxes Payable	0
Net Change in Working Capital	(3,625)
Cash Flow from Operating Activities	(8,125)
Investing Activities	
Fixed Asset Additions	(10,000)
Cash Flow After Investing Activities	(18,125)
Financing Activities	
Increase/(Decrease) Short-Term Debt	0
Net Proceeds (Payments) Long-Term Debt	0
Proceeds (Purchase) of Common Stock	0
Dividends Paid	0
Cash Generated/(Used)	(18,125)
Cash Flow Proof	
Beginning Cash Balance	29,000
Cash Generated/(Used)	(18,125)
Ending Cash Balance	10,875

TABLE CS 10-52 Gross Margin $(000)'s

Net Revenues	40,000
Cost of Goods Sold (COGS)	(17,000)
Gross Margin (GM)	**23,000**

Year 4 Income Statement

Year 4 pro-forma statements are prepared by referring to the assumptions in Tables CS 10-1 and CS 10-2. Year 4 is another year of revenue growth. The revenue and cost of goods sold (42.5%) during Year 4 are $40,000,000 and $17,000,000 ($40,000,000 * 0.425) respectively. Therefore, the gross margin as calculated by Equation [10-1] and tabulated in Table CS 10-52 is $23,000,000.

$$Gross\ Margin = Net\ Revenue - Cost\ of\ Goods\ Sold \qquad [10\text{-}1]$$

$$Gross\ Margin = 40{,}000{,}000 - 17{,}000{,}000 = \$23{,}000{,}000$$

In order to keep the Company on a high growth track, it is expected that expenditures on research and development, sales and marketing, and general and administrative will continue to increase as LTI continues to invest in new products and build infrastructure. During Year 4, R&D, S&M, and G&A expenses increase to $9,000,000, $8,000,000, and $3,000,000 respectively. Total operating expenses (Equation [10-2]) for the Year are $20,000,000.

$$\begin{aligned} Operating\ Expenses = {} & Research\ \&\ Development + Sales\ \&\ Marketing \\ & + General\ \&\ Administrative \end{aligned} \qquad [10\text{-}2]$$

$$Operating\ Expenses = 9{,}000{,}000 + 8{,}000{,}000 + 3{,}000{,}000 = \$20{,}000{,}000$$

Total operating expenses as they would appear in the Income Statement are shown in Table CS 10-53.

EBITDA is calculated with the use of Equation [10-3].

$$EBITDA = Gross\ Margin - Total\ Operating\ Expenses \qquad [10\text{-}3]$$

TABLE CS 10-53 Operating Expenses $(000)'s

Operating Expenses (OpExp)	Research and Development (R&D)	9,000
	Sales and Marketing (S&M)	8,000
	General and Administrative (G&A)	3,000
Total Operating Expenses		**20,000**

For Year 4, gross margin and total operating expenses are $23,000,000 and $20,000,000 respectively. Hence:

$$EBITDA = 23{,}000{,}000 - 20{,}000{,}000 = \$3{,}000{,}000$$

In order to accommodate its rapid growth, LTI continues to invest in plant and equipment during Year 4 and purchases $20,000,000 of fixed assets. Once again, Ms. Debson assumes this takes place at the beginning of the year. These assets also have a useful life of 10 years. Therefore, the annual depreciation of the assets purchased at the beginning of Year 4 is obtained with the use of Equation [10-4].

$$Depreciation = \frac{Total\ Cost\ of\ Asset}{Useful\ Life} \quad [10\text{-}4]$$

$$Depreciation = \frac{20{,}000{,}000}{10} = \$2{,}000{,}000/year$$

Ms. Debson realizes this is not the end of the depreciation story for Year 4. She recalls that $10,000,000 of fixed assets were purchased at the beginning of each of Years 2 and 3. These assets are only in the third and second year of their useful lives respectively and so they will each depreciate by an additional $1,000,000 during the current year. Therefore, the total depreciation for Year 4 will be $4,000,000, as shown in Table CS 10-54.

TABLE CS 10-54 Depreciation and Amortization $(000)'s

	Year 2	**Year 3**	**Year 4**	**Total Yr 4**
Fixed Asset Additions	10,000	10,000	20,000	40,000
Avg Useful Life in Years	10	10	10	
Year of Assets Depreciation	3rd	2nd	1st	
Depreciation	1,000	1,000	2,000	4,000
Amortization	0	0	0	0

There is no goodwill or intellectual property so the amortization is once again zero and the earnings before interest and taxes (EBIT) calculated by using Equation [10-6] is a loss of $1,000,000.

$$EBIT = EBITDA - Depreciation - Amortization \quad [10\text{-}6]$$

$$EBIT = 3{,}000{,}000 - 4{,}000{,}000 - 0 = -\$1{,}000{,}000$$

While LTI is profitable at the EBITDA line, it is still losing money after accounting for depreciation. Because the Company isn't profitable, it isn't generating enough cash to pay for the high level of investment in plant and equipment and escalating operating expenses. It's clear to Ms. Debson that additional financing is required so she works a five-year,

$12,000,000 term note bearing an interest rate of 10%, paid annually in arrears with a balloon payment at the end of the fifth year into her model.[33] Also, since the assets the loan will be used to partially finance are assumed to be in place at the beginning of the year, it is assumed that the entire amount is drawn down for the entire year. The interest on the note that has to be paid to the bank at the end of year 4 is:

$$Interest\ Expense = (Debt)\left(\frac{Interest\ Rate}{100}\right) \quad [10\text{-}8]$$

$$Interest\ Expense = (12{,}000{,}000)\left(\frac{10}{100}\right) = (12{,}000{,}000)(0.10) = \$1{,}200{,}000$$

Ms. Debson continues to assume that LTI receives no interest on its dwindling cash. Therefore, the company's EBT is as expressed by Equation [10-9]:

$$EBT = EBIT \pm Interest\ Income/Expense \quad [10\text{-}9]$$

$$EBT = -\ 1{,}000{,}000 + 0 - 1{,}200{,}000 = -\$2{,}200{,}000$$

LTI still isn't profitable and doesn't have any income tax obligations. Therefore, the net income (NI) is the same as the pretax income (Equation [10-10]).

$$NI = EBT - Taxes\ Paid \quad [10\text{-}10]$$

$$NI = -\ 2{,}200{,}000 - 0 = -\$2{,}200{,}000$$

Ms. Debson then prepared the Year 4 Income Statement for LTI by entering the results of these calculations into the Income Statement format she has been using (Table CS 10-55).

TABLE CS 10-55 Light Technologies Inc. Income Statement for Year 4 $(000)'s

Net Revenues			40,000
Cost of Goods Sold (COGS)			17,000
Gross Margin (GM)			23,000
Operating Expenses (OpExp):	Research and Development (R&D)	9,000	
	Sales and Marketing (S&M)	8,000	
	General and Administrative (G&A)	3,000	
Total Operating Expenses			(20,000)
Earnings before Interest, Taxes, Depreciation, and Amortization (EBITDA)			3,000
Depreciation and Amortization (D&A)			(4,000)
Earnings before Interest and Taxes (EBIT)			(1,000)
Interest Income/Expense (Int)			(1,200)
Earnings before Tax (EBT)			(2,200)
Taxes Paid (TaxesPaid)@ 40%			0
Net Income (NI)			(2,200)

[33]Given the current stage of LTI's development it's unlikely this loan could be obtained without a pledge of security. Best case would be an ABL (asset-based loan) from a bank. Another possibility would be a loan funded by current shareholders with warrants that could be converted to equity at some attractive rate at the end of the five-year period.

Next, she prepares the Year 4 Balance Sheet and Cash Flow as she did for prior years.

Year 4 Balance Sheet

No additional capital was raised during the year and the net income for the year was a loss of $2,200,000. The total shareholders' equity (Equation [10-27]) is the sum of paid-in capital (Equation [10-29]) and retained earnings (Equation [10-30]) and is shown in Table CS 10-56:

$$\begin{aligned} \textit{Total Shareholders' Equity}_{(\text{End Year 4})} &= \textit{Paid-in Capital}_{(\text{End Year 4})} \\ &\quad + \textit{Retained Earnings}_{(\text{End Year 4})} \end{aligned} \qquad [10\text{-}27]$$

$$\textit{Paid-in Capital}_{(\text{End Year 4})} = \textit{Paid-in Capital}_{(\text{End Year 3})} + \Delta \textit{Paid-in Capital}_{(\text{Year 4})} \qquad [10\text{-}29]$$

$$\textit{Paid-in Capital} = 50{,}000{,}000 + 0 = \$50{,}000{,}000$$ [34]

and

$$\begin{aligned} \textit{RetEarnings}_{(\text{End Year 4})} &= \textit{RetEarnings}_{(\text{End Year 3})} + \textit{NI}_{(\text{Year 4})} \\ &\quad - \textit{Dividends Paid}_{(\text{Year 4})} \end{aligned} \qquad [10\text{-}30]$$

$$\textit{Retained Earnings} = -18{,}500{,}000 - 2{,}200{,}000 - 0 = -\$20{,}700{,}000$$

Substituting these values in Equation [10-27], the total shareholders' equity is obtained and tabulated in Table CS 10-56.

$$\textit{Total Shareholders' Equity} = 50{,}000{,}000 - 20{,}700{,}000 - 0 = 29{,}300{,}000$$

TABLE CS 10-56 Shareholders' Equity $(000)'s

Paid-in Capital	50,000
Retained Earnings	(20,700)
Total Shareholders' Equity	**29,300**

[34] At the rate LTI was going through cash at the end of Year 2 it was clear that additional financing would be required. If the Company actually achieved this performance, it could probably go to the capital markets to raise more equity. Since debt is less expensive than equity and the Balance Sheet is relatively strong, the logical source of capital for the Company would be to take on long-term debt. Furthermore, if the Company had chosen to raise $12 million of equity, the paid-in capital at the end of Year 3 would have been $62,000,000 (50,000,000 + 12,000,000) and long-term debt would have been zero.

TABLE CS 10-57 Long-Term Debt $(000)'s

Long-Term Debt	12,000

As noted earlier, LTI borrowed $12 million at the beginning of Year 4 to finance its growth. Therefore, the long-term debt on the Company's Balance Sheet at year-end would be as shown in Table CS 10-57.

The Company continues to pay its vendors on a 45-day basis. Therefore, with the aid of Equation [10-39], the accounts payable at the end of Year 4 are $2,125,000.

$$Accounts\ Payable\ (AP) = (Annualized\ Cost\ of\ Goods\ Sold)\left(\frac{APDOS}{360}\right) \quad [10\text{-}39]$$

$$Accounts\ Payable = (17{,}000{,}000)\left(\frac{45}{360}\right) = \$2{,}125{,}000$$

Year 4 was another loss year for the Company and so it doesn't have any income tax obligations. Also, the growth was financed with a five-year term loan and thereby avoided taking on any short-term debt. Hence, the Current Liabilities section of the Year 4 Balance Sheet will be as shown in Table CS 10-58.

$$Current\ Liabilities = Accounts\ Payable + Taxes\ Payable + Short\text{-}Term\ Debt \quad [10\text{-}25]$$

$$Current\ Liabilities = 2{,}125{,}000 + 0 + 0 = \$2{,}125{,}000$$

TABLE CS 10-58 Current Liabilities $(000)'s

Accounts Payable	2,125
Taxes Payable	0
Short-Term Debt	0
Total Current Liabilities	**2,125**

Tables CS 10-56, CS 10-57, and CS 10-58 account for all of LTI's liabilities. Combining these tables and using Equation [10-32] to calculate the total liabilities, the liability side of the Year 4 Balance Sheet is created (Table CS 10-59).

$$Total\ Liabilities + TSHE = Current\ Liabilities + Long\text{-}Term\ Debt + Total\ Shareholders'\ Equtiy \quad [10\text{-}32]$$

$$Total\ Liabilities + TSHE = 2{,}125{,}000 + 12{,}000{,}000 + 29{,}300{,}000 = \$43{,}425{,}000$$

TABLE CS 10-59 Liabilities and Total Shareholders' Equity $(000)'s

Current Liabilities	
Accounts Payable	2,125
Taxes Payable	0
Short-Term Debt	0
Total Current Liabilities	2,125
Long-Term Debt	12,000
Total Liabilities	14,125
Shareholders' Equity	
Paid-in Capital	50,000
Retained Earnings	(20,700)
Total Shareholders' Equity	29,300
Total Liabilities + TSHE	43,425

The process of developing the asset side of the Balance Sheet begins with Equation [10-11]:

$$\textit{Total Assets} = \textit{Total Liabilities} + \textit{Total Shareholders' Equity} \qquad [10\text{-}11]$$

where:

$$\textit{Total Assets} = 14{,}125{,}000 + 29{,}300{,}000 = \$43{,}425{,}000$$

Following the practice she has been using of working from the bottom up[35] of the asset side of the Balance Sheet, the first asset class encountered is Intangible Assets. The company still does not have any goodwill. Nor are there any other intangible assets to amortize. Therefore, the net tangible assets are zero, as shown in Table CS 10-60.

TABLE CS 10-60 Intangible Assets $(000)'s

Goodwill and Other Intangible Assets	0
Less Accumulated Amortization	0
Net Intangible Assets	**0**

In order to keep up with demand for its products and accommodate the forecasted growth, Year 4 is another year of expansion of production facilities at a cost of $20,000,000. As Equation [10-15] indicates, the Property, Plant, and Equipment at

[35] Hopefully by now it is obvious that the liabilities + total shareholders' equity side of the Balance Sheet could be completed by starting anywhere. The practice of starting from the bottom and working upward is based on the notion of starting with what is known and consistently progressing upward until the cash balance is determined.

the end of Year 4 is the sum of the PP&E at the end of Year 3 ($20,000,000) plus the purchases during Year 4 ($20,000,000).

$$\textit{Property, Plant, and Equipment at Cost}_{(\textit{End Year 4})} = \textit{PP\&E@Cost}_{(\textit{End Year 3})} + \Delta \textit{PP\&E@Cost}_{(\textit{Year 4})} \quad [10\text{-}15]$$

$$\textit{Property, Plant, and Equipment at Cost} = 20{,}000{,}000 + 20{,}000{,}000 = \$40{,}000{,}000$$

When the Income Statement for Year 4 was prepared the assumption made for the average life of Year 4's additions was 10 years and the depreciation during Year 4 was the sum of the depreciation resulting from Year 2's PP&E purchases ($1,000,000) plus the depreciation emanating from Year 3's fixed asset additions ($1,000,000) plus the depreciation associated with Year 4's additions ($2,000,000), or $4,000,000. The accumulated depreciation or the sum of all depreciation since the beginning of the Company at the end of Year 4 is the accumulated depreciation at the end of Year 3 ($3,000,000) plus Year 4's depreciation as illustrated by Equation [10-16].

$$\textit{Accumulated Depreciation}_{(\textit{End Year 4})} = \textit{Accumulated Depreciation}_{(\textit{End Year 3})} + \textit{Depreciaton}_{(\textit{Year 4})} \quad [10\text{-}16]$$

$$\textit{Accumulated Depreciation}_{(\textit{EndYear 4})} = 3{,}000{,}000 + 4{,}000{,}000 = \$7{,}000{,}000$$

The net fixed assets are determined by substituting $40,000,000 (Year 2 = $10,000,000, Year 3 = $10,000,000, and Year 4 = $20,000,000) for PP&E at cost and the Year 4 accumulated depreciation into Equation [10-14]. The results are shown in Table CS 10-61.

$$\textit{Net Fixed Assets} = \textit{Property, Plant, and Equipment at Cost} - \textit{Accumulated Depreciation} \quad [10\text{-}14]$$

$$\textit{Net Fixed Assets} = 40{,}000{,}000 - 7{,}000{,}000 = \$33{,}000{,}000$$

TABLE CS 10-61 Fixed Assets $(000)'s

Property, Plant, and Equipment at Cost	40,000
Less Accumulated Depreciation	(7,000)
Net Fixed Assets	**33,000**

Two of the three asset classes on LTI's Balance Sheet, Intangible Assets, and Fixed Assets, are now known. The relationship of the third asset class, Current Assets, to intangible assets and fixed assets is defined by Equation [10-22], which is easily rearranged to solve for current assets (Equation [10-23]):

$$\textit{Total Assets} = \textit{Current Assets} + \textit{Net Fixed Assets} + \textit{Net Intangible Assets} \quad [10\text{-}22]$$

$$\textit{Current Assets} = \textit{Total Assets} - \textit{Net Intangible Assets} - \textit{Net Fixed Assets} \quad [10\text{-}23]$$

The total assets, net intangible assets, and net fixed assets are $43,425,000, $0, and $33,000,000 respectively. Entering these values in Equation [10-23] gives the value for the current assets.

$$\textit{Current Assets} = 43{,}425{,}000 - 0 - 33{,}000{,}000 = \$10{,}425{,}000$$

LTI's current assets consist of cash, accounts receivable, and inventory (Equation [10-12]).

$$\textit{Current Assets} = \textit{Cash} + \text{Accounts } \textit{Receivable} + \textit{Inventory} \qquad [10\text{-}12]$$

And by rearranging,

$$\textit{Cash} = \textit{Current Assets} - \textit{Accounts Receivable} - \textit{Inventory} \qquad [10\text{-}13]$$

In the assumptions table (Table CS 10-2), the accounts receivable days outstanding (ARDOS) are 45 days. The currency value of the accounts receivable is determined with the aid of Equation [10-35].

$$\textit{Accounts Receivable (AR)} = (\textit{Annualized Net Revenues})\left(\frac{\textit{ARDOS}}{360}\right) \qquad [10\text{-}35]$$

$$\textit{Accounts Receivable} = (40{,}000{,}000)\left(\frac{45}{360}\right) = \$5{,}000{,}000$$

Inventory is forecasted to turn at four times per year. The year-end value of the inventory is determined by using Equation [10-37].

$$\textit{Inventory} = \frac{\textit{Annualized Cost of Goods Sold}}{\textit{Inventory Turns}} \qquad [10\text{-}37]$$

$$\textit{Inventory} = \frac{17{,}000{,}000}{4} = \$4{,}250{,}000$$

The cash that LTI has on hand at the end of Year 4 is calculated by substituting values for current assets, accounts receivable, and inventory into Equation [10-13].

$$\textit{Cash} = \textit{Current Assets} - \textit{Accounts Receivable} - \textit{Inventory} \qquad [10\text{-}13]$$

$$\textit{Cash} = 10{,}425{,}000 - 5{,}000{,}000 - 4{,}250{,}000 = \$1{,}175{,}000$$

The current assets as they will appear in the Balance Sheet are shown in Table CS 10-62.

$$\textit{Current Assets} = \textit{Cash} + \textit{Accounts Receivable} + \textit{Inventory} \qquad [10\text{-}12]$$

$$\textit{Current Assets} = 1{,}175{,}000 + 5{,}000{,}000 + 4{,}250{,}000 = \$10{,}425{,}000$$

TABLE CS 10-62 Current Assets $(000)'s

Cash	1,175
Accounts Receivable	5,000
Inventory	4,250
Total Current Assets	**10,425**

Combining Tables CS 10-60, CS 10-61, and CS 10-62 and the result of Equation [E-22] creates the asset side of the Balance sheet (Table CS 10-63).

$$\textit{Total Assets} = \textit{Current Assets} + \textit{Net Fixed Assets} + \textit{Net Intangible Assets} \qquad [10\text{-}22]$$

$$\textit{Total Assets} = 10{,}425{,}000 + 33{,}000{,}000 + 0 = \$43{,}425{,}000$$

TABLE CS 10-63 Total Assets $(000)'s

Current Assets	
Cash	1,175
Accounts Receivable	5,000
Inventory	4,250
Total Current Assets	10,425
Fixed Assets	
Property, Plant, and Equipment at Cost	40,000
Less Accumulated Depreciation	(7,000)
Net Fixed Assets	33,000
Intangible Assets	
Goodwill and Other Intangible Assets	0
Less Accumulated Amortization	0
Net Intangible Assets	0
Total Assets	43,425

Finally, as she did for the prior years, Ms. Debson prepares the pro-forma Balance Sheet for Year 4 by combining the total assets (Table CS 10-63) and total liabilities + TSHE (Table CS 10-59) sides of the Balance Sheet in Table CS 10-64.

After looking at the cash balance in Table CS 10-64, Ms. Debson was concerned that the long-term loan used in her model should have been larger because with just over $1 million of cash going into Year 5, the company would have to aggressively manage receivables, payables, and inventory. After thinking about it, she decided to deal with the potential problem by arranging a short-term loan at the beginning of Year 5.

TABLE CS 10-64 Light Technologies Balance Sheet for Year 4 $(000)'s

Current Assets		**Current Liabilities**	
Cash	1,175	Accounts Payable	2,125
Accounts Receivable	5,000	Taxes Payable	0
Inventory	4,250	Short-Term Debt	0
Total Current Assets	10,425	**Total Current Liabilities**	2,125
Fixed Assets		**Long-Term Debt**	12,000
Property, Plant, and Equipment at Cost	40,000		
Less Accumulated Depreciation	(7,000)	**Total Liabilities**	14,125
Net Fixed Assets	33,000		
Intangible Assets		**Shareholders' Equity**	
Goodwill and Other Intangible Assets	0	Paid-in Capital	50,000
Less Accumulated Amortization	0	Retained Earnings	(20,700)
Net Intangible Assets	0	**Total Shareholders' Equity**	29,300
Total Assets	43,425	**Total Liabilities + TSHE**	43,425

Year 4 Cash Flow Statement

As before, the first step in preparing the Cash Flow Statement for Year 4 is to adjust Year 4's net income for non-cash charges such as depreciation and amortization.[36]

Operations When the Income Statement for Year 4 was prepared the depreciation and amortization were calculated to be $4,000,000 and $0 respectively. Therefore, the Year 4 net cash flow from operations (net income adjusted for non-cash charges) is calculated by using Equation [10-59] and is shown in Table CS 10-65.

$$\textit{Net Cash Flow from Operations (CFfO)} = \textit{Net Income} + \textit{Depreciation} + \textit{Amortization} \qquad [10\text{-}59]$$

$$CFfO = -2{,}200{,}000 + 4{,}000{,}000 + 0 = \$1{,}800{,}000$$

[36]Year 3 was the first year LTI had any interest expense. Technically, interest is the result of the capital structure. Net income could be adjusted for interest by adding back the $1,200,000 interest expense in Table CS 10-64. However, it would also have to be included in the financing activities, the result of which would be a "+" in net cash flow from operations and a "−" of the same amount in financing activities, leaving the CGU unchanged. Since this is not done in practice and in the interest of simplicity, this step has been omitted.

TABLE CS 10-65 Operations $(000)'s

Net Income (Loss)	(2,200)
Depreciation	4,000
Amortization	0
Net Cash Flow from Operations	**1,800**

Working Capital Accounts The impact changes in the Working Capital accounts in the Balance Sheet have on cash is determined next.

At the end of Years 3 and 4, LTI's accounts receivable was $2,250,000 and $5,000,000 respectively. Therefore, the increase in accounts receivable is $2,500,000 and this represents money the company didn't collect for product shipped during the year and a use of cash (Equation [10-44]).

$$\Delta Accounts\ Receivable = Accounts\ Receivable_{(End\ Year\ 3)} - Accounts\ Receivable_{(End\ Year\ 4)} \quad [10\text{-}44]$$

$$\Delta Accounts\ Receivable = 2{,}500{,}000 - 5{,}000{,}000 = -\$2{,}500{,}000$$

Similarly, inventories at the end of Years 3 and 4 are $2,250,000 and $4,250,000 respectively. If the Company's inventory had remained unchanged, no cash would have been used to finance inventory. However, the reality is that inventory increased by $2,000,000 (Equation [10-45]). Therefore, like accounts receivable, the increase in inventory represents a commensurate use of cash.

$$\Delta Inventory = Inventory_{(End\ Year\ 3)} - Inventory_{(End\ Year\ 4)} \quad [10\text{-}45]$$

$$\Delta Inventory = 2{,}250{,}000 - 4{,}250{,}000 = -\$2{,}000{,}000$$

LTI continues to pay its suppliers on a 45-day basis. As pointed out earlier, the Income Statement assumes that everything purchased was paid for during the period in question. At the end of Year 4, LTI has $2,125,000 of accounts payable on its Balance Sheet compared to $1,125,000 at the end of Year 3. If LTI had decided just prior to the end of Year 4 to keep its accounts payable at the same dollar amount as at the end of Year 3, the Company would have used $1,000,000 of cash to do so and its accounts payable days outstanding (APDOS) would have been 26.5 days (Equation [10-38]).

$$Accounts\ Payable\ Days\ Outstanding = \left(\frac{Accounts\ Payable}{Annualized\ Cost\ of\ Goods\ Sold}\right)(360) \quad [10\text{-}38]$$

$$Accounts\ Payable\ Days\ Outstanding = \left(\frac{1{,}125{,}000}{17{,}000{,}000}\right)(360) = 26.5\ days$$

However, by choosing to keep its APDOS at 45 days, LTI's accounts payable grew to \$2,250,000, letting their suppliers help finance their business and by doing so created a source of cash and conserved \$1,000,000 of the Company's cash as calculated by the use of Equation [10-47]).

$$\Delta Accounts\ Payable = Accounts\ Payable_{(End\ Year\ 4)} - Accounts\ Payable_{(End\ Year\ 3)} \quad [10\text{-}47]$$

$$\Delta Accounts\ Payable = 2{,}125{,}000 - 1{,}125{,}000 = \$1{,}000{,}000$$

While Year 4 is another year of revenue growth, the Company once again lost money and did not incur any tax obligations. This is exactly the same situation the Company found itself in at the end of Year 3. Therefore, the change in the Taxes Payable account is zero and thereby represents neither a use nor a source of cash (Equation [10-49]).

$$\Delta Taxes\ Payable = Taxes\ Payable_{(End\ Year\ 4)} - Taxes\ Payable_{(Year\ 3)} \quad [10\text{-}49]$$

$$\Delta Taxes\ Payable = 0 - 0 = \$0$$

The result of all of the changes in the Working Capital accounts is calculated by Equation [10-61] and presented in Cash Flow Statement form in Table CS 10-66.

$$Net\ \Delta WC = \pm\Delta AR \pm \Delta INV \pm \Delta AP \pm \Delta TP \quad [10\text{-}61]$$

$$Net\ \Delta WC = -\ 2{,}500{,}000 - 2{,}000{,}000 + 1{,}000{,}000 + 0 = -\$3{,}500{,}000$$

TABLE CS 10-66 Working Capital Accounts \$(000)'s

	Year 3	Year 4	Change
(Increase)/Decrease Accounts Receivable	2,500	5,000	(2,500)
(Increase)/Decrease Inventory	2,250	4,250	(2,000)
Increase/(Decrease) Accounts Payable	1,125	2,125	1,000
Increase/(Decrease) Taxes Payable	0	0	0
Net Change in Working Capital			(3,500)

Cash Flow from Operating Activities Cash flow from operating activities is defined as the sum of net cash flow from operations and the change in working capital (Equation [10-51]). Since the cash flow from operations is \$1,800,000 and the net change in working capital is negative \$3,500,000, the CFfOA is equal to the sum of the two and is shown in Table CS 10-67.

TABLE CS 10-67 Cash Flow from Operating Activities \$(000)'s

Cash Flow from Operating Activities	(1,700)

$$Cash\ Flow\ from\ Operating\ Activities\ (CFfOA) = Cash\ Flow\ from\ Operations \pm Net\ \Delta WC \quad [10\text{-}51]$$

$$CFfOA = 1{,}800{,}000 - 3{,}500{,}000 = -\$1{,}700{,}000$$

Investing Activities At the beginning of Year 4, \$20,000,000 of fixed assets are purchased. The fixed asset additions amounted to \$20,000,000 during the year, Hence, the cash outlay for investing activities is \$20,000,000 (Table CS 10-68).

TABLE CS 10-68 Investing Activities \$(000)'s

Fixed Asset Additions	20,000

Cash Flow after Investing Activities Cash flow after investing activities (CFaIA) is defined as the sum of cash flow from operating activities (CFfOA) and the sum of all investing activities (Equation [10-62]). During Year 4, the cash flow from operating activities is a negative \$1,700,000. The investing activities resulted in an outlay of \$20,000,000 for asset purchases. Hence, the CFaIA is a negative \$21,700,000 (Table CS 10-69).

$$Cash\ Flow\ after\ Investing\ Activities\ (CFaIA) = CFfOA - Additions\ to\ Fixed\ Assets \quad [10\text{-}62]$$

$$CFaIA = -1{,}700{,}000 - 20{,}000{,}000 = -\$21{,}700{,}000$$

TABLE CS 10-69 Cash Flow after Investing Activities \$(000)'s

Cash Flow after Investing Activities	(21,700)

Financing Activities LTI hasn't raised any equity since it raised the \$50,000,000 of equity during Year 1. During Year 4 the Company negotiated and drew down on a \$12,000,000 five-year term loan and thereby brought \$12,000,000 of cash into the company. The impact of this term loan on the financing activities is shown in Table CS 10-70 and the cash flow after financing activities is –\$9,700,000.

TABLE CS 10-70 Financing Activities $(000)'s

	Year 3	Year 4	Change
Increase/(Decrease) Short-Term Debt	0	0	0
Net Proceeds (Payments) Long-Term Debt	0	12,000	12,000
Proceeds (Purchase) of Common Stock	0	0	0

$$CFaFA = CFaIA \pm \Delta STD \pm \Delta LTD \pm (Sale/Purchase\ of\ Common\ Stock) \quad [10\text{-}63]$$

$$CFaFA = -21{,}700{,}000 \pm 0 + 12{,}000{,}000 \pm 0 = -\$9{,}700{,}000$$

Cash Generated/(Used) As was the case in all previous years, the cash generated or used by LTI during Year 4 is simply the sum of the cash flow after investing activities and any cash generated or used as a result of financing activities and any dividends paid. The CFaIA is shown in Table CS 10-69. The financing activities are tabulated in Table CS 10-70. No dividends were paid during the year. The cash generated/(used) is calculated by using Equation [10-56] and shown in Table CS 10-71.

$$CGU = CFaIA \pm \Delta STD \pm \Delta LTD \pm \Delta TSHE - DP \quad [10\text{-}56]$$

$$Cash\ Generated\ (Used) = -21{,}700{,}000 \pm 0 + 12{,}000{,}000 \pm 0 – 0 = -\$9{,}700{,}000$$

TABLE CS 10-71 Cash Generated/(Used) $(000)'s

Cash Generated/(Used)	(9,700)

Cash Flow Proof The cash on hand at the beginning of Year 4 ("Beginning Cash Balance") was $10,875,000. During Year 4, $9,700,000 of cash was used. Therefore, the cash on hand at the end of the year ("Ending Cash Balance") is $1,175,000, which agrees with the cash shown in the Balance Sheet Account, Table CS 10-64. The ending cash balance is calculated with the assistance of Equation [10-58]. The results are displayed in Table CS 10-72).

$$Ending\ Cash\ Balance_{(Year\ 4)} = Beginning\ Cash\ Balance_{(Year\ 4)} \pm Cash\ Generated\ or\ Used_{(Year\ 4)} \quad [10\text{-}58]$$

$$Ending\ Cash\ Balance_{(Year\ 4)} = 10{,}875{,}000 - 9{,}700{,}000 = \$1{,}175{,}000$$

TABLE CS 10-72 Cash Flow Proof $(000)'s

Beginning Cash Balance	10,875
Cash Generated/(Used)	(9,700)
Ending Cash Balance	1,175

TABLE CS 10-73 Light Technologies Cash Flow Statement for Year 4 $(000)'s

Operating Activities	
Operations	
Net Income (Loss)	(2,200)
Depreciation	4,000
Amortization	0
Net Cash Flow from Operations	1,800
Working Capital Accounts	
(Increase)/Decrease Accounts Receivable	(2,500)
(Increase)/Decrease Inventory	(2,000)
Increase/(Decrease) Accounts Payable	1,000
Increase/(Decrease) Taxes Payable	0
Net Change in Working Capital	(3,500)
Cash Flow from Operating Activities	(1,700)
Investing Activities	
Fixed Asset Additions	(20,000)
Cash Flow after Investing Activities	(21,700)
Financing Activities	
Increase/(Decrease) Short-Term Debt	0
Net Proceeds (Payments) Long-Term Debt	12,000
Proceeds (Purchase) of Common Stock	0
Dividends Paid	0
Cash Generated/(Used)	(9,700)
Cash Flow Proof	
Beginning Cash Balance	10,875
Cash Generated/(Used)	(9,700)
Ending Cash Balance	1,175

Ms. Debson proceeds to complete LTI's Cash Flow Statement for Year 4 (Table CS 10-73) by simply combining the results shown in Tables CS 10-65 through CS 10-72.

Year 5 Income Statement

According to the assumptions in Table CS 10-1, Year 5 is expected to be a year of strong revenue growth with revenue and cost of goods sold reaching $80,000,000 and \$32,000,000 (\$80,000,000 * 0.40) respectively. Gross margin is calculated using Equation [10-1] and shown in Table CS 10-74.

$$\textit{Gross Margin} = \textit{Net Revenue} - \textit{Cost of Goods Sold} \qquad [10\text{-}1]$$

$$\textit{Gross Margin} = 80{,}000{,}000 - 32{,}000{,}000 = \$48{,}000{,}000$$

TABLE CS 10-74 Gross Margin \$(000)'s

Net Revenues	80,000
Cost of Goods Sold (COGS)	(32,000)
Gross Margin (GM)	**48,000**

The high growth is fueled by investments in research and development, sales and marketing, and general and administrative expenses. During Year 5 spending in R&D, S&M, and G&A increase to \$13,000,000, \$13,000,000, and \$5,000,000 respectively. Total operating expenses increase to \$31,000,000 (Equation [10-2]) and would appear in the Income Statement as shown in Table CS 10-75.

$$\textit{Operating Expenses} = \textit{Research \& Development} + \textit{Sales \& Marketing} + \textit{General \& Administrative} \qquad [10\text{-}2]$$

$$\textit{Operating Expenses} = 13{,}000{,}000 + 13{,}000{,}000 + 5{,}000{,}000 = \$31{,}000{,}000$$

Earnings before interest, taxes, depreciation and amortization (EBITDA) are defined by Equation [10-3]. For Year 5, the gross margin and total operating expenses are \$48,000,000 and \$31,000,000 respectively, leaving a \$17,000,000 EBITDA.

$$\textit{EBITDA} = \textit{Gross Margin} - \textit{Total Operating Expenses} \qquad [10\text{-}3]$$

$$\textit{EBITDA} = 48{,}000{,}000 - 31{,}000{,}000 = \$17{,}000{,}000$$

TABLE CS 10-75 Operating Expenses \$(000)'s

Operating Expenses (OpExp):	Research and Development (R&D)	13,000
	Sales and Marketing (S&M)	13,000
	General and Administrative (G&A)	5,000
Total Operating Expenses		**31,000**

LTI continues to invest in plant and equipment during Year 5 and purchases \$10,000,000 of fixed assets. As previously, the assumption is that these purchases take place at the beginning of the year. These assets also have a useful life of 10 years. Therefore, the annual depreciation of the assets purchased at the beginning of Year 5 is \$1,000,000 (Equation [10-4]).

$$Depreciation = \frac{Total\ Cost\ of\ Asset}{Useful\ Life} \quad [10\text{-}4]$$

$$Depreciation = \frac{10,000,000}{10} = \$1,000,000/year$$

The total depreciation during Year 5 is the sum of the depreciations of the assets purchased in each of the prior years. Recall that \$10,000,000 of fixed assets were purchased at the beginning of Years 2 and 3 and \$20,000,000 of assets were purchased at the beginning of Year 4. These assets are only in the fourth, third, and second years of their useful lives and will depreciate by an additional \$1,000,000, \$1,000,000, and \$2,000,000 respectively. Therefore, the depreciation shown in the Income Statement for Year 5 will be calculated as shown in Table CS 10-76.

TABLE CS 10-76 Depreciation and Amortization \$(000)'s

	Year 2	Year 3	Year 4	Year 5	Total Yr 5
Fixed Asset additions	10,000	10,000	20,000	10,000	50,000
Avg Useful Life in Years	10	10	10	10	
Year of Assets Depreciation	4th	3rd	2nd	1st	
Depreciation	1,000	1,000	2,000	1,000	5,000
Amortization	0	0	0	0	0

With \$5,000,000 of depreciation and no intellectual property to amortize, the earnings before interest and taxes (EBIT) is calculated by applying Equation [10-6].

$$EBIT = EBITDA - Depreciation - Amortization \quad [10\text{-}6]$$

$$EBIT = 17,000,000 - 5,000,000 - 0 = \$12,000,000$$

As can be seen, LTI is expected to generate substantial profits at the EBIT line during Year 5. But (as will be seen when the Cash Flow Statement is prepared) the Company is still not generating sufficient cash to finance its growth and so once again management will have to arrange additional funding. In this case it is assumed that an additional \$2,000,000 of borrowing is arranged with a bank in the form of an 18-month note bearing an interest rate of 8%.[37] Like the long-term debt that was taken on during Year 4,

[37] At the end of Year 5 the loan will be 6 months to maturity and therefore is classified as short-term debt.

interest is paid annually in arrears. Since this loan will be used to partially fund the fixed assets assumed to be in place at the beginning of the year, it is implicit that the entire amount is drawn down for the entire year. The interest on the short-term and long-term notes that has to be paid to the bank at the end of Year 5 is calculated as follows and summarized in Table CS 10-77.

$$Interest\ Expense = (Debt)\left(\frac{Interest\ Rate}{100}\right) \quad [10\text{-}8]$$

$$Interest\ Expense_{(LTD\ Year\ 5)} = (12{,}000{,}000)\left(\frac{10}{100}\right) = (12{,}000{,}000)(0.10) = \$1{,}200{,}000$$

$$Interest\ Expense_{(STD\ Year\ 5)} = (2{,}000{,}000)\left(\frac{8}{100}\right) = (2{,}000{,}000)(0.08) = \$160{,}000$$

TABLE CS 10-77 Interest Expense $(000)'s

	LTD	SD	Total
Loan Outstanding	12,000	2,000	na
Interest Rate	10.00%	8.00%	na
Interest	1,200	160	1,360

As stated earlier, LTI receives no interest on its cash. Interest expense is $1,360,000. Using this data the company's EBT for Year 5 is calculated with the aid of Equation [10-9].

$$EBT = EBIT \pm Interest\ Income/Expense \quad [10\text{-}9]$$

$$EBT = 12{,}000{,}000 + 0 - 1{,}360{,}000 = \$10{,}640{,}000$$

This is the first year that LTI has positive earnings before tax. However, LTI still doesn't have any income tax obligations because the Company is in a tax-loss carry-forward position by virtue of the fact the Company had accumulated $20,700,000 of losses by the end of Year 4 and this amount more than offsets Year 5's EBT of $10,640,000, as shown in Table CS 10-78.[38]

Therefore, net income (NI) for Year 5 using (Equation [10-10] is:

$$NI = EBT - Taxes\ Paid \quad [10\text{-}10]$$

$$NI = 10{,}640{,}000 - 0 = \$10{,}640{,}000$$

[38] LTI's tax-loss carry-forward at the end of Year 5 is still $10,060,000. This amount will offset an equivalent amount of EBT during Year 6. Anything earned in excess of this amount would be taxable.

TABLE CS 10-78 Tax-Loss Carry-Forward $(000)'s

	Year 1	Year 2	Year 3	Year 4	Year 5
Net Income	0	(12,000)	(6,500)	(2,200)	10,640
Tax-Loss Carry-Forward	0	(12,000)	(18,500)	(20,700)	(10,060)

Ms. Debson then enters the results of her calculations into the Income Statement format she has been using to produce Light Technologies Income Statements for prior years (Table CS 10-79).

TABLE CS 10-79 Light Technologies Inc. Income Statement for Year 5 $(000)'s

Net Revenues			80,000
Cost of Goods Sold (COGS)			(32,000)
Gross Margin (GM)			48,000
Operating Expenses (OpExp):	Research and Development (R&D)	13,000	
	Sales and Marketing (S&M)	13,000	
	General and Administrative (G&A)	5,000	
Total Operating Expenses			(31,000)
Earnings before Interest, Taxes, Depreciation and Amortization (EBITDA)			17,000
Depreciation and Amortization (D&A)			(5,000)
Earnings before Interest and Taxes (EBIT)			12,000
Interest Income/Expense (Int)			(1,360)
Earnings before Tax (EBT)			10,640
Taxes Paid (TaxesPaid) @ 40%			0
Net Income (NI)			10,640

Year 5 Balance Sheet

Net income for the year is a profit of $10,640,000. As before, the total shareholders' equity (Equation [10-27]) is the sum of paid-in capital (Equation [10-29]) and retained earnings (Equation [10-30]).

$$Total\ Shareholders'\ Equity_{(End\ Year\ 5)} = Paid\text{-}in\ Capital_{(End\ Year\ 5)} + Retained\ Earnings_{(End\ Year\ 5)} \quad [10\text{-}27]$$

$$Paid\text{-}in\ Capital_{(End\ Year\ 5)} = Paid\text{-}in\ Capital_{(End\ Year\ 4)} + \Delta Paid\text{-}in\ Capital_{(Year\ 5)} \quad [10\text{-}29]$$

Since no additional capital was raised from shareholders during Year 4, the paid-in capital at the end of Year 5 is:

$$Paid\text{-}in\ Capital = 50{,}000{,}000 + 0 = \$50{,}000{,}000$$

and

$$RetEarnings_{(End\ Year\ 5)} = RetEarnings_{(End\ Year\ 4)} \pm NI_{(Year\ 5)} - Dividends\ Paid_{(Year\ 5)} \quad [10\text{-}30]$$

$$Retained\ Earnings = -20{,}700{,}000 + 10{,}640{,}000 - 0 = -\$10{,}060{,}000$$

Substituting these values in Equation [10-27] obtains the total shareholders' equity, which is tabulated in Table CS 10-80.

$$Total\ Shareholders'\ Equity = 50{,}000{,}000 - 10{,}060{,}000 = \$39{,}940{,}000$$

TABLE CS 10-80 Shareholders' Equity $(000)'s

Paid-in Capital	50,000
Retained Earnings	(10,060)
Total Shareholders' Equity	**39,940**

As noted earlier, LTI borrowed $12 million at the beginning of Year 4 to finance its growth. This note is in its second year of a five-year term with a balloon payment due at the end of the fifth year. Therefore, the long-term debt on the Company's Balance Sheet at the end of Year 5 would be $12,000,000 (Table CS 10-81).

The Company's policy on paying its vendors does not change and so it continues to pay on a 45-day basis. With the aid of Equation [10-39] the accounts payable outstanding at the end of Year 5 is calculated to be $4,000,000.

$$Accounts\ Payable\ (AP) = (Annualized\ Cost\ of\ Goods\ Sold)\left(\frac{APDOS}{360}\right) \quad [10\text{-}39]$$

$$Accounts\ Payable = (32{,}000{,}000)\left(\frac{45}{360}\right) = \$4{,}000{,}000$$

TABLE CS 10-81 Long-Term Debt $(000)'s

Long-Term Debt	12,000

Year 5 was profitable but because the Company has prior-year losses that more than cover earnings, the Company doesn't have any income tax obligations. Also, they financed their growth with $2,000,000 of debt, which at the end of Year 5 will only have six months to maturity and so is classified as short-term debt. Therefore, the Current Liabilities section of the Balance Sheet will be as shown in Table CS 10-82.

$$\textit{Current Liabilities} = \textit{Accounts Payable} + \textit{Taxes Payable} + \textit{Short-Term Debt} \qquad [10\text{-}25]$$

$$\textit{Current Liabilities} = 4{,}000{,}000 + 0 + 2{,}000{,}000 = \$6{,}000{,}000$$

TABLE CS 10-82 Current Liabilities $(000)'s

Accounts Payable	4,000
Taxes Payable	0
Short-Term Debt	2,000
Total Current Liabilities	**6,000**

Tables CS 10-80, CS 10-81, and CS 10-82 and the result of Equation [10-32] account for all of LTI's liabilities, and by combining these tables the liability side of LTI's Year 5 Balance Sheet (Table CS 10-83) is created.

$$\textit{Total Liabilities} + \textit{TSHE} = \textit{Current Liabilities} + \textit{Long-Term Debt} + \textit{Total Shareholders' Equity} \qquad [10\text{-}32]$$

$$\textit{Total Liabilities} + \textit{TSHE} = 6{,}000{,}000 + 12{,}000{,}000 + 39{,}940{,}000 = \$57{,}940{,}000$$

Creating the asset side of the Balance Sheet for Year 5 begins with Equation [10-11]:

$$\textit{Total Assets} = \textit{Total Liabilities} + \textit{Total Shareholders' Equity} \qquad [10\text{-}11]$$

where:

$$\textit{Total Assets} = 18{,}000{,}000 + 39{,}940{,}000 = \$57{,}940{,}000$$

The company still does not have any intangible assets to amortize so the net tangible assets are zero, as shown in Table CS 10-84.

TABLE CS 10-83 Liabilities and Total Shareholders' Equity $(000)'s

Current Liabilities	
Accounts Payable	4,000
Taxes Payable	0
Short-Term Debt	2,000
Total Current Liabilities	6,000
Long-Term Debt	12,000
Total Liabilities	18,000
Shareholders' Equity	
Paid-in Capital	50,000
Retained Earnings	(10,060)
Total Shareholders' Equity	39,940
Total Liabilities + TSHE	57,940

As in previous years, Year 5 is also a year of investment with investments in PP&E of $10,000,000. As Equation [10-15] indicates, Property, Plant, and Equipment at the end of Year 5 is the sum of the PP&E at the end of Year 4 ($40,000,000) plus the $10,000,000 purchased during Year 5.

$$\textit{Property, Plant, and Equipment at Cost}_{(End Year\ 5)} = \textit{PP\&E@Cost}_{(End Year\ 4)} + \Delta \textit{PP\&E@Cost}_{(Year\ 5)} \quad [10\text{-}15]$$

$$\textit{Property, Plant, and Equipment at Cost} = 40{,}000{,}000 + 10{,}000{,}000 = \$50{,}000{,}000$$

Depreciation during Year 5 was $5,000,000. Hence, the accumulated depreciation[39] at the end of Year 5 is the accumulated depreciation at the end of Year 4 ($7,000,000) plus Year 5's depreciation of $5,000,000 and is calculated by using Equation [10-16].

$$\textit{Accumulated Depreciation}_{(End\ Year\ 5)} = \textit{Accumulated Depreciation}_{(End\ Year\ 4)} + \textit{Depreciaton}_{(Year\ 5)} \quad [10\text{-}16]$$

$$\textit{Accumulated Depreciation}_{(End\ Year\ 5)} = 7{,}000{,}000 + 5{,}000{,}000 = \$12{,}000{,}000$$

TABLE CS 10-84 Intangible Assets $(000)'s

Goodwill and Other Intangible Assets	0
Less Accumulated Amortization	0
Net Intangible Assets	**0**

[39] The sum of all depreciation since the beginning of the Company.

TABLE CS 10-85 Fixed Assets $(000)'s

Property, Plant, and Equipment at Cost	50,000
Less Accumulated Depreciation	(12,000)
Net Fixed Assets	**38,000**

The net fixed assets are calculated using Equation [10-14], as summarized in Table CS 10-85.

$$\text{Net Fixed Assets} = \text{Property, Plant, and Equipment at Cost} - \text{Accumulated Depreciation} \quad [10\text{-}14]$$

$$\text{Net Fixed Assets} = 50{,}000{,}000 - 12{,}000{,}000 = \$38{,}000{,}000$$

Of the three asset classes on LTI's Balance Sheet, intangible and fixed assets have been quantified. Total assets, net intangible assets, and net fixed assets are $57,940,000, $0, and $38,000,000, respectively. Rearranging Equation [10-22] and substituting these values into Equation [10-23] gives the value of the current assets.

$$\text{Total Assets} = \text{Current Assets} + \text{Net Fixed Assets} + \text{Net Intangible Assets} \quad [10\text{-}22]$$

$$\text{Current Assets} = \text{Total Assets} - \text{Net Intangible Assets} - \text{Net Fixed Assets} \quad [10\text{-}23]$$

$$\text{Current Assets} = 57{,}940{,}000 - 0 - 38{,}000{,}000 = \$19{,}940{,}000$$

LTI's current assets consist of cash, accounts receivable, and inventory (Equation [10-12]).

$$\text{Current Assets} = \text{Cash} + \text{Accounts Receivable} + \text{Inventory} \quad [10\text{-}12]$$

The cash component is obtained by rearranging Equation [10-12].

$$\text{Cash} = \text{Current Assets} - \text{Accounts Receivable} - \text{Inventory} \quad [10\text{-}13]$$

The assumption used throughout the process of preparing these pro-forma statements for ARDOS is 45 days. Therefore, with the assistance of Equation [10-35], accounts receivable at the end of Year 5 is calculated to be $10,000,000.

$$\text{Accounts Receivable (AR)} = (\text{Annualized Net Revenues})\left(\frac{ARDOS}{360}\right) \quad [10\text{-}35]$$

$$\text{Accounts Receivable} = (80{,}000{,}000)\left(\frac{45}{360}\right) = \$10{,}000{,}000$$

Applying Equation [10-37], the inventory at the end of the year, based on the assumption that it turns four times per year, is $8,000,000.

$$Inventory = \frac{Annualized\ Cost\ of\ Goods\ Sold}{Inventory\ Turns} \qquad [10\text{-}37]$$

$$Inventory = \frac{32,000,000}{4} = \$8,000,000$$

Recalling Equation [10-13] and substituting $19,940,000, $10,000,000, and $8,000,000 for current assets, accounts receivable, and inventory respectively calculates the cash at year-end to be:

$$Cash = Currents\ Assets - Accounts\ Receivable - Inventory \qquad [10\text{-}13]$$

$$Cash = 19{,}940{,}000 - 10{,}000{,}000 - 8{,}000{,}000 = \$1{,}940{,}000$$

The current assets as they will appear in the Balance Sheet are shown in Table CS 10-86.

$$Total\ Current\ Assets = Cash + Accounts\ Receivable + Inventory \qquad [10\text{-}12]$$

$$Total\ Current\ Assets = 1{,}940{,}000 + 10{,}000{,}000 + 8{,}000{,}000 = \$19{,}940{,}000$$

TABLE CS 10-86 Current Assets $(000)'s

Cash	1,940
Accounts Receivable	10,000
Inventory	8,000
Total Current Assets	**19,940**

Combining Tables CS 10-84, CS 10-85, and CS 10-86 with the result of Equation [10-22] creates the asset side of the Balance sheet (Table CS 10-87).

$$Total\ Assets = Current\ Assets + Net\ Fixed\ Assets + Net\ Intangible\ Assets \qquad [10\text{-}22]$$

$$Total\ Assets = 19{,}940{,}000 + 38{,}000{,}000 + 0 = \$57{,}940{,}000$$

Finally, the complete Balance Sheet for Year 5 is the combination of total assets (Table CS 10-87) and total liabilities + total shareholders' equity (Table CS 10-83) and is shown in Table CS 10-88.

TABLE CS 10-87 Total Assets $(000)'s

Current Assets	
Cash	1,940
Accounts Receivable	10,000
Inventory	8,000
Total Current Assets	19,940
Fixed Assets	
Property, Plant, and Equipment at Cost	50,000
Less Accumulated Depreciation	(12,000)
Net Fixed Assets	38,000
Intangible Assets	
Goodwill and Other Intangible Assets	0
Less Accumulated Amortization	0
Net Intangible Assets	0
Total Assets	57,940

TABLE CS 10-88 Light Technologies Inc. Balance Sheet for Year 5 $(000)'s

Current Assets		**Current Liabilities**	
Cash	1,940	Accounts Payable	4,000
Accounts Receivable	10,000	Taxes Payable	0
Inventory	8,000	Short-Term Debt	2,000
Total Current Assets	19,940	**Total Current Liabilities**	6,000
Fixed Assets		**Long-Term Debt**	12,000
Property, Plant, and Equipment at Cost	50,000		
Less Accumulated Depreciation	(12,000)	**Total Liabilities**	18,000
Net Fixed Assets	38,000		
Intangible Assets		**Shareholders' Equity**	
Goodwill and Other Intangible Assets	0	Paid-in Capital	50,000
Less Accumulated Amortization	0	Retained Earnings	(10,060)
Net Intangible Assets	0	**Total Shareholders' Equity**	39,940
Total Assets	57,940	**Total Liabilities + TSHE**	57,940

Year 5 Cash Flow Statement

Operations The first step Ms. Debson took preparing the Year 5 Cash Flow Statement was to adjust Year 5's net income for non-cash charges such as depreciation and amortization. Earlier, the depreciation and amortization charges for the year were determined

TABLE CS 10-89 Operations $(000)'s

Net Income (Loss)	10,640
Depreciation	5,000
Amortization	0
Net Cash Flow from Operations	**15,640**

to be $5,000,000 and $0 respectively. Therefore, net cash flow from operations (net income adjusted for non-cash charges) for Year 5 is once again calculated by using Equation [10-59] and is shown in Table CS 10-89.

$$Net\ Cash\ Flow\ from\ Operations\ (CFfO) = Net\ Income + Depreciation + Amortization \quad [10\text{-}59]^{40}$$

$$CFfO = 10{,}640{,}000 + 5{,}000{,}000 + 0 = \$15{,}640{,}000$$

Working Capital Accounts Accounts receivable at the end of Years 4 and 5 were $5,000,000 and $10,000,000 respectively. Since the increase in accounts receivable during Year 5 is $5,000,000 (Equation [10-44]), Ms. Debson concludes this represents a use of cash.

$$\Delta Accounts\ Receivable = Accounts\ Receivable_{(End\ Year\ 4)} - Accounts\ Receivable_{(End\ Year\ 5)} \quad [10\text{-}44]$$

$$\Delta Accounts\ Receivable = 5{,}000{,}000 - 10{,}000{,}000 = -\$5{,}000{,}000$$

Similarly, inventories at the end of Years 4 and 5 were $4,250,000 and $8,000,000 respectively. This represents an increase in inventory of $3,750,000, as calculated by Equation [10-45] and a corresponding use of cash.

$$\Delta Inventory = Inventory_{(End\ Year\ 4)} - Inventory_{(End\ Year\ 5)} \quad [10\text{-}45]$$

$$\Delta Inventory = 4{,}250{,}000 - 8{,}000{,}000 = -\$3{,}750{,}000$$

According to Ms. Debson's model, LTI continues to pay its suppliers on a 45-day basis. This results in the Company's accounts payable increasing from $2,125,000 at the

[40] Once again, interest expense has been ignored for the sake of simplicity. If it were included, it would be added to net cash flow from operations and subtracted in the Financing section of the Cash Flow Statement with no impact on cash generated/(used).

end of Year 4 to $4,000,000 at the end of Year 5 or an increase of $1,875,000 (Equation [10-47]). This is treated as a source of cash.

$$\Delta Accounts\ Payable = Accounts\ Payable_{(End\ Year\ 5)} - Accounts\ Payable_{(End\ Year\ 4)} \quad [10\text{-}47]$$

$$\Delta Accounts\ Payable = 4{,}000{,}000 - 2{,}125{,}000 = \$1{,}875{,}000$$

While Year 5 is highly profitable, the income is shielded by prior-year losses. Therefore, no taxes are payable for this year. This is exactly the same situation the Company found itself in at the end of Year 4. Therefore, the change in the "Taxes Payable" account is zero, thereby representing neither a use nor a source of cash (Equation [10-49]).

$$\Delta Taxes\ Payable = Taxes\ Payable_{(End\ Year\ 5)} - Taxes\ Payable_{(End\ Year\ 4)} \quad [10\text{-}49]$$

$$\Delta Taxes\ Payable = 0 - 0 = \$0$$

Using the results of these calculations, Ms. Debson was able to determine the change in working capital by using Equation [10-61] and presented it in the Cash Flow Statement format she had been using (Table CS 10-90).

$$Net\ \Delta WC = \pm \Delta AR \pm \Delta INV \pm \Delta AP \pm \Delta TP \quad [10\text{-}61]$$

$$Net\ \Delta WC = -5{,}000{,}000 - 3{,}750{,}000 + 1{,}875{,}000 \pm 0 = -\$6{,}875{,}000$$

TABLE CS 10-90 Working Capital Accounts $(000)'s

	Year 4	Year 5	Change
(Increase)/Decrease Accounts Receivable	5,000	10,000	(5,000)
(Increase)/Decrease Inventory	4,250	8,000	(3,750)
Increase/(Decrease) Accounts Payable	2,125	4,000	1,875
Increase/(Decrease) Taxes Payable	0	0	0
Net Change in Working Capital			**(6,875)**

Cash Flow from Operating Activities Cash flow from operating activities is defined as the sum of net cash flow from operations and change in working capital (Equation [10-51]). Since cash flow from operations is $15,640,000 and net change in working capital is negative $6,875,000, the CFfOA is equal to the sum of the two and Ms. Debson summarized the result in Table CS 10-91.

TABLE CS 10-91 Cash Flow from Operating Activities $(000)'s

Cash Flow from Operating Activities	8,765

$$Cash\ Flow\ from\ Operating\ Activities\ (CFfOA) = Cash\ Flow\ from\ Operations \pm Net\ \Delta WC \quad [10\text{-}51]$$

$$CFfOA = 15{,}640{,}000 - 6{,}875{,}000 = \$8{,}765{,}000$$

Investing Activities Next she addressed the investing activities of the Cash Flow Statement, noting that during Year 5, $10,000,000 of fixed assets are purchased and so the cash outlay for investing activities must be $10,000,000 (Table CS 10-92).

TABLE CS 10-92 Investing Activities $(000)'s

Fixed Asset Additions	10,000

Cash Flow after Investing Activities Cash flow after investing activities (CFaIA) is the sum of cash flow from operating activities and investing activities (Equation [10-62]). During Year 4 the CFfOA is a positive $8,765,000 and the result of the Company's investing activities is an expenditure of $10,000,000. Ms. Debson used this data to calculate the CFaIA to be a negative $1,235,000 (Table CS 10-93).

$$Cash\ Flow\ after\ Investing\ Activities\ (CFaIA) = CFfOA - Additions\ to\ Fixed\ Assets \quad [10\text{-}62]$$

$$CFaIA = 8{,}765{,}000 - 10{,}000{,}000 = -\$1{,}235{,}000$$

TABLE CS 10-93 Cash Flow after Investing Activities $(000)'s

Cash Flow after Investing Activities	(1,235)

Financing Activities In order to help finance its growth, LTI entered into a $2,000,000, 18-month term loan with its bank syndicate during Year 5, drew down on the loan at the beginning of the year, and thereby brought $2,000,000 of cash into the company.[41] Also during Year 5, the Company paid interest on its $12,000,000 five-year note (drawn down at the beginning of Year 4) but did not repay any principal. The result of utilizing the $2,000,000 term loan credit facility on the financing activities was tabulated by Ms. Debson in Table CS 10-94. The CFaFA was then calculated to be $765,000.

$$CFaFA = CFaIA \pm \Delta STD \pm \Delta LTD \pm (Sale/Purchase\ of\ Common\ Stock) \quad [10\text{-}63]$$

$$CFaFA = -1{,}235{,}000 + 2{,}000{,}000 \pm 0 \pm 0 = \$765{,}000$$

[41] The term loan was arranged at the beginning of the year and since it only has 6 months of tenor remaining at year-end it is classified as short-term debt.

TABLE CS 10-94 Financing Activities $(000)'s

	Year 4	Year 5	Change
Increase/(Decrease) Short-Term Debt	0	2,000	2,000
Net Proceeds (Payments) Long-Term Debt	12,000		0
Proceeds (Purchase) of Common Stock	0	0	0

Cash Generated/(Used) Cash generated or used by LTI during Year 5 is the sum of cash flow after investing activities and any cash generated or used as a result of financing activities (Equation [10-56]). During Year 5, there is $2,000,000 of cash generated from financing activities and so the negative CFaFA is more than offset and the cash generated (used) for the year is $765,000 (Table CS 10-95).

$$CGU = CFaIA \pm \Delta STD \pm \Delta LTD \pm \Delta TSHE - Dividends\ Paid \qquad [10\text{-}56]$$

$$Cash\ Generated\ (Used) = -1{,}235{,}000 + 2{,}000{,}000 + 0 \pm 0 - 0 = \$765{,}000$$

TABLE CS 10-95 Cash Generated/(Used) $(000)'s

Cash Generated/(Used)	765

Cash Flow Proof The cash on hand at the beginning of Year 5 ("Beginning Cash Balance") was $1,175,000. During Year 5, $765,000 of cash was generated. Therefore, the cash on hand at the end of the year ("Ending Cash Balance") is calculated by Ms. Debson to be $1,940,000 (Equation [10-58] and Table CS 10-96).

$$Ending\ Cash\ Balance_{(Year\ 5)} = Beginning\ Cash\ Balance_{(Year\ 5)} \pm Cash\ Generated\ or\ Used_{(Year\ 5)} \qquad [10\text{-}58]$$

$$Ending\ Cash\ Balance_{(Year\ 4)} = 1{,}175{,}000 + 765{,}000 = \$1{,}940{,}000$$

TABLE CS 10-96 Cash Flow Proof $(000)'s

Beginning Cash Balance	1,175
Cash Generated/(Used)	765
Ending Cash Balance	1,940

TABLE CS 10-97 Light Technologies Inc. Cash Flow Statement for Year 5 $(000)'s

Operating Activities	
Operations	
Net Income (Loss)	10,640
Depreciation	5,000
Amortization	0
Net Cash Flow from Operations	15,640
Working Capital Accounts	
(Increase)/Decrease Accounts Receivable	(5,000)
(Increase)/Decrease Inventory	(3,750)
Increase/(Decrease) Accounts Payable	1,875
Increase/(Decrease) Taxes Payable	0
Net Change in Working Capital	(6,875)
Cash Flow from Operating Activities	8,765
Investing Activities	
Fixed Asset Additions	(10,000)
Cash Flow after Investing Activities	(1,235)
Financing Activities	
Increase/(Decrease) Short-Term Debt	2,000
Net Proceeds (Payments) Long-Term Debt	0
Proceeds (Purchase) of Common Stock	0
Dividends Paid	0
Cash Generated/(Used)	765
Cash Flow Proof	
Beginning Cash Balance	1,175
Cash Generated/(Used)	765
Ending Cash Balance	1,940

Finally, Ms. Debson was able to finalize LTI's pro-forma Cash Flow Statement for Year 5 by combining Tables CS 10-89–CS 10-96, which she had prepared as she worked her way through the document (Table CS 10-97).

Comparative Statements

After completing the pro-forma financial statements for LTI, Ms. Debson proceeded to analyze the results. The first step in this process was the preparation of Comparative Income, Balance Sheet, and Cash Flow Statements (Tables CS 10-98, CS 10-99, and CS 10-100 respectively).

TABLE CS 10-98 Comparative Income Statements Years 1–5 $(000)'s

		Year 1	Year 2	Year 3	Year 4	Year 5
Net Revenues		0	0	20,000	40,000	80,000
Cost of Goods Sold (COGS)		0	0	(9,000)	(17,000)	(32,000)
Gross Margin (GM)						
Operating Expenses (OpExp):	R&D	0	6,000	7,000	9,000	13,000
	S&M	0	3,000	6,000	8,000	13,000
	G&A	0	2,000	2,500	3,000	5,000
Total Operating Expenses		0	(11,000)	(15,500)	(20,000)	(31,000)
Earnings before Interest D&A (EBITDA)		0	(11,000)	(4,500)	3,000	17,000
D&A		0	(1,000)	(2,000)	(4,000)	(5,000)
EBIT		0	(12,000)	(6,500)	(1,000)	12,000
Interest Inc/(Exp) NetInt		0	0	0	(1,200)	(1,360)
Earnings before Tax (EBT)		0	(12,000)	(6,500)	(2,200)	10,640
Taxes Paid (TaxesPaid) @ 40%		0	0	0	0	0
Net Income (NI)		0	(12,000)	(6,500)	(2,200)	10,640

Comparative Income Statement

One of the first observations was that despite the fact she had cut back the Company's sales forecasts her projections still had LTI's revenues growing at a *compound annual growth rate* (CAGR)[42] of 100%[43] and clearly that rate was unsustainable.

$$\%CAGR = \left[\left(\frac{V_{End}}{V_{Beg}}\right)^{\frac{1}{n}} - 1\right](100) \qquad \text{[C-8]}$$

$$Revenue\ CAGR = \left[\left(\frac{80,000,0000}{20,000,000}\right)^{\left(\frac{1}{2}\right)} - 1\right](100) = \left[(4)^{(0.5)} - 1\right](100)$$
$$= (2-1)(100) = 100\%$$

However, even if the growth rate slowed to 20% for the next 10 years, LTI would achieve revenues of approximately $500 million and, given the opportunities for this company, this could well be at the low end of the range.

$$Revenues_{(After\ 10\ Years\ @20\%)} = (80,000,000)(1.2)^{10} = (80,000,000)(6.19)$$
$$= \$495,339,000$$

[42]See Appendix C for derivation of Equation [C-8].

[43]Which is entirely consistent with the assumptions in Table CS 10-2.

TABLE CS 10-99 Comparative Balance Sheet, Years 1–5 $(000)'s

Current Assets	**Year 1**	**Year 2**	**Year 3**	**Year 4**	**Year 5**	**Current Liabilities**	**Year 1**	**Year 2**	**Year 3**	**Year 4**	**Year 5**
Cash	50,000	29,000	10,875	1,175	1,940	Accounts Pay	0	0	1,125	2,125	4,000
Accounts RX	0	0	2,500	5,000	10,000	Taxes Payable	0	0	0	0	0
Inventory	0	0	2,250	4,250	8,000	Short-Term Debt	0	0	0	0	2,000
Total Cur Assets	50,000	29,000	15,625	10,425	19,940	**Tot Cur Liabilities**	0	0	1,125	2,125	6,000
Fixed Assets						**Long-Term Debt**	0	0	0	12,000	12,000
PP&E at Cost	0	10,000	20,000	40,000	50,000						
Depreciation	0	(1,000)	(3,000)	(7,000)	(12,000)	**Total Liabilities**	0	0	1,125	14,125	18,000
Net Fixed Assets	0	9,000	17,000	33,000	38,000						
Intangible Assets						**Shareholders' Equity**					
Goodwill and OIA	0	0	0	0	0	Paid-in Capital	50,000	50,000	50,000	50,000	50,000
Amortization	0	0	0	0	0	Ret Earnings	0	(12,000)	(18,500)	(20,700)	(10,060)
Net Intang Assets	0	0	0	0	0	**Total SH's Equity**	50,000	38,000	31,500	29,300	39,940
Total Assets	50,000	38,000	32,625	43,425	57,940	**Total Liab's + TSHE**	50,000	38,000	32,625	43,425	57,940

Next she turned her attention to EBITDA and noted that according to her financial model the company would achieve an EBITDA of $17 million in Year 5 or approximately 21% (17,000/80,000 = 21.3%) of revenue. After thinking about this for some time, Ms. Debson concluded that as volume increased the COGS as a percentage of revenue should decrease and operating expenses as a percent of revenue would also decrease somewhat from the current run rate of 38.8% (31,000/80,000 = 38.8), making it highly likely that LTI's EBITDA margin could level out at 25% or higher and at this margin the Company's EBITDA would be approximately $125 million.

$$EBITDA_{(After\ 10\ Years\ @\ 20\%)} = (500,000,000)(0.25) = \$125,000,000$$

Next, she reasoned that with this kind of performance a company growing at 20% for such a period could well have an EBITDA multiple equal to the compound annual growth rate and that if the Company went public at that time, it would have a value of at least $2.5 billion, and this would represent a return of 50 times the original investment ($2,500,000,000/$50,000,000 = 50).

$$Future\ Value = (125,000,000)(20) = \$2,500,000,000$$

Then she wondered how this increase in value over the 15-year period would be expressed in terms of a compound annual growth rate. She obtained the answer by once again applying Equation [C-8].

$$\%CAGR = \left[\left(\frac{V_{End}}{V_{Beg}}\right)^{\frac{1}{n}} - 1\right](100) \qquad [C\text{-}8]$$

$$CAGR_{15\ Years} = \left[\left(\frac{2,500,000,000}{50,000,000}\right)^{\frac{1}{15}} - 1\right](100) = \left[(50)^{0.0667} - 1\right](100)$$
$$= (1.30 - 1)(100) = 30\%$$

So it seemed that investing in LTI could be very profitable. Next she turned her attention to the Comparative Balance Sheet (Table CS 10-99).

Comparative Balance Sheet

Her first concern about the Balance Sheet was the assumptions that produced the cash balances in Years 4 and 5, which in her view were on the low side of a CFO's comfort zone. Experience had taught her that depending on the company and the characteristics of the market it served, CFOs like to have cash availability of somewhere between 5% and 10% of revenues. In Year 4 the revenue was $60,000,000, implying a desired cash balance of between $3,000,000 and $6,000,000. Similarly Year 5's revenue would indicate a desired cash availability of $4 to $8 million. This would suggest that the long-term loan entered into in Year 4 should have been at least $14,000,000 to bring the year-end cash balance to $3,175,000, and the short-term loan put in place in Year 5 should have been at $3,000,000, or better still, $4,000,000. This didn't trouble her because if LTI could produce this kind of performance, the Company would be able to access the debt markets at very attractive interest rates.

Furthermore, she observed that the Balance Sheet didn't contain any intellectual property, which LTI would be accumulating at a considerable rate by virtue of its patent portfolio and therefore was understated. While this doesn't have any cash impact, she considered this to be an important factor in any decision as to whether to invest.

Comparative Cash Flow Statement and a Discussion of LTI's Ability to Generate Adequate Cash Flow to Finance Growth

When it came to the Comparative Cash Flow Statement (Table CS 10-100), Ms. Debson's main concern was LTI's ability to generate enough cash to finance the aggressive growth

TABLE CS 10-100 Comparative Cash Flow Statement, Years 1–5 $(000)'s

	Year 1	Year 2	Year 3	Year 4	Year 5
Operating Activities					
Operations					
Net Income (Loss)	0	(12,000)	(6,500)	(2,200)	10,640
Depreciation	0	1,000	2,000	4,000	5,000
Amortization	0	0	0	0	0
Net Cash Flow from Operations	0	(11,000)	(4,500)	1,800	15,640
Working Capital Accounts					
(Increase)/Decrease Accounts Receivable	0	0	(2,500)	(2,500)	(5,000)
(Increase)/Decrease Inventory	0	0	(2,250)	(2,000)	(3,750)
Increase/(Decrease) Accounts Payable	0	0	1,125	1,000	1,875
Increase/(Decrease) Taxes Payable	0	0	0	0	0
Net Change in Working Capital	0	0	(3,625)	(3,500)	(6,875)
Cash Flow from Operating Activities	0	(11,000)	(8,125)	(1,700)	8,765
Investing Activities					
Fixed Asset Additions	0	(10,000)	(10,000)	(20,000)	(10,000)
Cash Flow after Investing Activities	0	(21,000)	(18,125)	(21,700)	(1,235)
Financing Activities					
Increase/(Decrease) Short-Term Debt	0	0	0	0	2,000
Net Proceeds (Payments) Long-Term Debt	0	0	0	12,000	0
Proceeds (Purchase) of Common Stock	50,000	0	0	0	0
Dividends Paid	0	0	0	0	0
Cash Generated / (Used)	50,000	(21,000)	(18,125)	(9,700)	765
Cash Flow Proof					
Beginning Cash Balance	0	50,000	29,000	10,875	1,175
Cash Generated/(Used)	50,000	(21,000)	(18,125)	(9,700)	765
Ending Cash Balance	50,000	29,000	10,875	1,175	1,940

projections. To deal with this, she decided to generate Year 6 financial statements based on a slower growth in revenue.

Year 6 Income Statement

She began the process by taking the Years 3–5 Income Statements and converting the various line items to percentages of revenue. Next she assumed that revenue in Year 6 would only increase by 50% and the increase in volume would capture additional procurement and manufacturing efficiencies and result in a 2.5% improvement in the COGS, to 37%. Next she assumed that total operating expenses would remain high compared to the industry average but decrease to 35% of revenue. Depreciation and amortization in the industry was typically in the range of 3–5% but since LTI was still a relatively new participant it would have to invest at a rate somewhat higher than the high end of the range and so she settled on a level of 5.3% or 1% (percentage) point less than Year 5. When it came to interest she had a hunch the Company's debt would not change in any material way and settled on interest expenses of $1,360,000—the same as Year 5. Furthermore, since she was anticipating significant earnings and cash flow, she assumed that there would not be a need to raise more equity from the capital markets.

The line items for the Income Statement were calculated as follows:

Net Revenues

$$Net\ Revenues = (80{,}000{,}000)(1.50) = \$120{,}000{,}000$$

Cost of Goods Sold

$$COGS = (120{,}000{,}000)(0.370) = \$44{,}400{,}000$$

Gross Margin

$$Gross\ Margin = Net\ Revenue - Cost\ of\ Goods\ Sold \tag{10-1}$$

$$Gross\ Margin = 120{,}000{,}000 - 44{,}400{,}000 = \$75{,}600{,}000$$

Operating Expenses

$$Operating\ Expenses = (120{,}000{,}000)(0.350) = \$42{,}000{,}000$$

EBITDA

$$EBITDA = Gross\ Margin - Operating\ Expenses \tag{10-3}$$

$$EBITDA = 75{,}600{,}000 - 42{,}000{,}000 = \$33{,}600{,}000$$

Depreciation & Amortization

$$D\ \&\ A = (120{,}000{,}000)(0.530) = \$6{,}360{,}000$$

EBIT

$$EBIT = EBITDA - Depreciation\,\&\,Amortization \quad [10\text{-}6]$$

$$EBIT = 33{,}600{,}000 - 6{,}360{,}000 = \$27{,}240{,}000$$

Interest Income/Expense

$$Interest\ Income/Expense = -\$1{,}360{,}000$$

EBT

$$EBT = EBIT \pm Interest\ Income/Expense \quad [10\text{-}9]$$

$$EBT = 27{,}240{,}000 - 1{,}360{,}000 = \$25{,}880{,}000$$

The results of these assumptions and the Year 6 Income Statement are shown in Table CS10-101.

TABLE CS 10-101 Light Technologies Income Statement for Year 6 $(000)'s and %

		Year 3	Year 4	Year 5	Year 6 %	Year 6
Net Revenues		20,000	40,000	80,000	50%	120,000
Cost of Goods Sold (COGS)		45.0%	42.5%	40.0%	37.0%	44,400
Gross Margin (GM)		55.0%	57.5%	60.0%	63.0%	75,600
Operating Expenses (OpExp):	R&D	35.0%	22.5%	16.3%		
	S&M	30.0%	20.0%	16.3%		
	G&A	12.5%	7.5%	6.3%		
Total Operating Expenses		77.5%	50.0%	38.8%	35.0%	42,000
Earnings before Interest D&A (EBITDA)		–22.5%	7.5%	21.3%	28.0%	33,600
D&A		10.0%	10.0%	6.3%	5.3%	6,360
EBIT		–32.5%	–2.5%	15.0%	22.7%	27,240
Interest Inc/(Exp) NetInt		0.0%	3.0%	1.7%	1.1%	1,360
Earnings before Tax (EBT)		–32.5%	–5.5%	13.3%	21.6%	25,880
Taxes Paid (TaxesPaid) @ 40%		0.0%	0.0%	0.0%	–5.3%	(6,328)
Net Income (NI)		–32.5%	–5.5%	13.3%	16.3%	19,552

Before calculating the net income she toyed with the idea of ignoring the fact that LTI still had a tax-loss carry-forward position and applying the full 40% tax rate to the earnings before tax of $25,880,000. However, after thinking about it she concluded that the impact the tax-loss carry-forward of $10,060,000 would have on cash and net income was too great to ignore since it reduced the taxable income and income tax payable to $15,820,000 and $6,328,000, respectively (Table CS 10-102).

TABLE CS 10-102 Tax-Loss Carry-Forward and Taxable Income $(000)'s

	Year 5	Year 6
Earnings before Tax (EBT)	10,640	25,880
Tax-Loss Carry-Forward	(10,060)	0
Taxable Income	0	15,820
Income Tax Payable @ 40%	0	6,328

Having made her decision about using the tax-loss carry-forward she calculated the net income (NI) with the aid of Equation [10-10]:

$$NI = EBT - Taxes\ Paid \qquad [10\text{-}10]$$

$$NI = 25{,}880{,}000 - 6{,}328{,}000 = \$19{,}552{,}000$$

The result of these assumptions and the Year 6 Income Statement are shown in Table CS 10-102.

Year 6 Cash Flow Statement

Having roughed out an Income Statement for Year 6, Ms. Debson then proceeded to prepare an Estimated Cash Flow Statement. The first issue she had to deal with was depreciation and amortization.

In Year 5 the D&A was $5,000,000 compared to Year 6's $6,360,000. The impact of the $6,360,000 of depreciation on Year 6's net cash flow from operations is shown in Table CS 10-103.

$$Net\ Cash\ Flow\ from\ Operations\ (CFfO) = Net\ Income + Depreciation + Amortization \qquad [10\text{-}59]$$

$$CFfO = 19{,}552{,}000 + 6{,}360{,}000 + 0 = \$25{,}912{,}000$$

TABLE CS 10-103 Operations $(000)'s

Net Income (Loss)	19,552
Depreciation	6,360
Amortization	0
Net Cash Flow from Operations	**25,912**

The next thing Ms. Debson addressed was the impact of changes in working capital on Year 6 cash flow. Since she didn't have any reason to change the assumptions associated with accounts receivable, inventory, accounts payable, and taxes she proceeded to calculate the Year 6 ending account balances using the 45-day and four-turns assumptions for accounts receivable/accounts payable and inventory respectively. As for taxes payable, they would be zero since she assumed all taxes were paid.

$$Accounts\ Receivable\ (AR) = (Annualized\ Net\ Revenues)\left(\frac{ARDOS}{360}\right) \quad [10\text{-}35]$$

$$Accounts\ Receivable = (120{,}000{,}000)\left(\frac{45}{360}\right) = \$15{,}000{,}000$$

$$Inventory = \frac{Annualized\ Cost\ of\ Goods\ Sold}{Inventory\ Turns} \quad [10\text{-}37]$$

$$Inventory = \frac{44{,}400{,}000}{4} = \$11{,}100{,}000$$

$$Accounts\ Payable\ (AP) = (Annualized\ Cost\ of\ Goods\ Sold)\left(\frac{APDOS}{360}\right) \quad [10\text{-}39]$$

$$Accounts\ Payable = (44{,}400{,}000)\left(\frac{45}{360}\right) = \$5{,}550{,}000$$

The impact of the changes in the Working Capital accounts is calculated by using year-end amounts for Years 5 and 6 and is tabulated in Table CS 10-104.

As can be seen from Table CS 10-104 the accounts receivable and inventory increased in Year 6, representing a use of cash. The accounts payable also increased, thus creating a source of cash.

TABLE CS 10-104 Working Capital Accounts $(000)'s

	Year 5	Year 6	Change
(Increase)/Decrease Accounts Receivable	10,000	15,000	(5,000)
(Increase)/Decrease Inventory	8,000	11,100	(3,100)
Increase/(Decrease) Accounts Payable	4,000	5,550	1,550
Increase/(Decrease) Taxes Payable	0	0	0
Net Change in Working Capital			**(6,550)**

Next Ms. Debson obtained the cash flow from operating activities ($25,912,000 – $6,550,000) by adding the results of Tables CS 10-103 and CS 10-104 (Equation [10-51]). (See Table CS 10-105.)

$$Cash\ Flow\ from\ Operating\ Activities\ (CFfOA) = Cash\ Flow\ from\ Operations \pm Net\ \Delta WC \qquad [10\text{-}51]$$

$$CFfOA = 25,912,000 - 6,550,000 = \$19,362,000$$

TABLE CS 10-105 Cash Flow from Operating Activities $(000)'s

Cash Flow from Operating Activities	19,362

Recall that with no additional expenditures on property, plant, and equipment, Year 6's D&A would have been the same as Year 5's, or $5 million. However, as can be seen from the Year 6 Income Statement, the depreciation for the year was $6.36 million. Ms. Debson reasoned that the additional D&A must be the consequence of additional purchases of PP&E, and if the life of the Year 6 purchases was 10 years, then the additional $1.36 million ($6,360,000 – $5,000,000) of depreciation must be the result of $13,600,000 spent on PP&E in Year 6. Recalling Equation [10-4]:

$$Depreciation = \frac{Total\ Cost\ of\ Assets}{Useful\ Life} \qquad [10\text{-}4]$$

Rearranging,

$$Total\ Cost\ of\ Assets = (Depreciation)\ (Useful\ Life) \qquad [10\text{-}65]$$

Substituting,

$$Total\ Cost\ of\ Assets = (1,360,000)(10) = \$13,600,000$$

The consequences of Year 6's investing activities are shown in Table CS 10-106.

TABLE CS 10-106 Investing Activities $(000)'s

Fixed Asset Additions	13,600

With the use of Equation [10-62], the cash flow after investing activities was calculated and tabulated in Table CS 10-107.

$$Cash\ Flow\ after\ Investing\ Activities\ (CFaIA) = CFfOA - Additions\ to\ Fixed\ Assets \qquad [10\text{-}62]$$

$$CFaIA = 19,362,000 - 13,600,000 = \$5,762,000$$

TABLE CS 10-107 Cash Flow after Investing Activities $(000)'s

Cash Flow after Investing Activities	**5,762**

With nearly $6,000,000 of cash flow after investing activities, Ms. Debson validated her assumptions about no additional borrowing or the sale of common stock in her Year 6 model. The result of all this was there would be no proceeds from financing activities (Table CS 10-108) and the cash flow after financing activities and the cash generated/(used) (Table CS 10-109) would be the same.[44]

$$CFaFA = CFaIA \pm \Delta STD \pm \Delta LTD \pm (Sale/Purchase\ of\ Common\ Stock) \quad [10\text{-}63]$$

$$CFaFA = 5{,}762{,}000 \pm 0 \pm 0 \pm 0 = \$5{,}762{,}000$$

$$CGU = CFaIA \pm \Delta STD \pm \Delta LTD \pm \Delta TSHE - Dividends\ Paid \quad [10\text{-}56]$$

$$CGU = 5{,}762{,}000 \pm 0 \pm 0 \pm 00 = \$5{,}762{,}000$$

TABLE CS 10-108 Financing Activities $(000)'s

	Year 4	Year 5	Year 6
Increase/(Decrease) Short-Term Debt	0	2,000	0
Net Proceeds (Payments) Long-Term Debt	12,000	0	0
Proceeds (Purchase) of Common Stock	0	0	0

TABLE CS 10-109 Cash Generated/(Used) $(000)'s

Cash Generated/(Used)	5,762

Recalling that the cash balance at the end of Year 5 was $1,940,000, the cash generated during Year 6 was combined with this opening balance to produce a cash balance at the end of Year 6 of $7,702,000 (Table CS 10-110).

$$Ending\ Cash\ Balance_{(Year\ 6)} = Beginning\ Cash\ Balance_{(Year\ 6)} \pm Cash\ Generated\ or\ Used_{(Year\ 6)} \quad [10\text{-}58]$$

$$Ending\ Cash\ Balance_{(Year\ 6)} = 1{,}940{,}000 + 5{,}762{,}000 = \$7{,}702{,}000$$

[44]Note the STD at the end of Year 5 only had 6 months to maturity. Table CS 10-108 assumes this loan will be extended as will be seen when the Balance Sheet is prepared in the following section.

TABLE CS 10-110 Cash Flow Proof $(000)'s

Beginning Cash Balance	1,940
Cash Generated/(Used)	5,762
Ending Cash Balance	7,702

Finally, by combining Tables CS 10-103–CS 10-110 she was able to construct the Year 6 Cash Flow Statement (Table CS 10-111).

Noting that the cash balance at the end of Year 6 was expected to be nearly $7,702,000 (6.4% of revenue), she concluded that this was in the 5–10% range and cash should not be a problem.

TABLE CS 10-111 Light Technologies Inc. Cash Flow Statement for Year 6 $(000)'s

Operating Activities	
Operations	
Net Income (Loss)	19,552
Depreciation	6,360
Amortization	0
Net Cash Flow from Operations	25,912
Working Capital Accounts	
(Increase)/Decrease Accounts Receivable	(5,000)
(Increase)/Decrease Inventory	(3,100)
Increase/(Decrease) Accounts Payable	1,550
Increase/(Decrease) Taxes Payable	0
Net Change in Working Capital	(6,550)
Cash Flow from Operating Activities	19,362
Investing Activities	
Fixed Asset Additions	(13,600)
Cash Flow after Investing Activities	5,762
Financing Activities	
Increase/(Decrease) Short-Term Debt	0
Net Proceeds (Payments) Long-Term Debt	0
Proceeds (Purchase) of Common Stock	0
Dividends Paid	0
Cash Generated/(Used)	5,762
Cash Flow Proof	
Beginning Cash Balance	1,940
Cash Generated/(Used)	5,762
Ending Cash Balance	7,702

While she had satisfied her concerns about LTI's cash flow, she decided in the interest of completeness to wrap up the exercise by producing the Year 6 Balance Sheet.

Year 6 Balance Sheet

Given the work that had been done producing the Year 6 Cash Flow Statement, Ms. Debson already had a fix on the current liabilities and long-term debt. In order to complete the liabilities + total shareholders' equity side of the Balance Sheet she needed to fill in the shareholders' equity piece. Since no additional equity had been raised during the year, the paid-in capital remained at $50 million. LTI's Year 6 net income was $19,552,000 and once again no dividends were paid. Therefore, retained earnings at the end of Year 6 would be $9,492,000.

$$Ret\ Earnings_{(End\ Year\ 6)} = RetEarnings_{(End\ Year\ 5)} \pm NI_{(Year\ 6)} - Dividends\ Paid_{(Year\ 6)} \quad [10\text{-}30]$$

$$RetEarnings_{(End\ Year\ 6)} = -10,060,000 + 19,552,000 - 0 = \$9,492,000$$

Total shareholders' equity is the sum of paid-in capital and retained earnings, as shown in Table CS 10-112.

$$Total\ Shareholders'\ Equity_{(End\ Year\ 6)} = Paid\text{-}in\ Capital_{(End\ Year\ 6)} + Retained\ Earnings_{(End\ Year\ 6)} \quad [10\text{-}27]$$

$$Total\ Shareholders'\ Equity_{(End\ Year\ 6)} = 50,000,000 + 9,492,000 = \$59,492,000$$

TABLE CS 10-112 Shareholders' Equity $(000)'s

Paid-in Capital	50,000
Retained Earnings	9,492
Total Shareholders' Equity	**59,492**

Earlier Ms. Debson calculated the accounts payable to be $5,550,000 and assumed all taxes would be paid so there wouldn't be any accrued balance in the Taxes Payable account. The LTD ($12,000,000) has several years to go before maturity so it didn't have to be addressed. She also assumed the STD ($2,000,000) would be rolled over for another year or more, and this would not present a problem, so the liabilities + total shareholders' equity side of the balance sheet would be as tabulated in Table CS 10-113.

$$Total\ Liabilities + TSHE = Current\ Liabilities + Long\text{-}Term\ Debt + Total\ Shareholders'\ Equity \quad [10\text{-}32]$$

$$Total\ Liabilities + TSHE = 7,550,000 + 12,000,000 + 59,492,000 = \$79,042,000$$

TABLE CS 10-113 Liabilities and Total Shareholders' Equity $(000)'s

Current Liabilities	
Accounts Payable	5,550
Taxes Payable	0
Short-Term Debt	2,000
Total Current Liabilities	7,550
Long-Term Debt	12,000
Total Liabilities	19,550
Shareholders' Equity	
Paid-in Capital	50,000
Retained Earnings	9,492
Total Shareholders' Equity	59,492
Total Liabilities + TSHE	79,042

Proceeding to the asset side of the balance sheet Ms. Debson once again noted there is no goodwill or other intangible assets on the books, nor was any purchased during Year 6. Therefore, the net intangible assets remain as they were at the end of Year 5. (See Table CS 10-114.)

TABLE CS 10-114 Intangible Assets $(000)'s

Goodwill and Other Intangible Assets	0
Less Accumulated Amortization	0
Net Intangible Assets	**0**

During Year 6, $13,600,000 of PP&E was purchased and $6,360,000 of depreciation was incurred; hence, the PP&E increases from $50,000,000 to $63,600,000 and the Year 5 accumulated depreciation ($12,000,000) increases by $6,360,000 to $18,360,000 (at the end of Year 6), leaving net fixed assets for Year 6 at $45,240,000. (See Table CS 10-115.)

$$\textit{Property, Plant, and Equipment at Cost}_{(EndYear\ 6)} = PP\&E@Cost_{(End\ Year\ 5)} + \Delta PP\&E@Cost_{(Year\ 6)} \quad [10\text{-}15]$$

$$\textit{Property, Plant, and Equipment at Cost}_{(EndYear\ 6)} = 50{,}000{,}000 + 13{,}600{,}000 = \$63{,}600{,}000$$

TABLE CS 10-115 Fixed Assets $(000)'s

Property, Plant, and Equipment at Cost	63,600
Less Accumulated Depreciation	(18,360)
Net Fixed Assets	**45,240**

$$Accumulated\ Depreciation_{(End\ Year\ 6)} = Accumulated\ Depreciation_{(End\ Year\ 5)} + Depreciation_{(Year\ 6)} \quad [10\text{-}16]$$

$$Accumulated\ Depreciation_{(End\ Year\ 6)} = 12{,}000{,}000 + 6{,}360{,}000 = \$18{,}360{,}000$$

$$Net\ Fixed\ Assets = Property,\ Plant,\ and\ Equipment\ at\ Cost - Accumulated\ Depreciation \quad [10\text{-}14]$$

$$Net\ Fixed\ Assets = 63{,}600{,}000 - 18{,}360{,}000 = \$45{,}240{,}000$$

To complete the asset side of the Balance Sheet, she worked with the basic requirement of any Balance Sheet whereby total assets must equal total liabilities + total shareholders' equity. The total liabilities + total shareholders' equity at the end of Year 6 is projected to be $79,042,000. With this information and the assistance of Equation [10-23], she calculated the value of the current assets.

$$Current\ Assets = Total\ Assets - Net\ Fixed\ Assets - Net\ Intangible\ Assets \quad [10\text{-}23]$$

$$Current\ Assets = 79{,}042{,}000 - 45{,}240{,}000 - 0 = \$33{,}802{,}000$$

Having determined the value of current assets, Ms. Debson was able to calculate the year-end cash balance by rearranging Equation [10-12].

$$Current\ Assets = Cash + Accounts\ Receivable + Inventory \quad [10\text{-}12]$$

$$Cash = Current\ Assets - Accounts\ Receivable - Inventory \quad [10\text{-}13]$$

Recalling that the accounts receivable and inventory were earlier calculated to be $15,000,000 and $11,100,000 respectively, the cash is calculated to be $7,702,000.

$$Cash = 33{,}802{,}000 - 15{,}000{,}000 - 11{,}100{,}000 = \$7{,}702{,}000$$

The asset side of the Balance Sheet (Table CS 10-116) is prepared by combining the cash, accounts receivable, and inventory amounts with the data from Tables CS 10-114 and CS 10-115.

Then by combining Tables CS 10-113, CS 10-114, CS 10-115, and CS 10-116 she completed the Year 6 Balance Sheet (Table CS 10-117), noting that the cash balance on the Balance Sheet was identical to that calculated earlier for the Cash Flow Statement.

TABLE CS 10-116 Total Assets $(000)'s

Current Assets	
Cash	7,702
Accounts Receivable	15,000
Inventory	11,100
Total Current Assets	33,802
Fixed Assets	
Property, Plant, and Equipment at Cost	63,600
Less Accumulated Depreciation	(18,360)
Net Fixed Assets	45,240
Intangible Assets	
Goodwill and Other Intangible Assets	0
Less Accumulated Amortization	0
Net Intangible Assets	0
Total Assets	79,042

TABLE CS 10-117 Light Technologies Inc. Balance Sheet for Year 6 $(000)'s

Current Assets		**Current Liabilities**	
Cash	7,702	Accounts Payable	5,550
Accounts Receivable	15,000	Taxes Payable	0
Inventory	11,100	Short-Term Debt	2,000
Total Current Assets	33,802	**Total Current Liabilities**	7,550
Fixed Assets		**Long-Term Debt**	12,000
Property, Plant, and Equipment at Cost	63,600		
Less Accumulated Depreciation	(18,360)	**Total Liabilities**	19,550
Net Fixed Assets	45,240		
Intangible Assets		**Shareholders' Equity**	
Goodwill and Other Intangible Assets	0	Paid-in Capital	50,000
Less Accumulated Amortization	0	Retained Earnings	9,492
Net Intangible Assets	0	**Total Shareholders' Equity**	59,492
Total Assets	79,042	**Total Liabilities + TSHE**	79,042

Conclusion

Satisfied with the results of her analysis of the LTI investment opportunity, Ms. Debson concluded she would like to own part of this Company and called the investment banker responsible for raising LTI's capital to express an interest in taking up to 5% of the $50,000,000 the Company was planning to raise.

APPENDIX A

Present Value Models

PRESENT VALUE OF ANY STREAM OF CASH FLOWS[1]

The present value of any stream of cash flows can be calculated by using Equation [A-1] or [A-2].

$$PV = \sum_{i=1}^{n} \frac{E_i}{(1+k)^i} \qquad \text{[A-1]}$$

$$PV = \frac{E_1}{(1+k)^1} + \frac{E_2}{(1+k)^2} + \frac{E_3}{(1+k)^3} + \cdots + \frac{E_n}{(1+k)^n} \qquad \text{[A-2]}$$

where:

PV = Present value

$\sum_{i=1}^{n}$ = Sum of the periodic cash flows out to year n in increments i

n = The last period for which cash flow is expected

E_i = Expected cash flow in the ith period in the future

k = Discount rate (usually the company's weighted average cost of capital adjusted for risk as appropriate)

i = The period (usually in years) in the future in which the prospective cash flow is expected to be received

This series of cash flows is depicted in Figure A-1.

[1] General references for this appendix are: T. E. Copeland and J. F. Watson, *Financial Theory and Corporate Policy* (Reading, MA: Addison-Wesley, 1979); J. F. Watson and E. F. Brigham, *Managerial Finance*, 6th ed. (Hinsdale, IL: Dryden Press, 1978); and A. Damodaran, *Damodaran on Valuation, Security Analysis for Investment and Corporate Finance* (New York: John Wiley & Sons, 1994).

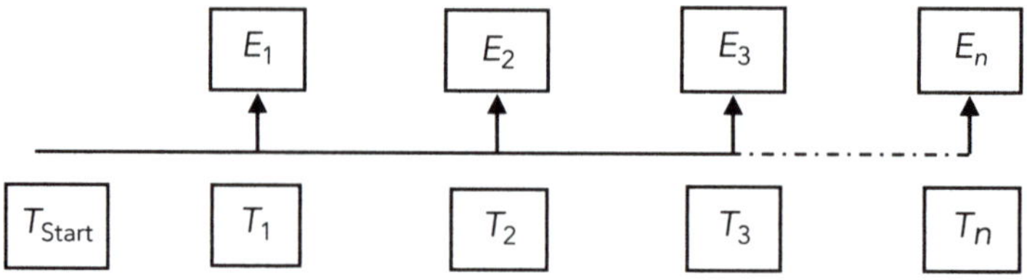

FIGURE A-1 Stream of Cash Flows

Equation [A-2] is the expanded form of Equation [A-1] and can be used in a wide variety of applications. However, since this is a book about value, it's important for the reader to understand the context in which they will be used. In this appendix the objective is to further develop and simplify the present value equations depicted by [A-1] and [A-2] so they can be used to estimate the value of cash flows during forecast and post-forecast periods.

Forecast Period Cash Flows

Business plans almost always have a set of pro-forma financial statements that represent management's best estimate of the financial consequences of the strategies and action plans that constitute the plan. Plans typically have financial statements that forecast three to five years out and it's the cash flows that eventuate during this period that are known as the *forecast period cash flows*.

Post–Forecast Period Cash Flows

Simply because a business plan doesn't forecast beyond some period of three to five years doesn't mean that cash flows end at that point. In most cases, the further out one goes to predict anything, the more the forecasts become less and less meaningful. Yet to value a business's cash flow stream beyond the forecast period requires some mechanism. This is accomplished by taking the present value equations in general form and imposing on them certain assumptions that result in expressions that depict and quantify post–forecast period cash flows for a variety of scenarios.

The simplest post-forecast model is an expression that calculates the present value of a single cash flow that takes place at some point n in the future.

PRESENT VALUE OF A CASH FLOW *E* THAT TAKES PLACE AT THE END OF YEAR *n*

In this case a single cash flow takes place at the end of year n. This means that the cash flows depicted in Equation [A-2] consist of a series of cash flows $E_1 = E_2 = E_3 = \dots E_{n-1} = 0$ and the only cash flow of interest is the final cash flow, as shown in Figure A-2.

$$PV = \frac{0}{(1+k)^1} + \frac{0}{(1+k)^2} + \frac{0}{(1+k)^3} + \cdots + \frac{0}{(1+k)^{n-1}} + \frac{E_n}{(1+k)^n} \qquad \text{[A-3]}$$

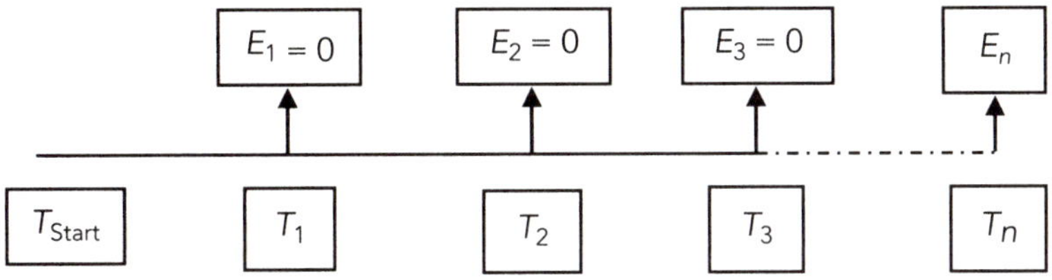

FIGURE A-2 Cash Flow *E* That Takes Place at End of Year *n*

Simplifying, Equation [A-3] becomes

$$PV = \frac{E_n}{(1+k)^n} \quad \text{[A-4]}$$

Equation [A-4], while simple, is not especially helpful in valuing post–forecast period cash flows. The reason is it's difficult to conceive of a business whose post–forecast period cash flow is simply a number with no rationale. However, [A-4] is useful when combined with a concept called *terminal value.*

PRESENT VALUE OF THE TERMINAL VALUE OF A CASH FLOW AT THE END OF YEAR *n*

Many cash flow valuation methodologies rely on a concept called terminal value. The Terminal Value Model assumes that the business is hypothetically sold at the end of the forecast period at market value. This doesn't mean the business is actually sold. It's simply a technique that ascribes value to the post–forecast period cash flows. Terminal values vary by industry, growth history and prospects, and attractiveness to potential buyers. There is a large body of knowledge that chronicles *Terminal Value Multipliers* (TVMs) for a wide variety of scenarios. Hence, if a willing buyer is prepared to pay eight times the most recent year's EBITDA (which is generally a surrogate for cash flow), then a business with $10 million of EBITDA in the last period of the forecasted cash flows would have a terminal value of $80 million.

This concept can be generalized by assigning E_{TY} to represent the last cash flow in a series of *n* cash flows and letting TVM represent the Terminal Value Multiplier that would be appropriate to value the *n*th cash flow. Then, multiplying E_{TY} by the TVM gives the terminal value in the terminal year TV_{TY} of the last cash flow and multiplying the E_{TY} by the expression $1/(1 + k)^n$ discounts the terminal value in the terminal year back to the present and is designated as the present value of the terminal value PV_{TVM}. In this way Equation [A-4] is easily modified to provide a useful expression that ascribes meaningful value to the last cash flow in a series. In Chapter 4, Equation [A-5] is referred to as the Terminal Value Model.

Terminal Value Model

$$PV_{TVM} = \frac{E_{TY}(TVM)}{(1+k)^N} = \frac{TV_{TY}}{(1+k)^N} \qquad \text{[A-5]}$$

PRESENT VALUE OF A STREAM OF FIXED CASH FLOWS *E* FOR *n* YEARS[2]

An annuity is a good example of a stream of fixed or constant cash flows and while this situation is seldom encountered in valuing a series of cash flows it is useful to develop an expression that simplifies the valuation of such a stream, as will be seen in the following section.

Refer to Figure A-3. For this model the cash flow in any given year is assumed to be the same as the cash flow in any other year. The result of this assumption is $E_1 = E_2 = E_3 = \ldots = E_n = E$ and Equation [A-2] becomes:

$$PV = \frac{E}{(1+k)^1} + \frac{E}{(1+k)^2} + \frac{E}{(1+k)^3} + \cdots + \frac{E}{(1+k)^n} \qquad \text{[A-6]}$$

The term $(1/(1 + k)$ makes Equation [A-6] a little awkward to work with. The algebra can be simplified by letting $u = 1/(1 + k)$ and substituting in Equation [A-6] to create Equation [A-7].

$$PV = uE + u^2E + u^3E + \cdots + u^nE \qquad \text{[A-7]}$$

Recalling that the objective is to get a simplified expression for a series of equal cash flows, Equation [A-7] is now manipulated to this end. The process starts by multiplying both sides of Equation [A-7] by u.

$$uPV = u(uE + u^2E + u^3E + \cdots + u^nE) = u^2E + u^3E + u^4E + \cdots + u^{n+1}E) \qquad \text{[A-8]}$$

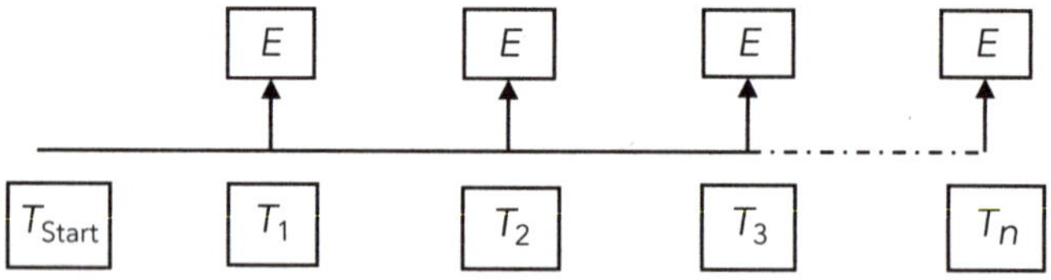

FIGURE A-3 Stream of Fixed Cash Flows *E* for *n* Years

[2] T. E. Copeland and J. F. Watson, *Financial Theory and Corporate Policy* (Reading, MA: Addison-Wesley, 1979), 523, Appendix A, "Constant Payment Annuities."

Next, in order to begin to eliminate some of the *u*'s, Equation [A-8] is subtracted from Equation [A-7].

$$PV - uPV = uE + u^2E + u^3E + \cdots + u^nE - u^2E - u^3E - \cdots - u^nE - u^{n+1}E) \qquad \text{[A-9]}$$

Careful inspection of the right-hand side of Equation [A-9] shows that all terms $u^3E \ldots u^nE$ cancel, leaving

$$PV - uPV = uE - u^{n+1}E \qquad \text{[A-10]}$$

Simplifying and rearranging,

$$PV(1 - u) = uE(1 - u^n) \qquad \text{[A-11]}$$

Dividing both sides of the equation by $(1 - u)$ creates an expression for PV in terms of u and E.

$$PV = \frac{uE(1-u^n)}{(1-u)} \qquad \text{[A-12]}$$

Recalling that $u = 1/(1 + k)$, substituting for u in Equation [A-12] and simplifying,

$$PV = \frac{\frac{E}{(1+k)}\left\{1-\left[\frac{1}{(1+k)}\right]^n\right\}}{\left[1-\frac{1}{(1+k)}\right]} = \frac{\frac{E}{(1+k)}[1-(1+k)^{-n}]}{\frac{(1+k-1)}{(1+k)}}$$

$$= \frac{\frac{E[1-(1+k)^{-n}]}{(1+k)}}{\frac{(k)}{(1+k)}} = \frac{E[1-(1+k)^{-n})}{(1+k)}\left[\frac{(1+k)}{k}\right] \qquad \text{[A-13]}$$

Finally, canceling like terms $(1 + k)$ in the last term in Equation [A-13] creates an expression that gives the present value of a "stream of finite fixed cash flows for *n* years."

$$PV = \frac{E[1-(1+k)^{-n}]}{k} \qquad \text{[A-14]}$$

In Chapter 4, Equation [A-14] is referred to as the Finite Fixed Model.[3]

[3]In finance texts this expression is also referred to as the "present value of an annuity."

Finite Fixed Model

$$PV_{FXM} = \frac{E_{FX}[1-(1+k)^{-NX}]}{k} \qquad \text{[A-14]}$$

where:

PV_{FXM} is the present value of the fixed cash flows E_{FX} that take place for NX periods

PRESENT VALUE OF A FIXED STREAM OF CASH FLOWS IN PERPETUITY (n = INFINITY)[4]

Earlier it was stated that a fixed or constant stream of cash flows is seldom encountered in valuation analysis and this is certainly true for the forecast period. However, when it comes to the post-forecast period this expression can be modified to be useful. There will be instances where a Terminal Value Multiplier is not available or appropriate to use for valuing post–forecast period cash flows. Rather than throw up one's hands or ignore the value these cash flows represent, it is sometimes helpful to ascribe value by assuming that some level of cash flow goes on forever. If the fixed stream of cash flows is expected to continue for a very long time (n = infinity), then in the limit the expression $(1 + k)^{-n}$ equals zero:

$$\lim_{n\to\infty}(1+k)^{-n} = \lim_{n\to\infty}\frac{1}{(1+k)^n} = \frac{1}{(1+k)^\infty} \to 0$$

and

$$\frac{E[1-(1+k)^{-n}]}{k}$$

becomes

$$\frac{E[1-0]}{k}$$

and

$$PV = \frac{E}{k} \qquad \text{[A-15]}$$

In Chapter 4, Equation [A-15] is referred to as the Perpetual Fixed Model.

Perpetual Fixed Model

$$PV_{PXM} = \frac{E_{PX}}{k} \qquad \text{[A-15]}$$

where:

PV_{PXM} is the present value of the fixed cash flows E_{PX} that take place for a very long time (infinity)

[4] T. E. Copeland and J. F. Watson, *Financial Theory and Corporate Policy* (Reading, MA: Addison-Wesley, 1979), 524, Appendix A, "Constant Payment Annuities."

TABLE A-1 Ratio of Equations [A-14] and [A-15]

k = 0.05		*k* = 0.10		*k* = 0.15		*k* = 0.20	
n years	Ratio of [A-14]/[A-15]	*n* years	Ratio of [A-14]/[A-15]	*n* years	Ratio of [A-14]/[A-15]	*n* years	Ratio of [A-14]/[A-15]
10	38.61%	10	61.45%	10	75.28%	10	83.85%
20	62.31%	20	85.14%	20	93.89%	20	97.39%
25	70.47%	25	90.77%	25	96.96%	25	98.95%
30	76.86%	30	94.27%	30	98.49%	30	99.58%
35	81.87%	35	96.44%	35	99.25%	35	99.83%
45	88.87%	45	98.63%	45	99.81%	45	99.97%
50	91.28%	50	99.15%	50	99.91%	50	99.99%
90	98.76%	90	99.98%	90	100.00%	90	100.00%
95	99.03%	95	99.99%	95	100.00%	95	100.00%
100	99.24%	100	99.99%	100	100.00%	100	100.00%

Requirements for *k* and *n*

Obviously, Equation [A-15] is simpler to use than Equation [A-14]. However, nothing goes on forever, so this gives rise to the question: "How large does *n* have to be before Equation [A-15] can be used without introducing significant error?" An answer is obtained by first running a large number of calculations for several *k*'s for various *n*'s in each of Equations [A-14] and [A-15]. The results are then compared as the ratio of [A-14]/[A-15]. The outcome of all of this is: The higher the *n*'s and *k*'s the closer the ratio of Equations [A-14] / [A-15] approaches 1, indicating that at that point Equations [A-14] and [A-15] give the same answer. Table A-1 tabulates these calculations and as can be seen the error introduced depends both on *k* and *n*, and if Equation [A-15] is used in the shaded area, the error introduced is less than 1%.

SINGLE-STAGE GROWTH MODELS

Single-stage growth models are used to value post–forecast period cash flows based on the assumption that the cash flows will grow in some defined way.

In the previous sections, models were developed to value the post-forecast cash flows by using a Terminal Value Multiplier or a Fixed (Constant) Stream of Cash Flows methodology. In reality, the TVM model is highly relevant and the fixed stream of cash flows less so. However, the fixed stream of cash flows can be made more useful by making some important assumptions. As will be seen, the price paid for this is that the subtleties underling the assumptions have to be kept in mind when the equations are applied. For this reason, in this section and those that follow, the important assumptions implicit in each model are summarized in a table and in the associated text to regularly remind the reader of their existence.

PRESENT VALUE OF A STREAM OF CASH FLOWS THAT GROW AT A FIXED RATE FOR A FINITE PERIOD[5]

One refinement to the Fixed (Constant) Stream of Cash Flows models (Equations [A-14] and [A-15]) is to assume that rather than remaining static the post-forecast period involves a series of cash flows that grow at some fixed rate for some finite period. For example, if it was reasonable to expect that the post-forecast cash flows would grow at a 5% rate and the beginning cash flow was 100, then the next would be 100*(1.05), followed by $100^*(1.05)^2$, and so forth.

Once again, Equation [A-2] is the starting point.

$$PV = \frac{E_1}{(1+k)^1} + \frac{E_2}{(1+k)^2} + \frac{E_3}{(1+k)^3} + \cdots + \frac{E_n}{(1+k)^n} \qquad \text{[A-2]}$$

In order to have a cash flow stream that grows at some fixed rate g it is necessary to have a starting cash flow that can grow at the fixed rate g. To deal with this, the starting cash flow is designated to be E_0.

The consequences of this assumption are that the cash flow at any time t is $E_1 = E_0(1 + g)^t$ as depicted in Figure A-4. If this cash flow took place just before period 1 starts, then the cash flow at the end of period 1 is $E_1 = E_0(1 + g)$, and E_1, E_2, E_3, ... expressed in terms of E_0 are:

$$E_1 = E_0(1 + g),\ E_2 = E_0(1 + g)^2,\ E_3 = E_0(1 + g)^3, \text{ etc.} \qquad \text{[A-16]}$$

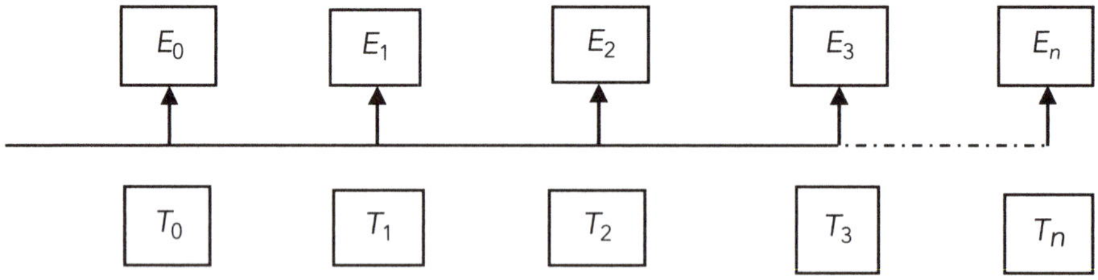

FIGURE A-4 Stream of Cash Flows That Grow at a Fixed Rate for a Finite Period

[5]T. E. Copeland and J. F. Watson, *Financial Theory and Corporate Policy* (Reading, MA: Addison-Wesley, 1979), 527, Appendix A, "Annuities with Growing Payments."

Using the results of Equation [A-16] and substituting for E_t in terms of E_0 and g, Equation [A-2] becomes:

$$PV = \frac{E_0(1+g)}{(1+k)^1} + \frac{E_0(1+g)^2}{(1+k)^2} + \frac{E_0(1+g)^3}{(1+k)^3} + \cdots + \frac{E_0(1+g)^n}{(1+k)^n} \quad \text{[A-17]}$$

Once again, in order to obtain the desired result, Equation [A-17] has to be algebraically manipulated. To do so, let $u = (1 + g)/(1 + k)$ and substitute in Equation [A-17]:

$$PV = uE_0 + u^2E_0 + u^3E_0 + \cdots + u^nE_0 \quad \text{[A-18]}$$

Factoring, Equation [A-18] becomes

$$PV = uE_0\,(1 + u + u^2 + \cdots + u^{n-1}) \quad \text{[A-19]}$$

Multiply both sides of Equation [A-19] by u:

$$uPV = u^2E_0(1 + u + u^2 + \cdots + u^{n-1}) \quad \text{[A-20]}$$

Now to simplify [A-20] it's necessary to get rid of some of the u's. As a first step, Equation [A-20] is subtracted from Equation [A-19]:

$$\begin{aligned} PV - uPV = {} & uE_0(1 + u + u^2 + \cdots + u^{(n-1)}) \\ & - u^2E_0(1 + u + u^2 + \cdots + u^{(n-1)}) \end{aligned} \quad \text{[A-21]}$$

Simplifying,

$$PV - uPV = uE_0(1 + u + u^2 + \cdots + u^{(n-1)}) - u^2E_0(1 + u + u^2 + \cdots + u^{(n-1)}) \quad \text{[A-22]}$$

$$PV(1 - u) = uE_0[(1 + u + u^2 + \cdots + u^{(n-1)}) - u(1 + u + u^2 + \cdots + u^{(n-1)}) \quad \text{[A-23]}$$

$$PV(1 - u) = uE_0[(1 + u + u^2 + \cdots + u^{(n-1)} - u - u^2 - u^3 - \cdots - u^n) \quad \text{[A-24]}$$

All u terms on the right-hand side of Equation [A-24] cancel out except u^n and the u associated with E_0. Therefore, [A-24] becomes:

$$PV(1 - u) = uE_0(1 - u^n) \quad \text{[A-25]}$$

Dividing both sides by the term $(1 - u)$ gives an expression for the present value PV in terms of E_0 and u.

$$PV = \frac{uE_0(1-u^n)}{(1-u)} \quad \text{[A-26]}$$

Recalling that $u = \frac{(1+g)}{(1+k)}$ and substituting for u in Equation [A-26], forming a common denominator and simplifying gives

$$PV = \frac{\frac{E_0(1+g)}{(1+k)}\left\{1-\left[\frac{(1+g)}{(1+k)}\right]^n\right\}}{\left[1-\frac{(1+g)}{(1+k)}\right]}$$

$$= \frac{\frac{E_0(1+g)\left\{1-\left[\frac{(1+g)}{(1+k)}\right]^n\right\}}{(1+k)}}{\frac{(1+k-1-g)}{(1+k)}}$$

$$= \frac{\frac{E_0(1+g)\left\{1-\left[\frac{(1+g)}{(1+k)}\right]^n\right\}}{(1+k)}}{\frac{(k-g)}{(1+k)}} \qquad \text{[A-27]}$$

Canceling the term (1 + k) from the numerator and denominator of [A-27], [A-27] becomes

$$PV = \frac{E_0(1+g)\left\{1-\left[\frac{(1+g)}{(1+k)}\right]^n\right\}}{(k-g)} \qquad \text{[A-28]}$$

But earlier it was said that $E_0(1 + g) = E_1$, which is the first cash flow that takes place after E_0, which may be the last cash flow that takes place during the forecast period. Substituting in Equation [A-28] and simplifying, an expression for the present value of a cash flow stream that grows at a fixed rate g for finite period n is obtained. It's important to note that g must be less than k ($g < k$); otherwise, the result is nonsensical. Also, Equation [A-29] present values the cash flow stream represented in Table Figure A-4 to time T_0, which was when E_0 occurred.

$$PV = \frac{E_1\left[1-\left(\frac{1+g}{1+k}\right)^n\right]}{(k-g)} \qquad \text{[A-29]}$$

In Chapter 4, Equation [A-29] is referred to as the Finite Growth Model.

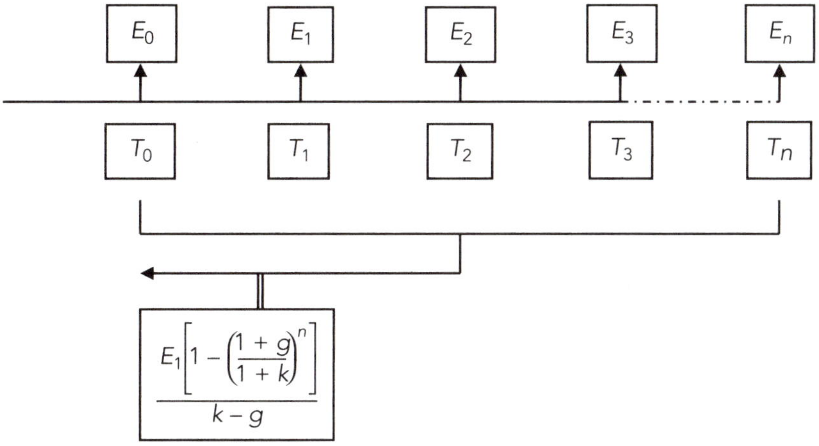

FIGURE A-5 Finite Growth Model

Finite Growth Model

$$PV_{FGM} = \frac{E_{FG}\left[1 - \left(\frac{1+g_{FG}}{1+k}\right)^{NG}\right]}{(k - g_{FG})} \qquad \text{[A-29]}$$

where:

PV_{FGM} is the present value of the cash flow E_{FG} (that takes place after the last forecasted cash flow) that grows at a fixed (constant) rate g_{FG} for a finite number of periods $_{NG}$

Equation [A-29] is a special equation and was derived based on a very important assumption. When applying it, it's important to remember that it gives the present value of a cash flow stream that had cash flow E_0 just prior to commencement of period 1 and the cash flow at the end of period 1 is given by $E_1 = E_0(1 + g)$. This concept is portrayed pictorially in Figure A-5. The assumptions are summarized in Table A-2.

TABLE A-2 Finite Growth Model Assumptions

Present Value of a Finite Cash Flow Stream That Grows at a Fixed Rate g_{PG} for *NG* Periods
Cash flow E_0 took place just prior to the commencement of the first period in the cash flow stream being evaluated.
The first cash flow in the stream of cash flows is E_1. It occurs at the end of period 1 at time T_1 and is quantified by the expression $E_1 = E_0(1 + g_{FG})$.
Like E_1, all subsequent cash flows also grow at a fixed rate g_{FG}, albeit compounded.
The last cash flow is E_n at time T_n.
The cash flow stream is *NG* periods long.
g_{FG} must be less than k; otherwise, the result is nonsensical.
All periods are usually expressed in years.

PRESENT VALUE OF A STREAM OF CASH FLOWS THAT GROW AT A FIXED RATE IN PERPETUITY[6]

Mathematically Equation [A-29] can be simplified for the special case when $g < k$ and n is large, by applying limits. An investigation of what this involves is of interest because there are companies that grow at modest rates for extended periods of time.

$$PV = \frac{E_1\left[1 - \left(\frac{1+g}{1+k}\right)^n\right]}{(k-g)} \quad \text{[A-29]}$$

In the limit, the expression $\left(\frac{1+g}{1+k}\right)^n = \lim_{n\to\infty}\left(\frac{1+g}{1+k}\right)^n = \lim_{n\to\infty}\frac{(1+g)^n}{(1+k)^n} \to 0$ and Equation [A-29] becomes [A-30].[7]

$$PV = \frac{E_1}{k-g} \quad \text{[A-30]}$$

In Chapter 4, Equation [A-30] is referred to as the Perpetual Growth Model.

Perpetual Growth Model

$$PV_{PGM} = \frac{E_{PG}}{k - g_{PG}} \quad \text{[A-30]}$$

where:

PV_{PGM} is the present value of the cash flow E_{PG} that takes place after the last forecasted cash flow E_0 and is equal to $E_0(1 + g_{PG})$ and grows at a fixed (constant) rate g_{PG} in perpetuity

At first glance, Equation [A-30] may not appear to be useful. However, this is not the case. There are many examples of companies that grow at some modest rate (which often is similar to the growth of the economy as measured by Gross National Product) with only spurts of higher growth driven by some innovation. So if there aren't any innovations on the drawing board that will drive a period of higher growth during the post-forecast period, then it may be perfectly logical to characterize the post–forecast cash flows as being slow "organic" growth for valuation purposes. When this is the scenario and the period of organic growth is large, then Equation [A-30] may be a perfectly valid model. However, as will be seen, it can be more useful when refined a little further.

---

[6] T. E. Copeland and J. F. Watson, *Financial Theory and Corporate Policy* (Reading, MA: Addison-Wesley, 1979), 528, Appendix A, "Annuities with Growing Payments."

[7] Remember when applying Equation [A-30], that g must be less than k. Otherwise, the equation gives meaningless answers. For example, if $g = k$, then the result is indeterminate, and if $g > k$, the result is negative.

GENERAL EQUATION FOR PRESENT VALUE OF SINGLE-STAGE CASH FLOWS THAT GROW AT A FIXED RATE

Equation [A-29] is satisfactory for some applications and, as will be seen, not so satisfactory for others. For example, if an investor wants to calculate the present value of a dividend on a stock that the investor is planning to purchase that will in the investor's judgment grow at some fixed rate for a period of time, then Equation [A-29] will be helpful since the investor is only concerned with the cash flows expected after the purchase of the stock.

On the other hand, if someone is trying to evaluate the present value of a stream of cash flows (like in a business) where the first cash flow E is followed by a stream of cash flows that are assumed to grow at a fixed rate g, Equation [A-29] doesn't quite do the job because it ignores the first cash flow.

A more general equation that gets around this problem and takes into account all of the cash flows can be derived by introducing a term to take care of the first cash flow and modifying Equation [A-29] so that its reference point is the beginning of the cash flow stream. The assumptions for the single-stage growth model are contained in Table A-3. The reader may find it helpful to refer to Figure A-6 during the following discussion.

Consider Period 0 Since E_0 is the first cash flow and it occurs at T_0, then the present value of E_0 at T_{Start} is $PV_{E_0 @ T_{Start}}$ and is obtained by multiplying the cash flow E_0 by the discounting term $[1/(1+k)]$. Hence:

$$PV_{E_0 @ T_{Start}} = \frac{E_0}{1+k} \qquad \text{[A-31]}$$

Next Consider Period A The first cash flow during period A is E_1 at T_1, one period after E_0, and is followed by a series of cash flows $E \ldots E_n$. Other than the terminology, this is identical to the situation encountered when the Finite Fixed Growth Model Equation [A-29] was developed except the period is now N_A in place of n. Therefore [A-29] becomes

$$PV = \frac{E_1\left[1-\left(\frac{1+g_A}{1+k}\right)^{N_A}\right]}{k-g} \qquad \text{[A-29]}$$

TABLE A-3 Single-Stage Growth Model Assumptions

Period 0	This period consists of a single period ending with cash flow E_0 at time T_0.
Period A	This period consists of N_A periods and begins immediately after cash flow E_0 has taken place. The first cash flow during this period is E_1 at time T_1. The last cash flow during this period is E_n at time T_n.
Duration	All periods constituting periods 0 and A are of equal length and usually expressed in years.

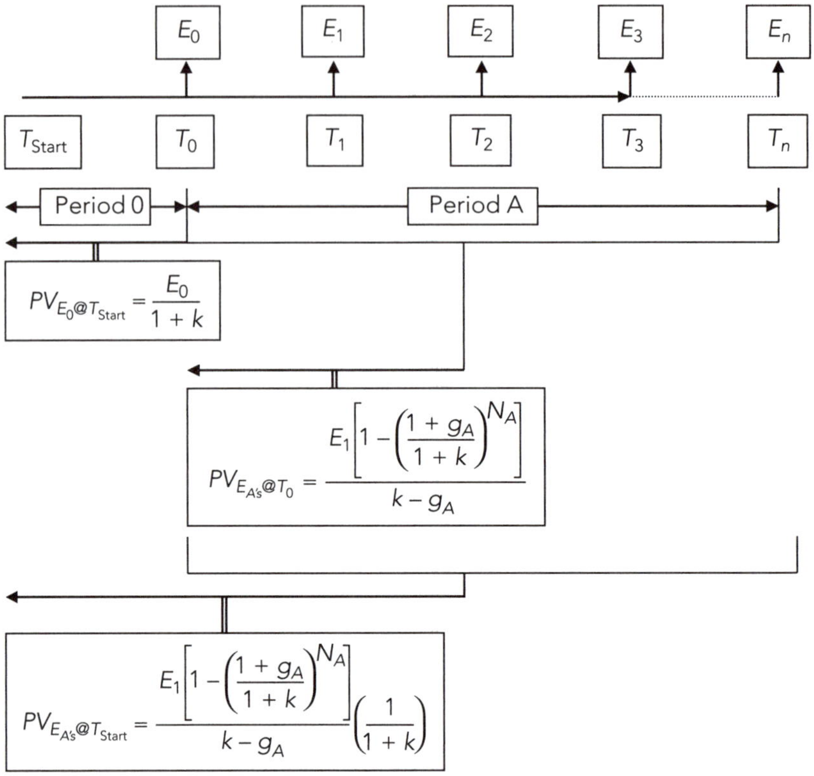

FIGURE A-6 Single-Stage Growth Model

and calculates the present value of cash flows $E_1 \ldots E_n$ at time T_0 that take place during the N_A periods of period A. The present value of this expression at time T_{Start}, is obtained by multiplying Equation [A-29] by the discounting factor $1/(1+k)$. Therefore, the present value of [A-29] at T_{Start} is $PV_{E_{A's} @ T_{Start}}$ and is given by Equation [A-32][8]:

$$PV_{E_{A's} @ T_{Start}} = \frac{E_1\left[1-\left(\frac{1+g_A}{1+k}\right)^{N_A}\right]}{k-g_A}\left(\frac{1}{1+k}\right) \qquad \text{[A-32]}$$

Simplifying,

$$PV_{E_{A's} @ T_{Start}} = \frac{E_1\left[1-\left(\frac{1+g_A}{1+k}\right)^{N_A}\right]}{(k-g_A)(1+k)} \qquad \text{[A-33]}$$

[8] Assuming that T_{Start} occurs one period before E_0.

As can be seen from Figure A-6, the present value of all of the cash flows is the sum of the present value of each component of the cash flows. Therefore, $PV_{(E_0+E_{A's})}$, the present value of the cash flows for periods 0 and A, present valued to time T_{Start} is

$$PV_{(E_0+E_{A's})} = PV_{E_0@T_{Start}} + PV_{E_{A's}@T_{Start}} \qquad \text{[A-34]}$$

Substituting the results of Equations [A-31] and [A-33] into Equation [A-34] yields Equation [A-35]:

$$PV_{(E_0+E_{A's})} = \frac{E_0}{1+k} + \frac{E_1\left[1-\left(\frac{1+g_A}{1+k}\right)^{N_A}\right]}{(k-g_A)(1+k)} \qquad \text{[A-35]}$$

By definition, $E_1 = E_0(1 + g_A)$. Substituting, Equation [A-35] becomes

$$PV_{(E_0+E_{A's})} = \frac{E_0}{1+k} + \frac{E_0(1+g_A)\left[1-\left(\frac{1+g_A}{1+k}\right)^{N_A}\right]}{(k-g_A)(1+k)} \qquad \text{[A-36]}$$

Now by referring to Figure A-6 the following can be noted:

- There are n periods.
- The first cash flow in period A is E_1 and it starts one period after E_0; hence, N_A actually consists of $n - 1$ periods and $N_A = n - 1$.
- E_0 is simply the first cash flow and it can be referred to as E.
- g_A is the growth of the cash flows after the first period and can be referred to as g.

Finally, the general Equation [A-37] is obtained by substituting E for E_0, $n - 1$ for N_A, and g for g_A in Equation [A-36]:

$$PV_{(E_0+E_{A's})} = \frac{E}{1+k} + \frac{E(1+g)\left[1-\left(\frac{1+g}{1+k}\right)^{(n-1)}\right]}{(k-g)(1+k)} \qquad \text{[A-37]}^9$$

where:

$PV_{(E_0+E_{A's})}$ is the present value PV of a stream of cash flows beginning with an initial cash flow E that grows thereafter at a fixed rate g for $N_A = (n - 1)$ periods

[9] Equation [A-37] can be further simplified. It is left in this form since the contribution made by each period and term in the equation to the present value being calculated is a little more obvious.

Special Case

Like Equation [A-29], Equation [A-37] can be simplified for the special case when $g < k$ and n is large, by applying limits.

In the limit, $\lim_{n \to \infty} \left(\frac{1+g}{1+k}\right)^{(n,1)} \longrightarrow 0$ the term $\left[1-\left(\frac{1+g}{1+k}\right)^{(n-1)}\right] = [1-(0)]$ and Equation [A-37] becomes

$$PV_{(E_0+E_{A's})} = \frac{E}{1+k} + \frac{E(1+g)[1-0]}{(k-g)(1+k)} \qquad \text{[A-38]}$$

Simplifying,

$$PV = \frac{E}{1+k} + \frac{E(1+g)}{(k-g)(1+k)} \qquad \text{[A-39]}^{10}$$

Factoring,

$$PV = \left(\frac{E}{1+k}\right)\left[1+\left(\frac{1+g}{(k-g)}\right)\right] \qquad \text{[A-40]}$$

Equation [A-40] can be further simplified by letting $1 = \frac{k-g}{k-g}$ and forming a common denominator.

$$PV = \left(\frac{E}{1+k}\right)\left[\left(\frac{k-g}{k-g}\right)+\left(\frac{1+g}{k-g}\right)\right] = \left(\frac{E}{1+k}\right)\left(\frac{k-g+1+g}{k-g}\right) = \left(\frac{E}{1+k}\right)\left(\frac{1+k}{k-g}\right) \qquad \text{[A-41]}$$

Finally,

$$PV = \frac{E}{k-g} \qquad \text{[A-42]}$$

which is identical to the expression obtained when Equation [A-29] was simplified for the special case when $g < k$ and n is large.

MULTISTAGE GROWTH MODELS

The single-stage growth models are suitable for a wide variety of valuation purposes. However, there are instances where they may not be adequate. For example, an aircraft manufacturer may have a business model that starts with a next-generation aircraft that is a game-changer and for a period of time the airlines rush to change out their fleet. This is followed by a period of slower sales where aircraft orders are driven by obsolescence and growth in air travel. Instances like this can be addressed with multistage growth models.

[10] Again note that Equations [A-37] and [A-39] require that $g < k$.

TWO-STAGE GROWTH MODELS

The simplest multistage growth model is the two-stage model. Essentially, it consists of a series of cash flows that take place during the first period (A) for a finite number of periods, followed by a second stream of cash flows (B) that can be perpetual or finite.

Present Value of a Cash Flow Stream That Grows at a Fixed Rate g_A for N_A Periods and Thereafter at a Fixed Rate g_B

An expression that accommodates two different growth rates can be derived by utilizing the principles developed in the previous section. Table A-4 summarizes the assumptions. Figure A-7 pictorially illustrates the components of the two-stage growth model.

Period 0 The first cash flow E_0 takes place at time T_0. This is identical to the situation encountered previously where an expression was developed for the present value of a cash flow stream growing at a fixed rate g and the present value of E_0 at time E_{Start} is $PV_{E_0@T_{Start}}$. Therefore, the first term in the two-stage growth model is:

$$PV_{E_0@T_{Start}} = \frac{E_0}{1+k} \qquad \text{[A-31]}$$

Period A Just as in the single-stage growth model, the cash flow during period A begins with E_1, which had cash flow E_0 just prior to commencement. If $g = g_A$, the growth during period A, and N_A is the number of periods during period A, then $PV_{E_{A's}@T_0}$, the present value of the cash flow stream during period A at time T_0, is again given by the Finite Growth Model, Equation [A-29]:

$$PV_{E_{A's}@T_0} = \frac{E_1\left[1-\left(\dfrac{1+g_A}{1+k}\right)^{N_A}\right]}{(k-g_A)} \qquad \text{[A-29]}$$

TABLE A-4 Two-Stage Growth Model Assumptions

Period 0	This period consists of a single period ending with cash flow E_0 at time T_0.
Period A	Period A consists of N_A periods and begins immediately after cash flow E_0 has taken place. The first cash flow during this period is E_1 at time T_1. The last cash flow during this period is E_{N_A} at time T_{N_A}. The growth rate during this period is g_A.
Period B	This period consists of a very large (infinite) number of periods N_B and begins immediately after cash flow E_{N_A} has taken place. The first cash flow during this period is $E_{(N_A+1)}$ at time $T_{(N_A+1)}$. The last cash flow during this period is E_n at time T_n. The growth rate during this period is g_B.
Duration	All periods constituting periods A and B are of equal length and usually expressed in years.

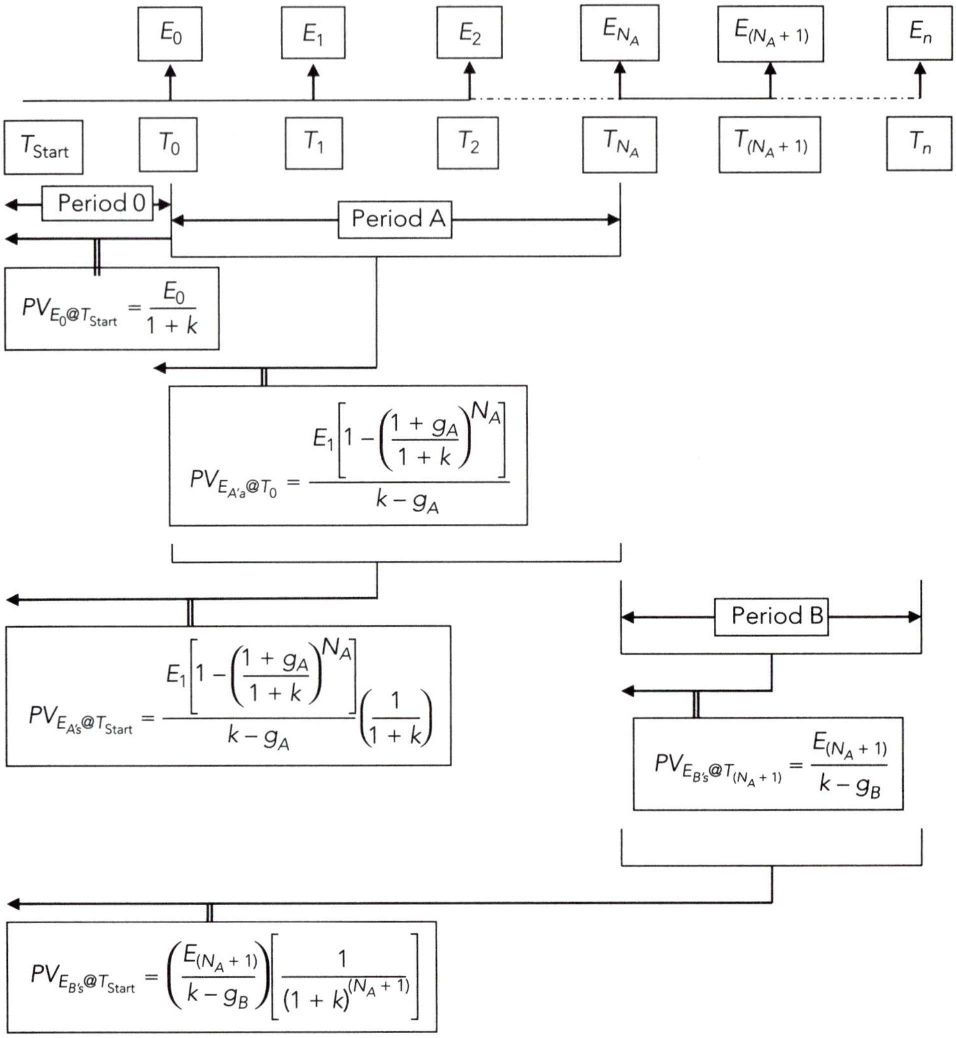

FIGURE A-7 Two-Stage Growth Model

And by reasoning identical to that used to develop Equation [A-32], the $PV_{E_{A's}@T_{Start}}$ is:

$$PV_{E_{A's}@T_{Start}} = \frac{E_1\left[1-\left(\frac{1+g_A}{1+k}\right)^{N_A}\right]}{(k-g_A)}\left(\frac{1}{1+k}\right) \qquad \text{[A-32]}$$

Simplifying,

$$PV_{E_{A's}@T_{Start}} = \frac{E_1\left[1-\left(\frac{1+g_A}{1+k}\right)^{N_A}\right]}{(k-g_A)(1+k)} \qquad \text{[A-33]}$$

Period B After period A, the cash flows grow at a fixed rate g_B throughout period B, which in this case continues forever. This is identical to the situation described by the Perpetual Growth Model, Equation [A-30],[11] except that the first cash flow during period B is $E_{(N_A+1)}$ and occurs one period after E_{N_A}. Therefore, the present value of the cash flows during period B at time T_{N_A} is:

$$PV_{E_{B's}@T_{N_A}} = \frac{E_{(N_A+1)}}{k-g_B} \quad \text{[A-43]}$$

Now E_{N_A} occurs (N_A + 1) periods after T_{Start}. To bring the value of the cash flows during period B back to T_{Start}, Equation [A-43] needs to be multiplied by the expression $1/(1+k)^{(N_A+1)}$. Therefore, $PV_{E_{B's}@T_{Start}}$, the cash flows that take place during period B, present valued to time T_{Start} is:

$$PV_{E_{B's}@T_{Start}} = \frac{E_{(N_A+1)}}{k-g_B}\left[\frac{1}{(1+k)^{(N_A+1)}}\right] \quad \text{[A-44]}$$

Simplifying,

$$PV_{E_{B's}@T_{Start}} = \frac{E_{(N_A+1)}}{(k-g_B)(1+k)^{(N_A+1)}} \quad \text{[A-45]}$$

Present Value of the Two-Stage Cash Flows

Now an expression for the present value of all of the two-stage-growth cash flows can be derived. As can be seen from Figure A-7, the present value of the cash flows is the sum of the present value of each component of the cash flows. Therefore, $PV_{(E_0+E_{A's}+E_{B's})}$, the present value of the cash flows for periods 0, A, and B, present valued to time T_{Start} is:

$$PV_{(E_0+E_{A's}+E_{B's})} = PV_{E_0@T_{Start}} + PV_{E_A@T_{Start}} + PV_{E_B@T_{Start}} \quad \text{[A-46]}$$

Next, use the results of Equations [A-31], [A-33], and [A-45] to substitute for $PV_{E_0@T_{Start}}$, $PV_{E_A@T_{Start}}$, and $PV_{E_B@T_{Start}}$ respectively in Equation [A-46].

$$PV_{(E_0+E_{A's}+E_{B's})} = \frac{E_0}{(1+k)} + \frac{E_1\left[1-\left(\frac{1+g_A}{1+k}\right)^{N_A}\right]}{(k-g_A)(1+k)} + \left[\frac{E_{(N_A+1)}}{(k-g_A)(1+k)^{(N_A+1)}}\right] \quad \text{[A-47]}$$

[11] See the Special Case, "Present Value of a Cash Flow Stream when $g<k$ and n Is Large," presented earlier in this appendix.

General Equation for the Present Value of Two-Stage Cash Flows That Grow at a Fixed Rate g_A for N_A Periods and Thereafter at a Fixed Rate g_B

Equation [A-47] is somewhat awkward since it is expressed in terms of E_0, E_1, and $E_{(N_A+1)}$. By definition:

$$E_1 = E_0(1+g_A) \qquad \text{[A-48]}$$

and

$$E_{(N_A+1)} = E_{N_A}(1+g_B) \qquad \text{[A-49]}$$

and

$$E_{N_A} = E_0(1+g_A)^{N_A} \qquad \text{[A-50]}$$

Therefore,

$$E_{(N_A+1)} = E_0(1+g_A)^{N_A}(1+g_B) \qquad \text{[A-51]}$$

Equation [A-52] is obtained by substituting Equations [A-48] and [A-51] for E_1 and $E_{(N_A+1)}$ respectively into Equation [A-47].

$$PV_{(E_0+E_{A's}+E_{B's})} = \frac{E_0}{(1+k)} + \frac{E_0(1+g_A)\left[1-\left(\frac{1+g_A}{1+k}\right)^{N_A}\right]}{(k-g_A)(1+k)} + \frac{E_0(1+g_A)^{N_A}(1+g_B)}{(k-g_B)(1+k)^{(N_A+1)}} \qquad \text{[A-52]}$$

Finally, if $E_0 = E$, the first cash flow in a stream that grows at a fixed rate g_A during Period A and at fixed rate g_B thereafter, then Equation [A-52] becomes:

$$PV_{(E_0+E_{A's}+E_{B's})} = \frac{E}{(1+k)} + \frac{E(1+g_A)\left[1-\left(\frac{1+g_A}{1+k}\right)^{N_A}\right]}{(k-g_A)(1+k)} + \frac{E(1+g_A)^{N_A}(1+g_B)}{(k-g_B)(1+k)^{(N_A+1)}} \qquad \text{[A-53]}[12]$$

THREE-STAGE GROWTH MODELS

The three-stage model is a two-stage model with a third period of growth (C) taking place after the second stage (B). Like the period B cash flows, period (C) can be either finite or perpetual. In practice, the cash flows that take place during period (C) may add little to the present value calculation even if period C has a long duration.

[12] Like Equation [A-37], Equation [A-53] can be further simplified. However, by leaving it in this form the contribution made by each period and term in the equation to the present value being calculated is a little more obvious.

Present Value of a Cash Flow Stream That Grows at a Fixed Rate g_A for N_A Periods, Fixed Rate g_B for N_B Periods, and Thereafter at a Fixed Rate g_C

Figure A-8 shows what a three-stage growth model can look like. The assumptions associated with this model are summarized in Table A-5.

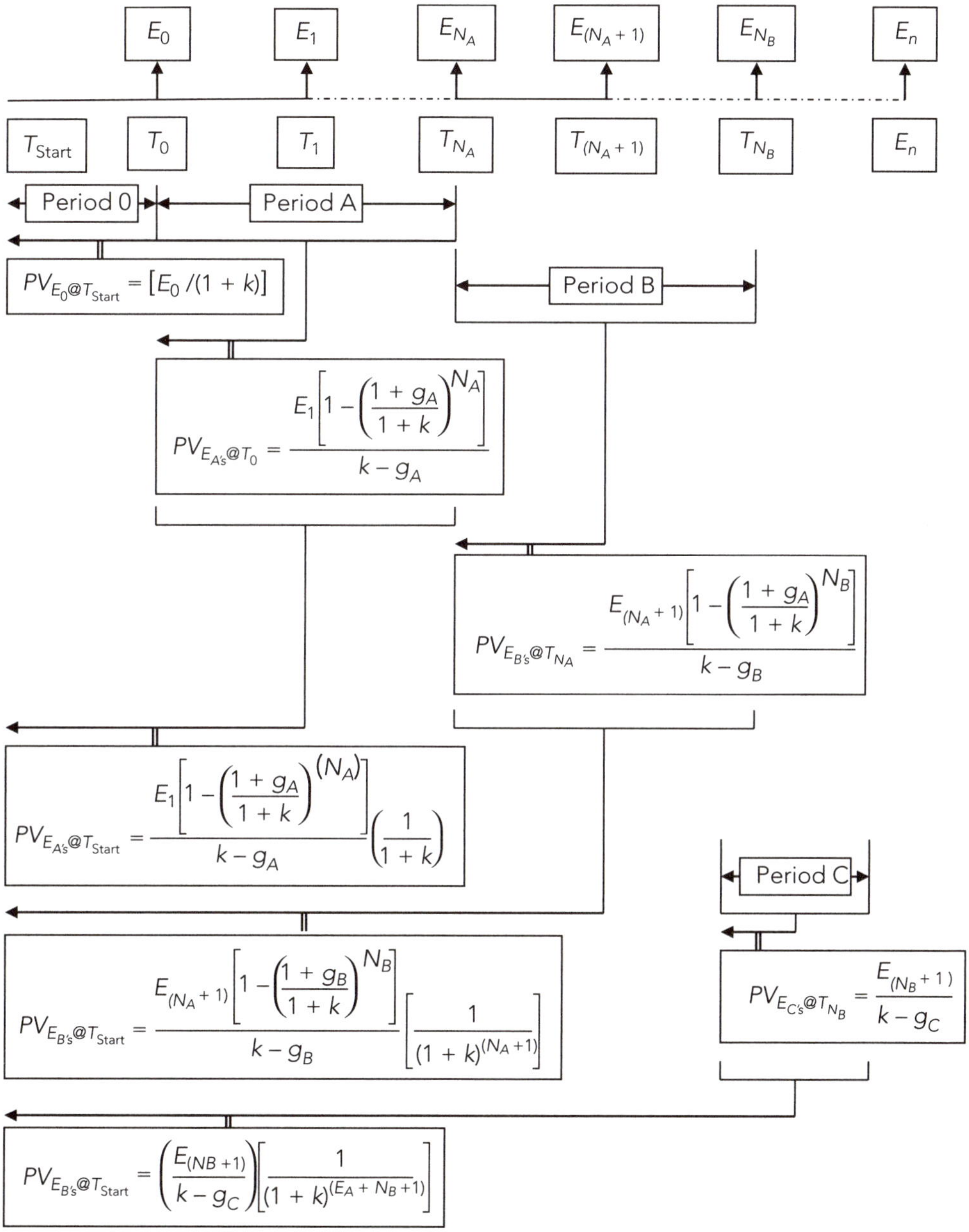

FIGURE A-8 Three-Stage Growth Model

TABLE A-5 Three-Stage Growth Model Assumptions

Period 0	This period consists of a single period ending with cash flow E_0 at time T_0.
Period A	This period consists of N_A periods and begins immediately after cash flow E_0 has taken place. The first cash flow during this period is E_1 at time T_1. The last cash flow during this period is E_{N_A} at time T_{N_A}.
Period B	This period consists of N_B periods and begins immediately after cash flow E_{N_A} has taken place. The first cash flow during this period is $E_{(N_A+1)}$ at time $T_{(N_A+1)}$. The last cash flow during this period is E_{N_B} at time T_{N_B}.
Period C	This period consists of a very large (infinite) number of periods N_C and begins immediately after cash flow E_B has taken place at time T_B. The first cash flow during this period is $E_{(N_B+1)}$ at time $T_{(N_B+1)}$ and grows forever.
Duration	All periods constituting periods 0, A, B, and C are of equal length and usually expressed in years.

The derivation of equations for the three-stage growth model is going to be approached a little differently than what was the case for other multistage models. Reference to the single- and two-stage models will show that in order to develop general equations it was ultimately necessary to express all cash flows in terms of E_0 and this was done at the end of each model. As will be seen, by expressing cash flows in terms of E_0 at the outset, developing the general equation becomes much simpler.

First Consider Period 0 As with the earlier examples, the first cash flow E_0 takes place at time T_0. The present value of this cash flow at time T_{Start} is given by Equation [A-31].

$$PV_{E_0@T_{Start}} = \frac{E_0}{1+k} \qquad \text{[A-31]}^{13}$$

Next Consider Period A[14] The first cash flow during period A is E_0 at time T_1. If period A is N_A periods long, then the present value of the cash flows that take place during period A at time T_0 is given by Finite Growth Model, Equation [A-29].

$$PV_{E_{A's}@T_0} = \frac{E_1\left[1-\left(\dfrac{1+g_A}{1+k}\right)^{N_A}\right]}{(k-g_A)} \qquad \text{[A-29]}^{15}$$

[13]See "General Equation for the Present Value of a Cash Flow Stream That Grows at a Fixed Rate g."
[14]The conditions encountered in this period are identical to those encountered in the comparable periods in the single-stage and two-stage growth models. The rationale and equations are repeated here.
[15]Refer to: "Two-Stage Growth Model," "Present Value of a Cash Flow Stream That Grows at a Fixed Rate g_A for N_A Periods and Thereafter at a Fixed Rate g_B."

And the present value of the cash flows during period A at time T_{Start} is obtained by multiplying Equation [A-29] by the term [1/(1 + k)] and simplifying, just as was done to derive Equation [A-33].

$$PV_{E_{A's}@T_{Start}} = \frac{E_1\left[1-\left(\frac{1+g_A}{1+k}\right)^{N_A}\right]}{(k-g_A)}\left(\frac{1}{1+k}\right) \qquad \text{[A-33]}$$

Equation [A-54] is obtained by substituting $E_1 = E_0\,(1 + g_A)$ in Equation [A-33] and simplifying.

$$PV_{E_{A's}@T_{Start}} = \frac{E_0(1+g_A)\left[1-\left(\frac{1+g_A}{1+k}\right)^{N_A}\right]}{(k-g_A)(1+k)} \qquad \text{[A-54]}$$

Period B Since the cash flows during period B grow at a fixed rate g_B for N_B periods with the first cash flow $E_{(N_A+1)}$ taking place at time $T_{(N_A+1)}$, the present value of the cash flows $PV_{E_{B's}@T_{N_A}}$ that take place during period B at time T_{N_A} is once again obtained by applying the Finite Growth Model, Equation [A-29]:

$$PV_{E_{B's}@T_{N_A}} = \frac{E_{(N_A+1)}\left[1-\left(\frac{1+g_B}{1+k}\right)^{N_B}\right]}{k-g_B} \qquad \text{[A-55]}$$

The objective for period B is to develop an expression that states the present value of Equation [A-55] at time T_{Start}. Reference to Figure A-8 shows that T_{N_A} occurs (N_A + 1) periods after T_{Start}. Therefore, $PV_{E_{B's}@T_{Start}}$, the present value of the cash flows during period B at time T_{Start}, is obtained by multiplying Equation [A-55] by the term $\left[1/(1+k)^{(N_A+1)}\right]$.[16]

$$PV_{E_{B's}@T_{Start}} = \frac{E_{(N_A+1)}\left[1-\left(\frac{1+g_B}{1+k}\right)^{N_B}\right]}{k-g_B}\left[\frac{1}{(1+k)^{(N_A+1)}}\right] \qquad \text{[A-56]}$$

Now recall Equation [A-51]:

$$E_{(N_A+1)} = E_0(1+g_A)^{N_A}(1+g_B) \qquad \text{[A-51]}$$

[16] Another way of looking at this would be to consider a two-step process. The present value of Equation [A-55] at time T_0 is obtained by applying the term [1/(1 + k)], N_A times. This is written mathematically as $\left[1/(1+k)^{N_A}\right]$. Then, to present value the expression to time T_{Start} from time T_0 it is necessary to discount the equation one more time and hence the term $\left[1/(1+k)^{(N_A+1)}\right]$.

Equation [A-57] is obtained by substituting $E_0(1+g_A)^{N_A}(1+g_B)$ for $E_{(N_A+1)}$ in Equation [A-56] and simplifying.

$$PV_{E_{B's}@T_{Start}} = \frac{E_0(1+g_B)(1+g_A)^{N_A}\left[1-\left(\frac{1+g_B}{1+k}\right)^{N_B}\right]}{(k-g_B)(1+k)^{(N_A+1)}} \qquad \text{[A-57]}$$

Period C The cash flows during period C commence right after E_{N_B} with the first one being $E_{(N_B+1)}$ at time $T_{(N_B+1)}$ and continue growing at fixed rate g_C forever. Once again this is an application of the Perpetual Growth Model, Equation [A-30]. Hence, $PV_{E_{C's}@T_{NB}}$, the present value of the cash flows during period C at time T_{NB}, is given by

$$PV_{E_{C's}@T_{NB}} = \frac{E_{(N_B+1)}}{k-g_C} \qquad \text{[A-58]}$$

As before, it is the present value of Equation [A-58] at time T_{Start} that is desired. Reference to Figure A-8 indicates that T_{NB} occurs (N_A+N_B+1) periods after T_{Start}. Therefore, $PV_{E_{C's}@T_{Start}}$, the present value of the cash flows during period C at T_{Start}, is obtained by multiplying Equation [A-58] by the term $\left[1/(1+k)^{(N_A+N_B+1)}\right]$.

$$PV_{E_{C's}@T_{Start}} = \frac{E_{(N_B+1)}}{k-g_C}\left[\frac{1}{(1+k)^{(N_A+N_B+1)}}\right] \qquad \text{[A-59]}$$

Now

$$E_{(N_B+1)} = E_{N_B}(1+g_C) \qquad \text{[A-60]}$$

and

$$E_{N_B} = E_{N_A}(1+g_B)^{N_B} \qquad \text{[A-61]}$$

Also recall that

$$E_{N_A} = E_0(1+g_A)^{N_A} \qquad \text{[A-50]}$$

Equation [A-62] expressed in terms of E_0 is obtained by first substituting for E_{N_A} in Equation [A-61], and then for E_{N_B} in Equation [A-60].

$$E_{(N_B+1)} = E_0(1+g_A)^{N_A}(1+g_B)^{N_B}(1+g_C) \qquad \text{[A-62]}$$

Finally, by substituting the results of Equation [A-62] in Equation [A-59] for $E_{(N_B+1)}$ and simplifying, the desired expression for $PV_{E_{C's}@T_{Start}}$ in terms of E_0 is obtained.

$$PV_{E_{C's}@T_{Start}} = \frac{E_0(1+g_A)^{N_A}(1+g_B)^{N_B}(1+g_C)}{(k-g_C)(1+k)^{(N_A+N_B+1)}} \qquad \text{[A-63]}$$

Present Value of the Three-Stage Growth Cash Flows

Figure A-8 illustrates that the present value of all of the cash flows in the three-stage growth model is the sum of the present value of each component of all of the cash flows.

Therefore, $PV_{(E_0+E_{A's}+E_{B's}+E_{C's})}$, the present value of the cash flows for periods 0, A, B, and C, present valued to time T_{Start} is:

$$PV_{(E_0+E_{A's}+E_{B's}+E_{C's})} = PV_{E_0@T_{Start}} + PV_{E_{A's}@T_{Start}} + PV_{E_{B's}@T_{Start}} + PV_{E_{C's}@T_{Start}} \qquad \text{[A-64]}$$

Using the results of Equations [A-31], [A-54], [A-57], and [A-63] to substitute for $PV_{E_0@T_{Start}}$, $PV_{E_{A's}@T_{Start}}$, $PV_{E_{B's}@T_{Start}}$, and $PV_{E_{C's}@T_{Start}}$, respectively in Equation [A-64] we get an expression for $PV_{(E_0+E_{A's}+E_{B's}+E_{C's})}$:

$$PV_{(E_0+E_{A's}+E_{B's}+E_{C's})} = \frac{E_0}{1+k} + \frac{E_0(1+g_A)\left[1-\left(\frac{1+g_A}{1+k}\right)^{N_A}\right]}{(k-g_A)(1+k)} + \frac{E_0(1+g_B)(1+g_A)^{N_A}\left[1-\left(\frac{1+g_B}{1+k}\right)^{N_B}\right]}{(k-g_B)(1+k)^{(N_A+1)}} + \frac{E_0(1+g_A)^{N_A}(1+g_B)^{N_B}(1+g_C)}{(k-g_C)(1+k)^{(N_A+N_B+1)}} \qquad \text{[A-65]}$$

General Equation for the Present Value Three-Stage Cash Flows That Grow at a Fixed Rate g_A for N_A Periods, Fixed Rate g_B for N_B Periods, and Thereafter at a Fixed Rate g_C

If $E = E_0$, the first cash flow after T_{Start}, which grows at a fixed rate g_A during period A and then at a fixed rate g_B throughout period B, followed by fixed growth rate g_C thereafter, Equation [A-65] becomes:

$$PV_{(E_0+E_{A's}+E_{B's}+E_{C's})} = \frac{E}{1+k} + \frac{E(1+g_A)\left[1-\left(\frac{1+g_A}{1+k}\right)^{N_A}\right]}{(k-g_A)(1+k)} + \frac{E(1+g_B)(1+g_A)^{N_A}\left[1-\left(\frac{1+g_B}{1+k}\right)^{N_B}\right]}{(k-g_B)(1+k)^{(N_A+1)}} + \frac{E(1+g_A)^{N_A}(1+g_B)^{N_B}(1+g_C)}{(k-g_C)(1+k)^{(N_A+N_B+1)}} \qquad \text{[A-66]}$$

APPENDIX B

Business Valuation Models

INTRODUCTION

In this appendix, models are developed that calculate the present value of various cash flow streams frequently encountered when valuing business plans. The theoretical framework for these models was developed in Appendix A. Where possible the models refer to the equation(s) in Appendix A that form the basis for the various business models that follow.

STREAM OF DISTINCT CASH FLOWS[1]

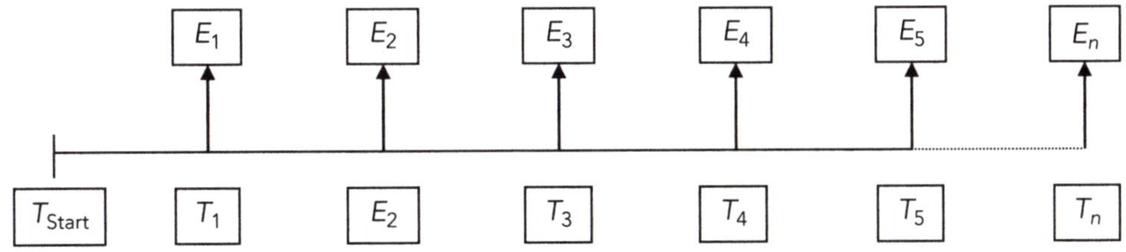

FIGURE B-1 Stream of Distinct Cash Flows

Application	
Equation [B-1] can be used to calculate the present value of any stream of cash flows that are based on estimates or growth assumptions for each period. In this sense [B-1] is completely general and in fact is the starting point for developing special cases such as the *perpetual* and *finite* models. Equation [B-2] is simply the expanded form of Equation [B-1].	

(continued)

[1]Also referred to as Forecast Period Cash Flows.

$$PV = \sum_{i=1}^{n} \frac{E_i}{(1+k)^i} \quad [B-1]$$

$$PV = \frac{E_1}{(1+k)^1} + \frac{E_2}{(1+k)^2} + \frac{E_3}{(1+k)^3} + \cdots + \frac{E_n}{(1+k)^n} \quad [B-2]$$

Where:

PV = Present value of a stream of cash flows

$\sum_{i=1}^{n}$ = Sum of the periodic cash flows in increments i for n periods

n = The last period for which cash flow is expected

E_i = Expected cash flow in the ith period

k = Discount rate (usually the company's weighted average cost of capital [WACC] adjusted for risk as appropriate)

i = The period in the future in which the prospective cash flow is expected to be received.

E_1 = The first distinct cash flow at time T_1

E_n = The last distinct cash flow at time T_n

Appendix A Reference:

Equations [A-1] and [A-2]

STREAM OF DISTINCT CASH FLOWS FOLLOWED BY A STREAM OF PERPETUAL FIXED CASH FLOWS

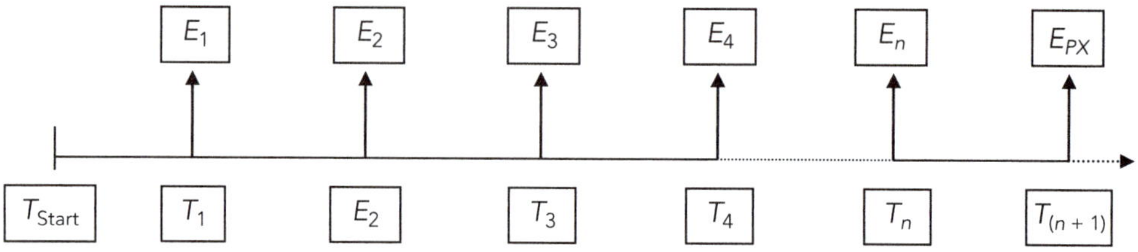

FIGURE B-2 Stream of Distinct Cash Flows Followed by Perpetual Fixed Cash Flows

Application

This is identical to the situation described for post-forecast finite fixed cash flows (discussed later) except that the business is expected to generate a fixed stream of cash flows in perpetuity after the period of distinct or forecasted cash flows ends. Basically, this model says: The business will generate a series of cash flows (during the forecast or discrete cash flow period) for some period of time and then becomes "annuity-like" and provides a cash flow stream at some fixed level thereafter forever.

In practice, a business must find a way to grow or it will die. However post–forecast period growth scenarios are not always easy to substantiate. This model is used in unusual situations such as those where it's difficult to predict growing cash flows after the period of distinct cash flows and there is a need to include something beyond management's forecast horizon.

Also see the discussion on:

Equations [B-4], [B-5], [B-6], and [B-7]

Equation [B-3] is the sum of equations [A-2] and [A-15] (which is adjusted for the time value of money by the term $(1 + k)^{(n+1)}$) and calculates the present value of a "stream of distinct cash flows followed by a stream of perpetual fixed cash flows that continue forever."	
$$PV_{FP+PX} = \frac{E_1}{(1+k)^1} + \frac{E_2}{(1+k)^2} + \frac{E_3}{(1+k)^3} + \ldots + \frac{E_n}{(1+k)^n} + \frac{E_{PX}}{k(1+k)^n} \quad [B\text{-}3]$$ Where: PV_{FP+PX} = Present value of forecasted cash flows plus post-forecast perpetual fixed cash flows E_1 = The first distinct cash flow at time T_1 E_n = The last distinct cash flow at time T_n n = The number of periods in the distinct cash flow stream k = Discount rate (usually the company's WACC adjusted for risk as appropriate) E_{PX} = The fixed cash flow that continues forever with the first cash flow taking place at time $T_{(n+1)}$ and present valued back to the start by the term $1/(1 + k)^n$	Appendix A Reference: Equations [A-2] and [A-15][2]

STREAM OF DISTINCT CASH FLOWS FOLLOWED BY A STREAM OF FINITE FIXED CASH FLOWS

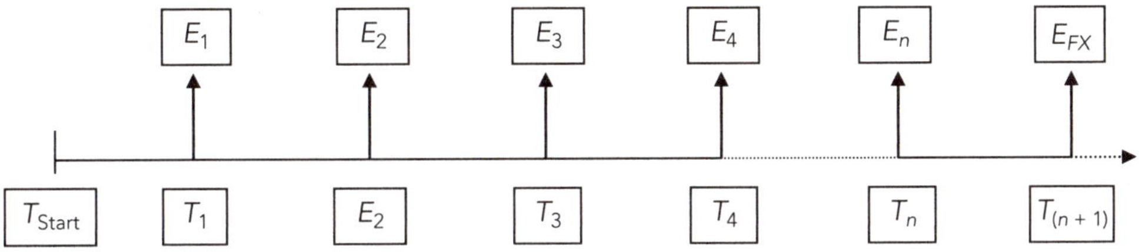

FIGURE B-3 Stream of Distinct Cash Flows Followed by Finite Fixed Cash Flows

Application This is identical to the situation described for the perpetual fixed stream of cash flows described elsewhere except that the business is expected to generate a fixed stream of cash flows for finite period NX after the period of distinct cash flows ends. Basically, this model says: The business will generate a series of cash flows (usually referred to as the *forecast* or *discrete* cash flow period) for some period of time and then it goes into a "cliff" mode whereby the cash flow stream continues at some fixed level for a finite period of time and then disappears (becomes zero).	Also see the discussion on: Equations [B-3], [B-5], [B-6], and [B-7]

(continued)

[2] The expression E_{PX}/k calculates the present value of a stream of perpetual fixed cash flows. In this example, the first one takes place at time $T_{(n+1)}$. Therefore, this expression present values the fixed cash flow stream that continues forever at time T_n. To value it at time T_{Start}, the term needs to be multiplied by the term $[1/(1 + k)^n]$. Also refer to the Perpetual Fixed Model in Chapter 4.

It is atypical to find a business that has such grim prospects. Therefore, this model is primarily used in multistage cash flow analysis or in unusual situations where there is a need to give some recognition to a flat level of cash flows that eventuate after the discrete/forecast period for a finite number of periods.

In summary, Equation [B-4] calculates the present value of "stream of distinct cash flows followed by a stream of finite fixed cash flows for NX years" and is the sum of Equations [A-2] and [A-14].

$$PV_{FP+FX} = \frac{E_1}{(1+k)^1} + \frac{E_2}{(1+k)^2} + \frac{E_3}{(1+k)^3} + \cdots + \frac{E_n}{(1+k)^n} + \frac{E_{FX}\left[1-(1+k)^{-NX}\right]}{k(1+k)^n} \quad \text{[B-4]}$$

Where:

PV_{FP+PX} = Present value of forecasted cash flows plus post-forecast finite fixed cash flows

E_1 = The first distinct cash flow at time T_1

E_n = The last distinct cash flow at time T_n

n = The number of periods in the distinct cash flow stream

k = Discount rate (usually the Company's WACC adjusted for risk as appropriate)

E_{FX} = The fixed cash flow that continues for NX years after period n with the first cash flow taking place at time $T_{(n+1)}$ and the last cash flow taking place at time $T_{(n+NX)}$

Appendix A Reference:

Equations [A-2] and [A-14][3]

STREAM OF DISTINCT CASH FLOWS FOLLOWED BY A STREAM OF PERPETUAL GROWTH CASH FLOWS

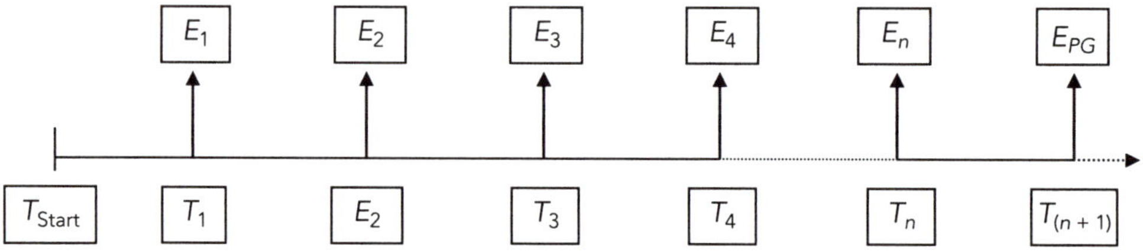

FIGURE B-4 Stream of Distinct Cash Flows Followed by Perpetual Growth Cash Flows

Application

While perpetual growth streams are hard to find, this model does find relatively widespread use. Typical applications are calculating post-forecast value after very long forecast periods or streams of discrete cash flows[4] and in multistage models. Like others, this model starts with management preparing a cash flow estimate going out several periods based on pro-forma financial statements.

Also see the discussions on:

Equations [B-3], [B-4], [B-6], and [B-7]

[3]The expression $E_{FX}[1-(1+k)^{-NX}]/k$ calculates the present value of a stream of perpetual fixed cash flows. In this example, the first one takes place at time $T_{(n+1)}$. Therefore, this expression present values the fixed cash flow stream that continues forever at time T_n. To value it at time T_{Start}, the term needs to be multiplied by the term $[1/(1+k)^n]$. Also refer to Chapter 4, Finite Fixed Model.

[4]Ten years or more.

Regardless of the application, this model makes a *fixed growth* assumption for all cash flows after cash flow E_n. When used on its own, it usually follows a long forecast period of cash flows because the impact that the growth rate assumption has on the value of post-forecast cash flows is mitigated to some extent by the fact that it doesn't start for many years. It is also used in multistage applications where a finite period of cash flows growing at growth rate g_1 is followed by a perpetual stream of cash flows growing at growth rate g_2. In either case, this approach has merit since one of management's responsibilities is to keep reinventing the business and continue to generate growth for a very long time.

The present value of a "stream of distinct cash flows followed by a stream of perpetual growth cash flows" is provided by the sum of equations [A-2] and [A-30] with the latter adjusted for the time value of money as is done in Equations [B-3] and [B-4].

$$PV_{FP+PG} = \frac{E_1}{(1+k)^1} + \frac{E_2}{(1+k)^2} + \frac{E_3}{(1+k)^3} + \cdots + \frac{E_n}{(1+k)^n} + \frac{E_{PG}}{(k-g_{PG})(1+k)^n} \quad \text{[B-5]}^5$$

Where:

PV_{FP+PG} = Present value of forecasted plus post-forecast perpetual growth cash flows
E_1 = The first distinct cash flow at time T_1
E_n = The last distinct cash flow at time T_n
n = The number of periods in the distinct cash flow stream
k = Discount rate (usually the company's WACC adjusted for risk as appropriate)
g_{PG} = Rate at which E_{PG} grows
$E_{PG} = E_n(1 + g_{PG})$, the cash flow that grows at a fixed rate g_{PG} and continues forever with the first cash flow taking place at time $T_{(n+1)}$

Appendix A Reference:

Equations [A-2] and [A-30]

STREAM OF DISTINCT CASH FLOWS FOLLOWED BY A STREAM OF FINITE GROWTH CASH FLOWS

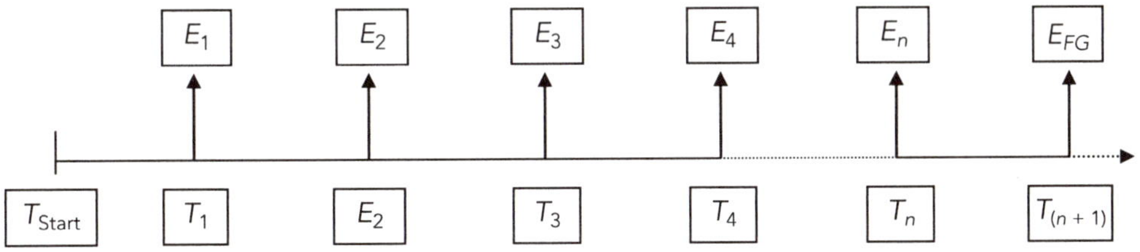

FIGURE B-5 Stream of Distinct Cash Flows Followed by Cash Flows That Grow for a Finite Period

[5]Care must be taken when applying this model. Note that g_{pg} must be less than k. Otherwise, the Continuing Value $(k - g_{pg})$ term will give nonsensical results. If g_{pg} is relatively large compared to k, Equation [A-30] can generate large present values, especially if n is relatively small. Also refer to the Perpetual Growth Model in Chapter 4.

<table>
<tr>
<td>

Application

The finite growth term in Equation [B-6] is usually a term in a present value model that has a period of forecasted cash flows followed by a period of fixed growth g_{FG} for a finite period of time. However, this need not be the case. It can be used on its own.

There are business applications where the assumptions and criteria the Finite Growth Model deals with are exactly what needs to be addressed. For example, if a business's (or some subset of the business's) cash flow is dependent on royalties from intellectual property that are expected to start at some level and grow at a fixed rate for a finite period of time, then this model can be used to present value the cash flows that are forecasted to eventuate.

When using Equation [B-6], keep in mind that the period of fixed growth starts right after the last discrete cash flow E_n takes place. This cash flow is E_{FG} and continues for NF periods. The term $E_{FG}\left[1-\left(\frac{1+g_{FG}}{1+k}\right)^{NF}\right]\Big/(k-g_{FG})$ in the equation present values the cash flow to the time when E_n occurs, which is at the end of period T_n. The term $[1/(1+k)^n]$ present values this term to time T_{Start}. Without it, it is only present valued to time T_n. A thorough discussion of this equation and its development is contained in Appendix A.[6]

</td>
<td>

Also see the discussions on:

Equations [B-3], [B-4], [B-5], and [B-7]

</td>
</tr>
<tr>
<td>

$$PV_{FP+FG}=\frac{E_1}{(1+k)^1}+\frac{E_2}{(1+k)^2}+\frac{E_3}{(1+k)^3}+\cdots+\frac{E_n}{(1+k)^n}+\frac{E_{FG}\left[1-\left(\frac{1+g_{FG}}{1+k}\right)^{NF}\right]}{(k-g_{FG})(1+k)^n} \quad \text{[B-6]}$$

Where:

PV_{FP+FG} = Present value of forecasted plus post-forecast finite growth cash flows

E_1 = The first distinct cash flow at time T_1

E_n = The last distinct cash flow at time T_n

n = The number of periods in the distinct cash flow stream

k = Discount rate (usually the company's WACC adjusted for risk as appropriate)

g_{FG} = Rate at which E_{FG} grows

$E_{FG} = E_n(1+g_{FG})$, the cash flow that grows at a fixed rate g_{FG} for NF periods with the first cash flow taking place at time $T_{(n+1)}$

</td>
<td>

Appendix A Reference:

Equations [A-2], [A-29], and [A-33]

</td>
</tr>
</table>

[6]Also refer to the Finite Growth Model in Chapter 4.

STREAM OF DISTINCT CASH FLOWS FOLLOWED BY A TERMINAL CASH FLOW

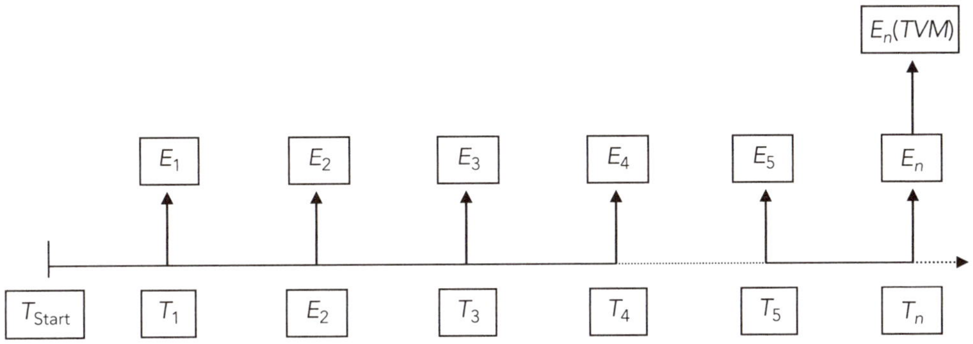

FIGURE B-6 Stream of Distinct Cash Flows Followed by a Terminal Cash Flow

Application

The Terminal Value Model is used for calculating the present value of a stream of cash flows for the purpose of valuing a business. Typically, management prepares cash flow estimates based on pro-forma financial statements. This model assumes that the business is sold at the end of the forecast period for some multiple of the last year's (year *n*'s) cash flow. This is known as the *terminal value*; hence, the *Terminal Value Multiplier* (TVM) used in the last term of Equation [B-7]. The TVM is usually obtained from industry statistics, comparable transactions, or expert advice.

It's not important that the business actually be sold or that the owners plan to sell it. The terminal value approach simply allows one to ascribe some value to the business by estimating what someone might pay for it at the end of the cash flow forecast period, assuming lots of things, including that all the value-added enhancements that management plans to put in place over the forecast period eventuate.

In this case, the present value of a "stream of distinct cash flows followed by a payout (terminal value)" is simply the sum of equations [A-2] + [A-5] as shown in [B-7]. Once again the term $[1/(1 + k)^n]$ present values the terminal value to time T_{Start}[7].

Also see the discussions on:

Equations [B-3], [B-4], [B-5], and [B-6]

$$PV_{FP+TV} = \frac{E_1}{(1+k)^1} + \frac{E_2}{(1+k)^2} + \frac{E_3}{(1+k)^3} + \cdots + \frac{E_n}{(1+k)^n} + \frac{E_{TY}(TVM)}{(1+k)^n} \qquad \text{[B-7]}$$

Where:

PV_{FP+TV} = Present value of forecasted cash flows plus a terminal value
E_1 = The first distinct cash flow at time T_1
$E_n = E_{TY}$ = The last distinct cash flow at time T_n
n = The number of periods in the distinct cash flow stream
k = Discount rate
TVM = Terminal Value Multiplier

Appendix A Reference:

Equations [A-2] and [A-5]

[7] Also see the Terminal Value Model in Chapter 4.

INITIAL CASH FLOW SEQUENTIALLY FOLLOWED BY A FINITE PERIOD OF CASH FLOWS THAT GROW AT A FIXED RATE g_{FG} AND A TERMINAL CASH FLOW

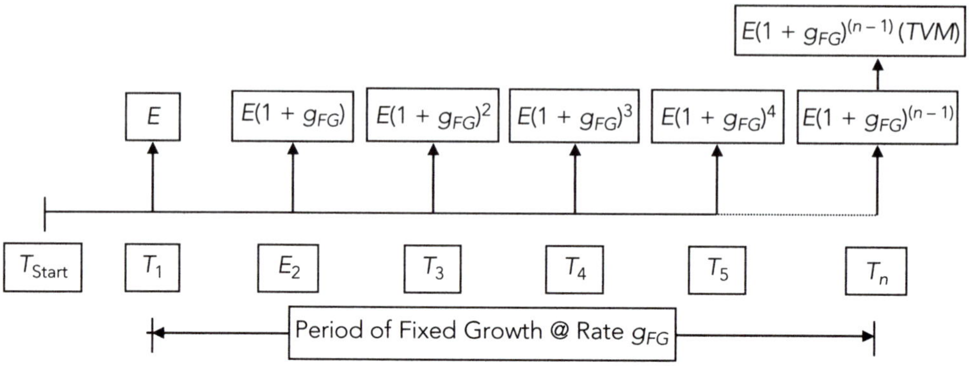

FIGURE B-7 Initial Cash Flow Sequentially Followed by Finite Period and Terminal Cash Flows

Application	Also see the discussion on:
This model assumes that after an initial cash flow E, the cash flow grows at a fixed rate for $(n - 1)$ periods and then the business is sold at some multiple of the cash flow achieved during period n. This is a very useful back-of-the-envelope business valuation model. All the user needs to do is to make some estimate of the cash flow during the first year and decide on a growth rate for a finite period of years. The value that is added during the owner's stewardship is evaluated by assuming the business is sold at the end of the finite period for some multiple of year n cash flow. Like the model quantified by Equation [B-6], the most difficult aspect of using this model is making sure that one understands how the fixed growth term works. n represents the total number of periods starting from T_{Start}. The first cash flow E takes place at the end of the first period. Therefore, the number of periods during which the cash flows grow at fixed rate g_{FG} is $(n - 1)$. The cash flow that is used to evaluate the terminal value is the same as the last cash flow during the period of fixed growth, that is, $E(1 + g)^{(n-1)}$. To present value the terminal value to T_{START}, it needs to be multiplied by $1/(1 + k)^n$.	Equations [B-3] and [B-7]

$$PV = \frac{E}{1+k} + \frac{E(1+g)\left[1-\left(\frac{1+g}{1+k}\right)^{(n-1)}\right]}{(k-g)(1+k)} + \frac{E(1+g)^{(n-1)}(TVM)}{(1+k)^n} \quad \text{[B-8]}$$

Where:

PV = Present value

E = The cash flow that grows at a fixed rate g

n = The number of periods in the cash flow stream

k = Discount rate

g = Rate at which E grows

$E_n = E(1+g)^n$ The last cash flow in the stream that has grown at a fixed rate g

TVM = Terminal Value Multiplier

Appendix A Reference:

Equations [A-4], [A-5], and [A-37]

INITIAL CASH FLOW SEQUENTIALLY FOLLOWED BY A FINITE PERIOD OF CASH FLOWS THAT GROW AT A FIXED RATE g_{FG} AND A PERPETUAL FIXED CASH FLOW

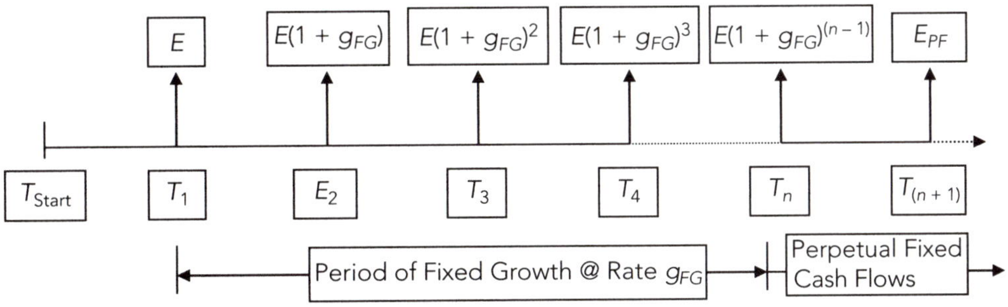

FIGURE B-8 Initial Cash Flow Sequentially Followed by Finite Period and Perpetual Fixed Cash Flows

Application

This model is identical to other models where the initial cash flow is followed by a finite period of cash flows that grow at a fixed rate except that second-stage cash flows are represented by a term that present values a stream of perpetual fixed cash flows. The first of the fixed cash flows E_{PX} that take place occurs at time $T_{(n+1)}$, the second E_{PX} occurs at $T_{(n+2)}$, and so on.

Also see the discussion on:

Equations [B-3] and [B-8]

(continued)

$$PV_{FG+PX} = \frac{E}{(1+k)} + \frac{E(1+g_{FG})\left[1-\left(\frac{1+g_{FG}}{1+k}\right)^{(n-1)}\right]}{(k-g_{FG})(1+k)} + \frac{E_{PX}}{k(1+k)^n} \qquad \text{[B-9]}$$

Where:

PV_{FG+PX} = Present value of a period of finite growth followed by a perpetual fixed cash flow

E = The cash flow that grows at a fixed rate g_{FG}

n = The number of periods in the cash flow stream leading up to the period of fixed cash flow in perpetuity

k = Discount rate

$(n-1)$ = The number of periods during which E grows at a fixed rate g_{FG}

g_{FG} = Rate at which E grows during the period of fixed growth

E_{PX} = The perpetual fixed cash flow with the first cash flow taking place at time $T_{(n+1)}$

Appendix A Reference: Equations [A-15], [A-37], and [A-53][8]

INITIAL CASH FLOW SEQUENTIALLY FOLLOWED BY A FINITE PERIOD OF CASH FLOWS THAT GROW AT A FIXED RATE g_{FA} FOR N_A PERIODS AND PERPETUAL CASH FLOWS THAT GROW AT A FIXED RATE g_{PB}

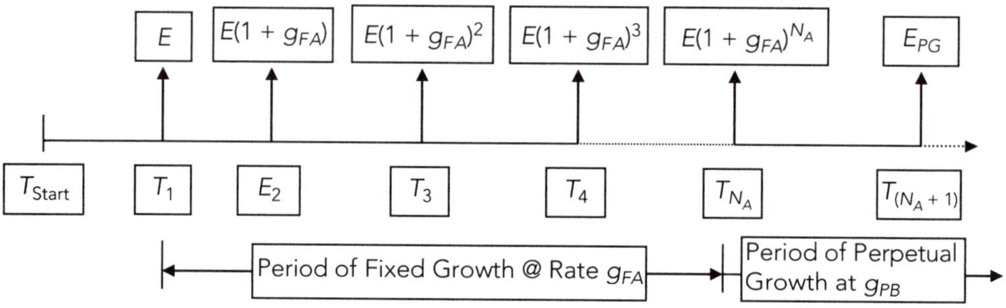

FIGURE B-9 Initial Cash Flow Sequentially Followed by Finite Period of Growth and Perpetual Growth Cash Flows

[8]Equation [B-9] is not developed in Appendix A per se. It can be easily deduced from Equation [A-53]. The first term in [A-53] is the now-familiar present value of the first cash flow E that immediately precedes the fixed period of fixed growth. The second term is the present value of the cash flows that grow at a fixed rate g_{FG} for N_A periods, where in this case $N_A = (n-1)$. To get Equation (B 9) from [A-53] the third term is replaced with the expression $E_{PF}/k(1+k)^n$, where in this application E_{PX}/k is the present value at time T_n of a stream of fixed cash flows with the first one occurring at time $T_{(n+1)}$ and continuing forever, and the multiplier $1/(1+k)^n$ present values E_{PX}/k to time T_{Start}.

Application The model defined by Equation [B-10] is a powerful business tool. It allows one to value cash flow streams that grow at different rates and is similar to that described earlier and defined by Equation [B-9], except the second term, where the cash flows grow at a rate g_{FA} for N_A periods, is followed by a stream of cash flows that grow at a fixed rate g_{PB} forever. This model can cater to situations where forecasted cash flows are followed by two growth streams by adjusting for the first term to represent a stream of discrete cash flows followed by fixed and perpetual cash flows that grow at rates g_{FA} and g_{PB} respectively. Equation [B-10] can be simplified further. However, in this form the contribution made by each period and term in the equation to the present value being calculated is a little more obvious.	Also see the discussion on: Equations [B-5] and [B-9]
$$PV = \frac{E}{(1+k)} + \frac{E(1+g_{FA})\left[1-\left(\frac{1+g_{FA}}{1+k}\right)^{N_A}\right]}{(k-g_{FA})(1+k)} + \frac{E(1+g_{FA})^{N_A}(1+g_{PB})}{(k-g_{PB})(1+k)^{(N_A+1)}} \quad [B\text{-}10]$$ Where: PV = Present value E = The first cash flow in a stream of cash flows that grow at a fixed rate g_{FA} for N_A periods and at fixed rate g_{PB} thereafter k = Discount rate N_A = The number of periods during which E grows at rate g_{FA} g_{FA} = Rate at which E grows for N_A periods g_{PB} = Rate at which E grows thereafter $E_{PB} = E(1 + g_{FA})^{N_A}(1 + g_{PB})$	Appendix A Reference: Equations [A-37] and [A-53]

STREAM OF CASH FLOWS THAT GROW AT A FIXED RATE g_A FOR N_A PERIODS, FOLLOWED BY A STREAM OF CASH FLOWS THAT GROW AT A FIXED RATE g_B FOR N_B PERIODS, AND A STREAM OF PERPETUAL GROWTH CASH FLOWS THAT GROW AT A FIXED RATE g_C

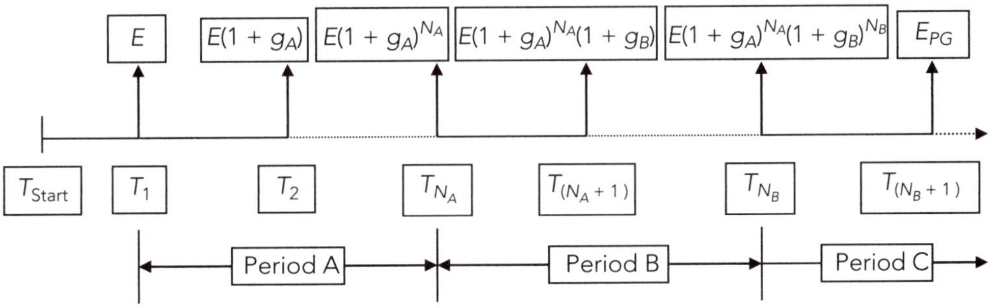

FIGURE B-10 Stream of Cash Flows That Grow at a Fixed Rate for a Period Sequentially Followed by a Finite Period of Growth and Perpetual Growth Cash Flows

Application

This model accommodates a growth cycle that has three distinct phases. It is designed to approximate the classical S-curve that portrays the way many business and product lines behave during the first three phases of their life cycle.

The first phase can be described as one of *incubation*. During this time the business (or some subset of the business, product line, etc.) is just getting started. This phase is characterized by relatively slow cash flow growth. Incubation is followed by a *growth* phase. This is the time when everything is expected to come together and the business takes off and cash flows grow at a higher rate. When growth slows down and "the pipeline has been filled," the business enters the third phase, *maturity*. During the mature phase of the cycle, growth typically slows down and, although often greater than what it was during incubation, is less than it was during the growth period.

There is, of course, a fourth phase (which this model doesn't address), *decline*. Hopefully, this phase will not eventuate because prudent management continues to reinvest part of the cash flow in the business and thereby keeps the business vibrant for a very long period of time.

While this is seemingly the most complicated model in this appendix, its application is relatively straightforward.

Like the previous fixed growth models, the first term in Equation [B-11] is the present value of the first cash flow E that immediately precedes the first period of fixed growth. The second term is the present value at time T_{Start} of the cash flows of period A that grow at a fixed rate g_A for N_A periods. Note that the first cash flow during period A is $E(1 + g_A)$. The third term is the present value at time T_{Start} of the cash flows of period B that grow at a fixed rate g_B for N_B periods. Also note that the first cash flow during period B is $E(1 + g_B)(1 + g_A)^{N_A}$. Finally, the fourth term is the present value at time T_{Start} of the cash flows of period C that grow at a fixed rate g_C forever. The first cash flow of period C is $E(1 + g_A)^{N_A}(1 + g_B)^{N_B}(1 + g_C)$:

Also see the discussion on:

Equations [B-5] and [B-10]

$$PV = \frac{E}{1+k} + \frac{E(1+g_A)\left[1-\left(\frac{1+g_A}{1+k}\right)^{N_A}\right]}{(k-g_A)(1+k)} + \frac{E(1+g_B)(1+g_A)^{N_A}\left[1-\left(\frac{1+g_B}{1+k}\right)^{N_B}\right]}{(k-g_B)(1+k)^{(N_A+1)}}$$

$$+\frac{E(1+g_A)^{N_A}(1+g_B)^{N_A}(1+g_C)}{(k-g_C)(1+k)^{(N_A+N_B+1)}} \qquad \text{[B-11]}$$

Where:

PV = Present value

E = The first cash flow in a stream of cash flows that grow at a fixed rate g_A for N_A periods, then at fixed rate g_B for N_B periods and at a fixed rate g_C thereafter

k = Discount rate

N_A = The number of periods in cash flow stream A

g_A = Rate at which E grows during period A

N_B = The number of periods in cash flow stream B

g_B = Rate at which E grows during period B; period C consists of an infinite number of periods

g_C = Rate at which E grows thereafter forever

Appendix A Reference: Equation [A-64] and [A-66]

APPENDIX C

Growth Models

INTRODUCTION

In this appendix, general expressions for estimating growth rates are presented.

- Compound annual growth (CAGR) rate model
- General model for estimating CFaIAg, the growth rate of Cash Flow after Investing Activities (CFaIA), and NIg, the growth rate of Net Income (NI), from the Investment Rate (IR) and Net Income Return on Capital Employed (NiROCE)

GENERAL COMPOUND ANNUAL GROWTH RATE MODEL

Let V_{Beg} and V_{End} represent the beginning and ending values of a series of numbers that develop over n periods. Then V_{End} can be expressed in terms of V_{Beg} and n by Equation [C-1].

$$V_{End} = V_{Beg}(1 + CAGR)^n \qquad [C\text{-}1]$$

where: *CAGR* is the compound annual growth rate[1]

Taking logarithms of both sides of Equation [C-1],

$$lnV_{End} = lnV_{Beg} + n\ ln(1 + CAGR) \qquad [C\text{-}2]$$

[1]CAGR is normally expressed as a decimal fraction.

Rearranging:

$$(n)\ ln(1 + CAGR) = lnV_{End} - lnV_{Beg} \qquad [C\text{-}3]$$

Multiplying both sides of [C-3] by n^{-1}

$$(n^{-1})\,(n)\ ln(1 + CAGR) = (n^{-1})\,(lnV_{End} - lnV_{Beg}) \qquad [C\text{-}4]$$

Since $(n^{-1})\,(n) = 1$ and $n^{-1} = \frac{1}{n}$, Equation [C-4] can be rewritten as,

$$ln(1+CAGR) = \left(\frac{1}{n}\right)\left(lnV_{End} - V_{Beg}\right) \qquad [C\text{-}5]$$

taking antilogarithms of both sides of [C-5]:

$$(1+CAGR) = \left(\frac{V_{End}}{V_{Beg}}\right)^{\frac{1}{n}} \qquad [C\text{-}6]$$

Finally, by rearranging, an expression for compound annual growth rate for a series of numbers covering n periods in terms of the ending and beginning values is obtained.

$$CAGR = \left(\frac{V_{End}}{V_{Beg}}\right)^{\frac{1}{n}} - 1 \qquad [C\text{-}7]$$

Or if it is preferred to express the CAGR as percentage:

$$\%CAGR = \left[\left(\frac{V_{End}}{V_{Beg}}\right)^{\frac{1}{n}} - 1\right](100) \qquad [C\text{-}8]$$

Example

If a retailer's sales in Years 1 through 5 are \$100, \$125, \$150, \$175, and \$200 million respectively, then $V_{Beg} = 100$, $V_{End} = 200$, and $n = 4$ periods.

By substituting in Equations [C-7] or [C-8], the CAGR from Year 1 to Year 5 is calculated to be 18.9%.

$$CAGR = \left(\frac{V_{End}}{V_{Beg}}\right)^{\frac{1}{n}} - 1 = \left(\frac{200}{100}\right)^{\frac{1}{4}} - 1 = (2)^{0.25} - 1 = 1.1892 - 1 = 0.1892$$

$$CAGR = 18.92\%$$

The result can be checked by substituting the value obtained for the CAGR in Equation [C-1].

$$V_{End} = V_{Beg}\,(1 + CAGR)^n = 100(1 + 0.1892)^4 = 100(1.9999) = 200$$

GENERAL EXPRESSION FOR CFaIAg, THE GROWTH RATE OF CFaIA

Let CFaIAg_n be the growth rate of CFaIA between any two years. Then in any year n, CFaIAg_n can be expressed by:

$$CFaIAg_n = \frac{CFaIA_n - CFaIA_{(n-1)}}{CFaIA_{(n-1)}} \quad \text{[C-9]}$$

Dividing the numerator of Equation [C-9] by the denominator, $\text{CFaIA}_{(n-1)}$,

$$CFaIAg_n = \frac{CFaIA_n}{CFaIA_{(n-1)}} - \frac{CFaIA_{(n-1)}}{CFaIA_{(n-1)}} = \frac{CFaIA_n}{CFaIA_{(n-1)}} - 1 \quad \text{[C-10]}$$

In Chapter 2, CFaIA_n was expressed in terms of NI and NIR as shown in Equation [C-11]:

$$CFaIA_n = NI_n(1 - IR_n) \quad \text{[C-11]}$$

Also in Chapter 2, NI_n was expressed in terms of NI, NetInvest, and NiROCE, as in Equation [C-12]:

$$NI_n = NI_{(n-1)} + NetInvest_{(n-1)}(NiROCE_n) \quad \text{[C-12]}$$

Substituting the result of Equation [C-12] in Equation [C-11],

$$CFaIA_n = [NI_{(n-1)} + NetInvest_{(n-1)}(NiROCE_n)](1 - IR_n) \quad \text{[C-13]}$$

In Chapter 2, it was demonstrated that $\text{NetInvest}_{(n-1)}$ can be expressed as:

$$NetInvest_{(n-1)} = NI_{(n-1)}(IR_{(n-1)}) \quad \text{[C-14]}$$

Rearranging,

$$NI_{(n-1)} = \frac{NetInvest_{(n-1)}}{IR_{(n-1)}} \quad \text{[C-15]}$$

Substituting for $\text{NI}_{(n-1)}$ in Equation [C-13] and forming a common denominator:

$$CFaIA_n = \left\{\left[\frac{NetInvest_{1(n-1)}}{IR_{(n-1)}}\right] + NetInvest_{(n-1)}(NiROCE_n)\right\}(1 - IR_n) \quad \text{[C-16]}$$

$$CFaIA_n = \left[\frac{NetInvest_{(n-1)} + NetInvest_{(n-1)}(IR_{(n-1)})(NiROCE_n)}{IR_{(n-1)}}\right](1 - IR_n) \quad \text{[C-17]}$$

Factoring Equation [C-17],

$$CFaIA_n = \frac{NetInvest_{(n-1)}[1 + IR_{(n-1)}(NiROCE_n)]\,(1 - IR_n)}{IR_{(n-1)}} \quad \text{[C-18]}$$

Similarly, Equation [C-11] can be restated as:

$$CFaIA_{(n-1)} = NI_{(n-1)}(1 - IR_{(n-1)}) \quad \text{[C-19]}$$

Again, recalling Equation [C-15] and substituting $\frac{\text{NetInvest}_{(n-1)}}{\text{IR}_{(n-1)}}$ for $\text{NI}_{(n-1)}$ in Equation [C-19],

$$CFaIA_{1(n-1)} = \frac{NetInvest_{(n-1)}(1 - IR_{(n-1)})}{IR_{(n-1)}} \quad \text{[C-20]}$$

Substituting for $\text{CFIA}_{(n-1)}$ (Equation [C-18]) and CFIA_n(Equation [C-20]) in Equation [C-10],

$$CFaIAg_n = \left\{ \frac{\dfrac{NetInvest_{(n-1)}[1 + IR_{(n-1)}(NiROCE_n)](1 - IR_n)}{IR_{(n-1)}}}{\dfrac{NetInvest_{(n-1)}(1 - IR_{(n-1)})}{IR_{(n-1)}}} \right\} - 1 \quad \text{[C-21]}$$

Canceling like terms,

$$CFaIAg_n = \frac{[1 + IR_{(n-1)}(NiROCE_n)](1 - IR_n)}{(1 - IR_{(n-1)})} - 1 \quad \text{[C-22]}$$

Special Case: CFaIAg_n, When IR and NiROCE Are Constant

If $\text{IR}_{(n-1)} = \text{IR}_n = \text{constant} = \text{IR}$, then Equation [C-22] becomes

$$CFaIAg_n = \frac{[1 + IR(NiROCE_n)](1 - IR)}{(1 - IR)} - 1 = [1 + IR(NiROCE_n)] - 1 \quad \text{[C-23]}$$

Canceling like terms and simplifying,

$$CFaIAg_n = IR(NiROCE_n) \quad \text{[C-24]}$$

Finally, if $\text{NiROCE}_n = \text{constant} = \text{NiROCE}$, then Equation [C-24] becomes

$$CFaIAg_n = IR(NiROCE) \quad \text{[C-25]}$$

Or, since CFaIAg_n is constant for all years, the subscript on *g* can be dropped.

$$CFaIAg = IR(NiROCE) \quad \text{[C-26]}$$

GENERAL EXPRESSION FOR NIg, THE GROWTH RATE OF NI

Let NIg_n be the growth rate of NI between any two years. Then in any year *n*, NIg_n can be expressed by:

$$NIg_n = \frac{NI_n - NI_{(n-1)}}{NI_{(n-1)}} \quad \text{[C-27]}$$

Proceeding as before and dividing the numerator of Equation [C-27] by the denominator:

$$NIg_n = \frac{NI_n}{NI_{(n-1)}} - \frac{NI_{(n-1)}}{NI_{(n-1)}} = \frac{NI_n}{NI_{(n-1)}} - 1 \qquad \text{[C-28]}$$

Equation [C-12] expresses NI_n as:

$$NI_n = NI_{(n-1)} + (NetInvest_{(n-1)})(NiROCE_n) \qquad \text{[C-12]}$$

and Equation [C-15] expresses $NI_{(n-1)}$ as:

$$NI_{(n-1)} = \frac{NetInvest_{(n-1)}}{IR_{(n-1)}} \qquad \text{[C-15]}$$

Substituting the results of Equation [C-15] in Equation [C-12] creates an expression for NI_n:

$$NI_n = \frac{NetInvest_{(n-1)}}{IR_{(n-1)}} + (NetInvest_{(n-1)})(NiROCE_n) \qquad \text{[C-29]}$$

Substituting the results of Equations [C-29] and [C-15] into Equation [C-28],

$$NIg_n = \left[\frac{\frac{NetInvest_{(n-1)}}{IR_{(n-1)}} + (NetInvest_{(n-1)}(NiROCE_n))}{\frac{NetInvest_{(n-1)}}{IR_{(n-1)}}}\right] - 1 \qquad \text{[C-30]}$$

Forming a common denominator for the numerator and factoring,

$$NIg_n = \left\{\frac{\frac{NetInvest_{(n-1)}[1 + IR_{(n-1)}(NiROCE_n)]}{IR_{(n-1)}}}{\frac{NetInvest_{(n-1)}}{IR_{(n-1)}}}\right\} - 1 \qquad \text{[C-31]}$$

Canceling like terms and simplifying,

$$NIg_n = [1 + IR_{(n-1)}\,(NiROCE_n)] - 1 \qquad \text{[C-32]}$$

Finally,

$$NIg_n = IR_{(n-1)}\,(NiROCE_n) \qquad \text{[C-33]}$$

Special Case: NIg_n, When IR and NiROCE Are Constant

If $IR_{(n-1)}$ = constant = IR, then Equation [C-33] becomes

$$NIg_n = IR(NiROCE_n) \qquad [C\text{-}34]$$

and, if $NiROCE_n$ = constant = NiROCE, then Equation [C-34] becomes

$$NIg_n = IR(NiROCE) \qquad [C\text{-}35]$$

Or, since NIg_n is constant between all years, the subscript can be dropped and [C-35] becomes

$$NIg = IR(NiROCE) \qquad [C\text{-}36]$$

Special Case: CFaIAg = NIg

Recall that in the special cases where the Investment Rate (IR) and Net Income Return on Capital Employed (NiROCE) were constant the expressions we derived for CFaIAg and NIg were:

$$CFaIAg = IR(NiROCE) \qquad [C\text{-}26]$$

and

$$NIg = IR(NiROCE) \qquad [C\text{-}36]$$

Under these conditions, Equation[C-26] = [C-36] and

$$CFaIAg = NIg \qquad [C\text{-}37]$$

and the growth rates in CFaIA and NI are the same and expressed by the product of the Investment Rate and Net Income Return on Capital Employed: IR(NiROCE).

APPENDIX D

General Equations for Estimating NI and CFaIA

INTRODUCTION

The equations developed in this appendix are intended for making quick estimates of net income and cash flows for business plans and early stage budgeting. Unlike the more familiar approach that involves detailed Profit and Loss Statements, Balance Sheets, and Cash Flow Statements, the Envelope Equations are based on the concepts of Net Income Return on Capital Employed (NiROCE), Net Investments (NetInvest), and the Investment Rate (IR).

ROCE AND NiROCE[1]

In Chapter 1 the Return on Capital Employed (ROCE) was defined as:

$$ROCE = \frac{NOPAT}{Capital\ Employed} = \frac{EBIT(1-TR)}{TSHE + Interest\text{-}Bearing\ Debt} = \frac{EBIT(1-TR)}{TSHE + IBD} \qquad [1\text{-}29]$$

Since the objective of the Envelope Equations is to make quick estimates of net income, the classical definition of ROCE does not suit our purpose because it deals with EBIT and

[1] T. E. Copeland, T. Koller, and J. Murrin, *Valuation, Measuring and Managing the Value of Companies*, 2nd ed. (New York: John Wiley & Sons, 1995), 137, "What Drives Cash Flow and Value"; and T. Koller, R. Dobbs, and B. Huyett, *The Four Cornerstones of Corporate Finance*, McKinsey and Company (Hoboken, NJ: John Wiley & Sons, 2011), 237, Appendix A.

to get to net income involves introducing additional complexity that isn't warranted. To get around this, the definition of ROCE is modified to use net income in place of NOPAT and designated as *net income ROCE* (NiROCE).[2]

$$NiROCE = \frac{NI}{CE} = \frac{NI}{TSHE + Interest\text{-}Bearing\ Debt} = \frac{NI}{TSHE + IBD} \quad [2\text{-}1]$$

In Chapter 2, the net investments and investment rate were defined as:

$$NetInvest = Investments - Depreciation\ \&\ Amortization = Investments - D\ \&\ A \quad [2\text{-}4]$$

$$IR = \frac{NetInvest}{Net\ Income} = \frac{NetInvest}{NI} \quad [2\text{-}7]$$

or

$$NetInvest = IR(NI) \quad [2\text{-}8]$$

The Envelope Equations that follow and utilize these concepts are valid to the extent the following conditions are reasonable for the intended application.

- A company has an existing asset base that produces a net income of NI_n during Year n and will continue to do so for subsequent years.

$$Net\ Income\ Year\ n = NI_n$$

- The cash flow during Year $n + 1$ is:

$$CFaIA_n = NI_n - NetInvest_n \pm NetInt_n \pm \Delta WC_n \quad [2\text{-}5]$$

- A fraction of net income called $NetInvest_n$ (net investments) is invested each year. This amount depends on the investment rate IR_n where:

$$IR_n = \frac{NetInvest_n}{NI_n} \quad [2\text{-}7]$$

- Net investments are defined as:

$$NetInvest_n = Investments_n - D\ \&\ A_n \quad [2\text{-}4]$$

[2]The reason ROCE uses NOPAT is that it excludes the impact of interest income or expense and since the cause of interest is the debt in the Balance Sheet, using NI would in a sense be double counting because it understates the NOPAT by an amount equal to the after-tax impact of interest. To the extent there is any interest expense, NiROCE would be less than ROCE and vice versa. If there isn't any interest, the NiROCE and ROCE would be the same.

- During Year n, net investments of a magnitude $NetInvest_n$ are made and these investments will produce the expected net income return on capital employed, $NiROCE_{(n+1)}$, the following year, creating *incremental net income* $\Delta NI_{(n+1)}$,

$$\Delta NI_{(n+1)} = NetInvest_n\,(NiROCE_{(n+1)})$$

which will also continue for subsequent years.

- This results in a net income in Year $n + 1$ of:

$$NI_{(n+1)} = NI_n + \Delta NI_{(n+1)}$$

or, substituting for $\Delta NI_{(n+1)}$,

$$NI_{(n+1)} = NI_n + NetInvest_n\,(NiROCE_{(n+1)})$$

This and subsequent net incomes become the basis for creating future cash flows. With this construct in mind, it becomes relatively easy to develop the general case for forecasting net income and cash flows.

THE GENERAL CASE FOR THE ENVELOPE EQUATIONS

The relationships between NI, NR, and NiROCE can be expressed in general form. This is done by assuming that the net income for Year n is NI_n and during the year the company makes net investments at a rate IR_n and these investments provide a return of $NiROCE_{(n+1)}$ the following year.

Net Income in Year *n*

The net income in Year n is:

$$Net\ Income\ Year\ n = NI_n \qquad \text{[D-1]}$$

CFaIA in Year *n*

In Chapter 2, it was shown that the *cash flow after investing activities* (CFaIA) can be expressed as:

$$CFaIA = NI - NetInvest \pm NetInt \pm \Delta WC \qquad \text{[D-2]}$$

Generalizing this equation, the CFaIA for Year n becomes:

$$CFaIA_n = NI_n - NetInvest_n \pm NetInt_n \pm \Delta WC_n \qquad \text{[D-3]}$$

Recall

$$IR_n = \frac{NetInvest_n}{NI_n} \quad \text{[D-4]}$$

Rearranging Equation [D-4],

$$NetInvest_n = NI_n\,(IR)_n \quad \text{[D-5]}$$

and substituting $NI_n\,(IR)_n$ for $NetInvest_n$ (Equation [D-5]) in Equation [D-3],

$$CFaIA_n = NI_n - NI_n(IR)_n \pm NetInt_n \pm \Delta WC_n \quad \text{[D-6]}$$

Factoring Equation [D-6] gives a general expression for the cash flow after investing activities in Year *n*:

$$CFaIA_n = NI_n\,(1 - IR_n) \pm NetInt_n \pm \Delta WC_n \quad \text{[D-7]}$$

Net Income in Year *n* + 1

A portion of the net income (defined as the *investment rate*) from Year *n* is invested in assets that will generate future net incomes and cash flows resulting in a net investment of:

$$NetInvest_n = NI_n(IR)_n \quad \text{[D-8]}$$

Since $NetInvest_n$ made in Year *n* provides a return of $NiROCE_{(n+1)}$ in Year $n + 1$, the incremental net income in Year $n + 1$ is:

$$\Delta NI_{(n+1)} = NetInvest_n\,(NiROCE_{(n+1)}) \quad \text{[D-9]}$$

And the net income in Year $n + 1$ will be the sum of the net income in Year *n* plus the incremental net income created by the net investments in Year *n*:

$$NI_{(n+1)} = NI_n + \Delta NI_{(n+1)} \quad \text{[D-10]}$$

The net income in Year $n + 1$ is obtained by substituting the result of Equation [D-9] in [D-10]:

$$NI_{(n+1)} = NI_n + NetInvest_n\,(NiROCE_{(n+1)}) \quad \text{[D-11]}$$

The result of Equation [E-8] is then substituted into Equation [D-11]:

$$NI_{(n+1)} = NI_n + NI_n\,(IR)_n\,(NiROCE_{(n+1)}) \quad \text{[D-12]}$$

The desired expression for the net income in Year $n + 1$ is obtained by factoring [D-12].

$$NI_{(n+1)} = NI_n \, [1 + (IR)_n \, (NiROCE_{(n+1)})] \qquad \text{[D-13]}$$

CFaIA in Year *n* + 1

From Equation [E-3] one can deduce that the CFaIA in terms of NetInvest in Year $n+1$ is:

$$CFaIA_{(n+1)} = NI_{(n+1)} - NetInvest_{(n+1)} \pm NetInt_{(n+1)} \pm \Delta WC_{(n+1)} \qquad \text{[D-14]}$$

Similarly, from Equation [D-8] it is noted that the NetInvest in Year $n + 1$ is

$$NetInvest_{(n+1)} = NI_{(n+1)} \, (IR)_{(n+1)} \qquad \text{[D-15]}$$

Substituting [D-15] into Equation [D-14],

$$CFaIA_{(n+1)} = NI_{(n+1)} - NI_{(n+1)} \, (IR)_{(n+1)} \pm NetInt_{(n+1)} \pm \Delta WC_{(n+1)} \qquad \text{[D-16]}$$

Factoring creates an expression for $CFaIA_{(n+1)}$ for Year $n + 1$ in terms of the investment rate IR:

$$CFaIA_{(n+1)} = NI_{(n+1)}[1 - (IR_{(n+1)})] \pm NetInt_{(n+1)} \pm \Delta WC_{(n+1)} \qquad \text{[D-17]}$$ [3]

Net Income in Year *n* + 2

Now, $NetInvest_{(n+1)}$ the amount invested during Year $n + 1$, provides a return (on the investment) of $NiROCE_{(n+2)}$ in Year n + 2, generating an incremental net income ΔNI_{n+2} of

$$\Delta NI_{(n+2)} = NetInvest_{(n+1)} \, (NiROCE_{(n+2)}) \qquad \text{[D-18]}$$

And since the net income in Year $n + 2$ is the continuing net income from Year $n + 1$ plus the incremental net income $\Delta NI_{(n+2)}$, the net income $NI_{(n+2)}$ in Year $(n + 2)$ is:

$$NI_{(n+2)} = NI_{(n+1)} + NetInvest_{(n+1)} \, (NiROCE_{(n+2)}) \qquad \text{[D-19]}$$

Again, by combining Equations [D-15] and [D-19] and factoring, a general expression for $NI_{(n+2)}$, the net income in Year $n + 2$, is obtained.

$$NI_{(n+2)} = NI_{(n+1)} \, [1 + IR_{(n+1)} \, (NiROCE_{(n+2)})] \qquad \text{[D-20]}$$

[3] Equations [D-8], [D-11], and [D-13] are powerful tools for doing quick estimates of a stream of net incomes. These equations together with the Cash Flow Equations [D-14] and [D-17] constitute five of a set of equations that are useful for predicting cash flows and therefore value.

CFaIA in Year $n + 2$

Once more by deduction and the use of Equation [D-3], the CFaIA for Year $n + 2$ in terms of the net investment is:

$$CFaIA_{(n+2)} = NI_{(n+2)} - NetInvest_{(n+2)} \pm NetInt_{(n+2)} \pm \Delta WC_{(n+2)} \qquad \text{[D-21]}$$

Also by deduction and Equation [D-5], the net investment in Year $n + 2$ based on an investment rate $IR_{(n+2)}$ is:

$$NetInvest_{(n+2)} = NI_{(n+2)}\,(IR_{(n+2)}) \qquad \text{[D-22]}$$

Substituting the result of Equation [D-22] into Equation [D-21] and simplifying, the CFaIA in Year $n + 2$ in terms of the investment rate $IR_{(n+2)}$ is obtained.

$$CFaIA_{(n+2)} = NI_{(n+2)}\,(1 - IR_{(n+2)}) \pm NetInt_{(n+2)} \pm \Delta WC_{(n+2)} \qquad \text{[D-23]}$$

Net Income in Year $n + 3$

Again, $NetInvest_{(n+2)}$, the amount invested during Year $n + 2$, provides a return (on the investment) of $NiROCE_{(n+3)}$ in Year $n + 3$, generating an incremental net income ΔNI_{n+3} of

$$\Delta NI_{(n+3)} = NetInvest_{(n+2)}\,(NiROCE_{(n+3)}) \qquad \text{[D-24]}$$

And since the net income in Year $n + 3$ is the continuing net income from Year $n + 2$ plus the incremental net income $\Delta NI_{(n+3)}$, the net income $NI_{(n+3)}$ in Year $n + 3$ is:

$$NI_{(n+3)} = NI_{(n+2)} + NetInvest_{(n+2)}\,(NiROCE_{(n+3)}) \qquad \text{[D-25]}$$

Combining Equations [D-24] and [D-25] and factoring, a general expression for $NI_{(n+3)}$, the net income in Year $n + 3$, is obtained.

$$NI_{(n+3)} = NI_{(n+2)}\,[1 + IR_{(n+2)}\,(NiROCE_{(n+3)})] \qquad \text{[D-26]}$$

CFaIA in Year $n + 3$

Once more by deduction and Equation [D-3], the CFaIA for Year $n + 3$ in terms of the net investment is:

$$CFaIA_{(n+3)} = NI_{(n+3)} - NetInvest_{(n+3)} \pm NetInt_{(n+3)} \pm \Delta WC_{(n+3)} \qquad \text{[D-27]}$$

Also by deduction and Equation [D-5], the net investment in Year $n + 3$ based on an investment rate $IR_{(n+3)}$ is:

$$NetInvest_{(n+3)} = NI_{(n+3)}\,(IR_{(n+3)}) \qquad \text{[D-28]}$$

Substituting the result of Equation [D-28] into Equation [D-27] and simplifying, the CFaIA in Year $n + 3$ in terms of the investment rate $IR_{(n+3)}$ is obtained,

$$CFaIA_{(n+3)} = NI_{(n+3)}\,(1 - IR_{(n+3)}) \pm NetInt_{(n+3)} \pm \Delta WC_{(n+3)} \qquad \text{[D-29]}$$

and so on.[4]

It is worthwhile to note that for the equations just derived, no restrictions were placed on what the investment rate and net income return on capital employed must be in any year or relative to any other year.

SPECIAL CASE: CONSTANT INVESTMENT RATE AND NET INCOME RETURN ON CAPITAL EMPLOYED

In many companies the investment rate and net income return on capital employed often tend to be relatively stable over time. Therefore, in situations where the investment rate and net income return on capital employed don't change significantly from year to year, the subscripts on these terms can be dropped and treated as constants. Applying the concept of constant IR and NiROCE to the general equations just developed yields Equations [D-30]–[D-49] respectively.

For Year *n*

For any year n with given net income NI_n:

NetInvest *n*

$$NetInvest_n = NI_n\,(IR) \qquad \text{[D-30]}$$

Cash Flow *n*

$$CFaIA_n = NI_n - NetInvest_n \pm NetInt_n \pm \Delta WC_n \qquad \text{[D-31]}$$

Or

$$CFaIA_n = NI_n\,(1 - IR) \pm NetInt_n \pm \Delta WC_n \qquad \text{[D-32]}$$

For Year *n* + 1

Net Income *n* + 1

$$NI_{(n+1)} = NI_n + \Delta NI_{(n+1)} \qquad \text{[D-33]}$$

$$\Delta NI_{(n+1)} = NetInvest_n\,(NiROCE) \qquad \text{[D-34]}$$

$$NI_{(n+1)} = NI_n + NetInvest_n\,(NiROCE) \qquad \text{[D-35]}$$

Or

$$NI_{(n+1)} = NI_n\,[1 + IR(NiROCE)] \qquad \text{[D-36]}$$

[4] It should be noted that it is not necessary to derive Equations [D-18]–[D-29] since these are general recursive formulas that are simply obtained by replacing the subscripts.

NetInvest $n+1$

$$NetInvest_{(n+1)} = NI_{(n+1)}\ IR \qquad [D\text{-}37]$$

Cash Flow $n+1$

$$CFalA_{(n+1)} = NI_{(n+1)} - NetInvest_{(n+1)} \pm NetInt_{(n+1)} \pm \Delta WC_{(n+1)} \qquad [D\text{-}38]$$

Or

$$CFIA_{(n+1)} = NI_{(n+1)}\ (1 - IR) \pm NetInt_{(n+1)} \pm \Delta WC_{(n+1)} \qquad [D\text{-}39]$$

For Year $n+2$

Net Income $n+2$

$$NI_{(n+2)} = NI_{(n+1)} + NetInvest_{(n+1)}\ (NiROCE) \qquad [D\text{-}40]$$

Or

$$NI_{(n+2)} = NI_{(n+1)}\ [1 + IR(NiROCE)] \qquad [D\text{-}41]$$

Net Invest $n+2$

$$NetInvest_{(n+2)} = NI_{(n+2)}\ IR \qquad [D\text{-}42]$$

Cash Flow $n+2$

$$CFalA_{(n+2)} = NI_{(n+2)} - NetInvest_{(n+2)} \pm NetInt_{(n+2)} \pm \Delta WC_{(n+2)} \qquad [D\text{-}43]$$

Or

$$CFalA_{(n+2)} = NI_{(n+2)}\ (1 - IR) \pm NetInt_{(n+2)} \pm \Delta WC_{(n+2)} \qquad [D\text{-}44]$$

For Year $n+3$

Net Income $n+3$

$$NI_{(n+3)} = NI_{(n+2)} + NetInvest_{(n+2)}\ (NiROCE) \qquad [D\text{-}45]$$

Or

$$NI_{(n+3)} = NI_{(n+2)}\ [1 + IR(NiROCE)] \qquad [D\text{-}46]$$

Net Invest $n+3$

$$NetInvest_{(n+3)} = NI_{(n+3)}\ (IR) \qquad [D\text{-}47]$$

Cash Flow $n+3$

$$CFalA_{(n+3)} = NI_{(n+3)} - NetInvest_{(n+3)} \pm NetInt_{(n+3)} \pm \Delta WC_{(n+3)} \qquad [D\text{-}48]$$

Or

$$CFalA_{(n+3)} = NI_{(n+3)}\ (1 - IR) \pm NetInt_{(n+3)} \pm \Delta WC_{(n+3)} \qquad [D\text{-}49]$$

and so on.[5]

SPECIAL CASE: FOCUS ON OPERATIONAL CASH FLOWS

The equations just developed deal with operational cash flows, interest (capital structure), and changes in working capital (Balance Sheet). However, as important as they are, net interest and working capital do not generate operating cash flow. Consequently

[5]Once again it is noted that Equations [D-40]–[D-49] are recursive and could have simply been obtained by replacing the subscripts.

in instances where the focus is on recurring operational activities that impact cash flow, one may not need to be concerned with ±NetInt and ±ΔWC. When interest and changes in working capital can be ignored these terms can be eliminated to further simplify the equations that have been developed. Applying this concept to the foregoing equations produces equations [D-50]–[D-64].[6]

For Year *n*

For any year *n* with given net income NI_n:

Net Invest

$$NetInvest_n = NI_n\,(IR) \qquad \text{[D-50]}$$

Cash Flow

$$CFaIA_n = NI_n - NetInvest_n \qquad \text{[D-51]}$$

Or

$$CFaIA_n = NI_n\,(1 - IR) \qquad \text{[D-52]}$$

For Year *n* + 1

Net Income

$$NI_{(n+1)} = NI_n + \Delta NI_{(n+1)} \qquad \text{[D-53]}$$

$$\Delta NI_{(n+1)} = NetInvest_n\,(NiROCE) \qquad \text{[D-54]}$$

$$NI_{(n+1)} = NI_n + NetInvest_n\,(NiROCE) \qquad \text{[D-55]}$$

Or

$$NI_{(n+1)} = NI_n\,[1 + IR(NiROCE)] \qquad \text{[D-56]}$$

NetInvest

$$NetInvest_{(n+1)} = NI_{(n+1)}\,(IR) \qquad \text{[D-57]}$$

Cash Flow

$$CFaIA_{(n+1)} = NI_{(n+1)} - NetInvest_{(n+1)} \qquad \text{[D-58]}$$

Or

$$CFIA_{(n+1)} = NI_{(n+1)}\,(1 - IR) \qquad \text{[D-59]}$$

For Year *n* + 2

Net Income

$$NI_{(n+2)} = NI_{(n+1)} + NetInvest_{(n+1)}\,(NiROCE) \qquad \text{[D-60]}$$

Or

$$NI_{(n+2)} = NI_{(n+1)}\,[1 + IR(NiROCE)] \qquad \text{[D-61]}$$

Net Invest

$$NetInvest_{(n+2)} = NI_{(n+2)}\,(IR) \qquad \text{[D-62]}$$

---

[6] It is also possible to apply this concept to the equations developed for the general case. In this instance the interest and working capital terms would disappear but the investment rate and net income return on capital employed terms would remain in the general form.

Cash Flow

$$CFaIA_{(n+2)} = NI_{(n+2)} - NetInvest_{(n+2)} \qquad \text{[D-63]}$$

Or

$$CFaIA_{(n+2)} = NI_{(n+2)}\,(1 - IR) \qquad \text{[D-64]}$$

and so on.

NET INCOME AND CASH FLOW GROWTH EQUATIONS

This appendix has dealt with five of the set of equations described as the Envelope Equations. The two remaining equations, the Net Income Growth Equation (NIg) and Cash Flow Growth Equation (CFaIAg), are developed and discussed in Appendix C.

APPENDIX E

R&D Growth and Investment Equation

INTRODUCTION

One of the challenges of deciding on appropriate amounts of R&D spending is estimating the cost of the next generation of product and the Revenue required to provide an adequate return. The R&D Growth and Investment Equation provides a simple way to quickly estimate what must be achieved.

In most companies one of the things that is known is the cost of the R&D effort to create the current generation of product. So it seems logical to use this as a starting point to make an estimate of the next generation's cost.

GENERATIONAL COST FACTOR

By definition, the Generational Cost Factor F is an estimate of the multiple by which the cost of the next generation will exceed the cost of the current generation. Then, if I_{current} is the R&D cost of the current generation expressed as a percentage of the lifetime revenues for the current generation LTRev_{CurGen} and I_{Next} the cost of the next generation also expressed as a percentage of the lifetime revenues, and the next generation is expected to generate $\text{LTRev}_{NextGen}$, then:

$$(I_{\text{Next}})(LTRev_{NextGen}) = (F)(I_{current})(LTRev_{CurGen}) \quad \text{[E-1]}$$

If the first-year revenue for the next generation is $\text{Rev}_{NextGen1}$ and $\text{Rev}_{LYCurGen}$ the Revenue for the last year of the current generation, and if the average lifetime growth rate for the next generation is g, then:

$$Rev_{NextGen1} = Rev_{LYCurGen}(1 + g) \quad \text{[E-2]}$$

Similarly, $Rev_{NextGen2} = Rev_{LYCurGen}\,(1 = g)^2$, $Rev_{NextGen3} = Rev_{LYCurGen}\,(1 + g)^3$, and so forth.

PRODUCT LIFE CYCLE

Now if the Product Life Cycle expressed in years for the next generation is PLC, then the next generation's lifetime revenue can be expressed as:

$$LTRev_{NextGen} = (Rev_{LYCurGen})(1 + g) + (Rev_{LYCurGen})(1 + g)^2 + (Rev_{LYCurGen})(1 + g)^3 + \cdots + (Rev_{LYCurGen})(1 + g)^{PLC} \qquad [E\text{-}3]$$

Factoring,

$$LTRev_{NextGen} = (Rev_{LYCurGen})[(1 + g) + (1 + g)^2 + (1 + g)^3 + \cdots + (1 + g)^{PLC}] \qquad [E\text{-}4]$$

or

$$LTRev_{NextGen} = (Rev_{LYCurGen}) \sum_{n=PLC}^{i=1} (1+g)^n \qquad [E\text{-}5]$$

where

$$\sum_{n=PLC}^{i=1} (1+g)^n = (1+g)+(1+g)^2+(1+g)^3+\cdots+(1+g)^{PLC} \qquad [E\text{-}6]$$

Equations [E-4] and [E-5] are awkward to work with and can be made more user friendly by simplifying the expression in Equation [E-6]. This is done by letting $(1 + g) = u$ and substituting in Equation [E-6].

$$\sum u^n = u + u^2 + u^3 + \cdots + u^{PLC} \qquad [E\text{-}7]$$

Factoring,

$$\sum u^n = u[1 + u + u^2 + \cdots + u^{(PLC-1)}] \qquad [E\text{-}8]$$

Multiplying both sides of Equation [E-8] by u,

$$u\sum u^n = u^2[1 + u + u^2 + \cdots + u^{(PLC-1)}] \qquad [E\text{-}9]$$

Subtracting Equation [E-9] from Equation [E-8],

$$\sum u^n - u\sum u^n = u[1 + u + u^2 + \cdots + u^{(PLC-1)}] - u^2[1 + u + u^2 + \cdots + u^{(PLC-1)}] \qquad [E\text{-}10]$$

Multiplying through by u in the last term of Equation [E-10] to eliminate u^2,

$$\sum u^n - u\sum u^n = u[1 + u + u^2 + \cdots + u^{(PLC-1)}] - u[u + u^2 + u^3 + \cdots + u^{PLC}] \qquad [E\text{-}11]$$

Factoring,

$$\sum u^n[1-u] = u\{[1+u+u^2+\cdots+u^{(PLC-1)}]-[u+u^2+u^3+\cdots+u^{PLC}]\} \quad \text{[E-12]}$$

Simplifying,

$$\sum u^n[1-u] = u[1+u+u^2+\cdots+u^{(PLC-1)}-u-u^2-u^3-\cdots-u^{PLC}] \quad \text{[E-13]}$$

Canceling like terms,

$$\sum u^n[1-u] = u(1-u^{PLC}) \quad \text{[E-14]}$$

Transposing,

$$\sum u^n = \frac{u(1-u^{PLC})}{(1-u)} \quad \text{[E-15]}$$

Multiplying through by u in the numerator,

$$\sum u^n = \frac{u-u^{(PLC+1)}}{(1-u)} \quad \text{[E-16]}$$

Substituting for u and simplifying,

$$\sum_{n=PLC}^{i=1}(1+g)^n = \frac{(1+g)-(1+g)^{(PLC+1)}}{[1-(1+g)]} = \frac{(1+g)-(1+g)^{(PLC+1)}}{(1-1-g)} = \frac{(1+g)-(1+g)^{(PLC+1)}}{(-g)} \quad \text{[E-17]}$$

Multiplying top and bottom by (–1) and simplifying,

$$\sum_{n=PLC}^{i=1}(1+g)^n = \frac{(-1)(1+g)-(1+g)^{(PLC+1)}}{(-1)(-g)} = \frac{-(1+g)+(1+g)^{(PLC+1)}}{g} \quad \text{[E-18]}$$

$$\sum_{n=PLC}^{i=1}(1+g)^n = \frac{(1+g)^{(PLC+1)}-(1+g)}{g} \quad \text{[E-19]}$$

DEVELOPING AN EXPRESSION FOR THE COST OF THE NEXT GENERATION

An expression for the cost of the next generation can be obtained by first substituting the expression developed in Equation [E-19] for $\sum_{n=PLC}^{i=1}(1+g)^n$ in Equation [E-5],

$$LTRev_{NextGen} = (Rev_{LYCurGen})\left[\frac{(1+g)^{(PLC+1)}-(1+g)}{g}\right] \quad \text{[E-20]}$$

and then substituting the results of Equation [E-20] into Equation [E-1].

$$(I_{Next})(Rev_{LYCurGen})\left[\frac{(1+g)^{(PLC+1)}-(1+g)}{g}\right]=(F)(I_{Current})(LTRev_{CurGen}) \qquad \text{[E-21]}$$

Transposing,

$$I_{Next}=\frac{(F)(I_{Current})(LTRev_{CurGen})}{(Rev_{LYCurGen})\left[\frac{(1+g)^{(PLC+1)}-(1+g)}{g}\right]} \qquad \text{[E-22]}$$

Inverting the term $\left[\frac{(1+g)^{(PLC+1)}-(1+g)}{g}\right]$ and rearranging an expression for the cost of the next generation expressed in terms of current generation parameters, the cost factor F is obtained.

$$I_{Next}=\frac{(g)(F)(I_{Current})(LTRev_{CurGen})}{\left[(1+g)^{(PLC+1)}-(1+g)\right](Rev_{LYCurGen})} \qquad \text{[E-23]}$$

In order to monetize Equation [E-23] it is necessary to calculate the lifetime revenue of the next generation. This can be done with a concept called the Lifetime Revenue Factor.

LIFETIME REVENUE FACTOR

Table E-1 consists of solutions to Equations [E-6] and [E-19].

$$\sum_{n=PLC}^{i=1}(1+g)^n=(1+g)+(1+g)^2+(1+g)^3+\cdots+(1+g)^{PLC} \qquad \text{[E-6]}$$

$$\sum_{n=PLC}^{i=1}(1+g)^n=\frac{(1+g)^{(PLC+1)}-(1+g)}{g} \qquad \text{[E-19]}$$

Hence each cell represents a value for a particular combination of g and PLC and, as will be seen, can be used in a number of ways.

By definition, the Lifetime Revenue Factor (LTRF) is the number by which the first year's revenue is multiplied to get the lifetime revenue. Table E-1 contains LTRFs for various growth rates g and product life cycles (PLCs). For example, if the average compound annual growth rate is 5% and the PLC is six years, then the LTRF is 7.142. Multiplying this number by the revenue that immediately preceded the period in question gives the lifetime revenue. This is illustrated by Equation [E-24].

$$LTRev_{NextGen}=LTRF(Rev_{LYCurGen}) \qquad \text{[E-24]}$$

TABLE E-1 Lifetime Revenue Factor for Various Growth Rates and Product Life Cycles

	Growth Rates g														
PLC	**1%**	**2%**	**3%**	**4%**	**5%**	**6%**	**7%**	**8%**	**9%**	**10%**	**11%**	**12%**	**13%**	**14%**	**15%**
1	1.010	1.020	1.030	1.040	1.050	1.060	1.070	1.080	1.090	1.100	1.110	1.120	1.130	1.140	1.150
2	2.030	2.060	2.091	2.122	2.153	2.184	2.215	2.246	2.278	2.310	2.342	2.374	2.407	2.440	2.473
3	3.060	3.122	3.184	3.246	3.310	3.375	3.440	3.506	3.573	3.641	3.710	3.779	3.850	3.921	3.993
4	4.101	4.204	4.309	4.416	4.526	4.637	4.751	4.867	4.985	5.105	5.228	5.353	5.480	5.610	5.742
5	5.152	5.308	5.468	5.633	5.802	5.975	6.153	6.336	6.523	6.716	6.913	7.115	7.323	7.536	7.754
6	6.214	6.434	6.662	6.898	7.142	7.394	7.654	7.923	8.200	8.487	8.783	9.089	9.405	9.730	10.067
7	7.286	7.583	7.892	8.214	8.549	8.897	9.260	9.637	10.028	10.436	10.859	11.300	11.757	12.233	12.727
8	8.369	8.755	9.159	9.583	10.027	10.491	10.978	11.488	12.021	12.579	13.164	13.776	14.416	15.085	15.786
9	9.462	9.950	10.464	11.006	11.578	12.181	12.816	13.487	14.193	14.937	15.722	16.549	17.420	18.337	19.304
10	10.567	11.169	11.808	12.486	13.207	13.972	14.784	15.645	16.560	17.531	18.561	19.655	20.814	22.045	23.349
11	11.683	12.412	13.192	14.026	14.917	15.870	16.888	17.977	19.141	20.384	21.713	23.133	24.650	26.271	28.002
12	12.809	13.680	14.618	15.627	16.713	17.882	19.141	20.495	21.953	23.523	25.212	27.029	28.985	31.089	33.352
13	13.947	14.974	16.086	17.292	18.599	20.015	21.550	23.215	25.019	26.975	29.095	31.393	33.883	36.581	39.505
14	15.097	16.293	17.599	19.024	20.579	22.276	24.129	26.152	28.361	30.772	33.405	36.280	39.417	42.842	46.580
15	16.258	17.639	19.157	20.825	22.657	24.673	26.888	29.324	32.003	34.950	38.190	41.753	45.672	49.980	54.717

The use of Equations [E-23], [E-24], and the Lifetime Revenue Factor are best illustrated with an example.

EXAMPLE E-1: CALCULATING THE R&D COST OF THE NEXT GENERATION

The data and expected performance of the next generation of product is presented in Table E-2. The value of Inext can be obtained by substituting the values from Table E-2 into Equation [E-23].

$$I_{Next} = \frac{(g)(F)(I_{Current})(LTRev_{CurGen})}{\left[(1+g)^{(PLC+1)} - (1+g)\right](Rev_{LYCurGen})} = \frac{(0.07)(2)(0.065)(140,000,000)}{[(1+0.07)^{(8+1)} - (1+0.07)](19,600,000)}$$

$$I_{Next} = \frac{1,274,000}{15,061,801} = 0.0846$$

$$I_{Next} = 8.46\%$$

which states that the R&D cost for the next generation will be 8.46% of the lifetime revenue of the next generation.

Now, according to the parameters given for the next generation in Table E-2, the average Compound Annual Growth Rate is 7% and this is expected to take place over eight years. The intersection of 7% and eight years in Table E-1 gives an LTRF of 10.978. Again, according to Table E-2 the revenue during the last year of the current generation was $19,600,000. Hence, the Lifetime Revenue of the next generation is:

$$LTRev_{NextGen} = LTRF(Rev_{LYCurGen}) = 10.978 * \$19,600,000 = \$215,170,000$$

and the total R&D Cost for the next generation is:

$$\$I_{Next} = I_{Next}(LTRev_{NextGen}) = 0.0846 * 215,170,000 = \$18,200,000$$

TABLE E-2 Parameters for Calculating the Cost of the Next Generation

Expected CAGR for Next Generation	g	7.00%
Generational Cost Factor	F	2.00
Cost of Current Generation as % of Lifetime Revenue	$I_{Current}$	6.50%
Lifetime Revenue of Current Generation	$LTRev_{CurGen}$	$140,000,000
Expected Product Life Cycle for Next Generation (Years)	PLC	8
Revenue for the Last Year of the Current Generation	$Rev_{LYCurGen}$	$19,600,000

GROWTH RATES AND PRODUCT LIFE CYCLES THAT SATISFY THE REQUIREMENT $I_{CURRENT} = I_{NEXT}$

Now there may be instances where there is a desire to estimate the growth rate g and product life cycle (PLC) required to make the percentage cost of the next and current generations the same. This can be accomplished by setting $I_{Next} = I_{Current}$. Under these circumstances Equation [E-23] becomes:

$$I_{Current} = \frac{(g)(F)(I_{Current})(LTRev_{CurGen})}{\left[(1+g)^{(PLC+1)} - (1+g)\right](Rev_{LYCurGen})} \qquad \text{[E-25]}$$

Dividing both sides by the term $I_{Current}$ and canceling like terms,

$$1 = \frac{(g)(F)(LTRev_{CurGen})}{[(1+g)^{(PLC+1)} - (1+g)](Rev_{LYCurGen})} \qquad \text{[E-26]}$$

Transposing,

$$\frac{[(1+g)^{(PLC+1)} - (1+g)]}{g} = \frac{(F)(LTRev_{CurGen})}{(Rev_{LYCurGen})} \qquad \text{[E-27]}$$

In practice, the term $\frac{(F)(LTRev_{CurGen})}{(Rev_{LYCurGen})}$ will be easily calculated since all of the variables are known. The challenge comes when trying to find the combination of g and PLC in the term $\frac{[(1+g)^{(PLC+1)} - (1+g)]}{g}$ that equals the numeric value of $\frac{(F)(Rev_{CurGen})}{(Rev_{LYCurGen})}$. This can be done with the assistance of Table E-1, which as stated earlier calculates the value of the term $\frac{[(1+g)^{(PLC+1)} - (1+g)]}{g}$ for various g's and PLCs.

The use of Equation [E-27] and Table E-1 can be illustrated by an example.

EXAMPLE E-2: DETERMINING g AND PLC WHEN $I_{CURRENT} = I_{NEXT}$

The first step is to determine the magnitude of the ratio $\frac{(F)(LTRev_{CurGen})}{(Rev_{LYCurGen})}$ in Equation [E-27]. Referring to Example E-1 and Table E-2 it is noted that $F = 2$, $Rev_{CurGen} = 140{,}000{,}000$, and $Rev_{LYCurGen} = 19{,}600{,}000$. Hence,

$$\frac{(F)(LTRev_{CurGen})}{(Rev_{LYCurGen})} = \frac{(2)(140{,}000{,}000)}{19{,}600{,}000} = 14.285$$

Referring to Table E-1 it is noted that the g and PLC that come the closest is 14.193, which is obtained with a g and PLC of 9% and nine years respectively.

The result can be checked by substituting these values in Equation [E-23],

$$I_{Next} = \frac{(g)(F)(I_{Current})(LTRev_{CurGen})}{\left[(1+g)^{(PLC+1)} - (1+g)\right](Rev_{LYCurGen})} = \frac{(0.09)(2)(0.065)(140,000,000)}{[(1+0.09)^{(9+1)} - (1+0.09)](19,600,000)}$$

$$I_{Next} = \frac{1,638,000}{25,036,328} = 0.0654$$

$$I_{Next} = 6.54\%$$

which agrees very closely with ($I_{Current}$) = 6.5%, the difference being the fact that the closest number to the 14.285 in Table E-1 was 14.193.

APPENDIX F

Inventory Considerations and the EOQ Model

INTRODUCTION

Inventory management and control is one of the business areas that has been extensively quantified and heavily impacted by operations research. The basic inventory model is known as the Economic Order Quantity Model, which has been used for many years for inventory management. The "gold standard" is an EOQ = 1. As will be seen in this appendix, there are many factors that impact the EOQ and complicate the task of minimizing inventory and make unitary EOQ's out of reach for most companies.

COMPONENTS OF INVENTORY COSTS[1]

Inventory represents a major investment for most manufacturing companies. The cost of inventory has three broadly defined components:

1. Carrying costs
2. Shortage costs
3. Procurement costs

Carrying costs represent the cost of physically having inventory on hand. They include costs such as financing, inventory management, facilities, insurance, depreciation, and obsolescence. These costs tend to mount as the quantity of inventory on hand increases.

Shortage costs are those costs incurred by a company when its production operations run out of parts and include such costs as idle direct labor, production disruption,

[1] J. F. Watson and E. F. Brigham, *Managerial Finance*, 6th ed. (Hinsdale, IL: Dryden Press, 1978), 201, Appendix A to Chapter 7, "The Basic Inventory Model."

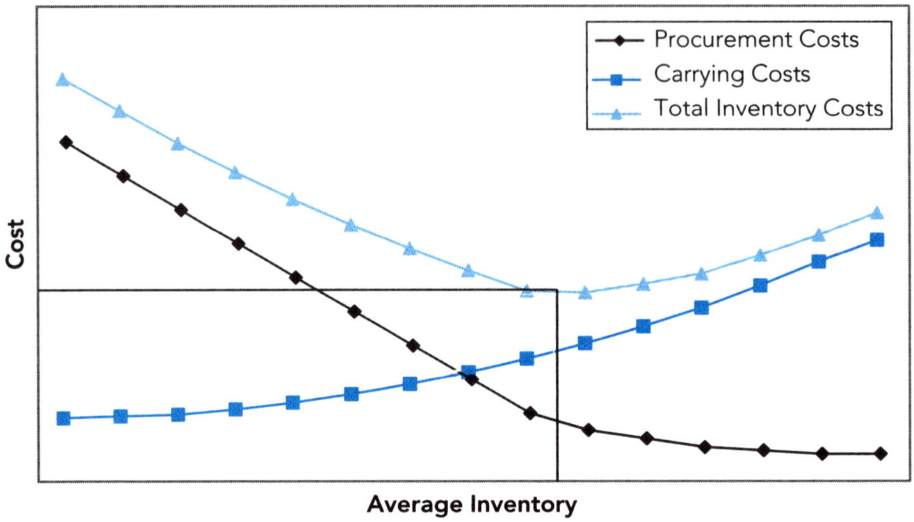

FIGURE F-1 Optimum Investment in Inventory

scheduling changes, diversion of sales and marketing efforts for customer hand-holding, lost sales, and loss of customer goodwill.

Procurement costs are those costs associated with ordering and receiving inventory, forgoing quantity discounts, and so on. These costs tend to decline as the average inventory increases because the number of orders and receipts per year will decrease and the company will capture the benefit of quantity discounts from its suppliers or experience lower unit costs for internally manufactured parts because of the longer production runs.

All three costs can be addressed in various ways. Shortage costs are usually addressed by adding safety stocks to an otherwise optimal inventory level.[2] Carrying and procurement costs are normally incorporated into a model that optimizes the trade-offs involved by trying to lower procurement costs by carrying a higher inventory level and the carrying costs associated with the higher inventory. The relationship between carrying costs, procurement costs, and total costs is shown in Figure F-1.

A look at Figure F-1 reveals three obvious points:

1. Carrying costs rise as the average inventory level increases.
2. Procurement costs decline as the average inventory level increases.
3. The *total inventory cost curve* is the sum of the carrying and procurement costs.

A closer look reveals three subtle and yet very important observations:

1. The absolute values of the slopes of the carrying cost and procurement cost curves are the same at a common average inventory level.

[2]The issue of safety stocks is dealt with later in this appendix.

2. At this point the marginal carrying costs are increasing as fast as the marginal procurement costs are decreasing.
3. The minimum value of the total cost curve occurs at the point where the absolute values of the slopes of the carrying cost and procurement cost curves are the same. This is also the point at which the slope of the total inventory cost curve equals zero.

The minimum value on the total cost curve represents the optimal size of investment in inventory and can be determined by an equation that quantifies the Economic Order Quantity (EOQ). This equation can be derived as follows.

Objective of the Economic Order Quantity–Based Inventory Model

As can be seen from Figure F-1, the total inventory cost curve, as defined by carrying and procurement costs, has a minimum point. The objective is to locate this point and the economic ordering quantity that will result in a minimization of total inventory costs.

Average Inventory

Fundamental to the notion of inventory minimization is the concept of average inventory. For example, if a company has an *annual usage* requirement of U units and places a single order for the year, then the order quantity is Q = U. This would result in having Q units and zero units on hand at the beginning and end of the year respectively. Based on this reasoning, the *average number of units* (Avg#U) would be:

$$Avg\#U = \frac{Q}{2} \qquad \text{[F-1]}$$

Similarly, if the same company that requires U units for a year places two orders, then the order quantity Q is $\frac{U}{2}$ and the average number of units is:

$$Avg\#U = \frac{\frac{U}{2}}{2} \qquad \text{[F-2]}$$

Following this logic, if a company has an annual usage requirement of U units per year and decides to order N times per year, then the order quantity Q is:

$$Q = \frac{U}{N} \qquad \text{[F-3]}$$

and the average number of units is:

$$Avg\#U = \frac{\frac{U}{N}}{2} \qquad \text{[F-4]}$$

or simply,

$$Avg\#U = \frac{U}{2N} \qquad \text{[F-5]}$$

Carrying Costs

As mentioned earlier, carrying costs represent the cost of physically having inventory on hand and involves the cost of money (interest), indirect labor (to manage and keep track of the inventory), facilities to store the inventory, insurance to protect against losses not normally incurred in the ordinary conduct of business, depreciation on the equipment and facilities, inventory management personnel, and benefit costs and inventory obsolescence.

Typically companies define the cost of carrying inventory as a percentage of the total investment in inventory. For example, if the cost of money is 8%, indirect labor to manage the inventory is 3%, facilities, insurance, and depreciation 4%, and obsolescence 7%, then the cost of carrying inventory as a percentage of total inventory investment is 23%. If this cost is defined as %CCost and the cost per unit and the average number of units are U Cost and AVG #U respectively, then the total carrying cost TCC is:

$$TCC = (\%CCost)(UCost)(Avg\ \#U) \qquad \text{[F-6]}$$

Procurement Costs

Unlike carrying costs, which are largely variable (because they rise in direct proportion to the size of the inventory), procurement costs have fixed and variable components. For example, in order to place purchase orders a company needs some basic level of staffing, equipment, and support services in its purchasing department. The most basic purchasing staff can process one or thousands of orders in a year and is relatively easy to augment with automation (computers and software). Furthermore, every time a part is to be manufactured or assembled, setup time for the machinery, jigs, and fixtures is required, and this time is independent of the number of units to be produced. *Handling costs* (shipping and receiving costs) are a mixed bag and usually have a fixed and variable component. The fixed part is associated with putting in place the capability to ship and receive parts. The act of handling material or parts that are going out for processing or received by a company is almost all labor, much more difficult to automate (compared to purchasing), and largely variable. If all of the fixed costs associated with ordering, setup, and handling are lumped together, then the *total fixed procurement costs* (TotFixPC) in a year is:

$$TotFixPC = (FixPCost)(N) \qquad \text{[F-7]}$$

where:

FixPCost = The fixed ordering and handling costs per order
N = The number of orders placed per year

Similarly, the total variable cost of ordering and handling parts, *total variable procurement costs* (TotVarPC), for a year is:

$$TotVarPC = (VarPCost)(U) \tag{F-8}$$

where:

VarPCost = The variable unit cost of ordering and handling parts
U = The total number of units ordered per year

Combining Equations [F-7] and [F-8] creates an expression for TPC, the total procurement cost per year.

$$TPC = TotFixPC + TotVarPC \tag{F-9}$$

Substituting,

$$TPC = (FixPCost)(N) + (VarPCost)(U) \tag{F-10}$$

Total Inventory Cost

The *total inventory cost* (TIC) is the sum of the total carrying costs TCC and the total procurement costs TPC. Combining Equations [F-6] and [F-10], we get:

$$TIC = [(\%CCost)(UCost)(Avg\#U)] + [(FixPCost)(N) + (VarPCost)(U)] \tag{F-11}$$

Recalling that $\text{Avg\#U} = \frac{Q}{2}$ (Equation [F-1]) and substituting into Equation [F-11] gives an expression with the first term expressed in terms of the variable Q and fixed costs.

$$TIC = \left[(\%CCost)(UCost)\left(\frac{Q}{2}\right)\right] + [(FixPCost)(N) + (VarPCost)(U)] \tag{F-12}$$

Equation [F-3] can be rearranged so that

$$N = \frac{U}{Q} \tag{F-13}$$

Substituting for N in Equation [F-12] yields Equation [F-14], which expresses the total inventory cost in terms of several variables. The cost of carrying inventory as a percentage of total inventory investment %CCost is not something a company can change on a day-to-day basis. Nor are the cost per unit UCost or the fixed or variable procurement costs FixPCost and VarPCost respectively. What management can impact on a day-to-day basis is the quantity Q per order and the variable of interest when it comes to minimizing total inventory investment.

$$TIC = \left[(\%CCost)(UCost)\left(\frac{Q}{2}\right)\right] + \left[(FixPCost)\left(\frac{U}{Q}\right) + (VarPCost)(U)\right] \tag{F-14}$$

ECONOMIC ORDER QUANTITY

The order quantity Q that defines the point at which total inventory cost is at a minimum can be found by differentiating Equation [F-14] with respect to Q and setting the result equal to zero.

$$\frac{\partial(TIC)}{\partial Q}=\frac{\partial\left[(\%CCost)(UCost)\left(\frac{Q}{2}\right)\right]}{\partial Q}+\frac{\partial\left[(FixPCost)\left(\frac{U}{Q}\right)+(VarPCost)(U)\right]}{\partial Q} \quad \text{[F-15]}$$

$$\frac{\partial(TIC)}{\partial Q}=\frac{\partial\left[(\%CCost)(UCost)\left(\frac{Q}{2}\right)\right]}{\partial Q}+\frac{\partial\left[(FixPCost)\left(\frac{U}{Q}\right)\right]}{\partial Q}+\frac{\partial[(VarPCost)(U)]}{\partial Q} \quad \text{[F-16]}$$

$$\frac{\partial(TIC)}{\partial Q}=\left(\frac{(\%CCost)(UCost)}{2}\right)-(FixPCost)\left(\frac{u}{Q^2}\right)+0 \quad \text{[F-17]}$$

Setting $\frac{\partial(TIC)}{\partial Q}=0$ and rearranging,

$$\left(\frac{(\%CCost)(UCost)}{2}\right)=(FixPCost)\left(\frac{U}{Q^2}\right) \quad \text{[F-18]}$$

from which

$$Q^2=\frac{2(FixPCost)(U)}{(\%CCost)(UCost)} \quad \text{[F-19]}$$

Taking the square root of both sides of Equation [F-19] gives an expression in terms of the order quantity Q.

$$Q=\sqrt{\frac{2(FixPCost)(U)}{(\%CCost)(UCost)}} \quad \text{[F-20]}$$

By definition, the order quantity Q when $\frac{\partial(TIC)}{\partial Q}=0$ (the rate of change of the total inventory cost with respect to Q is zero) is that order quantity that minimizes the total inventory cost TIC and is known as the Economic Order Quantity (EOQ). Hence,

$$EOQ=\sqrt{\frac{2(FixPCost)(U)}{(\%CCost)(UCost)}} \quad \text{[F-21]}$$

where:

EOQ = The Economic Order Quantity of the inventory item under consideration
FixPCost = The fixed procurement (ordering and handling) costs per order
U = The annual usage of the inventory item under consideration
%CCost = The carrying cost of inventory as a percentage of the total investment in inventory
UCost = The unit cost (cost per unit) of the inventory item under consideration

The messages from Equation [F-21] are:

- The EOQ increases when the fixed procurement costs FixPCost and/or the annual usage U increase.
- The EOQ decreases when the inventory carrying cost %CCost and/or the unit cost UCost increases.
- The EOQ is a function of the square root of these variables. Therefore, for example, if the annual usage doubles, the EOQ will increase by $\sqrt{2} = 1.414$, or 41.4%. Similarly, if the unit cost doubles, the EOQ will decrease by $\sqrt{\frac{1}{2}} = \sqrt{0.5} = 0.7071$, or 29.29%.

SHORTAGE COSTS

Earlier it was stated that a company would incur shortage costs if it runs out of inventory. These costs range from idle time in the factory and increased expediting efforts to lost sales and diversion of resources to mollifying disappointed customers. Equation [F-21] doesn't deal with these costs. In fact it is based on several assumptions that, if ignored, virtually assure that shortage costs will be incurred. The assumptions inherent in Equation [F-21] are:

1. Sales can be forecasted perfectly so that the exact annual usage U for every part can be accurately quantified.
2. Sales and therefore parts usage are evenly distributed over the sales cycle.
3. Lead time = 0 days (i.e., parts are delivered within moments of being ordered).

Since none of these assumptions are reasonable in most manufacturing environments, the Economic Order Quantity Model has to be modified to eliminate the built-in bias to creating shortage costs. Introducing the concepts of *lead time quantity*, *order point*, and *safety stock* does this.

Lead Time Quantity and Order Point

Just-in-time (JIT) manufacturing is based on the notion that parts are delivered just in time. Even if suppliers perform perfectly (which is very rare), they still require time to produce what has been ordered from them. For example, if the annual usage of a part is 720 units and the EOQ of that part is 20 units, then the company would place 36 orders in a year $\left(720/_{20}\right)$ or one every 10 days $\left(360/_{36}\right)$. This implies that the company will use 2 parts per day $\left(20/_{10}\right)$. By definition:

$$\textit{Lead Time} = (\textit{Time it takes to generate and order}) + (\textit{Time it takes to receive the order from a supplier}) \qquad \text{[F-22]}$$

If the lead time is four days, then the quantity of units required to be on hand to account for the time it takes to generate and receive an order is:

$$\textit{Lead Time Quantity} = (\textit{Normal Lead Time}) \times (\textit{Normal Daily Usage}) = 4 \times 2 = 8$$

Therefore, an order should be placed for the part when the shelf-count reaches eight units. Otherwise, manufacturing will be short of the part in question for four days.

The order point can be defined as:

$$\textit{Order Point} = (\textit{Lead Time Quantity}) + (\textit{Safety Stock}) \qquad \text{[F-23]}$$

In this case, since safety stock has not been dealt with at this point, the order point would be:

$$\textit{Order Point} = 8 + 0 = 8$$

With an order point system in place, the company will generate an order for 20 units when the shelf-count reaches 8 units. Four days later the shelf-count will be zero when the 20 units arrive from the supplier. Therefore, our inventory of this part will vary between 20 and 0 with the average inventory being 10 units. Hence, introducing an order point per se doesn't increase the average inventory. It simply takes into account lead time.

Safety Stock

While incorporating lead time into the inventory model is an improvement, it still doesn't deal with the other assumptions on which the EOQ model is based. For example, suppliers don't always deliver as promised, and therefore, in practice, lead times can vary. Also, there is always considerable uncertainty associated with any sales or usage forecast. Finally, orders don't come in at a uniform rate. To deal with these uncertainties, companies often add a safety stock to their inventory.

In most instances safety stocks are based on experience and determined empirically.[3] Safety stock can be defined as the units required in inventory to account for the uncertainties associated with the various assumptions made in the Economic Order Quantity Model. Stated simply, safety stock is a function of *annual usage uncertainty, usage rate uncertainty,* and *lead time uncertainty*. This concept can be expressed as:

$$\textit{Safety Stock} = \mathbb{F}\,[(\textit{Annual Usage Uncertainty}), (\textit{Usage Rate Uncertainty}), (\textit{Lead Time Uncertainty})] \qquad \text{[F-24]}$$

For example, if the annual usage forecast is considered to be accurate as an average, but peak daily usage is 50% higher than average daily usage and the lead time six days worst-case, then the maximum usage (and the order point) under the four possible scenarios is tabulated in Table F-1.

Equation [F-23] can be rearranged as follows:

$$\textit{Safety Stock} = (\textit{Order Point}) - (\textit{Lead Time Quantity}) \qquad \text{[F-25]}$$

[3]Theoretically, quantifying an appropriate level of safety stock involves incorporating statistical and probabilistic concepts into the inventory model. The author has chosen not to introduce this level of complexity into this discussion since it is felt that the principles involved can be adequately demonstrated by using a practical approach.

TABLE F-1 Order Point for the Four Scenarios

Average Daily Unit Usage Rate	Maximum Unit Usage = Order Point	
	Lead Time = 4 Days	Lead Time = 6 Days
2	8	12
3	12	18

TABLE F-2 Safety Stock for the Four Order Point Scenarios

Average Daily Unit Usage Rate	Safety Stock	
	Lead Time = 4 Days	Lead Time = 6 Days
2	0	4
3	4	10

Since the lead time quantity is eight units, substituting 8 for the lead time quantity in Equation [F-25] gives the safety stock required for each of the possible scenarios in Table F-1. The results are tabulated in Table F-2.

Table F-2 is quite informative. It says that if management wants to provide for:

- Normal usage and lead time, then no safety stock is required.
- Maximum usage (3 units/day) or maximum lead time (6 days), then the safety stock required is 4 units.
- Maximum usage (3 units/day) and maximum lead time (6 days), then the safety stock required is 10 units.

Table F-3 brings together numerically the concepts just discussed, which are indicative of issues associated with inventory management.

Table F-3 illustrates some important points:

- In Case 1, the initial order would be for 32 units. Thereafter, every time the shelf-count reached 12 units, an order for 20 units would be placed. Normally these units would be received four days later and at that time the shelf-count would be four units and equal to the safety stock.
- Case 2 is identical except that the initial order is for 38 units, an order for 20 units would be placed when the shelf-count reached 18 units, and assuming a normal lead time and usage, the shelf-count would be equal to the safety stock of 10 units when these units are received.
- While introducing an order point does not increase average inventory, safety stock does. For example, in Cases 1 and 2, if everything went as planned, the safety stock would not be used and the average inventory would be as shown in Table F-4.

TABLE F-3 Impact Inventory Variables Have on Inventory Management

Variable	Symbol	Case 1	Case 2
Annual Usage	U	720 units	720 units
Economic Order Quantity	EOQ	20 units	20 units
Number of Orders Placed per Year	N	36 orders	36 orders
Average Daily Usage Rate		2 units per day	2 units per day
Normal Lead Time		4 days	4 days
		Annual usage = as forecast	Annual usage = as forecast
		and	**and**
		Peak daily usage rate = 3 units	Peak daily usage rate = 3 units
		or	**and**
		Extended lead time = 6 days	Extended lead time = 6 days
Safety Stock		4	10
Lead Time Quantity		8	8
Order Point		12	18
Economic Order Quantity	EOQ	20	20
Initial Order		32	38

TABLE F-4 Impact of Safety Stock on Average Inventory

	Symbol	Case 1	Case 2
Average Inventory (No Safety Stock)	AvgU	10	10
Safety Stock (No Safety Stock Usage)		4	10
Total Average Inventory		14	20

- The guidelines that management sets to control safety stocks are very important. As can be seen from Table F-4, if the safety stock is intended to cover only "peak daily usage" or "extended lead time," then the maximum average inventory is 14 units, or an increase of 40%. On the other hand, if safety stock is intended to cover both possibilities occurring at the same time, then the average inventory can increase by as much as 100% (to 20 units).
- Safety stock would permit the company to exceed its planned production for short periods of time. For example, In Cases 1 and 2, assuming normal lead times, the company could sell an additional 1 $\left(^{4\ Units}/_{4\ Days}\right)$ and 2.5 $\left(^{10\ Units}/_{4\ Days}\right)$ unit(s) per day respectively and not run out of stock while it was waiting for its quantity of 20 units to be delivered.

Selected References

Copeland, T. E., T. Koller, and J. Murrin. *Valuation: Measuring and Managing the Value of Companies,* 2nd ed. New York: John Wiley & Sons, 1995.

Copeland, T. E., and J. F. Watson. *Financial Theory and Corporate Policy.* Reading, MA: Addison-Wesley, 1979.

Damodaran, A. *Damodaran on Valuation, Security Analysis for Investment and Corporate Finance.* New York: John Wiley & Sons, 1994.

Damodaran, A. *Investment Valuation.* New York: John Wiley & Sons, 1996.

Damodaran, A. *The Little Book of Valuation.* Hoboken, NJ: John Wiley & Sons, 2011.

Davidson, S., J. S. Schindler, C. P. Stickney, and R. L. Weil. *Financial Accounting.* Hinsdale, IL: Dryden Press, 1976.

Higgins, R. C. *Analysis for Financial Management.* New York: McGraw-Hill Irwin, 2007.

Koller, T., R. Dobbs, and B. Huyett. *The Four Cornerstones of Corporate Finance.* McKinsey & Company. Hoboken, NJ: John Wiley & Sons, 2011.

Pratt, S. P., R. F. Reilly, and R. P. Schweihs. *Valuing a Business: The Analysis and Appraisal of Closely Held Companies,* 3rd ed. New York: McGraw-Hill, 1996.

Watson, J. F., and E. F. Brigham. *Managerial Finance,* 6th ed. Hinsdale, IL: Dryden Press, 1978.

AUTHOR'S NOTE

I have endeavored to follow what is considered to be best practice for authors and that is to refrain from consulting other authors' material during the preparation of this book. The extent to which I have wavered has been the occasional need to consult various authorities from time to time.

The "Selected References" listed here are part of my library and are the references I consulted while writing this book. I have made an effort to reference specific material from these sources throughout this work. However, this book has been written and rewritten over a period of 15 years and so some specific references may have been omitted. To the extent this may have occurred, I apologize to the authors involved.

No part of this book has been previously published. It is based on my business experience over the past 50 years. While this approach has advantages it also presents a problem. During this period I earned my MBA from the Wharton School at the University of Pennsylvania. In addition I attended numerous Young Presidents Organization, World

Presidents Organization, and Chief Executive Organization educational events. And like all businesspeople I have read thousands of articles from numerous sources. All of these sources of learning and the people I have had the pleasure of working with have had a major impact on my career and accumulated knowledge. Unfortunately, any notes that I may have taken are long gone, so attribution to all the sources of my lifelong business education is impossible. I thank everyone who has had an impact on my career.

Lawrence C. Karlson
Palm Beach Gardens, Florida
February 2015

About the Author

Lawrence C. Karlson has broad experience investing in and building the corporate value of companies of all sizes, both public and private, through both internal growth and acquisition. In the late 1980s and early 1990s, Mr. Karlson served as CEO of Pharos AB, and after an acquisition, became chairman of Spectra Physics AB. Both were public companies listed on the Stockholm Stock Exchange with operations throughout Europe and North America. Spectra Physics was a high-technology conglomerate with companies specializing in lasers and optics, laser scanning, precision distance and temperature measurement, navigation aids, and process weighing systems using a wide range of technologies. He also served as CEO and chairman of Berwind Financial Group (a leveraged buyout fund) from 2001 to 2005.

Since his retirement in the early 1990s, Mr. Karlson has served on numerous boards and led various committees, including audit, finance, corporate governance, and compensation committees in these organizations. He also has provided consulting services to a broad spectrum of companies in Europe and the United States.

Mr. Karlson currently serves on the board of directors of a number of public corporations, including CDI Corporation, Philadelphia, Pennsylvania (CDI–NYSE) ($1.2 billion engineering and temporary placement business); Campbell Soup Company, Camden, New Jersey (CPB–NYSE) ($8 billion worldwide consumer packaged goods company); and H&E Equipment Services Inc., Baton Rouge, Louisiana (NASDAQ–HEES) ($1 billion national rental equipment company). He also currently serves on the board of directors of a number of private companies, including Berwind Corporation, Aegis Software Inc., Harris Group Inc., JEP Management Inc., and Hillview Capital Advisors LLC's advisory board.

Mr. Karlson completed undergraduate engineering studies at Ryerson University, Toronto, Canada, and was awarded a Master's Degree with Distinction in Business Administration by the Wharton School at the University of Pennsylvania, Philadelphia. He and his wife, Deborah, maintain residences in Palm Beach Gardens, Florida; London, England; and Toronto, Canada.

Index